Preaching the New Lectionary

# Preaching the New Lectionary

## Year A

Dianne Bergant, C.S.A.

*with*

Richard Fragomeni

## THE LITURGICAL PRESS

Collegeville, Minnesota

www.litpress.org

Year A: ISBN 0-8146-2472-3
Year B: ISBN 0-8146-2473-1
Year C: ISBN 0-8146-2474-X

| 1 | 2 | 3 | 4 | 5 | 6 | 7 | 8 |
|---|---|---|---|---|---|---|---|

**Library of Congress Cataloging-in-Publication Data**

Bergant, Dianne.
    Preaching the new lectionary / Dianne Bergant, with Richard Fragomeni.
      p.  cm.
    Includes bibliographical references and index.
    Contents:    —[v. 2] Year B.
    ISBN 0-8146-2473-1 (alk. paper)
    1. Lectionary preaching—Catholic Church.   2. Catholic Church.
Lectionary for Mass (U.S.). Sundays and feasts.   3. Bible-Homiletical use.
I. Fragomeni, Richard N.   II. Title.
BV4235.L43B47   1999
251'.6—dc21
                                                             99-16138
                                                               CIP

# Contents

**Ordinary Time (Part Two)**

**Ordinary Time (Part Three)**

**Ordinary Time (Part Four)**

**Solemnities and Feasts**

# Introduction

The Lectionary is a unique genre of ecclesial literature. It is part of the liturgical canon, a collection of books that also includes the Sacramentary, the Ritual Books for Sacraments, the Book of Blessings, the Pontifical, and the Liturgy of the Hours, to name a few. The Constitution on the Sacred Liturgy (no. 24) states that sacred Scripture is the source of the readings and prayers used in the liturgy. The Lectionary, while not identical to the Bible, is drawn from its contents, providing a kind of narrative infrastructure for celebration of the Liturgical Year. The Lectionary is drawn from sacred Scripture by selecting passages from the biblical material (decontextualizing) and then placing these readings within a new literary and liturgical context (recontextualizing), thus creating a new ecclesial genre.

This recontextualization of former biblical material calls for a new way of interpretation, one that takes into consideration the liturgical character and setting of the Lectionary readings. The present commentary is an example of this type of interpretation. It will be fundamentally a literary reading of the texts, but it will also provide historical information whenever something in the text might appear foreign to the contemporary believer.

## Features

This commentary is unique in several ways. First and foremost, it employs a literary-liturgical way of interpreting all three readings of each Sunday and major feast of the Liturgical Year. It also interprets the responsorial psalm, part of the liturgy that has seldom enjoyed the importance it deserves and has at times even been changed or eliminated. Second, it explicitly situates the interpretation of each day's readings within the theology of its respective liturgical season. This theology is drawn from the specific themes of the readings that make up that particular year rather than from general theological themes otherwise associated with the season. In this way the meaning of the entire season becomes the context for understanding its individual parts. Third, the lections of the season are also read in sequential order, from the first Sunday of that season to the last (all of the first readings, all of the second readings, and so on). This kind of reading creates a kind of mini-reading and provides yet another way of understanding the riches of the readings (charts at the beginning of each season demonstrate this).

## Limitations

The present commentary does have limitations. Unfortunately, it does not directly engage the other books of the liturgical canon, most importantly the Sacramentary. There are two reasons for this. First, various liturgical books are presently being revised. While the composition of the Lectionary has been determined, the form of the Sacramentary is still in transition. As important as this book is to full liturgical recontextualization, it did not seem appropriate to use the unrevised edition, nor was it deemed wise to delay the commentary until the revision of the Sacramentary appeared.

Second, inclusion of all the relevant liturgical material would have made the commentary unmanageable. The method employed here is a relatively new one and is offered in a limited fashion. Those who find it helpful are encouraged to use it in other liturgical contexts.

## Uses

The commentary is ordered in the following way. Each lectionary season is first presented by way of a chart showing readings for the entire season. This is followed by the Initial Reading of that season, which explains how the lections can be read sequentially across the season from the first Sunday to the last. This procedure is carried out with each of the four readings so the theological patterns that are unfolding within the weeks of the seasons can be seen. Because of its length, Ordinary Time has been divided into four sections: Sundays 1–9 (before Lent); Sundays 10–17; Sundays 18–24; Sundays 25–34 (the remainder of the year). Each of these sections has a particular thematic focus. After the theological themes of the season are uncovered a literary reading of the lections of each respective Sunday is provided, and some of the theological themes of that Sunday are brought into dialogue with one another.

Reading the Lectionary in the various ways provided here has great potential for many forms of liturgical ministry. It can quicken the religious imagination of homilists, thus providing fresh new possibilities for liturgical preaching. It can offer creative insights for those involved in the liturgical preparation for the celebration of feasts and seasons. It can also act as a valuable resource for liturgical catechesis. In so many ways the material in this commentary can contribute toward enhancing the liturgical lives of the faithful.

## Development

It is important to acknowledge those upon whose groundbreaking work this approach is built. They are David N. Power, O.M.I., the inspiration of such an approach, and Bishop Blase Cupich, who wrote his doctoral dissertation under the direction of Professor Power on the topic of the Advent Lectionary.[1] In this work he laid the foundations for the literary-liturgical method employed here.

In the recent past, three books have appeared that can act as companions to this commentary. Two of them suggest a way of understanding the Lectionary that corresponds to the one advanced here. In *Scripture and Memory*[2] Fritz West recounts the way lectionary patterns have been developed and are interpreted by various Christian denominations. He also explains the three-year cycle of readings, which originated within the Roman Catholic tradition but which then spread to the wider Church. In *The Sunday Lectionary*[3] Normand Bonneau provides an overview of the principles that determine the selection of lectionary readings and an outline of the patterns that shape the seasons of the Liturgical Year.

Very recently a third resource has appeared. In *Preaching Basics*[4] Edward Foley works from many of the same principles noted here as he provides a new way of thinking about preaching. Together these four studies offer a new way of understanding the Lectionary and of opening its riches.

Finally, a debt of gratitude belongs to Richard N. Fragomeni, who introduced me to this approach. He is the one who explained the textual mosaic that introduces each season, and his creative interpretations form the basis of the **Themes of the Day**, which complete the commentary of the Sunday or feast. His contribution to this project has been invaluable.

1. Blase J. Cupich, "Advent in the Roman Tradition: An Examination and Comparison of the Lectionary Readings as Hermeneutical Units in Three Periods" (Ph.D. diss., The Catholic University of America, 1987).

2. Fritz West, *Scripture and Memory: The Ecumenical Hermeneutic of the Three-Year Lectionaries* (Collegeville: The Liturgical Press [A Pueblo Book], 1997).

3. Normand Bonneau, *The Sunday Lectionary: Ritual Word, Paschal Shape* (Collegeville: The Liturgical Press, 1998).

4. Edward Foley, *Preaching Basics* (Chicago: Liturgy Training Publications, 1998).

# Advent

| | | | |
|---|---|---|---|
| **First Sunday**<br><br>Isaiah 2:1-5<br>Reign of peace | Psalm 122:1-9<br>Go rejoicing to the house of the LORD | Romans 13:11-14<br>Our salvation is near | Matthew 24:37-44<br>Stay awake; be prepared |
| **Second Sunday**<br><br>Isaiah 11:1-10<br>The peaceable kingdom | Psalm 72:1-2, 7-8, 12-13, 17<br>Justice shall flourish | Romans 15:4-9<br>Christ saves all | Matthew 3:1-12<br>The kingdom is at hand |
| **Third Sunday**<br><br>Isaiah 35:1-6a, 10<br>The desert will flourish | Psalm 146:6-10<br>The LORD will save us | James 5:7-10<br>Be patient | Matthew 11:2-11<br>John questions the messiahship of Jesus |
| **Fourth Sunday**<br><br>Isaiah 7:10-14<br>The child is the sign | Psalm 24:1-6<br>Ascend the mountain of the LORD | Romans 1:1-7<br>Descendant of David, Son of God | Matthew 1:18-24<br>The virgin shall conceive |

# Advent

## Initial Reading of the Advent Lectionary

### Introduction

In order to introduce us to the rich themes of the season this section provides an initial reading of the mosaic formed from the texts of the Sundays of Advent. It offers us a context for examining the individual lections of the season. It is based on the literary forms of the readings as well as on a preliminary interpretation of their content. In a sense it presents the meaning of the entire season as the context for our understanding of the individual parts.

### First Testament Readings

Reading the First Testament lections in sequential order, from the first to the fourth Sunday, gives us a glimpse into the anticipated eschatological age. All of the readings come from the prophet Isaiah, and all of them look to a future time marked by peace and tranquility.

The readings for the First and the Third Sundays describe the long-awaited era itself. The first scenario is one of political accord. At that time warring nations will be at peace, and Jerusalem, the city of peace, will be the rallying point where this peace will be accomplished. The scenario depicts a transformed world bursting with life. The forces of death will have lost their grip and miracles of healing will abound. Once again Jerusalem plays a prominent role as the place where praise and rejoicing will take place. The readings for the Second and Fourth Sundays also speak of peace, but they describe an individual through whom this peace will be established, a descendant of David who will signal the fulfillment of the promises made to the people through the dynasty.

The flavor of anticipation in these four readings implies that the people are in dire straits, suffering some form of deprivation, discouraged with life. It is important to note that here they are not crying out to God. Rather, it is God who initiates the prophetic proclamation of hope. It is God who promises a new era of peace and harmony.

1

*Psalms*

The psalm responses for this Liturgical Year continue the theme of anticipation. Here too Jerusalem, the city of peace, plays an important role. It is the site where all the peoples of the earth gather; it is the place where the Law will be taught and judgment executed; it is the sacred dwelling place of God. The responses for the First and Fourth Sundays provide us with songs of rejoicing to be sung as we join the pilgrimage to the city of God, there to relish the blessings God has promised.

On the Second Sunday we turn our attention again to the anointed of God, the long-awaited king of peace. We look to his universal reign of justice for all and tender consideration of the vulnerable. The response for the Third Sunday clearly states that this kind of rule comes not from some human monarch but from God, who alone is sovereign and who reigns in undisputed glory.

All of the psalm responses clearly remind us that the blessings of peace for which we pray and which we anticipate come from God. The harmony and healing for which we long may come to us through the agency of another and may be associated with Jerusalem, but they originate in the heart of God.

*Epistles*

Anticipation for the coming age of fulfillment dominates the readings for this season of Advent. However, the principal focus here is the manner of living expected of believers as they await the dawning of the eschatological age. Although the establishment of this new age is the work of God and only God has the power to bring it to birth, believers have the responsibility of living in a manner that demonstrates their commitment.

The difference between the present age and the age to come is clearly delineated in the reading for the First Sunday as it contrasts the opposites sleep and wakefulness, night and day, darkness and light. The advent of the eschatological age presents us with a choice: Within which age do we wish to live? The reading for the Second Sunday teaches us that this new life is offered to all. Some may have been invited earlier than others. In fact, the invitation of some may actually flow from the invitation of others. However, all are invited and so all must be welcomed. Differences such as race or nationality or social status or gender or physical condition are not important to God, and so they should not be important to God's people. All have been called to glorify God in this new age.

The delay in the final coming of Christ challenged the endurance of the anxious Christians. When would he come? How long would they have to wait? We today may experience a similar anxiety. The length of his delay might even make us wonder whether he is coming at all. With the early Christians we are told in the reading for the Third Sunday to be faithful to our Christian responsibilities and to be patient. The reading for the last Sunday is a kind of introduction to the one who is about to come. All of the waiting and anticipation is now brought to a conclusion. The promises are now fulfilled, the religious hopes are now realized. The eschatological age has dawned. We have at last been blessed with the grace and peace of God.

## Gospels

The four Advent gospel readings from Matthew together create a kind of gospel in itself. Each in its own way is a stage in the dawning of the eschatological age of fulfillment. On the First Sunday we are reminded of the hidden moment of this dawning. The situation in which we find ourselves today is probably more like that of the time of Noah than of the earliest Christians. The people of the latter period were expecting some great advent of God, while those of the former went about their lives oblivious of the events that would soon overtake them. With their fate as a stern warning to us, we are told in no uncertain terms: Be prepared!

In the gospels for the Second and Third Sundays we encounter the figure of John the Baptist, a man of remarkable strength and conviction. His voice echoes down through the ages: Repent! The kingdom of God, the eschatological age, is at hand! John insisted that if we are to enter into this new age we must leave behind the works of the old age. He also knew that the repentance he preached was only a kind of preface to the real thing. He was merely the herald, not the promised one. And not even he was certain about the person he preceded, about what he would look like, how he would act, what he would require of us. Even John had to be enlightened.

With the gospel of the Fourth Sunday we are brought to the threshold of the new age. We are told that the promises are being fulfilled, even though the circumstances of their fulfillment are not at all what we expected. God is with us in a new and wondrous way, yet it looks so common, so ordinary. All we can do is stand in awe.

## Mosaic of Readings

This mosaic of readings shows that God has planned a wonderful experience of peace and harmony for us and, step by step down through the ages, has prepared us for the advent of that experience. All of the readings contain a very positive note of promise. A new age will come; all people will be gathered together and God will be in their midst; a leader will appear who will accomplish this for God and for us. Advent is the time for us to open ourselves to this mystery of divine love.

# Readings

## *First Sunday of Advent*

### Isaiah 2:1-5

The first reading of the first Sunday of this Liturgical Year contains a vision of universal peace and an invitation to participate in that peace by fidelity to the word of God. The prophetic oracle opens with a standard superscription that identifies both the prophet and the subject of his pronouncement. Although Isaiah mentions Judah, the southern region of Israel, the focus of his words is the city of Jerusalem. Like most major cities of the land, for reasons of protection it was built on a mountain. However, the image depicted here is not one of a city known for its political prominence or military might. This is not a nationalistic dream of unchallenged superiority that was realized by a king or by some other official of the state. The vision is of a city revered because it is the dwelling place of God.

In the ancient world high mountains were believed to be the homes of the gods. The higher the mountain, the more important the god. The highest mountain was also considered the *axis mundi*, the center of the universe from which all blessings flow. In vision, Isaiah claims that Mount Zion, a mount that is actually of medium height, will be established as the highest mountain. Regardless of its physical proportions, it will enjoy religious stature because it is the site on which is built the Temple of the LORD, the place where God dwells in a special way in the midst of the people. It is to this mountain that all nations will stream as if in religious pilgrimage or procession, for it will be from this mountain that the word of the LORD will proceed. It is clear that this is the reason Zion is the center of the universe.

The invitation posed (v. 3) contains expressions associated with the Wisdom tradition of Israel: that he may instruct us in his ways *(derek)*; that we may walk in his paths *('ōrah)*. The parallel construction that follows further emphasizes the centrality of this instruction:

| from Zion | instruction *(tôrâ)* | |
| | word *(dābār)* | from Jerusalem |

Those who come to the mountain of the LORD willingly comply with God's instructions. It is clear that it is the moral force of the word of the LORD and not the military might of the monarchy that draws "all nations" (v. 3) and "many peoples" (v. 4). Obedient to this word, the nations will convert all their weapons of war and death into implements of peace and life. The earth will no longer be a battlefield but a place that will once again bring forth fruits of life.

This is a vision of the future. All of the verb forms indicate this. It speaks of the eschatological age of complete faithfulness to God and the peace and harmony among people that will flow from it. Because it promises peace we can presume the people to whom it was first spoken were not then enjoying peace. Although the peace depicted here can come only from God, people do play a very important role in its advent. They are invited to approach God and to conform their lives to the instructions God has given them. Because this eschatological age has not yet come in its fullness this vision is a promise and an invitation that will continue to be relevant to each succeeding generation. The final exhortation is spoken to all: Let us walk in the light of the LORD!

## Psalm 122:1-9

The responsorial psalm, referred to by some as a song of Zion, is an individual hymn of joy and praise of one who had the opportunity to go to the Temple in Jerusalem. Its association with pilgrimage is seen in the mention of approaching the Temple and of setting foot within the gates of the city (vv. 1-2). The images it contains are vibrant, and the sentiments it expresses are profound. Glorious temples were not only evidence of the wealth and importance of the rulers who were responsible for their construction. More importantly, they were concerned with constituting the dwelling place of God on earth. For this reason an opportunity to go to Jerusalem and to enter the courts of the Temple was considered a great honor, and it often resulted in a religious experience.

The city of Jerusalem was itself something to behold. It was built on Mount Zion, a hill that towered above much of the neighboring low-lying terrain. This not only gave it a vantage point from which one could survey the surrounding territory, an important asset in case of possible attack, but its height enabled it to be seen from a distance, thus creating the impression of watchfulness and protection. Jerusalem was a city with walls and gates, suggesting both significant size and military fortifications. The strong fortifications of the city and its reputation as the site of the Temple and the place where God dwelt gave Jerusalem the reputation of being invincible (v. 3). It was the seat of royal political power, and it became the religious center of the tribal confederacy that was bound together by common allegiance to God (v. 4). In this capacity it also became the center of the administration of justice during the time of the monarchy (v. 5). When one arrived at Jerusalem one was visiting the center of every facet of Jewish life.

The psalmist calls the audience to pray for the peace of the city (v. 6). It was customary to offer greetings of peace as one entered a home or addressed a group (cf. Rom 1:7; 1 Cor 1:3; Gal 1:3; etc.). Such a prayer might seem especially pertinent in this instance given the etymological similarity in the words "peace" *(shālôm)* and "Jerusalem" *(yᵉrûshālayim)*. Peace, as spoken of here, incorporates more than the absence of war or strife. It includes prosperity, well-being, and completeness. It is for this peace that the psalmist requests prayer. Speaking of Jerusalem, the psalmist requests blessings on those who love the city. In essence, may those prosper who pray for the prosperity of Jerusalem. Such blessings will indeed be enjoyed by the Jerusalemites, for those within the city itself will certainly participate in its peace and prosperity.

The sentiments found in the last verses (8-9) form a kind of *inclusio* with those of the opening verses (vv. 1-2). Although the city has strong fortifications, it is the presence of the house of the LORD that makes it worthy of the peace it enjoys and provides for those within its gates. It is also because of the Temple that the psalmist offers prayer in the first place. This reference to the Temple, and the male privilege associated with it, could explain the clear male exclusiveness found in the last verses (brothers and friends). It is the men who entered into the sacred precincts of the Temple and performed those duties required by the cultic tradition of the people. However, women and children accompanied the men as they went in pilgrimage to the Holy City (cf. Luke 2:41), and so they did participate in the excitement of the procession and the praise of the city.

## Romans 13:11-14

Paul here speaks about the decisive time of fulfillment, the *kairós,* the period of transition from the present age of sin to the long-awaited age of fulfillment. His words reflect Jewish eschatological thinking: alone, human beings were powerless to bring about the realization of the promises God had made in the distant past and renewed with each succeeding generation of believers. Instead, it would be necessary for God to intervene and provide new avenues for the accomplishment of the marvels that had been planned. The intervention of God, anticipated by the Jewish community though not clearly understood, would be the event that separated "this age" from "the age to come." The fundamental Christian claim is that "the age to come" has dawned with the coming of Jesus.

Paul employs several images to characterize this division of time: "this age" is like slumber, or night and darkness; "the age to come" is like wakefulness, or day and light. He first exhorts the Christians to wake from sleep. As used here, the image does not suggest that they have been negligent but that they have been living in the old age. There seems to have been an interval between the time of their first believing and the time of this exhortation (v. 11). This apparent incongruity could be an example of the paradox expressed by the eschatological statement "already but not yet." It is a way of acknowledging that the age of fulfillment has already dawned, but it has not yet been brought to completion. The incongruity might also suggest Paul's belief that the coming of Christ was imminent and that it was imperative that Christians take resolute steps to reform their lives. They are urged to leave their former manner of living behind, just as one leaves the world of sleep behind when awakened. Like the world of sleep, the present age is the realm of unreality, but the age of fulfillment is the realm of attentiveness and reality.

Night, the time for sleep, is over; day, the time for wakefulness, is now at hand. Night is also the time when darkness conceals sinful behavior. Paul uses three couplets to sketch some of the evils of "the present age." They include forms of intemperance, of sexual excess, and of social disharmony. These are the kinds of sins that not only undermine personal integrity but also erode the foundations of society. When Paul speaks of the desires of the flesh *(sárx)*, he is referring to anything associated with human frailty, not merely with physical weaknesses. Desires of the flesh are whatever militates against life in the spirit. Just as one leaves the world of sleep, so one must put aside the works of darkness.

The two images used to speak of the new life that Christians are called to live are both metaphors of clothing. Armor comes from the military realm. It suggests spiritual warfare, indicating the hardships Christians must be prepared to face. The defensive covering is "armor of light." It is protective clothing one wears in the daytime. The metaphor is even more telling. The Christians are exhorted to put on the Lord Jesus Christ. In this instance the clothing does indeed make the person. To put on Christ is to become identified with him, to live his life in one's own flesh. To live in this way is to live fully in the new age. It is important to note that such a manner of living does not bring forth salvation. Rather, the salvation that comes from God determines the Christian manner of living. Everything is gift from God.

## Matthew 24:37-44

The reading for this Sunday opens with a statement that identifies the audience to whom Jesus speaks. This is not a public discourse, as are so many of his sermons. This is a private instruction given by Jesus to his disciples. It is a lesson on eschatology, on the character of the *parousía*, or future coming of the Son of Man. Although the Greek word *parousía* simply means "coming" or "presence," it soon took on eschatological significance in Christian theology.

The ancient Israelites believed there would be a time in the future when the designs of God would be ultimately fulfilled. Not even their own human sinfulness could prevent this from happening. The question was not *if* this time would come but *when* it would come. They were well aware of their own inability to inaugurate this time of fulfillment. Instead, they believed God would send someone to do it in God's name. Several traditions grew up surrounding this eschatological (end-time) hope. One claimed a descendant of David would come who, as king, would set up the reign of God. Others believed a priest would fashion them into a truly holy people. Yet another tradition envisioned a mysterious being "like a Son of Man," who would come on the clouds to establish the reign of God (cf. Dan 7:13-14).

The reading for today speaks of the suddenness of this imminent time of fulfillment and of the need to be ready at all times for its dawning. Jesus is portrayed as an extraordinary teacher. In order to impart his message he first draws an analogy with one of the stories of ancient Jewish tradition. He then sketches two very ordinary experiences of life as demonstrations. The gender balance here should be noted: the responsibility of preparedness is all-inclusive. Finally, he concludes with a kind of parable that teaches a lesson. All of these teaching devices follow the same twofold pattern: (1) the people had no idea of what was in store for them; (2) calamity befell them because they were unprepared.

The people at the time of Noah were oblivious of the danger that faced them, and so they did not ready themselves. The same is true in the analogies of the men and women, and the parable of the householder, all of whom blindly go about their daily lives. We don't know whether the first two were prepared, but we see clearly how important it is that they should be. As for the householder, we know he was not prepared, because the text says the thief did break into the house. There is a bit of ambiguity in the reports of the man taken from the field and the woman taken from the mill. Because elsewhere the verb *(paralambánetai)* is translated "take you to myself" (John 14:3), some maintain that is the meaning intended here. This has given rise to the notion of what some Evangelicals refer to as "the rapture," God's scooping the faithful up and carrying them into heaven. However, since the consequence of the approaching day is negative in both the story of Noah and the experience of the householder, the verb should probably be understood in a negative way here as well. In other places the coming of the Son of Man might be seen as a time of salvation. Here, it is portrayed as a time of calamity.

There are two strong exhortations in this passage: "Stay awake!" "Be prepared!" What might that have meant in each of the situations? Was everyone expected to build a boat as Noah did? At least they should not have ignored the warning he gave. What made one of the men and one of the women different from the others? We do not know, but whatever it was, it does not seem to have prevented them from living normal lives. Was the householder expected to keep constant watch? Obviously the answer is: Yes! Each depiction in its own way says: Be ready! You never know when the time will come!

## Themes of the Day

Pilgrimage is the overarching theme for the First Sunday of Advent. This theme not only addresses the message of this particular Sunday, it also sets the tone for the entire Advent season. We may be accustomed to think of Advent as the time when we prepare for the coming of God, but the readings also train our attention on our own journey to God. We see this most clearly in this First Sunday with readings that tell us the identity of the pilgrims, the destination toward which they travel, and the way of life required of them on their journey. As the Vatican Council has proclaimed: We are a pilgrim people.

## The Pilgrims

The very first reading for this Sunday, for this season, underscores the universality of the invitation to approach the mountain of the LORD, the place where God dwells in the midst of the people. All nations, many peoples, gather together and approach as one community of believers. There is no discrimination here, no restriction of gender, race, culture, age. No one who wants to undertake this pilgrimage will be prevented from doing so. The other readings do not explicitly identify the audience to which they were intended and so do not really exclude any individuals or groups. The only qualifications for participation in this journey to God are found in the manner of life required while on the pilgrimage itself. All are invited. All are welcome. All have a place on the mountain of the LORD.

## The Destination

Both the reading from Isaiah and the psalm response speak of the pilgrimage to the mountain of the LORD, the place where God can be found. Although the psalm speaks about Jerusalem and refers to the Temple there, the broader theological significance of the mountain, the city, and the Temple is one and the same. They represent the presence of God in our midst, and this presence is the goal of our striving.

The city and the Temple may have been the destination of the early Israelites or even the people at the time of Jesus, but what is our destination? A pilgrimage is neither a random wandering nor an escape. It is not a trip that moves away from some place but a religious journey toward a specific destination. Where are we heading? Our Advent pilgrimage is toward eschatological fulfillment. And where is this fulfillment to be found? Not in some distant place, not somewhere beyond us, not in another world. We will find fulfillment where we live and work; we will find God deep within us; we will find God in our midst, in the new world of justice and peace that we fashion with each other.

## Life on the Pilgrimage

The readings provide us with clear directions about how we are to live while we are on this pilgrimage to God. In Isaiah we learn that we must put away our instruments of violence and hatred, our swords and our spears. Lest we pick them up again, we are told to convert them into life-producing implements, into plows and pruning hooks. Paul exhorts us to put away our deeds of darkness and self-indulgence and to clothe ourselves instead in the deeds of Jesus Christ. Matthew points out the need for alertness, attentiveness, and a disposition open to a change of heart.

The life we must live must be lived in the actual world in which we find ourselves. We are called to journey deeper into our lives, not outside of them. That is where God is present. And if we are truly alert and attentive we will discover that it is in our own lives, as ordinary as we may think they are, that we will discover God. There we will find eschatological fulfillment, and there the Son of Man will come to us.


## Second Sunday of Advent
### Isaiah 11:1-10

The oracle of salvation, which constitutes the first reading for this Sunday, is enclosed by references to "the root of Jesse" (vv. 1, 10) and can be divided into two major sections. The first section (vv. 2-5) lists various divinely bestowed gifts enjoyed by a new Davidic king; the second section (vv. 6-9) describes a realm of remarkable peace in the world of nature. Together they provide us with a picture of social and ecological tranquility and harmony. The future character of this realm is seen in the very first words: it will come to pass "on that day," a phrase used by the prophets to refer to the eschatological time of fulfillment. Everything about this prophetic vision bespeaks a time quite different from the present.

"Stump" implies that the house of Jesse, the father of David, has been cut down; the monarchy has been conquered, and it appears there is no hope for a future king. However, appearances are deceiving, for out of this stump sprouts a shoot. This is not a completely new plant, for it grows out of Jesse's roots. Upon him rests the spirit of the LORD, that divine force bestowed on certain individuals enabling them to accomplish feats they would never be able to accomplish on their own. The bestowal of the spirit of the LORD suggests there is a return to the charismatic character of the monarchy.

The gifts bestowed upon this ruler are listed in pairs, each pair pointing to one of the major responsibilities of the monarchy. Wisdom and understanding enable the king to rule with competence and insight; counsel and strength are necessary for the administration of justice, whether this is executed judicially through the courts or militarily on the battlefield; knowledge and fear of the LORD dispose the ruler to humble reverence toward God, ensuring that the reign is faithful to God's will. It will be only through these extraordinary gifts from God and not through any personal competence that the new monarch will be able to rule appropriately. Furthermore, he will be able to see beyond appearances, and he will be the champion of the poor and the meek. He will be girded about with righteousness *(ṣedeq)* and faithfulness *('ōmen)*, two characteristics that belong to God but are bestowed upon God's covenant partners. This is clearly God's king.

The scene of "the peaceable kingdom" is reminiscent of the primal paradise of Eden (cf. Genesis 2). The animals do not follow their predatory instincts, and natural enemies live in harmony with one another. Mention of nursing and weaned children who have no fear of snakes suggests that human beings live in a state of innocence and safety. All of creation has been either transformed or re-created. This vision is not a return to the past but one of future peace and fulfillment. These two scenes are joined by mention of the safety on the holy mountain, most likely a reference to Zion, the mount upon which Jerusalem was built and from which the new Davidic king will rule. There will finally be peace on this mountain, for the knowledge of God will fill the entire earth like life-giving waters over the chaotic waters of the sea. In other words, God will ultimately reign over the earth. The final verse declares the universality of this wonder. On that day of fulfillment the new Davidic ruler will stand as a rallying point for the people of all nations to assemble. Since these marvels have been God's doing, through this extraordinary descendant of David they will all be drawn to God.

## Psalm 72:1-2, 7-8, 12-13, 17

In this royal hymn the psalmist is asking God to bless the king so the king in turn can bless the people. Ancient monarchs exercised incredible control over the lives of their subjects. Despite the scope and depth of this influence the authority described here is not unregulated. Rather, it is under the jurisdiction of God.

The psalmist begins with a prayer asking God that the king be given a share in God's own justice (vv. 1-2). This is the same justice with which God governs the world and all of the people in it. It is the justice that gives birth to harmony and to the peace (v. 7) that embodies complete well-being. This justice will enable the king to govern in a way that will provide the people with the peace and well-being God wills for them.

These people are explicitly identified as belonging to God, presumably the people of the covenant. Thus this is no ordinary king; he is one who has been placed over the covenanted people to rule them as God would, in justice and righteousness. The test of the character of the royal rule is the care given to the most vulnerable of the society, the poor. The psalmist asks God to grant righteousness to the king so he can protect the defenseless and guarantee for them a share in the prosperity of the nation.

The psalmist turns to the rule of the king itself (v. 7). He prays first for its steadfastness: may it last forever, until the moon is no more. Actually, it is not the reign itself that is the object of his prayer but the righteousness of the reign. Since it is really God's righteousness, he prays that it will take root and flourish throughout the rule of this particular king and that it will even outlast him, enduring along with peace until the end of time.

The psalmist next prays that this rule of justice be extended to include the entire world and all the nations within it (vv. 8). Since the sea frequently symbolized chaos (cf. Ps 89:9-10), the expression "from sea to sea" (v. 8a) delineates the inhabitable land that lies securely and thrives peacefully within the boundaries of chaotic waters. "The River" (v. 8b) suggests a specific waterway that marks a land that stretches to the end of the earth. Both of these sweeping images sketch a reign that encompasses all the world.

The prayer continues with a picture of righteousness in action (vv. 12-13). If the test of justice is the solicitude shown the needy, the prayer of the psalmist has been answered. The kingdom is rooted in the righteousness of God, and the most vulnerable in the society have an advocate in the king.

It was believed that the name of a person contained part of that person's identity and personality. The more important the person, the more powerful was the name. From this it is easy to see why the name of the king was held in such high regard, particularly the name of a righteous king. The prayer ends with a plea that this name, and therefore the power and influence of this king, remain forever. Thus his reputation of righteousness will be a model for other nations, and through him they too will be blessed by God (this is reminiscent of the promise of universal blessing made to Abram; see Gen 12:2).

## Romans 15:4-9

The principal theme of this reading is the universality of the blessings won by Christ and the unity within the believing community that results from this inclusiveness. Paul begins his teaching by attesting to the perennial value of the Scriptures. Referring to what we today call the First or Old Testament, he insists that though its contents originated from people who faced a very different world and different concerns than did his audience, its message continues to provide instruction to the people of his day, and by implication to the people of our day as well. He does not elaborate on the nature of the instruction it contains, but he does maintain that the Scriptures offer encouragement, and this encouragement should enable us to hope. The rest of the passage shows that Paul is talking primarily about the promises made to the ancestors of Israel.

Paul bases this particular teaching on God's original promise that Abram and his descendants would be a source of blessing for others (cf. Gen 12:2; 22:18). From this he argues that it was in fulfillment of this promise that the Gentiles have been brought into the family of God. Although Christ himself preached to his own people (Paul uses the male-biased expression, "the circumcised"), the Scriptures' promise of universality becomes the hope of inclusion of the Gentiles and the harmony they will enjoy with the Jews. All, Jew and Gentile alike, have been welcomed by Christ, and this universal welcome should stand as the model of the openness they extend to each other. (The verb "welcome" *[proslambánō]* means "to take to oneself.")

In his prayer for the community (vv. 5-6) Paul asks for three different expressions of unity: "to think in harmony," to be in "one accord," and to glorify God in "one voice." The thinking *(phrónēsis)* is more than merely the intellectual faculty. It is the highly prized practical reasoning, the right state of mind, and the source of virtue. The word translated "one accord" *(homothymadón)* denotes a unity that springs from an external interest rather than from some shared personal inclination. In other words, they are of one accord because of something outside themselves rather than something they hold in common. The unity for which Paul prays in no way obliterates the differences between Jew and Gentile; it is a unity in diversity. Christ Jesus is both the source and the model of their unity, and they glorify God by accepting those who, though different from themselves, have also been called by God in Christ. Finally, so united these very different people can praise God as if with one mouth *(stóma)*.

Just as he begins this instruction with a reference to Scripture, so Paul brings it to a conclusion with a quote found in two places (2 Sam 22:50; Ps 18:49). In the original contexts it is David (and the psalmist) who praises God for having protected him from the danger posed by other nations, and thereby the favor David enjoyed with God is demonstrated. By taking the verse out of its original contexts and placing it in this instruction Paul reinterprets its meaning. It is now a praise of God for having included the other nations in the company of those who are favored.

## Matthew 3:1-12

From the outset the description of the baptism performed by John the Baptist has an eschatological character to it. It is preceded by a terse exhortation: Repent! Change your heart. The reason for this challenging admonishment is the imminent appearance of the reign of heaven. Though unique to Matthew, this phrase is a reference to the eschatological reign of God long awaited by the Jewish people. The exhortation suggests that a change of heart *(metánoia)* is required at the dawning of this new age. John is cast in the role of its precursor. His life-style in the wilderness prompts the gospel writer to revise slightly a passage from the prophet Isaiah (40:3) in the description of him. However, in Isaiah it is the way of the LORD that is in the wilderness; here it is John's voice calling for renewal. John's attire resembles that of a prophet (cf. 2 Kgs 1:8), and his diet, which certainly corresponds to one that might sustain a wilderness dweller, suggests to some that he belonged to a sect like the Nazirites, who for religious reasons abstained from wine and meat.

John's baptism was neither one of incorporation, the kind that proselytes to Judaism underwent, nor the repeated ritual cleansing the Essene community of Qumran practiced. It was a devotional rite with eschatological significance, administered to Jews, accompanied by an acknowledgment of sinfulness and a resolve to live an ethical life. Although he was away from the major cities in the wilderness of Judea, the region that sloped down from the highlands to the Dead Sea, John attracted large groups of people from the entire vicinity. Even members of the Pharisees and Sadducees, two prominent religious groups, came to him. The text does not say they actually submitted themselves to his baptism. Some think they came to spy on him. However, his condemnation of them suggests they were not there simply for political reasons.

John's criticism of these religious leaders is fraught with animosity. He accuses them of coming to him because they seek to flee from the wrath of God associated with the coming of the eschatological age. It may be they are interested in the rite he performs but not in the repentance he preaches. He further accuses them of considering their identity as children of Abraham as a privilege that protects them from this wrath. Playing on the similarity between the Hebrew words for child *(bēn)* and stone *('eben),* he lays bare the shallowness of such claims. At the time of the new age only righteous lives will account for anything. Everything else will be destroyed as if by fire.

John admits his subordinate role when compared with Jesus. He is the voice that announces the coming of another. Though John precedes the other one in time, he follows him in importance. He, John, is not worthy to perform for him the menial tasks of a servant. Applying the Isaian passage to Jesus in this way suggests that Jesus is actually the LORD (in Hebrew it is the personal name of God) who is coming in salvation. John's baptism is a baptism of water for repentance; it is a preparation. The one to come will baptize with the Holy Spirit and fire, a symbol of both cleansing and refinement (Zech 13:9; Mal 3:2-3) and also of destroying fire. Mention of the winnowing fork introduces the theme of harvest. The fork itself is a symbol of separation that takes place then. The harvester uses it to throw the grain into the air. The kernels of wheat fall to the ground, while the lighter chaff is blown away. The context of this passage suggests that the winnowing refers to the separation of those who respond to John's call to repentance from those who do not. John does not act as judge; the one who is to come will do the judging. In other words, the time of the Messiah will be a time of both redemptive and destructive judgment.

### Themes of the Day

We examine the theme of pilgrimage on the Second Sunday of Advent as well, but this time from a slightly different perspective. Taken together, the three readings remind us of Chaucer's famous *Canterbury Tales*. In that literary work of art various pilgrims step forward to tell their stories, stories from which we are meant to derive lessons for our own lives. Here the biblical authors sketch profiles of individuals after whom we can model our lives as we embark on our pilgrimage to eschatological fulfillment. Isaiah depicts the righteous messianic king; Paul provides us with a glimpse of Jesus, the one who ministers to all; Matthew describes John the Baptist, the prophet who prepares for the advent of Christ.

### *The Messianic King*

The gifts Isaiah attributes to the messianic king are the same gifts we receive with the anointing of the Spirit: wisdom, understanding, counsel, fortitude, knowledge, piety, and fear of the LORD. We may not exercise them in the same way ancient Israelite royalty might, but we must admit how important they are to us as we progress on our journey. We certainly need competence and insight in every walk of life; we are all responsible for establishing and safeguarding justice in society; we all owe God our humble reverence and our commitment to God's reign. The image of the messianic king may have been fulfilled in Jesus, but it is also offered to us as a model after which we can pattern our lives.

### *The Minister to All*

The universality of God's call, a theme we contemplated last week, is placed before us again today. At a time when there was struggle between Jewish Christians and members of the believing community who came from a Gentile background, Paul declares that Christ came for all. Just as *The Canterbury Tales* describe pilgrims of all backgrounds and characters, so our companions on the pilgrimage come from diverse circumstances. Since the invitation to participate was extended to all, we are expected to welcome all and, like Jesus our model, minister to them in their need, whatever that need may be. Some of Chaucer's characters were quite unpleasant, but they were part of the group. Many of the people to whom Jesus ministered were quite unpleasant, but this did not deter him. His example is set before us today. All have been called to sing praise to God's name. They are invited to joins us; we are invited to join them.

## The Herald of Good News

The third role model offered to us for our imitation is John the Baptist, the one who announced the advent of Jesus. He himself lived a life of radical self-denial, but he did not require this of those who came to hear his message. What he preached was repentance, *metánoia* or change of heart, not a rejection of the circumstances of life but of the character of that life. The message he preached resembled that of the prophets of old. Like them, he called for a return to righteousness, to lives of integrity, to relationships rooted in honesty and respect. He spoke against presumption and arrogant reliance on one's religious origin, against complacency and the shirking of responsibility, against disinterest in the welfare of others.

This is a powerful image in a world such as ours, where we are tempted to compromise our principles in favor of enhancing our status, where we are instructed to get what we want with the least amount of effort, where we are encouraged to disregard the needs of others and take care of "number one." We may not be called as was John to proclaim this message to a broad audience, but as pilgrims on the journey to eschatological fulfillment we are certainly challenged to heed his message in our own lives and to do what we can to instill it in the lives of those with whom we live and work and for whom we may be responsible.

## Third Sunday of Advent
### Isaiah 35:1-6a, 10

In this oracle of salvation Isaiah depicts two ways in which the renewal promised by God is manifested: the barren wilderness will be filled with new life, and those who suffer physical maladies will be healed of their infirmities. The prophet is the messenger of this good news and is told to announce this message to those who have been broken by the hardships of life, who are weak and filled with fear, who have been snatched from their homeland and are suffering exile in a foreign land.

The salvation promised will be seen first in the regeneration of the natural world. Creation will be renewed. This promised renewal is characterized by images of wastelands bursting forth with life. It is amazing what a little water can effect in dry and barren land. It can work miracles; deserts can be transformed into oases. Three images of lifelessness are here replaced by three images of fruitfulness. The desert *(midbār)*, the parched land *(ṣîyâ)*, and the steppe *('ărābâ)* all refer to the rift of the Jordan valley, especially south of the Dead Sea in the region of the Negev desert. The promise states that land such as this will be blessed with the kind of fertility for which the northern part of the country was renowned, particularly the lush forest growth of Lebanon and Carmel, and with the fecundity of the land found in the Plain of Sharon. What was lifeless will now be abundantly fruitful, a sign of God's blessing. "Glory" and "splendor" are divine attributes revealed in the actions of God, which are reminiscent of the first creation of life.

The proclamation "Fear not" is a common expression found in many accounts of divine revelation (cf. Gen 15:1; Josh 8:1; Isa 41:10). It is spoken by God or a messenger of God in an attempt to assuage the very natural trepidation one experiences in the presence of a supernatural phenomenon. Here, as part of a promise of salvation, it is meant to encourage the fainthearted. It precedes the announcement of the coming of God as vindicator. While in some situations this can be a terrifying announcement, here it is a message of salvation. God may be coming in judgment for some, but for those to whom the prophet speaks, God is coming to bring new life.

In a world that believes God has created everything in proper order, imperfection of any kind is often perceived as a consequence of some form of human transgression. This is particularly true of physical infirmity, which is often considered evidence of the presence of evil forces in the world. The person with the infirmity may be innocent of serious transgression, but it is believed that someone or something is responsible. In such a world healing can be seen as the restoration of the proper order of creation. In vivid language this oracle describes four healing situations (eyes, ears, legs, tongue), which are probably representative of any or all cures, whether physical or spiritual. The cures symbolize the transformative power of God, who comes to save the people.

Just as deprivation and infirmity were considered signs of evil in the world, so the restoration described here was perceived as a sign of the transformation only God can effect. It was a testimony to God's presence in the world and to God's victory over evil. God had reestablished the original order of creation, and all life began again to flourish.

Ransom *(pādâ)* is a legal term implying transfer of ownership and became associated with the cultic redemption of the firstborn. Here the term signifies the unearned nature of their release. Like the transformation and rejuvenation described earlier, their release and return is a free gift from God.

## Psalm 146: 6-7, 8-9, 9-10

The responsorial psalm is a hymn of praise of the LORD (*Hallelujah* in Hebrew). Such hymns have a definite pattern. The summons itself *(hallelu)* appears in a plural verb form, suggesting a communal setting, and contains an abbreviation of the divine name *(jah)*. In this psalm the word is used as a refrain, a response to a series of statements that offer examples of God's indescribable graciousness.

Although covenant is never explicitly mentioned, various themes seem to point to it. The very first verse mentions God's faithfulness *('ōmen)*, one of the principal characteristics of covenant commitment. Then there is an allusion to God's deliverance of the people from the bondage of Egypt and to God's providential care of them during their sojourn in the wilderness. Throughout all of Israel's history God has been faithful. This is reason enough to praise the LORD.

God's graciousness to the vulnerable is next extolled (vv. 8-9). There are many situations in life that can force one to be bowed down, whether a physical disability, a mental or emotional affliction, an economic or social disadvantage. Whatever it might be, God raises up the needy, enables them to stand with pride, reestablishes them in security. Strangers or aliens lack certain legal rights, and since where they are living is not their own nation, they may not be familiar with the rights they do have. Insensitive or unscrupulous people can very easily take advantage of them. These vulnerable strangers are precisely the kinds of people the God of Israel chooses. Israel itself is the prime example of this. It was when they were aliens in Egypt that God took them and made them God's own people. This is certainly reason to praise God.

In patriarchal societies only adult free men enjoy certain privileges. As part of the household, women and children are under the jurisdiction and care of such men. Women belong to the households either of their fathers, their brothers, or their sons. In this psalms response, "widows" probably refers to women who cannot return to their home of origin because they have married but whose husbands are now dead and they have no adult son to care for them. Such women are marginal in society and need some patron to care for them. Likewise, it is presumed that the orphans referred to here have no extended family within whose jurisdiction they might take refuge. These are the ones for whom God cares.

The final verse praises God as sovereign and eternal ruler in Jerusalem. All of the other verses of the psalm testify to the glory of this God who reigns forever from the very hill that is at the center of the lives of the people. This is not a God who is far off. Rather this God has entered into their history and into the very social fabric of their existence. Such a God deserves praise.

## James 5:7-10

Patience is the controlling theme in this short passage. The author both exhorts believers to be patient in waiting for the coming of the Lord and offers for their imitation examples of patient waiting. *Parousía,* which means "coming" or "presence," became a technical term for the future coming of Christ to inaugurate the definitive manifestation of God's eternal dominion. Because the exact time of this advent was unknown, patience would be necessary until that day of fulfillment dawned. Such is the essence of the exhortation found in this passage.

The example of the farmer waiting for the crop to grow and mature high-lights some important aspects of this waiting. First, the ripening of the crops depends upon seasonal rains over which farmers have no control. The early rains fell in the autumn, around October and November. They softened the parched ground so that sowing could take place. The late rains came in the spring, between March and May, before the ripening was complete. Farmers scheduled sowing and reaping in accord with these climatic patterns, but the approach, duration, and extent of the rains themselves were out of their hands. Once the sowing had been completed, the farmers could only oversee the field and wait for the rains to come. However, farmers were not entirely passive. They had to work hard to prepare the fields, removing stones and plowing the land prior to sowing the seed. Farming was not an easy occupation.

So it would be with the coming of the Lord. Living a life in accord with Christian principles is not easy. There is seldom immediate gratification for such righteousness. Farmers at least knew when the rains could be expected, but the Christians really had no idea of the time of the coming of Christ. The author insists that the *parousía* is at hand, but we know that eventually they had to reinterpret just what this might mean. As it stands, there is an urgency to this exhortation (the Lord is at hand). However, the longer they had to wait for his coming, the more significant patience became.

A second admonishment warns against complaining about one another. The reason for such complaint is not given, but that is not necessary because people can always find something to complain about. Whatever the case may be, they are told not to judge lest they themselves be judged (cf. Matt 7:1; Luke 6:37). Once again, the imminence of the *parousía* is suggested. This time Christ is characterized as a judge standing at the door (*thýa*; cf. Rev 3:20). The image suggests some kind of final judgment.

Finally, believers are instructed to take the prophets as their models in bearing the hardships of life and in waiting patiently for the coming of the Lord. The author could be referring to the ancient prophets of Israel, whose devotion to God was revered by all who cherished the religious tradition. Or the reference could be to those faithful Christians who went before them or who were even at that time proclaiming the gospel of God. Calling on such witnesses as models of virtuous living served as a reminder of the unavoidable hardships of life that every person must endure and the patience required of those who in the midst of such hardships wait with excitement for the *parousía* of the Lord.

## Matthew 11:2-11

The gospel passage for this Sunday can be divided into two distinct sections. One recounts the exchange between Jesus and some of the disciples of John the Baptist (vv. 2-6); the other reports Jesus' own praise of the Baptist (vv. 7-11). The response Jesus delivers to John's disciples is really intended for the Baptist himself. It seems that John had heard of the works of "the Christ" (the Greek equivalent for "Messiah"). This does not mean he had heard of the ministry of Jesus. John is probably referring generally to the Messiah, whoever that might be. He knew the teachings of the prophets regarding this person; he was aware of the signs that were to signal the dawning of the time of fulfillment to be inaugurated by the Messiah. The fact that he sent disciples to find out whether Jesus was indeed this person suggests that either he knew nothing of the wonders Jesus had already performed or he did not see all of the eschatological signs he had expected to see. After all, release of the captives was one such sign (cf. Isa 61:1), and he (John) was still imprisoned.

In his response to the query, Jesus links some of his own wondrous deeds with prophetic allusions to eschatological visions of the time of fulfillment: sight has been given to those who were blind and hearing to those who were deaf (cf. Isa 29:18); those who were lame now leap like deer (cf. Isa 35:6); those who were dead now live (cf. Isa 26:19); finally, those who are poor hear the good news (cf. Isa 61:1). These were all signs of the dawning of the eschatological age. They were also indications of the type of Messiah Jesus would be. Those who were expecting a political or military leader who would free them from Roman domination or a priest who would bring them together as a cultic community might not be pleased with Jesus. Perhaps even John would be disappointed. To this Jesus replies: Blessed is the one who is not scandalized *(skándalízō)* in me.

The scene shifts sharply. Jesus no longer speaks to John's disciples about himself as Messiah; he now speaks to the crowds about John as precursor. Once again the discourse is a response to a question: What did you go out to the desert to see? The reference to desert is significant. You would expect to find a fierce and resolute man there, not one that resembles an unstable reed shaken by the wind. You would expect to find someone dressed simply, perhaps in camel's hair with a belt around his waist (cf. 3:4), not one attired in the fine clothing associated with the palace. You would expect to find a prophet, and that is exactly what you found.

Jesus points out the excellence of John the man, yet at the same time the limitations of his office as precursor of the age of fulfillment. John receives the highest praise given by Jesus to any man: No human being was greater than John the Baptist! He was the messenger promised by God to prepare God's way (cf. Mal 3:1; in the prophet it is God who comes; in Matthew it is Jesus.). As important as this is, John merely prepared the way, he did not follow Jesus along that way. From an eschatological point of view John stood on the threshold of the new age; he did not cross over into it. On the other hand, anyone who accepted Jesus' invitation into the reign of heaven belonged to the new age. Regardless of how insignificant they might be in this new age, as citizens of the reign of heaven they enjoyed a privilege John did not know.

## Themes of the Day

Halfway through our Advent pilgrimage to eschatological fulfillment we pause for a moment to celebrate Gaudete Sunday, a Sunday for rejoicing. The readings provide us with a glimpse of our destination. A wonderful sight is set before us, a sight that is truly a reason for rejoicing. However, the readings are not all scenes of peace and tranquility. There is a paradox here. On the one hand there is a scene of burgeoning life and restoration; on the other there is a picture of John the Baptist languishing in prison. It seems that the reality toward which we are traveling is not devoid of hardships, and the journey itself can at times seem endless. Patience is also an Advent theme.

### Restoration and New Life

Isaiah paints a picture of regeneration. The desert that once seemed to be dead is now bursting with life; eyes that lacked sight, ears incapable of capturing and holding sound, limbs without strength, and tongues devoid of speech are all given new life. There will be no death in that age of fulfillment, no limitations, no mourning. The world will be again as it was when it first came forth from the divine womb. It will be young and vibrant, innocent and brimming with promise. This fulfillment is the goal of our pilgrimage.

As we move deeper and deeper into the reality of God's presence in our midst we will discover the meaning of true fulfillment. We will realize that there is life in what we thought was death; there is strength in what we thought was weakness. The barrenness of the world's pretensions will be revealed and the paucity of its standards will lie bared before us. The eschatological age will turn things upside down, but we will recognize our place in the world and see it in a new way.

### The Kingdom of Heaven

John the Baptist plays a double role in the drama that unfolds in the gospel reading. He is a kind of standard for judging the privilege of entering, here and now, the kingdom of heaven. There is no doubt that in death he has joined the communion of saints and does indeed enjoy the fullness of God's kingdom, but during his lifetime he never saw its dawning. He was the herald of the coming of Jesus, the one who prepared for him, but John himself died before the death and resurrection of Jesus opened the floodgates of the eschatological tide. By comparison, the privilege of being even the least in the kingdom of God is far greater than being the prophetic herald of its coming. It is our good fortune to have been invited to join the pilgrimage, to have been baptized into the kingdom of God.

John also serves as a model of patience in suffering. His circumstances teach us that moving toward eschatological fulfillment is not without cost. The road we are asked to travel may not always be clear. Like John, we might be filled with doubts. Like John, we might fail to recognize the signs of the eschatological age. Even in such straits John is a model for us. He shows us how to remain loyal even during these times of hardship. He is not only the herald of the eschatological age, he is an example of faithful endurance. This same theme is expressed in the letter of James. That writer exhorts the Christians of his time to follow the example of the prophets, who suffered hardship for their proclamation of the word of God. According to Jesus himself, of all the prophets there is none greater than John.

### Patience

Just as Matthew presents us with the example of John the Baptist, so James describes the patience required of the farmer. The farmer not only toils arduously but must wait to see the fruits of that toil. The farmer exemplifies the Advent theme of the woman who is heavy with child, who endures the pains of childbirth, but whose pain is overcome by joy when the child is brought forth into the world. It is to this farmer that we look to see how we should proceed on the pilgrimage with determination and steadfastness. The eschatological day of fulfillment will dawn in its time; all we can do is discharge our responsibilities regardless of how demanding they might be and wait for that day patiently, convinced that it will come in God's due time.

### Fourth Sunday of Advent
#### Isaiah 7:10-14

This passage from Isaiah may be one of the best known yet least understood passages from the great sixth century prophet. The passage itself contains many ambiguities, but the predominant way it has been understood may result more from its New Testament reinterpretation (cf. Matt 1:23) than from the Isaian context.

Ahaz, king of the southern nation of Judah, is told to ask for a sign that will confirm earlier promises made either to him personally or to the Davidic dynasty of which he is the present heir. There seem to be no bounds to the character of the sign he is allowed to request. "The sky's the limit!" Actually, the scope is even vaster. The sky is only one limit; the other is the netherworld *(sheʾôl)*. Ahaz can go as high or as low as he wishes. He is given every opportunity to trust that God will be faithful to promises given. However, he chooses not to trust in God's faithfulness, and he compounds his lack of faith by feigning piety; he insists that he will not tempt the LORD.

The prophet Isaiah responds in apparent exasperation. His formal address (house of David) indicates that what is at issue has to do with the monarchy and not merely with the personal life of the king. Ahaz' behavior has not only piqued the people, but God is tired of it as well. Nevertheless, although the king may not be faithful, God's fidelity endures and God will give a sign even though Ahaz has refused to request one. The sign that will be given and the meaning it carries are the heart of this prophetic utterance.

Two Hebrew words are translated "virgin": *beṯûlâ* and *ʿalmâ*, the word used here. The first is the more technical term, usually referring to one who has not had any sexual encounter; the term here denotes a young woman of marriageable age, perhaps a virgin, perhaps not. The identity of the young woman in this passage has been variously interpreted as the wife of the king, the wife of the prophet, or some unidentified young woman. The last option is discounted by most interpreters, but as many opt for the second as the first. Because the name "Emmanuel" translates as "God with us" and because the king was believed to be a sign of God's presence with the people, the first option has been held by commentators to be the most obvious. However, neither the identity of this young woman nor her virginal status is the focus of the prophecy.

The child and the implication of his name are the real issues here. It should be noted that the mother ultimately names the child Emmanuel. The king plays a rather insignificant role. One might think that a royal child who signifies the presence of God with the people would indeed be a sign of God's fulfillment of the promise made to David concerning the perpetuity of his dynasty (cf. 2 Sam 7:12-16). Still, this passage is more concerned with the sign than with anything else. At issue is the fulfillment of God's promise to be present with the people, regardless of the situations within which they find themselves. This prophecy encourages the king to place his trust in God, not in the child himself.

## Psalm 24:1-2, 3-4, 5-6

The psalm response consists of a hymn of praise of God the Creator (vv. 1-2) and a section suggesting the question-response ritual associated with a liturgical pilgrimage (vv. 3-6). An interesting feature of this response is the variety of images of God it contains: creator, savior, patron deity.

Behind the imagery of the opening verses is ancient Near Eastern cosmology. In various myths from that tradition we find a primeval struggle between gods of chaos and deities who would establish order. Chief among the former were Yam (the Hebrew word for sea) and Nahar (the Hebrew for river). In the myths a vibrant, young warrior god conquers the chaotic waters, establishes dominion over the universe, and assigns the celestial bodies their places in the heavens. The similarities, both linguistic and in content, between such a myth and the picture painted in the psalm response are obvious. However, in this psalm response the focus is the earth, which, the ancients believed, floated like a saucer on the cosmic waters. This earth and all those who live on it belong to or are under the protection of the LORD. Such a claim would not be made if there were any doubt about the LORD's sovereignty. This is the deity who exercises dominion, and this would only be the case if the LORD were the victorious warrior who conquered the chaotic cosmic force.

The liturgical portion of the response opens with an exchange of question and answer. In the mythological tradition the high god dwelt on the highest mountain. In Israel's liturgical tradition, Jerusalem with its Temple was identified with this high mountain. Therefore, as the pilgrims approached the walls of the city, certain persons (probably priests) inquired about the suitability of those who would enter the sacred precincts. According to the strict regulations in Israel's cultic tradition, only those who conformed to the prescriptions of holiness or cultic purity were allowed to enter. These prescriptions generally governed external regulations. Hands that had not touched forbidden objects were considered "sinless." However, here external conformity is not enough. An appropriate inner disposition is required as well. The polarities of chaos-order have been transformed into those of unclean-clean and then unworthy-worthy.

The male bias in Israel's liturgical participation is seen in the reference to those who receive blessing. This notwithstanding, God is further identified as God of Jacob and savior, clear allusions to both the ancestral and the exodus traditions of Israel. These epithets are not only divine titles but are also reminders of God's special election and care of this people. Fidelity to the prescriptions of the religious tradition was the primary way to live out faithfully one's role as covenant partner of God—the covenant associated either with the ancestors (cf. Gen 17:2) or with the exodus tradition (cf. Exod 19:5). The blessings and reward mentioned flowed from such fidelity. This was all dependent upon the people's desire to seek the face of God, to be united to God through commitment and devotion.

One very important final point must be made. The two sections of this psalm response may at first glance appear to be quite separate. However, joined together as they are, they interpret each other. In other words, the God who first called and then saved Israel is none other than the Creator who vanquished the cosmic powers of chaos; the God who exercises dominion over all creation is the one who established an intimate covenant with this people.

## Romans 1:1-7

This passage follows the standard literary pattern of the introduction to a letter of the Hellenistic period. It consists of the name of the sender (v. 1), the name of the recipient (v. 7a), and a brief greeting (v. 7b). What makes this introduction unique is the extended statement of faith that follows Paul's self-identification. In the Greek the entire passage is but one sentence consisting of ninety words. There is a formality to this introduction not found in Paul's other letters. Some commentators suggest this might be the case because he was writing to a church he had not established or even visited. Paul did not know these Christians, so he did not write to them in a familiar fashion.

Paul identifies himself in a threefold manner. He is a slave *(doúlos)*, an apostle *(apóstolos)*, and one set apart *(aphorisménos)*. It is unusual that a Roman citizen such as Paul would refer to himself as a slave and glory in this designation. However, this is a way of proclaiming the lordship of Christ in his life, and according to Paul there could be no higher honor than to be so known. He is also an apostle, one who has been called by another and sent out to deliver a message. It was not through his own initiative that he became an apostle but by God's election, and as an apostle he delivers the message determined by God and not by himself. Finally, Paul maintains he has been set apart for the service of the gospel. Each of these self-designations contains a humble acknowledgment of God's initiative in Paul's calling and of Paul's own subordination to Christ Jesus.

Paul relates the gospel he preaches to the promises made by God through the prophets (vv. 2-3). In this way he highlights the link between the message of Jesus and the ancient traditions of Israel. The christological formula that follows (v. 4) continues this linkage. By stating that Jesus was a descendant of David, Paul is attributing to him all the promises and blessings ascribed to the person of David and to the dynasty he had established. As descendant of David, Jesus is a member of the people of Israel and placed squarely in the fold of human nature. However, he is more than human. Through his resurrection he has been established Son of God in power. Paul is not here suggesting that Jesus became Son of God through his resurrection but that the resurrection uniquely manifested his divine sonship. Finally, this was all accomplished according to the Spirit of holiness. Here we find the foundation of Paul's trinitarian faith.

Paul next describes his understanding of the ministry to which he has been called (vv. 5-6). He considers his apostleship a grace from God, bestowed upon him through the agency of Christ. He maintains it will be through the agency of his own apostleship that the Gentiles will be brought to faith in Jesus. He personalizes this message by singling out the Christians in Rome to whom he is writing the letter. They are beloved of God, called to be holy people *(hagíois)*. The lines of initiative and responsibility are clear. God has called Paul and set him apart for the ministry of the gospel. Paul is sent to the Gentiles in order that they too be set apart for God.

The extended statement of faith is concluded, and Paul completes the formal epistolary introduction with a salutation composed of the Greek expression "grace to you" and the Hebrew greeting "peace." The salutation is really a prayer for grace and peace, coming conjointly from God and from Christ. This is more a christological than a trinitarian statement. Christ is divine, for he too is the source of blessing. Furthermore, Paul calls God "our Father," an allusion to Christian adoption through baptism rather than to the union of the Father and the Son.

## Matthew 1:18-24

Although the gospel reading for today purports to be an account of the birth *(génesis)* of Jesus, it is really an explanation of his descent *(geneá)*. It comments on his conception and on the early days of Mary's pregnancy. The passage describes how Jesus, though not the natural son of Joseph, can through him be legitimately considered a son of David.

The marriage customs of the day are clearly sketched. Betrothal, which usually lasted about a year, was a legal agreement conferring on the couple the status of marriage. The woman remained in the home of her father until the public ceremony, within which the man came in procession to bring her into his own home. The union was usually consummated after this. At this time the man and woman were given the titles "husband" and "wife," and the commitment and fidelity associated with those titles were expected of them. In fact, infidelity on the part of the woman was regarded as adultery. If one of them died before the final celebration, the survivor was considered a widow or widower. It was during the time of betrothal that Mary conceived.

When it became clear that Mary was carrying a child, Joseph was faced with a dilemma. Since the child was not his, it would appear that Mary had committed adultery and, according to the Law, should be stoned (cf. Deut 22:23-24). Joseph was a righteous man *(díkais)*, an observer of the Law. What was he to do? Jewish Law did allow a man to divorce his wife (cf. Deut 23:13-21; *Mishnah Sotah* 1.1, 5), and not wanting to expose Mary to shame, this was the course of action he chose. The Bible contains many stories of divine revelations, either in dreams or through the mediation of heavenly messengers. Both means of communication are employed here. In a dream an angel reveals the true origin of the child and exonerates Mary of any impropriety. Joseph is encouraged to embark on the final phase of the marriage. He does so, and thus the child becomes his legal son.

Several features of the angel's message call for serious consideration. First, the mention of the Holy Spirit is probably less a question of trinitarian theology than of eschatological fulfillment. In Jewish prophetic theology the spirit of the LORD was believed to be the renewing force in the future messianic era. Here, at the dawning of that era, the power of the spirit is manifested in an extraordinary way. It should be noted that the angel announces the child's name. "Jesus" is the Greek form of the Hebrew *Yᵉhōšuʿa*, which means "YHWH is salvation." The name is further explained: *yōšîʿa*, or "he will save." Third, a solemn formula of fulfillment is proclaimed. This formula highlights the connection between what has been described and something significant in the earlier tradition of Israel. Fourth, the child is given a name that indicates his role in history, Emmanuel *(ʿimmânû-ʾēl)*, "God with us." These two names identify Jesus as the saving power of God and the presence of God in the midst of the people.

The Emmanuel citation from the prophet Isaiah (7:14) comes from the Septuagint, the Greek version of the Bible. There the Hebrew *ʿalmâ* (young woman of marriageable age) is translated as *parthénos* (virgin). Regardless of how the tradition of Mary's virginity eventually developed within Christian theology, the content of this passage indicates the concern is less with Mary's actual perpetual virginity than with the origin of Jesus in God. He comes from God; he is the salvation from God; he is the presence of God; the new age will be born through him.

## Themes of the Day

With the Fourth Sunday of Advent we are on the threshold of the eschatological age of fulfillment. Today's readings tell us that faith is required for us to step over that threshold. Before us are set two figures, two examples of human response to the call to faith: Ahaz, who failed the test, and Joseph, who despite his quandary was a paragon of faith. Paul offers us three ways of living out this faith: as a slave of Christ Jesus; as an apostle; as one set apart for service. The psalm response tells us that we end the Advent season where we began, in procession to the mountain of the LORD, the holy place of God.

### Faith

Despite all the excitement associated with our pilgrimage to eschatological fulfillment, despite all the assurances it will be an experience of peace and abundant life, the mystery for which we long requires the risk of faith. Despite all the times we have celebrated the nativity, we still do not have full comprehension and understanding. Ahaz was unable to take the blind step of faith into trust of God, and he tried to hide his weakness behind false piety. In contrast, Joseph's piety precipitated the dilemma in which he found himself. Which course of action was the faithful way to go? We are not required to set in motion events of the future as were these two men. Rather, we are invited to enter deeply into the event before us. Will we step into a life of deeper faith and commitment, or will we merely participate in the external celebration of the feast? Only we can decide, and only we will really know the decision we make.

### Slave, Apostle, One Set Apart

The circumstances of our lives influence the way we live out our faith. We may not like the word "slave" *(doúlos)*, but it refers to one who is devoted to the service of another. This is precisely what Christians are called to be and do, to be devoted to the service of Christ. Our primary commitment must be to Christ and to the way of being human he has shown us. We must be committed to what enriches life and not to what diminishes it. We must be committed to the good of people and not to the hoarding of things. To be a slave of Christ means we will be decent, upright women and men, people of integrity. This is certainly the kind of life we really want to live, and as we step into the eschatological age, we are called to recommit ourselves to this way of being human.

The apostle *(apóstolos)* is one sent to deliver a message. Again, all Christians are somehow called to be apostles. We may not be official heralds of the gospel, but we proclaim our faith in the way we live our lives, in the kindness with which we treat others, in the honesty of our business transactions. We proclaim the gospel when we stand for justice, when we forgive those who have offended us, when we show compassion to those who suffer. As we step into the eschatological age, we are called to recommit ourselves to genuine Christian living.

At baptism we were all set apart *(aphorízō)* for service. When we love, it is not difficult to serve the loved one. Friends, lovers, spouses, and parents do this without question. Service of others is perhaps the most common way of living out our faith. We serve others when we teach children how to live in our world, when we dedicate quality time to our primary relationships, when we visit the sick, when we care for the elderly, even when we car-pool. As we step into the eschatological age, we are called to recommit ourselves to others and to deepen our service of them.

### The Mountain of the LORD

With the completion of the Advent season we have arrived at the mountain of the Lord, the place where God dwells. Like T. S. Eliot, we may discover we have arrived at the place where we began, but we now see it in a new light. We ascend the mountain and enter into the presence of God at the same time God comes into our lives. We are on the threshold of the new age. How will we enter this moment?

# The Nativity of the Lord (Christmas)

| | | | |
|---|---|---|---|
| **Mass at Midnight** | | | |
| Isaiah 9:1-6<br>A Son is given to us | Psalm 96:1-3, 11-13<br>Let the heavens be glad | Titus 2:11-14<br>The grace of God has appeared | Luke 2:1-14<br>Today a Savior has been born |
| **Mass at Dawn** | | | |
| Isaiah 62:11-12<br>Behold, your Savior comes | Psalm 97:1, 6, 11-12<br>A light will shine on us | Titus 3:4-7<br>Out of mercy, he saved us | Luke 2:15-20<br>The shepherds came |
| **Mass During the Day** | | | |
| Isaiah 52:7-10<br>Announce the good news | Psalm 98:1-6<br>All have seen God's salvation | Hebrews 1:1-6<br>God has spoken through the Son | John 1:1-18<br>The Word became flesh |
| **The Holy Family of Jesus, Mary, and Joseph** | | | |
| Sirach 3:2-6, 12-14<br>Honor your parents | Psalm 128:1-5<br>Blessed are those who fear the LORD | Colossians 3:12-21<br>Over all these, put on love | Matthew 2:13-15, 19-23<br>Flight into Egypt |
| **January 1, Solemnity of the Blessed Virgin Mary, Mother of God** | | | |
| Numbers 6:22-27<br>The LORD bless you and keep you | Psalm 67:2-3, 5, 6, 8<br>May God bless us | Galatians 4:4-7<br>God's Son was born of a woman | Luke 2:16-21<br>The shepherds came to Bethlehem |

| | | | |
|---|---|---|---|
| **Second Sunday After Christmas**<br><br>Sirach 24:1-2, 8-12<br>Wisdom lives with God's people | Psalm 147:12-15, 19-20<br>God's Word became human | Ephesians 1:3-6, 15-18<br>We are children of God through Christ | John 1:1-18<br>The Word became flesh |
| **January 6,<br>The Epiphany of the Lord**<br><br>Isaiah 60:1-6<br>God's glory shines on us | Psalm 72:1-2, 7-8, 10-13<br>All nations will adore God | Ephesians 3:2-3a, 5-6<br>Gentiles are coheirs of the promise | Matthew 2:1-12<br>We saw his star |
| **Sunday After January 6,<br>The Baptism of the Lord**<br><br>Isaiah 42:1-4, 6-7<br>Behold my servant | Psalm 29:1-4, 3, 9-10<br>The LORD will bless with peace | Acts 10:34-38<br>Anointed with the Spirit | Matthew 3:13-17<br>The beloved Son |

# The Nativity of the Lord (Christmas)

## Initial Reading of the Christmas Lectionary

*Introduction*

Employing the same method of reading the Lectionary that was used in the Advent season, we interpret the constellation of readings the Christmas season offers. While the Advent season incorporates three cycles of the Lectionary, the Christmas readings, with the exception of the choices for the feast of the Holy Family and the Baptism of the Lord, do not vary. Each group of readings will be examined and interpreted. A presentation of the entire mosaic of readings will follow this exercise.

*First Testament Readings*

The Midnight Mass at Christmas begins the season. It is a word of emancipation. The people in darkness now see, for the child is born. The close of the season, the feast of the Baptism of the Lord, identifies the child as the servant, the one who brings about this liberation by the word of God proclaimed with power. The child-servant heralds a profound and wonderful reversal. Something cosmic has happened at Christmas. In the midst of the darkness, the light that emanates from the child-servant reveals God's intentions to the ends of the earth.

The other First Testament readings in this season unpack the richness of the transformation this birth brings about. The people who were lost are no longer forsaken. The glad tidings of this good news will be sung by the servant, who proclaims liberty to captives and sight to the blind, who gives a name to the nameless and a voice of significance to women and children and to those who are forsaken. The transformation touches the very heart of the domestic world of parents and children and calls for an ordering based in love and the promise of the world made new. In this order the blessing of peace is found, a blessing that is both a hope and a charge. It is a hope for God's peace among the people, while at the same time it is a charge to live in such a way as to make the blessing of wisdom real in their lives and in their worlds.

At the end of the Christmas season we are told that God's glory goes forth from the city to the ends of the earth. All nations, races, peoples, tribes, and languages will proclaim the wisdom of God. The mystery of Christmas will gather all people into the promise of God. This is the work of the child-servant. It is a work caught up into the wonderful reversal of justice and compassion that still whispers in the night.

## Psalms

The lectionary refrains for the Christmas season fall into three categories: declarations of the wonderful work of God among the people, the implications of these works in the lives of those who call upon the LORD, and the universality of these works and the extension of God's glory.

Some of the refrains speak of the reality of the birth of a Savior. They declare that the birth takes place today; it is the present moment that knows the wonder of the Word made flesh. Other psalms are shouts of exultation and praise in face of this wonder. They express the unimaginable joy of those who receive God's gift and find in it their fulfillment.

Toward the end of the season the refrains move us into an understanding of the specific implications of the gift of the child that is born among us. They voice the happiness of those who know the Lord. The blessings of God abound, and this elicits the praises of all the people. The ultimate blessing given is peace.

## Epistles

An examination of the epistles of the season shows they are an extended meditation on salvation. In these Christmas readings we are told that salvation has been given and now has appeared among us. It is offered to all people, and it brings with it the hope and promise of righteousness. Salvation is not our achievement; it is a gift that comes from God's Spirit.

The implications of this salvation are demonstrated in several epistle readings. Relationships change when salvation is received. First, we are called into forgiveness, patience, and the meekness that allows us to embrace one another in love and mercy; second, the relationship with God is made intimate, and we are able to call God *Abba*. This new way of naming God allows us the inheritance of God, for we find ourselves to be children of God and sisters and brothers in Christ. All of these new relationships take place within the Church, which is not only the place of salvation but, more importantly, the people of salvation. The beauty of God and the wealth of the inheritance are ours in the community of faith.

Salvation is not confined; God's salvation is for all, Jew and Greek alike, and the wealth of it is to be shared among the nations. Peter preaches the universality of this gift in the name of Jesus, who was anointed by the Spirit. In the power of the same Spirit we are called to the same universality. In our day it takes the form of inter-religious dialogue and recognition of the religious value present in other religions of the world.

The epistles offer an ever-widening understanding of salvation, from the first appearance of the gift of Christmas, to the preaching of the apostles, to our own appreciation of it.


*Gospels*

The gospels for the Christmas season remain somewhat narrative, punctuated by passages from the Prologue of the Gospel of John, which reveals the theological significance of the Christmas story itself. There are two ways of viewing the gospels of the season. The first is a simple narrative reading that begins with the birth of Jesus, moves through the visit of the shepherds, to a reading that provides a theological interpretation of the events recounted. The narrative continues with episodes from the life of the young Jesus followed by a theological interpretation. It concludes with two accounts of the manifestation of Jesus' true identity; the first is to the Magi and the second is at his baptism.

The gospels move from the birth to the baptism. They invite the religious imagination to accept the baby as the gift to the nations, the one whose ministry in the Spirit will make him a servant of God and of humanity. The Christmas season ends with us poised for Jesus' mission and his entry into the place of testing, which will begin the lenten season.

The way of reading recognizes a kind of chiastic structure:

> a) birth
>> b) shepherds
>>> c) theological interpretation
>>>> d) visit to Temple
>>>> d¹) visit to Temple
>>> c¹) theological interpretation
>> b¹) Magi
> a¹) baptism

The birth and the baptism are both forms of manifestation; the shepherds and the Magi represent all those to whom the revelation is given, both the poor and the prosperous, the Jews and the Gentiles. The theological interpretations can be matched, leaving the visits to the Temple as the focal point of the chiasm. In such a structure the accent of importance is placed on the texts at the center. In this case, the religious observances in the Temple offer a key insight into the season.

Both accounts show that Jesus is grounded in the practices of his religious tradition. He is willing to be consecrated to God and to be incorporated into God's people. Both accounts also mention Mary's unique role in the drama of the incarnation. She realizes the uniqueness of her child when he is found in the Temple with the teachers and when the shepherds come prior to his circumcision. In both instances she stands in awe, not quite understanding. Jesus is the Lord who comes to his Temple; God has visited us in the form of a little child. Mary is the image of the Church; we rejoice in the birth of the child, but we do so not quite understanding the depth of this mystery. The child is born and redeemed but only so that we can be redeemed and reborn.

### Mosaic of Readings

The Christmas cycle is a proclamation of the presence of God in human history. The Lectionary weaves narrative, prophecy, and exhortation together, producing a tapestry of breathtaking beauty. A threefold message is contained in this work of art: (1) something definitive has happened in history, and it is the work of God; (2) this marvel is a gift that can be received by all people of goodwill, a universal gift extending to all the nations; (3) when received, this gift forms us into a community that lives by it and shows itself to be the place where God has pitched a tent among us. The Church is the community of grace and compassion for the life of the world. Christmas is the promise of Easter in the lives of those who receive the child-servant.

# Readings

### The Nativity of the Lord (Mass at Midnight)
#### Isaiah 9:1-6

The reading begins with the announcement of deliverance. Its message of hope and consolation is expressed through the contrast between light and darkness (v. 1). The darkness does not seem to be merely a temporary clouding of the light. Rather, the entire land is in darkness, and the people seem fixed in it. It is to them that a great light comes. This light ushers in a complete reversal of fortune, which the rest of the reading describes. The people did not bring this reversal on themselves; they are the recipients of God's good pleasure (v. 6).

After the initial announcement the prophet speaks directly to God, enumerating examples of God's acts of graciousness toward the people. First, the people embrace the entire experience of salvation with unbounded joy (v. 2). The rejoicing is of the kind that follows either an abundant harvest, when there is enough yield to satisfy the needs of all, or an assessment of the spoils of war after the battles have been won. In each instance there is a sense of relief that the hardships of the venture are over as well as great satisfaction with the respective fruits that accrued from it.

The prophet next describes how God liberated the people from oppression (vv. 3-4). In the past they were shackled like oxen, forced to do arduous, ignoble tasks. They were subjected to physical abuse at the hands of another. But God intervened and destroyed the instruments of their servitude. The reference to Midian calls to mind the defeat of that nation under the leadership of Gideon (Judg 7:15-25). Not only was that defeat absolute, it was also miraculous, accomplished through divine power. Mention of this battle along with the military title LORD of hosts may also explain the reference to spoils of war. The comparison is clear. God and only God has gained salvation for the people, and that salvation is absolute.

The final verses of the reading sketch a picture that is most astounding. The salvation reported is realized through the agency of a child (vv. 5-6). The responsibility for establishing the peace described here rests on his shoulders. The names ascribed to him signify the feats expected of him. Like every good leader he will make wise decisions, and he will be able to guide others in their judgments. However, he will surpass all others in this regard; he will be a wonder! God-Hero comes from the Hebrew word *gibbor*, another term with military connotations. This child will be a divine warrior, capable of withstanding all the evil cosmic forces. He will be Father Forever, unfailing in providing for those under his care. He is Prince of Peace, the one who both secures and safeguards it. This peace is more than the absence of war. It means wholeness, completion, harmony. It is a condition in which all things, human beings, animals, and plants, follow their God-given destinies undisturbed.

All of these titles were in some way associated with the Davidic king. He was expected to be a wise ruler, mighty in battle, a father to his people, and the guarantor of peace. However, a more-than-human dimension has been added to them here. This child may belong to the line of David, but he is an extraordinary descendant. The exercise of his dominion is the saving action of God.

### Psalm 96:1-2, 2-3, 11-12, 13

The psalm calls upon the people to praise God for the wonderful acts of salvation that God has performed (vv. 1-3). Three times the psalmist calls them to sing God's praises, each time highlighting a different aspect of the song. First, they are called to sing a new song. This is only appropriate, since their salvation has transformed them into a new people. No longer will laments be acceptable. The only kind of song worthy of the event of salvation that has unfolded before their very eyes is a hymn of praise.

Next, there is a note of universality to the singing. Not just Israel but all the earth is called upon to sing this song of praise. Finally, along with the call to sing is a summons to bless the name of the LORD. Since a name was thought to contain part of the very essence of the person, a call to bless God's name is really a summons to give praise to some aspect of God's character. The aspect to be praised is the salvation God has brought about for the sake of Israel. All the earth is called to announce the good news of this salvation and to announce it unceasingly, day after day.

God is here portrayed enthroned as lord of the entire earth, accomplishing wondrous deeds that all the nations have been able to witness. The final verses (vv. 11-13) show that these deeds include the creation and governance of all the earth as well as the direction and judgment of all nations. Such universal power and dominion could only be wielded by a God who is above all other gods, one who reigns supreme in the heavens but who executes authority on earth as well. God not only performs these marvelous feats, but he does so with justice and faithfulness. This God is indeed powerful, but he is also trustworthy. Such is the portrait of the God of Israel painted in the psalm.

The reasons for the praise for which the psalmist calls are specifically laid out. God is acclaimed as the ruler of the heavens and the earth. It is quite understandable to claim dominion over the earth for God. Even minor gods were thought to exercise some power on earth. Since heavenly beings were frequently personified as deities in other ancient Near Eastern religions, it is a bit more difficult, though not impossible, to ascribe rule over them to God. It is clear from the early verses of this psalm that here the heavens are merely regarded as elements of natural creation. As such, they join in honoring the Creator. What is interesting is the inclusion of the sea and all the watercourses over which it has control in this chorus of praise, since the sea was traditionally considered a mythological force of evil. That it is regarded as merely a creature of God is quite significant.

All the rejoicing is focused on an upcoming event, the advent of the LORD. The rejoicing itself does not overshadow the reason for the LORD's coming, which is judgment. God will judge the earth. As harsh as the notion of judgment may be, God judges with righteousness and truth (v. 13). Divine judgment is less a question of power than one of harmony and right order. God's

rule is one of right order. Salvation itself is really a return to this order. Therefore, the judgment of God is really the establishment of harmony, the establishment of peace.

## Titus 2:11-14

This short excerpt from one of the Pastoral epistles is a confession of faith in the
saving grace of God. The verb "appeared" (v. 11) is testimony to divine revelation. The reading proclaims that God's grace is no longer something for which
the people wait with longing. It has arrived; it is an accomplished fact. Furthermore, the universality of this salvation is clearly stated. It is not merely for an
elect group, whether Jewish or Christian; it is for all humans *(ánthrōpois)*.

This grace, or good favor, takes the form of salvation, a theological concept
with profound Jewish and Hellenistic connotations. In Jewish thought salvation was seen as rescue from the perils of life, and it was accomplished by God.
Many narratives of the First Testament recount such salvation. In the Hellenistic mystery religions, which were so prominent at the time of the writing of
this letter, the initiates shared in the mythical divine being's victory over
death, and they were thereby assured a share in blissful life in the hereafter. In
this particular passage the concept of salvation includes aspects of both views.
It is because they have been saved from the perils of evil that the Christians
have been empowered to live lives of moral integrity in this world. On the
other hand, their salvation has come to them through the sacrifice of Christ
Jesus, and they still await a future divine manifestation.

The reading also declares that God's saving grace imparts the kind of
training necessary to combat the forces of a godless world and to live truly
Christian lives (v. 12). The author of the epistle does not enumerate what
these evil forces might be. (Discerning them may well be even more of a challenge than opposing them.) What *is* confidently stated is the assurance that
the power of divine grace will adequately prepare believers to live in modera-
tion, righteousness, and piety, regardless of the opposition within themselves
and from others they may have to face. Such a courageous way of living is evidence that the age of fulfillment has indeed arrived. However, this indication
of "realized eschatology" does not erase the expectation of a "future eschatology." Christians live an "already but not yet" existence. Their moral lives are
both signs of and expectation of the final fulfillment.

Christ Jesus has achieved this great grace. His sacrifice of himself has redeemed and cleansed those who have accepted him. The moral character of
this salvation is apparent in the final verse of the reading. The Christians are
redeemed from lawlessness, and they are purified as a people who then perform good works. There is no doubt this is God's saving grace, but it comes to
the people through Christ Jesus. The Pastoral epistles generally identify God

as the savior of all. The Greek in this passage is quite awkward. It reads: "great God and savior of our Jesus Christ" (v. 13). It is only in translations that Jesus is identified as the Savior. Whatever version is chosen, the intimate relationship between God and Christ is obvious, and that is the point of the reading.

This passage does not call for hope. As a profession of faith, it affirms a tenet of belief and holds it out as a truth that calls for commitment. Salvation has been won by Christ and offered to all. We decide how we will respond to it.

## Luke 2:1-14

Luke's version of the birth of Jesus is one of the best-known stories of the Bible. It has inspired both paintings and music down through the ages. Even small children know about the census, the swaddling clothes and manger, the shepherds and the angels' song. Our critical examination of the text should not so demythologize the imagery that we undermine popular religious imagination and overlook the power of its message.

The details of the story serve two very important purposes: they situate Jesus in first-century history, and they link him with the house of David. The miraculous incidents that accompany this birth might lead some to conclude that the event recounted was too other-worldly to be genuinely historical. Such a position throws into question the very heart of the doctrine of the incarnation. Situating the birth within the world of real Roman rulers underscored its claim that God was indeed born at this time, in this place, among these people.

The details also identify Jesus as the Davidic Messiah. Since the gospel tradition maintains that Jesus was from Nazareth, it was important somehow to establish him in Bethlehem. The account of the census, regardless of how inaccurate its details may be, explains how his parents happened to be in Bethlehem at the time of his birth. The Davidic link is made again and again. Joseph was of the house of David, and so he traveled to the town of David to be registered (vv. 4f). The first to pay homage to the newborn were Bethlehemite shepherds, simple herders not unlike David himself. Mary and Joseph do not play the central roles here. Joseph is important because of his Davidic lineage, and Mary is identified as Joseph's pregnant wife. The entire focus of the story is on the child.

A related theme is God's choice of the most unlikely and frequently overlooked members of society to accomplish God's will. From the outset this child was treated like an unwelcome stranger, almost an outcast. He was deprived of the comforts that normally surrounded a birth, born away from the home of his parents, away from the warmth and love of an extended family. He was not visited by friendly neighbors but by shepherds, a class of people considered unclean because their occupation often required that they deal with both the birth- and the death-blood of their flocks. The stage is set to tell the story of God's predilection for the poor, the overlooked, and the forgotten. Like his ancestor David, the one who was destined for great things had a humble, even despised, beginning.

Despite the unconscionable affront by human beings, the birth of this extraordinary child was surrounded by celestial grandeur. An angel announced the wondrous event to the lowly shepherds and was then joined by countless other angelic beings who filled the night with their song of praise of God. The glory of God could not be contained, and it burst forth encompassing the shepherds with its brilliance. The disregard of the human community was outstripped by a display of heavenly exaltation.

This simple yet beloved Christmas story contains a complex christology. On the one hand, the author takes great pains to situate Jesus squarely within the human family of David. On the other hand, he identifies Jesus as Savior and Lord, and he paints a picture of heavenly celebration. Such is the mystery of Christmas.

## Themes of the Day

The Church commemorates the birth of Christ with three celebrations of the Eucharist: at midnight; at dawn; and during the day of Christmas. These inaugural celebrations usher in the Christmas cycle with themes that will be revisited several times before the season ends. In the middle of the night the community gathers to meditate on three of these themes: the historical birth of Jesus; the liberating king; and the new age of fulfillment of God's promise inaugurated by this king.

### The Birth of Jesus in History

The gospel clearly situates the birth of Jesus within a historical epoch, that of the Roman rule of Israel in the first century. The proclamation announced on this day places Jesus' birth within the affairs of human life with its struggles and cares. These historical and human details indicate that this birth is not simply an otherworldly event; it happened at a specific time and in a specific place. The incarnation of God happened among us! God comes to us in our time, in our place, and in our history.

Once the historical reality is established, the story reveals another dimension of this birth. The ordinary becomes transparent and reveals the extraordinary; the divine is known in the child. Angels appear in order to declare that this is so. Night glows with the radiance of daytime, and the midnight hour is the breakthrough of everlasting light. Only those of humble heart come to know this wonder. The reality of the mystery is offered, but its significance is missed by many. In this case it is not the influential who recognize the gift but those society forgets. It is the shepherds, the poor and forsaken subjects of history, who happen upon this birth and who believe. They behold it, and they come to embrace it. In fact, it is the nature of this child, born in history, to reverse the orders of power.

## The Liberating King

The readings contain strong images of the royalty of Lord. God is portrayed as a valiant liberator worthy of praise and worship. It is God who champions the cause of justice and who brings a liberation that can reverse history and the ways of war, power, and oppression. The coming events will satisfy the needs of all. However, the reversal of the fate of history is made more shocking by the fact that the one who is the mighty warrior and conqueror of the nations is a child, one who rules with peace and integrity.

This child is Jesus. However, the child is the servant who can conquer the alienating forces of history, the one whose life is destined to change the fate of humanity. Furthermore, it is the child as the weak and voiceless one, the one who has neither power nor legal rights, who will shake the empire. God's reversal of the long-standing realities of this world is accomplished through the apparently insignificant, through the gift of this child, who is given to us in the middle of the night.

## The Age of Fulfillment Has Begun

With the birth of the child, something new has happened: the age of God's fulfillment has arrived. This is an age of grace and fresh hope, made available to all people of good will. It is an era of redemptive presence, because now all people can walk in the newness of life and grace. This age has come about by the gift of Christ poured out for us. We can see it, touch it, taste it. It is a time when justice and mercy appear, when nations seek the ways of peace, and when reconciliation transforms us. And yet, while the age has begun, it is not yet fully realized.

We live in the traces of this hope, believing in its presence and awaiting its fulfillment. In a real sense, although we are celebrating Christmas we are still an advent people who await the coming of the Lord in the abundance of mercy yet to erupt in history. We are a tensive people, not tense with the cares of this age but poised to receive the gift of the ever-deepening promise that was born among us and whose birth continues to astound us at every appearance of hope.

## *The Nativity of the Lord (Mass at Dawn)*
### Isaiah 62:11-12

The message of these two short verses is extraordinary in several ways. First, it has been prescribed by the LORD. Second, it concerns the redemption of Israel and is to be proclaimed to the whole world. Third, it deals less with the promise of a future salvation than with the announcement that salvation is already on its way. Fourth, it includes new names for the people and for the city of Jerusalem, names that show that both the people and the city have been radically transformed.

This prophetic notice repeats some of the content of an oracle that appears elsewhere in the book of the prophet Isaiah (40:10). In the earlier oracle it was the LORD God who was coming in might with reward and recompense. Here God is identified with salvation, and it is this salvation that comes with reward and recompense. Salvation has been accomplished. The new names for the people and the city make this clear.

In order to appreciate the significance of the title "the holy people," we must remember that ancient Israel was a nation whose political and social exile was interpreted by the people themselves as punishment for their sins. Now they have a new name, and that name implies they are not only forgiven, but they enjoy a new identity as if newly born. The people are also called "the redeemed of the LORD," a title that marks a double relationship with God. The obvious meaning points to a bond between redeemer and redeemed. The former is someone who pays the debt of another and thereby provides deliverance from any kind of servitude; the latter is the one released from debt. The less obvious relationship implied in the title is one of kinship. Normally, it was a close relative who paid the debt. These titles point to the intimate and remarkable attachment God has for this people.

Zion/Jerusalem is also given new names (cf. 62:2-4), indicating a new identity. The city that was overthrown, depopulated, and plundered will once again attract people to it. It will then be called "Frequented" or "Not Forsaken." The name declares that the desolation of the past is forgotten. Salvation has come to the city.

### Psalm 97:1-6, 11-12

The psalm opens with the traditional enthronement declaration. "The LORD is king!" It is appropriately followed by the exclamation: "Rejoice, and be glad!" The response suggests that the manner of God's rule calls for celebration, and this celebration extends beyond the confines of Israel to the entire world (v. 1).

A report of the manifestation of God's glory, composed of several commanding images, follows. It begins with a description of the divine king's throne, which is established on the firm foundation of justice (v. 2b). Unlike other regimes built merely on brute force or military victory, both of which might fail and result in dethronement, God's rule is constructed in the permanence of justice and right order. It is not only impregnable, it is immutable. It stands secure, enabling God to govern undisturbed by any threat and assuring reliable protection to all those under God's jurisdiction. The throne is surrounded by clouds and darkness (v. 2a), reminiscent of the theophany that took place on Mount Sinai (Exod 19:16-19) and the signs of the presence of God when the ark of the covenant was finally installed in the Temple in Jerusalem (1 Kgs 8:10-12). The cloud itself obscures the glory of God, leaving everything else in darkness.

Along with the image of a securely erected throne is a description of a royal procession (v. 3). A raging fire, symbolizing the purifying presence of God, is in the lead of this entourage, consuming all the enemies of God in its path and purging the land as it proceeds. The verbs in this verse are in the Hebrew imperfect tense, suggesting that this refining manifestation is an event in the future.

The report of the dramatic features of the theophany continues (vv. 4-6). The verbs in this section are in the Hebrew perfect tense, implying that what is portrayed has already taken place or is presently unfolding before the eyes of those witnessing the spectacle. The event described resembles a forceful upheaval of nature, something like an earthquake that makes the whole world tremble. This disturbance is accompanied by an enormous display of lightning, enough to illumine the entire sky and all the earth below it. In many ancient Near Eastern religions these spectacular demonstrations were frequently associated with a storm god or variously credited to minor gods, offspring of the principal deity. In this psalm they are nothing more than natural phenomena that accompany the theophany of the God who reigns as king of all creation.

The massiveness of mountains has led people to believe that they are also invulnerable. Such is not the case here. Instead, their durability is negligible, and they melt like wax before the intensity that attends the manifestation of God. The heavens, celestial beings considered divine in some religions but regarded in Israel as merely awesome creatures of God, join in praise of God's righteous rule. This colossal theophany is a phenomenon observed by all, and it challenges all to live righteously in accord with the righteousness of God that has been manifested (vv. 11-12). The psalm concludes with a glimpse into the lives of those who accept this challenge.

## Titus 3:4-7

The appearance of the saving love of God is the theme of this passage, which was probably part of an early Christian baptismal hymn. The salvation achieved through Jesus Christ completely changed the lives of the newly baptized, drawing a striking contrast between the way they lived before their conversion and the way they live now. As in the reading for the Christmas Mass at Midnight, this passage announces what has already taken place. The love and kindness of God have appeared; it is not a future event for which believers ardently long. Furthermore, it has appeared in time, in history. The coming of Christ coincides with the ultimate manifestation of God's love.

It is clear that this love is a free gift springing from the mercy of God and not simply compensation for righteous living. On the contrary, salvation is bestowed first, so that, having received it, Christians might then be able to live virtuously. It is this saving grace that justifies them, not any moral effort on their part. Everything is a free gift bestowed out of divine largesse. This includes love, mercy, and justification in this life, and the inheritance of eternal life. God's magnanimous giving is celebrated here.

A rudimentary trinitarian formula appears in the reference to baptism. The text explicitly states that it is God's love that appears and it is God who saved us through the washing of baptism. It was God who poured out the Spirit through Jesus Christ. As with the passage from Titus read at the Mass at Midnight, there is no clear line drawn here between God as savior and Christ as savior. It may be that such distinctions had not yet been sharply made. What is clear in this reading is that rebirth and renewal come through the Spirit, and divine titles (savior) and activities (saving) are attributed to Christ.

Although the author uses commonplace Hellenistic religious language such as "rebirth" and imagery such as cleansing through water, the theology of justification is drawn from Jewish thought. There the righteous are those who, though unfaithful, have been acquitted by God. The initiative is always God's, and it is usually exercised in the face of human infidelity. From a human point of view the absurdity of such a situation is unmistakable. Still, accepting the opportunity of freely given justification is not an easy thing to do, and many people do not even believe it is possible. For those who believe it is both possible and desirable, reluctance to avail themselves of salvation is the real absurdity.

This baptismal hymn both proclaims tenets of faith and indirectly exhorts believers to embrace a life of virtue. Since they have been born anew, they can now act in a new way, walking blamelessly in this world in anticipation of the next. Christians are radically changed because God has entered their lives. The appearance of God's love has accomplished this.

## Luke 2:15-20

It is because of the gospel reading that this Mass was formally referred to as the Shepherds' Mass. The passage itself is rich with theological themes: response to divine revelation, theological insight, evangelization, praise of God, contemplative reflection.

One of the reasons shepherds were considered irreligious by the self-righteous of the time was their failure to participate in regular ritual observance. Their occupation required them to be with the flocks, supervising their grazing and growth and protecting them from harm. This responsibility prevented them from being part of the worshiping community. That they would leave their flocks in the hills and go into Bethlehem in search of a newborn was extraordinary. Should anything happen to the sheep while they were gone, they would suffer a financial setback if the flock was theirs, or they would be liable to the owner if the flock belonged to another. The shepherds were most likely poor, and they would be well aware of the risk they were taking.

This did not deter them. They were responding to divine revelation and had received a heavenly directive. Rather than being irresolute they went in haste, leaving behind what gave them the little security they may have enjoyed. These humble shepherds were the first to respond to the divine invitation to leave all for the sake of this child. While it is true that they did return to their flocks, their willingness to initially leave them has religious significance.

When they saw Mary and Joseph and the baby, they understood what the angel had said. What was it that gave them insight? What enabled them to recognize their Messiah and Lord in this unlikely situation? What is it that enables any of us to see traces of the divine in the very ordinary of life? Might it be openness to God and willingness to accept the unexpected that provides eyes of faith that can see beyond appearances?

Themselves convinced of the arrival of the long-anticipated Messiah, they proclaimed this to all they met. Such behavior must have compounded the jeopardy into which they had placed themselves. They had not only abandoned their responsibilities and put their own futures at risk, they were now making incredible claims. The text does not say those who heard them were convinced by their words. It says they were astonished. Evangelization does not itself guarantee success.

The shepherds do not seem to have been influenced one way or another by the reactions of others. They return to their flocks praising God. Their lives may have resumed their normal pattern, but the shepherds themselves could not have been the same. They had had a profound religious experience; they had heard and understood a startling religious truth; they had placed this religious truth above their own personal needs and aspirations. These humble, probably uneducated, people had been transformed into believers, and their final response was praise.

The author inserts one sentence that has little to do with the shepherds. Mary reflected on all of this. She is the believer who has already experienced the power of God, and she stands silently before the mystery of what God has done. She treasures these things in respectful contemplation.

## Themes of the Day

Traditionally, the Mass at dawn is called the Shepherds' Mass, because the gospel text recounts the visit of the shepherds. The readings highlight four themes: God's initiative of universal transformation; the profound gratitude that ensues in face of this gift; the life of baptism that is receptive to God's initiative; and solidarity with outcasts as a sacrament of God's presence.

### God's Initiative of Universal Transformation

God has taken the first step in our redemption, and the offer of grace is made to all people who can hear and who will embrace the gift. As a season, Christmas is really a time of universal goodwill. Widespread change seems to occur at Christmas; human hearts appear to soften, and we greet each other with good wishes and cheer. Because we remember the gift of God's love and receive it anew in our hearts, our interactions are transformed.

Left to our own designs, we tend to set limits and to remain caught in the status quo of our lives and our answers. God disrupts the order of life and, by a divine undertaking of grace, starts something that can impact the universe. The declaration of Christmas is bold: all this possibility has already been realized; we can already live by the new name of God's compassion and justice. Transformative love comes alive in our midst, in the city where people dwell. The possibility of a new way of life happens now, and the future will usher it in among us. Receptivity is all that is asked of us.

### A Matter of Great Gratitude

In response to God's gracious gift of transformation we are invited to rejoice with grateful hearts. The royal infant whose birth we celebrate is the one who was promised, the one who inaugurates the age of transforming grace. The child is, in fact, the long-awaited messianic king. He is the source of rejoicing in those who receive him with great gratitude. He is recognized by the angels and by the shepherds but not by the power structures of the city. Only those who are open to God's gift can receive it with thanksgiving. When it is received, however, marvelous things happen. Our identities are changed, all the cosmos joins in the festivity, and righteousness blossoms in history.

### The Life of Baptism

For Christian believers the life of baptismal fidelity is the grateful response to the gift of God's initiative. This baptismal life is rooted in the mystery of the triune

God, the God in whom believers are baptized. It is a life lived in the rebirth of the spirit of God that animates us to live blamelessly, to live in a way that shows our appreciation of this gift, to live lives that are manifestations of holiness.

It is by living such lives that Christians are able to proclaim that God has truly appeared and to become the place of the ongoing appearance of God's gift of transformation. What becomes clear is that this is not our work, it is the work of God, who has come to dwell with us and in whom we find our cause for celebration. The baptismal life is a life of gratitude for the gift we have received, a gift whose fulfillment will be realized by God in the future.

## Solidarity with the Poor

While Christmas morning may be a time for opening gifts and for family celebrations, it is also a time when people of means reach out to those who are less fortunate. Christmas celebrates generosity, first the generosity of God and then our generosity with each other, especially with the poor. Solidarity with the outcasts of society, with those who are barred from the power structures of society, is in keeping with the spirit of Christmas.

The birth of the baby is the source of joy for the poor and those who are scandalously forced to the fringes of Bethlehem. The despised shepherds become the privileged ones to whom the message is announced. God's gift finds a place among the outcasts and continues to dwell at home there. It is indeed a Christmas grace to be able to find God there, to rejoice in the gift, and creatively to respond to it. Thus we become the place where shepherds and kings meet in adoration and where the future of God's justice dawns.

## The Nativity of the Lord (Mass During the Day)
### Isaiah 52:7-10

The proclamation of good news is dramatically portrayed in this passage in several ways. It begins with a sketch of a messenger running swiftly over the mountains with the message of peace and salvation (v. 7). The focus here is on the feet of the runner. This highlights his speed and determination. They are beautiful feet because of the message of deliverance they carry. There is an excitement in this scene; the message holds such promise. There is an urgency as well; the people to whom the messenger runs have been desolate for so long, waiting for a ray of hope. The content of the message is peace, good news, and salvation. The messenger announces to Zion that its God is king, the one who rules and controls the circumstances of its existence. By implication this means that the city will be able to partake in the victory of its God.

The first to see the runner are the sentinels who stand watch on the walls of the city (v. 8; cf. 40:9). Since a messenger can bring either good news or bad news, from a distance these sentinels cannot be certain of the content of the message. However, their joyful reaction to the approach indicates that it signals not only a proclamation but the very actualization of the message that will be proclaimed. In a way, the coming of the runner is itself the promise to be proclaimed. The people know what the coming of the messenger means, for what they have longed to see now unfolds before their eyes, and they shout for joy. As is so often the case with the prophetic word, its very proclamation effects the salvation it announces. Seeing the runner and hearing his words of peace and salvation are themselves the good news. With the announcement of peace and salvation, the LORD has indeed returned to the city.

First the sentinels cry out with joy. Then the very ruins of the city are exhorted to break forth in song (vv. 9-10). No longer need they lie destitute, unable to stand with dignity or protected with honor. God comforts and redeems the people dwelling within them. The inhabitants are now a renewed people, and so the city itself is renewed. Peace is no longer a hoped-for dream, nor is salvation only a promise for the future. They are now accomplished facts for which to rejoice.

The prophet sketches yet another dynamic picture. In it we see the arm of God bared, revealing the source of the divine power that effected the deliverance the city now enjoys. This demonstration of strength serves to remind the people of the might of their protector. It also alerts the other nations to the seriousness with which God acts as protector of this people. It is not enough that Zion is rescued. The other nations of the world must see and acknowledge this power. They must recognize both the scope of God's power and the identity of the people who most benefit from it. Just as the messenger heralds peace and salvation to Zion, so the deliverance of the city heralds the mighty power of God to the ends of the earth.

## Psalm 98:1, 2-3, 3-4, 5-6

The psalm belongs to the category of enthronement psalms, praising God as king over all (v. 6). It opens with a summons to sing a new song to God (cf. Psalm 96). The reason for this new song is the marvelous new things God has done. The psalmist follows this summons with an enumeration of some of the acts of God (vv. 1b-3).

God is first depicted as a triumphant warrior whose right hand and outstretched arm have brought victory. The victory sketched in these verses seems to have been historical, one that transpired on the stage of Israel's political experience. However, it is not too difficult for a god to defeat human forces. If God is to be acclaimed as king over all, there must be a more comprehensive victory, one that demonstrates preeminence on a cosmic scale. Behind the image of the triumphant warrior is just such an understanding. The divine warrior is the one who conquers the forces of chaos. This is a cosmic victory. These verses do include mention of a sweeping victory (v. 3). Thus it is correct to say that God's triumph is universal and undisputed.

The focus here is on the particularity of Israel's salvation by God. Two aspects of this victory are mentioned. First, the victory, or demonstration of righteousness, is really vindication meted out in order to rectify a previous injustice. Second, the victory follows God's recall of the covenant promises made to the house of Israel. Lovingkindness *(ḥesed)* and faithfulness *(ĕmûnâ)* are closely associate with these promises (v. 3). It is important to remember that this particular psalm praises God as king precisely as a triumphant warrior. This implies that either the righteous character of God's rule or its universal scope was challenged, so any victory here is really a reestablishment of right order. In other words, it is vindication.

An important feature of this reading is its statement about the relationship that exists between God's saving action and the promises God made. The psalmist claims it was remembrance of the covenantal lovingkindness *(ḥesed)* that prompted God to save Israel. It was because of the promise made to the ancestors that the divine warrior stepped in and triumphed over Israel's enemies. That triumph, which was revealed to all the nations, is the reason for the psalmist's call to praise God in song.

The final verses elaborate on the musical element of the praise. The instrumental directions are quite specific. They could have originated in an actual enthronement ceremony. Two instruments are explicitly mentioned, the lyre and the trumpet. The first was frequently used as accompaniment for singing; the second might really be a reference to the ram's horn, which, like a clarion, announced days and seasons of ritual celebration. Here, as at the foot of Mount Sinai, it announces the coming of the LORD in glory (Exod 19:16).

## Hebrews 1:1-6

This confessional hymn celebrates Christ as the agent of revelation, creation, and salvation. It begins with a comparison of the ways God communicates with humankind. In the past God spoke to the ancestors through the prophets; in the present God speaks a definitive word to the believers through God's own Son. Without disparaging the former way, it is clear that the author of this letter considers divine revelation through Christ far superior to the earlier method. The former method of revelation was fragmentary, incomplete. As a reflection of God's glory and an exact representation of God's being, Christ could be called the perfect revelation of God.

The Father-Son language found in most translations of this passage does not appear in the Greek, with the exception of the references included at the end of the reading (1:5-6). It is the sense of the overall passage that suggested the translations. Because of the Father-Son covenantal relationship, the Son of God enjoys a position of unrivaled privilege. This Son is the heir of all things and the agent through which the world was made and through which it continues to be sustained. Besides preeminence, this assertion suggests preexistence.

The description of the relationship between the Son and God borrows elements from two very different yet related Jewish traditions: the monarchy and Wisdom. The first originated in the ancient Near Eastern world where people believed their kings were either human manifestations of the deity or their actual physical offspring. "Son of God," a royal title usually conferred on the king at the time of his coronation, was understood literally. Such royal ideology was a serious religious threat to Israel, and many within the nation objected to the establishment of the monarchy (cf. 1 Sam 8:1-22). Political circumstances compelled the people to reconsider, and eventually Israel was able to reconcile having a monarchy within a monotheism (cf.2 Sam 7:8-17). "Son of God" was demythologized, and the title was understood figuratively rather than literally.

Two of the references at the end of the reading (vv. 5-6) belong to this royal tradition. The first comes from an enthronement psalm (Ps 2:7), the second from the Davidic covenant passage (2 Sam 7:14). When this ideology is applied to Christ a very interesting reinterpretation takes place. The title "Son of God" is remythologized and understood literally once again. This is the meaning intended here.

The author also reinterprets the Wisdom tradition. There we find that it was through Wisdom that God created (Prov 8:22-31; Wis 9:9), and Wisdom is the pure emanation of the glory of God (Wis 7:25-26). In this tradition the line between Wisdom as creation of God and Wisdom as attribute of God cannot always be clearly detected. This very ambiguity lends itself to christological interpretation.

Since the Son is indeed the Son of God as well as the Wisdom of God, it stands to reason that he would be superior even to the angels. As the agent of salvation, he sits enthroned in the place of greatest honor, at the right hand of God. The author of this letter has used the royal theology of Israel to illustrate his christological faith. Jesus is indeed the Son of God, the Wisdom through whom all things came to be and remain.

## John 1:1-18

The Gospel of John begins with one of the most profound statements about Jesus found in the entire Second Testament. Its lofty christology is comparable to that found in the reading from Hebrews. Both characterize Christ as preexistent; both depict Christ as an agent in the creation of the world. The reading itself falls easily into five parts: a description of the role the Word played in the creation of the world (vv. 1-5); a brief sketch of a witness named John (vv. 6-8); an account of the Word's entrance into the world (vv. 9-14); a report about John (v. 15); an acknowledgment of our participation in Christ's glory (vv. 16-18).

The opening statement, "In the beginning," recalls a comparable statement in Genesis (1:1). This parallel may be the author's way of implying that the coming of the Word into the world is as momentous as was the first creation. The Word is then described in language reminiscent of the figure of Wisdom personified (Prov 8:30; Wis 7:25). Like Wisdom, the Word was actively involved in creation. Unlike Wisdom, the Word is explicitly identified as divine. In a free-flowing manner the author ascribes life-giving power to the Word, life that gives light. The mention of light enables the author to draw one of his many contrasts. This particular contrast is between light and darkness. At times the light is synonymous with life (v. 5a). At other times it represents truth (v. 5b). At still other times, the Word is the light (vv. 7-9).

The witness named John is not further identified. However, it is presumed that it is the Baptist, since the words that appear here are later ascribed to him (v. 15; cf. 1:30). There seems to be a definite need to contrast the Word and John. While the Word is the true light that comes into the world, John is merely the witness who testifies to the authenticity (vv. 7-9) and superiority of this light (v. 15). Though designated by God as a witness to the Word (v. 6), John is neither a peer nor a rival of the Word.

Up to this point only John is clearly a historical person. The Word resides in some primordial place. Now the Word enters human history, and the next section describes both the incarnation and the rejection by human beings that the Word faced (vv. 9-14). In a third contrast, the author distinguishes between those who were somehow intimately associated with the Word but did not accept him and those who did accept him and thereby became children of God. "His own" may be a reference to other members of the Jewish community. Here ancestry does not make one a child of God; only faith in the Word made flesh can accomplish this.

Several translations state that the Word "made his dwelling among us" (v. 14). A better reading of the Greek might be "tenting." It calls to mind the tabernacle in the wilderness where God dwelt among the people (Exod 40:34) as well as the tradition about Wisdom establishing her tent in the midst of the people (Sir 24:8). The Word of God, who is also the holiness of God and the Wisdom of God, now dwells in the midst of humankind. Women and men have been greatly enriched by this divine presence, transformed by the love that first prompted God's revelation and Christ's incarnation.

### Themes of the Day

With this set of readings the Christmas celebration gains a new depth of theological meaning. There is progression of insight from the midnight gathering to the assembly that takes place during the daytime hours. At midnight the birth in history was proclaimed. At dawn the initiative of God's gift was declared, and the baptized community's joyful gratitude was announced. In this third celebration, we meditate on the identity of Christ and on our own new way of life in the Word made flesh. Four themes can be identified: salvation takes place before our eyes; salvation is universal; the child is the reflection of God's glory; it is with eyes of faith that we recognize the Word of God made flesh.

### *Salvation in Our Midst*

If our eyes are open and alert, we can see marvelous things. We can see that God has won a victory for us. The victory is tangible; it is realized in our midst. What kind of victory is it? It is an overwhelming victory, one that conquers the enemy and conquers permanently. Strong military language accents this victory. The power of God brings about a sweeping triumph that is unparalleled. What is conquered is evil itself, the disruptive powers of sin that choke off life and bring unbearable suffering to weak and strong alike. God has won victory for us, and blessed are those who have eyes to see the messenger and ears to hear the glad tidings of triumph. When the victory is experienced, salvation is ours. We can take it in and make it our own. By this victory God is glorified, the past is made right, and there is righteousness for all.

### *A Universal Salvation*

God's victory has a profound impact upon every place, every time, every people. The birth of the infant, who is a king in David's line, promises salvation to all who long for it. This salvation is a new vision of wisdom, one that has been realized in Christ, who is God's agent of grace in the world. This means that we humans have another chance at living lives of righteousness. We are now able to be forgiven and to forgive. We have been graced with the presence of one who can make a difference in our lives, if only we would be attentive to what is in front of us. It is a new world, one of inclusivity and righteous honor. It is a new age, ushered in by the child who is leading a victory procession.

### *The Glory of the Child King*

Christ is the source and signal of God's universal salvation. The child king is the reflection of God's glory, and we are in awe of the wonder made known to us. What we need are eyes of faith to see this marvel of God's wisdom, this reflection of God's glory in the fragility of the child of Bethlehem. The clouds of heaven are opened for just a moment, but it is enough time for us to catch a glimpse of the divine character of this mysterious child. He is the exact representation of God; he sits at God's right hand; he is God's Word made flesh.

### The Word of God Made Flesh

Ultimately, the eyes of faith allow us to see the fullness of God's revelation. The glory of the infant king is the very presence of God made flesh. Jesus is the eternal incarnate Word who has pitched his tent among us. Ours is not a distant God. Rather, the incarnate Wisdom of God is among us, and we are called to a change of heart that will allow us to see this wonder. But something more happens. In this turn of events, the participation in the mystery can be so complete that we can know a deep communion in the reality offered in Christ. The marvel is that the child who was born among us can be born again and again in those who believe. The divine Word continues to draw close to those who seek to live lives of sincerity and truth. We too can be children of light. Grace becomes incarnate in those who believe, for the salvation of God is made flesh in us. The tent of God is pitched wherever salvation is offered, and the ways of evil and death are overturned. All of this takes place right before our eyes.

## The Holy Family of Jesus, Mary, and Joseph

### Sirach 3:2-6, 12-14

The book of Sirach (or Ecclesiaticus) belongs to ancient Israel's Wisdom tradition. Unlike the prophets, who either call the people back to the religious traditions from which they have strayed or console and encourage them to be faithful in the face of overwhelming suffering, the Wisdom tradition is a collection of insights gleaned from the successful living of life. It is instruction that provides a glimpse into a way of living that has brought happiness in the past, but it describes it in order to encourage similar behavior that will bring corresponding happiness in the present or future.

The reading for today is instruction about family life, identifying the kind of living that will result in family harmony. Although the teaching originated with a society that was patriarchal (the father is the head) and a perspective that was androcentric (male-centered), it continues to have value for societies that do not share these biased points of view. The focus is the respect and obedience that children (both male and female) owe their parents (both mother and father). Finally, it is presumed that the children are adults, not young children. The final verses (vv. 12-14) make this clear.

In the face of the patriarchal nature of the original society, the admonition to honor one's mother (vv. 2-7) takes on added importance. The parallel construction within which each of these references to the mother is found suggests that respect and obedience are due both of the parents, not just the dominant father. The text states that the mother has authority over her sons and that this authority was confirmed by the LORD (v. 2). In the face of the androcentric bias found in the text, this point is quite significant.

True to the character of Wisdom instruction, Sirach lists the blessings that follow such a way of life. The dutiful child is promised life itself (vv. 1, 6), remission of sins (vv. 3, 14), riches (v. 4), the blessing of children (v. 5a), and the answer to prayer (vv. 5, 6).

The final verses exhort the adult son to care for his father in his declining years. The picture portrayed is quite moving. The weakness of the elder is contrasted with the strength of the son, who presumably is at the height of his own powers (v. 13b). This son is told not to use his strength against his frail, elderly father but rather for the older man's benefit. This should be the case whether the father's infirmity is physical or mental. There is no mention of caring for his mother in the same way. This may be because in patriarchal societies it was presumed that women would be cared for by their fathers or brothers, then by their husbands, and finally by their sons. The head of the family was normally not so vulnerable as to be in need of care. At issue is not a question about which parent needs care; the admonition is to give it where needed.

Finally, the entire teaching about respect for parents, from the commandment (cf. Exod 20:12; Deut 5:16) to this admonition in Sirach, takes on a completely different perspective when we remember it is addressed to an adult child, and the responsibilities of respect and obedience are those of offspring who are mature.

## Psalm 128:1-2, 3, 4-5

This psalm is classified as a Wisdom psalm. It is clearly descriptive instruction that teaches rather than an address directed to God in praise or thanksgiving. The psalm contains themes and vocabulary associated with the Wisdom tradition such as reward and punishment; happy or blessed; ways or path. It begins with a macarism (v. 1), which is a formal statement that designates a person or group as blessed (or happy). This statement includes mention of the characteristic that is the basis of the happiness and then describes the blessings that flow from that characteristic. In this psalm those called blessed are the ones who fear the LORD, who walk in God's ways (vv. 1, 4) The blessing that flows from this attitude of mind and heart is a life of prosperity (vv. 2-3).

In the Wisdom tradition fear of the LORD is the distinguishing characteristic of the righteous person. It denotes profound awe and amazement before the tremendous marvels of God. While this may include some degree of terror, it is the kind of fear that accompanies wonder at something amazing rather than dread in the face of mistreatment. The one who fears the LORD is one who acknowledges God's sovereignty and power and who lives in accord with the order established by God. If anyone is to be happy and enjoy the blessings of life, it is the one who fears the LORD.

The blessings promised here are both material good fortune and a large and extended family. Large families, like vast fields, were signs of fertility and prosperity. They not only provided companionship through life and partnership in labor but also were assurances of protection in a hostile world. The promise of future generations (v. 6) guaranteed perpetuity for the family; its bloodline and its name would survive death and would endure into the next generation. Although the androcentric bias in the psalm is seen in its reference to the fruitful wife and numerous children (the Hebrew reads "sons"), the concern is really with the family as a cohesive and abiding unit.

The last verses of the psalm (vv. 12-14) redirect the focus from the good fortune of the individual to the blessing enjoyed by the nation. Mention of Zion, Jerusalem, and Israel indicates this (vv. 12-14). The reference to children's children holds both familial and civic importance. It bespeaks long life and the continuation of the family, but it also implies that the nation is prospering and will endure. The blessings come from God, but God resides at the heart of the nation in Jerusalem, the city of Zion (v. 5). The good fortune of the individual is really a share in the good fortune of the nation.

The final statement (v. 6b) is less a prayer than an exclamation: "Peace upon Israel!" Peace, *shalom*, is fullness of messianic blessings. This includes personal contentment, harmony with others and the rest of creation, adequate material resources. And all of this is the result of right relationship with God. The psalm begins and ends on the same note: "Happy are those who fear the LORD" and "Peace."

## Colossians 3:12-21

An exhortation to virtuous living is introduced with the stated rationale for such a manner of life. Because the Christians are God's chosen, holy and beloved, they should act accordingly. This moving characterization is followed by a very demanding program of behavior. The notion of clothing oneself with virtue does not suggest such behavior is superficial or merely outward show. It refers to the practice of wearing a uniform of some kind that readily identifies the role one plays in society. Christians are to be recognized on sight by their manner of living.

The virtues themselves (vv. 12-15) are all relational. They are directed toward others, requiring unselfish sensitivity. They may demand great sacrifice. This is especially true about bearing with the annoying and even repugnant behavior of others and forgiving them when they have been offensive. The motivation for such self-sacrifice is the forgiveness the Christians have received from God. The list continues with an admonition to love, the highest of all virtues. The peace of Christ, which is placed before them, should not be confused with mere tolerance or control imposed from some outside force. It is an inner peace that comes from right relationship with God and, therefore, true harmony with others.

The author seems to provide directives for some kind of communal practice. The Christians are urged to open themselves to the transforming power of the word of Christ, to instruct and advise one another, to join in praising God through psalms and other religious songs. These activities might take place during some kind of liturgical event or as part of everyday life. Whatever the case, the virtues that are fostered and the manner of living that is encouraged are all communal.

The final directives (vv. 18-21) reflect the household codes prevalent in the Greco-Roman world of the time (cf. Eph 5:22-29). This was a patriarchal world where the men who headed the families exercised total control over their wives, their children, and their slaves. There certainly must have been mutual concern within the families themselves, but it was not mandated by law. The heads of households held the lives of the members in their hands, to do with them what they deemed fit. In such a social context, the admonitions found in this passage are quite revolutionary.

While the author still insists that wives must be subject to their husbands, he instructs the husbands to act toward their wives with love and thoughtfulness. Children are still told to obey their parents, but fathers are advised to be moderate in the training of their children lest discipline become oppressive. The Christian virtues listed at the beginning of the reading, when practiced within the context of the family, appear to have transformed the patriarchal social customs of the day. What is emphasized in this Christian household code is not patriarchal privilege but male responsibility in the familial relationships. This means that, in Christ, the relationships between man and woman and child have been radically altered.

## Matthew 2:13-15; 19-23

The gospel reading for this Sunday consists of two discrete narratives, both of which are structured in the same way. They both begin with the form of the verb that indicates that the event described is contingent on the termination of an earlier event (when the Magi had departed; when Herod had died). This is followed by the exclamatory word "behold" *(idoú)* and the phrase "the angel of the Lord appeared to Joseph in a dream." Directives are then given, indicating both divine guidance and divine providence. Joseph's compliance with these directives results in situations the author regards as the fulfillment of prophetic sayings. In each instance the movement of the Holy Family is in direct response to the initiative of God.

The first narrative contains so many echoes of the exodus tradition that it is safe to say they were specifically chosen for that very reason. First, the family's flight into Egypt, precipitated by the hatred of Herod, recalls Joseph's escape to that same land because of the hatred of his brothers. Second, both the Holy Family and the family of Jacob/Israel remained in Egypt until the death of a ruler persuaded them to leave that country and return to their land of origin. The passage from the prophet Hosea (11:1) is meant to link these two returns. Finally, just as Israel returned to the land of its ancestors, there to be shaped into the People of God, so Jesus returns to his homeland, there to eventually establish the reign of God.

Through the agency of an angel, God first led Joseph and his family into Egypt and then later directed him to return to Israel. By means of yet a third dream Joseph was warned of the dangers present in the region of Judea, so he turned to the region of Galilee, specifically to the town of Nazareth. The gospel writer states that this decision was also in fulfillment of the prophets: "He shall be called a Nazorean." However, this claim of origin has raised more questions than it might answer. First, such a prophetic proclamation is found nowhere in the Scriptures. Nor is it considered a reference to any particular prophet. The plural "prophets" suggests that no specific passage was intended but rather that the important aspects about Jesus' identity, ministry, and destiny all somehow fulfill the expectations of Israel.

Read literally, the designation simply means that Jesus is a resident of the city. The word itself *(nazoraios)* is also the name of a Christian sect (Acts 24:5). However, both the name and the sect might be related to Nazirite, a group known from earlier biblical tradition (Samson in Judg 13:4-5), a group that some believed later had an influence on John the Baptist. Since Jesus did not observe the rigorous life associated with the Nazirites, this explanation of the name as attributed to him is unlikely. A final explanation links the designation with the Hebrew word *nēṣer* (branch). This position traces the gospel reference back to the Isaian prophecy about the messianic descendant of David: "A shoot shall come out from the stump of Jesse, and a branch shall grow out of his roots" (Isa 11:1). The image suggests the destruction of the great organization set up by David, the son of Jesse, and transferred to his heirs. What struggles to emerge from this ruin is insignificant in comparison with what once was prominent. Such an understanding corresponds to the insignificance with which Nazareth was viewed (cf. John 1:46; "Can anything good come out of Nazareth?").

This reading emphasizes the early Christian community's belief in the active presence of God in the events of the life of Jesus. It was God who directed Joseph and who saw to the safety of the child. The time of Jesus' rejection and death had not yet come.

## Themes of the Day

All of the major themes found in today's readings highlight the relational character of family life. In Sirach some of the dynamics of family living and responsibility as exercised in the ancient world unfold before our eyes. The rewards of faithfully observing these family codes are showcased in the responsorial psalm. Paul directs our attention to the manner of relational living to which we are summoned as members of the family of God, a manner of living that flows from the bond of perfection that unites us. The gospel narrative paints a picture of a family that follows the directives of God.

### Family Living

So much has been said recently about family values. But what exactly are they? The specifics of family customs and roles played within the family may be culture-bound, but it seems that the values out of which they emerge and that inform them are not. Sirach sketches a picture of ancient family customs, but it is easy to look beneath them and find values that are enduring and speak to us today. There we clearly discover the values of mutuality, respect, and service between wives and husbands, between parents and children, and between the young and the old. This does not mean there are no roles of dominance. However, these roles often disappear or, because of circumstances, revert to another family member. As Sirach demonstrates, the son who was once dependent on the father now becomes his caretaker. Despite the nature of the roles and the way they move from one person to another, mutual respect and care for those in need remain a constant.

These values challenge us today. Because of cultural differences we may not be inclined to live them out in the same way, but mutuality, respect, and care for others should still be the backbone of our living together. The challenge before us is to devise ways for husbands and wives to live in mutual esteem; for parents to honor the dignity of their children at the same time as children obey and show respect for their parents; for the elderly to protect the young even as the young watch over the elderly. Abuse occurs in far too many corners of the world, and no group seems to be spared its horror. The message from Sirach speaks to us today.

## The Family of God

While this feast considers the family unit as such, it also celebrates the Church as the family of God. Thus the values of mutuality, respect, and service become characteristics of the Church or the ecclesial family. What binds the family of God together are virtues as relational as are the ties that bind the members of the natural family together. While we use the metaphor of family and relate it to the Church, this does not mean that some within the community are mature and others are not. Within the family of God, the virtues outlined by Paul are to be lived in a mature manner, not one that is infantile. The Church is a community of adults who are called in one body to live in a collaboration of love, mutuality, and service. They are joined in a bond of perfection, not in subservience or neurotic antagonism.

It may be more challenging to live out these values within the Church, for those who are called to put on Christ, bearing with one another in compassion, kindness, humility, gentleness, and patience, must relate in this way with people who may be strangers. The natural family bonds are absent. Within the family of God there is great diversity; there are often significant differences. There it is neither blood nor marriage that binds, only the word of Christ in the hearts of the believers. It is no wonder that more than once in the reading for today Paul admonishes the Christians to forgive. The Church may be a different kind of family, but the values of mutuality, respect, and service are as essential here as anywhere.

## The Holy Family

The model for both the natural family and the family of God is the Holy Family. There we find mutuality in the relationships; we find compassion, kindness, and humility, gentleness and patience. In this portrait of the Holy Family, people do not claim privilege. Jesus, who was the Son of God, was cared for and protected by his mother and father. In today's reading it is Joseph, who is the head of the family, who is approached by the divine messenger.

Today the breakdown of family structure and the erosion of true family values have left many fathers and mothers adrift on the sea of confusion. Ours is a dangerous world for children. The gospel reading depicts Joseph as one who is open and obedient to the directives of God. For the sake of the safety of the child, he willingly leaves behind the familiar life he must have known and with Mary journeys to a foreign land. He is the model of a parent who puts the needs of the child before his own. Our children are not our possessions; they are our treasure and our legacy. They have been entrusted to us by God. In Joseph we see one who took this trust very seriously. This story is a marvelous example of family values in operation.

## A Celebration of Wisdom

It is not by accident that several of the readings for today deal with the theme of wisdom, which can be understood as seeking and savoring those insights gained from the experience of life that enable us to live fully and with integrity. In each reading we see that we arrive at wisdom through the way we live out the relationships closest to us. In the family we discover that while children are taught and molded by parents, it is the children themselves that teach the adults what it means to be a real parent. In the family we discover that husbands and wives fashion and shape each other into caring, loving, and forgiving partners. So it is in the family of God. There we discover that it is only in trusting relationships that we can live lives of mutuality, respect, and service. Modeling ourselves after Jesus, we learn to be compassionate, kind, humble, gentle, and patient. In the family of God we take on the most basic family characteristic—we put on love.

## January 1, Solemnity of the Blessed Virgin Mary, Mother of God

### Numbers 6:22-27

The blessing found in this reading may be one of the oldest pieces of poetry in the Bible. It is introduced by a statement that gives the content of the blessing both Mosaic and divine legitimation. Although it is the priests who ultimately bless the people, it is Moses who receives the blessing from God and who delivers it to Aaron and his sons (vv. 22-23). These are examples of mediatorial roles, one played by Moses and another played by Aaron and the priests.

YHWH, the personal name of God, is repeated three times in the blessing (vv. 24-26). There is some question about the actual use of this blessing, since there is a tradition, standing to this day, that forbids the use of the personal name of God. People believed that a name possessed some of the very identity of the person named. To know someone's name was to possess intimate knowledge of and to enjoy some form of control over that person. To know and use God's name presumes this kind of intimacy and control. In order to guard against such presumption, some other word or title was pronounced in place of God's name. According to the Mishnah, an ancient collection of Jewish Law that dates back to about the third century of the common era, God's personal name was pronounced only when the blessing was used in the Temple. Whatever the case may be, the power of the personal name of God cannot be denied.

The blessing itself is quite crisp and direct. It is addressed to "you," a singular pronoun that can refer to an individual or to the entire nation understood as one. Each line invokes a personal action from God: to bless with good fortune and to keep from harm; to look favorably toward and to be gracious; to look upon and to grant peace. Actually, there is very little difference in the petitions. They all ask for the same reality, that is, the blessings that make life worth living. This could mean different things to different people at different times, but basically, they are asking for peace. Peace is the fundamental characteristic of Jewish blessing, the condition of absolute well-being.

The reading opens with God giving directions to Moses. It closes with a final word from God. The priests are told to invoke God's name on the Israelites. The Hebrew would be better read "put my name" on them. This evokes the image of placing one's name on property in order to certify ownership. The priests are instructed to put God's name on the Israelites, indicating that they belong to God and that God will certainly bless them.

## Psalm 67:2-3, 5, 6, 8

The verb forms in this psalm make it difficult to be categorized. Some commentators believe the verbs are in past tense, and they classify the psalm as a prayer of thanksgiving for blessings already received. Others consider them a form of wish or bidding prayer, a moderate request for blessings not yet enjoyed. However the verbs are read, it is safe to consider the psalm as a prayer of blessing.

The psalm begins with a slight adaptation of the first words of the blessing used by Aaron and the priests who descended from him (v. 2; cf. Num 6:24-26). This use of this Aaronic blessing in a congregational prayer suggests the favors once promised to that particular priestly family are now sought for the entire people. The metaphor of God's shining face refers to the favorable disposition a smiling countenance reflects. The psalmist asks that God look favorably upon the people, that God be benevolent toward them.

God's goodness toward this people will redound to God's reputation among other nations. They will see the people's good fortune and will interpret it as the fruit of God's saving power on their behalf and God's continued rule over them. These other nations will conclude that only a mighty and magnanimous God would be able to secure such good fortune. Here prosperity is not used as leverage against others. Quite the contrary, it benefits even those who may not be enjoying it. It does this because it is perceived as coming from God and not merely as the product of human exploits or ingenuity.

The psalm moves from an acknowledgment of divine rule over one people (v. 3) to an announcement of universal divine governance (v. 5). All nations will not only rejoice over God's goodness, they will also be guided by that same God and ultimately will praise that God (vv. 6, 8). In other words, the good fortune of one nation is testimony to salvific activity of God. This in turn becomes the occasion of salvation for all the earth. One nation is the source of blessing for all. This is the fulfillment of the promise made to Abraham (cf. Gen 12:2-3).

The psalm ends with a prayer for continued universal blessing. It is the past tense of the verb in this verse that had led some commentators to conclude that all of the blessings referred to earlier were also bestowed and enjoyed in the past. They maintain that the plea here is that God continue to bless the people so that all nations will continue to revere God. Whether past or future, the psalmist believes that all good fortune comes from God. Others see this and praise God, and in this way God is made known to all the earth.

## Galatians 4:4-7

The mission of Christ to the world is the major focus of Paul's teaching in the verses that make up this reading. "The designated time" refers to that time in history when God brought the messianic expectations to fulfillment by sending his Son into the world. The word for "send" *(apostéllō)* carries the idea of authorization, as in the case of an envoy. The primary stress of this verb is less on the actual sending than on the commission, especially when it is God who sends. This passage, then, is concerned with the mission entrusted to Christ by God. Referring to Christ as God's Son establishes his divine nature; acknowledging that he was born of a woman establishes his human nature. The christology in this passage is rich and complex.

According to Paul, the goal of Christ's mission is to transform the Galatians from being slaves under the Law to being adopted sons of God. Normally in patriarchal societies only male offspring can inherit. Since legal status is the primary focus of this passage, the androcentric bias here becomes obvious. In a more egalitarian society the fundamental message of change of status, while inclusive, would remain basically the same.

Paul is here setting up the contrast between servitude under the Law and freedom in Christ. In order to do this he uses a social custom of his day. If an heir was too young to claim inheritance a legal guardian was appointed until the heir came of age. Paul compares the believers to underage minors, who, until "the designated time had come," could not claim what might be rightfully theirs. The Law acted as legal guardian. All of this changes with the coming of Christ. Christians are no longer minors bound to the tutelage of the Law. They are legal heirs, adopted children, because Christ is the only true Son. Does anyone need proof of this? The very fact that they are filled with the spirit of Christ and dare to call God by the intimate term *Abba* should be evidence enough.

Paul's attitude toward the Law is not as negative as it appears elsewhere (cf. Rom 7:7-24). Here it is a necessary guardian that carefully watches over minors until they are mature enough to take care of themselves. It is binding in order to teach; it restricts in order to instruct. Though it is inferior to the Spirit of Christ, it is faithful and trustworthy. However, once the Spirit takes hold of the believer, dependence on the Law ends and freedom in the Spirit, the rightful inheritance of the children of God, begins.

The reading ends as it began, declaring that all of this is God's doing according to God's plan. God sent the Son to make sons and daughters of the rest of us. This is accomplished by means of the indwelling of the Spirit, which empowers us to call God *Abba,* tender Father.

## Luke 2:16-21

This reading for the feast of the Solemnity of Mary is essentially the same as that of the Christmas Mass at Dawn. However, these verses include mention of the circumcision and naming of Jesus. Although this is a slight difference, the addition shifts the focus of the passage away from the shepherds to the child and his parents. First, the sight of this lowly family opened the eyes of the shepherds so they could understand the meaning of the message announced by the angels. Then, Mary took all of these mysterious events into her heart and there pondered their meaning. Finally, Mary and Joseph arranged for the child to be circumcised and named.

Circumcision was the ritual that initiated the males into the community of Israel. It was enjoined by God on Abraham and all his descendants, and from that time forward it was considered a sign of the covenant (Gen 17:9-11). As observant Jews, Mary and Joseph fulfilled all the prescriptions of the Law, seeing that the child was circumcised as custom dictated.

In addition to being circumcised, the child was named. When the angel appeared to Mary and announced that she had been chosen to be the mother of the long-awaited one, the angel also told her that the child would be named Jesus (1:31), which means "savior" (cf. Matt 1:21). Now almost everything the angel had announced has come to pass. Mary would have to wait to see how he would acquire the throne of his father David and rule the house of Jacob forever (cf. 1:32f).

## Themes of the Day

Liturgically, the Octave of Christmas commemorates several celebrations: the Solemnity of the Mother of God; the day designated for prayers for global peace; the beginning of the New Year. The Lectionary contains a variety of themes that resonate with these celebrations. The major themes are the person of Mary as the example of faith and contemplation and the blessing of peace for the New Year.

*Mary*

The gospel story, with the addition of the mention of the circumcision and naming of Jesus, is the same passage that was read for the celebration of the Christmas Mass During the Day. Placed within the context of the Solemnity of the Mother of God, however, the reading has a different emphasis. Here Mary is the focus, not the child. Although the shepherds are depicted as gaining insight into the presence of God by seeing this Holy Family, it is Mary who is described as holding all these things in her heart. She is the one who ponders the significance of these events.

By her willingness to hold all things in her heart, Mary becomes to Christians an inspiration of contemplation and reflection. She inspires us to consider deeply the significance of events rather than to go blandly through life without meaning or direction. She inspires us to constant reflection on the truths of the faith, which continue to be made real in life's experiences. She inspires us to fidelity to the practices of our faith, practices that are the disciplines of soul that lead the community to a clearer focus on God's presence in human affairs.

*Blessings and Prayers for Peace in the New Year*

The theme of peace appears on many levels. Its meaning, "fullness of life," bursts forth in every reading for today. The ancient prayer/blessing of peace is an appropriate start for the New Year. In personal affairs, family concerns, in community and world organizations, peace is at a premium. We long for it; we pray for it. When God blesses us with peace, hearts are stilled and souls are at rest. This blessing of peace resonates well with the angels' wish for people of goodwill. The beginning of a New Year is a good time to reach out to others and to pray for God's blessing of peace for each dimension of human encounter.

Peace is also our inheritance in Christ. As adopted children of God we have been given the freedom to live in a godly manner, calling God our *Abba*. If we are resolved to live this new identity, we will be granted the freedom of heart that shows itself in works of peace and justice. Right relationships in the covenant activity of God are the pathways of peace. Our commitment to respond to God's initiatives in Christ and our willingness to be a new creation are solid New Year's resolutions for all who are interested in peace on earth.

## Second Sunday After Christmas
### Sirach 24:1-2, 8-12

In many ways this reading from Sirach resembles a poem found in the book of Proverbs (8:22-31). The characterization is quite interesting. First, Wisdom is personified as a woman. This is significant when we remember the high regard within which wisdom was held. Second, she is not dependent on another to pay her homage. She sings her own praises, and she does this publicly, both before her own people and in the midst of the very court of God. From the outset it is clear that this Woman Wisdom is no ordinary being. She is revered both on earth and in the heavens.

As a creature of God, Wisdom's glory is really derived from the excellence of her creation. It is this she praises, and she does so among her people and within the divine court. It is unusual that a woman, even Woman Wisdom, should be granted admission to the court of God and be allowed to speak about anything, much less herself, before the high God and the hosts or courtiers of God. The origin and identity of this mysterious woman has challenged commentators from the beginning. The image has been interpreted in various ways. Some believe she was originally an ancient Israelite goddess. However, as Israel developed a monotheistic faith, she lost her divine prerogatives.

Other commentators consider Woman Wisdom a personification of a divine attribute. In this view she is not an independent deity but a characteristic of God. Although she is a creature of God, she enjoys extraordinary privileges. She exists before anything else has been created and she does not seem to face death or destruction. The ambiguity of the text does not provide a definite explanation of this mysterious figure.

This reading from Sirach adds an element not found in earlier portraits of Woman Wisdom. It states that although she was free to roam throughout the universe she was in search of a dwelling place for herself, a place where she would be able to rest. Her role in creation seems to have provided her some measure of universal influence, so she could have decided on almost anyplace. However, it was the Creator God who determined where she would abide, and God decided it would be in Israel that she would dwell (vv. 8-12).

Deciding the proper place for Woman Wisdom to settle was not a divine afterthought. It seems to have been part of primordial creation itself. One can conclude from this that the establishment of cosmic Wisdom in the midst of Israel, decreed as it was at the primordial event, is here seen as part of the very structure of the created cosmos. Wisdom was there from the beginning, ministering to God but waiting to be revealed in a special way to the children of Israel. Once she is revealed to this people, she is exalted and admired, she is praised and blessed.

## Psalm 147:12-13, 14-15, 19-20

This passage is from the final stanza of a hymn of praise of God. It highlights God's protection of and solicitude toward the people of Israel. Both Jerusalem, the capital of the nation, and Zion, the mount upon which the city was built, came to represent the people. They are called upon directly to praise

God (v. 12). This summons is followed by a listing of some of the many wonderful works of God that elicit such praise. All of them point to the uniqueness of the bond that holds God and this people together.

God protects the people by fortifying the city. The ancient practice of building walls around cities provided them with a defense against possible attack and gave them a vantage point from which to observe the activity outside the walls (v. 13a). As strong as these walls might have been, the gates of the city put it in jeopardy, for they had to provide entrance for the normal traffic of the city, for travelers and traders, for those who farmed outside the walls. The city was somewhat vulnerable at its gates. The psalmist calls the people to praise God, who has strengthened them precisely at this their most vulnerable spot (v. 13).

Walls also act as borders. They define the limits of personal property, and they determine the sweep of the city. Protected as they are, the people of Jerusalem/Zion are truly blessed. They can go about their daily lives with a sense of security, for the fortification provided by God has assured them of peace (v. 14). Furthermore, this peace has enabled them to prosper, since they do not have to invest time or resources into defense measures.

Prosperity is symbolized by the wheat, which is abundant and of the finest quality. Both these characteristics represent the blessing bestowed by God. The abundance suggests either expansive fields that were never ravaged by wild animals or invading enemies, or an extraordinary yield from a smaller plot of land. In either case the people would consider themselves singularly blessed by God. The exceptional quality of the wheat demonstrates the fertility of the land. Again, this is a land that has been spared the despoiling that usually accompanies war. This is a land that has known peace.

The psalmist paints a dynamic picture of the powerful word of God. It is like an emissary who runs swiftly throughout the earth, both proclaiming and bringing about what has been proclaimed. God speaks, and it is accomplished. God promises to protect and to provide for the people, and it is done.

This same powerful word is spoken to Israel, but with a different emphasis and with different consequences (vv. 19-20). It is God's special word, God's law, the law of life that will ensure God's continued protection and care. Just as Jerusalem/ Zion (the people) is singled out for special consideration, here Jacob/Israel (the nation) is chosen for a unique relationship. No other nation has been so blessed. No other nation has been given God's law of life. This is the People of God. This privilege is the reason to praise God. The psalm ends as it began. "Praise the Lord!"

## Ephesians 1:3-6, 15-18

The reading opens with a benediction (vv. 3-6), a common way to open letters as well as prayers (cf. 1 Kgs 5:7; 2 Cor 1:3-11). It also serves as a solemn, courtly form of congratulation (Ruth 4:14). This benediction blesses God, who has blessed us with "every spiritual blessing." As is always the case in Christian theology, the blessing of God comes to us through the agency of Christ. This agency is important enough to be mentioned in every verse of the benediction.

The blessings themselves are distinctively of a spiritual, even cosmic, nature. First is election in Christ. The theme of election has its origins in Jewish tradition (Exod 19:5-6; Deut 14:2). What is unique here is the idea of primordial predestination. Predestination refers to that act whereby God's love, from all eternity, determines salvation in Christ. Although the author is writing to specific individuals, there is no sense that some are predestined for salvation and others are not. The point is that salvation in Christ is not an afterthought; it was in God's plan from the beginning.

The believers were not chosen *because* they were holy and blameless, but *that they might be* holy and blameless. Once again it is clear that salvation is the cause and not the consequence of righteousness. The reading goes on to say that believers were chosen for adoption into the family of God. It is through Christ, the only real Son of God, that others can become God's adopted children. Although it is not explicitly stated here, the implicit baptismal theme is in the background of this passage. The benediction ends as it began, with a reference to praising God.

This part of the reading is a twofold prayer: first, of thanksgiving that the baptismal grace referred to in the benediction has taken effect in the lives of the believers, and second, of petition that the believers will grow more and more into the kind of people they were predestined to become.

The author acknowledges the faith and the love of the members of the community. Although there is warmth in this greeting, one does not get the sense the author knew this community intimately. He has heard about them, commends them for their devotion by thanking God for it, and includes them in his own prayers.

The prayer itself is for wisdom, one of the primary baptismal gifts. The tradition of praying for wisdom can be traced as far back as Solomon (cf. 1 Kgs 3:5-9). Unlike this royal prayer, which asks for the ability to govern well, the goal, wisdom, for which the author prays, is spiritual: to know God; to understand the hope within the great call of election; to appreciate the excellence of the inheritance that comes with adoption as children of God.

## John 1:1-18

The Gospel of John begins with one of the most profound statements about Jesus found in the entire Testament. Its lofty christology is comparable to that found in the reading from Hebrews. Both characterize Christ as preexistent; both depict Christ as an agent in the creation of the world. The reading itself falls easily into five parts: a description of the role the Word played in the creation of the world (vv. 1-5); a brief sketch of a witness named John (vv. 6-8); an account of the Word's entrance into the world (vv. 9-14); a report about John (v. 15); and an acknowledgment of our participation in Christ's glory (vv. 16-18).

The opening statement "In the beginning," recalls a comparable statement in Genesis (1:1). This parallel may be the author's way of implying that the coming of the Word into the world is as momentous as was the first creation. The Word is then described in language reminiscent of the figure of Wisdom personified (Prov 8:30; Wis 7:25). Like Wisdom, the Word was actively involved in creation. Unlike Wisdom, the Word is explicitly identified as divine. In a free-flowing manner the author ascribes life-giving power to the Word, life that gives light. The mention of light enables the author to draw one of his many contrasts. This particular contrast is between light and darkness. At times the light is synonymous with life (v. 5a). At other times it represents truth (v. 5b). At still other times the Word is the light (vv. 7-9).

The witness named John is not further identified. It is presumed that it is the Baptist, since the words that appear here are later ascribed to him (v. 15; cf. 1:30). There seems to be a definite need to contrast the Word and John. While the Word is the true light that comes into the world, John is merely the witness who testifies to the authenticity (vv. 7-9) and superiority of this light (v. 15). Though designated by God as a witness to the Word (v. 6), John is neither a peer nor a rival of the Word.

Up to this point only John is clearly a historical person. The Word resides in some primordial place. Now the Word enters human history, and the next section describes both the incarnation and the rejection by human beings that the Word faced (vv. 9-14). In a third contrast, the author distinguishes between those who were somehow intimately associated with the Word but did not accept him and those who did accept him and thereby became children of God. "His own" may be a reference to other members of the Jewish community. Here ancestry does not make one a child of God, only faith in the Word made flesh can accomplish this.

Several translations state that the Word "made his dwelling among us" (v. 14). A better reading of the Greek might be "tenting." It calls to mind the tabernacle in the wilderness where God dwelt among the people (Exod 40:34) as well as the tradition about Wisdom establishing her tent in the midst of the people (Sir 24:8). The Word of God, who is also the Holiness of God and the Wisdom of God, now dwells in the midst of humankind. Women and men have been greatly enriched by this divine presence, transformed by the love that first prompted God's revelation and Christ's incarnation.

## Themes of the Day

This Sunday could be called "Wisdom Sunday." It celebrates Christ, God's incarnated gift, who comes to dwell in our midst. The divine Word, who has pitched a tent among us, is associated with the fulfillment of Wisdom and with our participation in her power. Several themes emerge from this association: Wisdom was present from the beginning of time as a cosmic force; Wisdom lives in the midst of the people; Christ is the fulfillment of Wisdom and the agent of our salvation.

### Wisdom as Cosmic Force

Wisdom is part of creation from the beginning and holds sway over cosmic affairs. She inspires the praise of all creation. Told by God to live among the people, she is in their midst as a source of inspiration and encouragement for them. When joined with the Prologue of the Gospel of John, Wisdom is seen as incarnate in Jesus. In Jesus, Wisdom is the divine Word that dwells among us. In this Word all creation has come to be and is sustained in life and destiny.

### Wisdom Lives Among the People

Wisdom dwells in Zion, in the Holy City of Jerusalem, in the midst of the city of God. When Wisdom dwells at the heart of the community, three changes occur. First, protection is offered to the people. There is no fear, no threat. All are secure in Wisdom's abiding presence. Second, with Wisdom comes a sense of God's sustaining mercy and love. Third, the protection and blessing that Wisdom brings draw forth the praises of God. The people, all of the city, are inspired to give praise and thanks to God for Wisdom's wondrous gifts.

### Christ, the Agent of Salvation

God is praised and blessed for the wonders of the divine gifts offered to us. Within this blessing there is the profound awareness that it is Christ who makes all good things possible. Christ is the agent of our salvation. In fact, the promise of salvation is proclaimed from the beginning of creation. Just as Wisdom was told by God to pitch her tent among the people, so the divine Word, bringing the gift of salvation, has pitched a tent amidst the people. This gracious act of God is an assurance that salvation is offered to all who are willing to receive it. Thus Christ, divine Wisdom and God among us, is the promise that all creation can be regenerated. This new life is the way of peace, the way of gratitude. It is the way of praise and thanks for the protection and blessing of God.

## *January 6, The Epiphany of the Lord*

### Isaiah 60:1-6

The reading opens with a twofold summons: "Arise!" "Shine!" The feminine form of the verbs suggests the city of Jerusalem is being addressed. Although it had been downtrodden and enshrouded in darkness, it is now called out of this desperate state. The illumination into which it emerges is not merely the light of a new day, a new era of peace and prosperity. It is the very light of God, it is the glory of the LORD. This expression usually refers to some kind of theophany, some kind of manifestation of divine majesty. The oracle that follows the summons suggests the divine majesty that is revealed is the restoration of Zion/Jerusalem.

The assertion, that Jerusalem enjoys the light of divine glory while everyone else is wrapped in a darkness that covers the entire earth (v. 2), is reminiscent of one of the plagues that befell Egypt when the pharaoh refused to release God's people from their confinement in that land (Exod 10:21-23). Certainly the allusion was not lost on those for whom this prophetic announcement was intended. The privilege Israel enjoyed in the first instance and the benefits this privilege afforded them serve here as incentive for relying on God's continued care of Israel.

This prophet states again and again that other nations will witness the glory of the LORD as it is revealed through the salvation of Israel (cf. 40:5; 52:10; 61:11; 62:11). Here the prophet makes the same claim (v. 3). The light Jerusalem provides for others is really the radiance of God's glory, and that glory is in fact the manifestation of its deliverance. Thus Jerusalem's redemption enables others to behold and to walk in God's light. It is now the messenger of good news for others. This is why Jerusalem is summoned, "Arise and shine forth!"

Jerusalem is not only delivered from its misfortune by God, it is reestablished as a thriving city. Its dispersed inhabitants return; its destroyed reputation is restored; its despoiled prosperity is reconstituted (vv. 4-5). This is not a promise to be fulfilled in the future; Jerusalem's salvation is an accomplished fact. It is happening before its very eyes. The major centers of wealth and wisdom once again send their wares to Jerusalem. Wealth from land and sea pours into the city. Such good fortune is evidence of God's favor. This is another reason the city is summoned, "Arise and shine forth!"

### Psalm 72:1-2, 7-8, 10-11, 12-13

In this royal hymn the psalmist is asking God to bless the king so the king in turn can bless the people. Ancient monarchs exercised incredible control over the lives of their subjects. Despite the scope and depth of this influence the authority described here is not unregulated. Rather, it is under the jurisdiction of God.

The psalmist begins with a prayer, asking God that the king be given a share in God's own justice (vv. 1-2). This is the same justice with which God governs the world and all the people in it. It is the justice that gives birth to harmony and to the peace (v. 7) that embodies complete well-being. This justice will enable the king to govern in a way that will provide the people with the peace and well-being God wills for them.

These people are explicitly identified as belonging to God, presumably the people of the covenant. Thus this is no ordinary king; he is one who has been placed over the covenanted people to rule them as God would, in justice and righteousness. The test of the character of the royal rule is the care given to the most vulnerable of the society, the poor. The psalmist asks God to grant righteousness to the king so he can protect the defenseless and guarantee for them a share in the prosperity of the nation.

The psalmist turns to the rule of the king (v. 7). He prays first for its steadfastness: may it last forever, until the moon is no more. Actually, it is not the reign itself that is the object of his prayer but the righteousness of the reign. Since it is really God's righteousness, he prays that it will take root and flourish throughout the rule of this particular king and that it will even outlast him, enduring along with peace until the end of time.

The psalmist next prays that this rule of justice be extended to include the entire world and all the nations within it (vv. 8, 10-11). Since the sea frequently symbolized chaos (cf. Ps 89:9-10), the expression "from sea to sea" (v. 8a) delineates the inhabitable land that lies securely and thrives peacefully within the boundaries of chaotic waters. "The River" (v. 8b) suggests a specific waterway that marks a land that stretches to the end of the earth. Both of these sweeping images sketch a reign that encompasses all the world.

The kingdoms listed provide a specific profile to this universal rule (vv. 10-11). Tarshish is thought to have been a Phoenician commercial center in southern Spain; Sheba was in southern Arabia; Seba was a royal Ethiopian city in southern Egypt. If the River refers to the Euphrates, these sites trace the outline of the ancient Near Eastern world. The cities not only provide the borders of the reign of righteousness, they also signify its good fortune. They are all well-established and are flourishing internationally respected centers of commerce and trade. If they are the outposts of this remarkable kingdom, how successful its center must be!

The reading ends with a picture of righteousness in action (vv. 12-13). If the test of justice is the solicitude shown the needy the prayer of the psalmist has been answered. The kingdom is rooted in the righteousness of God, and the most vulnerable in the society have an advocate in the king.

### Ephesians 3:2-3a, 5-6

The preaching of the gospel is the major focus of this reading. However, there are four very significant themes connected with it and interwoven in the passage: ministry or commission; revelation; mystery; and co-heir.

*Oikonomía* (ministry) comes from two Greek words: *oíkos,* meaning "house," and *nomós,* meaning "law." It means the law of the house. The word itself might be better translated "administration" or "management." This is because "ministry" has too often been understood as "works" rather than deputized responsibility for some aspect of the household, as is the meaning here. In this reading the *oikonomía* was assigned directly by God, thus making the writer of the letter both responsible for the believers and accountable to God.

The gospel message the author preached, specifically that in Christ the Gentiles are co-heirs, co-members, and co-partners with the Jews (v. 6), had been revealed to him by God. This is an important point, for within the early Church the gospel message was usually handed down from one member to another (cf. 1 Cor 11:23). It may be that new insights into God's plan were considered new revelations, and it might have been necessary to regard them in this way in order that they be deemed genuine.

According to the author the status of the Gentiles had to be revealed because it had been secret until now (cf. Col 1:25-26). The apostles and prophets, to whom the Spirit revealed this message, constitute the foundation of the Church (cf. Eph 2:20). In other words, it is through this appointed messenger that the Spirit has revealed a new revelation to the established Church. The message of this new revelation is this: In Christ the Gentiles are co-heirs, co-members, and co-partners with the Jews.

Since what qualifies one an heir is life in the Spirit of Christ and not natural generation into a particular national group, there is no obstacle in the path of Gentile incorporation. The body to which all belong is the body of Christ, not the bloodline of Abraham. The promise at the heart of gospel preaching is the promise of universal salvation through Christ, not of descendants and prosperity in a particular land. This is a radical insight for a Church with Jewish roots and traditions.

The early Church may have cherished the hope and conviction of universality, but it seems that it had to rethink what this might mean. The message of this passage claims the Gentiles are co-heirs precisely as Gentiles and not as initiates who have come to Christ through the faith of Israel. This new revelation does not demean the importance of the Jewish faith for Jewish Christians. It respects it but does not insist on it as a prerequisite for admission into the Church. The one thing necessary is to be "in Christ."

## Matthew 2:1-12

As we near the end of the Christmas season we read another popular Christmas story: that of the Three Kings or Three Wise Men. Actually, they were astrologers, men who studied the heavenly bodies and there discovered the meaning of human life on earth. The account is a kind of *haggadah,* a Jewish story fashioned from diverse biblical material intended to make a theological point. This does not mean the story is not true. It means that the truth of it is more in the total story and its meaning than in any or all of its details.

The story itself has developed a *haggadah* through which we now understand it. For example, the text says there were three gifts, not three men. It identifies the three gifts, but does not relate gold with kingship, frankincense with divinity, or myrrh with suffering. It does not name them (Caspar, Balthasar, and Melchior), nor does it say one was black. All this is haggadic addition.

Modern astrologers tell us there actually was an unusual astral phenomenon around this time. It is likely the author of this account provided a theological explanation of it. This story itself is dependent on elements from several earlier biblical traditions: the fourth oracle of Balaam the Moabite speaks of a star rising out of Jacob (Num 24:17); a reference to the kings of Tarshish, Sheba, and Seba, who render tribute and bring gifts (Ps 72:10-11); the promise that gold and frankincense will be brought on camels from Midian and Ephah and Sheba to Jerusalem (Isa 60:6).

Lest the astrological details lead us to believe this is a myth, the author situates the events squarely in time and place: the reign of Herod, Bethlehem, and Jerusalem. Since they believed astral marvels frequently accompanied the birth of great kings, it is understandable that the astrologers would go straight to the Judean king. The entire royal establishment (all Jerusalem) was frightened by news of this birth, for the child would be a potential rival. The learned of the court (chief priests and scribes) knew where to find the child. They relied on the prophetic message to tell them where to look, but they rejected its identification of the child as a legitimate ruler. Knowing the tradition is no guarantee of loyalty to it.

The report of the astrologers' veneration of the child is brief, yet stirring. The star actually led them to where he was. Finding him, they prostrated themselves before him and paid him homage. The text does not say they honored Herod in this way, so this should not be seen as tribute for a king. It is probably the kind of veneration they reserved for a god. The astrologers were adept at discerning truth. They read the astral signs; they recognized the true identity of the child; they understood a message in a dream that told them to return home another way.

These anonymous men come out of obscurity and they return to obscurity. All we know is that they were not Israelite, and this is the whole point of the story. It illustrates that people of goodwill, regardless of their ethnic or religious background, are responsive to the revelation of God. Their openness brought the astrologers to the child, and they did not go away disappointed. This child draws Jew and Gentile alike.

## Themes of the Day

The Christmas season reaches an apex on the Solemnity of the Epiphany. Traditionally known in many parts of the world as "Little Christmas," it is a commemoration of the manifestation of God to all the nations. In some liturgical traditions this feast is the central celebration of Christmas. It commemorates not only the birth of Christ and the visit of the Magi but also his baptism in the Jordan and the manifestation of his glory at the wedding feast of Cana. In the Roman Catholic tradition the focus is on the first of these commemorations: the visit of the Magi and the implications of that visit for the glorious manifestation of God to all the peoples of the world. The readings develop the importance of this manifestation. Three themes dominate: Jerusalem is the source of light for the nations; Christ is the revelation of God to all the nations; new relationships are established in Christ between Jew and Gentile.

### Jerusalem Is the Source of Light

There is a wonderful summons to alertness and presence of mind and heart, a call for all the nations to witness the marvelous works of God that shine as light in the midst of the surrounding darkness. This is no ordinary light. It is a light that has God's Holy City Jerusalem as its source. The people of Israel have enjoyed the radiance of God's glory and are now set as a beacon for the nations. All the ends of the earth can witness the wonder of God's light in the midst of the city, its people, its rulers, and its way of life.

The light of God is known in the ways in which the most vulnerable in the city are cared for and acknowledged. In just action and righteousness the city becomes the beacon of God, and all the nations are attracted by this light. The quality of the light leads the way through the darkness and sustains the world in goodness and peace.

### Christ as the Light to the Nations

Led by a star, the astrologers come in search of the infant king. They have been attentive to the marvels of the universe, and there they have read signs in the heavens. They represent all who search for truth in the wonders of creation and in the wisdom of their own cultures of origin. Because they searched with eyes of faith they were able to recognize the gift of God when they found him, even though he did not conform to their initial perception of a royal heir.

They came from the far corners of the earth, Gentiles who followed the light and who found the new king whose reign would bring justice and righteousness into human affairs. They returned home, enlightened by their visit to God's place of revelation. Their encounter shows that in Christ the light of God is given to all people of goodwill, Jew and non-Jew alike.

## The New Relationships Between Jew and Gentile

The manifestation of God among us changes the ways in which we perceive one another. Christ's birth provides us with the light by which we see a new criterion for relating. The Magi who come in faith to worship the child represent the multi-ethnic and cultural diversity in civic and parish situations as well as the many religions of the world. To us who are related no longer merely by blood affiliation or national origin, Christ offers the spirit of holiness as the ground for our relationships. This new universal belonging will be manifest in the community of believers, who live no longer in the darkness of exclusivity and sin but by a new dispensation of grace. All people, regardless of race or ethnic origin, can be co-heirs with Christ.

## Sunday After January 6, The Baptism of the Lord
### Isaiah 42:1-4, 6-7

This is the first of four passages (49:1-6; 50:4-9; 52:13–53:12) traditionally known as the Servant Songs. They constitute a unique set of poems that identify a mysterious figure who acts as a pious agent of God's compassionate care. Presumably it is God who speaks, and it is God who singles out this servant and gives him a special function to perform within the community. The uniqueness of this person can be seen in the title bestowed on him by God: "my servant." Very few people were so called by God: Abraham (Gen 26:24); Moses (Num 12:7); Caleb (Num 14:24); Job (Job 1:8). The one most frequently referred to in this way was David (2 Sam 3:8). The parallel construction in this first verse further identifies the servant as someone chosen by God and one with whom God is pleased.

Most significant in this description of the servant is his having been endowed with God's own spirit. Earlier Israelite leaders were thought to have been seized by the spirit: judges (Judg 6:34; 11:29, 32; 14:19); kings (1 Sam 16:13); prophets (Mic 3:8; Ezek 11:5). Those who received the spirit were thus empowered to act within the community in some unique fashion. The particular needs of the community determined the character of the action. God's saving power was brought to the community through the agency of various individuals. The servant in this song has received the spirit of the LORD in order to bring forth justice to the nations.

The manner in which this justice is executed is quite extraordinary (vv. 2-4). It is not harsh and exacting, making a public pronouncement of God's judgment of Israel. Instead, it is gentle and understanding, willing to wait for the establishment of God's universal rule. This justice will not compound the distress of an already suffering people. Rather, it will be a source of consolation.

God speaks again, this time directly to the servant (vv. 6-7), indicating the role the servant is to play in the life of the community. All the verbs used reveal the deliberateness of God's choice: "I called you; I grasped you; I formed you and set you." The mission of the servant is clearly determined by God, not by the servant himself. The parallelism between "covenant of the people" and "light to the nations" suggests that covenant is to be understood in a general sense, underscoring the universalism referred to elsewhere (vv. 1, 4) rather than in the exclusive sense usually associated with biblical covenant.

The responsibilities that flow from the servant's election are aspects of the commission to bring forth justice (vv. 1, 6). Although these tasks single out specific situations of human suffering, they probably stand for any form of darkness and confinement. Several themes converge here. The servant is called to bring forth justice to the nations and to be a light to the nations. This light will open the eyes of those relegated to the darkness of confinement. Most likely the reference here is not to the release of Israelites but of those outside the believing community. The passage describes the deliverance of the whole world, not the rescue of Israel from its particular bondage. The universalism cannot be denied.

## Psalm 29:1-2, 3-4, 3, 9-10

This hymn of praise describes the LORD as sovereign over the heavens and the earth. It begins with a call to praise (vv. 1-2). Unlike most psalms of this kind, here the call is addressed to heavenly, not human, beings. The scene is the celestial court with the divine council (the Hebrew reads "sons of God") assembled (cf. Job 1:6; 2:1). They are there in attendance, and they are called on to render honor to God. The imperative verb form used here indicates this is not an invitation, it is a command. These heavenly beings are charged to sing praise to God's glory and might.

The glory of God usually refers to some kind of divine manifestation. The psalmist declares that this glory is revealed in God's name. Traditional people believe there is power in a person's name, since the name embodies part of that person's very essence. How much more is this the case with the name of God. The great respect in which God's name was held explains why the people of Israel were forbidden to pronounce it. The psalm reports that this wondrous name was revered in heaven as well as on earth. The entire council is enjoined to pay homage to God, who is revealed as sovereign.

God's sovereignty is further manifested in the power God exercises over the forces of nature (vv. 3-4, 9-10). The voice of the LORD thunders over the waters (v. 3). This is a description of the mighty storm god whose voice is the thunder itself, who in the beginning conquered the forces of chaos, characterized as ruthless, destructive water. Although the characterization within the psalm suggests that God acts here as a mighty warrior, the imagery paints a slightly different picture. According to this psalm, God did not need a heavenly army to quell the chaotic waters. God's commanding voice was powerful enough. As in the first account of creation (Gen 1:1–2:4a), God's voice is itself creative power and divine splendor (v. 4).

God thunders. While this may appear to be a demonstration of the devastating power of God's voice, the context of the psalm reminds us that its focus is God's superiority over the forces of destruction. Therefore this verse is a reminder that the power of God's word can be felt both in heaven and on earth. In calling the heavenly beings to praise God, the psalmist is calling them to acknowledge all these marvels.

The last scene brings us back to the divine council, to the heavenly temple and the throne of God. (vv. 9c-10). All who are present there praise God with the joyous acclamation: "Glory!" There God sits triumphant above the floodwaters. (The only other place in the Bible where the word "flood" is found is in the Genesis account [7:17].) The scene is majestic. God's thunderous voice has silenced the forces of chaos, and now God reigns supreme forever as king of heaven and earth.

## Acts 10:34-38

The scene is the house of Cornelius, a newly converted Roman centurion. Normally an observant Jew like Peter would not enter the home of a Gentile. The first words of his discourse ("I begin to see") indicate that he was not always open to association with Gentiles as he is now. It was a newly gained insight about God that changed his view of those who did not have Jewish ancestry. He realized that "God shows no partiality" (vv. 34-35; cf. Deut 10:17; 2 Chr 19:7), and therefore, neither should he. All are acceptable to God, Jew and Gentile alike.

According to Peter, God's message of peace was given initially to Israel, but this does not cancel that fact that it is meant for all. Inclusivity is the centerpiece of this reading. God shows no partiality, and Christ is Lord of all. Not even Peter, who knew the historical Jesus intimately and should have understood the implications of the message he preached and the example he gave, originally understood the radical nature of this gospel. But now he can testify that it is truly "good news of peace."

Peter presumed that although they were Gentiles, they were living in Judea, so his audience would have heard something about the life and ministry Jesus, if only in the form of gossip. As a Roman centurion stationed in this small country, Cornelius certainly must have known something, for his station would have required that he be informed of anything that might threaten the Roman Peace. Mention of Jesus' baptism by John (v. 37) would have called to mind another disturber of the peace. Even though John was an irritant to the Jewish leadership, the unrest he caused would have been known to the Roman officials.

Although each of these incidents had a political side, this does not seem to have been Peter's motivation for referring to them. It seems, instead, he was recalling incidents that manifested the power evident in the ministry of Jesus and the universal scope of that ministry.

The power of Jesus' ministry flowed from his having been anointed by God with the Holy Spirit. This reference to anointing is probably an allusion to his baptism, when the heavens opened and the Spirit descended upon him (Luke 3:21-22; 4:14, 18; cf. Isa 61:1). It was in and through this power that he had performed such miracles as releasing those who were in the grip of the devil. Peter makes a point of this last particular miracle, probably because those possessed by demons were considered the most unclean of the unclean. Despite this, Jesus did not relegate them to the margins of society as the self-righteous purists might have done. He touched them, he healed them. Like Jesus, Peter was now moving in circumstances (contact with Gentiles) considered by some as being unclean. Like Jesus, he disregarded such a judgment and refused to conform to such a manner of estrangement. Peter was convinced that with God there is no partiality.


## Matthew 3:13-17

The gospel reading opens with a statement about Jesus' leaving the familiarity and security of his home in the region of Galilee and his journeying to the Jordan River where John was baptizing. We are not told how John came to know who Jesus was, but we do know that when he recognized Jesus he resisted baptizing him. The reading recounts an exchange that took place between the two men. In it, John questions the appropriateness of Jesus' submission to the baptism John performs. He states that he should be baptized by Jesus instead. It is not clear from the text whether this is a reference to the excellence of the baptism Jesus will establish—a baptism with the Holy Spirit and fire rather than one of repentance—or if John is acknowledging the superiority of Jesus himself, one whose sandals John is not even worthy to carry (cf. Matt 3:11). Whichever the case may be, initially John is not willing to baptize Jesus.

Jesus insists, giving as his reason for being baptized that it is necessary to fulfill all righteousness. The gospel writer's intent in using "righteousness" has been disputed. It certainly does not imply that Jesus needs to experience the righteousness that comes from repentance. Most commentators maintain that he is probably referring to the plan of God for salvation. It is important that all things be accomplished in order that the reign of God be established. Although he will make different claims about himself and his ministry and will require different things of his followers, by participating in John's baptism Jesus associates himself with the message of repentance and the need for renewal that John represents. In this way, he himself enters into God's plan, which has already been unfolding. Later he will bring this plan to its fulfillment in most extraordinary ways.

There is no description of the actual baptism, but we do have an account of what happened after the baptism had occurred. All the verbs indicate the events happened *to* Jesus; they were not accomplished *by* him or *through* him. Jesus was the recipient of these extraordinary events. First, the heavens were opened. This suggests some kind of apocalyptic phenomenon (cf. Ezek 1:1). Here it is the prelude for the descent of the Spirit of God. John had declared that the one to come would baptize with the Spirit. Here, before Jesus embarks on his ministry the Spirit descends upon him. This is not to suggest that in this way Jesus was filled with the Spirit, which does not seem to have been necessary. However, the fact that the Spirit comes upon him indicates Jesus is somehow intimately associated with the Holy Spirit. There are two ways of understanding the phrase "like a dove." It could refer to the manner of the descent of the Spirit, a gentle manner like that of a dove. Or it could suggest the form the Spirit took in its descent. Though the Greek formulation allows for either meaning, the understanding has been the traditional one. Religious art frequently depicts the Spirit in the form of a dove.

The trinitarian scene is completed with the voice from heaven, which identifies Jesus as "Son." The words spoken combine an allusion to the "servant of the LORD" (cf. Isa 42:1) and the enthronement of the messianic king (cf. Ps 2:7). Together they provide an insight into the character of Jesus' ministry. While he will be the messianic fulfillment of the royal tradition, the words of the voice from heaven are spoken about him rather than to him. Some believe this is an indication of the catechetical intent of the gospel writer. The episode has also been considered by many as the depiction of the divine commissioning of Jesus.

## Themes of the Day

This christological feast is the celebration of Jesus as the anointed servant of God. It brings to a close the Christmas season, which reveals who God is for us and who we are to be for others in Christ. The readings bring together various aspects of this mystery. As though in a montage of snapshots we are introduced to the image of the Isaian servant of God; we catch sight of Jesus, who fulfills the role of that servant; we see the fruits of Jesus' messiahship in the person of Cornelius; and we are brought to see the cosmic wonders of God's re-creative power revealed in this mystery.

## The Baptism of Jesus

The baptism of Jesus inaugurates his ministry as the anointed one, or the Messiah of God. The passage from Isaiah indicates the kind of Messiah God intends Jesus to be. He will not exercise harsh justice as a mighty judge would. Nor will he wield the sword of vengeance on the battlefield. The Messiah of God will be a servant, one who, though mighty, is gentle; one who is chosen by the high God, yet committed to the needy and the marginal; one who is the proclaimed Son of God and who still attends to the least within the human community. The Messiah of God may have come from an insignificant village like Nazareth, but he was anointed with the Holy Spirit and with power. He taught the coastlands and he healed those under the power of the devil. The Messiah of God does not conform to the expectations of a proud and self-absorbed society. Filled with the Spirit of God, the Messiah of God acts out of that gentle, compassionate spirit.

## For Whom Did He Come?

For whom did the Messiah of God come? For those whom the society discarded. He came for the people who were broken and suffering, for those who were blind, for those who were imprisoned. He came for people who are so easily pushed to the margins, beyond our view, where the circumstances of their lives will not trouble us—the homeless, the unemployed, the abandoned children, the helpless elderly, the mentally and chronically ill. He also came to people who, like Cornelius, do not belong to our inner circles, people who for any number of reasons threaten us, people we might actually despise. He came for the strangers among us, those who have different cultural customs, those who worship in different ways. He came for people we have pushed out as well as for those we have refused to let in. The Messiah of God came for all people without distinction.

## Cosmic Ramifications

While the psalm praises God the Creator, on this feast joined with the other readings, it proclaims God's re-creative power. Through the servant in Isaiah God fashioned a new society, one of justice and compassion and healing and liberation. In Jesus, the Messiah who came as a servant, the creative majesty of God is revealed in its premier form and all creation is made new. Walls of enmity tumble, and all people are bound together in the peace of Christ. We who are baptized share in this new creation and in the messianic responsibility of declaring the good news to the coastlands. As disciples of Jesus, the servant Messiah, we continue the ministry he first took upon himself. Now it is through us that God re-creates society. Like Paul, we bring the good news of the gospel to all people. The Christmas season ends with us facing our challenge to be participants in the servant messiahship of Jesus.

# Lent

| First Sunday | | | |
|---|---|---|---|
| Genesis 2:7-9; 3:1-7<br>Creation and sin | Psalm 51:3-6, 12-13, 14, 17<br>Be merciful, O LORD | Romans 5:12-19<br>Where sin decreased, grace increaced | Matthew 4:1-11<br>Jesus is tempted |
| **Second Sunday** | | | |
| Genesis 12:1-4a<br>Blessings of Abram | Psalm 33:4-5, 18-20, 22<br>Let your mercy be on us | 2 Timothy 1:8b-10<br>Salvation through Christ | Matthew 17:1-9<br>Jesus is transfigured |
| **Third Sunday** | | | |
| Exodus 17:3-7<br>Give us water | Psalm 95:1-2, 6-9<br>Hear the voice of God | Romans 5:1-2, 5-8<br>God's love is poured out | John 4:5-42<br>Water of eternal life |
| **Fourth Sunday** | | | |
| 1 Samuel 16:1b, 6-7, 10-13a<br>David is anointed | Psalm 23:1-6<br>The LORD is my shepherd | Ephesians 5:8-14<br>Live as children of light | John 9:1-41<br>The blind man sees |
| **Fifth Sunday** | | | |
| Ezekiel 37:12-14<br>I will open your graves | Psalm 130:1-8<br>With you is forgiveness | Romans 8:8-11<br>The Spirit is alive | John 11:1-45<br>I am the resurrection |
| **Palm Sunday of the Lord's Passion** | | | |
| Isaiah 50:4-7<br>I gave my back to those who beat me | Psalm 22:8-9, 17-20, 23-24<br>Why have you abandoned me? | Philippians 2:6-11<br>Christ humbled himself | Matthew 26:14–27:66<br>Passion |

# Lent

## Initial Reading of the Lent Lectionary

### Introduction

The comprehensive lenten Sunday readings can be viewed as a theological matrix serving as a source for interpreting the readings of the individual Sundays of Lent and as a key for an appreciation of the lenten season itself. The matrix presented here is based on the patterns of meanings offered in the literary forms and the content of the readings themselves. When read in columns, beginning with the first Sunday of Lent and concluding with Palm Sunday, the lections provide an overview of the meaning of the entire lenten season.

Although Lent has traditionally been understood as a time of repentance and penance, the liturgical readings of the season focus our attention on the goodness of God and the blessings that flow from this into our lives rather than on human sinfulness and any attempts to make amends for it through lenten practices. The readings for the Third, Fourth, and Fifth Sundays of Lent for Year A are the preferred readings for all three years when there are catechumens journeying with us toward Easter. These readings present, for them in particular but also for the entire believing community, the christological hope and end of the Christian faith.

### First Testament Readings

The first readings for the Sundays in Lent provide us with a very interesting insight into the meaning of the season. On the First Sunday we consider the goodness of God in creating the first human being and placing that first creature in a garden filled with trees delightful to look at and good for food. Despite this graciousness on the part of God, the first woman and man disobeyed the divine injunction and sinned. This first reading ends without any mention of repentance on the part of those who sinned or of forgiveness of them by God.

Having set the tone for the drama of human history, all the first readings for the next four Sundays give examples of God's loving providence in the face of human sinfulness. On the Second Sunday we see Abram, a man chosen by

God to be both beneficiary of God's blessing and agent of blessing for others. There is no mention of sin here, only blessing. The graciousness of God is even more evident on the Third Sunday. There we read of the ingratitude of those who were brought out of Egypt. They murmur against the God who saved them. God does not punish them for their thanklessness. Instead, God gives them the refreshment they demand.

The anointing of David as king, the reading for the Fourth Sunday, demonstrates God's continued care for this people. Their leader is one who has been especially chosen by God. We read on the Fifth Sunday that, even after their infidelities brought the nation to complete ruin, God promised to re-create this people, to open their graves and to fill them with God's own spirit so that they might live. The ultimate example of God's graciousness is seen in the reading for Palm Sunday. There we behold the willingness of the prophetic figure to allow himself to be the object of the hatred of others. Though he is devout, he suffers at the hands of others, and he does so without offering any defense. All these readings suggest that not even our sinfulness can cause God to turn away from us. Instead, we are inundated with divine blessings. This is a profound if often overlooked lenten message.

*Psalms*

The responsorial psalms for the season of Lent, though intended to be responses to themes found in the respective first readings, provide us with a broad selection of religious sentiments. They include three laments, two of which belong to a collection known as the Penitential psalms; a hymn of praise; an enthronement song; and a psalm of trust.

On the First Sunday we pray one of the most familiar psalms. In it we acknowledge our sinfulness and beg for God's mercy. We also ask for a transformed heart that will enable us to proclaim God's praise. The righteousness and trustworthiness of God are praised on the Second Sunday. When directed toward us, these divine characteristics instill confidence in God's mercy. The enthronement psalm of the Third Sunday extends an invitation to approach this God who has forgiven us despite the fact that it is we who have turned away from divine comfort. Probably the best expression of the tenderness and comfort God offers us is found in the response for the Fourth Sunday. There we see God's unconditional love and care laid out before us.

As we come closer to Holy Week, we return to the sentiments of lamentation. On the Fifth Sunday we pray another Penitential psalm, crying to God from the depths of our misery. Our attention makes a dramatic shift on Palm Sunday. All the readings for that day turn our attention to the sufferings of Jesus. Therefore, although in the responsorial psalm the psalmist is bemoaning his own situation, the focus of the readings suggests the sentiments be placed into the mouth of the suffering Jesus.

## Epistles

The selections from the epistles considered individually and collectively place before us a major lenten theme—the unconditional love God has for us as demonstrated in the salvation won for us by Christ. The focus during the lenten season is not on our sinfulness or on the penance required to atone for it. We are not directed in these readings to look at ourselves but rather to concentrate on God. There we are assured that sin cannot imperil grace. Instead, the obedience of Jesus has made even sinners righteous (First Sunday). We are told that God saved us and called us to a life of holiness, and we received this grace through Christ Jesus (Second Sunday). Our thoughts next move from the righteousness of Jesus to the love of God, poured out into hearts (Third Sunday). We also see that it is because of Jesus that we can live as children of light (Fourth Sunday). Finally, we are comforted by the news that all of this will be accomplished by the Spirit who dwells within us (Fifth Sunday). These readings clearly point to divine graciousness as a major theme of the season.

As with all the other readings for Palm Sunday, the epistle selections rivet our attention on Jesus. There the way he humbled himself is offered as the model for our own behavior.

## Gospels

Read together, the lenten gospels invite us to fix our attention on one aspect of the personality of Jesus, his extraordinary reality. We read about his temptation in the wilderness on the First Sunday. However, this reading very clearly shows that Jesus himself exerted definite power over the devil. He did not succumb to the temptations that assailed him. Then, on the Second Sunday we behold him transfigured before three of his closest disciples and conversing with Moses and Elijah. This is clearly an astonishing man.

The Third, Fourth, and Fifth Sundays of Lent mark the period of scrutiny for the catechumens. The gospel readings for these Sundays have a special catechetical significance. The stories found within them include Jesus' encounter with the woman of Samaria and his revelation of himself to her as the Messiah; the miracle of his giving sight to the man born blind and his eventual revelation of himself to him as the Son of Man; and finally, Jesus' raising of Lazarus from the dead and his revelation of himself to Martha as the resurrection and the life.

When one reads these stories of the extraordinary nature and miraculous power of Jesus, the account of his passion takes on a very different character.

Jesus could not possibly be the powerless victim of treachery or circumstances. Instead, his suffering and death could have happened only because he allowed them to happen. This is precisely the message we find in the passion narrated on Palm Sunday.

### Mosaic of Readings

This mosaic of readings shows that Lent is a time to consider the graciousness of God toward us despite our own sinfulness. It begins with examples of this goodness evident at various times in the history of the chosen people. And it finds its culmination in the blessings won for us by Christ Jesus. Without denying our infidelity, we are invited to contemplate God. Only after we are seared by the fire of divine love will any kind of penance be seen in its proper light. Finally, the passion of Jesus is presented as the freely given gift of himself for the salvation of all.

# Readings

### First Sunday of Lent

## Genesis 2:7-9; 3:1-7

This reading features three episodes: the creation of the first man, his placement in the garden, and the sin. The man *('ādām)* is formed of the ground *('ǎdāmâ,* v. 7) as are the trees of the garden (v. 9), thus establishing from the beginning a physical bond between humans and other creatures of the earth. This bond notwithstanding, the man's creation is completed when, with a divine act, God breathes the breath of life into him.

The story is filled with allusions to wisdom. First, Eden is in the east, considered the place of enlightenment because the sun rises there. In the middle of this garden, which was the source of delight and nourishment, was the tree of life. The Hebrew construction suggests that mention of the tree of knowledge, a second allusion to wisdom, was an addition, probably included when the originally separate stories of the garden and the sin were brought together.

The major focus of the reading is the account of the sin. This story does not describe a fall from grace. There is no loss of supernatural or preternatural gifts, as some much later interpretations contend. The sinful act itself was one of disobedience, but the inclination that gave rise to it was a form of hubris—

the desire to be like gods. The connection with the tree of knowledge suggests this desire was somehow associated with wisdom.

The cunning serpent, another allusion to wisdom, should not be confused with the devil, who appears much later in the biblical tradition. This is a creature whose mysterious character has been used by the writer to point out how vulnerable humans are to temptation. Like temptation itself, the exchange between the serpent and the woman is more subtle than direct. The wily creature leads the woman on but does not really lie to her. It tells her that if she and her husband eat the fruit they will not die but their eyes will be opened and they will know good from evil. That is exactly what happened. However, as is often the case with temptation, what happens is unexpected, and it is only afterwards that the tempted realize they have allowed themselves to be deceived.

The tree of knowledge plays no role in the story except as the object of temptation. It was very enticing, but forbidden. Did God put the tree in the garden for the express purpose of testing the couple? Or was it to establish limits to human freedom and ingenuity, to remind them that, despite their incredible abilities and potential, they are, after all, only creatures of the dust and not gods?

The wisdom character of the account is quite clear. Its setting is a garden in the east, the place of wisdom; the cunning serpent pointed out the possibility of being like God, knowing good from evil; the woman was overcome by the desire for wisdom; both she and her husband ate the forbidden fruit and their eyes were opened to the experiential knowledge of good and evil. Once again the subtlety of temptation is obvious. It is admirable to want to be like God, but it is hubris to take things into one's own hands and make decisions contrary to God's will.

## Psalm 51:3-4, 5-6, 12-13, 14, 17

This is one of the most familiar of the Penitential psalms. The response for today consists of a plea for mercy (vv. 3-4); a confession of sin (vv. 5-6); a prayer for transformation (vv. 12-13, 14); and a request for the opportunity of praising God. In the initial plea the psalmist appeals to God's covenant dispositions: goodness (*ḥesed*) and compassion or womb-love, the kind of attachment a mother has to the child she has carried in her womb (*raḥămîm*). The first refers to the steadfast love that characterizes that relationship between covenant partners; the second is the attitude God has toward those who have violated the covenant bond. The psalmist probably appeals to these dispositions of divine graciousness in order to set the context for the confession of sin and for prayer for transformation.

Three different words are used to characterize the sinfulness of the psalmist. "Evil" (*raʿ*, v. 6) is a very general term and can refer simply to behavior that is unacceptable. A second, and the most frequently used word for sin (*hattā't*, vv. 4, 5, 6), is a much more technical term. It comes from the verb that means "miss the mark," and it connotes transgression of some Law or statute. The third term (*pesha'*, vv. 3, 4, 5) denotes rebellion of the gravest nature, such as a violation of the covenant bond.

Realizing that the seriousness of the offenses call for a thorough transformation, a total *metanoia* of the offender, the psalmist prays for a clean heart and a right or true spirit (cf. Ezek 11:19). The technical verb for create *(bārā')* is used, indicating that the psalmist is asking for a transformation that possesses a kind of pristine quality. The same prayer is then made, but in a manner that might be called completely opposite. "Do not cast me from your presence; do not take your holy spirit (here used as a synonym for presence) from me." The psalmist is here praying for the reestablishment of the covenant relationship that was shattered by the psalmist's own sins. This becomes clear in the plea for a return of the joy of salvation (v. 14).

The response ends with a prayer that the psalmist might be empowered by God to praise God. This request shows that the covenant relationship, forgiveness of sin, transformation of heart, and the ability to praise God are all gifts of grace from God.

## Romans 5:12-19

The point of the teaching in this passage is the incomparable nature of God's salvific grace. In order to illustrate the scope and force of this grace Paul uses a diatribe, a form of argument used by the Greek Stoics. He sets up a comparison between the universal effects of sin and death and the all-encompassing power of forgiveness and life. He does this by contrasting the actions of Adam, "the type of the one who was to come," and Christ, his unrivaled counterpart. While it may appear the contrast is between Adam and Christ, it is really between the epochs each inaugurated. Adam inaugurated the era of sin and death; Christ established the eschatological era of acquittal and life. At each stage of Paul's comparison we see the surpassing power of the salvation won by Christ.

Although the name "Adam" often refers to the individual depicted in the creation accounts, throughout this passage the corresponding word for "man" is *ánthrōpos* (humankind) rather than *anēr* (singular male). Paul seems to be talking about the individual who represents the entire race of women and men.

The epoch Adam inaugurated is sketched first. Paul uses both the account of the first sin (Gen 3:6) and the common experience of all people to explain the pervasive presence of sin and death in the world. Adam may have been the first to sin, but subsequently all have sinned. In one sense there is no transgression if there is no law to transgress. However, according to Paul the power of sin and death are independent of the Law. He maintains that indeed there was sin in the world before Moses received the Law. It entered the world through Adam. The evidence of this is the universal reign of death, which according to the Genesis narrative follows sin. All die, therefore all must have sinned.

Paul uses an *a fortiori* argument to make his point about the excellence of Christ: if this is the way it was with sin, how much more it is with grace (v. 15). Although Paul earlier insisted that all have sinned, his primary comparison is between Adam and Christ. As death for all entered the world through the sin of one—Adam, so grace was won for all through the gift of one—Christ. However, there is a significant difference; grace is much more powerful than sin. Grace does not merely acquit the sin of Adam, it acquits all sin. With an *a fortiori* argument Paul insists that as death reigned through the one sin, how much more will life reign through the one Jesus Christ.

In his conclusion, Paul draws the lines of comparison quite clearly: condemnation came through one sin, acquittal comes through one righteous act; disobedience brought death, obedience brought life. However, even in this comparison, the act of Christ was and is so much more powerful than any act of Adam. Grace surpasses all sin.

## Matthew 4:1-11

The gospel passage is an account of the temptation of Jesus. While the story appears to report an event in Jesus' life, certain details bring into question its historical character, particularly his transport from the wilderness to the pinnacle of the Temple and then to a high mountain. The significance of the narrative is probably to be found less in its historical accuracy than in its theological meaning. Jesus' responses to the temptations posed by the devil all come from the Deuteronomy version of Israel's testing in the wilderness. This suggests that Jesus is here being compared with that ancient community.

The similarities between Jesus and the wilderness community are striking. Most obviously, the place of testing is the desert, traditionally believed to be the abode of evil spirits. There the normal supports of life are absent, and one is forced to turn elsewhere for sustenance. Reminiscent of Israel's forty years in the wilderness, Jesus fasted for forty days and forty nights, and then he encountered the devil *(diábolos)*, the tempter *(peirázōn)*, the one he finally calls "Satan." The temptations should not be understood as hallucinations brought on by hunger. Rather, the fasting was a spiritual discipline that strengthened him for his confrontation.

Twice the devil challenges Jesus' identity as Son of God, a reference that for ancient Israel had royal connotations but in the gospels always points to divine origin. If Jesus is the Son of God and he wishes to establish the reign of God in a world that seems to be under the control of evil forces, he should dramatically demonstrate his power. In days gone by God rained bread from heaven. Jesus is told to do something even more spectacular: miraculously to turn stones into bread. His response shows that, unlike the murmuring Israelites of old, he heeds the words of God (cf. Deut 8:3).

Next the devil proposes that Jesus test God's promise of protection (cf. Ps 91:12) and throw himself from the pinnacle of the Temple. If he is the Son of God, he will certainly be saved from injury. Jesus refuses to put God to the test, as the wilderness community had done (cf. Deut 6:16). Finally, the devil, the one who seems to hold sway over all the world, offers Jesus dominion over this world. Jesus exerts his authority over Satan by dismissing him with words that demonstrate his allegiance to God alone. Jesus has passed the final test, reversing the pattern set by the wilderness community.

This account is replete with messianic meaning. It suggests that the Son of God has chosen not to use divine power to establish his reign on earth. Jesus' responses outline a very different approach. He will be open to the word of God, allowing it to direct his actions; he will rely on God's providence and not put God's promises to the test; he will not compromise his fidelity to God regardless of the price he might have to pay. Unlike the wilderness community that proved faithless when put to the test, Jesus is steadfast in the face of temptation.

## Themes of the Day

The readings for the First Sunday of Lent act as a kind of overture to the entire season. They enable us to engage in a double confession: a confession of sin and the repentance that follows; and a confession of praise for the mercy of God, which is shown us in spite of our sin. Specifically, they sketch the contours of the human condition—broken and death-bound; they give us a glimpse of God's unqualified mercy; and they invite us to look to Jesus, who is our way to God's mercy.

### The Human Condition

The first reading reminds us of the fragility of the human condition. We are made of the dust *('āpār)* of the ground, the very stuff that represents death and decay (cf. Gen 3:19). We were reminded of this when ashes were used to sign us on Ash Wednesday. The creation narrative reports that an additional act of God was necessary to enliven this lifeless material. As with all mythic narratives, ambiguity is present rather than logical development. Here it agrees in the connections among the stuff out of which humans are made, the sin of which they are guilty, and the death they must face. On the one hand the text implies that the human creatures return to dust because it was from dust that they came; on the other hand, it suggests that they must die because of their death-dealing sin. This latter is the view expressed in the reading from Romans. In either case, the reading confronts us with both our mortality and our sinfulness.

At the beginning of Lent we are invited to acknowledge honestly and realistically our fundamental human weakness. This is particularly true with regard to the psalm response. No excuse for human weakness is given there. Rather, responsibility is straightforwardly and humbly accepted. We are guilty, and consequently we are in need of God's mercy.

## The Compassion of God

Despite the fundamental weaknesses of the human condition, the situation in which we find ourselves is not hopeless. Somewhere deep within ourselves we know we are not helpless prisoners of our limitations. God has not deserted us to our guilt. With the psalmist we hopefully plead: "Have mercy *(ḥānan)*; be gracious; grant this favor." For what do we pray? God's compassion *(raḥămîm)*, a word derived from the Hebrew for "womb" *(raḥem)*. The root of this word suggests that compassion might accurately be described as "womb-love," an attachment like that which exists between a woman and the child she has borne or between two people born of the same womb. Such is the posture we are asking of God. Although today "compassion" often refers to the sentiment of deep sympathy felt for the suffering of another, the word appears in biblical texts that describe the attitude of mercy God has toward sinners. As a response to the first reading, which states that we are created from the lifeless dust of the earth, the psalm reminds God that we have come forth from the divine womb, and for this reason we boldly lay claim on the compassion that springs from that intimate connection.

The form God's compassion takes is outlined in the reading from Romans. It is in the death and resurrection of Jesus that we see the extent of this divine compassion. Its scope is first measured by the yardstick of human sinfulness, and then it outstrips those dimensions. God's gracious gift *(cháris)* far exceeds the effects of human transgression. On this First Sunday we are not allowed to linger over thoughts of human frailty and sinfulness. In fact, they seem to be placed before us only to enable us to reflect on the mercy of God.

## Choose Christ

The gospel reading moves us from both the anthropological and theological considerations to the crowning christological reflections. Let us look to Jesus. There we see humanity at its best, tempted but not overcome. There will certainly always be human limitations, human weaknesses that will open the door to temptation. But Jesus shows us we are not thereby doomed. The God we are called to serve is the God who serves us by showing us compassion and by giving us Jesus as a model for our own journey to new life.

## *Second Sunday of Lent*
### Genesis 12:1-4a

The first reading for this Sunday tells us something about Abram (Abraham), but it tells us more about the plan of God. Abram is the one who is chosen, the one directed by God to pull up stakes and move to another place, the one to whom the promises of blessing are made. It is only in the very last verse that he acts, and his action is that of following the directions given him. In a way this is really a narrative about God, or about how the Israelites perceived their God. It is a picture of God's choice of one family among many and of the good fortune and fame with which this family will be blessed.

Abram seems to have been securely settled in his land of origin as part of the patriarchal household of his father. In traditional societies one would not move out of this kind of social enclave without some weighty reason, such as war or famine. The account expressly states the reason for Abram's departure: he was directed by God to do so. He is told to travel from the land of his kinfolk to one that presumably is foreign to him. Since the ancients often believed that land was under the jurisdiction of various gods, to leave a land was tantamount to leaving the domain and protection of the god of that land. It is clear from this narrative that the God of Abram is not bound to such territorial restrictions. This God exercises authority over Abram while he is in his land of origin and promises to bless him when he is in another land.

The promise of blessing is fivefold: I will make you a great nation; I will bless you; I will make your name great; I will bless those who bless you; I will curse those who curse you. God promises to make Abram a great nation. The word used *(gôy)* refers to the political, ethnic, or territorial aspects of the group rather than merely the people *('am)*. This will be a nation, like the other nations of the world. God further promises to bless this nation with prosperity and with a name (reputation) that will be respected by others. These are all blessings any nation would expect of its patron god. However, this God makes another promise, one that at first glance appears to be unusual. God promises that Abram and his descendants will be mediators of God's blessing to others. Actually, these last two promises fit together. They indicate how God will respond to the treatment Abram's nation will receive from others. Those who treat it with respect will be blessed; those who disdain it or abuse it will suffer the wrath of God. Abram's family has been chosen by God, and God will protect this chosen family.

The directives from God require profound faith on Abram's part. He is being asked to sever himself from the most fundamental ties an individual has—the ties of origin. These were not merely family attachments, they were social and ethnic bonds. They determined his identity (his past), his place in society (his present), and his inheritance (his future). God was asking him to start anew. Actually, it was God's plan to start something new through Abram. What would be his response? The words of the text are straightforward and unembellished: "Abram went as the LORD directed him." No questions were asked; no long period of preparation is suggested. The tone of the entire ancestral narrative is set: God directs, and the People of God respond.

## Psalm 33:4-5, 18-19, 20, 22

The verses of this psalm response contain a collection of themes. The passage opens with a statement that reflects the basis of ancient Israel's faith in God (vv. 4-5). This faith is rooted in the truth of God's word, in the faithfulness of God's works, in the justice of God's covenant, and in the steadfastness of God's love. These four attributes encourage the people to place their trust in God. The attributes themselves connote the magnanimity of God's love. Each describes something of God's manner of relating with others.

The fear of the LORD is the posture of respect with which one stands before the awe-inspiring God (vv. 18-19). Those who possess this kind of fear are committed to God and to the ways of God. They are wise and righteous because they live their lives before the constant gaze of God. The virtuous attitude of fear delights God, who is then inclined to attend to the needs of those who fear. Famine and death, the evils from which the psalmist pleads to be delivered, represent all the dangers that intrude into the lives of women and men. Those who fear the LORD turn to God for relief in their distress, and they are rescued. Those without faith look elsewhere for help, and they are confounded.

The psalm ends with a final reference to covenant commitment, or lovingkindness (*ḥesed*, v. 22). Because of this bond God will act as a protecting shield, warding off dangers and bestowing kindness and blessing.

## 2 Timothy 1:8b-10

In this brief passage from one of the Pastoral letters Paul exhorts Timothy his disciple to suffer with Paul (*synkakopathéō*) the misfortunes that come from fidelity to the gospel. Paul is not here thinking merely of the hardships that stem from the ministry. The call of which he speaks (*kaléō*) is the call to holiness, which is extended to all. In this case, the hardships are those that accompany righteous living.

The kerygmatic character of what follows has led some to classify the next section as a Christian hymn (vv. 9-10). It outlines what God has done for us and what Christ has done on our behalf. It begins with a double statement of God's graciousness toward us: God saved us from a life of sin and called us to a life of holiness. We have been rescued from one life and invited into another. There is no question in Paul's mind as to the source of these wondrous blessings; they are all God's doing. Neither salvation nor the call to holiness is the fruit of any deed we might have performed. They are not rewards for good behavior; they come to us freely out of the goodness of God. They are part of God's plan; they are *cháris* (grace).

Though this grace comes to us from God, it comes to us through Christ Jesus. Thus Christ is the mediator through whom God blesses us. There is an allusion to the preexistence of Christ in this statement about the grace of God. Grace was given through Christ before the ages of time, but it was only made manifest through Christ's appearance *(epipháneia)*. This Greek word usually refers to the coming of Christ, his future eschatological manifestation. Here it probably refers to Jesus in his earthly appearance as the agent of eschatological grace.

Paul concludes this Christian hymn by proclaiming that the grace of God is made manifest through Christ Jesus our Savior. His saving action is described as twofold: he destroyed death; he brought life and immortality to light. He destroyed death by not letting death destroy him. He first endured it, and then he threw off its hold on him and rose to new life. Through his resurrection he gave new meaning to both life and immortality (the Greek word is *aphtharsía*—incorruptibility).

The reading closes as it began, with a reference to the gospel. In the first instance Paul refers to the suffering fidelity to the gospel brings. Here the focus is on the gospel as glad tidings; it announces our salvation through Christ Jesus. It is through this gospel we are brought to see the eschatological hope of new life.

## Matthew 17:1-9

The gospel narrative recounts a theophany, a self-revelation of God. There are really two dimensions to this event: the experience of Jesus himself, and the experience of the apostles who accompanied him up the mountain. Several elements in the account place the event squarely within the company of other significant theophanies. The first characteristic is its location. It takes place on a mountain whose significance is less in its name than in its height. High mountains were thought to be places where the gods dwelt. Hence people often traveled to such spots in order to have some experience of that god. It was on a mountain that Jesus was transfigured. There a bright cloud engulfed the apostles, and a voice from the cloud addressed them.

Jesus is transformed before Peter, James, and John, the apparent inner circle of the apostles. The Greek word *metamporphóō* can refer to a change that is merely external or to one that is actually a change of state or being. The once-popular interpretation of this account as a post-resurrection story read back into the time of the public ministry of Jesus has been challenged by most commentators today. In its place is the opinion that the account is not a vision of the future glorification of Jesus but an insight into his identity during his public life. From this point of view, the transformation would be a change that took place when Jesus' inner reality shone forth and transfigured his outer appearance. Like Moses before him (cf. Exod 34:35), Jesus' face shines brightly. However, in this instance his attire is also brilliant. Jesus is seen to be conversing with Moses and Elijah, the representatives of the Law and the Prophets, respectively. These are the men who stood for the entire religious tradition of ancient Israel. The topic of their conversation is not given. It may be their presence confirms the authority of Jesus and the legitimacy of his teaching.

The importance of this teaching is evident in the words spoken from the cloud: Listen to him! As with other incidences in the biblical tradition, the cloud symbolizes the presence of God (cf. Exod 40:35). Here the description of the cloud is curious. One would expect a brilliant cloud to illuminate everything upon which its rays fell. Here it is said to have cast a shadow. Furthermore, it is not clear over whom this shadow is cast. Presumably it is the apostles. Whatever the case may be, from this cloud God both identifies Jesus as Son and gives authority to his teaching. While Moses and Elijah converse with Jesus, the voice from the cloud speaks to the apostles. They are the ones who seem to need the identification of Jesus and the directive from God.

The apostles' response to this two-dimensional experience is also twofold. They would like to prolong Jesus' transfiguration and conversation with the ancient heroes, and they seem eager to participate in such a venture. At least Peter, who acts as spokesperson, is of this mind. However, the voice from heaven strikes fear in their hearts, and they fall prostrate. They may have witnessed Jesus' initial transformation, but they seem not to have seen his return to normal appearance. Using words that frequently accompany an awe-inspiring experience of God, the Jesus they have always known reassures them: Do not be afraid. However, identifying himself as the mysterious Son of Man, he directs them to remain silent about this experience until after his resurrection. It should be noted that the transfigured Jesus was identified as Son of God, while it is as Son of Man that he will be raised from the dead. Though very different, both titles boast an aspect of divinity.

## Themes of the Day

The theme of the mercy of God seen in the First Sunday of Lent carries over into the Second. The account of God's promise to Abram of blessing for himself and through him for the rest of the world is a specific manifestation of this mercy. It signals a new start not merely after the repentance but despite sin (cf. Genesis 11). The unmerited character of God's graciousness is clearly stated in the passage from 2 Timothy. Finally, the christological importance of these lenten Sundays becomes clear in the gospel. It is the death and resurrection of Jesus and not any acts of devotion on our part that will bring about the ultimate blessing of God.

### *Divine Blessings*

The blessings referred to in these readings and upon which we meditate on this Sunday in Lent are undeserved gifts from God. They were not earned. Abram was called out of his family of origin because God had a plan for him, not because Abram had already performed some noteworthy work. In the reading Paul is very clear about the reason for our salvation: it was not because of any works of ours but because of the grace bestowed by God. The three apostles did nothing to warrant the privilege of witnessing the transfiguration of Jesus. They did not even understand its significance, wanting to remain in its magnificence rather than return to the hardships of the ministry. In each case God is not only liberal in bestowing particular blessings, but God seems always ready to lavish us with even more. What alone is required of us is openness to receive the blessings.

### *A New Beginning*

The graciousness of God transforms us in such a way as to effect new beginnings. It can be seen in the promises made to Abram. He leaves the past behind and moves into a new future. It can be seen in the psalm response. The LORD delivers us from death and inspires us to look to the future. We see it in the reading from 2 Timothy. Through Christ Jesus we are called to a new life of holiness; we escape the fetters of death and are brought into the freedom of the resurrection. We see it in the gospel, a glimpse into the future glory of Jesus, which through grace we will be able to share. Lent is a time of new beginnings that find their origin in the abundant blessings of God.

### *Choose Christ*

The ultimate blessing of God is Jesus himself. As Abram was called to be the source of blessing for all others, as Peter, James, and John were chosen to witness the transfiguration of Jesus, so today we too are invited to look to Jesus for inspiration during this holy season. Paul speaks of the salvation Jesus brings as having come not because of any works of righteousness we might have performed but because of the grace of God. The gospel account of the transfiguration confirms the authority of Jesus and the legitimacy of his teaching. Through Moses and Elijah it links him with the cherished tradition of the Jewish nation, while the voice identifying him as beloved Son makes a claim not even ancient Israel dared to make. This vision is a kind of proleptic glimpse into the future. It reveals the glory which is already with Jesus but which will be revealed to all in the future. Once again the lenten readings focus on the merciful action of God in our lives, and in the end they point to Jesus. In them we see the fullness of what it means to be human as well as the unexpected graciousness of God in the lives of the faithful.

## Third Sunday of Lent
### Exodus 17:3-7

The story recounts the murmuring of the people in the wilderness and the miracle of water from the rock, which is God's response to their rebellion. While the people were indeed suffering from thirst, their reaction to the lack of water laid bare their resistance to the leadership of Moses and the shallowness of their trust in God. These were the very people God had miraculously delivered out of Egyptian bondage. Yet they suggest that it was done not out of God's lovingkindness but so they will die of thirst in the wilderness. In their insolence they cry out their challenge: "Is the LORD in our midst or not?"

The mediatorial role of Moses can be plainly seen. It is the authority of Moses that receives the direct attack. However, although the people murmur *(lûn)* against him for having led them out of Egypt and into the desert, they are really rebelling against God. And it is to God that Moses turns in his plight. The seriousness of the situation is seen in his fear that he will be stoned by this rebellious mob. Nonetheless, just as God had delivered the people from the bondage of Egypt through the leadership of Moses, so now, again through the actions of Moses, God gives them the water they demand.

The miracle itself demonstrates that God is indeed in their midst. God responds to their defiance by giving in to their demands. They are in the wilderness where water is scarce, and God has Moses bring forth life-giving water from a lifeless rock. Since the people did not recognize God's reassurance in the signs and wonders of the past, God performs yet another sign. It is as if the miracles are intended merely to meet the physical needs of the people and not necessarily to bring them to faith in God.

Lest the people forget the marvels of the past or question whether Moses is still the agent of God, Moses is instructed to employ again the very staff he used to perform the signs and wonders that surrounded the liberation from Egypt. This staff was a symbol of his own authority and of the divine power it could wield. Since both his and God's role in the lives of the people have here been challenged, using the staff again will reinforce their authority. When Moses strikes the rock in Horeb, the mountain whose name means "dry" or "desolate," life-giving water flows forth. Once again, God brings life out of what is lifeless.

This is a curious story. One wonders how a people who have been the beneficiaries of God's abiding concern and miraculous protection can be so faithless and lacking in trust. After all that God has done, they still put God to the test. The place in the wilderness where this happened is called Massah, which means "testing," and Meribah, which means "dissatisfaction." It is remembered not for the manifestation of divine power that met the people's need but for the murmuring that demonstrated their rebellion. One also wonders about God. Why does God endure such thanklessness, rebellion, and audacity? This is but another example of God's boundless and compassionate love for sinners.

## Psalm 95:1-2, 6-7, 8-9

The responsorial psalm combines an invitation to praise, a plea for openness, and a word from God. The invitation is given three times: Come, let us sing joyfully (v. 1); Let us come into his presence (v. 2); Come, let us bow down (v. 6). Together they seem to be a reenactment of some liturgical movement. There is the initial summons to praise followed by an invitation to enter the presence of God (presumably the Temple), there to bow before God in worship. God then addresses the reverent community.

The relationship that exists between God and the people is characterized by means of several metaphors. God is the Rock of their salvation (v. 1). A rock is solid and secure. It affords grounding for whatever relies on it. A large rock or formation of rocks also provides refuge and shelter from inclement weather and various dangers. It is an apt image to refer to God as the protector of the people. God is also clearly identified as Creator (v. 6). This can be a reference to God as Creator of the universe and everything within it, or it can be a more personal reference to the fashioning of a disparate group of individuals into a coherent community. The image that follows suggests the latter interpretation.

The psalmist identifies the community as the flock and God as the shepherd (v. 6). In a pastoral community such a relationship was quite intimate. Shepherds took total responsibility for their sheep, caring for them and protecting them even at the risk of their own lives. For reasons such as this, the shepherd became a fitting metaphor to describe the monarch, who was expected to act in this same way on behalf of the people of the realm. In this psalm the images of rock and shepherd illustrate the people's perception of God as protector.

Having depicted God as a caring and devoted protector, the psalmist turns again to the people and issues a serious plea that they be open to the voice of God. This plea suggests that "today" the people who have been gathered together will hear God's voice. Since this gathering is clearly liturgical in character (v. 6), it is safe to conclude that the word from God will be a part of the actual liturgical celebration. The people have come to worship God and to receive some word from God that will comfort them or set a direction for their lives.

The word that follows is an appeal by God to respond positively to God, not in the spirit of rebellion that governed their ancestors while they were in the wilderness (cf. Exod 17:1-7; Deut 6:16). During that earlier time the people had demanded signs that would prove the presence and power of God acting on their behalf. They dared to be so demanding despite the fact that they had witnessed God's gracious deliverance of them from Egyptian bondage. God desires hearts that are open, not hearts hardened by selfishness or lack of faith. "Today" the descendants of those rebellious wanderers are called upon to respond with open faith and willing obedience.

## Romans 5:1-2, 5-8

Paul's teaching on justification, though complex and sometimes difficult to understand, is quite clear in this passage. He tells the Christians in Rome they have been justified through the actions of others; they have not justified themselves. The word itself *(dikaióō)* is relational. It is based on the righteousness that originates in God, a righteousness that gives and sustains life, security, and well-being. Human beings are said to be righteous when they respect and enhance the life, security, and well-being that is given and sustained by God. Strictly speaking, they can only do this if they are in right relationship with God and, through this relationship, share in God's righteousness.

According to Paul we have no right to this relationship with God. It has been given to us, won for us by the Lord Jesus Christ. In fact, we did not even deserve it. We were sinners, alienated from God, when Christ died for us and gained access for us to the grace that places us in right relationship with God. Paul tries to explain the astonishing character of this gesture when he says that it is hard enough to die for a good person; to die for someone who is not good is almost unthinkable. Yet that is exactly what Christ did. He died for us while we were yet sinners; he died for us before we had been justified, and his dying gave us access to God.

There is a subtle suggestion here of the place where God sits enthroned in glory. Through his sacrifice Jesus opened the way for us to approach God. We may be brought by Jesus to the threshold of God's presence, but we ourselves must take the step over that threshold. We do this by faith. With this step of faith we no longer stand in enmity; we now stand in grace, in peace with God. The form of the verbs indicate this justification has already been accomplished by the Lord Jesus Christ. He has already gained our salvation, but we have not yet completely worked it out, and so we live in hope.

The last theme Paul develops is that of hope. He maintains that its foundation is the love God has for us. This love was first shown to us in Christ's willingness to die on our behalf even when we were still alienated from God. It is further poured into our hearts through the Spirit, who has been given to us. The prodigality of God's graciousness is beyond comprehension. It is poured out like water, life-giving, enriching, overflowing. Anticipation of the trinitarian theology is unmistakable.

## John 4:5-42

The story of Jesus' encounter with the Samaritans can be divided into three parts. The first is the discourse on living water (vv. 7-15); the second is the discussion about true worship (vv. 19-26); the third recounts the acceptance of Jesus by the people of the town (vv. 39-42). The Samaritan woman plays a significant role throughout the entire account. She is first the one with whom Jesus enters into dialogue, and she is the messenger who heralds the good news to the other townsfolk.

The fatigue of Jesus and his request for a drink from the well set the stage for his exchange with the woman. He asks for water when in fact he is the one who will give water, which he calls the "gift of God." "Living water" could refer to running water, especially a kind of font that bubbles up from a spring. However, "gift" *(dōrea)* is used almost exclusively to refer to divine bounty, suggesting that this living water seems to have a very special character. The living-water metaphor itself has a long and rich history in the religious tradition of Israel. The prophets used it to refer to the spiritual refreshment that flowed from the Temple (cf. Ezek 47:1; Zech 14:80). It is also a reference to the teaching of the wise (Prov 13:14) or to Woman Wisdom herself (Sir 24:21, 24-27). In each of these instances living water is a principle of spiritual life.

It should have been clear from what Jesus said that he was not talking about the kind of water that could be drawn from the well. However, his real meaning was not immediately evident, so the woman continued in the original vein of the conversation. Her misunderstanding was the opening for Jesus' instruction. The water from Jacob's well, considered a sacred ancestral spot, was merely water. It could not permanently quench the thirst of those who drank from it. On the other hand, one drink of the water Jesus gives is enough to satisfy one forever. The woman's response is cryptic. Does she still misunderstand? Or is she merely playing with the metaphor?

Jesus' unexplained knowledge of the woman's marital situation prompts her to call him a prophet and to engage him in a discussion about the proper place to worship God. Biblical Law prescribed a single site without naming it (Deut 12:5-6). The Jews believed Jerusalem was this favored place, and they pointed to the prophetic tradition to substantiate their claim (cf. Isa 2:3; 24:23). The Samaritans worshiped on Mount Gerizim, a magnificent elevation from which one could see both the Jordan River on the east and the Mediterranean Sea on the west.

Once again Jesus moves the conversation away from what is merely perceptible to the level of deep spiritual meaning, from a discussion of the place of worship to one that characterizes the manner of worship. Before he does this he draws a significant theological distinction between these two religious groups, which have common ancestry. He insists that the promises of salvation were fulfilled through the Jews, while the Samaritans believed that only the Torah (Five Books of Moses) was revealed, and so they rejected prophetic messianic promises. Jesus declares that when the eschatological hour arrives all religious observance, regardless of how noble and efficacious it may have been, will be superseded by worship animated by the Spirit. The trinitarian character of this statement is clear. In the age of fulfillment God will be worshiped in the Spirit that will be given by Jesus.

The account goes to great lengths to contrast the Jews and the Samaritans. The character of the Samaritan woman is questionable. She is alone at the well at a time when women do not normally draw water, and she engages in conversation with a strange man. She has had five husbands, when the Law of Moses frowned on more than three marriages. Even her Samaritan religion is described as inferior to the religion of the Jews.

The author draws the lines so starkly in order to underscore the universality of the invitation of Jesus. The woman is a questionable member (a sinner) of a subordinate group (a woman) of a despised people (a Samaritan). Yet she is the one Jesus approaches, and she is the one to whom he reveals himself as Messiah; she is the one who heralds this good news to the people in the town. They listen to her testimony but then are convinced by the teaching of Jesus himself. The word of salvation takes root in the hearts of the despised and marginalized, and it grows into a great harvest.

## Themes of the Day

The lectionary readings for the first two Sundays of Lent were arranged in such a way as to call our attention to the relationship between sin and grace. Now the readings begin to exhort us to make a choice. These are the Sundays that include the scrutinies, the Sundays when we uncover the secret sins that might keep us from committing ourselves wholeheartedly to the gospel of Jesus. The readings are intended primarily for instruction of the catechumens, a preparation for their incorporation into the People of God. However, they also provide us with an opportunity to recommit ourselves to the values and responsibilities that captured our religious imaginations when we first made our choice for Christ.

## Scrutinies

There is a kind of progression in the focus of the three scrutiny Sundays. In each instance it is the reading from the Gospel of John that determines the principal dimension of our consideration. On the First Sunday we are invited to rivet our attention to personal matters. The reading from John recounts Jesus' encounter with the Samaritan woman, the character of her life, and the step that she would have to take in order to move beyond that life and venture into the new life of grace. The Second Sunday is more ecclesial in nature. The leaders of the people represent the perspective taken by the community of believers. On the Third Sunday our concerns are more universal. There we consider life and death, matters with which all peoples of all times, places, and cultures are concerned. In each instance we are told once again to look to Jesus to see what insight is being revealed or what response would be appropriate.

## For What Do We Thirst?

All people thirst for meaning, but of what does that meaning consist? Or where is that meaning to be found? The people in the desert thirsted for water, but it is clear they misunderstood their thirst. Did they think there would be no thirst in the wilderness? Did they expect God to exempt them from such a fundamental response to need? The woman of Samaria thirsted. That is precisely why she went to the well in the first place. Her conversation with Jesus showed that she thirsted for understanding and insight as well.

For what do we thirst in this world of such great excess and unmeasured need? Life has not become simpler with all the advances of which we are the recipients. And still we thirst for more—for the newest, the fastest, the best. How much is enough, and when do we cross the line into "too much"? If possessions are not our concern, might we be thirsting for acclaim, for prestige, for status in the community? Or are our desires lodged in areas of comfort, of pleasure, or of satisfaction? For what do we thirst, and what will we choose?

*Choose Christ*

The gospel readings for the scrutiny Sundays very clearly lay out the choices placed before the catechumens and the rest of the believing community as well. This Sunday it is between water that quenches thirst and water that does not. Jesus identifies himself as the source of water that guarantees eternal life. He places before the Samaritan woman a choice that requires a step of profound faith. She knows the thirst-quenching quality of the water from Jacob's well, but she is not acquainted with the water promised by this stranger, a stranger who is also an enemy of her people. The choice is not an obvious one. It is a choice made in faith.

A similar choice is placed before us. We know the demands of our culture; we are acquainted with the circumstances of our lives. Are we able to acknowledge the sins of which we are guilty, recognize the grace being offered to us, and make the right choice?

## Fourth Sunday of Lent
### 1 Samuel 16:1b, 6-7, 10-13a

The search for the new king and the choice and anointing of David open a new chapter in the story of the people of Israel. Each step of the way is determined by God, making the history of Israel a history of salvation. In this episode it is God, through the prophet, who decides from which family the kings will come, and even which son in that family. The account opens with a statement of divine election and closes with a report of divine confirmation.

David is the last son to be presented to the prophet because his father does not even think he is a viable consideration. The symbolism in this account is telling. Jesse brought seven sons to the prophet, a number long considered a sign of completeness. David is the eighth son, the one who is something of an outsider. He is obviously considered too young or unimportant to be part of the pool of candidates. He has not even been invited to participate in the sacrifice. Yet he is the one into whose heart the LORD has looked, and obviously God has been pleased with what is there. The young shepherd will be God's king. Once again, God has chosen the weak things of the world to confound the strong.

When David is finally brought to Samuel, the prophet is struck by his appearance. Samuel had been instructed earlier by God not to consider the lofty stature of Eliab, yet he is taken by the attractiveness of his younger brother. There may be another meaning to the description of David's appearance. He is said to be ruddy (*'admônî*) of complexion. Those who heard the story would have thought immediately of the first man *('ādām),* for the two words come from the same stem. The storyteller may have wanted to draw parallels between David and Adam. Just as the first man was formed out of the dust, so this young man was chosen out of obscurity. The first man was the progenitor of the race; the second man would be the founder of a dynasty. The future of the People of God rested on the shoulders of both men.

Samuel's choice of David was by direct command of God. The anointing was a solemn and sacred action that ceremonially sealed God's election. Following the ritual, the spirit of the Lord rushed upon David. Within the early traditions of Israel the spirit of the Lord was understood as a principle of dynamic divine action, a force that had unique effects in human history. Those who were seized by the spirit were thus empowered to act within the community in some unique fashion. In this way God's saving power was brought to the community through the agency of certain individuals. The particular needs of the community determined the character of this action. The spirit took hold of judges (cf. Jdg 3:10) and prophets (cf. Isa 61:1). This story recounts how it took hold of a future king.

### Psalm 23:1-3a, 3b-4, 5, 6

This responsorial psalm is one of the most familiar and best loved psalms of the entire Psalter. It paints vivid pictures of a carefree existence, peaceful rest, and abundant fruitfulness. Although "shepherd" suggests a flock rather than merely one sheep, here the focus is on the individual. In addition to this image God is characterized as a host, one who supervises a banquet and within whose house the psalmist ultimately dwells.

The psalm opens with a metaphor that sets the tone of the entire song. It is the responsibility of the shepherd to find pastures that will provide enough grazing and abundant water for the entire flock, to lead them there without allowing any of the sheep to stray and be lost, to guard them from predators or dangers of any kind, and to attend to their every need. To characterize the Lord as a shepherd is to trust that God will discharge all these responsibilities. The personal dimension of the psalm shifts the care given to the entire flock to concern for one individual, making God's care a very intimate matter. Not only are the physical needs of the psalmist satisfied, but the soul, the very life force *(nepesh)* of the person, is renewed.

The guidance of the shepherd is more than provident, it is moral as well. The psalmist is led in the paths of righteousness (v. 3), and this is done for the sake of the Lord's name. Since one's name is a part of the very essence of the person, this indicates that the way of the Lord is the way of righteousness. Following this we can say that the magnanimous care shown by the shepherd flows from enduring righteousness rather than from some passing sentiment of heart. This is confirmed by the reference to the covenant kindness *(ḥesed)* that surrounds the psalmist (v. 6). In other words, the divine shepherd's tender commitment to the flock and to each individual within it is as lasting as is God's covenant commitment.

The psalmist is confident of the Lord's protection, as demonstrated in his mention of the shepherd's rod and staff, which were used to ward off wild animals as well as poachers. The valley of deep darkness, can be a reference to the darkest part of the terrain or to the gloom that can overwhelm an individual. However, it also has a mythological connotation and is frequently interpreted as death. Whichever meaning is intended here, the psalmist claims to be unafraid, for the presence of the LORD is reassuring.

The image of the shepherd securing nourishment for the flock suggests another metaphor, that of the host who prepares a lavish banquet for guests. Many societies have a very strict code of hospitality. The people are obliged to provide the very best provisions they have, even for their enemies. The LORD spreads out such a banquet here, which not only affords nourishment but also is a public witness to God's high regard for the psalmist, who will continue to enjoy God's favor in God's house. Whether this indicates the Temple or is merely a reference to the place where God dwells, the fundamental meaning is clear. The psalmist has been under the loving guidance of the LORD and will remain there forever.

## Ephesians 5:8-14

The move from darkness to light is the principal metaphor used by the author to describe the radical change that has taken place in the lives of the Christians as a result of their commitment to Christ. The seriousness of their original plight is evidenced in the way in which they are characterized. They were not merely surrounded by darkness or in the midst of darkness. They were so much a part of that darkness they were actually identified with it. But no more. As identified as they had been with darkness, so are they now identified with light, the light that comes from the Lord.

The catechesis that follows revolves around two major imperatives. The first (v. 8) is a standard Christian exhortation: If you are in the light, live ("walk," from the Greek *peripatéo*) as children of the light! This admonition comes from the Wisdom tradition, which maintains there are only two courses of life: the wise way of the righteous and the foolish way of the sinner. The light-darkness binary opposition is another way of representing this contrast. The author is drawing this contrast in order to inspire the Christians to hold fast to the new life that has been given to them.

The three qualities produced by the light—goodness, righteousness, truth—are merely symbolic of the complete transformation of character this light can effect. Goodness is a quality of moral excellence; it is one of the fruits of the Spirit (cf. Gal 5:22). Although righteousness is really a divine attribute, humans share in it as long as they live lives in harmony with God's plan. Truth connotes sincerity, genuineness, the absence of sham or pretense. These three qualities describe a life lived openly in the light that comes from Christ.

In the imperative (v. 11) the Christians are not only warned about the works of darkness but urged to expose them. The author is not suggesting that Christians set out to disclose what is even too shameful for mention. Instead, the counsel given here is a play on the difference between virtuous behavior, which can be plainly seen because it is done in the light, and shameful behavior, which is hidden in the secret of darkness. The author has already said that the Christians themselves *are* light in the Lord. Earlier they were encouraged to live honest and open lives. It is these lives that are the light that exposes the works of darkness. In other words, authentic Christian living will itself illumine the darkness and expose the shameful behavior performed in its shadows.

The passage ends with a cryptic saying. It contains three phrases closely associated with Christian initiation. All three phrases describe the transition from a state of inertia or restriction to one of vibrancy. From sleep to wakefulness; from death to new life; from darkness to illumination. It is clear from these metaphors that the Christians have entered into a new state of being that will require of them a new way of living.

## John 9:1-41

The account of the healing of the man born blind consists of the report of a miraculous cure; the interrogation of the healed man, during which he refuses to repudiate Jesus; Jesus' identification of himself; and the man's confession of faith. Throughout the account the lines are drawn between darkness and light, between blindness and sight. The cause-and-effect relationship between sin and suffering is behind the initial inquiry of the disciples. Whose sin caused this man's blindness? Jesus responds that the impairment is the occasion for the power of God to be manifested.

The cure itself is not a restoration, for the man was born blind. It is more of a new creation. The author takes advantage of the belief that saliva has curative properties. His use of the ground is reminiscent of one of the ancient creation accounts (cf. Gen 2:7). Jesus, who was sent by God (v. 4), sends the man to the pool named "One who has been sent." There the waters wash away his blindness; by means of the waters he is made a new creation.

The cured man now becomes the subject of a series of interrogations. The first one is carried out by the people who knew him as a begging blind man. They are astonished at his transformation, and they inquire as to its source. His initial testimony is merely a report of the events that had occurred along with the name of the healer. He is next questioned by the Pharisees, who are divided over their opinion of the righteousness of one who would heal on the sabbath. The man himself professes that Jesus is a prophet. A third interrogation follows, this time it is of the parents of the man. They are afraid to accord any kind of acclaim to Jesus lest they lose their standing in the religious community. Finally, the man is brought forward again. Unlike his parents, he boldly proclaims that his cure is evidence that Jesus is from God. The man pays the price for his confession of Jesus; he is expelled.

The man has progressed from simply knowing the name of the one who cured him to professing that Jesus is a prophet, then to proclaiming that he comes from God. The final stage in his profession of faith occurs when he encounters Jesus a second time. When Jesus reveals his identity to him, the one whose eyes have been opened attests to his faith in Jesus and accords him the kind of reverent adoration that belongs to God.

As mentioned above, the struggle between darkness and light, between blindness and sight, is a thread that runs throughout this account. First, Jesus uses a binary form to underscore the urgency of his ministry. He and the disciples with him must do God's work while it is yet day, for the night will come when such work will have to cease. Jesus identifies himself as the light of the world. Next, the man, who is gradually brought from physical blindness to sight, also progressively moves from spiritual blindness to religious insight. This is not true about the Pharisees. Those who prided themselves for being disciples of Moses were blind to the truth that the newly cured man saw so clearly. The one who was blind sees, and those who can see are blind.

## Themes of the Day

The Fourth Sunday of Lent is also the second of the scrutiny Sundays. The principal theme today is seeing. Although physical sight is very important, in both the first readings and the gospel such sight is really the point of entry into a much deeper theme, that of religious insight. These readings also play on the themes of darkness = blindness and light = sight.

### As God Sees

Humans see and judge by appearances, but God looks into the heart and there finds the real person. David was the youngest son of a family of many sons. According to the custom of the time he would have been the last person to be chosen as leader. However, as the Scriptures tell us so often, God's ways are not our ways. God turns things upside down; God chooses the weak things of the world to confound the strong.

The standards by which God judges are not superficial, as are so many of the standards of the world. It is not age, beauty, or physical strength that is important; it is not social position or religious role that is preferred. God chooses whom God chooses. God saw in David, the insignificant shepherd, the potential for being the chief shepherd of his people. The man who was born blind became the one through whom others would see the mighty works of God. Yet neither young David nor the man in the gospel made the initial step; each simply responded with openness to God's choice of him.

By what criteria do we judge others? Do we consider some people too insignificant for greatness? Are we overly concerned with status? Do we categorize people according to the disease or physical limitation they must endure? Do we sometimes blame them for their disability? The readings for this Sunday offer us an opportunity to look carefully at how we perceive others. Do our eyes perceive life in accord with the standards of a materialistic, body-orientated, pleasure-seeking society? Or do we look into the other's heart, as God does?

## Does the Community See?

The man in the gospel narrative was given his sight, and he believed. In fact, in this story seeing is believing; sight stands for faith. There is a paradoxical shift here: the man who was blind is the one who has real sight; those who can see are blind to the power of God. Although this is a story of an individual, it is also a report of the faith of a community. The community of which the man was a member did not believe, so it did not see the deep meaning of his cure. It judged by appearances: someone must have sinned to cause this blindness. Even the apostles thought in this way until Jesus explained it was otherwise. This religious community had no idea that human weakness or vulnerability was the doorway through which the power of God would enter someone's life.

This lenten season invites the religious community to examine how it perceives reality. In what areas is our community of faith blind? Have we excluded people from membership because they do not seem to fit? Are we afraid of what we do not understand? Do we have inappropriate expectations? Are we unwilling to change our minds? Does our community of faith look beyond the external appearances and perceive the inner reality?

## Choose Christ

As with the other scrutiny Sundays, catechumens and long-standing members alike are exhorted to make a choice. Jesus is the one who gives sight to blind eyes, who gives religious insight to those who are open to receive it. However, it is very clear there is a price one is called upon to pay. Not only must we put away the works of darkness—our blindness to the needs of others, our prejudices, our complacency—but we must be ready to suffer for our choice. We might lose status in the community, we might be ostracized. We must choose. Will it be the standards of the world or the power of God in Jesus Christ?

## Fifth Sunday of Lent
### Ezekiel 37:12-14

In this oracle of salvation Ezekiel uses bodily resurrection as a metaphor for the reestablishment of the nation after its exile in a foreign land. The standard prophetic declaration, "Thus says the LORD," indicates the resolute nature of the message. If God says it, regardless of how incredible it might appear it will surely happen. This decisiveness is underscored in the last words of the passage, "I have promised, and I will do it."

The scene is a graveyard, the ultimate place of death and decay. Three divine statements of reversal are made: the sealed graves will be opened; those who are dead will rise; the exiled will return home. The fact that the metaphor describes resurrection from the dead does not necessarily mean the people believed it might actually happen. In fact, its improbability may be one of the strongest reasons for employing it here, for then God's wondrous power over death itself could be revealed. Resurrection would proclaim that God can bring life out of death, can make the impossible possible.

The restoration envisioned is likened to creation. In the beginning, the creature that had been formed from the dust of the ground became a living being when God breathed the breath *(nᵉshāmâ)* of life into it (cf. Gen 2:7). Here, those in the grave live again when they are raised from the dust of death and are given God's own spirit *(rûaḥ)*. Both original creation and this resurrection from the dead are unconditional gifts from a magnanimous God. This feature of the metaphor is remarkable when applied to the reestablishment of the nation, especially since the people believed their exile had been a punishment for their sins. This suggests they viewed their restoration as yet another pure gift from God.

The passage testifies to God's absolute and unconditional control over the powers of life and death, destruction and restoration. Just as the metaphor of bodily resurrection illustrated the incredible nature of the restoration of the nation, so its reestablishment might have led the people to believe resurrection itself was possible as well. Whatever God promises will come to pass.

### Psalm 130:1-2, 3-4, 5-6, 7-8

The psalm response comes from one of the seven psalms known in Christian devotion as the Penitential psalms. It opens with a cry for relief (vv. 1-2) followed by an acknowledgment of the helplessness of sinful human beings in the presence of the righteous God (vv. 3-4); a confession of faith (vv. 5-6); and an acknowledgment of God's covenant love (vv. 7-8).

The psalmist has been cast into the very depths of misery. Depths refers to deep waters, the place of ultimate chaos, the place where death reigns and life has no power. This misery could be a form of physical affliction, an interior torment, or some kind of hardship brought on by another. The psalm itself is not specific. Whatever the case may be, the psalmist knows where to look for help. He prevails upon God to turn an open ear to this fervent supplication. This in itself is an act of faith and trust. Faith that God *can* come to the psalmist's aid, and trust that God indeed *will*. There is no direct correlation made between the psalmist's misfortune and possible personal sin, but what follows suggests some kind of connection.

The psalmist contrasts two ways of understanding God's manner of dealing with sinners. The first focuses on strict retributive justice. If God ever meted out the exact punishments that human sin deserves, no one would be able to endure it. This admission asserts not only the character of human culpability but also its scope. Rebellion against God is a serious matter, and all women and men are guilty of it. Even those who are fundamentally upright deviate at times from the path of righteousness.

The psalmist insists that God acts toward sinners in a very different way. Moved by compassion, God shows mercy to those who have sinned and grants them forgiveness. There is no way human beings can earn this forgiveness. It is a free gift from God, granted so God may be revered or feared *(yārē')*. While the expression "fear of God" includes the notion of dread and terror, its principal connotation is reverence and awe in the face of God's majesty and power. Here it is God's willingness to forgive that evokes such awe.

The proper attitude of one who fears God is trust (the verb is also translated "wait for"). Trust requires that we bide our own time until God's designated time. Willingness to wait is frequently the measure of one's trust. The psalmist is willing to wait but not without eager anticipation. In fact, the psalmist waits for God to put an end to the terrors that accompany misery and the afflictions that characterize life—more than a sentinel waits for the dawn to extinguish the darkness and terror of night and bring to conclusion the arduous time of watching.

The psalmist maintains that God will surely act in the future because God is committed to Israel with covenant love *(ḥesed)*. This love is the basis of God's mercy and forgiveness, of God's willingness to redeem Israel from all its sins. It is also the basis of the psalmist's own trust in God's graciousness.

## Romans 8:8-11

Paul contrasts two ways of living: life in the flesh and life in the spirit. Although "flesh" and "spirit" can refer to two distinct aspects of human nature, they both can also connote the whole human being, but from a particular point of view or with a certain life-direction. It is in the latter manner that Paul uses the concepts. When Paul refers to the flesh, he is not thinking of specific bodily or sexual behavior. He is speaking of human nature in all its limitations, limitations that sometimes incline one away from God and the things of God. On the other hand, life in the spirit is attuned to God. It is, in fact, that dimension of the human being that can be joined to the very Spirit of God.

Paul's denunciation of life in the flesh is unqualified. Such a life-direction cannot please God. Life in the spirit, on the other hand, is a form of union with God. He assures the Christians they are in the spirit if the Spirit of God dwells within them. He does not state when or how this indwelling may have occurred. However, in true trinitarian fashion, he does liken the Spirit of God to the Spirit of Christ, and he maintains it is through this Spirit that resurrection is promised.

The real point of this passage is the resurrection of those who are in union with God. Paul speaks of life and death in two ways. Reversing the metaphor slightly, he states that those who live in the Spirit have Christ living in them. This is the same Christ who, through his own death, has vanquished the powers of death. Although sin can still exact physical death as a punishment, it cannot quench the spirit that lives because of righteousness. Therefore, just as Christ conquered death and lives anew, so those joined to Christ will share in his victory and enjoy new life.

Paul does not deny that Christians are under the same sentence of death as are all other people. However, he contends that sin and death are not the ultimate victors. The Spirit of God raised Jesus, and that same Spirit will raise those who here and now live in the Spirit of Christ.

## John 11:1-45

The death and resurrection of Lazarus proleptically point to the death and resurrection of Jesus and of everyone who believes in him. Lazarus is a shortened form of Eleazar, which means "God helps," a name that foreshadows the events that will take place. Various aspects of the motif of life-and-death run through each scene of this dramatically recounted incident, revealing its many-faceted character.

It is clear that Lazarus' illness was fatal. Knowing this, Jesus declares its real purpose was not the death of Lazarus but the glory of God and of the Son of God. He waits until there is no question about the irreversibility of this death, which will really be a condition for the manifestation of Jesus as the resurrection and the life. When he finally decides to go, the disciples remind him of the jeopardy in which he will be placing his own life and perhaps theirs. His death could be the price he will pay for Lazarus' life.

Jesus' response to their objections is an enigmatic parable about day and night, which can be understood in at least three ways. The first is the obvious and literal meaning. During the day we see where we are going; at night we can stumble and fall. The second capitalizes on the fact that the light is not outside but within the person. It is an inner light that guides rather than the light of day. One stumbles when there is no inner light. Finally, the light can also refer to Jesus. This interpretation would suggest the disciples will be safe as long as they remain united to Jesus. If they desert him, they risk stumbling in the dark.

Whether or not the disciples understood this saying, it is only when he straightforwardly announces Lazarus' death that they realize Jesus has been speaking cryptically. They have no idea of the irony in their words (*sothésetai* can mean both "will recover" and "will be saved"). They think Lazarus will recover; Jesus knows he will be saved from death. Irony is also present in Thomas' exclamation. He probably does not realize the implications of his words when he suggests to the others that they accompany Jesus, even to his death. Their misapprehension emphasizes the unfathomable nature of Jesus' future actions.

All of this prepares for the instruction Jesus gives to Martha. Along with her sister, Mary (v. 32), she had hoped Jesus would come to heal her brother. She has no idea he has come to bring Lazarus back from the dead. Her response to Jesus' assurance that Lazarus will rise shows that she shares the Pharisee's view of a general resurrection and judgment at the end of time (cf. Dan 12:2). With a self-revelatory exclamation (*egó eími*) Jesus proclaims that *he* is the resurrection and the life, and faith in him will guarantee life for others. The explanation of this claim is the heart of Jesus' teaching here. Belief in Jesus establishes a bond of life that not even death can sever. Although believers die physically, this bond will bring them back to life. Furthermore, this bond will survive physical death and keep believers from an eternal death.

The solemn question is posed: "Do you believe?" Martha's answer is immediate and unequivocal: "Yes, Lord!" She elaborates on her faith, assigning three messianic titles to Jesus: Christ, Son of God, the one who is to come. She may not know Jesus is about to accomplish the impossible, but her faith and trust in him are secure. Having explained to Martha what he meant when he claimed to be the resurrection and the life, Jesus next acts it out. He first prays to God, not in petition for divine power, for having been sent by God, he already possesses it. He prays in thanksgiving, for he knows God always hears him. His prayer is really a public testimony to his relationship with God, and it is prayed for the sake of those around him.

The marvel he has performed cannot be denied, but it can be misunderstood. Jesus is not merely a wonder-worker; he himself has the power of resurrection, and he is the source of eternal life. Although Lazarus' raising is merely a temporary resuscitation, the new lease on life given to him is a powerful sign of the eternal life that faith in Jesus guarantees.

## Themes of the Day

The themes for this Sunday add a third dimension to the reflections of the scrutiny Sundays. On the Third Sunday of Lent we considered the plight of the individual (the Samaritan woman), and we saw Jesus as the source of living water. On the Fourth Sunday we encountered the blindness of the believing community, and we watched Jesus give the man both sight and insight. Today we consider the universality of death, and Jesus is revealed to us as the resurrection and the life.

### Death

The first theme for this Sunday recalls the beginning of Lent. On the First Sunday we reflected on death, and we return to that reflection today. Death is the fate of all human beings. No one is spared. The grave swallows up the righteous and the sinner alike. As a metaphor, death can stand for many things. The prophet Ezekiel witnessed the death of the nation. The gospel reports the death of Lazarus. Although Paul refers to the mortal character of our physical bodies, he is more concerned with spiritual life and death. Death attacks each of us in all three of these ways. We are all mortal and subject to physical death; we are all sinners and must deal with the implications of spiritual death; we are all subject to the consequences of social sins such as terrorism, violence, group hatred, greed, and ecological exploitation. The question before us is whether we are going to allow death to reign in our lives and our communities.

### God's Offer of New Life

All three readings for this Sunday, as well as the psalm response, point out our inability to raise ourselves out of the deaths that afflict us. In the passage from Ezekiel it is God who promises to open the graves of the people; the people are helpless to do anything. The psalmist cries to God from the depths of pain and helplessness. Acknowledging human propensity to sin, Paul credits the Spirit of God with transforming death into life. Finally, Jesus calls Lazarus out of the grave and returns him to his life. As with the First Sunday of Lent, so today we see that God does not leave us to languish in our various deaths. Instead, God offers us new life out of the tombs. In some instances it is another chance at the life that was once enjoyed; in others it is an opportunity to enter into an entirely new way of living.

Throughout the lenten season the readings have invited us to meditate on the mercy and compassion of God, on God's willingness to give us chance after chance despite our unrighteousness. There has been no insistence on penitential practices. Instead, it is almost as if God is asking for another chance, another chance to shower us with mercy. If we but accept the new life offered us we can be reconciled with the people from whom we are alienated. We can throw off the burdens of resentment and forgive those who have offended us. We can be released from our preoccupation with ourselves and be attentive to the needs of others. Even when we experience in our bodies the approach of death itself, we can cherish in a new way the life we have and the people that are in that life.

### Choose Christ

In the face of death we are encouraged to choose life. This is particularly strong in the reading from Romans and in the gospel. In both readings we see that this life can be found only in Christ. Paul draws a sharp contrast between the flesh (human limitations) and the spirit (the power that comes from God). It is the Spirit of God at work in us through Christ that transforms us. In the gospel Jesus holds life and death in his hands because he is the "resurrection and the life." These readings are placed before us today so that once again we can make a choice. Will we choose death or life? Will we choose our own willfulness or Christ?

### Palm Sunday of the Lord's Passion
### At the Procession
## Matthew 21:1-11

The account of Jesus' entry into Jerusalem can be divided into two parts: a description of the directions given to his disciples to procure the ass and the colt on which Jesus will ride into the city (vv. 1-5), and his actual entry into the city (vv. 6-11). His actions in this account have symbolic meaning, since they reinterpret several royal messianic traditions. This is particularly true regarding the details surrounding the acquisition of the animals. Jesus does not enter the Holy City on foot as a pilgrim would. Instead, he rides in as a messianic king (cf. Zech 9:9). There is some confusion about the number of animals used. Surely Jesus would not ride in on two animals. There is also question about the species—an ass and a colt. Actually, "colt" could refer to the young of any number of animals, therefore, to the young of an ass. If the colt was as yet unbroken and therefore somehow ritually clean, mention of two animals could be a reference to the custom of bringing a parent animal along when introducing a colt to service.

Two other features of the account contain royal allusions. First, kings had the right to press privately owned animals into their service whenever the situation seemed to warrant such action. (Even today, in an emergency, officials can similarly appropriate what they need.) This practice could explain both Jesus' directive and the subsequent compliance of those who initially questioned the disciples' behavior. Second, the explanation given, "The Master (*kýrios*) needs it!" suggests that some kind of prerogative on Jesus' part is in the background. Finally, Jesus is in complete control of this incident. He knows in advance what is available, what can be done, and what should be said. He gives his disciples directions to follow, and they find that in each instance he had foreknowledge and authority.

The event occurred at Bethphage, a village east of Jerusalem. The narrative describes a dramatic scene of Jesus coming over the crest of the eastern hill at the Mount of Olives, a place long associated with the appearance of the Messiah (cf. Zech 14:4). The people along the path spread their cloaks on the ground before Jesus as their ancestors had formerly done in deference to a king (cf. 2 Kgs 9:13), and they praise him with an acclamation taken from one of the psalms (cf. Ps 118:25-26). This psalmic blessing became part of the liturgical greeting of those who met pilgrims as they entered the Temple. Here the bystanders direct the acclamation to Jesus, thus making it a cry of homage and not merely one of greeting. In this portrayal the one who comes in the Lord's name is the one who inaugurates the coming kingdom of David. These features point to Jesus as the fulfillment of the Davidic messianic expectations. This is reason to exult "in the highest!"

Contrary to those who have claimed such a festive procession was commonplace, the reading states that the entire city was electrified by the occasion. Those within the city inquired as to the identity of the one who created such a stir. The people who accompanied Jesus stated that he was the prophet from Nazareth in Galilee. The designation "prophet" may refer to Jesus' own ministry. On the other hand, it could be an allusion to "the prophet," one of the messianic figures of Israel's tradition (cf. John 1:21). Whichever the case, the crowds recognize Jesus' prophetic character.

## *At the Mass*

### Isaiah 50:4-7

The dynamics of hearing and speaking focus prominently in this passage. The claim is made that God has both appointed the speaker to a particular ministry and provided him with what is essential if the ministry is to be effective, namely ears to hear God's word and a well-trained tongue to speak that word to others. This word is alive and fresh each day, for God opens the speaker's ears morning after morning. This means the latter must be always attentive to hear the word that is given. Although the speaker is identified as a disciple (one who is well-trained), the description is precisely that of the prophet, one who hears God's word and proclaims it.

The ability to speak and the words spoken all come from God. They are given to the speaker, but they are for the sake of the weary. Although the text does not indicate who these weary might be or the character of the words themselves, it does seem to presume these people are in some way downtrodden, and the words are words of comfort.

A heavy price is exacted of the speaker. He suffers both physical attack and personal insult. He is beaten, his beard is plucked, he is spit upon. Despite all of this he does not recoil from his call. Moreover, he does not even seem to ward off the blows that come his way. He willingly accepts what appears to be the consequence of his prophetic ministry to the weary. No explanation is given as to why this activity should precipitate such a violent response from others, or even who these persecutors might be. All we know is that the ministry generates such a response and the speaker does not abandon it or take himself out of harm's way. The suffering endured is willingly accepted.

In the face of all of the affliction the speaker maintains that God is his strength. This is an unusual statement, for such maltreatment would normally have been interpreted as evidence God was on the side of his persecutors. Although he has been assaulted the speaker declares that he is not disgraced and will not be put to shame. There are no grounds for the speaker to make these claims other than utter confidence in God, certainty of the authenticity of his call, and a conviction of the truth of the words he communicates.

Much of the content of this passage resonates with that found in many of the laments. However, there is really no complaint here, just a description of the sufferings that accrue from faithfully carrying out the mission assigned by God. If anything, this passage resembles a declaration of confidence in God's sustaining presence.

### Psalm 22:8-9, 17-18, 19-20, 23-24

The psalm is a combination of a lament (vv. 8-9; 17-20) and a thanksgiving song (vv. 23-24). The imagery used is both vivid and forceful. In some places it is so realistic that one cannot distinguish with certainty factual description from poetic metaphor. While the psalm may have grown out of the struggle of one person, mention of the assembly *(qāhāl)* adds a communal liturgical dimension to its final form.

The opening verses describe the derision the psalmist must endure from onlookers. These spectators are not explicitly identified as enemies. They are merely people who look upon the affliction of the psalmist and revile him rather than comfort him. The actual taunt is graphically described. Those who mock him part their lips to sneer at him, perhaps to hiss. They wag their heads in ridicule. The most cutting derision may be the words they hurl at him. He is reviled not only because he suffers but primarily because in his suffering he clings to God in confidence. It appears the onlookers are mocking what they consider to be the psalmist's misplaced trust. Their taunt throws into question whether there is any point to such trust. Does God really care what happens to this pitiful man?

The metaphors used to describe the bystanders are trenchant. They are characterized as encircling dogs or some other type of predatory pack ready to tear him limb from limb. They are bloodthirsty assailants assaulting his body. They are rapacious thieves stripping the very clothes off his back. Nothing is safe from their savagery, neither the psalmist's person nor his possessions. In the end, he lies humiliated, stripped, and wounded. His integrity has been challenged and his trust in God ridiculed.

Neither the mockery nor the brutality of these onlookers can undermine the devotion of the psalmist. In the face of all this suffering he clings to hope. Turning to God, he prays for a sense of God's presence and for deliverance from his misery. He does not seek reprisals; he seeks relief. These verses do not tell us whether the psalmist perceives his suffering as punishment for some offense, but they do indicate the psalmist does not believe his unfortunate predicament should keep him separated from God. Suffering and devotion are not incompatible.

The reading ends with an exclamation associated with thanksgiving. This implies either that the psalmist's entreaties have been heard and he has been granted relief from this suffering or that he is convinced it will happen and he rejoices in anticipation. Since one's name holds part of the essence of a person, to proclaim the name of God is to recognize and praise the greatness, in this case the graciousness, of God. The text suggests this acclamation will take place within a liturgical assembly. The psalmist will make a public declaration of gratitude and praise. Although the identification of the assembly as a gathering of brothers (v. 23) reveals a clear gender bias, the further mention of the descendants of Jacob (the Hebrew has "seed"; v. 24) indicates the intended inclusivity. The psalmist will proclaim his praise and thanksgiving before all the people, so that all of the people can join him in praising God.

## Philippians 2:6-11

This christological reflection on the nature and mission of Jesus can be divided into two parts. In the first (vv. 6-8) Jesus is the subject of the action; in the second (vv. 9-11) God is. The first part describes Jesus' humiliation; the second recounts his exaltation by God.

The first verse sets the tone for the actions of Christ Jesus. He did not cling to the dignity that was rightfully his. Two phrases identify this dignity: he was in the form of God; he was equal to God. Since the form of something is its basic appearance from which its essential character can be known, if Christ was in the form of God he enjoyed a Godlike manner of being. The parallel phrase restates this in a slightly different way: he is equal to God. The verb reports that Christ did not cling to this prerogative; he did not use his exalted status for his own ends. Christ freely gave up the right to homage that was his.

Once again the verb plays an important role in this recital. Not only did Christ relinquish his Godlike state, he emptied himself of it. The contrasts drawn here are noteworthy. Though in the form of God, he chose the form of a servant or slave. Without losing his Godlike being he took on the likeness of human beings. This does not mean he only resembled a human being but really was not one. Christ did take on human form, but the qualification suggested by "likeness" points to the fact that he was human like no one else was human. Although the word "Lord" (*kýrios*, a word also applied to God) is not found in these early verses, the contrast between Lord and servant stands conspicuously behind it.

Christ emptied himself and took on the human condition. The final verb states he then humbled himself and became obedient. Having taken on the form of a slave, he made himself vulnerable to all the particulars of that station in life. For a slave, obedience is the determining factor. The extent of his obedience is striking. Compliance to God's will in a world alienated from God requires that one be open to the possibility of death. In a sense, Christ's crucifixion was inevitable. It was common punishment for slaves, the nadir of human abasement. Such ignominy was a likely consequence of emptying himself and taking on human form.

The exaltation of Christ is as glorious as his humiliation was debasing. It is important to note that while Christ was the subject of his self-emptying, his superexaltation is attributed directly to God. Once again there is a play on words and ideas. Just as "form" and "appearance" denote being, so "name" contains part of the essence of the individual. In exalting Jesus, God accords his human name a dignity that raises it above every other name. It now elicits the same reverence the title "Lord" (*kýrios*) does. Every knee shall do him homage and every tongue shall proclaim his sovereignty.

The extent to which Christ is to be revered is total. The entire created universe is brought under his lordship. This includes the spiritual beings in heaven, all living beings on earth, and even the dead under the earth. Distinctions such as spiritual or physical, living or dead, are meaningless here. All will praise Christ, whose exaltation gives glory to God.

## Matthew 26:14–27:66

The passion narrative found in Matthew's gospel is really a collection of episodes that together tell the story of Jesus' last days from particular theological perspectives. Although in several of these episodes, especially those that describe events that transpired after Jesus' capture, Jesus appears to be the passive object of the actions of others, it is quite clear to the reader that he is really in charge of his destiny. He makes many of the major decisions, and he hands himself over to others, allowing them to decide his fate in those cases. The section of the passion read today begins and ends on notes of treachery or animosity: Judas betrays Jesus and puts into motion the events that result in his death; some of those who oppose Jesus insist that the grave be secured lest the claim of resurrection be made by Jesus' disciples. Despite themselves, these adversaries become the agents through whom the plan of God unfolds.

Jesus declares that the time of his death and resurrection is the *kairós* time (26:18), that decisive moment when the promises of God will be brought to fulfillment (26:54, 56). As part of this unfolding Jesus himself predicts that certain things will come to pass. For example, he tells his disciples about the man who will offer his room for the celebration of the Passover (26:18); about his own betrayal by one with whom he shared food (26:21-25); and about Peter's denial (26:31-34). More importantly, he shows that his suffering is in fulfillment of prophecies made long ago: the desertion of his followers (26:31; cf. Zech 13:7) and the purchase of a field with Judas' blood money (27:15; cf. a combination of Zech 11:13; Jer 36:6-15).

The titles that identify Jesus play an important role in this lengthy narrative. The man in whose room the Passover was celebrated has known him as "the teacher" (26:18), while Judas calls him "Rabbi" (26:25, 49). Jesus consistently refers to God as "Father," but when referring to himself he uses the eschatological designate "Son of Man" (26:24, 45, 64) rather than the divine title "Son of God." However, there is an oblique allusion to it, for Jesus answers yes when asked if he is the "Christ (Messiah), the Son of God" (26:63), or the "king of the Jews" (27:11). This latter is the title with which the soldiers mock

Jesus (27:29) as well as the title on the inscription above the cross (27:37). Finally, it is the Roman centurion and the men with him who, seeing the earthquake that accompanies the death of Jesus, recognize him as "Son of God" (27:54). All of these titles reveal a dimension of the christology upon which the passion narrative is built.

The reading closes at the site of the sealed tomb. Pilate has met his obligation; the threat to Roman peace and stability has been removed. A contingent from the Jewish ruling body has also accomplished its goals; the contentious wonder-working preacher has been silenced, and any possibility of future upheaval has been sealed in the tomb with his body. Neither Pilate nor the Jewish leaders realize that in reality everything is now in place for the eschatological event of the resurrection.

## Themes of the Day

In this final lenten Sunday as we prepare to enter the sacred time of Holy Week, we look again at the significance of Christ in our lives. We recognize him as our Savior, but we look more closely in order to discover just what kind of Savior he is. We find he has taken the form of a slave; he has been glorified with a name above all other names; he continues to suffer with us.

### A Self-Emptying Savior

We have not been saved through military power but through the kenotic humility of Jesus. Though he was really in the form of God, Jesus came in the form of a slave. We have a Savior who was crushed for our iniquities, nailed to a cross as a convicted felon, and who there endured the sense of abandonment. Why has God stooped so low? Why did Christ empty himself so completely? We could say all of this happened because Jesus was obedient to God's will in his life, regardless of where this led him. This may be true, but it does not answer the fundamental question: Why does God love us with such abandon?

### A Highly Exalted Savior

We have a Savior who was lifted up and exalted precisely because he emptied himself of his divine prerogatives. He became one of us in order to show us how we are to live. Unlike conquerors who triumph by putting down their opponents, Jesus was raised up because he himself was first willing to be put down. The passion recounts the extent to which he willingly offered himself. Because of this he has been exalted above everyone and everything else. His glorification was won at a great price, but it is his by victory and not by mere bestowal. His name commands the homage no other name can claim, and it does so because he first handed himself over to us.

### An Example for Us

We have a Savior who first offered himself *for* us and then continues to offer himself *to* us as an example to follow. As he was willing to empty himself for our sake, so we must be willing to empty ourselves for the sake of others. The best way to enter Holy Week with him is in the company of those with whom he has identified himself: the poor and the broken; the humiliated and the marginalized; those who suffer the abuse of others; those who never use rank to force their will. If we are to be saved we must go where salvation takes place: in our streets and in our homes where violence rages; in the dark corners of life where despair holds sway; wherever the innocent are abused or the needy neglected; wherever there is misunderstanding or fear or jealousy. We must go wherever Christ empties himself for our sake.

**Triduum**

| | | |
|---|---|---|
| **Holy Thursday**<br>Exodus 12:1-8, 11-14<br>Passover meal | **Psalm 116:12-13, 15-18**<br>Our blessing cup is a communion | **1 Corinthians 11:23-26**<br>Proclaim the death of the Lord | **John 13:1-15**<br>He loved them to the end |
| **Good Friday**<br>Isaiah 52:13–53:12<br>He was wounded for us | **Psalm 31:2, 6, 12-13, 15-17, 25**<br>Into your hands | **Hebrews 4:14-16; 5:7-9**<br>Jesus learned obedience | **John 18:1–19:42**<br>Passion |
| **Holy Saturday**<br>Vigil readings<br>Romans 6:3-11<br>Christ will die no more | **Psalm 118:1-2, 16-17, 22-23**<br>Give thanks to the LORD | | **Matthew 28:1-10**<br>The crucified is raised |

# Triduum

## Initial Reading of the Triduum

*Introduction*

The readings for the Triduum offer us a very different kind of mosaic. This is because of the unique character of the readings of the Easter Vigil. While the epistle and gospel passages of all three days can be read in columns, the readings from the First Testament and the psalm responses for the vigil constitute a unit in itself. Despite this slightly different configuration the patterns can be traced, and the meanings that emerge can provide a theological matrix for the Triduum.

*First Testament Readings*

The readings for Holy Thursday and Good Friday offer us two examples of vicarious sacrifice. The Paschal Lamb was slain as a substitute for the lives of the people. The Suffering Servant was also sacrificed that others might live. Both were innocent victims; both were led silently to slaughter. While these images might point implicitly to Jesus, the First Testament readings of the vigil service take us in another direction: they recapitulate the story of salvation that leads us to the waters of baptism.

Our reflection begins in the darkness of chaos out of which God calls light. Human beings are created and history begins. A hint of the intensity of God's desire to provide a future that far exceeds anything we might imagine can be seen in the story of Abraham and Isaac. That God does not really want the children of promise to perish is clear from the account of their crossing through the sea into freedom. God's love has the passion of a spouse. Even if the covenant relationship is threatened, this love will remain steadfast. God will provide for these people in all their needs, quenching their thirst with waters of life. They have but to turn and walk in God's ways and they will find peace. Even if they turn away and are unfaithful, God will pour clean water over them and give them new hearts.

*Psalms*

The psalm responses are variously songs of thanksgiving for the amazing care and protection we have received from God; hymns of praise of the graciousness of God, who has saved us and led us into a place of peace and prosperity; cries for help when we face insurmountable challenges or adversities; promises of fidelity to God and to the ways of God; and prayers that spring from hearts that long to rest in God. They are all brought to conclusion with a psalm that rejoices in the victory of the one who was rejected but has been exalted at the right hand of God.

*Epistles*

The mini-epistle created when the three readings are placed end-to-end develops the theological meaning of the sacrifice of Jesus. It begins with the official Christian proclamation of the eucharistic meal as the reenactment of the death of the Lord. This is followed by a priestly interpretation of the meaning of his death. It concludes with an explanation of our participation through baptism in Jesus' death and resurrection. We begin with a report of events that transformed a festive meal; we end with a reminder of how we are transformed by the saving action of God, which comes to us through these events.

*Gospels*

The gospel passages trace the theme of Jesus' selfless sacrifice of love. We begin with an account of his self-emptying service of others. Though he has the power of God at his disposal, he strips himself, gets on his knees before his disciples, and renders a service only the humblest servants perform. The passion narrative details the extent to which he was willing to humble himself. He endured rejection, ridicule, and abuse, and he did it with the dignity of a king and the beloved Son of God. Having been lifted up on the cross, he was also lifted up from the dead. The one who was cast down has now been raised up.

*Mosaic of Readings*

These three days have traditionally been set aside for our reflection on the most sacred mysteries of our faith, namely the suffering, death, and resurrection of Jesus. However, the readings offer us a slightly different picture to consider. Just as contemplation of his suffering and death always includes some mention of his resurrection, so the readings that report the events of his life all include mention of our participation in these mysteries. We do not sit on the sidelines as uninvolved spectators. This is our story, and we are part of it whether we accept the love offered to us or not. We are the ones who are cared for and nourished by God; we are the ones God lifts out of darkness and leads through the struggles of life. Even in his resurrection Christ beckons us to join him.

# Readings

## *Holy Thursday, Evening Mass of the Lord's Supper*
### Exodus 12:1-8, 11-14

The reading sets forth the ritual prescriptions for the annual celebration of the feast of Passover. The very first verse states that the establishment of the memorial, the determination of its date, and the details of the rite itself were all decreed by God. Since the event of the Exodus marked Israel's beginning as a people, it is only fitting the feast that commemorates this beginning be positioned at the head of their year.

The first words of the passage assert that the power of God is effective even in the land of Egypt. This is a profound theological claim for several reasons: (1) it means that rule of the God of Israel is not limited to the boundaries of the land of Israel itself; (2) it describes Israel's God as superior to the gods of Egypt, ruling where these other gods do not; (3) it implies that Israel's God exercises authority over the lives of the Egyptians themselves, striking down their firstborn.

The celebration takes the form of a meal, at the center of which is a lamb. Because of the significance of this ceremony the selection, slaughter, and consumption of this lamb are carefully determined by ritual ordinance. The lamb must be male, because the people cannot afford to lose the reproductive potential of the females of the flock. It must be a year old, so it has enough maturity to embody the salvific significance that will be placed upon it, yet not so old as to have lost its fundamental vitality. Like everything set aside for consecration to God, it must be free of all blemish.

The passover lambs must be slaughtered in the presence of the entire community and then eaten in the respective households. Presumably this is an evening meal, since the lambs are to be slaughtered at twilight. The entire household must join together for this feast, men and women, children and servants. The lambs must be eaten in their entirety; nothing of the sacrifice can be left over lest it be thrown out like refuse. For this reason, small households should join together to ensure total consumption of the animal. Even the manner of dress is prescribed. They must be clad like those in flight.

The ritual itself may have originated from an ancient nomadic ceremony. Herders frequently moved during the night from winter pasturage to places of spring grazing. Before their move, one of the choicest members of the flock was sacrificed in order to ensure the safety of the rest of the flock. Its blood was then somehow sprinkled around the camp. This was done because of blood's apotropaic value, that is, it could ward off any threatening evil.

Elements of this ritual can be seen in the passover ceremony. The night travel, the slaughter, and the marking with blood have now taken on historical meaning. What was initially a sacrifice for pacification of an evil deity is now a memorial of God's protection and deliverance. The blood of the lamb, which originally warded off night demons, was now a sign of salvation for all those whose doorposts were marked with it. The night journey in search of new pasturage became the flight for safety into the wilderness. This ritual was to be a perpetual memorial of the time when the LORD passed over the Israelites.

## Psalm 116:12-13, 15-16bc, 17-18

This psalm is an example of a temple service of thanksgiving. In it someone who made an appeal to God and promised to perform some act of devotion when the request was granted now comes to the Temple and, before God and the assembly of believers, gives thanks for the favor granted and fulfills the vow that was made. Most vows were promises to offer some form of sacrifice (cf. Ps 56:13): holocaust (cf. Ps 66:13; Lev 22:18-20; peace offerings (cf. Ps 50:14; Lev 7:16; 22:21-22); cereal offerings and libations (cf. Num 15:3, 8).

The psalm response opens with an acknowledgment that there is nothing the psalmist can do and no gift that can be offered that will even begin to compare with the favors received from God. Inadequate as it is, the psalmist still renders what can be offered, expressing devotion by offering a cup of salvation. It is not clear exactly what the cup of salvation is. It might be a libation offered in thanksgiving. Or it could be a festive drink, the wine that was shared at a sacred meal, a symbol of the joy God's graciousness has produced. Whatever its identify, it serves as a cup of joy for having been saved.

Along with the offering of this wine is the proclamation of the name of God. Since God's name holds part of the divine essence, to proclaim that name is to recognize and praise God's greatness, in this case the graciousness of God's saving action. The cup is taken up and God's name is proclaimed.

The psalmist insists that, contrary to any appearances, God is concerned with the fate of the righteous. The psalmist's own situation is an example of this. The psalmist may have suffered, but ultimately God did intervene. Mention of the righteous *(ḥāsîdîm)* indirectly identifies the psalmist as one of this group. The psalmist could be making another point here: virtue and misfortune are not incompatible; good people do in fact suffer. Still, the point of this psalm is not the sufferings the psalmist had to endure but the deliverance that came from God and the psalmist's response to this divine graciousness.

The relationship between the psalmist and God is strikingly characterized in the metaphor "servant" and its parallel "son of your handmaid." Although the first image has taken on a profound theological connotation (servant of God), the second clearly identifies both images as classifications within a structured household. A slave born into a household had neither a justified claim to nor any guaranteed likelihood of emancipation. By using these legal metaphors to characterize his relationship with God, the psalmist is dramatizing his own situation. Like a slave with no hope of lease, he was bound to a life of great difficulty. However, God looked kindly upon him and loosed him from his servitude.

The last verses (vv. 17-18) clearly identify the ceremony that will take place as a public ritual. A sacrifice of thanksgiving will be offered (cf. Lev 7:11-18); the name of the LORD will be proclaimed; vows will be paid in the presence of the People of God. The psalmist, who once faced the prospect of death, now stands in the midst of the assembly, humbled and grateful to God.

## 1 Corinthians 11:23-26

This account of the institution of the Lord's Supper draws on the "Jesus tradition." The language used is technical and formulaic; what Paul received he now hands down (cf. 1 Cor 15:3). This does not mean that he received this tradition in direct revelation from the Lord but that he received it by word of mouth, the usual way a religious heritage is transmitted. This manner of expression establishes the ecclesial authority of the teaching. It also demonstrates Paul's own conviction that the risen Christ transmits the tradition through the agency of the members of the body of Christ, the church. Since such transmission of tradition was a custom both in the Greek schools and the Jewish synagogue, the audience would understand what Paul was doing regardless of their ethnic or religious background.

That the account comes specifically from the Jesus tradition, and not from the early Christian tradition generally, is evident in the recital of the words of Jesus. They actually give instruction for the continual celebration of the liturgical reenactment. The fact that they are the words of Jesus gives divine legitimation to the *anámnēsis* (ritual of remembering) enjoined upon the community of believers. The words themselves are found within a succinct account of Jesus' Last Supper, wherein he draws lines of continuity between the old and new covenants and makes clear their differences.

Jesus' attention is on the bread and the wine. Faithful to Jewish table etiquette, as either the head of the household or the host he gives thanks and breaks the bread (v. 24). He identifies the bread as his body about to be given vicariously on behalf of those present. The fact that Jesus was actually with them when he said this makes the meaning of his words quite enigmatic. Was this really his body? Or did it represent his body? Believers have interpreted this in various ways down through the centuries. One thing is clear. They were charged to repeat among themselves what he had just done.

When the supper was over Jesus took the cup and pronounced words over it as well (v. 25). This cup is identified with the new covenant (cf. Jer 31:31-34) and with the blood of the Lord, which, like sacrificial blood, ratifies the covenant. This statement shows how the Jesus tradition has taken the new-covenant theme from Jeremiah and blood ratification from the Jewish sacrificial system, incorporated them, and reinterpreted them. This verse ends as did the previous verse, with a charge to repeat the memorial.

Jesus' sharing of the bread and the cup was a prophetic symbolic action that anticipated his death. The ritual reenactment of this supper would be a participation in his death and a sharing in the benefits that would accrue from it. In it the risen, exalted Lord continually gives what the dying Jesus gave once for all. In the memorial celebration the past, present, and future are brought together: the past is the commemoration of his death; the present is the ritual of remembrance itself; the future is his *parousía*, his coming again.

The reason for repeating Jesus' actions and words is that they signify his salvific death. Believers live an essentially eschatological existence, anticipating the future as they reenact the past.

## John 13:1-15

The account of the washing of the feet is introduced by a few references. They include identification of the time of year as that of the feast of Passover; a note about Jesus' relationship with God and his foreknowledge of his own death; a statement about his love for those called "his own"; and a report about Judas' complicity with the devil. All of this information sets the context for the narrative that follows.

The washing of feet was unusual for several reasons. Although it was a common practice of Eastern hospitality, it should have been done upon arrival at the house and not when everyone had already reclined at table. It was normally done by people of negligible social station—by slaves in a class-conscious household or, in a patriarchal society, by women. Here it was done by the one who could boast divine origin and who was both Lord and teacher of those at table. While foot-washing was a common social practice, as a symbolic action it here had theological significance and was intended as an example to be followed by all those present.

What looks like self-abasement by Jesus is really an expression of his love. By washing their feet Jesus showed the extent of the love he had for his disciples. Because of his love, he was willing to empty himself of all divine pre-rogatives and to assume the role of the menial household slave. Because of his love, he was willing to empty himself of his very life in order to win salvation for all. The love he had for his disciples is the model of the love they were to have for one another. In other words, they were to be willing to empty themselves for the sake of one another.

This symbolic action of foot-washing was misunderstood by Peter. He saw the humiliation in such behavior, but he did not perceive its real meaning. He would not allow Jesus, his Lord, to abase himself in this way. But Jesus would not allow Peter to refuse the gesture without dire consequences. To reject the symbolic action was to reject its profound theological significance. If Peter would not participate in Jesus's self-emptying, he could not enjoy the blessings it would guarantee.

In trying to explain the meaning of his action, Jesus played on the ideas of clean and unclean. Customary washing of feet could make the disciples physically clean, but this foot-washing could make them clean in a spiritual way, that is, all of them but Judas. Jesus knew that Judas had turned traitor and so was not clean. On one level Peter understood this explanation; on another level he did not. He seems to have thought that the more he washed the more he would be spiritually cleansed. Since their being washed symbolized their participation in Jesus' self-emptying, limited washing was adequate. Jesus assured Peter he would understand later, presumably after Jesus' resurrection.

Never did Jesus deny the dignity that was his as God, but he did not use it to safeguard his own comfort or well-being. Instead, it became the measure of his own self-giving and the example of the extent of self-giving his disciples should be willing to offer to others. During his Last Supper Jesus gave himself completely to those present and charged them to give themselves completely as well.

## Themes of the Day

This is the first day of the solemn Triduum, the most sacred moment of the Liturgical Year. On each of the three days we meditate on some aspect of the same question: What is the meaning of Passover? Holy Thursday opens this meditation by considering God's initiative in these wondrous events. Three themes are prominent: the Passover, which is the saving action of God; our response to God's Passover; the wonder of God's love.

### God's Passover

Here at the beginning of our meditation of the Passover, we see that it is God who passes over, saving us, nourishing us, serving us. The initiative is God's; the magnanimity is God's; the self-emptying is God's. We have nothing to contribute to these amazing happenings. We have only to open ourselves to receive the wondrous gifts that have been won for us.

God passes over us as a protective angel, preserving us from harm, leading us out of bondage into freedom. All we have to do is accept the salvation offered us through this spectacular act of love. God also passes through mere human companionship and becomes the covenantal meal that sustains us. Along with this heavenly bread comes the guarantee of eternal life. It is ours only if we accept it. Finally, Jesus passes beyond being Lord and master and kneels before us as our humble servant. If we are to belong to him we must allow him to wash our feet. In each instance, the saving action is God's. For no other reason but love, God offers us salvation, nourishment, and service.

## Our Response

"How shall I make a return to the Lord?" On this day of Eucharist, our only response is thanksgiving. When we give thanks we are merely opening ourselves to the graciousness of God. We are giving God the opportunity of overwhelming us with blessings. We participate in God's many passovers by accepting God's magnanimity. Our sacrifice of thanksgiving is really our openness to receive the sacrifice of God—the sacrifice of the lamb, whose blood on the doorpost liberated our future; the sacrifice of Christ's Body and Blood, which became our food and drink; the sacrifice of Jesus' self-emptying service, which stands as a model for our own service of others.

## The Wonder of It All

Who could have imagined that any of this would happen? A motley group of runaway laborers escapes from the clutches of their super-powerful overlords; bread and wine is changed into the Body and Blood of a man who is being hunted down; the Son who was sent by God into the world washes the feet of his disciples. This is all incredible; it is no wonder Peter initially resisted. It is so difficult for self-possessed, self-directed human beings to relinquish control of their lives and to stand ready to receive the gift of God. We do not question whether God *could* do such marvels, but we stand in awe that God *would*. God's love for us is beyond comprehension.

Finally, on the first night of this holy Triduum we are left with a directive: "As I have done, so you must do." The graciousness of God toward us prompts us to pass over from being served to serving others. Our thanksgiving is expressed in our own self-emptying service of others. Having received the gifts of God, we give them away; they flow from God through us to others.

## *Good Friday of the Lord's Passion*

### Isaiah 52:13–53:12

An account of the afflictions of a righteous man (53:1-11b) is here framed by two utterances of God (52:13-15; 53:11b-12). This portrait of innocent suffering challenges the traditionally held conviction that evil brings on its own penalty and therefore misfortune is evidence of sinfulness. In place of this view of retribution is a picture of one who not only suffered at the hands of others but did so for the very people who had unjustly afflicted him. The framework of God's words serves to legitimize this unconventional theological position.

It is clear that God is speaking in the closing verses, because only God would be able to bless the servant in the manner described (53:12). Since the servant is similarly identified in both of the framing parts, it is safe to conclude it is God who speaks in the introduction as well. The overriding theme in both parts is the relationship between the humiliation of the servant and his exaltation.

The opening verses do not suggest the servant's exaltation is reward for his humiliation. Rather, it is precisely *in* his humiliation that he is exalted. He is raised up even as the bystanders are aghast at his appearance (52:13-15). The closing words explain how this can be the case. The will of God is accomplished in his willingness to bear his afflictions at the hands of and for the sake of others (53:11b-12).

The actual account of the servant's suffering is narrated from the perspective of those who have been granted salvation through his tribulations. It begins with an exclamation of total amazement. Who would have ever thought the power of God (the arm of the LORD) would be revealed in weakness and humiliation? The details of this humiliation are then sketched (53:2-9). Unlike many righteous individuals whose lives contain episodes of misfortune, this servant lived a life marked by tribulation from beginning to end. Added to his physical distress was rejection by a community that held him in no regard.

The account is interrupted by a confession of the narrator's personal guilt and an acknowledgment of the servant's innocence. The narrator first states the traditional way of understanding the servant's plight: "we thought of him . . . as one smitten by God" (v. 4). Then a new and astonishing insight is proclaimed: "he was pierced for our offenses" (v. 5). This startling insight contains two important points: innocent people do in fact suffer for reasons that have nothing to do with their own behavior; the suffering of one can be the source of redemption for another.

The account of the servant's sufferings continues (vv. 7-9). Here his nonviolent attitude is clearly defined. He did not retaliate; he did not even defend himself. In fact, he willingly handed himself over to those who afflicted him.

The image of a lamb led to slaughter suggests the servant knew that he too would die at the hands of his persecutors. Still, he chose to be defenseless. Even in death he was shamed, buried with the wicked. There was nothing in this appalling life or death that served as a clue to the significance of this suffering, or its redemptive value, or the source of exaltation it would become. God's ways are astounding.

## Psalm 31:2, 6, 12-13, 15-16, 17, 25

The theme of trust permeates this psalm response (vv. 2, 15). Although it contains elements of complaint or lament and of petition, it opens with a testimony to the psalmist's conviction that there is refuge in God (v. 2). The image suggests he (identified as a male servant, v. 17) is fleeing some kind of peril, and he turns to God as a sanctuary in this flight. Further in the psalm (v. 16) he pleads to be rescued from his enemies and persecutors. Thus, threatened by such dangers the psalmist seeks protection in God, and he is certain he will find it there.

The covenant relationship between God and the psalmist is apparent in several places. First, he appeals to God's justice or righteousness, a characteristic of the covenant. This appeal also suggests the innocence of the psalmist. He would hardly call upon God's justice if he were in any way guilty. Evidence of the relationship can also be seen in the way the psalmist identifies both God and himself: You are my God (v. 15); I am your servant (v. 17). Finally, the psalmist appeals to God's lovingkindness (*ḥesed*), a technical term describing covenant loyalty. It is clear this relationship is the reason for his confidence; it is why he flees to God.

Complete confidence in God does not prevent the psalmist from pleading with God. His first concern is shame. This is not an inner attitude or state of mind. It is public disgrace. In many eastern societies it is referred to even today as "losing face." It is the opposite of possessing honor, an attribute more important than riches. A man without honor is an outcast in society, and for many people death is preferred to such disgrace.

The psalm does not clearly explain the initial cause of the psalmist's loss of honor. In a society that believed suffering was the consequence of wickedness, it could have been almost any kind of misfortune. Whatever it was, the psalmist was regarded as someone who was not only dead but who was then forgotten (v. 13). Since in this culture at this time the only way an individual could survive after death was in the memory of the living, to be forgotten was doubly deplorable. The psalmist was also treated like a broken dish, not only shattered but also discarded. Whatever the misfortune was, it was regarded as shameful.

The description of his shame is a collage of metaphors that characterize his disgrace. He is an object of reproach, a laughingstock, a dread. He is shamed before everyone, enemies, neighbors, even friends. He has already lost his honor. What will reinstate it is vindication, and only God can accomplish this. Only God can show that the psalmist was innocent in the first place.

The psalmist prays that God's face might shine upon him. Since the face identifies the person and reflects the attitudes and sentiments of that person, seeing the face of God would be a kind of divine manifestation. The psalmist is probably not asking for such a revelation but rather for the light that comes from God's face. In other words, he is asking for God's good pleasure. His last words are an exhortation to others to trust in God as he has. To the end, his confidence will not be swallowed up by any disgrace he might have to endure.

## Hebrews 4:14-16; 5:7-9

This reading consists of two distinct yet related parts. The first (4:14-16) contains a double exhortation: Hold fast to faith; approach the throne of grace with confidence. It develops the theme of Jesus the high priest who intercedes for us. This is a high priest who was tempted in all things and who therefore can sympathize with our struggle.

The basis of constancy in the confession of the community is the identity of Jesus. He is Son of God as well as the great high priest. Just as the high priest passed through the curtain into the presence of God in the Holy of Holies, there to sprinkled sacrificial blood on the mercy seat (Heb 9:7), so Christ, exalted after shedding his own blood, passed through the heavens into the presence of God. Being the Son of God, his sacrifice far exceeds anything the ritual performed by the high priest might have hoped to accomplish.

His exalted state has not distanced him from us. On the contrary, he knows our limitations. He was tried to the limit but did not succumb. Furthermore, it is precisely his exalted state that gives us access to the throne of God. Unlike former high priests, who approached the mercy seat alone and only on the Day of Atonement, Christ enables each one of us to approach God and to do so continually. This first section of the reading ends with the exhortation. The confidence we have in our relationship with Christ should empower us to approach the throne of God boldly, there to receive the grace we need to be faithful.

The second section (5:7-9) is confessional in character. Each of the three verses offers a slightly different view of biblical christology. The first refers to the depth of Jesus' suffering; the second to a major lesson he learned through suffering; the third to the mediatorial role he gained by that suffering.

"Days when Christ was in the flesh" is an allusion to Jesus' humanity. In the biblical sense of the term, flesh (*sárx*) is not evil but is fraught with limitations and weaknesses. Because it is subject to deterioration and death, it came to signify many things associated with human frailty, such as vulnerability and fear. For Jesus to have taken on flesh was to have taken on these limitations and weaknesses as well.

The reference to his anguished prayer calls to mind his agony in Gethsemane (Matt 26:36-46; Mark 14:32-42; Luke 22:40-46). The reference here is probably to a traditional Jewish image of the righteous person's impassioned prayer. Its sentiments are reminiscent of those found in the psalms that describe agony, terror, and depression (cf. Psalms 22, 31, 38). Jesus offered these prayers as a priest offers sacrifice, and he was heard because of his reverence, or Godly fear.

Though Son of God, Jesus learned what every human has to learn, namely, acceptance of God's will in the circumstances of life. The surest way to learn this lesson, though perhaps the hardest, is through suffering. This notion points once again to Jesus' willingness to assume every aspect of human nature. As mediator of salvation, Jesus endured torment of body and anguish of soul. He knew agony, terror, and depression. He could fully understand human distress and the desire to escape it. He was truly one with the human condition.

## John 18:1–19:42

This passion narrative can be divided into three parts: the arrest of Jesus and his examination by the high priest (18:1-27); the trial before Pilate (18:28–19:16a); the crucifixion, death, and burial (19:16b-42). Throughout this account Jesus is portrayed as serenely in control of the events that eventually culminate in his death. Again and again his kingship makes itself evident until he is finally lifted up in exaltation on the cross. Unbelief is exposed as resistance to God, and those who condemned him by this fact condemn themselves. Blame is placed more on the Jewish authorities than on the Romans, not out of any deep-seated anti-Semitism but because the Christian community at the time of the writing of the gospel was in desperate need of Roman approval in order to survive.

The undisputed sovereignty of Jesus is seen from the first to the last episode. A cohort of Roman soldiers, a group of about six hundred, along with representatives of the religious leaders of Israel, come to arrest Jesus. Not until he provides a display of his divine power does he allow them to take him. Later, he stands with authority before Annas, the high priest, insisting he has been arrested without cause. He acknowledges his authority to Pilate, pointing out that his rule is not of this world. He further announces that, while authority is his by right, Pilate's is merely by appointment. Finally, only when all things have been accomplished does he hand over his spirit. From beginning to end Jesus is in complete control.

The divine identity of Jesus is the fundamental reason for both his authority and the calm he exhibits. This identity is established at the outset. In the garden, three times (18:5, 6, 8) he responds to those who have come out after him with a simple self-identification: *Egó eimi!* I AM [he]! This is not lost on his accusers, who argue with Pilate that to claim to be Son of God makes Jesus liable to death. This claim strikes fear into Pilate's heart, and instead of releasing Jesus he hands him over to be crucified.

The title of king is an explicit point of much controversy. It is the center of the discussion with Pilate, who questions Jesus about it and then retreats somewhat when Jesus openly admits his royal status. Jesus' claim to kingship becomes the occasion for the mockery of the soldiers, the rejection by the religious leaders, and the crowd's choice of Barabbas rather than Jesus. This possible conflict with imperial sovereignty influences Pilate to capitulate to the people's angry demands and to hand Jesus over to be crucified, but not without asserting this kingship by means of the inscription on the cross. The kingship of Jesus plays a pivotal role in this drama.

There is no misunderstanding in the accusations made against Jesus or in the execution of the plan to put him to death. Those responsible know what they are doing. Judas, an intimate companion, betrays him; the same Roman soldiers, who had been thrown back by his power, arrest him; the religious authorities condemn him for the very messianic posture they should have recognized in him; Pilate hands him over to the Jewish authorities even though he finds no fault in him. In this account, unbelief is exposed as resistance to God. Despite this, God's plan of salvation moves inexorably forward.

## Themes of the Day

We continue our meditation on the meaning of Passover. On Good Friday we discover that Jesus is our Passover. Three different faces of Jesus our Passover are offered for our reflection: the prophetic Suffering Servant, the great high priest, and the triumphant king. Today's meditation ends with reflection on the power of the cross.

### *The Prophetic Suffering Servant*

Silent, like the paschal lamb that was sacrificed on behalf of the people, the Suffering Servant of the LORD allows himself to be handed over to the slaughter. Though innocent, he takes upon himself the guilt of the very ones victimizing him. We marvel at the willingness of those who place themselves at risk in order to save anyone who is vulnerable or anyone they love. But to do so for one's torturers is beyond human comprehension. Yet that is what Christ our Passover has done. He is the true Suffering Servant; he is the one who has allowed himself to be taken, to be afflicted, to be offered as sacrifice for others. It is his blood that spares us; it is his life that is offered. Through his suffering, this servant justifies many. He is our true Passover.

### The Great High Priest

Jesus is not only the innocent victim, he is also the high priest who offers the passover sacrifice. Because he is one of us he carries many of our own weaknesses. But it is because he is without moral blemish that, in him, we all stand before God. On this solemn day we behold his battered body, but we also look beyond it to the dignity that is his as high priest. Garbed as he is in wounds that rival the ornate garments of liturgical celebration, he offers himself on the altar of the cross. He is our true Passover.

### Triumphant King

"King of the Jews" was the crime for which he was tried and sentenced and executed. It was the title inscribed above his bloody throne. To those passing by he appeared to be a criminal, but he was indeed a king. His crucifixion was his enthronement. Lifted up on the cross, he was lifted up in triumph and exaltation. He was not a conquered king, he was a conquering king. He willingly faced death and stared it down. As he delivered over his spirit, death lay vanquished at the foot of the cross. Within a few days this would begin to become clear to others. He is our true Passover.

### The Power of the Cross

On Good Friday the cross gathers together all three images of Christ. It is in the light of this cross that we see clearly how all three must be accepted at once, for we never contemplate one image without contemplating the others. In the midst of the passion we see the victory; when we celebrate Easter we do not forget the cross. As we venerate this cross, we gather together the memory of all the living and the dead. With our petitions we bring to the cross all the needs of the world. In this way, the cross becomes the true *axis mundi*, the center of the universe, and Christ is revealed as the true Passover.

## Easter Vigil

### Genesis 1:1–2:2 (First Reading)

This first creation account is remarkable in several ways. It is replete with measured literary patterns. Each act of creation begins with the phrase "And

God said" and ends with the temporal designation "evening . . . morning . . . day one . . . two . . ." and so on. First the universe is fashioned, then it is appointed with all the heavenly luminaries. Next the sea and the sky and the earth are prepared as resourceful habitat for various animals. The appearance of these living things is described with another pattern: "And God said . . . and God made . . . and God blessed" (vv. 20-22, 24-28). The very structure of the narrative bespeaks order and rhythm, interdependence and care. Again and again an evaluation is pronounced: "And God saw that it was good!"

According to this account order is brought forth from chaos, light is summoned from the darkness. God's creative activity is effortless. It is all accomplished by divine word. God speaks and creation appears; the word is the deed. The universe moves according to unwritten yet well-known laws. One word from God sets it all in motion. The potential for life seems to be in the waters of the sea and in the earth itself. All it needs is a word from God and it will burst forth.

The most extraordinary creature is humankind. The woman and the man are the only creatures made after the image and likeness of God and given the responsibility to manage (subdue and have dominion) the rest of creation as caretakers. Only when all is completed and deemed "very good" does God rest.

## Psalm 104:1-2, 5-6, 10, 12, 13-14, 24, 35

The nature hymn from which the psalm response is taken recalls the Genesis story of creation and is certainly one of the most beautiful psalms in the entire Psalter. It begins with a self-summons to sing the praises of God. It is clear the psalmist is overwhelmed by the splendor of the universe and is brimming with praise for the Creator of such grandeur. In fact, this awesome experience of creation is itself a revelation of God. The brilliance of nature is God's glorious robe. To behold creation is to encounter God.

Of all the creation motifs present in the psalm, the most prominent is water. The earth itself was established amidst cosmic water and then covered with protective ocean water as with a garment. Hearty spring waters refresh the earth as well as the animals that find their home both on the land and in the sky. Water brings vegetation to life on the earth, making it a steady source of food. Although it was initially chaotic and threatening, through God's gracious act of creation water has become the indispensable source of life for all living creatures.

The creation narrative and this psalm response both underscore the fact of God's activity. None of this happens haphazardly, nor is there any struggle between God and the forces of nature. All nature serves the designs of God. In fact, in the psalm it is God who acts through nature; God sends the springs and raises the grass. God has created these marvels and then works through them for the benefit of all. No wonder the psalmist is inspired by creation to sing the praises of the Creator.

## Psalm 33:4-5, 6-7, 12-13, 20-22

The verses of this psalm response contain a collection of various themes. The passage opens with a statement that reflects the fundamental basis of ancient Israel's faith in God. This faith is rooted in the truth of God's word, in the faithfulness of God's works, in the justice of God's covenant, and in the steadfastness of God's love. Everything else flows from these convictions.

The psalm picks up the theme of God's word and carries us with it back to the creation account of Genesis, where this word establishes the heavens and separates the waters of the deep. The stability of natural creation is evidence of God's power and faithfulness. God's creation provides a welcoming and sustaining home for all living beings. Creation is so vast that the psalmist's gaze cannot even begin to encompass all the reasons for praising the great creator-God.

The psalmist moves from creation in its universality to history in its particularity. One people has been chosen by this creator-God to be a special people, to be God's own inheritance. The *macarism* ("Blessed [Happy] the nation!") denotes election, returning us to the themes with which this response opened. The placement of these themes is significant. Creation imagery is bracketed by covenant language. This literary arrangement makes two quite startling theological statements. First, it implies that the covenant God made with this special people is as firm and reliable as is creation. Second, it suggests that from the very beginning creation actually serves the goals of the covenant.

## Genesis 22:1-18 (Second Reading)

This passage is an account of the testing of Abram. However, here the son takes center stage. This is not some anonymous offspring; it is Isaac, Abram's only son, the one he loves. Abram may have had another son (Ishmael), but Isaac was the only son upon whom his dreams were pinned. He was the hope of the future, not only of his father but of the entire people who would eventually trace their ancestry back to Abraham. Isaac was the child of destiny, both of his father and of the entire race.

Just as Abram appears to be willing to sacrifice his beloved son, so Isaac seems to be willing to allow this to happen. There is no mention of struggle on his part. Though he inquires about the sacrifice, the answer given him by his father seems to satisfy him. Isaac is the innocent victim, the one who carries the wood of the sacrifice on his back up to the mountain where his life will be offered.

The fact that in this story Isaac is spared does not mitigate the horror of the scene depicted, nor does it alter the portrait of a brutal deity. God requires the innocent blood of the beloved son, and the father is willing to comply.

Abram relinquished his natural claim on this child of promise, and at the end of the account he is blessed with a promise of more children than he can count (cf. 12:2-3; 13:16; 15:5; 26:4, 24). We may not understand God's plan, but we cannot deny that though God may at first appear to demand the impossible of us, in the end God will not be outdone in generosity.

## Psalm 16:5, 8, 9-10, 11

The psalm verses speak of the covenant relationship with God and the confidence that abounds from it. Two images express this relationship. The allotted portion of land is the inheritance which each tribe was given and which was handed down within the tribes generation after generation. This land provided the people identity and membership, sustenance and prosperity. Without land they had no future, and they would not last long in the present. Here the psalmist is claiming that God has replaced the land in the religious consciousness of the people; the blessings and promises customarily associated with land are now associated with the LORD.

The second image is the cup. This might be the communal cup passed around from which all drank. Such an action solidified the union of those who drank from the common cup. When this action took place at a cultic meal, those participating in the feast were joined not only to one another but to the deity as well. The psalmist declares that this unifying cup is really the LORD. In other words, the psalmist is joined so closely with God as almost to defy separation. God is there at the psalmist's right hand, standing as an advocate or a refuge.

Such protection is reason for profound rejoicing. Regardless of the terrifying, even life-threatening ordeals the psalmist must endure, God is steadfast. In the face of things, this kind of confidence in God may appear foolhardy, but the psalmist's trust is unshakable. Ultimately the fullness of joys will abound in the presence of God.

## Exodus 14:15–15:1 (Third Reading)

We have come to that point in the story of liberation where God takes complete control of the situation. This divine leadership was exercised under several different forms: the words of God, the angel of the LORD, the pillar of cloud. First, God gives specific directions to Moses. Next, the angel leads the people to the sea and then moves behind them as they pass through the parted waters. Finally, the column of cloud, which originally led the people, moves to the rear of the company. There, along with the angel, it serves as a buffer between the fleeing Israelites and the pursuing Egyptians. The escape from Egypt has been accomplished through the power of God.

While this narrative may appear to be an account of the struggle between the people of Israel and the Egyptian pharaoh, it is really a battle between divine forces. The pharaoh, thought by his people to be a god, is in mortal combat with the God of Israel, and it is the God of Israel who emerges triumphant. Not only is the LORD able to protect the Israelites and secure their release, but this is accomplished in Pharaoh's own land and against his own armies. The religious establishment of Egypt is no match for the God of Israel.

The waters of the sea represent the waters of chaos. God parts them just as the great Creator parted the carcass of the monster of the deep at the time of creation. The jubilation that follows this defeat is not so much because of the death of the Egyptians as because of the victory of God over the forces of chaos, be they political or cosmic.

## Exodus 15:1-2, 3-4, 5-6, 17-18

This is a hymn of thanksgiving for deliverance and guidance. It recounts the miracle at the sea, the event that demonstrated God's mighty power and put an end to Israel's bondage in Egypt, and it reports Israel's entrance into and establishment in the land of promise. Recalling these marvelous feats, the poet praises God's glorious triumph.

As comments on the preceding reading stated, this is less a description of violence and the destruction of enemies than of deliverance of a favored people. The characterizations of God underscore this; they all represent some kind of relationship with the people. God is a savior; a patron God who guided and protected the ancestors; a warrior who conquered cosmic evil; a divine ruler who reigns forever and ever.

There is an explicit cultic dimension to this hymn. It contains a threefold mention of the sanctuary: the mountain of God's inheritance, the place of God's throne, the sanctuary itself (vv. 17-18). This sacred place was important because it was the spot where the people offered sacrifice to God. More than this, it was the privileged place on earth where God dwelt in the midst of the people. It was usually erected on that site believed to be the center of the universe, the place where heaven, earth, and the underworld met. The poet is thanking God for deliverance but also for God's perpetual presence among the people. This presence is important because it will ensure God's continued protection.

## Isaiah 54:5-14 (Fourth Reading)

Metaphors taken from familial relationships in a patriarchal household are used to characterize the covenant bond that exists between God and the people. Both God's love and God's wrath are portrayed in terms of a marriage bond that was established, then violated, and finally reestablished. Although the reading does not say Israel has been unfaithful, the implication is there. God is a loyal but dishonored husband, and Israel is an unfaithful wife. The male bias here is obvious.

Looking past these narrow and offensive gender stereotypes, we can still appreciate the underlying description of God's love. It is intimate, like a marriage bond (v. 5); it is forgiving and tender (vv. 7-9); it is everlasting (vv. 8, 10). Just as God originally created a covenant bond, so now God lovingly re-creates it. The reference to Noah and the new creation after the Flood suggests this (v. 9), as does the description of the reestablishment of the people in a city decked out in precious jewels (vv. 11-12).

Covenant language is very strong in this psalm. The reconciliation promised is called a "covenant of peace" (v. 10). "Lovingkindness" or "enduring love" (*ḥesed*, vv. 8, 10) denotes loyalty to covenant obligations. "Compassion" or "great tenderness" (vv. 7, 10) comes from the word *rāḥam* (womb) and might be translated "womb-love." It refers to a deep and loving attachment, usually between two people who share some kind of natural bond. It only appears as a characteristic of God's love after the human covenant partner has sinned. Hence, there is an aspect of forgiveness in the very use of the word.

## Psalm 30:2, 4, 5-6, 11-12, 13

This is a psalm of thanksgiving for deliverance from the peril of death, the netherworld, the pit (v. 4). The reference to death can be to illness, to depression, or to any serious misfortune that can threaten life itself. Whatever it might have been, the danger is now past; God intervened and saved the petitioner. In addition to the actual calamity, the psalmist is concerned with enemies who would take delight in the misfortune. The prayer asks to be preserved from this insult as well. Following the initial plea is an acknowledgment of deliverance. God has heard the petition and has granted the request.

The psalmist next turns to the congregation of believers and calls on them to praise God. As with the preceding reading, the psalm does not explicitly state that the suffering endured was the deserved penalty for some wrongdoing. However, since that was the customary explanation of misfortune, such a conclusion could be drawn. Still, retribution is not the point of the prayer. Rather, the psalm compares the vast difference between God's wrath and God's graciousness. The former is short-lived, the latter is everlasting.

The psalmist turns again in prayer to God, pleading for pity. There is no suggestion that God has turned a deaf ear to earlier cries. Quite the contrary. The psalmist announces that grief and mourning have been turned into relief and rejoicing. This is the reason for the thanksgiving in the first place. Regardless of the nature of or reason for the misfortune, God can be trusted to come to the aid of one who cries for help.

## Isaiah 55:1-11 (Fifth Reading)

This powerful prophetic oracle contains some of the most moving sentiments placed in the mouth of God. First, God's invitation is extended both to those who are able to pay for food and drink (v. 2) and to those who are not (v. 1). All are invited to come to the LORD in order to be refreshed and nourished. The reference is probably to something more than ordinary food and drink, since those called are also told to listen. The word of God is itself a source of rejuvenation.

The real object of the invitation is God's announcement of the reestablishment of a covenant bond (v. 3). The reference is to the royal covenant made with David and his house. Although it was instituted as an everlasting covenant, the people broke the bond by their sins. God is now eager to restore this bond. The oracle states that just as David's success proclaimed God's majesty to the nations, so the people called here will be witness of God's mercy and love. Just as David was the source of blessing, peace, and fullness of life for his own nation, the people called here will be a comparable source of blessing for nations they do not even know.

After this bold promise is made, the people are told to turn to the LORD; sinners are exhorted to reform their lives and seek forgiveness from God. These are not suggestions; they are imperatives. The people are summoned to repentance. Then God's plans will take effect, just as the rain accomplishes what it is intended to accomplish. Unlike human beings who work for justice and reparation, God's way is compassion and re-creation, and this renewal will last forever.

## Isaiah 12:2-3, 4, 5-6

This hymn of thanksgiving anticipates favors that will be granted and enjoyed in the future. Therefore one might consider it a hymn of confidence as well. God is declared "savior," and it is because of this characterization that the writer is unafraid and takes courage. The theme of water appears here as it did in the preceding reading. Though the imagery is slightly different, in both cases the water is transformative. Earlier it represented new creation; here it is water of salvation.

The theme of witness reappears here as well (vv. 4-5). The writer calls on the community to praise the glorious name of God, the name that represents the very character of God. They are to extol the marvels God has accomplished and to proclaim them to the nations. The most celebrated of these wondrous works is the transformation of the people themselves. In other words, the transformed lives of God's people will announce to the nations the marvels God has accomplished.

The third and final theme found in this response highlights the importance of Jerusalem. This city was both the royal capital of the Davidic dynasty and the site where the Temple was built. It is the second aspect that is the focus here. The city itself is called upon to rejoice. The reason for this exaltation is the presence of God in its midst. Although the Temple was the concrete representation of this divine presence, it is the presence of God and not the temple building that is fundamental (cf. Jer 7:3-4). The theology of the passage has come full circle. The presence of God in the midst of the people is the source of the writer's confidence in future deliverance.

### Baruch 3:9-15, 32–4:4 (Sixth Reading)

This passage, taken from a book attributed to the secretary of Jeremiah (cf. Jer 36:4), is considered one of the Bible's hymns of praise of wisdom (cf. Proverb 8 and 9; Sir 24:1-22; Wis 7:22–8:21). It begins with the characteristic summons "Hear, O Israel" (v. 9; cf. Deut 6:4) and continues with an explanation of the reasons for the nation's exile in the land of its foes. Basically it was because the people had turned from the Law, the fountain of wisdom (vv. 10-13).

The mysterious female figure that appears in these verses is more than a wise woman, she is Wisdom itself. This representation of Wisdom should not be considered a figure of speech. While many passages maintain that one of the chief characteristics of God is divine wisdom, the image found here suggests more. Wisdom Woman appears to enjoy an existence intimately associated with yet clearly distinct from God.

The description of Wisdom is reminiscent of images found elsewhere in the Wisdom literature. First, the question is posed: Where can Wisdom be found? (cf. Job 28:12, 20). In answer, the poet sketches an account of primordial creation. Wisdom was there with the Creator (vv. 32-35; cf. Prov 8:22-31; Wis 8:1), and only the Creator knows the way to her (v. 31).

Although she is inaccessible to all but God, she is given by God to Israel (3:36; cf. Sir 24:8-12). Because Wisdom is the way of God (3:13), she is also identified with the Law (v. 4:1; cf. Sir 24:23). Ultimately the way of Wisdom is conformity to the Law; conformity to the Law is the way to life; those who follow this way will be happy.

### Psalm 19:8, 9, 10, 11

Six different synonyms are used to extol the glories of the Law (*tôrâ,* meaning "instruction" or "teaching." The psalm describes the blessings that acceptance of the Law can impart, but it does so not merely to describe the Law but also to persuade the people to embrace it as the will of God and to live in accord with it. What is described here is not just any religious law; it is uniquely Israel's, because in a very specific way it represents the will of the God of Israel.

In a unique way the Law is that point where an encounter with God takes place. It consists of directives for living a full and God-fearing life. The qualities associated with fulfillment of the Law are some of the most highly prized attributes found in any religious tradition. The Law is perfect, or complete; it is trustworthy, upright, and clean; it is pure and true. Fidelity to the Law should lead one to the godliness enshrined within it.

The effects of the Law are all relational, enhancing human life itself. The Law imbues the soul with new vitality; it gives wisdom; it delights the heart; it enables the eyes to recognize truth; it generates awe; it is a path to righteousness; it is more valuable than gold; it is sweeter than honey. The Law of the LORD is something greatly to be desired. This description of the Law shows clearly that the psalmist found it life-giving and not restrictive, ennobling and not demeaning. Reverence for the Law seems to promise the best things life has to offer.

## Ezekiel 36:16-17a, 18-28 (Seventh Reading)

The prophet claims the Israelites brought on their own downfall through lives of violence and idolatry. Their sinfulness polluted the land, and so they were expelled. What is more despicable according to this prophet, is the fact that their shameful behavior and the punishment they had to endure because of it doubly dishonored the holy name of God. It was for this reason God relented and gave them another chance.

The renown among the nations of God's holy name is an important theme in this reading. The spectacular events of Israel's initial election and the prosperity with which the nation was subsequently blessed should have been a witness to the surrounding nations of the unbounded generosity of God. Because the people failed in this, God decided to re-create the nation and to do it in a way that the name of the God of Israel would be synonymous with mercy and compassion.

The regeneration of the nation is accomplished in several steps. The first is a ritual of cleansing. The people have polluted themselves, so God washes them with clean water. This symbolic action represents the inner cleansing that takes place. Next, God takes away their hard hearts and gives them tender hearts and a new spirit, which is God's own spirit. This new heart and new spirit will transform the inner being of the people, enabling them to live lives of integrity. Although the verbs are in a perfect or future form, it is a special prophetic perfect, implying that this future transformation has already been accomplished. God's regeneration of the people has already taken place.

## Psalm 42:3, 5; 43:3, 4 (A: When baptism is celebrated)

These two psalms really constitute one song, and so they are often linked together. The first is a lament, expressing the longing for God the psalmist experiences. This is a profoundly spiritual thirst, probably a desire for some form of worship in the Temple. The liturgical imagery is obvious: procession to the house of God, keeping festival. It seems the psalmist even exercised some form of leadership within the worshiping community, leading the procession. The context of this lament could be exile, making it a fitting response to the preceding reading. Despite the evident suffering, there is no despair there. The psalmist seems to anticipate ultimately standing in God's presence, beholding God's face.

The lament of the first psalm is replaced in the second by the petitions addressed to God. Whatever the suffering may be, the psalmist experiences it as darkness and, consequently, pleads with God to send light, which will lead the psalmist to God's presence (another reference to the Temple?). There is confidence here; God's fidelity is invoked. Where earlier the psalmist nostalgically remembered the house of God, here return to that house seems to be a future possibility.

The last verses of the psalm response resemble a prophetic announcement. It is cast in the future form, but it is less a hesitant hope than a confident expectation. The grief and lament of the opening verses have given way to gladness and rejoicing. God has heard and answered the prayer of the psalmist.

## Isaiah 12:2-3, 4bcd, 5-6 (B: When baptism is not celebrated)

This hymn of thanksgiving anticipates favors that will be granted and enjoyed in the future. Therefore one might consider it a hymn of confidence as well. God is declared savior, and it is because of this characterization that the writer is unafraid and takes courage. The theme of water appears here as it did in the preceding reading. Though the imagery is slightly different, in both cases the water is transformative. Earlier it represented new creation; here it is water of salvation.

The theme of witness reappears here as well (vv. 4-5). The writer calls on the community to praise the glorious name of God, the name that represents the very character of God. They are to extol the marvels God has accomplished and to proclaim them to the nations. The most celebrated of these wondrous works is the transformation of the people themselves. In other words, the transformed lives of God's people will announce to the nations the marvels God has accomplished.

The third and final theme found in this response highlights the importance of Jerusalem. This city was both the royal capital of the Davidic dynasty and the site where the Temple was built. It is the second aspect that is the focus here. The city itself is called upon to rejoice. The reason for this exaltation is the presence of God in its midst. Although the Temple was the concrete representation of this divine presence, it is the presence of God and not the temple building that is fundamental (cf. Jer 7:3-4). The theology of the passage has come full circle. The presence of God in the midst of the people is the source of the writer's confidence of future deliverance.

## Psalm 51:12-13, 14-15, 18-19
### (When baptism is not celebrated)

This may be the best known of the penitential psalms (cf. Psalms 6, 32, 38, 51, 102, 130, 143). Although it is considered a lament, it also contains elements of a confession of sin and a prayer for forgiveness. This passage opens with a plea for restoration. The clean heart and new spirit spoken of correspond to the same themes in the prophetic reading for which this psalm is a response. Such a prayer could be considered a veiled confession of sin, for it is a request for inner transformation. This is reinforced by the plea that God not cast the psalmist out but rather grant again the joy of salvation.

The psalmist next promises to announce to other sinners the salvation of God. Gratitude for having been forgiven becomes active service to others. The new life that results from the clean heart and steadfast spirit becomes an outward proclamation of God's gracious mercy. Others will see it and themselves be converted and return to God.

The interior nature of this transformation can also be seen in the character of worship that flows from it. External performance, regardless of how faithfully done, is not enough. The psalmist goes so far as to say that God is not even pleased with practices of worship. This may sound exaggerated, but it is in keeping with the theme of inner transformation so prominent in the prophetic reading and psalm response. Once again heart and spirit are the focus of the psalmist's attention. The clean heart is now also a humble heart; the steadfast spirit is now contrite. The inner renewal effected by God is now complete.

## Romans 6:3-11

Paul here explains how baptism has enabled the Christians to participate in the death and resurrection of Jesus. As they were engulfed in the water, they were buried with him in death; as they emerged from the water, they rose with him into new life. Paul's real intent in drawing these lines of comparison between the death and resurrection of Jesus and the baptism and new life of the Christians is ethical exhortation. He seeks to encourage them to set aside their old manner of living and to take on the new life of holiness.

While the descent into baptismal waters can symbolize Christ's descent into death, there is another dimension of the water imagery that strengthens Paul's argument. There is a long tradition that cosmic waters were chaotic and therefore death-dealing (cf. Genesis 6–9; Job 22:11; Ps 73:13-14; Isa 27:1). To be engulfed by water is to be swallowed by chaos and death. Christ is plunged into the chaos of death; the Christians were plunged into the death of chaos. By the power of God Christ rose to a new life of glory; by the power of God the Christians are raised to the glory of a new life.

Paul characterizes their former lives as slavery to sin. This old enslaved self has to be crucified. Just as death had no power over the resurrected Christ, so sin would have no power over the baptized Christian. Crucifixion is a fitting image for Christian conversion, not only because of the role it played in Christ's death but because the torment it entails exemplifies the suffering a change of life will exact of the Christians. However, the cross is the only way to new life.

### Psalm 118:1-2, 16-17, 22-23

The refrain ("His mercy endure forever") indicates this thanksgiving psalm was intended for congregational singing. The psalm itself is a song in praise of God's power and victory. God is depicted as a mighty warrior whose strong hand prevails over forces that can threaten the life of the psalmist. God's goodness and mercy toward the house of Israel are seen in this victory. The communal character of these sentiments suggests that the threat from which the people have been saved is some kind of national enemy. Having been spared, the psalmist extols God's good favor, actually becoming a witness to the grandeur of the saving works of the LORD. The gift of salvation by God engenders witness to others of the graciousness of this saving God.

The final image is the metaphor of reversal of fortunes found so often in religious literature. The situation is always the same. A righteous person is rejected, sometimes even persecuted, by other members of the community. When the patron steps in to correct this unjust situation, the righteous one is not only vindicated but is also elevated to a position of great importance. Here the stone that was rejected becomes the very foundation of the entire building. Applying this metaphor to the psalmist, one is led to conclude that the suffering endured was unwarranted. The stability of the entire community is dependent on the innocent one who was originally rejected. This individual was first a witness to salvation by God and is now the agent of salvation for others.

### Matthew 28:1-10

Many scholars believe the earliest resurrection accounts recalled the appearances of the risen Lord and only later did the tradition of the empty tomb arise. This is probably true because, given their understanding of the unity of human nature, the earliest Palestinian believers would not have conceived of a resurrection that did not include the physical body. Nonetheless, while appearances of the risen Lord in themselves are difficult to verify, an empty tomb really proves very little, for the body could have been stolen. The passage read today contains an account of the empty tomb as well as a resurrection appearance.

The reading is not a report of the resurrection itself but of some of the circumstances that surrounded it. First there is a great earthquake, signifying that this event had repercussions in the very foundations of the earth. Next we read of heavenly involvement. An angel rolls back the stone, striking fear into the guards. The heavenly brilliance of the angel resembles the appearance of Jesus at the time of the transfiguration (cf. Matt 17:2). The women who have come to the tomb are reassured with words meant to dispel their anxiety: Do not be afraid! The angel then reminds them of Jesus' own prediction of his resurrection and invites them to examine the empty tomb.

These women were devout followers of Jesus. Mary Magdalene plays a prominent role in other resurrection narratives (cf. Mark 16:1-7; Luke 24:1-2; John 20:11-18). The other Mary is probably the mother of James (cf. Mark 16:1; Luke 24:10). It was to these women that the proclamation of Jesus' resurrection was first announced: He is raised; he is living! The words of the heavenly messenger are both a proclamation of the resurrection and a commission instructing the women to announce this wondrous event to Jesus' disciples and to direct them to go to Galilee to meet their risen Lord. Although the witness of women was discounted in rabbinic Law, the witness of these women becomes the foundation of resurrection proclamation. This witness will be confirmed in Galilee by Jesus' appearance to the disciples.

As they hasten to obey the commission given them, the women encounter Jesus. They recognize him and pay him the homage accorded a deity. He speaks the same words as did the angel: Do not be afraid! He repeats the commission to direct the disciples to meet him in Galilee. Why they are to assemble there is not explained. It may be the political situation in the city of Jerusalem was still too dangerous for them. More than likely the reason is theological. The ministry of Jesus is directed back to Galilee, the place where it began. There it will be brought to completion.

## Themes of the Day

During the Easter Vigil on Holy Saturday evening, we complete our reflections on the meaning of Passover. On Holy Thursday we saw that God is the one who passes over; on Good Friday we recognized that Jesus is our Passover. Today we ourselves are drawn into the mystery as we contemplate our own passing over. Holy Saturday is a time of liminality. We are no longer in one place, but we have not yet arrived at the other. We are in the crossing. We are moving from darkness into light, and we do this by passing through water.

## The Passage Through Water

The vigil readings recount our journey from darkness into light, from the chaotic waters of creation to the saving waters of baptism. We begin at the dawn of creation, when God separated the waters and called light out of the darkness, ordered the world and made it pulsing with life. The unfathomable nature of the trust exacted of us as we embark on and remain faithful to this journey is seen in the test to which Abraham is put. In order to embrace the new life God has planned for us we must be willing to relinquish all that we hold dear in this life. This includes all of our hopes and dreams and even those upon which we have based our future. God must be our hope and our dream; God must be the foundation of our future.

In the dark of the night we must be willing to follow God into the un-known. If we can do this, if we can risk all and leave behind the life to which we have grown accustomed, we will be able to survive in this period of limi-nality. All we need to sustain us at this time is the confidence of knowing that God, who is our redeemer, loves us with indescribable passion. Secure in this love, we will be able to turn to God for all that we need. Embraced by God's everlasting covenant, we believe that we are being led to a land abundantly fer-tile and secure from all that might harm us. It is in this liminal stage that we can accept God's commandments of life and promise to live according to God's plan for us.

The vigil readings end with a promise of regeneration. Waters that first threatened us now cleanse us. We are given new hearts to enable us to live the life of faith to which we will soon again commit ourselves. We now stand at the threshold of a new creation. The period of liminality is over. Our next step is into the waters of baptism, there to be re-created, to be born anew, to die and to rise in Christ. Then our passing over will be complete, and we will be embraced by Christ our true Passover.

# Easter

| | | | |
|---|---|---|---|
| **Easter Sunday**<br>**Acts 10:34a, 37-43**<br>We ate and drank with him | **Psalm 118:1-2, 16-17, 22-23**<br>The day the LORD has made | **Colossians 3:1-4**<br>Seek what is above<br>(or)<br>**1 Corinthians 5:6b- 8**<br>Clear out the old yeast | **John 20:1-9**<br>He is risen |
| **Second Sunday**<br>**Acts 2:42-47b**<br>They held things in common | **Psalm 118:2-4, 13-15, 22-24**<br>His mercy endures forever | **1 Peter 1:3-9**<br>A rebirth through the resurrection | **John 20:19-31**<br>Receive the Holy Spirit |
| **Third Sunday**<br>**Acts 2:14, 22-23**<br>Death could not hold him | **Psalm 16:1-2, 5, 7-11**<br>Show me the path to life | **1 Peter 1:17-21**<br>Saved by the blood of the lamb | **Luke 24:13-35**<br>Were not our hearts burning |
| **Fourth Sunday**<br>**Acts 2:14a, 36-41**<br>Jesus is made both Lord and Christ | **Psalm 23:1-6**<br>The LORD is my shepherd | **1 Peter 2:20b-25**<br>He bore our sins | **John 10:1-10**<br>I am the gate |
| **Fifth Sunday**<br>**Acts 6:1-7**<br>Seven men filled with the Spirit | **Psalm 33:1-2, 4-5, 18-19**<br>Let your mercy be on us | **1 Peter 2:4-9**<br>Living stones | **John 14:1-12**<br>The way, the truth, and the life |

| | | | |
|---|---|---|---|
| **Sixth Sunday** | | | |
| Acts 8:5-8, 14-17<br>Samaria accepts the word of God | Psalm 66:1-7, 16, 20<br>Cry out to God with joy | 1 Peter 3:15-18<br>Give a reason for your hope | John 14:15-21<br>I will not leave you orphans |
| **Ascension** | | | |
| Acts 1:1-11<br>He was lifted up | Psalm 47:2-3, 6-9<br>God is king of all the earth | Ephesians 1:17-23<br>Jesus sits at God's right hand | Matthew 28:16-20<br>All power in heaven and earth |
| **Seventh Sunday** | | | |
| Acts 1:12-14<br>Devoted with one accord in prayer | Psalm 27:1, 4, 7-8<br>The LORD is my life's refuge | 1 Peter 4:13-16<br>Rejoice in the sufferings of Christ | John 17:1-11a<br>The hour has come |
| **Pentecost** | | | |
| Acts 2:1-11<br>Filled with the Holy Spirit | Psalm 104:1, 24, 29-31, 34<br>Send out your Spirit | 1 Corinthians 12:3b-7, 12-13<br>Different gifts but one Spirit | John 20:19-23<br>As the Father sent me, I send you |

# Easter

## Initial Reading of the Easter Lectionary

### Introduction

Throughout the entire Easter season the Church celebrates the membership of the newly initiated people. Within the context of the liturgy the texts read during this time constitute a mystagogical catechesis—formative instructions for neophytes. One of the distinctive features of the season is the inclusion of selections from the Acts of the apostles rather than readings from the First Testament.

### First Testament Readings

Taken together, the first readings tell us the story of the early Christian community. This story begins on Easter Sunday with the proclamation of the gospel message, an overview of the life of Jesus, and the meaning of that life. This is a fitting beginning for the season because it was just such proclamation that planted the seeds of faith out of which the community emerged. The Third Sunday of Easter also contains a gospel proclamation. Though slightly different in style, it interprets the life and death of Jesus from the perspective of ancient Israelite tradition. On the Fourth Sunday we see the fruits of such proclamation. Many Jews heard and heeded the words of the apostles, and the early Christian community grew in number.

The communitarian character of this new family of believers was extraordinary. They prayed together and held possessions in common. When there was internal dissension, they did what was necessary to repair the rift, keeping members apart. In accord with the commission they had received from Jesus, they dared to bring the message of the gospel to distant places despite the dangers involved. Finally, they were together when the Spirit took possession of them, filling them with courage and determination.

## Psalms

The excerpts that serve as responsorial psalms allow us to express sentiments appropriate to this joyous season. At the outset we cry out in thanksgiving for the wondrous blessings that have come to us through the resurrection of Jesus. We realize that it was only through the mercy of God that we have been so blessed. Our gratitude is a recognition of our total dependence. When we reflect on the goodness of God, we sing songs of praise. When our thoughts turn to ourselves, we realize anew our dependence, and our prayers express our trust in God. If God was willing to accomplish the marvel of the resurrection, surely we can trust that God will continue to care for us.

## Epistles

The epistle readings, while they extol various aspects of the resurrection, really describe some of the blessings enjoyed by Christians because of it. Raised with Christ, our lives are now hidden with Christ in God. For this reason we must cast out any old yeast of malice or darkness. Through the resurrection we have been granted a new birth. We have been saved through the precious blood of Christ. As our shepherd, Christ will lead us to safety and guard us from harm. Through Christ we have been made a chosen race, a royal priesthood. We must be ready to give an explanation for the hope that is in us. Christ is the head of the body that is the Church.

## Gospels

The gospel readings are all resurrection narratives. Beginning with the account of the empty tomb, they lead us first to the locked room into which the risen Lord came and finally to the disciples' reception of the Holy Spirit. In each instance we see doubt and ignorance transformed into Easter faith. We accompany the disciples as they travel to Emmaus, where they recognize the Lord in the breaking of the bread. We hear him describe himself as the gate of the sheepfold, and as the way and the truth and the life. He assures his disciples that, despite his ascension to the right hand of God, they will not be left without comfort. On Pentecost, this promise is fulfilled.

## Mosaic of Readings

These Easter readings remind us of the overwhelming love God has for us. Jesus was sent to earth to bring us all to heaven. The resurrection is the triumph of divine power that made this possible, and the community is the place where we continue to experience the effects of this power. The Easter season proclaims aloud the fact of eschatological fulfillment. Begun at the empty tomb, it continues on the roads of our lives, at the tables where we commune with God and with each other. It dissipates our fears and strengthens our resolve. Easter is the season of unbounded joy, of realized hope, of heartfelt gratitude, of firm determination.

# Readings

## *Easter Sunday*

### Acts 10:34a, 37-43

Peter's discourse is really an announcement about the scope and spread of the gospel. The story of Jesus from his baptism, through his ministry, to his death and resurrection has been reported all over the land. The power of Jesus' ministry flowed from his having been anointed by God with the Holy Spirit. The reference to anointing is probably an allusion to his baptism, when the heavens opened and the Spirit descended upon him (Luke 3:21-22; 4:14, 18; cf. Isa 61:1). It was in and through this power that Jesus performed good works and healings. Peter lists himself as a witness to all these wonders.

The text suggests Peter is speaking to a Gentile audience. Judea is referred to as the "land of the Jews," and the rejection Jesus experienced at the hands of his own people is mentioned. This indicates that "the Jews" were a group other than those being addressed. The allusion to the message of the prophets implies that the hearers would have known to whom Peter refers. However, this does not mean they were Jews, since there were many Gentiles in Judea at this time who were interested in Jewish tradition and practice and who would have been acquainted with the important prophetic teaching.

Although Jesus' ministry had a beginning, namely his baptism by John, it does not seem really to have had an ending. It continues through those who were commissioned to preach the gospel and to bear witness to it. This is precisely what Peter is doing in this reading, bearing witness to the resurrection of Jesus (v. 40) and proclaiming the universality of its effects (v. 42).

Peter's teaching regarding the resurrection includes several important components. First, it is clearly a work of God. Second, it is a genuine resurrection from the dead and not merely a resuscitation. That it occurred three days after Jesus' death is evidence of this. Third, Jesus was seen by some and then ate and drank with several of his followers, Peter among them. This demonstrates that the appearances of the risen Christ were genuine physical experiences and not some kind of hallucinations.

Finally, the fruits of the resurrection are both transformative and all-encompassing. Peter claims that Jesus, appointed by God, is the one who fulfills the role of the eschatological arbiter, judging the living and the dead (v. 42; cf. Dan 7:1). He further asserts that this judgment scene was the wondrous event to which the prophets testified. Peter is here explaining the mystery of Jesus in terms of prophetic expectation and thus is at once both reinterpreting earlier prophetic tradition and developing new theological insight. With just a few words Peter has placed Jesus at the heart of both the prophetic and the apocalyptic traditions of Israel.

The judgment Jesus brings is one of forgiveness of sin. He judges not to condemn but to save and transform. Furthermore, though born from the people of Israel and rooted within that tradition, he was raised up by God to bring forgiveness to all. The power of the resurrection is not circumscribed by ethnic or religious origin. It is open to all who believe in Jesus. This is truly good news to the Gentiles.

## Psalm 118:1-2, 16-17, 22-23

The responsorial psalm is a song in praise of God's power and victory. The refrain ("His mercy endures forever") indicates this thanksgiving psalm was intended for congregational singing. The communal character of these sentiments, seen in the reference to the house of Israel, suggests the threat from which the people have been saved is some kind of national enemy. God's goodness and mercy toward the house of Israel are made manifest in this victory. The Hebrew word for mercy (*hesed*) is a technical theological term denoting God's steadfast love for the partners in the covenant, the chosen people of the house of Israel. Having been spared, the psalmist extols God's good favor, actually becoming a witness to the grandeur of the saving works of the LORD.

God is depicted as a mighty warrior whose strong right hand prevails over forces that can threaten the security of the people and the very life of the psalmist. The bias for right-handedness is obvious. The right side of a person was considered the stronger side, the honorable side. Conversely, the left side was weak, untrustworthy, sinister. The image of God's right hand connotes strength and triumph. It suggests that God's victory was won in a righteous manner.

This divine achievement in itself made God deserving of praise and thanksgiving. However, there seems to be a personal element in this victory. In the wake of God's triumph the psalmist is preserved from death. As a result of this magnanimous deed the psalmist will publish abroad the mighty works of the LORD. Here again the individual and communal aspects of this thanksgiving psalm are intertwined.

The final image is the metaphor of reversal of fortunes found so often in religious literature. The situation is always the same. A righteous person is rejected, sometimes even persecuted, by other members of the community. When the divine patron of the sufferer steps in to correct this unjust situation, the righteous one is not only vindicated but is also elevated to a position of great importance. In this psalm the stone that was rejected becomes the very foundation of the entire building. The Hebrew identifies this stone as "the head of the corner." Although some interpret it as the capstone that completes the building, the reference is probably to the cornerstone that links two walls at right angles, thus holding up a significant part of the building's weight.

It is not clear to whom this metaphor of the cornerstone refers. However, as the verses of this psalm are arranged for our liturgical use, it seems the speaker who survived the threat of death is the referent. This salvation was brought about by God, and it is recognized as a marvel for which to give praise and thanks.

## Colossians 3:1-4 (A)

The passage, short as it is, contains the fundamental teaching about the resurrection and the way the death and resurrection of Christ transform the lives of Christians. It is set against the backdrop of ancient cosmology. The verbs used are quite telling. Besides the imperatives, which both address the present and remain open to all future moments, there are verbs in the perfect tense denoting the finality of some actions.

Two different realms are delineated: the world above and the world below. In a three-tiered cosmology this delineation has two possible meanings. On the one hand, it could refer to the earth and the netherworld, on the other, to the heavenly realm and the earth. Although early Christian theology spoke of Christ descending to the netherworld after his death, there to release the souls of the righteous awaiting resurrection, the reference in this passage to God's right hand indicates that the second interpretation is the one intended. The earth is the world below and the heavenly realm is the world above.

Christ rose from the dead and is now in the realm of heaven. Two images characterize the relationship between the risen Christ and God. First, Christ is seated at God's right hand. This suggests a heavenly imperial throne room where God reigns supreme and Christ sits next to God in the place of honor. The bias for right-handedness is clear. As explained above, the right side was considered the strong side, the side of goodness and favor. Enthroned there, Christ both enjoys God's favor and, as God's "right hand," bestows blessings on others and administers God's righteousness. The second image states that Christ is "in God." This means that having died to human life, Christ has been raised to a new life. In a new and total way Christ's being is rooted in God.

The admonition to the Christians flows out of belief in this reality. As believers they are joined to Christ. Consequently, they have died with Christ and have risen with Christ. Therefore they should turn their attention away from the things of this world and commit themselves to the things of heaven. They are called to a life that reflects this new reality. The specifics of such a life are outlined elsewhere, but one can presume that being joined to Christ would result in behavior like that of Christ.

While the admonitions are explicit imperatives, the statements about dying with Christ and being raised with Christ are in the perfect tense. This is not a dimension of Christians' future expectation, it is an accomplished fact. They are indeed joined with Christ, and so joined they are already with Christ in God. They have not left this world, but they are summoned to be attentive to the things of another world. In fact, they live in two worlds, or to use eschatological language, they have already entered "the age to come."

The passage ends with mention of Christ's ultimate appearance and a promise that those joined with Christ will also appear in glory. Here is an example of a complex eschatological view: "already, but not yet." Joined to Christ, Christians are already living in the final age, but this age of fulfillment is not yet complete.

## 1 Corinthians 5:6b-8 (B)

The reference in this reading to yeast calls to mind the Jewish feast of Unleavened Bread (cf. Exod 12:3-10; Deut 16:3-4), which marked the beginning of the barley harvest. Though originally an agricultural celebration, it was eventually joined to the herding feast of Passover, and together they became a commemoration of God's deliverance of the people from the bondage of Egypt. The reference to Christ our Passover marks this combining of festivals.

During the first seven days of the feast only bread made from the flour of the new grain was to be eaten. It was prepared without leaven, the dough that was left over from the previous baking. Because leaven ferments and also causes ingredients around it to break down, it was considered both corrupt in itself and an evil influence. Nothing from the old year, and certainly nothing corrupt, was to be brought into the fruits of the new harvest.

Paul uses this abstention from leaven, which marked the transition from one year to the next, as a metaphor for the Christians' conversion from life before Christ to life with Christ, from the old age to the age of fulfillment. He exhorts them to rid themselves of their former way of life, for even the slightest trace of corruption can undermine the good they might do. "A rotten apple spoils the whole barrel."

Continuing with imagery taken from these combined Jewish festivals, Paul emphatically states: "Christ our Passover has been sacrificed!" The allusion is to the death of Jesus, which, like the sacrifice of the Passover lamb, saved the people by vicariously assuming the guilt of the community. In order fittingly to celebrate this Passover the Christians must now purge themselves of all leaven of the past. They must put aside works of corruption and wickedness and commit themselves to lives of sincerity and truth.

## John 20:1-9

The resurrection stories begin with a report of Mary Magdalene's visit to the tomb. It is the first day of the week, while it is still dark. Reference to darkness rather than the dawn of a new day, which would be traditional, may be the author's way of incorporating the light/darkness symbolism. In other words, lack of faith is a life in darkness. Identifying the day as the first of the week will take on significance in subsequent Christian theology. It will be likened to the dawning of a new creation, or to the eschatological time of fulfillment.

No explanation is given for Mary's visit. The text does not say she came to weep or to anoint the body. It simply says she came to the tomb. Seeing that the stone had been moved, she presumed the body of Jesus had been taken away. She seems to have entertained no thought of his resurrection, only the removal of his body. She ran off to tell Peter and "the other disciple." The text is rather cryptic. For some reason Mary speaks in the plural: "We don't know. . . ," and the disciple who was with Peter is not named.

The reading contains a definite bias in favor of this other disciple. He is referred to as the one that Jesus loved (an allusion to John?), and he is the only one in the account who is said to have believed. He is beloved, and he is faith-filled. The text also hints at Peter's privileged status within the community. He is the one to whom Mary runs, and when the two men hurry to the tomb, the other disciple waits until Peter enters before he himself goes in.

The details about the burial wrappings are significant. They are still in the tomb, though the body is not. If the body had been merely transported to another tomb, burial wrappings would still have been needed and presumably would have been taken along. However, if the body had been carried away in order to desecrate it, the cloths would probably have been discarded. No explanation is given for why the head cloth was rolled up separately. The interpretation of these details seems to have been left to the character in the narrative. We are not told what Peter thought about them, but the Beloved Disciple noted these things and believed. It is unusual that resurrection faith would spring forth from an experience of the empty tomb rather than from an appearance of the risen Lord, but such is the case here.

The reading ends on a curious note. The reason for the general lack of faith of the disciples is given: they did not understand the Scriptures concerning the resurrection of Jesus. Regardless of how Jesus might have instructed his followers while he was still with them, they were ill equipped to comprehend his suffering and death, to say nothing of his rising from the dead. They would need both a resurrection experience and the opening of their minds to the meaning of the Scriptures.

The choice of this reading for Easter Sunday highlights the incomprehensibility of the event. The fact that neither Mary, probably Jesus' closest female disciple, nor Peter, the leader of the Christian community, was prepared spontaneously to embrace the truth of the resurrection should caution us lest we too glibly presume to grasp it. There is much in the reality of the resurrection that continues to challenge as well as sustain us.

## Themes of the Day

Easter is the season of mystagogical catechesis, the instruction that unpacks the hidden mystery experienced in the sacraments of initiation received or renewed on Easter. The readings of each Sunday concentrate on some aspect of this mystery. The central theme of this Sunday is newness of life in Christ. This newness is not without its historical context. It burst forth first in the resurrection of Christ and then through the preaching of the first Christians. History is broken open by this newness in unimaginable ways.

### Newness in Christ

In the Northern Hemisphere the world is coming alive. You can see it in the trees; you can smell it in the air. There is a freshness about to burst forth. Newness seems to be standing on tiptoes, eager to reveal itself, ready to be born. The life that was hidden in the darkness of winter is impatient to appear in all its glory. Nature itself seems poised to reenact the drama of death and resurrection.

On Easter Sunday the changes in nature all point to the transformation par excellence, the death and resurrection of Christ and the transformation that takes place in us as we participate in that resurrection presence. The readings testify that if we die with Christ we will appear with him in glory; if we cast out the old yeast we will be fresh dough. When this wondrous transformation takes place, everything is new, everything is fresh.

To what newness are we called? To what must we die in order to rise transformed? What old yeast of corruption must be cast out in order that we might be fresh dough? On Easter we renew our baptismal vows. What is it we really renounce? Ours is a world of violence, of prejudice, of indifference. Too often we harbor feelings of anger and resentment, of selfishness and disdain. Easter proclaims that Christ has died and has risen; with him we die to all the wickedness in our lives and in our world, and we set our hearts on higher things, on sincerity and on truth.

*History Is Broken Open*

Though we know well the Easter story, we never fully grasp its meaning. The stone has been rolled back and the tomb is empty; resurrected life cannot be contained. Like the first believers, we so often must continue to live even with our dashed hopes and our misunderstanding of God's mysterious power. Like the first believers, we come to the tomb and expect to find death, but instead we find signs of a new life we cannot even begin to comprehend. Like the first believers, we do not realize that history has been broken open and is now filled with the resurrected presence of Christ.

History no longer makes sense. The one who was maliciously singled out and shamefully hung on a tree was really the one set apart by God to judge the living and the dead. Who can comprehend such a paradox? But then, who goes to a tomb expecting to find life? History has been broken open, and now we really do not know what to expect!

This same resurrection power works in own lives today. "This is the day the LORD has made . . . it is wonderful in our eyes!" We too hear the Easter proclamation. By it, we too are brought into the power of the resurrection.

## Second Sunday of Easter

### Acts 2:42-47

On this Second Sunday of the Easter season we are given a glimpse of the Christian community after the Pentecost experience. It is an idealized picture, a kind of utopian dream. It depicts the primitive Church more in its eschatological fulfillment than as it probably really was. Other passages from the Acts of the Apostles provide us with a very different picture of the community, one that reveals its flaws and its struggles. The picture we are given today shows us features of the community that were certainly present during the apostolic age. We see only positive features, those associated with the age of fulfillment. Four features seem to be basic: apostolic teaching, community, Eucharist, and prayer.

Apostolic teaching refers to the authoritative teaching of the apostles, teaching that formed the basis of what ultimately became the New Testament. It included the teaching of Jesus as well as cherished yet interpreted accounts of the wonders he performed. It also included various aspects of the ancient Israelite tradition, which Christians believed was brought to fulfillment in Jesus. (An example of this kind of teaching can be seen in Peter's speech on Pentecost, cf. Acts 2:14-36, and that of Stephen before the council of Jewish leaders, Acts 7:1-50.)

The community life of the early Church *(koinōnia)* was one of communal sharing. This sharing had a social dimension, manifested in the members holding possessions in common, as well as a religious dimension, expressed in their celebration of the Lord's Supper. Unlike the practice observed by the Essenes and the community at Qumran, sharing within the Christian community was voluntary. Many people of means retained their own possessions. (An example is Lydia; Acts 16:14-15. Ananias and Sapphira were punished because they lied to the Holy Spirit, not because they withheld the proceeds of the sale of their property; cf. Acts 5:1-6.)

It is clear from this passage the earliest Christians did not consider themselves as separated from the larger Jewish community, for they regularly participated in temple prayer (cf. Acts 3:11; 5:12). This was probably because they believed they were the true Israel, in whose midst were being fulfilled the promises made to their ancestors, so there was no reason to cease participation. In the New Testament "breaking of bread" is a technical term for the celebration of the Lord's Supper. Most likely this service took place in the homes of Christians (house church). Later texts suggest its format followed a Jewish model, but its content centered around the memorial of the death of Jesus.

The signs and wonders performed by the apostles were primarily cures (cf. Acts 3:1-10), evidence the eschatological age of fulfillment had dawned. This miraculous activity filled the bystanders with awe, the conventional response of human beings who have witnessed the extraordinary power of God. Although wonders were worked by the apostles, this text makes it very clear that it was the power of God at work through them. It was the Lord who brought others into their midst and made their numbers increase.

## Psalm 118:2-4, 13-15, 22-24

The responsorial psalm consists of excerpts from a song of thanksgiving that seems to be part of a liturgical celebration. The psalm contains both individual and communal features: the language in the first and third sections (vv. 2-4; 22-24) is plural, while the speaker in the middle section (vv. 13-15) is clearly an individual. The refrain ("His mercy endures forever") establishes the psalm's congregational liturgical character.

The psalm itself begins with a call to give testimony to the goodness of God. This call is threefold in structure and inclusive in nature. The "house of Israel" designates the people of the covenant; the "house of Aaron" refers to the priesthood; "all who fear the LORD" is probably a reference to "God-fearers," or prose lytes of non-Israelite origin (cf. Ps 115:9-11). The Hebrew word for mercy (*ḥesed*) is a technical theological term denoting God's steadfast love for those in covenant with God. Presumably the leader of the liturgical assembly calls out to the members of each respective group, and they in turn declare God's faithfulness.

The voice is singular in the second section of the responsorial (vv. 13-15). It testifies to a time when the psalmist was under great duress, suffering at the hands of others and being overpowered. In the face of this oppression God stepped in and saved the psalmist from ultimate defeat. The acknowledgment of deliverance is followed by an individual song of praise (v. 14), which uses the language of one of Israel's oldest hymns of victory (Exod 15:2a). The song, long associated with God's deliverance of the people from Egyptian bondage, acclaims the faithfulness of God: "My strength and my courage is the LORD."

The rescue of the individual is linked to the salvation of the entire community. They are the righteous who live in tents (v. 15). This reference to tents could be another allusion to the exodus experience and the sojourn in the wilderness, or to the feast of Tabernacles, when the people remembered and celebrated this emancipation and sojourn. In whichever case, the shout of victory proclaims God's deliverance of the people.

In the third section (vv. 22-24), the congregation speaks again, announcing the reversal of fortune that has taken place. The one who had been rejected and hard pressed by enemies has now been saved and exalted by God. Throughout this account of suffering and salvation, it is very clear that deliverance and exaltation are the works of God and not the accomplishments of human beings. This saving act may have happened to an individual, but the entire congregation has witnessed it and marvels at it.

In genuine liturgical fashion, the responsorial psalm brings us to the present moment. Although the salvation described occurred in the past, the psalmist insists that *today* is the day the LORD made, *today* is the day we rejoice in God's saving work. This liturgical perspective enables believers of any generation to identify their own time as the day of salvation and to rejoice in it.

## 1 Peter 1:3-9

This short reading consists of two distinct yet intimately related focuses. The first is doxological—a hymn of praise to God for the wonderful things God has done in the lives of believers (vv. 3-5). The passage then shifts our attention to the suffering that Christians must endure while still in this life (vv. 6-9). The hope described in the first verses is the basis of the strength required for the experience described in what follows. The entire passage is remarkable for the variety of themes it weaves together. They include praise of God, christology, soteriology, and eschatology.

The opening doxology *(eulogētós)* is patterned after a Jewish hymn of praise. It is theocentric in perspective, praising God for the blessings bestowed upon believers through Christ. Although most translations speak of "new birth," the Greek verb *(anagennáō)* really refers to the function of the father in the process of procreation, suggesting that this new existence might be described better as being begotten anew rather than born anew. The author may have chosen this rather awkward expression so the new life of which he spoke would not be confused with the newness promised the Jewish proselyte or the rebirth claimed by the mystery religions of the time. He wanted his readers to realize that the new life that comes from God through Jesus Christ is of a nature completely different from these others. It defines the Christian as one who has been born into an otherworldly existence.

It is out of this theocentric perspective that the author develops his christology. He declares that Jesus is the mediator of the salvation that comes from God. It is through his resurrection that all enjoy new life. However, this salvation is not without cost. It was purchased through the death of Jesus, and it requires suffering on the part of those who have been begotten anew as well. It is through this suffering that faith is tested, like precious metal is tested by fire. In the present time Christians live lives of faith, believing in Christ even when they do not see him, but the fullness of salvation is about to be revealed. In the end suffering will have refined their faith, and they too will enjoy praise and glory and honor at the final revelation of Jesus their Savior. The idea of joy in the midst of suffering may seem strange at first sight. However, the joy is not in the suffering itself but in the new birth and in the blessings it promises.

The new life that believers receive from God is eschatological in nature. It looks to the future for the fulfillment of God's promise. Ancient Israel had been promised the land as an inheritance. There is an inheritance promised here as well. However, this inheritance is not of this world; it belongs to heaven and is safeguarded by God. It shares in many of the characteristics of heaven: it will not be conquered by death; it will be free from any form of pollution; it will not wither or dry up. Thus we see that the hope to which the new birth looks is eschatological, the inheritance that accompanies it is eschatological, and the salvation it guarantees is eschatological. This is the living hope to which Christians are born.

## John 20:19-31

Two resurrection appearances form a kind of diptych. The hinge that connects them is the person of Thomas. Absent for the first event, he is the central character of the second. His absence is curious, since on both occasions the doors of the room where the disciples were gathered were securely locked, "for fear of the Jews" (v. 19). Why had Thomas not gathered with the rest of the disciples? Was he not afraid? Or was he too afraid to be associated with them? The reason for his absence is never given. However, it does provide an occasion for another encounter with the risen Lord and the demonstration of faith that ensues.

The two resurrection appearances have several details in common: both occur on the first day of the week; despite the closed doors Jesus appears in their midst; he addresses them with a greeting of peace; he calls their attention to his wounds. Each of these details is laden with theological meaning.

The first day of the week is the actual day of the resurrection (v. 19) or the day that will eventually commemorate it (v. 26). The entire reckoning of time has been altered. Where previously the conclusion of the week had religious meaning, now the focus is on the beginning of the week, on the future. The closed doors not only secure the disciples from those who would be hostile toward them, but they also underscore the mysterious character of Jesus' risen body, which is not impeded by material obstacles. The wish of peace, the common greeting of the day, is also a prayer for the eschatological blessings of health, prosperity, and all good things. Finally, by calling attention to the wounds in his hands and side Jesus shows the disciples he is really the crucified one, now risen.

According to this account it is on the evening of the resurrection itself that the Holy Spirit is bestowed on the disciples. They are commissioned to go forth, to declare salvation and judgment. Though this charge comes from Jesus, it is a continuation of the commission he received from God. The trinitarian testimony is clear. The image of breathing life into another is reminiscent of the creation of Adam (cf. Gen 2:7) and the restoration of Israel (cf. Ezek 37:9). This very act by the risen Lord casts him in a creative/re-creative role.

Thomas represents the second generation of Christians, those who are called to believe on the testimony of others. The faith required of him is, in a way, more demanding than that required of those who actually encountered the risen Lord. Viewed in this way, his doubt is understandable. While we may judge him harshly for it, Jesus does not. Instead, he invites Thomas to touch him, an invitation not extended earlier to the other disciples. The story does not say Thomas actually touched the wounds, only that he cried out in faith: "My Lord and my God." The other disciples recognized that the one in their midst was their Lord. Thomas declared that the risen Lord was God, a profession of faith that outstrips the others.

According to Jesus, as profound as was Thomas' ultimate faith, it does not compare with the faith of those who do not enjoy the kind of experience of the Lord described here. Thomas should be remembered not because he was absent or because he doubted but because, like us, he was called to believe on the word of others. And like Thomas, we know how difficult that is.

## Themes of the Day

The themes for the Second Sunday of Easter set the tone for the entire Easter season. They are all geared toward the mystagogical instruction, primarily of the neophytes, who were baptized during the Easter Vigil, but also that of the whole Christian community. The readings for this season provide us an extended meditation on the mystery of the resurrection and on our own incorporation into that resurrection through the mysteries of initiation.

*The Sacred Mysteries*

All three readings for this Sunday invite us into the sacred mysteries of the season. Most of us are like Thomas, who looked for some tangible evidence of the resurrection. We may not be as straightforward in our demands as he was, but we are frequently no less resolute. We do not find it any easier to live by faith than he did. We are no more willing to listen to the good news that comes from others than he was. However, as obstinate as he first appeared, he was open to the power of the resurrection, and he ultimately entered into the depths of its mystery. Thomas is the model of those who come to the sacred mysteries through the words of others.

We find the same situation in the reading from Acts. The fledgling Christian community grew in number as a result of the teaching of the apostles. So it has always been down through the ages. Although we were not eyewitnesses of the actual events, we are the ones called through the teaching of others to witness to the power of the resurrection in our day. Regardless of how often we hear this Easter message proclaimed, we will never plumb the depths of its mystery. The mystagogical catechesis found in the letter of Peter invites all of us to stand beside Thomas, proclaiming with him the humble prayer: My Lord and my God!

*Tangible Proof*

We search for tangible proof of the resurrection, and we are told to live by faith. Remarkably, when we do live by faith, we discover tangible proof. This proof is found in the Christian community itself. Here we find people devoted to the teaching of the apostles, living a communal life, breaking bread together, and praying. Here we find people sharing their possessions with others and living in peace. Here we find people dedicating their lives to the work of reconciliation in families, among races and nations. Here we find people involved in works of justice as well as charity. Here we find people feeding the hungry, clothing the naked, sheltering the homeless, visiting the sick, comforting those in sorrow. Here we find people devoted to issues of life and health and well-being. These are all tangible proofs of the resurrection.

Jesus extends his wounded hands to us as he did to Thomas, and the community is invited to touch his wounds as we touch the wounds of our world. Today these wounds can be seen in the victims of war or racial violence, in those suffering debilitating illness, in those ostracized from society, in the vulnerable who are abused, in the disadvantaged who are exploited. The tangible proof of the resurrection can be seen in the way the community reaches out to others in care and support.

*The Cost*

Although the blessings we derive from the resurrection are clearly a gift from God, they are nonetheless a costly gift. They have been won through the blood of Christ, and we may have to pay dearly for having received them. Our faith may be tested by fire. Our commitment to the well-being of others may meet with rejection and opposition. Anyone who has set out to correct social ills knows this is not only a thankless job, but at times it can also be dangerous. Yet even these trials can be seen as tangible proof of the resurrection, for they remind us that the glorious wounds of Christ are still wounds. It was only through suffering that new life sprang forth.

## Third Sunday of Easter
### Acts 2:14, 22-33

The first reading for this Sunday is the speech of Peter, which proclaims Jesus as Lord and Messiah. It follows the pattern of early missionary preaching, which consisted of four major elements: an announcement of the arrival of the age of fulfillment; a summary of events in the ministry, death, and resurrection of Jesus; recourse to the Old Testament to show how Jesus fulfilled what it promised; and a call to repentance. It is clear from the text that Peter is speaking to a Jewish community. They are explicitly identified (vv. 14, 22) and later referred to as brothers (v. 29). The knowledge of Scripture presumed of them is further indication that Peter is talking to his compatriots, members of his own religious community. This should be remembered lest we allow his accusation to be interpreted in an anti-Judaic manner.

The Jewish nation believed that the eschatological age of fulfillment would be inaugurated by signs and wonders, by miracles that demonstrated the mighty power of God. Jesus himself appealed to this belief when earlier in his public ministry he responded to the question posed by John the Baptism (cf. Matt 11:5; Isa 35:5). Peter asserts that Jesus performed such works. This is no empty claim, for the people to whom Peter is speaking know this. If they had not witnessed Jesus' works themselves, they certainly had heard about them from others. Since such power could come only from God, such action was proof that God was working through Jesus and that the eschatological age of fulfillment was dawning.

Miraculous deeds exemplified the ministry of Jesus. Peter next describes his death and resurrection. He places responsibility for Jesus' death at the feet of both the Jewish people and the Roman officials. The first group handed him over; the second put him to death. However, Peter insists this all happened according to the plan and with the foreknowledge of God. God was at work in the ministry of Jesus as well as in his death, and finally, it was God's working that raised Jesus from the dead.

A passage from the Old Testament is called upon as testimony to the resurrection of Jesus. It comes from the Greek version of Psalm 16:8-11. Peter argues that the original Davidic reference is questionable because David did in fact die and was buried. His tomb at Siloam was well known to Peter's audience. Therefore, the psalmist must have been referring to a messianic descendant of David. This idea is reinforced by means of a second reference, which alludes to a promise made by God to David concerning such a descendant (cf. Ps 132:11). Following this line of rabbinic argumentation, a method of interpretation that may be foreign to us today, Peter maintains that David had the resurrection of Christ in mind when he spoke prophetically.

This passage does not contain a call to repentance, but it does insist that Peter and the eleven with him are witnesses to Jesus' resurrection. He proclaims that God both raised Jesus and exalted him in the place of honor at God's right hand. Throughout the speech it is clear Jesus is subordinated to God. He performed miracles through the power of God; he was raised and exalted by God; he received the promise of the Holy Spirit from God. This speech proclaims the resurrection, the ascension, and the descent of the Spirit. It also provides us with an early statement about the inner workings of the Trinity.

## Psalm 16:1-2, 5, 7-8, 9-10, 11

This psalm of confidence opens with a declaration of trust that God will protect the psalmist from danger (v. 1) and ultimately from death (v. 10). A confession of faith follows: The LORD is the only God for the psalmist. The psalm speaks of a covenant relationship with God and the confidence that redounds from it.

Two images express this relationship. The allotted portion of land is the inheritance each tribe was given, which was handed down within the tribes generation after generation. This land provided the people with identity and membership, sustenance and prosperity. Without land they had no future, and they would not last long in the present. Here the psalmist is claiming it is God who has replaced the land in the religious consciousness of the people; the blessings and promises customarily associated with land are now associated with the LORD. Furthermore, this portion of the inheritance is safe, for it is the LORD who holds it fast.

The second image is the cup. This may refer to the cup passed around from which all drank. Such an action solidified the union of those who drank. When this action took place at a cultic meal, those participating in the feast were joined not only to one another but to the deity as well. The psalmist declares that the unifying cup of which he speaks is really the LORD. In other words, the psalmist is joined so closely with God as almost to defy separation.

Three strong features suggest that the context of this psalm is the cult. The psalmist is counseled by the LORD. This could refer to the practice of a worshiper approaching a priest in order to receive counsel in a particular matter. A second feature is mention of prayer at night. This is probably an allusion to night vigil, the devotional ritual of spending the entire night at the sanctuary or in the Temple praying for a favor from God. Finally, the psalmist mentions the joy experienced in the presence of the LORD, what might be considered another allusion to the sanctuary. The psalmist clearly respects the importance of the cultic practices of the people.

The psalmist's entire being is filled with confidence and gladness. Two major dimensions of the human person are joined here in order to demonstrate the comprehensiveness of the psalmist. They are the heart, which, understood figuratively, refers to the inner or spiritual dimension of the person, and the flesh, the physical or exterior dimension of the person. The reason for this rejoicing is the rescue from death that God granted the psalmist. Regardless of the fact that Christians consider these as strong proleptic references to resurrection, the psalmist was probably merely thinking of being rescued *from* death, rather than *after* death.

The protection represented in these verses is reason for profound rejoicing. Regardless of the terrifying, even life-threatening ordeals that must be endured, the psalmist proclaims that God is steadfast. In such difficult circumstances this kind of confidence in God may appear to be foolhardy, but the psalmist's trust is unshakable. Ultimately the fullness of joy will abound in the presence of God.

## 1 Peter 1:17-21

The author of the letter from which this passage is taken looks carefully at the cost of salvation and the responsibilities that accompany it. He begins by reminding the audience of the implications of calling God "father." The masculine character of this appellation has caused some contemporary believers to refrain from using it. On the other hand, many others value it because of the intimate nature of the relationship it denotes. Its use here underscores a very different aspect of the notion. In strict hierarchal societies it was the responsibility of the head of the household to oversee the order of that household. In patriarchal societies this responsibility would fall to the male head of the family. (Presumably, in matriarchal societies it would fall to the female head.) This passage shows that to invoke God as father is comparable to asking God to act as disciplinarian. This presents a picture different from that of a tender parent, a picture to which we may have accustomed ourselves in recent times.

In situations where the welfare of the household was at stake, the head of that household could not afford to show partiality. Neither age nor social status nor even personal loyalties could compromise the well-being of the entire group. The author insists that if God is called "father," that very father will judge the members of his household according to the merit of each one's works. This in no way challenges the notion of the mercy and forgiveness of God. Rather, it points to the obligation that one has to live one's new life in Christ with integrity. Divine mercy can still be shown after divine judgment has been executed. The time on earth is referred to as a sojourn, a journey to a clearly defined destination. In a very real sense believers do not belong to this world. Instead, they belong to the world to which they sojourn. Even though they had already been ransomed, or redeemed, while on the journey of this life, they have very specific obligations to accomplish, the failure of which makes them liable to judgment.

The death/resurrection of Christ has ransomed believers from the vain or futile manner of living they inherited from their ancestors, the patterns of living into which they had been socialized. The price of this redemption was neither gold nor silver but the blood of Christ. Ancient Israelite Law stated that the passover sacrifice was to be a spotless unblemished lamb (cf. Exod 12:5). Christian faith maintains that Christ was the only perfect lamb, and it was his blood that ransomed us.

The participial structure of the next verse (v. 20) and its formulaic character support the idea that the death and resurrection of Christ were in the plan of God from the beginning and were not merely a remedy for the state of human sinfulness. The eschatological parameters of God's plan are explicitly sketched here. Redemption through Christ was determined before the foundation of the world, but it will be revealed fully in the final age. And when will the final age dawn? The Jews believed the Messiah would usher it in. The Christians reinterpreted this expectation a bit. While they maintained it had indeed burst forth with the coming of the Messiah, it had not yet totally unfolded. For this reason the Christians are exhorted to live in faith with hope.

## Luke 24:13-35

The report of the encounter with Christ on the road to Emmaus is probably one of the best-known resurrection stories. Besides being a piece of exquisite literary narrative, it is rich with theological themes. It depicts the unfolding character of revelation, a christology somehow rooted in the traditions of ancient Israel, and the revelatory nature of "breaking bread," to name but two.

The chronological sequence of the gospel resurrection narratives is impossible to trace. This may be because in one sense each experience of the risen Lord is a new beginning in itself. The events described here are said to have happened on the very day of the resurrection (v. 13), three days after the death of Jesus (v. 21). The tomb had already been discovered empty, but the reliability of the report of the women who found it so had apparently been questioned (vv. 22-23). In other words, the two disciples on the road had not heard of any actual experience of the risen Lord. It would only be upon their return to Jerusalem that they would hear such news (v. 34).

The disciples were probably returning home from the celebration of Passover, and they most likely assumed that the unrecognized Jesus was on the road for the same reason. Emmaus was only seven miles from Jerusalem, a distance that could be covered on foot in a relatively short span of time. This was their city of destination, their hometown. The character of the hospitality they extended to Jesus demonstrates this. Although Cleopas' companion is not named, there are several clues that suggest it is his wife. First, one of the women who stood at the foot of the cross was Mary the wife of Clopas (cf. John 19:25). Although this name is a corrupted form of a Semitic name, the similarity cannot be denied. Second, missionary couples were well known in the early Church (cf. Prisca and Aquila in Acts 18:2). Third, it sounds like the disciples are offering hospitality jointly, as husband and wife might.

The revelatory features of the account are quite interesting. At first the two do not recognize Jesus. However, they are not reluctant to describe the events of the past few days and to admit they had considered Jesus the fulfillment of their messianic expectations. At a time when those closest to Jesus seem to have withdrawn in fear for their own safety, these disciples are telling a perfect stranger they had believed in him. The ground is ready for a revelation of God. As Jesus interprets the Scriptures to show that they had really pointed to him, the hearts of the disciples burn within them. Their religious tradition is being interpreted for them in a new and revelatory way. At the same time, Jesus is showing how his death and resurrection were truly in accord with those Scriptures. Finally, it is in the breaking of the bread that their eyes are opened and they recognize him. The revelatory unfolding is finished.

The movement of the narrative follows the pattern of early Christian worship: the Christian story is remembered; it is then interpreted; the breaking of the bread follows. Whether or not the meal should be considered a genuine celebration of the Eucharist, Christians then and now certainly make that connection, for the words of the Last Supper are in the account: "He took the bread, said the blessing, broke it, and gave it to them" (v. 30; cf. Luke 22:19). The account itself underscores several important issues: glory comes by way of suffering; remembering the tradition is not enough; in a new situation it must be interpreted; we come to know Christ in the breaking of the bread.

### Themes of the Day

The Easter mystagogical instruction continues. This Sunday we reflect on the fact that life itself is a journey, the parameters of which we do not determine but which have been determined for us. While we may have some sense of where we are going, the journey holds many surprises that may completely alter how we travel along the way.

## Life as a Journey

This has become a very popular theme in certain circles of the Church today. It really expresses well the notion that life is not a static reality but rather a movement from one point to another. It is not so much that we make the journey but that we join one already in progress. We join those who have gone before us, those who have forged a path, those who have discovered the dark valleys as well as the places of refreshment. Even the unfolding of our religious tradition can be characterized as a journey. It is the path of meaning that we take throughout life.

We are not on this journey alone. We have companions with whom we can discuss all that has occurred. In fact, we need each other. We cannot journey alone. We need their encouragement and support; we need their talents and insight; we need their company. Journey is a rich and challenging metaphor for life.

## Surprises Along the Way

Today's readings show us that the way we ordinarily negotiate the journey of life is really not the way the journey is negotiated. The two disciples traveling to Emmaus admitted they had certain expectations that Jesus did not fulfill. They had hoped he would redeem Israel. They did not expect him to be put to death. Furthermore, they thought they were merely talking with a fellow traveler. They did not realize that Jesus had indeed redeemed Israel, and all other people as well. They did not realize that it was through his death that he accomplished this. Finally, they did not realize that the risen Lord himself was their traveling companion.

As with them, so with us. Something is happening beneath what we are able to observe. Christ is with us as an intimate traveling companion along the way. After all, it was God who laid out the parameters of the journey of life, and it is God who is at work beneath and within what we can observe. Perhaps we don't recognize this because, like the disciples on the way to Emmaus, we are "slow of heart to believe." We do not see the extraordinary in the ordinary. We do not see the hand of God in our lives. Perhaps we need someone to interpret for us both the tradition and the events of life.

*With Hearts Burning Within Us*

Once we realize who our traveling companion really is, our hearts will burn within us, our eyes will be opened, and we will look at life with eyes of faith. We will be able to recognize the working of God in the ordinary events of life, and we will proclaim this insight to others. This Easter faith will transform our disillusionment into missionary zeal. Some of us may be called upon to give more public witness, as was Peter. Most of us will preach with the example of our lives, as the words of Francis of Assisi suggest: Preach the gospel always; if necessary, use words. All of us can enter into this mystery as we recognize him in the breaking of the bread.

## Fourth Sunday of Easter
### Acts 2:14a, 36-41

The speech of Peter that was begun last Sunday is continued today. Accompanied by the other eleven apostles, Peter addresses a large crowd of Jewish people referred to here as the "house of Israel." This phrase is important not only because it marks the religious identity of his audience but because it stands in contrast to the reconstitution of the People of God, described later in this passage. Though placed in the mouth of Peter, the speech is probably an example of the early Church's confession of faith.

When Peter declares that God has made Jesus both Lord and Christ, he is alluding to two pivotal themes of the Jewish faith. Lord *(kýrios)* was a term of respect used for someone in a position of authority. It was also the Greek word used in the Septuagint as a substitution for YHWH, the personal name of God. Since the Septuagint was the version of the religious tradition most commonly read in synagogue services of the time, the Jews to whom Peter was speaking would have made the connection quite readily. Christ *(christós)* is the Greek translation for Messiah, anointed one. By employing these two titles Peter is making astounding claims about Jesus. He follows these claims by laying the guilt for Jesus' death at the feet of those who are listening to him.

The people are cut to the heart, not in anger or rage but with remorse. They had put to death the Holy One, God's anointed. The openness with which they receive Peter's words of testimony and accusation indicates that all the Jewish people were not hardhearted, as some have suggested. Indeed, these are eager to follow Peter's direction. What are they to do? In response, he exhorts them to repent and be baptized. Repentance *(metánoia)* is a total change of heart, an interior disposition that would result in a new way of life. Baptism was a recognized external rite that would mark the inner change. Peter's exhortation was not something entirely new to these people. A similar message and rite was the core of the ministry of John the Baptist (cf. Luke 3:3), and some form of baptism was also required of Gentile proselytes to the Jewish faith. What was new, however, was the name in which they were to be baptized and the gift they would then receive. They are told to be baptized in the name of Jesus, who is both Lord and Christ, and they are promised the gift of the Holy Spirit.

The promise of which Peter speaks is probably a reference to the promise of the Spirit that is found in the prophetic words of Joel (3:1-2 [Hebrew]); Isa (44:3); and Ezekiel (36:26-27). Initially this promise was made to the ancestors of the people in Peter's audience. However, it is now made to them; they too are offered the gift of the Spirit. This promise is not limited to them but will be offered to generations after them and to people who do not belong to the house of Israel. Here we get a glimpse of the reconstitution of the People of God. Jew and Gentile alike are invited to repent, be baptized in the name of Jesus, and be incorporated into the community through the gift of the Spirit.

Peter continues his testimony and his exhortation, and the membership of believers is abundantly increased. Three thousand may seem to be an excessive number. It might simply characterize the success of early apostolic preaching.

## Psalm 23:1-3a, 3b-4, 5, 6

The responsorial psalm is one of the most familiar and best loved psalms of the entire Psalter. It paints vivid pictures of a carefree existence, peaceful rest, and abundant fruitfulness. Although "shepherd" suggests a flock rather than merely one sheep, the focus here is on the individual. In addition to this image God is characterized as a host, one who supervises a banquet and within whose house the psalmist ultimately dwells.

The psalm opens with a metaphor that sets the tone of the entire song. It is the responsibility of the shepherd to find pastures that will provide enough grazing and abundant water for the entire flock; to lead them there without allowing any of the sheep to stray and be lost; to guard them from predators or dangers of any kind; and to attend to their every need. To characterize the LORD as a shepherd is to trust that God will discharge all these responsibilities. The personal dimension of the psalm shifts the care given the entire flock to concern for one individual, making God's care a very intimate matter. Not only are the physical needs of the psalmist satisfied, but the soul, the very life force *(nepesh)* of the person, is renewed.

The guidance of the shepherd is more than provident; it is moral as well. The psalmist is led in the paths of righteousness (v. 3), and this is done for the sake of the LORD's name. Since one's name is a part of the very essence of the person, this indicates that the way of the LORD is the way of righteousness. Following this, we can say that the magnanimous care shown by the shepherd flows from enduring righteousness rather than some passing sentiment of heart. This is confirmed by the reference to the covenant kindness *(ḥesed)* that surrounds the psalmist (v. 6). In other words, the divine shepherd's tender commitment to the flock, and to each individual within it, is as lasting as is God's covenant commitment.

The psalmist is confident of the LORD's protection, as demonstrated in his mention of the shepherd's rod and staff, which were used to ward off wild animals as well as poachers. The valley of "deep darkness," can be a reference to the darkest part of the terrain or to the gloom that can overwhelm an individual. It also has a mythological connotation and is frequently interpreted as death. Whichever meaning is intended here, the psalmist claims to be unafraid, for the presence of the LORD is reassuring.

The image of the shepherd securing nourishment for the flock suggests another metaphor, that of the host who prepares a lavish banquet for guests. Many societies have a very strict code of hospitality. They are obliged to provide the very best provisions they have, even for their enemies. The LORD spreads out such a banquet here, which not only affords nourishment, but also is a public witness to God's high regard for the psalmist, who will continue to enjoy God's favor in God's house. Whether this indicates the Temple or is merely a reference to the place where God dwells, the fundamental meaning is clear. The psalmist has been under the loving guidance of the LORD and will remain there forever.

## 1 Peter 2:20b-25

The following of Christ is the theme that connects the two parts of this reading. In the first part (vv. 20b-24) the disciples are exhorted to imitate Jesus' manner of suffering when misfortune overtakes them. In the second (v. 25) the image of the shepherd is placed before them to exemplify the solicitude of the one whom the disciples follow.

Suffering of some kind finds its way into the life of every human being, whether that person is religious or not. At times misfortune may have been brought on by the one suffering; at other times the afflicted one appears to be innocent of anything that could have precipitated the misfortune. Therefore, all are expected to bear the consequences of their actions. To endure misfortune that is either unwarranted or unjustly imposed calls for virtue. There is yet another kind of suffering, the kind inflicted upon one precisely for having done good. It is this latter form to which the author of the letter of Peter refers. He realizes it might take a special grace from God to be patient in such straits, but he believes the Christian calling requires just such a disposition.

In this kind of situation Christians have the example of Christ, an example after which they can pattern their behavior. They have Christ, in whose footsteps they can walk. The word for "example" *(hypogrammós)* refers to a child's writing exercise. In it the letters of the alphabet from alpha to omega (A to Z) are copied stroke by stroke from a pattern. By using this image the author is suggesting that, like this child, Christians can trace their own manner of suffering from the pattern set by Christ. A second but very similar metaphor follows almost immediately. The word for "footstep" *(íchnos)* might be better translated "footprint." When Christians follow Christ, they not only go where he went, but they also step right into the prints made by his feet. Walking in his footprints, they follow Christ as exactly as if they were tracing their lives after the pattern of his.

It is Christ's innocence and lack of vengeance that constitute this pattern. The innocent suffering of Christ is described in terms that recall a passage from one of the Suffering Servant Songs of the prophet Isaiah (53:4-7). The images and words of these two passages are almost identical. However, it is not that Isaiah had Christ in mind when he described this anguished individual. Rather, it is that the author of 1 Peter had Isaiah's servant in mind when he spoke of Christ. This is the pattern after which Christians are to model their lives. When they are persecuted for the good they have done, they must be willing to bear this suffering, perhaps even for the sake of the very ones who have victimized them.

The final image in this passage is that of the shepherd. This was a vital image because at this time in this place shepherding was a major occupation. The metaphor is used here to indicate that Jesus is the shepherd and his Christian disciples are the sheep. Although at times they wander away from him, they will be safe and will prosper only if they follow his lead. He alone knows what is in their best interest; he alone knows where they will be safe; he alone knows how to find the best pasturage.

## John 10:1-10

The imagery from which this passage is constructed presumes the practice of sheepherding in the Near East. At the outskirts of the village one would find a large sheepfold or pen in which were kept several flocks of sheep. Someone was hired to guard this enclosure, which had only one entrance, secured by some form of gate. Jesus uses several of these elements in his teaching about the relationship between himself and his followers. He describes himself first as shepherd (vv. 1-6), then as gate to the sheepfold (vv. 7-9).

The author of this gospel prefers the expression "figure of speech" *(paroimía,* v. 6) to the term "parable" *(parabolē)*, which is found in the Synoptic Gospels. However, both expressions denote the same very general literary device. The specific form of this device used here is the allegory, the figurative description of one subject under the guise of another. There are actually two brief allegories, each of which is introduced with the solemn words "Amen, amen, I say to you" (vv. 1, 7).

In the first figure of speech Jesus contrasts himself, the shepherd, with those who try to enter the sheepfold stealthily. They do not come through the gate because the gatekeeper would realize they do not belong. Unlike the shepherd, who is committed to guiding, guarding, and nurturing the sheep, these others regard the sheep only as potential objects of immediate ill-gotten profit. They are interested either in fleecing or in snatching the sheep. The true shepherd will not only be recognized by the gatekeeper but by the sheep as well. In the Near East sheepfolds often held more than one flock. When shepherds came to collect their flock they would stand at a distance and call out in a particular way. The sheep would recognize the sound of their shepherd's voice and follow him. They would not recognize the call of strangers, so they would not follow them.

The shepherd Jesus is describing does not simply call his sheep. He knows them so intimately he calls each by name, and they recognize this intimacy by responding appropriately. Although Jesus is obviously comparing true shepherds and thieves, the passage implies that he is really contrasting himself and the Pharisees. He is the true shepherd; he is the one the sheep will follow. The religious leaders of his day were not interested or invested in the welfare of the people as Jesus was. He judged them quite harshly when he cast them in the guise of thieves and robbers.

In the second figure of speech Jesus uses the technical phrase "I am" (*égō eími*) in his characterization of himself as the gate. Earlier it was the shepherd or the thieves who went in and out of the sheepfold. Here it is the sheep. Those who go through Jesus will be safe within the pen. Any other entrance will be the way taken by thieves, and the sheep will be in jeopardy. In like manner, if the sheep exit through the gate, which is Jesus, they will be led safely to pasture.

As both shepherd and gate of the sheepfold, Jesus is concerned with the welfare of the sheep. He has come that they may have life and have it more abundantly. The reference here is certainly to something more than peace and prosperity in this life. Some commentators believe it is a reference to a deep spiritual life lived in union with God. Others maintain it refers to eternal life.

## Themes of the Day

The Fourth Sunday of Easter has traditionally been known as "Good Shepherd Sunday." The readings chosen support this theme. The particular focus taken today is the question of leadership. Which voices do we follow today, and why do we follow these voices and not others?

## The Voices We Follow

We all look for leaders who can guarantee our safety and happiness. For many people this means someone who promises well-being and prosperity, someone who will eliminate the hardships we face and make life easier for us. It also means someone who will encourage us and affirm us in our endeavors, someone who will tell us we are on the right path. There is nothing wrong in wanting leaders, both political and religious, who will speak to us in these ways, but these are only half of the responsibilities of leadership.

Some, though not all, would also like a leader who can challenge them to be their better selves, to go beyond the present confines of possibility and attain a greater degree of self-realization, someone who can show them how to live graciously with the burdens of life and the disappointments all women and men must face. They want a leader who will help them recognize and admit when they are in error and help them correct it. They want a leader who is honest about the complexities of life and is able to guide them in dealing with these complexities.

## Authentic Leadership

It has been said many times that authentic leadership is rooted in authority. But then we must ask: Of what does authority consist? It must be more than might or control, because those are often resented and not really followed. Authentic authority is said to be the ability to author or bring life to birth. We recognize the voice of genuine authority because it cherishes, guards, and encourages the best in life. The psalm lists the characteristics of authentic authority: it provides rest and refreshment; it guides our steps; it nourishes us; it leads us to God. Peter, as portrayed in the Acts of the Apostles, is an example of authentic authority: he proclaims the truth even if others find it hard to hear; he denounces error even when this places him in jeopardy; he calls for a change of heart even when it makes great demands.

Authentic leadership is patterned after the leadership of Jesus. It is gentle and familiar, as is the voice of the true shepherd; it has won the confidence of those who follow, as did the true shepherd; it is committed to the enhancement of the lives of others, as was Jesus. Authentic leadership is willing to forgo its own needs and to deny its own interests in favor of the needs and interests of others.

## Those Who Follow

Heavy demands are placed on those who would follow the kind of leadership depicted in these readings. Peter's audience is told to admit their mistakes and repent of them, to turn aside from the corruption of the world in which they live. Those who would follow the Good Shepherd must follow him in the dark valleys as well as to the refreshing streams. They must be willing to relinquish some of their own plans and self-determination and entrust themselves to his leadership. They must never forget they are following a shepherd who has paid the ultimate price on their behalf. This should be both comforting and challenging. Comforting that we have a shepherd that loves us with such devotion; challenging because we might be called upon to follow him to death. Even in the joy of Easter we must remember that the price Jesus paid was his own blood.

## Fifth Sunday of Easter
### Acts 6:1-7

The episode recounted in the first reading for this Sunday furnishes us with a picture of the early Christian community quite different from those of the preceding Sundays of Eastertime. In previous scenes we saw a community of one mind and one heart (Acts 32); we were told that the preaching of Peter resulted in numerous conversions (Acts 2:41). Today we observe tension within the community itself and how the members resolved that tension.

What catches our attention is the makeup of the community. There are Hellenists and Hebrews. These were probably constituencies of Jewish Christians who were separated by language rather than religious background. While there may have been Gentile converts in the group (Nicholas of Antioch is an example of one), most of the community was probably Palestinian in origin. Why the widows of the Greek-speaking members were slighted is not stated. At issue is some practical matter, not a point of doctrine. It is interesting that the complaint came from the Hellenists, and the seven men who were appointed to remedy the situation all had Greek names. It is as if the mixed community chose members from the complaining segment in order to make sure there would be no reason to complain in the future.

The reading also gives us insight into the lines of authority that existed within the community. Peter does not stand as sole leader as he is depicted in the readings of previous Sundays. Instead, the entire group of apostles, known as the Twelve, addresses the problem. They are the ones who distinguish between various ministries and who establish a group to meet the need that was brought before them. Besides this example of collegiality, we see principles of subsidiarity at work. It is the community who selects the men to exercise the ministry; the apostles commission them.

It would be inaccurate to consider this account the description of the establishment of the order of deacons as we know it today. Although "laying on hands" eventually came to refer to ordination, that is probably not its meaning here. The practice was also a recognized ritual for investing someone with power or authority. These men had already received the Holy Spirit. This was a prerequisite for their selection. Here the practice is most likely a form of commissioning. In addition to this, the Greek work *diakonía* (service) is used in three different ways. Daily "distribution" (v. 1), "ministry" of the word (v. 4), and "serve" at table (v. 2) all come from the this word. The first suggests distribution of alms; the second refers to evangelization; the third describes the distribution of food. We know that both Stephen (cf. Acts 7:2) and Philip (cf. Acts 8:5) preached, so these ministries cannot be rigidly classified as priestly or diaconal.

The reading ends with a statement about the growth of the company of believers, as did the first readings of the last two Sundays. There are two aspects of growth mentioned here but not elsewhere. The increase mentioned here includes the idea of diversity, and diversity brings tension. The reading does not question the value of diversity. Rather, it demonstrates how the tensions that inevitably accompany it can be dealt with in an equitable and satisfactory manner. The second aspect addresses the inclusion of Jewish priests. The passage tells us nothing about the social or religious status of these men, only that they became obedient to the faith. Their mention adds another dimension to the complexity of this community.

## Psalm 33:1-2, 4-5, 18-19

The basic structure of a hymn of praise can be seen in the responsorial psalm for this Sunday. It opens with an invocation to praise God (vv. 1-2) followed by the reasons for such praise. This second feature is introduced by the standard particle *kî* (for), which expresses the causal relationship. This psalm praises God for the blessings of creation (vv. 4-5) as well as for the care shown human beings. The verses chosen for this response do not include the customary closing invocation of praise. Although the psalm itself does not include the ,kind of refrain that was used at cultic celebrations, the mention of lyre and harp does suggest congregational participation. Much of the language used throughout the psalm is describing preeminent absolutes and behavior very closely associated with ancient Israel's covenant theology: righteous (*ṣādēq*, vv. 1, 5); upright (*yāshar*, vv. 1, 4); trustworthy (*'āman*, v. 4); justice (*mishpāt*, v. 5); lovingkindness (*ḥesed*, vv. 5, 18).

The first theme emphatically stated is the trustworthiness of God's word. This word is as firm as God's own self. It was by this word and this word alone that the universe was created (cf. Genesis 1). The order and stability manifested through these marvels of creation not only stem from God's power and faithfulness, they are witnesses to it as well. If we rely on the firmness and regularity found in the natural world, surely we can trust the creative word from which it issues. All of this is grounded in God's kindness, which is more than simple benevolence or thoughtful consideration. It is the steadfastness of covenant loyalty (*ḥesed*). The trustworthiness of God's word parallels the constancy of God's covenant.

The psalmist moves from consideration of covenant commitment to consideration of divine providence. For whom does God care? For all those who fear the LORD. Fear means standing in awe of and wonder at someone or something, trembling in the presence of a great power or majesty. The psalm states that the LORD looks upon the people, presumably with eyes of compassion and love. God is characterized as a savior, one who will deliver them, one who will preserve them in the face of great need.

Although this is a psalm of praise, the characteristics of God that it acclaims suggest it is also meant to instill confidence into the minds and hearts of those who pray it. God has done wonderful things in the world, and we rejoice in them. In addition to this, these wonderful things encourage us to trust in this God, who is not only powerful but loving as well.

## 1 Peter 2:4-9

Using an image from the realm of building construction, the author develops both a christological theme and an ecclesiological one. He characterizes Christ as a living stone, and he describes Christians as living stones as well. Although the opening words appear to be an imperative (Come to him), the Greek form is really participial (Coming to him). Likewise, the second imperative (let yourselves be built) might be better translated as indicative (you are being built). With this rendition the author would be saying that by coming to Christ the living stone, Christians, as living stones themselves, are being built into a spiritual house.

Stone is used as a metaphor in different yet related ways. It is said to be living, a characteristic that sets this stone apart from all other stones. When describing Christ it pertains to his essence and not merely to his function. The stone is living because of who Christ is and not because of what he does, though what he does is influenced by the fact of his being a living stone. Despite this wondrous quality he was rejected by human beings. However, he was chosen by God for a particular purpose. When "living" describes Christians, it refers to the life that is theirs because of their relationship with Christ. A second use of the stone metaphor suggests the purpose for which God chose the living stone; it describes a particular function Christ performs. He is the cornerstone of the building constructed out of the living stones that are the Christians.

The author employs a technique similar to one used by the rabbis. They developed what has been referred to as a chain quotation, stringing biblical passages together one after another. We see this where "spiritual house" (a new kind of temple) invites mention of a holy priesthood, which suggests the offering of spiritual gifts. There is no logical progression of thought here. It is instead a rich tapestry of related themes.

A clearer example of this technique is seen in the author's use of passages from the Scriptures to illustrate his christology. The first citation (v. 6) comes from the prophet Isaiah 28:16. This stone is a foundation stone, one that acts as the underpinning of the building. Applied to Christ, this feature would illustrate the building's (the Christian community) total dependence on Christ. The origin of the second citation is Psalm 118:22. However, it appears to be closer to the Synoptic tradition's use of it (cf., Matt 21:42-44; Luke 20:17-18). There it refers to the capstone of a building, a stone, perhaps the stone that holds the two pillars of an arch together. Applied to Christ, this features demonstrates the interrelationship present within the community and the unity they enjoy as members through Jesus. Christ the cornerstone becomes the focus of judgment. Those who believe in him are not put to shame; those who reject him will stumble.

Having developed the christological theme, the author puts up again the ecclesiological theme. Earlier he called the Christians a holy priesthood; here he elaborates on that theme, expanding the language of Mosaic covenant theology (cf. Exod 19:6). Those who have accepted the living stone are not only a spiritual house, they are also the People of God. They have been brought out of darkness into the wondrous light of faith in Christ. Once again the author applies elements of the Israelite tradition to the Christian experience.

## John 14:1-12

This section of Jesus' discourse develops two major theological themes: eschatology (vv. 1-4) and christology (vv. 5-12). The first theme is introduced by Jesus himself. The second stems from questions posed by two of the apostles, Thomas and Philip.

The discourse opens on a note of tender concern. Jesus seeks to strengthen his followers, who appear to be troubled at the thought of his departure. He attempts to calm their hearts by urging them to trust, first in God and then in himself. (Since the verbs can be read as either imperative or indicative, the forms of the verb have been rendered in various ways.) Jesus does not conceal his imminent departure, but he interprets it in a very positive way. He is indeed leaving, but he is going to the dwelling place *(oikía)* of God in heaven. He uses the image of a large mansion with many guest rooms to describe this place. It is almost as if Jesus is simply going ahead to get places prepared for the others. He promises to return to get them, and then they will all be together again. The end-time is characterized as a community occupying a place in the residence of God. It would all sound so benign were it not that the manner of his leaving will be a brutal execution.

Jesus does not focus on the end of his life, only on the joyful events that will follow it. There is a bit of ambiguity in this eschatological picture. He leaves to prepare a place for the others with God. Is this a reference to heaven in the next life? He says he will return and will take his followers to himself. If he is referring to his return at the end of time, then the answer to the question is yes, the faithful followers will live with God in the next life. However, if his death is his departure and his resurrection is his return, then his union with his followers could well be the mutual indwelling enjoyed in this life by those united with him. The passage is open to both the apocalyptic and the mystical interpretations. The ambiguity of his words causes Thomas to question him.

There is a play on the meaning of "way." Understood literally, it is the path one takes in order to reach one's destination. This is probably the way Thomas understood it. In the Wisdom tradition it refers to the manner of living: the way of the wise (Prov 4:11) and the way of the wicked (Prov 4:19). This seems to be the way Jesus intended it to be understood. In response to Thomas, Jesus uses the "I am" *(égō, eími)* formula to identify himself as "the way and the truth and the life." The one he calls Father is the destination, and he, Jesus, is the way to that destination. Only by living life in conformity with Jesus can one hope to arrive at God. The kind of union with God that Jesus claims is often referred to as high christology, christology that focuses on Jesus' divine prerogatives.

Thinking he has understood Jesus, Philip asks to be shown the Father. In response, Jesus reiterates his explanation, claiming a manner of union with God that implies mutual indwelling and equality. Aware of the boldness of his words, Jesus invites Philip and all who are listening to recall the wondrous deeds he performed. If they cannot grasp the meaning of his words, they certainly cannot deny the significance of his deeds. Jesus ends his discourse with a promise: Those who believe in him will be able to perform deeds that are even more wondrous than those he performed. They will be able to do this because Jesus is going to the Father. Said in another way, they will be able to do this in the power of his death and resurrection.

## Themes of the Day

The gospel readings for the last Sundays before the feast of Pentecost are all taken from Jesus' last discourse as found in the Gospel of John. In them, Jesus prepares his followers for his death and resurrection but also for his ultimate exaltation. The entire Easter season is really a celebration of this exaltation.

### The Exaltation of Jesus

Jesus died, rose, and is exalted at the right hand of God in glory. This is the heart of the gospel message. It has already happened; it is a fact. Only in the gradual unfolding of the Liturgical Year do we commemorate separately each stage in this drama as if the reality were being revealed step by step before our eyes. These fifty days of Easter provide us with an opportunity to probe the depths of this mystery and to savor the insights we discover. It is a time to celebrate the glorification of Jesus as we await the time of his final glorification.

The exaltation of Jesus should cause us to wonder by what standards God chooses to glorify. This Sunday he speaks of going to the God that he calls Father. However, it is through his death that he goes to God. In John's Gospel Jesus is exalted as he is raised up in crucifixion. The author of the epistle declares him "chosen and precious in the sight of God," but it is as the stone that was rejected that he is so honored. Although some claim Jesus is exalted as a reward for having suffered such disgrace, these readings suggest he is exalted by God despite the fact that he was rejected by others. This should encourage us who might be tempted to fall victim to the standards of acceptability espoused by the world.

## Life in Community

It we ever wonder how the exaltation of Jesus will affect us, we have Jesus' own words of explanation. He promises to go ahead of us and make arrangements for us to share in his exaltation in the house of the one he calls Father. All we need do is follow him. The epistle reading characterizes him as the cornerstone that holds the house together. The first reading shows us how the reconciliation of tensions within the community can prevent the house from being divided. Taken together, these readings suggest that the exaltation of Jesus is most dramatically manifested in the character of the community of those called by his name. It is revealed in the way Christians settle their differences so that all parties are treated fairly. Jesus is the cornerstone upon which this community is built, and the community mirrors his influence in its life.

## Proclaim His Praises

Not only do the Christians participate in the exaltation of Jesus by living as a community of reconciliation, they also do it by spreading the good news to others. The reading from Acts shows how the witness of their lives and their preaching of the word of God increased their number. The gospel may be using hyperbole, but in it Jesus claims that his followers will accomplish deeds even greater than those he himself performed. This promise remains a challenge for followers of every age. What is the challenge for Christians today in a world broken to pieces by war, a world that values possessions more than people, a world that finds it difficult to admit its limitations? What in the gospel message for today is *good* news? And how can today's Christians proclaim it?

## *Sixth Sunday of Easter*

### Acts 8:5-8, 14-17

The description of the early Christian community, which has been the theme of the first readings of this Eastertime, continues with an account of the spread of the gospel. Philip, one of the seven men appointed by the Jerusalem community to attend to the needs of the widows of the Hellenists, travels north to Samaria. (Regardless of the geographic direction, one always traveled up to Jerusalem and down from it.) The animosity between the Jews and the Samaritans can be traced back to the period after the death of Solomon when the northern Israelite tribes withdrew their allegiance from the southern Judean monarchy (ca. 722 B.C.E.). This breach was reinforced when those who returned from exile in Babylon rejected the Samaritans' offer to help in the rebuilding of the Temple in Jerusalem.

Although in various ways the two groups pursued different paths, they retained many of their common traditions. One of these was messianic expectation (cf. John 4:25). This explains their openness to Philip when he proclaimed Christ (*christós,* the anointed one) to them. His proclamation was supported by exorcisms and healings, wondrous signs of the dawning of the eschatological age. Many people believed that possession by the devil and physical infirmity were evidence of sin's hold on the world. Release from this bondage was considered a sign of the new age. The wonders wrought by Philip would have convinced them of the trustworthiness of his words. The joy they experienced would have sprung both from their happiness for having been cured and from the knowledge that the new age had come.

The centrality of the Jerusalem community is seen in its response to the news of the Samaritan conversion. The ruling body sends Peter and John to Samaria. Perhaps it would have been easier for a Hellenist like Philip to go to the Samaritans than for men like these two who probably belonged to the "Hebrew" segment of the Jerusalem church. Whatever the reason, there is no evidence that the delegation from Jerusalem has been sent out to ensure proper protocol in the conversion. This is clearly a mission of goodwill, a demonstration of Christian solidarity. The visit itself shows that the conversion has been sanctioned by Jerusalem.

Once again there is a question about the function of the laying on of hands. The Samaritans had been baptized in the name of Jesus, and so they had already been incorporated into the People of God. Some commentators claim the Spirit was conferred upon them when the apostles laid hands on them. Others maintain that the gift of the Spirit comes with baptism, and the imposition of hands was simply a gesture that connected the believers in Samaria with the mother church. They further maintain that when the Spirit took hold of the new converts they would manifest the power of the Spirit, thus providing external evidence of possession by the Spirit. However this element is understood, the principal focus of the account is on the reconciliation in Christ between Jews and Samaritans.

## Psalm 66:1-3, 4-5, 6-7, 16, 20

Today's responsorial psalm consists of two major parts. It begins with a threefold summons to praise God followed by reason for giving such praise (vv. 1, 7), and it ends with individual expressions of thanksgiving. Although the summons is directed to all the earth, it is clear from the content that follows that the intended audience was the people who dwelt in the lands. Each part of the summons adds a slightly different dimension to the praise that is sought. First, it is universal in scope; all the earth is called to praise the God of Israel. Second, the object of the praise is the name of God, the name being identified as the very essence of God. Third, the praise given to God is glorious, weighty, not to be dismissed casually. The psalmist then gives the reason for glorifying God in the first place. It is because of the wondrous feats God has accomplished.

The works of God to which the psalmist refers are the wonders God has accomplished in the history of Israel. Although the text leads one to believe the deeds were done for all women and men, the deeds mentioned are specific to Israel. It may be the psalmist believes that what was done explicitly for Israel would redound to the benefit of all. Using a literary form known as merism (the first in a list of several consecutive items represents all the others), the author recalls Israel's history, from its release from Egyptian bondage to its entrance into the land.

Since subduing chaotic waters was at the basis of all creation activity in the ancient Near Eastern creation tradition, historical water crossings always contained a dimension of creation in them. This bears out in the stories under consideration. It was in the wilderness that the motley group of slaves was fashioned into a nation. The water passages that frame this chapter in their history act as the boundaries in a rite of passage. At both ends of the chapter they moved from one stage of existence to another. Thus, while the reference itself describes the historical event, it can serve to characterize any other event of passage. This is certainly cause for praise. Furthermore, in the creation story, after the forces of evil have been vanquished, the victorious warrior is acclaimed king over all creation. Traces of this royal acclamation are found here (v. 7; cf. Exod 15:1-8).

The communal dimension of the first section of the responsorial psalm gives way to an individual focus. Perhaps it means the psalmist benefits from the blessings bestowed on the nations. Or it may be the psalmist has been a recipient of some particular individual blessing. In either case, others are invited to join the psalmist in grateful praise of God.

## 1 Peter 3:15-18

The sufferings Christians must endure for their faith is the subject of the teaching in this passage. The author of the letter instructs them to respond to their suffering in a particular manner and to use this suffering in a way that will enhance the spread of the gospel. Finally, the sufferings of Christ are offered as an example for them to follow and in which they can place their trust.

The reading opens with an exhortation to sanctify *(hagiázō)* Christ in their hearts, to acknowledge his holiness. It ends with a reference to his resurrection. In this way, consideration of the sufferings of Christians is placed within the context of the holiness of Christ. It is this holiness that gives Christians both strength to endure patiently and courage to give witness to their faith. It seems their suffering has not squelched their hope, and this has raised questions in the minds of others: What motivates these Christians to live such hopeful lives? The author of the letter exhorts them to be ready to offer an explanation *(apología)* whenever asked. Though they are asked to defend, they should not be defensive. Christ should be their model in this. He suffered for his principles; he did not strike back.

The Christians are also told to keep their consciences clear, to give no one justification for finding fault with them. The reason given is that they will then be regarded as innocent sufferers, and those who might accuse them will have done so unjustly. Such behavior will reflect favorably on the Christians but shamefully on their accusers. It will also provide support for the defense of their hope; they will give witness to their righteousness through both words and deeds.

The author next turns to the example of Christ, who also suffered innocently. Aspects of his suffering are considered. First, his death was a kind of sin-offering, a vicarious sacrifice for the sins of others. Second, it was inclusive, effecting redemption for all. No other sacrifice of atonement need be offered in the future. If there is no need for another offering, this means the effects of Christ's sacrifice will be efficacious for all. Finally, it is because of his sacrifice that Christ can now provide access to the royal throne of God. All of this is explained so that Christians can be reminded of the good that can be brought about through innocent suffering, both that of Christ and of themselves.

The reading ends with a traditional formula of Christian faith in the resurrection built on the classical contrast between flesh *(sárx)* and spirit *(pneúma)*. The focus here is not anthropological, concerned with two aspects of human nature. It is a christological statement, referring to the human and the divine in Christ. It means that though dead in the human sphere, Christ is alive in the sphere of the spirit. Once again Christ can be set before Christians, this time as a reason for their hope. If they continue to follow his example, even though they should die in their suffering they can hope they will be brought to life in the spirit.

## John 14:15-21

This gospel passage contains several major theological themes. It emphasizes the link between love and obedience; it articulates a very complex eschatological perspective; it speaks of the presence of God with the one who loves; it provides us with a partial view of the internal relationships within the Trinity.

Love is the fundamental message of Jesus. However, he calls for a demanding love, one that is as self-sacrificing as was the love of Jesus himself. Only those who follow his example and obey his directives can be said to truly love, and those who love as Jesus did will in turn be loved by his Father. Obedience is not the requirement for love, it is the consequence of it. If the disciples truly love Jesus they will keep his commandments. And if they keep his commandments Jesus will ask his Father to send another advocate, the Spirit of truth, who will not leave them as Jesus is about to do but will remain with them forever.

The departure of Jesus will leave the disciples feeling abandoned. Jesus is aware of this and assures them he will return. Of which return does he speak? Is he referring to his resurrection, after which the bond between master and disciples will be forged in such a way as to endure all things? Or is his return to be seen in the gift of the Spirit for which he has prayed, the gift that promises the abiding presence of God? Might Jesus be speaking of his final coming at the end of the age, when believers will be united with him forever? Actually, it would be better not to choose one interpretation to the exclusion of the other two, for each one opens an aspect of Jesus' relationship with us. Together, they offer an insight of rich theological meaning.

Two other themes are woven throughout this reading: the breach between the world and the things of God, and the eschatological perspective. The dualism of John is obvious as he pits the world against both the Spirit of truth and the disciples of Jesus. The world is captive to materialism, open only to what is tangible. It cannot see the Spirit, and after Jesus leaves (dies) they will not be able to see him either. This is because Jesus will have been transported to the realm of the Spirit. The disciples, on the other hand, are motivated by love, and they respond to Jesus in obedience. The phrase "on that day" has definite eschatological connotations. It refers to the time of eschatological fulfillment. Used here it implies that the day of Jesus' return is in fact the dawning of the eschatological age.

While this passage cannot provide us with a complete trinitarian teaching, it does offer us some insight into the mystery of God. There is definitely an intimate relationship between Jesus and his Father. The very metaphor of father, which he uses to speak of God, is evidence of this. Although they are intimate, they are distinct. Jesus prays to his Father, and the Father hears his prayer. The Spirit, who is sent by the Father, is not a substitute for Jesus but is sent to abide with the believers.

Perhaps the real marvel of this passage is found in the description of the mutual indwelling. Jesus is in the Father; Jesus is in the disciples and they are in him; both the Spirit and Jesus will remain in the disciples. This is the manifestation of the love mentioned that begins and ends this reading.

## Themes of the Day

The reading from the farewell discourse continues, as does our concentration on the exaltation of Jesus. Our participation in this exaltation is translated into a way of living in this world that is extraordinary, a way of living that requires that we give a reason for the hope within us.

### Hope

It is because we have been blessed with the opportunity of participating in the exaltation of Jesus that we live in the hope that this exaltation will be brought to its final conclusion at the end of this age. This is extraordinary, because we possess a vision of an end-time of fulfillment in a world that has no hope. This is why we are called upon to give an explanation of this hope. We live in a hope based on promises: the promise that we will not be left orphaned when Jesus returns to his Father; the promise that we will be comforted by the Spirit, whom Jesus will send. We hope, not because we are trusting people but because God is trustworthy. It is trust in God that enables us to live in this world as if the promises have already been fulfilled, for in fact, it is precisely such living that fulfills them. That is why true Christian hope is so remarkable.

### The Spirit

We have not yet celebrated the feast of the Ascension, yet all three readings speak of the Spirit. It was the Spirit who quickened the resurrected life of Jesus, and it is the same Spirit who enlivens us. The Spirit is our Paraclete, our Advocate, the reason for our hope. It is the Spirit who strengthens us, comforts us, guides us, and inspires us. It is the Spirit who enables us to interpret the signs of the times in ways very different from the ways of the world. It is the Spirit who works through us for the transformation of the world. It is because the Spirit has already been given to us that, in the midst of our journey of life, we are able to live the promises into fulfillment. The exaltation has already taken place; the glory has already been given; the Spirit has already been bestowed upon us; we are already living in the new age. We may be considered foolish by those who live without this hope, but it is the foolishness of the Spirit of God.

## Life in the Spirit

Life in the Spirit requires that we conform our lives to the commandments of God, not in a legalistic or constraining way but out of love. Love prompts us to pattern our lives after the model of Jesus, the one we love. This means we will live with clear consciences, with gentleness and reverence. The love that comes to us through the Spirit will overflow into the lives of others. We will be agents of God's love in the world. Through our kindness and our commitment to righteous living we will cast out the unclean spirits that inhabit our world, the spirits of greed and selfishness, the spirits of deceit and manipulation, the spirits of hatred and violence, the spirits of disinterest and disdain. Our lives will be evidence of the presence of the Spirit in our midst.

The Spirit given by Christ is mediated through the laying on of hands. This still happens in our day in the gentle touch of friends, in the loving touch of parents, in the healing touch of those who cure both the body and the spirit. The Liturgical Year is preparing us for the ascension of Jesus into heaven, and Jesus is preparing us for life in the Spirit here on earth. This is the reason for our hope.

## The Ascension of the Lord
### Acts 1:1-11

The opening verses of the reading relate the book of the Acts of the Apostles to an earlier work, presumably the Gospel of Luke. Mention of the person of Theophilus (v. 1; cf. Luke 1:3) makes this clear. This man, whose name means "lover of God," may have been a patron of the author, one responsible for the circulation of the writings. In this introduction, known as a proem, the author identifies the scope of the contents of the first book and then recounts the event of the ascension of Jesus, an event described at the end of the first book as well. The ascension thus becomes the transition from the earthly ministry of Jesus to the experiences of the early Church. The author further links these two moments in history with the activity of the Holy Spirit, through whom Jesus previously instructed his apostles (v. 2) and in whose power they were to be witnesses to Jesus throughout the entire world (v. 8).

This author claims the risen Jesus remained on earth for forty days, appearing to his apostles and speaking about the reign of God. While this account suggests that only the apostles experienced the risen Lord (cf. vv. 2-3) and only they were present at his ascension (cf. "Men of Galilee," v. 11), other accounts describe a larger and more inclusive groups of followers. The number forty is the same as the number of days during which Moses was instructed in the Law (cf. Exod 34:28) and Elijah journeyed toward the mountain of God (1 Kgs 19:8). This correspondence may be one of the details of the account whereby the author connects Jesus with the expectations of Israel. The importance of remaining in Jerusalem is another. The mission must go forth from that sacred city to the ends of the world (v. 8; cf. Isa 2:3). Finally, Jesus' announcement of the apostles' baptism in the Holy Spirit recalls an earlier statement of John the Baptist (cf. Luke 3:16). These lines draw the continuity between Israel and the Church.

In most eschatological passages, the Spirt is identified with the end-time. Here the activity of the Spirit is a characteristic of the new age, the time between the resurrection and the time of complete fulfillment. The author reports that the apostles confused these two moments as well as the nature of the new age that has dawned. Their misunderstanding presented an opportunity for the risen Jesus to instruct them one final time. They are to concern themselves with being Jesus' witnesses to the ends of the earth and not with the limited restoration of one nation. Furthermore, it is not for them to know God's timing. They will have the power of the Spirit to guide them for whatever length of time God desires.

When their responsibilities had been sufficiently explained, Jesus was taken from their sight. Several features underscore the supernatural nature of this experience. The cloud is a traditional symbol of the presence of God. The two men in white garments who interpreted the ascension are reminiscent of the two men in similar garb who were at the tomb and who announced the resurrection (cf. Luke 24:4-5). Though these men state that Jesus will return as he has left them, the symbolic nature of this description prevents us from knowing just what that might mean. With the apostles, we will have to depend upon the Spirit.

### Psalm 47:2-3, 6-7, 8-9

A ritual of enthronement clearly unfolds in the verses of this psalm. It begins with a call to praise God with both a ringing cry and with clapping of hands. The cry *(rinnâ)* is a shout of jubilation connected with a divinely appointed sacrifice. Clapping hands is also a common ritual action. One of the derivatives of the Hebrew word for clap *(tāqaʿ)* is "trumpet." Perhaps the liturgical clapping of hands is a substitute for the blowing of the trumpet. These two words clearly situate the psalm in a cultic setting.

The occasion for the liturgical celebration is the enthronement of God. Two very significant divine titles are used in this passage: LORD and Most High. LORD

(YHWH) is the personal name of the God of Israel; Most High *(ʿelyôn)* is an ancient Semitic title that first appears in the Abraham-Melchizedek narrative (Gen 14:18-22). In that narrative it is the name of the god of Salem, a shortened form of Jerusalem. When the city became the center of Israelite worship, the title was applied to Israel's God. It now signifies the superiority of YHWH.

The enthronement itself appears to establish YHWH's sovereign reign. The LORD rules over all the earth (vv. 3, 8), over all nations (v. 9). In a world that believed each nation had its own divine patron, this was either a claim of the preeminence of YHWH over all other gods or an assertion of monotheistic faith. In either case, all people are called to acclaim the kingship of God (v. 8).

The notion of the kingship of the LORD has cosmic and mythological underpinnings. The ancients believed that before creation the forces of good were in mortal combat with the forces of evil. A great cosmic battle ensued from which good emerged triumphant. The divine leader of this victorious company assumed the role of creator and reordered the cosmos. When this was completed, a heavenly palace was constructed for this great god, who then ascended the throne, there to rule over the entire universe, maintaining the order that had been established. In Babylon, the enthronement of their god was repeated each year during the New Year festival.

While there is no explicit mention of cosmic victory in this psalm, there are reasons why this understanding lies close to the surface of interpretation. The most obvious is the title "Most High." In the earlier tradition this was the name given to "the creator of heaven and earth" (Gen 14:19). When this title was applied to the God of Israel, all the attributes associated with that name were appropriated as well. Therefore, if and when the kingship of God was commemorated, even though the primary focus was God's national or political significance, this cosmic dimension would be in the consciousness of the people. In their minds, their God was not only king over all the earth and the peoples that dwelt there but was also king over all the powers of heaven.

## Ephesians 1:17-23

This reading, though addressed to believers, is a series of intercessions. While the gifts for which the petitioner prays flow from faith in "our Lord Jesus Christ," the relevance of the Wisdom tradition is clear. The prayer is for a spirit of wisdom and revelation, gifts necessary for insight and understanding. Although this may sound a bit like Gnosticism, the belief that special God-given knowledge *(gnōsis)* set some people apart from the rest, it is clear that union with Christ is what sets Christians apart. The revelation referred to here is really the kind of enlightenment necessary for understanding the mysteries that have already entered human history. The verb forms used in the passage indicate the action has been completed and the results of the action are effected in the present.

The prayer is for a threefold spiritual enlightenment, an enlightenment of the inner eyes. The petitioner asks that the believers may know (1) the hope of the calling they have received from God, (2) the riches of the glory of God's inheritance in the holy ones, and (3) the surpassing greatness of God's power to those who believe. These marvels have already taken place; it is for the believers to acknowledge them in awe.

The power referred to throughout the reading belongs to God. It was God's power that raised Christ from the dead and seated Christ in the place of honor in heaven; it was God's power that made all things subject to Christ and exalted Christ as head of the Church. It is this same power that is now called upon.

The view of Christ contained in this passage is exalted. Having been raised from the dead, Christ now sits at God's right hand, high above all other heavenly creatures. Most likely, principality, power, virtue, and dominion are references to celestial beings once thought to be divine but now considered merely classifications of angels. However they are understood, they were certainly considered superior to human creatures. The marvel is that a human creature has been exalted above them. The mention about names being given in this age or in the age to come means that nothing is beyond Christ's rule (cf. Ps 110:1). His rule is universal in scope and duration.

The body metaphor characterizing the Church is introduced at the end of the reading. Exalted by God, Christ is made the head of the Church, which is the body of Christ. As members of this exalted body believers share in Christ's fullness, in Christ's exaltation. Seated in the heavens above all other creatures, Christ's glory fills the universe. This reading is a prayer asking that the believers be granted the wisdom and insight to reverence these mysteries and to live lives informed by them.

## Matthew 28:16-20

This account of the commissioning of the disciples by Jesus is replete with familiar theological themes. The disciples returned to Galilee, the place where the ministry of Jesus had begun. This was to assure those who still harbored doubts that this mysterious person was indeed the same Jesus with whom they had previously walked. We are not told the name of the mountain to which they had been directed, but the relationship between this commissioning on a mountain and Jesus' earlier sermon on the mountain could not have been lost on them.

They see him on the mountain and they worship him, but not with full understanding. This is all reminiscent of his earlier transfiguration. Jesus declares that all power in heaven and earth has been given to him, a reference to the Son of Man who was exalted by God and granted eschatological authority (cf. Dan 7:14). Employing that power, he commissions them. The text does not explicitly state he conferred his power upon them. Instead, it closes with an assurance that he will remain with them until the end of the age. He was Emmanuel, God-with-us, while in the flesh; he will continue to be Emmanuel until the end of time.

The great missionary commission is straightforward and all-encompassing. The disciples are told to go out and make other disciples of all nations. All social or cultural boundaries are dissolved; ethnic and gender restrictions are lifted. The universality of this commission has challenged believers from the time of its utterance to our very day. Different ages confront various aspects of it. The early Church experienced tension as it moved from an exclusively Jewish context into the Gentile world. Today we struggle with the diversity at the heart of inculturation. The commission remains the same: Make disciples of all nations.

The way to accomplish this is twofold: by baptizing and by teaching. The trinitarian formula for baptism gathers together elements already found in Jesus' teaching. Throughout his ministry he spoke of God as Father (cf. Matt 11:25-27), indicating the intimate relationship that exists between them. He also spoke of the Spirit, who came upon him at his baptism (cf. Matt 3:16) and through whose power he cast out demons (cf. 12:28-32). It is in this threefold name (one name, not three) that the disciples are to baptize. True to the Jewish roots of this community, the divine name is not actually given; it is enough to refer to it. Those to be baptized are plunged into the mystery of that name and re-created as new beings. While the elements of the baptismal formula may have come from Jesus, the formula itself does not appear again except in a second-century church manual (cf. *Didache* 7.1), leading some to question its actual dating.

The specific teaching alluded to here is moral rather than doctrinal. Those who hear the teaching are to observe what Jesus commanded. He inaugurated the reign of God, at the heart of which is a radically different way of life. This is to be the essence of the teaching of the disciples. Jesus assures them he will be with them until the end of the age. Although the text does not say it, we can presume that after this, all who have been baptized and have accepted this teaching will be with him.

## Themes of the Day

The feast of the Ascension is really a kind of liminal moment in the Easter season. It is a time between times; a moment when we have left one place in our journey but have not yet arrived at a second. While the narratives that describe the ascension fit well into the unfolding story of redemption, the feast itself celebrates one aspect of the resurrection itself, namely, the exaltation of Jesus. The readings help us through this paradox. They allow us to focus on this theological point while we commemorate a turning point in the life of the Church. We do this by considering the enthronement of Christ in the heavens and the new body of Christ on earth.

## The Enthronement of Christ

Many of the Easter accounts have directed our attention to the appearances of Jesus, which were intended to strengthen the Christians' belief in his bodily resurrection. The emphasis was frequently on certain physical characteristics: he ate food, he invited Thomas to touch him. In many of these accounts Jesus seems to have been saying: "I am the same one who walked with you before. This is the body you have always known." Today we stand awestruck, watching Jesus ascend into the clouds of heaven, there to be enthroned at the right hand of God. Today is a day to be overwhelmed by the reality of the divinity of the one we have known in his humanity.

Amidst shouts of joy and exaltation, Christ is enthroned in heaven in both his divinity and his glorified humanity. Like the conquering creator-god, he has overcome his enemy (death) and now reigns over his new creation (the Church). For our part, we live between the time of his departure and the time of his return. Today we rejoice in one aspect of this mystery, his triumphant ascension; soon we will celebrate the second, the coming of his Spirit. Even though he has left us physically, we do not live without him as we wait. He is present with us in a new way, in a new body, in the Church.

## The New Body of Christ

Christ, who ascended into heaven in his body, carries on what he began on earth through his new body, the community of believers. He teaches through its apostles and evangelists. He ministers through its prophets and pastors. In and through the Church Jesus continues to heal and to comfort; to forgive and to include. We have not been left alone; we have his power, the same power with which he performed marvels when he walked the earth. We have not been left alone; we have each other. Together we make up the new body of Christ. Together we await the fullness of this body. It is this new body that stands in between the times, secure in what we have, confident of what we will be given.

## Seventh Sunday of Easter

### Acts 1:12-14

The reading for this Sunday is anticlimactic. Jesus has ascended into heaven. Those who were with him on the mount return to the city, enter the place where they were staying, and devote themselves to prayer. A chapter in the story of salvation has closed and another has not yet opened. His followers are not described as bereft or bewildered. Neither are they waiting in anxious expectation. The passage simply says that they devote themselves to prayer.

Those who witnessed the ascension have not traveled very far. Mount Olivet is east of Jerusalem, across the Kidron valley on the way to Bethany. It is said to be the distance Jews were allowed to travel on the sabbath, one kilometer, or three-quarters of a mile. Although the text is not explicit about this, a long-standing tradition identifies the upper room as the place Jesus celebrated the Last Supper with his disciples (cf. Luke 22:12), the house of the mother of John Mark (cf. Acts 12:12). Exactly how all these people were accommodated is not stated. The important point of the account seems to be their gathering together for prayer.

The list of apostles corresponds with other lists found in the gospel accounts (cf. Luke 6:14-16) with the exception of Judas Iscariot. Simon is identified as a member of the Zealots, a militant wing of the Jewish independence movement. The women who accompany these men might be their wives or women followers of Jesus who had come with him from Galilee and who attended to his burial (cf. Luke 23:55). His mother was there along with his brothers. These latter no longer questioned the authenticity of Jesus' ministry (cf. John 7:5). They now join his disciples in prayer, open to the unfolding of God's plan.

## Psalm 27:1, 4, 7-8

The psalm response is a prayer of profound confidence in God. Unlike most prayers of this type, which begin with a plea for help and follow immediately with expressions of confidence that God will indeed hear the cry for assistance or relief and will grant the petitioner's request, this prayer begins with the expression of confidence (v. 1) and only then moves to the pleas for help (vv. 7-8). The form of the pronouns serves to divide the psalm into two sections. The initial acclamation of confidence and the description of the psalmist's wish for union with God are third-person indirect descriptive language. The supplication is addressed to God in second-person direct language.

God is initially characterized as using three distinct metaphors: light, salvation, and refuge. In a world where darkness was not only a danger to one's safety but also symbolized the forces of evil, light was seen as the force that dispelled any kind of danger. Because it also regularly conquered cosmic darkness, light enjoyed mythological prominence as well. Salvation, or deliverance, was always granted out of the beneficence of another; one did not save oneself. The misfortune from which God might save could be personal or communal, physical or spiritual. In any case, God was the savior. Finally, a refuge is a place of safety to which one in danger could flee for protection. All three metaphors characterize God as one holding unparalleled power and exercising this power on behalf of the psalmist, who was not only vulnerable but somehow besieged.

The supplications begin (v. 7) with the same invocation as does Israel's foremost prayer, the *Sh<sup>e</sup>ma<sup>c</sup>* (Hear, O Israel). The verb itself carries the meaning "to hear and respond favorably." The idea of being heard is reiterated in the plea for pity that follows immediately. The particular verb used *(ḥānan)* denotes a heartfelt response by one who has something to give another who is in need. God has been identified earlier in the psalm as light, salvation, and refuge. This might lead some to expect the psalmist is asking for some form of protection. Such is not the case here. The psalmist is pleading for the presence of God.

Since it was believed that God was experienced at shrines or during some ritual enactment, many commentators believe there is a cultic dimension to this psalm. This is reinforced by the statement of the psalmist's desire to dwell in the house of the LORD. While this could be a reference to actual residence in the temple precincts, it is more likely a prayer for intimacy with God. The psalmist is praying for an enduring realization of divine presence such as one would expect if living within the house of God itself. Such a realization would flower into a contemplative attitude that would enable the psalmist continually to delight in the glory of God.

On the other hand, it may be the petitioner, filled with confidence in God's solicitude, has brought her or his concerns to the sanctuary (women too prayed at the sanctuaries [cf. Hannah, 1 Sam 1:9-19]), where the petitioner hopes for some reply.

## 1 Peter 4:13-16

On this last Sunday before the feast of Pentecost we read again of the connection that exists between the suffering of Christ and that of the Christian followers. Those who share in his suffering will also share in his glory. This is the reason for the Christians' rejoicing. The eschatological character of this message can be clearly seen in the language used. Although *apokálypsis* simply means "revelation," it has come to be associated with the end-time. That is the way it is used in this passage. However, it is not clear which eschatological tradition the author is espousing here. Is it the inauguration of the new age, which was accomplished through the resurrection of Jesus? Or is it the culmination of time as we know it and the advent of life after this life? Whether one thinks of resurrection glory or the final and perfect glory at the end of time, those who share in the suffering with Christ will share in his glory. A second word charged with eschatological meaning is the term for time itself *(kairós)*. This is not ordinary chronological time *(chrónos)*. It is the decisive moment, the divinely ordained time when all will be fulfilled.

The author of the letter is very clear about the reason for the suffering of the Christians. They are either defamed for the name of Christ (v. 14) or harassed, even persecuted, for being Christians (v. 16). The author provides one form of personal injury that fits these categories, reproach *(óneidos)*, "to make another the object of disgrace." Since their religious teaching and values frequently prevented the Christian believers from engaging in behavior that was part of pagan culture, they often had to endure misunderstanding, mistrust, and resentment. Their way of living was considered antisocial at best, treasonable at worst. It is out of the question to think that suffering, which is the penalty for wrongdoing, could be associated with the suffering of Jesus. In order to make clear what he means here, the author gives some examples of the behavior that will not earn future glorification for the Christians. It includes murder, theft, wrongdoing, and acting as a busybody. This kind of behavior does not merit eschatological glory.

This is one of only three places in the Bible where the followers of Jesus are called "Christians" (cf. Acts 11:26; 26:28). While the term marks one as a supporter or follower of Christ, it may well have been intended as a name of scorn. Although it might be interpreted as "Messiah follower," the Christians claimed the Messiah they followed was a man who had been executed as a felon. To call them "Christian" might have been comparable to calling them "felon-follower." In the face of this, the author of the letter tells them to bear this name proudly and to endure any misfortune that might befall them because of it.

## John 17:1-11a

From the time of Cyril of Alexandria this passage from John's gospel has been known as the High Priestly prayer. Although it is an example of intercessory prayer, this designation comes more from an interpretation from outside the text than from a close reading of it. Since within it Jesus speaks of having accomplished his work (v. 4) and of returning to his Father (v. 11a), it is clearly a farewell message. In it Jesus prays first for himself (vv. 1-5) and then for his disciples (vv. 6-11a). The interweaving of various theological themes makes it a rich yet complex prayer.

One theme, upon which most of the others depend, is the nature of the relationship that exists between Jesus and God. It is one of father to son and son to father. This is the title with which Jesus addresses God (vv. 1, 5), and he refers to himself as "son" (v. 1). It was from this Father that Jesus came (v. 3), and it is to this Father that he returns (v. 11a). The glory for which Jesus prays is the glory he shared with his Father before the creation of the world (v. 5). Jesus' authority came from his Father (v. 2), and he in turn delivered the Father's word to his disciples (v. 8) and revealed the Father's name to them (v. 6). Though in some ways Jesus appears to be subordinate to his Father, yet they share all things (v. 10). This passage leaves no doubt in our minds about the divine character of Jesus.

The glorification for which Jesus prays can now be seen within the context of this unique relationship. He does not pray for a glory that is not already his. On the contrary, he enjoyed this glory before the world existed (v. 5). It is as if he laid it aside when becoming human, and now the hour has come for him to take it up again. The glorification *of* Jesus is linked to the glorification of God *by* Jesus. It is in the accomplishment of God's work that he glorifies God, and it is in the accomplishment of this same work that God glorifies him. Most commentators agree that the culmination of this work is the crucifixion, when Jesus is lifted up (cf. John 12:32). The crucifixion will be the ultimate moment of Jesus' glorification.

While on earth Jesus revealed the name of his Father through the life he lived and the ministry he performed. By means of the authority he received from God he was empowered to grant them eternal life. He did not promise eternal life as if it were something in the future. He granted it by revealing his Father (vv. 6-7), for this passage identifies eternal life as knowledge of God and of Jesus as the one sent by God (v. 3).

A final theme in this reading is Jesus' attitude toward the world *(kósmos)*. He mentions this world in several places, but he does not intend the same meaning in each instance. The first time the word is used (v. 5) Jesus is referring to the created universe. There is no moral judgment passed on the world in this case. However, it is clear that in the next two instances (vv. 6, 9) he is pitting himself and his followers against this world. Here he is referring to that realm of human life and reality that is antagonistic toward God and the things of God. Jesus' followers have been taken out of this world. Finally, Jesus is leaving the world, although his disciples remain within it (v. 11a). The reference here is probably to human life in general. He faces death, while they continue in this life the work he has begun.

## Themes of the Day

As we come to the end of the Easter season, we realize that we are in a liminal time, a time "in-between." Even the readings do not present a consistent representation of time. In the gospel Jesus prepares his disciples for his departure; in the first reading he has already ascended into heaven; the second reading speaks of the revelation of his glory. Time has been radically changed for us. We are now living in God's time, when future fulfillment has already come to pass.

### Already, but Not Yet

This last Sunday of Easter sums up the tension we have felt throughout the entire season. In one way, we have celebrated the mystery of the resurrection and the exaltation of Jesus as if it were a progressive unfolding. In another way, we have celebrated it as an event that happened once for all. There is no confusion here. Rather, the apparent disparity points to the fact that we always live in the tension of "already, but not yet." We see this tension in the readings; we see it in the liturgical season; we see it in life itself. We wait in anticipation for something already in our midst. In a very real sense the unfolding occurs within us. We are the ones who have been saved already but have not yet experienced the fullness of that salvation. We have already been transformed into Christ, but this transformation has not yet been complete. The glory of the risen Christ has already been revealed in us, but not yet totally. "Already, but not yet" is the way we live out our lives in God, not the way God lives in us. The tension is ours, not God's.

This tension is at the core of much of our frustration and suffering. We think we have made some progress in reforming our lives only to realize that with each step forward we discover more steps that need to be taken. We resolve to eliminate from our lives those attitudes and habits of behavior that diminish our character—impatience, resentment, small-mindedness—only to find that wholehearted commitment has not yet eradicated them from our lives. Because we live in the tension of "already, but not yet" we are always in need of salvation; we must always plunge ourselves into the death of Jesus so we can rise again with him. While in this liminal state we must remember that even if we become frustrated God does not. God is always at our side.

## Living In-Between

Living in-between the times is a special kind of living. It is a combination of rejoicing in the future that has already come and waiting for it to dawn. Though Christ is exalted in the heavens, the glory of Christ shines forth in us through our commitment to the message of the gospel. The readings for today show us that the radical nature of this in-between living requires the support of a community. After Jesus ascended into heaven the apostles returned to Jerusalem as a community, and they gathered as a community in prayer. Knowing the difficulties his followers would have to face, Jesus prayed for them. This prayer was made within the context of Jesus' declaration of oneness, oneness between him and the one he called Father. At this same time he described the participation of his followers in this oneness.

We need community, but not only for help in the ordinary experiences of life. We need a community of believers with whom we can pray, who will understand our spiritual aspirations, who will support us in our Christian commitment, who will challenge us when we stray from the right path. We need a community of believers who are companions with us on our journey through this in-between time, who experience the same struggle to be faithful in a world that does not share our values or our insights. We need a community of believers through whom shines the glory of the exalted Lord.

## Pentecost Sunday

### Acts 2:1-11

The Jewish feast of Pentecost was one of the three major pilgrim festivals of Israel. Originally an agricultural feast marking the end of the grain harvest, it was also called the feast of Weeks because it was celebrated seven weeks, or fifty days, after the feast of Unleavened Bread. As with the other two pilgrim festivals it eventually took on historical importance, commemorating the giving of the Law at Sinai. The fact that it was a pilgrim feast explains why devout Jews from every nation were in Jerusalem at this time. Although only devout men are mentioned (v. 5), we know that women and children also made the pilgrimage. This is an example of the author's gender bias.

The reading from Acts does not tell us precisely who was in the room when the Spirit descended. Was it the one hundred twenty that had gathered earlier (cf. Acts 1:15)? Was it only the twelve apostles (cf. 2:14)? Contrary to some translations the Greek does not use gender-specific language, so we cannot say it was a gathering made up exclusively of men. (The later reference to the Joel passage would suggest it was not; cf. 2:17-18.)

The external manifestations that accompanied the outpouring of the Spirit were all phenomena associated with a theophany, an experience of God. For example, thunder accompanied God's revelation at Sinai (cf. Exod 19:16); God spoke to Job from the whirlwind (Job 38:1) and to Moses from the burning bush (Exod 3:2). The text reports that these phenomena were audible and visible while the actual outpouring of the Spirit was not. However, as those in the room were filled with the Spirit they began to speak in other languages, a feat that could only have some supernatural origin.

The same Greek word (*glōssa*) is used for the tongues of fire that appeared above each one and for the foreign tongues that were subsequently spoken. There is question whether the reference here is to communicative speech (foreign tongues) or ecstatic speech, called "glossolalia." Since the people who came to see what had happened understood the bold proclamations of these Spirit-filled preachers, the meaning here seems to be communicative rather than ecstatic speech (vv. 6-11).

The crowd that gathered because of the loud noise were confused, astonished, and amazed. They knew those speaking were Galileans, presumably because of some feature of their speech. Yet the hearers were able to understand the message in their own dialect. Because the Galileans spoke in tongues and those in the crowd heard in their own speech, some commentators have suggested there was a miracle in hearing as well as in speaking.

The exact nature of this marvel is less significant than is its meaning. It was clearly a manifestation of the universal presence and power of the Spirit. Some commentators believe it demonstrated the reversal of the fragmentation of peoples that occurred when languages were confused after the people attempted to construct the tower of Babel (cf. Gen 11:1-9). The outpouring of the Spirit and the preaching of the gospel to all nations are seen by some as the reuniting of the human race and the gathering of all into the reign of God.

## Psalm 104:1, 24, 29-30, 31, 34

This hymn is remarkable in its depiction of God as Creator and sustainer of all life. It begins, as do other hymns of its kind, with a summons to praise. The call to "bless the LORD" is normally addressed to someone other than the psalmist. Twice a self-address is used (vv. 1, 35). This forms a kind of *inclusio* that divides the responsorial psalm into two parts. The first treats God as the wondrous Creator; the second describes God's providential care.

The Hebrew word translated "soul" *(nepesh)* comes from the word for breath. It yields over twenty meanings, chief among them are "life-breath" (or soul), "life," "living person." The reference here is probably to that center within the psalmist from which flows all life forces. This is not merely a spiritual or immaterial reality; it encompasses every aspect of the person. Every aspect of the psalmist's being is called upon to give praise to God.

God is described as robed in majesty and glory, wrapped around with radiant light. This is the way the commanding gods of the ancient Near East were depicted. The psalmist does not claim that God is visible but that God's garments are discernible. In other words, the splendor the psalmist beholds is an indication of God's presence. God is perceived through the glories of creation.

The natural world is not only marvelous in its appearance, it is diverse in its manifestations. The variety and complexity of its forms are astounding. This splendor is attributed to the wisdom of the Creator. In the biblical tradition there is an intrinsic link between creation and Wisdom (cf. Prov 8:22-31; Wis 9:9). Wisdom was understood as insight into, harmony with, or power over the orders of reality. These orders were established by God at the time of creation, and they are sustained by the same creative power.

In the second part of the psalm God is extolled as the one who cares for all living things. All creatures look to God for sustenance. From a human point of view creation is not a static act completed once for all in the distant past. We experience creation as an ongoing event. The act of creation and power of the Creator are perceived in the constant renewal of life, which unfolds before our eyes. In a very real sense creation is more than a primordial event, it is a personal experience.

The psalm then shows that the life forces of the natural world do not operate in a manner independent of the divine will. God sustains life by providing food, but God can also bring on death by taking back the breath of life. When this happens the creature returns to the dust from which it was initially taken (cf. Gen 2:7; Job 12:10). God is both the original Creator and the one who continues to control the forces of nature.

Finally, God not only creates but re-creates. The ongoing forces of nature are re-creative. Life is sustained and perpetuated. The word for "spirit" *(rûah)* is the same as that found in the story of creation, where a mighty wind swept over the waters (Gen 1:2). That was the first creation. The psalm claims that the spirit of the LORD can bring about a new creation. This is reason enough to bless the LORD.

## 1 Corinthians 12:3b-7, 12-13

This reading consists of three different yet related themes: an acclamation of the lordship of Jesus, a defense of diversity within the community, and the body metaphor that characterizes that diversity.

The acclamation "Jesus is Lord!" is rich in both Jewish and early Christian meaning. Lord *(kýrios)* was the official title of the Roman emperor. To proclaim Jesus as Lord was to set up a rivalry between the followers of Jesus and the ruling political authority. Since most if not all of the emperors claimed to be somehow divine, this rivalry was both political and religious. Furthermore, because the Roman government was involved in the death of Jesus, such a challenging claim would place those who made it at great risk for their lives.

The word "Lord" is also used in the Septuagint, the Greek version of the First Testament, as a substitute for God's personal name. To use this title for Jesus is to ascribe to him the attributes of God. This use may not have set up a political rivalry between Jesus and God, as was the case with the Roman emperor, but it certainly did make serious religious claims. It is important to note the acclamation uses the name of the man Jesus, not his religious title, Christ. It is this man who is placed on the same level as the God of ancient Israel. No one would make such a claim were it not for the promptings of the Holy Spirit. This is a cry of faith, a testimony to the divine character of this man from Galilee.

Paul next launches into a discourse on the varieties of functions within the Christian community. In sketching this diversity he uses two triads: gifts, ministries, and works; Spirit, Lord, and God. Although the latter triad suggests a trinitarian perspective that associates one set of functions with each of the divine persons, it is clear from the text that all the activities are manifestations of the Spirit (v. 7).

Gifts *(chárisma)* refers to those operations of the Spirit, notably speaking in tongues and prophesying, that were usually operative during worship. Ministry *(diakonía)* was service within the community. It included duties often considered menial, like serving at table or collecting money. Paul may have included this reference in order to show that within the community of believers no task is ignoble. Works *(enérgēma)* were feats of great energy or divine power. Since all these gifts or ministries or works were manifestations of the Spirit, no one was to be considered superior to another. Further, they were not given for the self-aggrandizement of the one who received them. All were given for the benefit of the entire community.

The diversity found within the community is compared to the complexity of the human body. Each part has its own unique function, but all parts work for the good of the whole. This metaphor characterizes several aspects of the community. First, it portrays unity in diversity, a unity that is far from uniformity. Second, it underscores the lack of competition among members, one activity elevating itself above the others. Lowly service is no less important than charismatic gifts. Third, it points up the interdependence that exists within the community. In this community there are no more stratifications, whether religious (Jew or Greek) or social (slave or free).

## John 20:19-23

This appearance account treats the resurrection and the bestowal of the Spirit upon the disciples of Jesus as having occurred on the same day, for the event described took place "on the evening of that first day of the week" (v. 19). The account contains several salient details. First, the incident took place on the first day of the week. Second, it occurred despite the doors being closed. Third, Jesus appears in the midst of the disciples. Fourth, he addresses those present with a greeting of peace. Fifth, he calls their attention to his wounds. Sixth, he confers the Spirit on them and entrusts them with the power of binding and loosing. Each of these details is laden with theological meaning.

This first day of the week is the actual day of the resurrection (v. 19). It is clear that the entire reckoning of time has been altered by the event that occurred early in the morning. Where previously religious meaning was given to the sabbath, the conclusion of the week, now the focus is on the beginning of the week, on the future. The locked doors secured the disciples from those who had had some part in the arrest, trial, and crucifixion of Jesus. His followers had reason to fear these people might be hostile toward them as well. The closed doors also underscore the mysterious character of Jesus' risen body. It is not impeded by material obstacles; it can move as it wishes and where it will.

The wish of peace, which was the common Jewish greeting of the day, was also a prayer for the eschatological blessings of health, prosperity, and all good things. When Jesus wishes peace for his disciples, he is proclaiming the arrival of this time of fulfillment. By calling attention to the wounds in his hands and side, Jesus shows the disciples he is not a figment of their imaginations or some kind of ghost from the netherworld. He is the same man who was crucified, but now he is risen. Apparently the disciples recognized the Lord, because they rejoiced at the sight of him.

The bestowal of the Holy Spirit is introduced by a second salutation of peace. The image of breathing life into another is reminiscent of the creation of Adam (cf. Gen 2:7) and the restoration of Israel after the Exile (cf. Ezek 37:9). By breathing in this way the risen Lord portrays himself as one who can create or re-create. One of the Hebrew words for breath *(rûah)* is also translated "spirit," so there is a long tradition of linking spirit and breath. The Spirit of God is also the breath of God.

The disciples are commissioned to go forth, to declare salvation and judgment. The language describes the activity of a judge, who decides whether the defendant is bound to the consequences of the charges or loosed from them. Most likely, the authority here given to the disciples is much broader than this. The phrase "bind and loose" (or forgive) is similar to "flesh and blood," or "left and right." Each expression names the opposite pole, but together they are meant to include everything between them as well. These are ways of describing totality: "flesh and blood" refers to the whole body; "left and right" includes the entire horizon; "bind and loose" suggests complete authority. With the bestowal of the Spirit the disciples are authorized to continue the mission of Jesus.

## Themes of the Day

The community has been living in the in-between time since the ascension of the Lord. Today it celebrates the dramatic inbreaking of the time of fulfillment. The feast celebrates the fullness of the Spirit and the great gathering together of nations. The feast also brings the Easter season to its conclusion. Like the finale of a majestic symphony, the readings for today recapitulate many of the themes that appeared throughout the Easter season: christology, trinitarian theology, reign of God, repentance, salvation, mission, universality. All are brought together as we are brought together into the body of Christ.

### In the Fullness of the Spirit

At last the plan of salvation has been brought to conclusion. The risen Lord has been exalted to his rightful place next to God, and he has sent his Spirit to fill the earth with God's power. The world is charged with divine energy; it needs but a spark to ignite it with life and excitement. This vitality explodes into the extraordinary: tongues are loosed, and speech overflows its linguistic constraints; charismatic gifts flood the valleys of human habitation; barred doors are burst open, and frightened hearts are calmed. The Spirit of the Lord fills the whole world.

## The Great Gathering

Once again we gather together for one reason, only to discover God has gathered us for another. Strangers assemble to fulfill personal obligations, and they experience a phenomenon that bonds them together for life. Individual religious devotion is swept up into communal divine revelation. Through the Spirit of God we are reconciled to one another, and then together we spend ourselves for the common good. Through the Spirit of God the world is renewed, the community is revitalized, and we come to know the mysterious yet all-pervasive peace of Christ.

If this has all really happened, why does our world look the same? Why is there so much religious and ethnic rivalry? Why do we continue to make distinctions between Jew and Gentile, slave and free, woman and man, distinctions that favor one at the expense of the other? Why is there so little peace, or comfort, or solace? Why do we refuse to forgive or to be reconciled? Is Pentecost merely a feast we celebrate in red vestments? Has the face of the earth really been renewed?

The answer is yes! Resoundingly, yes! The Spirit has been poured forth and works wonders wherever human hearts are open to its promptings. The earth is renewed each time rivalries are resolved; distinctions are recognized as merely expressions of diversity; peace is restored; comfort and solace are offered; forgiveness is granted. We are immersed in the vigor of the Spirit of God; all we have to do is open ourselves to it and the reign of God will be born in our midst.

# Ordinary Time (Part One)

| | First Reading | Psalm | Second Reading | Gospel |
|---|---|---|---|---|
| **First Sunday** (Baptism of the Lord) | | | | |
| **Second Sunday** | Isaiah 49:3, 5-6<br>The servant of the LORD | Psalm 40:2, 4, 7-10<br>I come to do your will | 1 Corinthians 1:1-3<br>Called to be an apostle | John 1:29-34<br>Behold the Lamb of God |
| **Third Sunday** | Isaiah 8:23–9:3<br>The people have seen a great light | Psalm 27:1, 4, 13-14<br>The LORD is my light and my salvation | 1 Corinthians 1:10-13, 17<br>Let there be no divisions | Matthew 4:12-23<br>Repent. . . . Come . . . Follow me |
| **Fourth Sunday** | Zephaniah 2:3; 3:12-13<br>A people humble and lowly | Psalm 146:6-10<br>The LORD is good and gracious | 1 Corinthians 1:26-31<br>The weak things of the world | Matthew 5:1-12a<br>Blessed are you |
| **Fifth Sunday** | Isaiah 58:7-10<br>Attend to the needs of others | Psalm 112:4-9<br>Shine like light in the darkness | 1 Corinthians 2:1-5<br>Christ, the mystery of God | Matthew 5:13-16<br>Let your light shine |
| **Sixth Sunday** | Sirach 15:15-20<br>Keep the commandments | Psalm 119:1-2, 4-5, 17-18, 33-34<br>Walk in the Law of the LORD | 1 Corinthians 2:6-10<br>The joys of the age to come | Matthew 5:17-37<br>But I say to you |

| Seventh Sunday | | |
|---|---|---|
| **Leviticus 19:1-2, 17-18**<br>Love your neighbor | **Psalm 103:1-4, 8, 10, 12-13**<br>The LORD is kind | **1 Corinthians 3:16-23**<br>You are the temple of God | **Matthew 5:38-48**<br>Love your enemies |
| Eighth Sunday | | |
| **Isaiah 49:14-15**<br>I will not forget you | **Psalm 62:2-3, 6-9**<br>God is my rock and salvation | **1 Corinthians 4:1-5**<br>We are servants of Christ | **Matthew 6:24-34**<br>You cannot serve<br>God and mammon |
| Ninth Sunday | | |
| **Deuteronomy 11:18, 26-28**<br>I set before you blessing and curse | **Psalm 31:2-4, 17, 25**<br>In you, O LORD, I take refuge | **Romans 3:21-25, 28**<br>Justified by faith | **Matthew 7:21-27**<br>A house built on rock |

# Ordinary Time (Part One)

## Initial Reading of the Ordinary Lectionary (Part One)

### Introduction

This period of Ordinary Time is really an interlude between seasons. Christmas is behind us, and in a few weeks we will be entering the season of Lent. Although time and again we might catch a glimpse of the future, a hint of what lies ahead for Jesus and for those who are his disciples, during this interim period our readings invite us to reflect on various aspects of our discipleship.

The number of Sundays in this period prompts us to divide Ordinary Time into four sections. The absence of specific seasonal themes makes this division somewhat arbitrary. Since there is consecutive reading from the epistles, we could have allowed these readings to determine the divisions. However, we felt that since there is significant reading from some epistles and much less from others, such divisions would be quite uneven in size. Therefore we simply divided the thirty-four Sundays by four and grouped the readings accordingly.

### First Testament Readings

Although they originate from various books of the First Testament, all the first readings for these Sundays of Ordinary Time are somehow related to the theme of covenant, the intimate relationship initiated by God that binds God to the people in both love and responsibility. The unfaithfulness of the people put the existence of the covenant in jeopardy. The conditions of the pact included punishment for disloyalty, but there was no guarantee God would give the people another chance. Still, another chance was given. The mysterious figure of the Servant of the LORD was believed to be an agent of the establishment of this covenant, one who would somehow bring an erring people back into the embrace of its God. Just as separation from God is likened to living in darkness, so this return is described as moving from darkness into light. The people are promised survival not because they deserve it but because God is faithful to covenant promises.

The newly established faithfulness of the people will be demonstrated in the way they live out their responsibilities. Having been shown compassion by their God, in their turn they are called to attend to the needs of others, to live in obedience to the commandments, and to love their covenant companions as God loves them. Perhaps one of the most touching statements found in the prophets is God's covenant promise: I will never forget you!

## Psalms

The psalm responses are appropriate to the covenantal sentiments expressed in the first readings. They include a hymn of praise (Fourth Sunday), which acknowledges the blessings that come to God's people because of the covenant; prayers of thanksgiving for the goodness God has shown (Second and Seventh Sundays); expressions of trust based on God's faithfulness to the covenant (Third, Eighth, and Ninth Sundays); and instructions on how to live so the people might carry out their own covenant responsibilities (Fifth and Sixth Sundays). This collection of psalm responses ends with a prayer used during covenantal renewal ceremonies.

## Epistles

Read in consecutive fashion, the passages from the first letter to the Corinthians all contrast the wisdom of God with that of the world. The tensions in the Christian community warrant this comparison, for they show the Christians are following the world's practice of pitting one person against another rather than adhering to the gospel's injunction to communal unity. Paul first establishes his own credentials. He has been called by God, and as an apostle he speaks with the authority given him by God. It behooves the Corinthians to heed his words.

Contrary to the manner of the world God chooses those who are considered foolish as well as the weak and the lowly. Thus it is not likely anyone will have anything to boast about. God acts like this so all will recognize the power of God at work in these "little ones." So it was with Christ, who, as the mystery of God, redeemed us precisely through the weakness of his death rather than through any show of strength or force. Because God's wisdom is so different from the wisdom of the world, only those who are mature in faith will understand or even recognize it. Paul returns to the internal rivalry that precipitated the letter in the first place, and he exhorts the Corinthians to preserve the unity that is theirs because the Spirit of God lives in them as in a temple.

The readings from the letter to the Romans develop Paul's insistence that faith is the only avenue to justification. This theme will be further developed in future Sundays.

## Gospels

With a few exceptions, the Sunday gospel readings for Ordinary Time of this Liturgical Year are taken from the Gospel of Matthew. The reading for the Second Sunday, which is taken from the Gospel of John, is one of those exceptions. Actually, Ordinary Time of each of the three cycles begins with a reading from John's gospel. In each case John the Baptist directs discipleship away from himself ("Behold the Lamb of God") and toward Jesus ("Repent . . . Come follow me"). Thus Ordinary Time considers various aspects of this discipleship.

The seven remaining gospel readings come from the Sermon on the Mount, that long instruction Jesus directed to his disciples rather than to the crowds. In it he sketches the manner of behavior required of those who would enter the reign of heaven. This includes the Beatitudes as well as Jesus' own interpretation of earlier Jewish traditions. It is clear he is asking more than the Law dictates. He insists on total commitment, not mere external conformity or superficial adherence.

## Mosaic of Readings

The readings for these Sundays provide us with a glimpse into the nature of a community of disciples. They show us what it should be and what it should not be. It is the call of God and not human accomplishments that invites us into the community of the covenanted. As members of that community we are challenged by standards that seem to be diametrically opposed to those that govern the world. The most basic attitude required is openness to receive. This is very difficult for those of us accustomed to striving to be wise, to be competent, to be independent. God is not impressed with these attitudes. God does indeed desire to accomplish great things through us, but these accomplishments must be seen as the working of the power of God in us, not our own power. This is the real challenge of discipleship.

# Readings

*First Sunday in Ordinary Time*
*The Baptism of the Lord*

*Second Sunday in Ordinary Time*

## Isaiah 49:3, 5-6

The verses for the first reading for this Sunday belong to the literary form known as "prophetic speech" ("The LORD said to me"). In this speech it is God who refers to the speaker as "my servant." Hence the designation "Servant Song." However, the actual identity of this servant is quite mysterious. At first reading it sounds like the prophet is the servant ("The LORD said to *me:* You are my servant). But then the servant is identified as Israel. Even this causes confusion, because the servant is called to accomplish the return of Jacob, the gathering back together of Israel (v. 5). Because the servant is said to have been formed as a servant from the womb, reminiscent of the call of the prophet Jeremiah (cf. Jer 1:5), some think the servant is Isaiah himself. Commentators are hard pressed to discover the precise identity of this individual. Most of them direct the reader to lay aside the search for the exact identity of the servant and instead to concentrate on his mission.

The text states that Israel is the servant, and it is through this people that God will be glorified *(pāʾar).* Since the verb suggests a kind of boasting, we can say that God boasts through Israel. But why? "Jacob" and "Israel" are two terms that at this time in the history of the people refer to the entire nation itself. The poem states that Jacob will be brought back and Israel will be gathered together. The prediction implies that at this time the people are some distance from their home; they are scattered. This is probably a reference to the Exile. It will be the mission of the servant, whoever that is, to bring them back to the LORD. The accomplishment of this mission will make the servant glorious in the sight of God. This is the cause for the boasting mentioned earlier. The spectacular return of the scattered exiles and their reestablishment as a people will be seen as the work of God. The glory that will shine forth will not be in their own accomplishments but in what God has accomplished in them through the agency of the servant.

The commission of the servant shifts dramatically (v. 6). Once again it is the LORD who speaks, so the words are authoritative. Gathering the dispersed people of Israel, as important as it may be, is a matter with too narrow a scope, so the mission of the servant will be expanded to include all the nations to the ends of the earth. A mission that originally focused on the rebirth of one nation has been broken open to include the salvation of all. It is noteworthy that a people struggling with its own survival because of its defeat at the hands of a more powerful nation should envision its God as concerned with the salvation of all, presumably even the nation at whose hands it suffered. Yet this is precisely what "light to the nations" suggests.


## Psalm 40:2, 4, 7-8, 8-9, 10

The psalm response contains three principal themes: thanksgiving for release from some difficulty; dedication to God, who is the savior; personal witness in the midst of the community. It begins with a report of the psalmist's past deliverance by God (v. 2). Though in distress, the psalmist waited in expectant hope and with patient trust. Hearing the cry for help, God first stooped down and drew the suffering believer out of the troubling situation, then put a new song into the psalmist's mouth. The former lament or cry for help had been heard and was now replaced by a grateful song of praise (v. 4).

The psalmist claims that in this situation God does not want the customary sacrificial rituals that form the basis of the cultic tradition. (The rituals include a sacrifice or communal meal, which was part of the festival of thanksgiving; a gift-offering, which was presented as an act of homage to God; a holocaust, or burnt offering, of an entire animal; and a sin-offering, which was a sacrifice of expiation.)

This apparent dismissal of the ritual should not be seen as a repudiation of the sacrificial system. Instead, it indicates that a deeper commitment is required here. Public worship, as important as it is, can become mere external ceremony. What God wants is an ear open to obedience (v. 7) and a willingness to delight in God's Law (v. 9), an interior commitment that will result in a life of righteousness and faithful worship.

The responsorial verses end with the psalmist standing before the worshiping assembly (*qahal*) and publicly proclaiming the wondrous acts of salvation God has accomplished. It is through this kind of testimony rather than in the conventional cultic manner that the psalmist shows gratitude for having been delivered from distress. Such witnessing not only proclaims the goodness of God, it can also inspire others within the community to turn to God with the same kind of hope and trust so they too may enjoy deliverance by God. It can encourage them to open their ears in obedience and to delight in God's Law.

The subject of the psalmist's public proclamation is the justice or righteousness of God. This characteristic is fundamental to God's very nature. It means that because of God all things are in order, in right relationship. It signifies God's faithfulness to all promises made to women and men. God's rewards and punishment flow from this sense of right order and fidelity. The psalmist's proclamation contends that commitment to God and reliance on God's adherence to covenantal promises will assure blessing.

Having been delivered, the psalmist is now at the disposal of God, has now an ear open to obedience and a tongue loosed for proclamation, and is now a herald of the righteousness of God.

## 1 Corinthians 1:1-3

The letters to the Corinthians are some of the most important Pauline correspondence we have. Today's reading is a perfect example of the greeting of a Greek letter: "Paul" is the superscription that identifies the writer; "to the church in Corinth" is the address; "grace and peace" is the salutation. Much of Paul's theology is found in the modifying words and phrases of this greeting.

Paul begins his self-identification by applying to himself the designation "apostle" *(apóstolos)*. The word means one who is sent by another, sent with a commission. Strictly speaking, an apostle is more than a disciple or follower. It is one who is sent with the full authority of the sender. Paul further states he was called to be an apostle. He did not volunteer; the initiative was not his. Moreover, he is an apostle of Jesus, who is called the Christ (the anointed one). This means that Jesus, the one who died before Paul came to know him, called Paul and sent him out as an apostle. Therefore, as an apostle, Paul exercises the authority of Christ. To be called is to be chosen, and this is how Paul perceives his apostleship. Finally, he maintains that all of this transpired because it was God's will. In a very real sense, this official greeting is really a proclamation of faith on Paul's part.

A reference in the Acts of the Apostles might tell us something about Paul's companion, Sosthenes (cf. Acts 18:17). There we read of a synagogue official in Corinth with the same name who, in the presence of the Roman tribunal that governed that city, was flogged by the Jews who had been enraged by Paul. The suffering he endured for the name of Christ must have gained him high regard in the Christian community of that city. Paul proclaims that this community has already been sanctified in Christ, redeemed through the sacrifice of his blood, and constituted a community of believers through baptism. Just as he had been called to be an apostle, so the members of the Corinthian church had been called to be holy. Although they constitute a local church, they are part of a much larger congregation, an assembly consisting of all those who profess faith in the name of Jesus, the Lord.

Finally, Paul's customary salutation, "Grace and peace," is a combination of Greek and Jewish greetings. "Grace" means "blessing" or "gift"; "peace" *(shalom* in Hebrew) is a wish for all good things. As part of his standard greeting these words are also expressions of faith, for they acknowledge that all good things come from God, whom Paul calls Father, and from Jesus, who is Lord and Christ.

In these three short verses we can see the outline of Paul's christology. He never uses Jesus' personal name without also identifying him as Christ, the anointed one. Furthermore, he professes that Jesus is the source of the sanctification and well-being of others. It is from the base of the theology expressed in this greeting that Paul speaks to the Christians of Corinth.

## John 1:29-34

The scene portrayed in today's gospel reading is familiar to many of us. While the reading is not an actual account of the baptism of Jesus, it includes John's report of that event along with his interpretation. In the incident depicted John points Jesus out from those around him and identifies him as the Lamb of God. Calling him the Son of God, he further seems to allude to a divine dimension in Jesus.

John contrasts the person of Jesus and himself as well as the efficacy of their respective baptisms. The ordinariness of Jesus is seen in the fact that twice John admits that initially he did not know *(oída)* Jesus. In fact, he only came to recognize who Jesus was by means of divine revelation. He states that God told him the one upon whom the Spirit would descend in the form of a dove would be the long-awaited one. It was when this happened at the baptism of Jesus that John knew he was the one. No longer would he see Jesus as ordinary. Now he identifies him as the Lamb of God and even as the Son of God.

The title "Lamb of God" is most likely a reference to the Suffering Servant found in Isa 53:7-10. Jewish theology of the time contained a very rich and complex collection of messianic expectations. Some of them were rooted in Davidic theology, and they looked for a royal leader (cf. Matt 27:11). Others thought the Messiah would be more prophetic (cf. Matt 16:14) or even that he would emerge from the priestly circles (a Qumran expectation). Still others believed the Messiah would be an otherworldly individual, one who would break into ordinary time and space in some extraordinary manner (cf. Matt 24:30). Few, if any, envisioned a Messiah who would suffer at the hands of the people. While this Isaian passage was held in high regard by the Jewish community, its imagery made it particularly popular with the followers of Jesus. The prophet's description of the Servant fit their interpretation of the events of the death of Jesus. Both the Servant and Jesus were led to slaughter like innocent lambs, and they handed over their lives as sin-offerings for others.

John states that he was called by God to baptize and that the purpose of his baptism was that Jesus might be made known to Israel, clearly a messianic hope. By contrast, the baptism Jesus would bring was one of messianic fulfillment rather than preparation. John baptized with water; Jesus would baptize with the Spirit. Reference to the Spirit recalls the prophetic promise of future cleansing with water and the gift of God's spirit (cf. Ezek 36:25-26).

Although the gospel narrative depicts Jesus as still alive, the christology within it is clearly resurrectional. While John may well have perceived Jesus as the fulfillment of messianic expectations, it is unlikely he would have expressed this faith in Christian theological terms. He would certainly consider the Messiah as ranking ahead of him. There was even a tradition claiming the Messiah was created by God at the beginning of time and therefore preexistent (v. 30). However, as the good Jew he was, John would probably not refer to Jesus as Son of God. That is a Christian title. The writer of the gospel has given John the faith we now profess.

## Themes of the Day

The readings for this Sunday lay the ground for our reflections on discipleship. In the gospel reading John the Baptist directs the crowds that have gathered around him to the person of Jesus. He is the one they should follow. In the second reading we find Paul boasting of his own apostleship. The sketch of the servant of the LORD becomes the lens through which we view discipleship these first Sundays of Ordinary Time.

### A Man of History

Ours is a historical religion. It not only unfolds within the joys and disappointments of time and place, but it is rooted in actual events that took place in the lives of real people. The Christ to whom we commit ourselves is not a mythic character, a figment of communal religious imagination. He is someone who was born into history, at a specific period of time, in a particular place. He was known by real people like John the Baptist; he submitted himself to historical rituals like baptism. He had followers who testified to the truth of both his existence and his life. Jesus was a man of history.

What does this tell us? It tells us that history is important. It tells us that the ordinary events that make up a life are sacred. Too often we look for the extraordinary, the spectacular, and we fail to appreciate the God-filled familiar moments of the day. Actually it is within these moments that our salvation unfolds. It is within these moments that we love those in our lives with the love of God, that we treat others with the compassion of God. We preach the gospel through the way we live these moments. The Buddhists speak on mindfulness, the deep living into the moments of life. The gospels show that Jesus' life was one of mindfulness. If we are to be his disciples, we too must learn to be mindful of the sacredness of our own history.

## Called to Be an Apostle

Paul situates the gospel squarely within the Corinthian church. It is a different time than the time of Jesus; it is a different place and a different culture. Yet in a sense the message is the same because it is grounded in the life and teaching of Jesus. The challenge Paul faces is the interpretation of the gospel of Jesus for a new historical moment. He does not merely repeat what he has heard. Because of the sacredness of the present moment of the Corinthians, Paul reinterprets the message for their unique time.

Like Paul, we too have been called to be apostles. We received this call when we were baptized. The beginning of the year, with its custom of making new resolutions, is a wonderful time to remember to what we have committed ourselves. At times it seems our own apostleship is no less daunting than was Paul's. However, it is no less immediate either. Whether the period of history is the first half of the first century, as was the time of Jesus, of the second half, as was the time of Paul, or the twenty-first century, as is our time, salvation unfolds within the events of time. Furthermore, the followers of Jesus always return to the events of his life in order to discover the meaning of the events in their lives. These past events are reinterpreted in the ongoing present. Discipleship is never otherworldly.

## The Servant of the LORD

Jesus was not only the Lamb of God, he was the Servant of the LORD as well. He came to unite all people, to bring new life to those who suffer defeat, to be a light to the nations. Paul's apostleship moves the servant ministry of Jesus forward into the Gentile world. It is now our turn to step into the role of servant—to work to unite families that have been torn apart, to bring new life to those on the brink of despair, to be a light in the midst of darkness. We all know situations in our very ordinary lives to which we can bring the saving grace of God. In this way we too can testify that Jesus is the Son of God.

## Third Sunday in Ordinary Time
### Isaiah 8:23–9:3

This description of the reversal of the fortunes of Israel can be divided into two sections. The first two verses (8:23–9:1) describe this reversal in third-person forms, while the last two verses (9:2-3) are directed toward God in second-person forms. The geographic references help us to ascribe the events depicted within the text to the time of the Syro-Ephraimite crisis, when the

Assyrian forces invaded and took over the territory of the northern tribes (ca. 733 B.C.E.).

The first verse contrasts the former times of hardship with the present experience of salvation. Then Zebulun, an area in southern Galilee that lies east of Carmel, and Naphtali, the northernmost territory of the kingdom of Israel, were overrun by foreigners. The Assyrian provinces of Dor, Meggido, and Gilead were carved out of Israelite lands known as the Way of the Sea, Transjordan, and Galilee of the Nations, respectively. It was a dark time for the People of God. But in the end the land was returned to Israel; the hardships that accompanied defeat and occupation were lifted; and the darkness was dispelled.

The common word for darkness *(hōshek)* is used figuratively in this passage. The darkness that came over the people would have included social disintegration, political collapse, and religious devastation. The use of the word here could be a reference to extinction, to the land of death. The reversal of fortunes is characterized by light. The salvation that came with God dispelled the darkness and burst upon the land with the brightness of shining light.

The words of the psalmist are next directed toward God. Salvation has embraced the people, and through it they are granted a threefold joy. This joy is compared to the excitement of harvest time, which included the deep satisfaction of accomplishment, the savoring of luscious fruits, and the assurance of new life. The joy is also compared to the headiness experienced when one has been victorious in battle and is allowed to divide the spoils that go to the vanquisher. Finally, the joy is compared to the relief experienced when one is freed from the yoke of military servitude, the pole of national discipline, and the rod of social oppression. God's saving grace smashes the yoke, the pole, and the rod. The reference to Midian recalls the repression the Israelites had to endure from the Midianites until God chose to raise up Gideon, who would miraculously defeat the enemy (cf. Judg 6:2-6). Truly the fortunes have been reversed, and the saving grace of God has taken over the world.

## Psalm 27:1, 4, 13-14

The psalm response is a prayer of profound confidence in God. The actual prayer begins with the expression of confidence (v. 1), moves to a petition that expresses the devotion of the psalmist (v. 4), and ends with a final declaration of confidence (v. 13). The psalm itself concludes with an exhortation addressed to the psalmist (v. 14).

God is initially characterized through the employment of three distinct metaphors: light, salvation, and refuge. In a world where darkness was not only a danger to one's safety but also symbolized the forces of evil, light was seen as the force that dispels any kind of danger. Because it was also believed to have conquered cosmic darkness, light enjoyed mythological prominence as well. Salvation, or deliverance, was always granted out of the beneficence of another; one did not save oneself. The misfortune from which God might save could be personal or communal, physical or spiritual. In any case, God was the savior. Finally, a refuge is a place of safety to which one in danger could flee for protection. All three metaphors characterize God as one holding unparalleled power and exercising this power on behalf of the psalmist, who was not only vulnerable but actually somehow besieged.

The focus of the psalm changes slightly. The sentiments of confidence are replaced with those of devout petition (v. 4). Since it was believed God was experienced at shrines or during some ritual enactment, many commentators believe there is an actual cultic dimension to this psalm. This is reinforced by the statement of the psalmist's desire to dwell in the house of the LORD. While this could be a reference to actual residence in the temple precincts, it is more likely a prayer for intimacy with God. The psalmist is praying for an enduring realization of divine presence, such as one would expect when living within the house of God itself. Such a realization would flower into a contemplative attitude that would enable the psalmist continually to delight in the glory of God. On the other hand, it may be that the petitioner, filled with confidence in God's solicitude, has brought her or his concerns to the sanctuary (women too prayed at the sanctuaries [cf. Hannah, 1 Sam 1:9-19]), where the petitioner hopes for some reply.

The prayer ends with a final expression of confidence (v. 13). Where the opening verses spoke of confidence in divine protection, here the psalmist speaks of divine blessing. The blessing will be enjoyed in this lifetime, in the land of the living. The final verse (v. 14), though clearly an injunction, can also be seen as an answer to the psalmist's prayer. One does not encourage another unless one fosters some hope of being heard. To wait for the LORD (*qāwâ*) means to look for with eager expectation. It involves the very essence of one's being. It is based on trust that all that God has promised will eventually be realized. Every aspect of this psalm response proclaims trust in God.

## 1 Corinthians 1:10-13, 17

The picture of the Corinthian church presented to us in this reading is one of bickering and pettiness. The natural differences that existed in the group have degenerated into rivalry. If left unchecked this rivalry could develop into serious divisions *(schismata).* Paul calls upon his authority as representative of Christ and addresses the situation.

Paul's appeal implies urgent entreaty. He addresses the Corinthians as brothers (and sisters), indicating he considers them as companion members of the Christian community. However, using the formal expression "in the name of our Lord Jesus Christ," he lets them know he is writing to them in an official capacity and not merely out of personal interest. His exhortation is threefold: agreement in matters of faith; unity, not schism; oneness in mind and purpose. His words do not imply that these features are absent from the community, but that they are at risk because of the rivalry.

Paul did not witness this bickering. He has been informed by others. Chloe is not further identified in the text, but she seems to have been head of a household in Corinth. Some of her servants have probably recently visited Paul and described the situation to him. Factions are forming. It is not unusual that people of common thinking join together and claim the leadership of a prominent person. That person may have influenced their thinking, gaining their loyalty because of an action performed or a promise made. The person may not even be aware of the attachment that has been formed. This occurs even today with religious or political leaders, sports figures, or entertainers, and we know how avid such supporters can become. This seems to have been the situation in Corinth.

Groups within the community claimed allegiance to various individuals. Those who rested on Paul's authority probably reflected the kind of freedom in Christ that was at the heart of his teaching. They could have been brought to the faith by Paul himself. Apollos was a Jewish native of Alexandria in Egypt. His knowledge of the Scriptures and the eloquence with which he explained them caught the attention of Priscilla and Aquila, who converted him to Christ (cf. Acts 18:24-28). He was certainly a worthy person to be revered. Those who claimed Cephas (Paul's preferred name for Peter) may have been Palestinian Jewish Christians or espoused that way of living out their Christian commitment. This would have included prescriptions such as were decided by the church in Jerusalem (cf. Acts 15:28-29). Such loyalty was also commendable. If there actually was a group that claimed a special commitment to Christ (cf. 2 Cor 10:7), they may have preferred an exalted Christ rather than the crucified one Paul preached.

Whatever the actual case may have been, there was inner strife in the Corinthian church. To this Paul poses rhetorical questions, which elicit only negative answers. No! Christ cannot be divided. No! Paul was not crucified for their salvation. No! They were not baptized in the name of Paul. He insists that neither the teachings nor the personal characteristics of a religious leader can be allowed to rival their allegiance to Christ. To demonstrate what he means, Paul minimizes his own ministerial approach. Allegiance belongs to the cross of Christ, not to human eloquence.

### Matthew 4:12-23

The gospel reading for this Sunday introduces Matthew's version of the public ministry of Jesus. The announcement of the arrest of John the Baptist prompts

Jesus to leave the vicinity and journey to Galilee. This should not be interpreted as an escape motivated by fear. On the contrary, John's imprisonment signaled both the end of his ministry and the beginning of Jesus' ministry. It was not Jesus' intent to pick up where John left off. Although he preached the same message as did the Baptist (Repent, for the kingdom of heaven is at hand [cf. Matt 3:2]), he did it in fulfillment of the prophecies rather than in anticipation of a future event. Further evidence that Jesus did not go to Galilee in search of safety is seen in the fact that he took up residence in Capernaum rather than Nazareth, where he had been raised and where he could find refuge.

The gospel writer makes a point of the geography by quoting a passage from the prophet Isaiah. There seems to have been a tradition that the first place that suffered occupation at the hands of the Assyrians (ca. 732 B.C.E.) would be the first place that would experience the redemption of God. Zebulun and Naphtali were districts in northern Galilee. They had been among the first to be overrun by the enemy from the north. These were the people who in the past had sat in darkness; they would be the first people to see the light of salvation. Galilee was a perfect place to begin a ministry. It was far enough away from the control of the leading party in Jerusalem, and in its own way it could boast of being at the crossroads of the world. This was because international trade routes to Damascus and Syria, Phoenicia, and even Egypt passed through the area.

The stage is now set for Jesus to begin. The first move he makes is to call some followers. Two sets of brothers—Simon and Andrew, James and John—are called away from their occupation. The play on the idea of fishing is clear: Now you cast your nets to catch fish; I am asking you to cast another kind of net in order to "catch" followers. The radical nature of their response should not be overlooked. These men are not poor beggars. They are all gainfully employed in one of the most stable occupations of the area. They have a lot to lose by following him, yet they drop everything and follow Jesus. James and John even leave their father, an unusual move in a society where kinship ties were very strong and loyalty to one's father was of paramount importance.

It should be noted that these men were called. They did not initiate their own discipleship as followers of rabbis normally did. However, what they witnessed more than rewarded their immediate response. Jesus' ministry is described as being threefold: he taught in the synagogues; he proclaimed the good news; and he cured those suffering from disease and illness. The proclamation of the good news and the healing of the sick were believed to be signs of the advent of the age of fulfillment (cf. Isa 61:1; 35:5-7). Jesus announced that this age, this kingdom of heaven, had come. The new disciples were witnesses of its appearance.

## Themes of the Day

The readings for this Sunday continue the theme of discipleship that we examined last Sunday. They address various aspects of the question of call. They depict discipleship as a call from God, and they help us to see that discipleship calls us *from* certain situations and calls us *to* others.

### The Call

Discipleship is not something we take upon ourselves. We are called to it. Some people are very conscious of this call. They are aware of it in their aspirations and dreams; they recognize it in the events of their lives. They hear the call as clearly as Simon, Andrew, James, and John heard the voice of Jesus. For others, the call to discipleship is not so clear. They may experience an undefined restlessness, a dissatisfaction with their lives. Or they may be very satisfied with life when they hear the call, as the four in the gospel seem to have been. People can respond to the call in one of two ways. They consider the mere suggestion of discipleship an intrusion into their plans, or they drop what they are doing, leave their former concerns behind, and follow Jesus. In either case, the call to discipleship originates with God.

### Called From

There seems to be a misunderstanding about being called and leaving everything behind. Although the gospel says the four men left their occupation of fishing in order to follow Jesus, this kind of "leaving behind" was not, and still is not, required of all. We saw in the readings of last week that it was in the ordinary events of life that our salvation unfolds. For most people this is precisely where they are to function as disciples. Still, disciples of Jesus are called to leave behind certain ways of living as they follow him. They are called away from lives of pettiness and division. They are called away from the kind of factionalism that seems to have threatened the unity of the Corinthian community. They are called away from narrow-mindedness and mean-spirited competition. They are called away from absolutizing their interpretation of the gospel message. It is in fact much easier to leave one's nets than to leave the web of one's prejudices. This is the darkness out of which disciples are called.

Today we live in a very complex Church. Some would say it is a divided Church. However, diversity need not be divisive. Like the Christians in Corinth, we have been baptized in the name of Christ, and in Christ there is no division. If we are to be faithful disciples of Christ we too must leave behind our inclination to take sides, to pit one religious position against another, to dismiss as disloyal or narrow-minded those who understand our common faith in quite different ways than we do. Discipleship calls us away from such a point of view.

## Called To

Disciples of Jesus are called to lives of servanthood. They are called to proclaim the gospel of the kingdom of heaven, whether that be in public ministry or in the circumstances of everyday life. They are called to heal disease and illness of mind and body and spirit. They are called to smash the yoke that burdens others and, if it cannot be smashed, to help carry the load. They are called to work for unity and peace even in the midst of diversity and misunderstanding, or better, precisely in the midst of diversity and misunderstanding. They are called to respect the struggles and commitment of others. Disciples of Jesus are called to be light in a world of darkness and gloom. This calling does not mean they have all the answers. They may not even know the questions. However, they have the assurance of God, who is our light and our salvation. The disciples of Jesus are called to continue in their time and place the ministry of the Servant of the LORD.

# Fourth Sunday in Ordinary Time
## Zephaniah 2:3; 3:12-13

The reading from this little-known prophet uses bold lines to sketch two very different scenes. In the first (2:3) the prophet exhorts the people to reform their lives. The second (3:12-13) is an oracle of salvation that promises a smaller but renewed community. Though the verses originate from different sections of the prophet's proclamation, placed together as they are in this reading they interpret each other. The opening exhortation sets the stage for the oracle; the oracle addresses the situation presumed in the exhortation.

The prophet addresses the people with a threefold exhortation: Seek the LORD! Seek righteousness! Seek humility! The verbs are intensive imperatives in form, indicating the urgency of the search. They imply that the search is necessary because something has been lost or in some way has disappeared. The admonishment "Seek the LORD" is usually a call to worship; however, that does not seem to be its meaning here. The threefold exhortation itself and the content of each admonition suggest that what is being required is a complete change of heart. Israel is being told to seek the LORD after having violated the covenant; to seek righteousness after having turned to sin; to seek humility after having acted arrogantly.

Israel's degenerate behavior seems to have been in the past, since the people are now called "humble of the earth" and are described as those who "observe the Law." However, there is still an edge to this exhortation, a sting of uncertainty. The prophet cannot guarantee forgiveness and salvation. All he can say is "Perhaps" *('ûlay).* Perhaps they will be protected from the wrath of God.

The second part of the reading provides us with a very different picture. This section is an oracle of salvation, loving words of God that offer assurance and hope. Once again Israel is addressed, but this time there is a definite promise rather than a hint at a vague possibility. Here God promises there will be a remnant. A portion of the people will not only survive, they will faithfully conform to the dictates of the covenant. This remnant will be humble and lowly. It might be better to say it will have been humbled, perhaps sobered, by the suffering it had to undergo. Aware of their own dismal situation, these people have taken refuge in God. Since the name represented the essence of a person, the name of the LORD represented the essence of God. Therefore, to take refuge in that name is to take seek shelter in God.

The path of righteousness the remnant will follow will be the consequence of their deliverance, not the cause of it. There is no thought that the blessings they will enjoy are rewards for their fidelity. Rather, every good that comes to them is a gift from God. It is God who promises there will be a remnant; It is God who will shelter them; it is God who will make sure they are not disturbed. Salvation and prosperity come from the hand of God.

## Psalm 146:6-7, 8-9, 9-10

The responsorial psalm is a hymn of praise of the LORD *(Hallelujah* in Hebrew). Such hymns have a very definite pattern. The summons itself *(hallelu)* appears in a plural verb form, suggesting a communal setting, and contains an abbreviation of the divine name *(jah).* In this psalm the word is used as a refrain, a response to a series of statements that offer examples of God's almost indescribable graciousness.

Although covenant is never explicitly mentioned, various themes seem to point to it. The first verse mentions God's faithfulness *('ōmen),* one of the principal characteristics of covenant commitment. Then there is an allusion to God's deliverance of the people from the bondage of Egypt and to God's providential care of them during their sojourn in the wilderness. Throughout Israel's history God has been faithful. This is reason enough to praise the LORD.

God's graciousness to the vulnerable is next extolled (vv. 8-9). There are many situations in life that can force one to be bowed down, whether a physical disability, a mental or emotional affliction, an economic or social disadvantage. Whatever it might be, God raises up the needy, enables them to stand with pride, reestablishes them in security. Strangers or aliens lack certain legal rights, and since they are not living in their own nation, they may not be familiar with the rights they do have. Insensitive or unscrupulous people can very easily take advantage of them. These vulnerable strangers are precisely the kinds of people the God of Israel chooses. Israel itself is the prime example of this. It was when they were aliens in Egypt that God took them and made them God's own people. This is certainly reason to praise God.

In patriarchal societies only adult free men enjoy certain privileges. As part of the household, women and children are under the jurisdiction and care of such men. Women belong to the households of either their fathers, their brothers, or their sons. In this psalm response, "widows" probably refers to women who cannot return to their home of origin because they have married, but their husbands are now dead and they have no adult son to care for them. Such women are marginal in society and need some patron to care for them. Likewise, it is presumed that the orphans referred to here have no extended family within whose jurisdiction they might take refuge. These are the ones for whom God cares.

The final verse praises God as sovereign and eternal ruler in Jerusalem. All the other verses of the psalm testify to the glory of this God, who reigns forever from the very hill that is at the center of the lives of the people. This is not a God who is far off. Rather this God has entered into their history and into the very social fabric of their existence. Such a God deserves praise.

## 1 Corinthians 1:26-31

The focus of the teaching found in this section from Paul's letter to the Corinthians is the question of honor and shame. Paul reminds the Christians that, judged by the standards of society at that time, they are unimportant; they are really nobodies. They lack education and do not belong to the intellectual elite; they do not exercise political clout; they are not wellborn in the social sense. They have little if anything about which they can boast.

While there is evidence that even from the beginning some prominent people did join the church, there is a very good reason why Paul's evaluation of the makeup of the community of believers was probably an accurate one. At the heart of Jesus' teaching was the promise of a new age, a time of eschatological fulfillment when wrongs would be righted and society would be reshaped so all would gain access to the blessings life has to offer. Although his interpretation of this promise was radically different from the overriding view of the people of his day, Jesus inherited this religious teaching from ancient Israel. He saw himself as the fulfillment of messianic expectation. Promises such as these would attract people who were oppressed or felt themselves dispossessed of the things of the world. The prosperous and otherwise privileged would not be apt to look favorably at a promise to revamp the very social structures benefiting them. It is no wonder those who were needy flocked to Jesus and, after his death and resurrection, to those who preached his message of hope.

Besides this possible sociological explanation of the cultural makeup of the church, there is also a theological reason given. According to Paul God chooses the nobodies of the world in order to shame those who think they are somebodies. Those who lack honor in the eyes of the world are highly honored by being chosen by God, while those the world honors are shamed by being overlooked by God. Paul says that God acts in this way so no one can boast of her or his own accomplishments. Whoever boasts, should boast in God. In other words, when God does wondrous things through the foolish or the weak or the lowly, it is very clear to all that it is the power of God at work and not merely the abilities of the human beings.

Paul's argument next turns from ecclesiology to christology. He insists that Christ Jesus is the real wisdom of God (cf. 1 Cor 1:24), the depository of righteousness (cf. 2 Cor 5:21), the source of our sanctification (cf. 1 Cor 6:11), and the one responsible for our redemption (cf. 1 Cor 6:11). Every good thing we have, we have received because of Christ. It would seem it is not so bad being nobodies after all, because nobodies give witness to the glory of Christ Jesus. "Who ever boasts, should boast in the Lord."

## Matthew 5:1-12a

The preaching and miracles of Jesus attracted crowds of people, making it necessary for him to leave the area and take his disciples up a mountain. There he taught them. The instruction known as the Sermon on the Mount was directed to his close followers, not to the broader crowds. The first part of that sermon, the Beatitudes, constitutes the gospel reading for today. By form and content, the Beatitudes themselves are Wisdom teaching, not Christian law, as is sometimes claimed. Most, if not all, of the sentiments expressed are found somewhere in ancient Jewish teaching.

The beatitude, or macarism, is a literary form belonging to the Wisdom tradition. It takes its name from the Greek word *makários* (happy or blessed). It is a descriptive statement intended for teaching purposes. Like most Wisdom literary forms, it describes a life situation that draws a connection between a particular manner of behavior and the consequences that flow from such behavior. Though it is a simple description, it is meant to encourage the behavior if the consequences are satisfying and to discourage it if they are not. These beatitudes follow this pattern exactly: a group of people who act in a particular way are said to be happy; the blessings they will enjoy are stated.

It is important to remember that while the teachings of Jesus are all in some way directed toward the establishment of the reign of God, the type of behavior or values he advocates is frequently the opposite of those espoused by society at large. This fact offers us a way to understand the challenges set before us in the Beatitudes. Perhaps the way to interpret them is to look first at the blessings promised. We may see that the behavior Jesus is advocating is at odds with what society would say will guarantee the blessing we seek.

The first and third beatitudes are similar. They treat the notion of power, which is often determined by the extent of one's material possessions. Societies are usually ruled by those with power and means. The reign of God, however, will be in the hands of the powerless (the meek) and those who have no means with which to exert power (the poor). The second and fourth beatitudes promise alleviation of some form of inner turmoil. A strict reading of the theory of retribution insists that suffering is usually the consequence of sin or some kind of inappropriate behavior. According to this theory, those who grieve do so because of something they have brought on themselves, and those who hunger for justice need only live justly to enjoy it. On the contrary, these beatitudes suggest that those suffering are not only not responsible for their misfortune, but the situations in which they find themselves will be remedied for them.

The fifth, sixth, and seventh beatitudes treat aspects of religious piety. Mercy is the disposition God has for sinners (cf. Exod 34:6). Those who seek this attitude from God are exhorted to extend it to others. Already in Israel's religious tradition we read it is not ritual conformity but a simple yet open heart that gives one entrance to the presence of God (cf. Ps 24:4). Finally, peace and tranquil order have been God's desire for us from the beginning. It is sin that disrupted this order and destroyed the peace. Those who overcome evil with good in order to reestablish peace are doing God's work and will be known as God's children.

The last beatitude clearly underscores the reversal referred to above. Commitment to Jesus and to his cause are bound to bring insult and persecution. When this happens the disciples should rejoice, knowing that the world is persecuting them because they belong to a kingdom not of this world, a kingdom with values the reverse of those espoused by this world. It is clear that each and every beatitude invites us to turn our standards and our way of life upside down and inside out.

## Themes of the Day

Last Sunday we reflected on various aspects of the disciple as one who is called. This Sunday we see that the disciple is also one who learns. For the next six Sundays we see Jesus giving his disciples private lessons in the art of discipleship.

## The Learner

To follow Jesus does not mean merely that one travels with him from place to place. It means that one learns from him, that one follows his manner of life and his way of thinking. To follow Jesus means to follow his example in the way he respects himself and other people, in his use of the things of the natural world. It means that one listens to what he says and asks for an explanation when what he says is not understood. All of this requires that the disciple be a learner, one who can learn from the life of Jesus as well as from his teaching.

In order to be a good learner the disciple must have the requisite inner attitudes; the disciple must be humble and open and willing to be coached. This should not be hard, because as Paul reminds us, God calls those who are foolish and weak and lowly. It may be that God calls all to be disciples but only those with the inner attitude of the learner are willing to follow. It is very difficult for those who consider themselves powerful and of noble birth to place themselves in the position of follower, to consider themselves foolish or weak or lowly.

## The Lessons

The first lessons the disciples must learn are found in the Beatitudes. The same lessons are placed before us, the modern-day disciples. We must all look honestly into our minds and hearts to discover how we manage the goods of this world. Do we hoard them? Do we use them as leverage against others? In other words, how can we learn the lessons of poverty and meekness? Suffering is an integral part of life. How do we react to it? And do we suffer for the right reasons? Do we grieve because we are petty and feeling sorry for ourselves or because we long for a world of justice and peace? How can we learn the lessons that suffering has to teach?

As disciples our inner dispositions must be patterned after those of Jesus, the one we follow. As disciples we are taught to forgive those who have wronged us, whether those be family members, neighbors, partners at work, or members of other races, cultures, or nations. We are taught to be single-minded and not duplicitous in our dealings with others, whoever they may be. We are taught to work for peace rather than revenge. However, this peace cannot be bought at any price. It must be coupled with righteousness, and this may exact a price that is dear.

The setting of Jesus' teaching is so serene—a mountain apart, a teacher with his disciples gathered around him, simple statements coupled with glorious rewards. However, the reality of the lessons is in stark contrast with this tranquil scene. These Beatitudes, these blessings, call for profound inner transformation.

## The Program

The gospel outlines the kind of person the disciple is to become; the psalm sketches the program to which the learner is called. The disciples of Jesus are not merely his followers; they also continue the work he began. And the work that Jesus took upon himself is the work of God. First God, then Jesus, and then the disciple work to secure justice for the oppressed, gives food to the hungry, gives sight to the blind, protects strangers, sustains the fatherless and the widowed. In other words, in whatever circumstance of life we find ourselves, as disciples of Jesus we work to sustain the good that is in the world and to transform whatever needs transformation. We do this as parents, as teachers, as health-care personnel, as people in business or commerce or any kind of service of others. This period of Ordinary Time provides us with a moment to listen to the lessons Jesus would teach us.

## Fifth Sunday in Ordinary Time
### Isaiah 58:7-10

The opening words of the prophet ("Thus says the LORD") give divine legitimation to the injunctions that follow. The passage maps out the kind of behavior required if one is to enjoy the blessings promised through the covenant. What are listed are ethical mandates rather than religious practices. It is clear from this passage that communion with God is dependent on the fulfillment of social responsibility (cf. Matt 25:35-36). The blessing that follows such a life is frequently described as some form of light. Light can be a symbol of deliverance, of prosperity, of truth, of God's favor. It is associated with life and all the good things that come with it. Because its meaning here is not explicitly stated, the reference can include all the richness of the symbol.

The first set of mandates addresses some of the most basic human needs: food, shelter, and clothing. The original Hebrew version highlights the personal involvement required in meeting the needs of others. This involvement does not take place at a distance, through an agency, but face to face. Share (*pāras*) means "to break in two." There is no thought here of merely giving from one's surplus. Rather, both giver and recipient eat of the same loaf. Sheltering the homeless is also a very personal act. The Hebrew states that the poor who have been cast out are to be brought into one's own house. The naked are to be covered whenever they are encountered. Finally, those who hear the words of the prophet are told that they are not to hide themselves from the demands made on them by their kin (their own flesh). They must be open to any and all requests made of them.

The blessings that follow this kind of selfless living all suggest some form of deliverance. Those who care for others will be drawn from the darkness of night or fear or suffering of any kind into the dawn of hope or happiness; their wounds of mind or soul or spirit will be healed; their righteousness (vindication) will be known to all; and they will be under the protection of God. The "glory of the LORD" suggests the cloud that led the Israelites out of Egyptian bondage (Exod 13:21-22). Here that glory gathers them in (*'āsap*). Finally, their prayers and cries will be heard by God. If they are attentive to the needy in their midst, God will be attentive to them.

A second set of injunctions addresses still other social concerns. Oppression (*môtâ*) is really the weighty crossbar of a yoke. Here it could be a reference to economic burdens, political repression, or social abuse. False accusation and malicious speech are other evils that undermine the fabric of social life. Those who have been admitted into the embrace of the covenant are expected to care for the needs of their covenant sisters and brothers in both body and soul. If they are faithful to this manner of living, they will be brought into the light and will be richly blessed by God. The communitarian dimension of living is at the heart of this prophetic message.

## Psalm 112:4-5, 6-7, 8-9

There is a type of psalm that instructs the human community rather than praises God. To this end it is more descriptive than exhortatory. Although it contains many of the same theological themes and concerns as do the hymns, laments, and songs of thanksgiving, this type of psalm belongs to a classification known as the Wisdom psalms. The Wisdom teaching arises from the interaction of the experience of life and the religious tradition and is a collection of the priceless gems born of this interaction. It is from this theological category that today's responsorial psalm comes.

In this responsorial psalm the image of the righteous person is placed before us for our imitation. This image is grounded in the theology of retribution, the theory that claims the virtuous will be rewarded and the wicked will be punished. The righteous or upright (*yāshār*) are said to be gracious (*ḥannûn*), merciful (*raḥûm*), and righteous (*ṣaddîq*, v. 4). These are characteristics that belong to God. They manifest themselves in the way God relates to human covenant partners. By applying these divine characteristics to the righteous ones, the psalmist is implying that these people are righteous precisely because they mirror the nature of the God with whom they are in covenant. The theory of retribution maintains that it is because of these very traits that the righteous one will be blessed. The blessings mentioned include light in the midst of darkness; well-being; security; remembrance even after death; fearlessness; and the acclaim of others.

Although the theory of retribution promises reward for upright living, these blessings/rewards do not come without a price. The psalm itself suggests that a righteous person has been repudiated but that this repudiation has been challenged (vv. 6-7). This would be a very serious situation in a society that holds to a strict honor/shame code. Because of the vital role that community plays in the safety and prosperity of the psalmist, loss of status within that community certainly would be something to fear. However, the righteous one described in this psalm does not submit to such fear. This is not because he is so strong but because the power of God is. It sounds like this person is beset with other difficulties as well, difficulties that are not explicitly reported but that might cause him to fear. However, even in the face of such trouble the righteous one is filled with trust in the LORD.

## 1 Corinthians 2:1-5

In the epistle read last Sunday Paul reminded the Corinthian Christians of their lowly status in society. He did this not to insult them but to explain that their lowliness enabled the power and glory of God to shine forth unimpeded through them. In today's reading Paul continues his discussion of this theme but here applies it to himself and to his manner of ministry. He maintains that the fact that there is nothing extraordinary about him will not hamper the spread of the gospel. Quite the contrary, it will advance the manifestation of the power of God.

Greek orators of the day were renowned for their eloquence and their devotion to wisdom *(sophía)*. Paul insists this was not the approach he took in his proclamation of the gospel. In verse 1 some ancient manuscripts have "testimony" *(martýrion)*, others have "mystery" *(mystērion)*. In either version the meaning seems clear. Paul did not try to impress his hearers with his intelligence or his clever speech. He was more concerned that they be touched by the power of the gospel itself. From the outset he was committed to the crucified Jesus Christ, and this became the hallmark of his preaching.

Paul's commitment to the crucified Jesus was not merely an example of pious devotion. On the contrary, he took a tremendous risk in this regard. The proclamation of Christ crucified was the most scandalous feature of the Christian message for Jew and Greek alike, yet it was the heart of Paul's teaching, a theme that was always in the forefront of his message. The Jews expected a Messiah who would be victorious, not one who would be convicted of a felonious act and subsequently executed. The Greeks would be repelled by an unlettered peasant, especially one who appears to have been a failure. This is the paradox of the gospel: what appears to be failure is really victory; what seems foolish is consummate wisdom.

Paul's message was bold, but his ministerial approach was humble and unassuming. He decided upon this approach because he did not want his manner of delivery to get in the way of the dynamism of the gospel, for that dynamism was the power of the Spirit. He wanted the faith of the community to be grounded in God, not in the cleverness of some preacher.

## Matthew 5:13-16

The instructions given to the disciples in last Sunday's gospel continue in today's. Jesus employs two metaphors to characterize the essence of discipleship: salt and light. In each case the metaphor points to what the disciples do for others rather than what discipleship does for the disciples themselves. Each metaphor gives us a glimpse of some of the broader consequences of living in this world according to the principles of the reign of heaven.

The importance of salt cannot be questioned by anyone. It is not only essential for life itself, it is also valuable for preserving, seasoning, and purifying food, and for fertilizing. Because of its significance it was used in various sacrifices (cf. Lev 2:13) and as a means of sealing certain covenants (cf. Num 18:19). Some of the sages also considered salt as a symbol of wisdom (cf. Col 4:6). Although the primary value referred to in this passage is found in its taste, all its other properties are in the background of our understanding when salt is used as a metaphor. In a sense, salt loses its separate identity when it salts something else. Its value resides in the way it acts on another substance. This is what Jesus is alluding to when he says that salt is worthless if it loses its taste. It can no longer act on anything. This is an important characteristic to remember when we apply this metaphor to the disciples. Their worth is gauged according to the influence they have on one another.

The second metaphor is light. The disciples are told that they are the light of the world, a designation that characterized Isaiah's Servant of the LORD as well (cf. Isa 42:6; 49:6). This was an eschatological title, and so whatever the metaphor might mean in itself, it also marks the disciples as the fulfillment of that particular eschatological expectation. Two distinct images are used to exemplify the role played by light. These are a city on a mountain and a lamp on a stand in a house. The first calls to mind a countryside at night. There are no lights on the road to dissipate the darkness. Then on a hill in the distance one can see the lights of a city. The surrounding darkness only accentuates the light from the city, which serves as a beacon leading the traveler to a place of safety. The second image is a lamp intended to provide light in a house. The flame is uncovered and held high so its rays light up the entire room.

The apostolic meaning of the metaphor of light is further explained. True disciples are the light that shines forth in the darkness of ignorance or faithlessness. They enlighten others not by words but by their manner of living. It is this manner of living that declares to the world that the reign of God has indeed been established in their midst and that the age of fulfillment has dawned.

### Themes of the Day

The Sermon on the Mount continues to instruct us in the meaning of disciple-ship. Today we look again at the wisdom of this teaching. With the metaphors of light and salt Jesus reveals the intimate connection between what a disciple is and what a disciple does. Once again we reflect on the ordinariness of life per-meated with the extraordinariness of grace. Yet we see that true wisdom is found in that which is very ordinary, an apt reflection for a Sunday in Ordinary Time.

### Action Follows Being

We live in a world where appearances frequently matter more than they should. We are often overly concerned with how we look and with how im-pressive what we do appears to be. Contrary to this predominating tendency, Jesus teaches us that what we do flows from who and what we are. We can en-lighten the world with the message of the gospel because our lives have been transformed by that gospel, and now we ourselves are light for others. We can serve others in various ways only because we have been saved by God's grace, and now we are agents of that grace in the lives of others. Our own renewal be-comes the means through which God renews the world.

### The Weak Things of the World

This may sound grandiose, but it isn't. It is the truth about the way God works. Extraordinary things are accomplished through ordinary people. Jesus grew up as the son of a carpenter; some of the apostles were fishermen; Paul was a tentmaker; we are store clerk and teachers, bus drivers and doctors, bank tellers and engineers. Like Paul, we come to ministry in weakness and fear and much trembling. It is the Spirit and power of God that works the wonders, and God works them through mundane elements of life such as light and salt.

Again and again in these Sundays of Ordinary Time we see how God chooses the weak things of the world to confound the strong; the insignificant people to outstrip those who are celebrities. Unfortunately we do not always appreciate the significance of this in our own lives. Either we want to do spec-tacular things for God or we ignore the possibilities for good that common things can provide. If we could once really realize that our ordinary lives are waiting to break forth with the brilliance of God, with the essence of the di-vine, we would embrace that life with enthusiasm and gratitude.

### Works of Mercy

As children many of us learned the corporal and spiritual works of mercy. We learned that we can practice them in every walk of life. Today's readings remind us of this. These works can be as simple as sharing food with neighbors when they are suffering from illness or death in the family; opening our homes to sick or elderly relatives; giving directions for strangers when they seem to be in unfamiliar situations; taking time out to help a child accomplish a task. We can comfort and encourage people with cards and flowers; we can share the wisdom we have learned from life with those who have not yet trod the path we know so well. We may not be asked to perform extraordinary feats, but all disciples of Jesus are called upon to do the ordinary things of life in an extraordinary way.

## Sixth Sunday in Ordinary Time
### Sirach 15:15-20

The book of Sirach, from which the first reading of this Sunday is taken, is a collection of proverbial teachings. The legitimacy of its instruction is grounded in the theology of retribution, which maintains that wise or righteous living will result in happiness or blessing, and foolish or depraved living will meet with misfortune or punishment. The ancients believed that certain actions had within them the very seeds of their consequences. In other words, life itself had been fashioned at the beginning in such an ordered way as almost to guarantee the consequences of behavior. The proverb, the literary technique in which most of this teaching is found, is descriptive in form but admonitory in function. While it indicates how a particular situation in life may readily unfold, it does so in order to encourage conformity to the order that undergirds that situation.

The Wisdom tradition presumes a fundamental order in creation and life, but it does not maintain that human beings are predestined to conform to this order. On the contrary, its very nature as an admonition or warning shows that it presumes humans are free. Women and men can decide to live in conformity with the way life unfolds, and this is wisdom, or they can choose to disregard this order, and that is foolishness. Today's reading addresses human freedom and human choice.

The choices mentioned are extreme poles: fire and water, life and death (cf. Deut 30:15), good and evil. Each pair sets the limits in a particular sphere, but taken together they also include everything that exists between these poles. It is a way of expressing totality (e.g., night and day, from left to right, etc.). In other words, what is placed before us is destruction and salvation, those realities that are life-giving and those that are death-dealing, what is good and what is evil. It is for us to decide which path we will take.

Our attention is next directed toward God, who is described as wise, powerful, and all-seeing. At times human freedom appears to be a challenge to all three of these divine characteristics. When we are confronted with misfortune and human suffering, we frequently wonder why God made this particular world in which we live. Could there not have been a better plan? One that did not include adversity? But such a world would have no provisions for human choice. Or could it be that the workings of the world are now out of God's control, out of God's foresight? Cannot God step in and take control? But such a world would have no provisions for human choice. The apparent tension between order and choice is evidence of the scope of God's wisdom and power. Humans cannot even understand how these two realities can be held together, while God seems to have no trouble balancing them. God is not only in control, but God is aware of everything that occurs.

The reading refers to "fear of the Lord," the expression found in the Wisdom tradition that characterizes the fundamental attitude we should have toward God. It is rooted in the recognition of divine grandeur and power, and it presumes people's conformity to God's will. Those who fear the Lord are the faithful. The eyes of God look on them with pleasure, just as they look to God in fidelity. The reading concludes with a disclaimer. Although it is God's desire that all will live in conformity to the order established, God has predestined no one to sin. All have been given freedom of choice. It is up to us to use it wisely.

## Psalm 119:1-2, 4-5, 17-18, 33-34

In form, this responsorial psalm is both an instruction and a prayer. The opening verses (vv. 1-2) employ a macarism, or beatitude, to describe the rewards that attend righteous living. This is a teaching technique meant to encourage imitation. The remaining verses are addressed to God in some kind of petition. The focus of both the teaching and the prayer is adherence to the Law (*tōrāh*, a word that might best be translated "instruction"). In fact, each verse of the psalm response contains either the word "law" or a synonym of it. The language used throughout is typical of that found in the Wisdom psalms. That sapiential tradition is characterized by a clear delineation of two ways of living: the way of the righteous and the way of the wicked. This psalm response is only concerned with the way (*derek*, v. 1) of the blameless.

From the outset we can see that the way or path of blamelessness is adherence to the Law of the LORD. This is the gist of both the opening beatitude and the prayers that follow. These prayers are generally petitions for constancy in obedience. Although the psalmist identifies himself as a servant of the Law (v. 17), it is important to note that here the Law is not regarded as restrictive or oppressive. Rather, the psalmist asks to be shown the wonders of that Law (v. 18). Furthermore, the commitment he seeks is not merely external observance. He prays for discernment, in order to keep the Law with his whole heart (v. 34). It is clear the psalmist aspires to a life of holiness, one which is certainly lived in conformity with God's command (v. 4) but which is set on that path out of devotion and not out of fear of punishment.

## 1 Corinthians 2:6-10

The Jewish apocalyptic perspective is the context within which Paul develops his instruction on wisdom. That particular worldview maintained that the secrets of the future had been written down at the beginning of time and were preserved somewhere safe from the eyes of humankind. When the fullness of time would at last dawn, these secrets would be revealed *(apokalýptō)*. Time was thus divided into "this age" of waiting and "the age to come," when all things would be made known. This thinking is reflected here in Paul's references to a hidden wisdom, predetermined before the ages, and to the rulers of this age.

The Jewish apocalyptic worldview shared various features with Gnosticism, a way of thinking with which the Greek Corinthians would have been familiar. There were various forms of Gnosticism in the world at this time, but they were generally all a way of interpreting mystery religions, which were also current. The mystery cults promised their devotees salvation by initiating them into the dying and rising of gods associated with the seasons of the year. These initiates, frequently called *teleíoi*, were thus brought into the heavenly world where the mysteries of that world were revealed to them. The disclosure of these mysteries was itself believed to be redemptive. Gnosticism emphasized the privilege attached to such secret knowledge *(gnōsis)*. That this type of knowledge corresponds to Paul's reference to wisdom that is hidden and mysterious is obvious. Furthermore, Paul employs the same word *teleíoi* when referring to the Christians in Corinth as the "mature."

These similarities notwithstanding, Paul contrasts the wisdom of which he speaks with the wisdom of this age. The plan of God may have been hidden in the past, but it has been clearly revealed in the present, and it has been revealed to all. The secrets are no longer secret, and there are no privileged seers. Those who are mature are those who have entered into the dying and rising of Christ by accepting the wisdom of the gospel. However, everything hinges on the essence of the mystery that has been revealed. This mystery is the death and resurrection of Christ. Paul maintains that had the rulers of this world known that the glory of God resided in the man Jesus, they would not have crucified him. But of course, they should have known, because Jesus did not keep this secret.

Paul cites a verse from the prophet Isaiah (64:4) and then elaborates on it in order to underscore the difference between Gnosticism and the revelation of God. He insists that what inaugurates one into the new age is not some form of secret knowledge but love of God. Furthermore, it is not a mystery rite that confers wisdom but the Spirit of God, the Spirit that knows even the depths of God. Paul may have used Jewish apocalyptic thinking as the framework of his argument, but there is no doubt about the Christian interpretation he makes.

## Matthew 5:17-37

This Sunday's gospel reading is a continuation of Jesus' instruction of his disciples. Although his teaching is based in the common tradition of Israel found in the Law and the Prophets (the two major sections of the Bible), his interpretations seem to have been so unprecedented that some accused him of having rejected that tradition. Jesus insists that this accusation is false. Furthermore, while his interpretations do indeed provide a new perspective, they really offer the fuller meaning of the tradition.

The gravity of Jesus' words is signified by his introductory statement: Amen, I say to you. "Amen" stresses the truth and validity of his words. The phrase "I say to you" emphasizes the authority with which he speaks. The contrast Jesus sets up is not between himself and the Law but between his interpretation and that of the scribes and Pharisees, the interpreters of the Law for the people of that day. Jesus has criticized them for their insistence on the minutiae of the Law at the expense of the righteousness that is at its heart. Some people believed that God's will is to be found in fidelity to the markings of the text, the actual letters of the Law. They went so far as to insist that even a mistake made when copying a text was a violation. Jesus uses this very point of view to argue that he is not abolishing anything. He respects even the smallest part of the smallest letter, and he teaches others to do the same. He insists that everything within the tradition will stand until it has all been fulfilled. Since he has inaugurated the eschatological age of fulfillment, that time has now dawned.

Jesus uses the formula: You have heard it said. . . . But I say to you. His interpretation is really radical. He demands much more than mere external conformity. While the Law bans murder, Jesus forbids anger and even insult. Anger with a member of the community will make one liable to judgment. Calling someone "fool" or "idiot" *(raqa)* warrants an even harsher penalty, the fires of Gehenna (the Jewish equivalent to hell). We must remember the significance in this society of both one's name and of honor and shame. The name contained the very essence of the individual. To publicly call another an insulting name was to shame that person and to deprive that person of an honored place in society.

Harmony within the community introduces the need to be reconciled with other community members. It is important to note that the grievance is against a disciple who has come to perform an act of religious devotion. Jesus states that reconciliation is the responsibility of that disciple, and this reconciliation even supersedes the act of devotion. Social discord must be attended to before it gets out of hand.

Jesus returns to his interpretation of the Law. It prohibits adultery, while Jesus forbids lustful desire. Jesus uses standard Near Eastern exaggeration to underscore the need for self-discipline. It is better to mutilate oneself than to suffer total annihilation in Gehenna. Jesus continues his discussion of adultery with another solemn pronouncement. It is clear he is talking about contemporary marriage regulations, for this particular injunction is not found in the Ten Commandments, as were the previously discussed laws. The religious leaders allowed divorce, sometimes for very trivial reasons. Jesus insists that divorce was allowed only in the case of *porneía*. Although the reference is to some form of sexual sin, the text is not clear about the nature of that sin. Some commentators believe it refers to premarital or extramarital affairs. Several Catholic scholars suggest it refers to an unlawful incestuous union. Whatever this exception to the Law may be, Jesus' basic position on divorce is much more demanding than the common practice.

The final contrast regards oaths. They were generally taken when the word of the person was not reliable. In such a situation, a person who was reliable was called upon to stand for the trustworthiness of the one taking the oath. Jesus here forbids taking frivolous oaths and thereby implicating God in any way in doing so. One's word should be honest and straightforward, and when given it should have the force of an oath.

These four examples demonstrate the radical nature of Jesus' reinterpretation of the Law.

## Themes of the Day

Jesus continues to instruct the disciples in the mysteries of the kingdom of heaven. The readings for today focus our attention on the nature of true wisdom. It is this true wisdom that prompts us to choose the right course of action. It is true wisdom that directs us in our interpretation of the Law. It is true wisdom that opens for us a world we could never have imagined without it.

### True Wisdom

The longer we live, the more we realize that life opens for us a series of choices. With these choices we chart the path we will take. Circumstances might be thrust on us, but we can still make choices about how we will deal with them. Obedient people do what they are told; wise people choose what good they will do. To say we choose life over death or good over evil does not take into consideration the complexity of the situations within which we choose. In the first reading Sirach exhorts us to true wisdom; in the gospel Jesus gives us a demonstration of it. There we see that service of people is to be preferred to service to the Law. Jesus' insistence is not a repudiation of the Law, nor does it necessarily make life easier. In fact, it might make life more difficult. Nonetheless, true wisdom calls us to choose life and whatever enhances life.

## Fulfill the Law

If we are truly wise we will come to realize that what was acceptable and life-enhancing in one situation may not be appropriate in another. Life is fluid, and our thinking and acting must be flexible enough to adapt to it when necessary. This is what Jesus did, and it is what he taught his disciples to do. He did not abolish the Law; he brought it to fulfillment when he reinterpreted it to meet the needs of the people of his day. For the Law to be a wise law it must be grounded in the adaptability of wisdom, not in the inflexibility of legislation.

Legal formulations that grew out of one period in history may not adequately address the needs of another period. However, the values and aspiration out of which the Law emerged can still inspire us in our age, as long as we are faithful to both the values we have inherited and the world in which we live. In today's reading from the Sermon on the Mount, Jesus teaches his disciples and us to interpret the Law in view of these new experiences. When we engage in such reinterpretation, we must always ask ourselves this very important question: How will this enhance the lives of others?

## Eye Has Not Seen

True wisdom, which comes to us through the Spirit, will enrich us with insight into life in ways we never thought possible. We will realize where and how we fit into the vast and interrelated ecosystems of the universe, and we will be overawed with the majesty and intricacy of its workings. We will recognize that we are all bone of the same bone and flesh of the same flesh, and we will honor and care for the common humanity that binds us together. We will understand once and for all that the value of anything is determined by its ability to enrich life, and we will cherish every manifestation of that life. No longer will we view others as competitors but as companions on the same journey. No longer will we be tempted to hide behind the doors of our homes or our hearts lest we be called upon to engage in the unfolding of life. Instead, we will stand on the threshold of new life facing the horizon of undreamed of possibilities. True wisdom, which comes through the Spirit, will open these vistas for us if we but follow the example of Jesus, our teacher.

## *Seventh Sunday in Ordinary Time*

### Leviticus 19:1-2, 17-18

The command to love as found in the book of Leviticus is quite familiar to most Christians because of its appearance in the gospels. However, if we were only to understand it in contrast to Christian love, we would risk misunderstanding its original meaning. This command is the second of a two-part passage that serves as the first reading for this Sunday. The first part is a prior command, an injunction to be holy as God is holy. It is from this disposition of divine holiness that the contrast of love and hate must be understood.

The holiness of God is the ground of all religious living. God is holy, and the people with whom God is in covenant are required to be holy as well. But what does this mean? Holiness is really the quintessential characteristic of God. It is much broader in scope than mere goodness. It might best be understood as "godness," as divine majesty. God's holiness is made visible as divine glory, which is awe-inspiring. Everything else is holy only as it stands in relationship to God. Even this explanation leaves us with questions. The meaning of divine holiness is really beyond our grasp, yet we are required to model our lives, both individually and communally, after it. The laws we find in the traditions of Israel, particularly those referred to as the Holiness Code (Leviticus 17–26), are directives that outline for us the way we are to accomplish this. We should not think our own holiness is the consequence of obedience to these laws. Rather, holiness is an all-inclusive way of life, and our conformity to the directives is our way of entering into the life of holiness.

This reading reveals that the life of holiness, which is patterned after the holiness of God, is a life lived in community. It requires integrity, honesty, and faithfulness to one another. In order to be holy as God is holy we must refrain from nursing hatred in our hearts; if we see someone doing wrong we are required to rebuke them or we will share their guilt; we are forbidden to entertain any form of vengeance; and we are told to love others as we love ourselves—their well-being must be as important to us as our own. These are very demanding directives, but they give us a glimpse of what the holiness of God is like. The language used suggests that this kind of behavior is required within the covenant community. It says nothing about relationships outside that community. The "brother" (*'āḥ;* the Hebrew does not include sister) is either a blood relative or a countryman. The two words used for neighbor (*'āmît* and *rēʻa*) mean "close companion." At issue here are the responsibilities that exist among and between those bound together in covenant with God, not the possible exclusiveness of that community.

As stated above, everything is holy only as it stands in relationship to God. The directives from the Holiness Code show us ways of standing in that relationship. It should be noted that these directives are communal in nature. In other words, our likeness to God is determined by the way we relate to others. The reading ends with the solemn divine self-proclamation: I am the LORD! This is the way I want it. This is the way it is to be.

## Psalm 103:1-2, 3-4, 8, 10, 12-13

The responsorial psalm begins with a summons to bless the LORD. Although the word "bless" is often used as a benediction, a prayer for God's presence, or grace for the future, in this case it is a call to praise or to thank God for blessings already received. The call to "bless the LORD" is normally addressed to someone other than the psalmist. Here it is a self-address (vv. 1-2). The Hebrew word translated "soul" (*nepesh*) comes from the word for breath. It yields over twenty meanings, chief among which are life-breath (or soul), life, living person. The reference here is probably to that center within the person from which all life forces flow. This is not merely a spiritual or immaterial reality; it encompasses every aspect of the person. This understanding is corroborated by the phrase "all my being."

In the biblical world a person's name was an expression of that person's unique identity. In many ways names held more significance for people then than they do today. One could exercise power over another simply by somehow controlling the name of that person. There were times during Israel's history when, in their attempt to show great reverence for God, the people paid homage to God's name rather than directly to God (cf. Deut 12:11, 21; 14:23f.; 16:2, 6, 11). Even when they did this they were very careful to avoid using the divine name itself. Today we show the same respect when we merely use the consonants YHWH or substitute LORD (small upper case letters) rather than using the divine name itself.

The reason for praising or thanking God, the benefits to which the psalmist refers, is God's willingness to pardon, to heal, and to redeem or save. These are all acts that flow from God's lovingkindness (*ḥesed*) and compassion (*raḥămîm*, vv. 3-4). These two attributes are not only closely associated with covenantal commitment, but, as is seen in exodus tradition, are integral aspects of God's own name and identity (v. 8; cf. Exod 34:6). It is out of this mercy that God acts, not requiring the harsh punishment the sins of the people would warrant.

The extent of God's mercy is further sketched by means of the figure of speech "east to west," which denotes immeasurable distance. Human eyes can only envision a fraction of the stretch that lies between the horizons. What is perceived is only infinitesimal; the reality is beyond comprehension. Using this figure of speech, the psalmist is claiming the same limitlessness for the compassion of God. Out of covenant love, God puts our transgression so far from us that the distance cannot even be imagined. This is reason to praise and bless the LORD.

Finally, the psalmist uses a familial image to characterize God's compassion. Although the reference is to the compassion of a father for his children, the word itself comes from the word for womb *(reḥem)*. Here "compassion" is much more intimate than empathy felt for those who suffer. It is womb-love. In other words, the love God has for us is the love a mother has for the children of her womb. This explains God's commitment to us, and it is certainly reason to bless the LORD.

## 1 Corinthians 3:16-23

Today's reading from the first letter to the Corinthians is made up of three themes. Paul first describes the community as the temple of God. He then contrasts the wisdom of the world with the wisdom of God. The reading ends with a discussion of boasting.

The method of argument with which Paul introduces his instruction resembles the Greek rhetorical style of diatribe. In it he addresses his audience, referring to assumptions they share but do not seem to be living out. These assumptions have to do with the holiness of the temple of God. In Paul's thinking the temple is no longer a material building. It is, rather, the collection of people who gather in God's name. Paul declares that the Corinthians are this temple. This notion was not original with Paul, for it is found in the literature of the Qumran community as well. There we find the members referred to as a "holy house" *(bêt qôdeš,* cf. 1 QS 5:5; 8:4). However, the general community was only the "holy house," while the priestly members were considered the "holy of holies," the inner sanctum where the presence of God resides. The word Paul uses for temple *(naós)* really refers to the sanctuary rather than to the broader temple precincts. Thus, in his thinking the entire assembly is the "holy of holies." Just as the presence of God made the Temple in Jerusalem holy, so it is the presence of the Spirit of God that makes this new temple holy, and the Spirit dwells in all of the members.

Those who defiled the Temple in Jerusalem were liable to death. Outside the inner court of the Temple a sign was posted that excluded Gentiles from entering and warned of severe consequences for violation of this prohibition. Why such a harsh penalty? Because the Temple of God is holy, and only those people and things that have been set aside as holy can enter it. With this regulation in mind, Paul plays with the meaning of the Greek word *phtheirō*, which can be translated both "to corrupt" and "to destroy." Those who corrupt or defile God's Temple will be destroyed.

Paul returns to an earlier discussion about the wisdom of this age or of this world (cf. 1 Cor 2:6-10, Sixth Sunday). The standards the world uses to determine wisdom are frequently diametrically opposed to the standards of God. This is exemplified in Jesus. Therefore those who wish to be wise with the wisdom of God will have to choose a path that will be judged foolish by the standards of the world. Once again Paul appeals to the Scriptures. The first passage is from the book of Job (5:13); the second comes from the Psalms (94:11). Each in its own way challenges the merit of human insight. As necessary and valuable as that may be, it is nothing when compared with God's knowledge.

Although the third theme appears distinct from the other two, it can be connected to both. The boasting of which it speaks refers to the false pride the Corinthians took in identifying with various religious leaders (cf. 1 Cor 1:10-13, Third Sunday). Such boasting is evidence of the wisdom of the world, a wisdom that must be overturned. It is also at the heart of the conflict that threatens the unity of the Corinthian community. It undermines the holiness of the Temple of God and could even lead to its ultimate corruption. The Corinthians are reminded that they do not belong to their heroes. They belong to Christ, and Christ belongs to God. It is in this wisdom that they must live.

## Matthew 5:38-48

The contrast between Jesus' interpretation of the religious tradition and the one current at the time is continued in this Sunday's gospel reading. The two injunctions treated in today's passage address the way the disciples are to interact with people with whom they share a strained relationship. The first deals with retaliation for an evil perpetrated against them; the second discusses love of enemy.

The policy "an eye for an eye and a tooth for a tooth," known as *lex talionis*, was found as early as the eighteenth century B.C.E. in the code of the Babylonian ruler Hammurabi. It was really a moral advance over the common custom of blood vengeance, which would exact a price that far exceeded the wrong done. Jesus says that even this more humane form of justice should not be practiced by his followers. In fact, he instructs his disciples to offer no resistance at all when someone tries to take advantage of them, and, as was the case in earlier teaching (cf. Matt 5:17-37; Sixth Sunday), he employs Near Eastern exaggeration to make his point. He gives three examples to illustrate what he means.

The disciples are told that if someone insults them, striking them on the right cheek with the back of the hand, they should allow themselves to be injured with the full force of the palm of the hand on the left cheek. There is more in this example than merely striking. One strikes a subordinate with the back of the hand but an equal with one's palm. Jesus is telling his disciples they should not retaliate when insulted but should offer nonviolent resistance in such a situation. The disciples are further told that if the court requires that they hand over their clothing in order to pay a debt, they should be willing to relinquish even the cloak they might use at night as a blanket. Finally, if a soldier of the occupying forces compels them to carry his gear for a mile (as the Romans often did), they should be willing to carry it twice that distance. The point of these three examples can be summarized in Jesus' final admonition: Give to whoever asks. In fact, give more than is asked. Disarm them with your willingness to go beyond what is required. This will shame them and you will gain honor in their sight.

The second contrast treats the matter of love, the love of volition *(agápē)* and not that of passion *(érōs)* or friendship *(philía)*. Although Leviticus exhorts the Israelites to "love your neighbor" (19:18), nowhere are they told to hate their enemy. However, such hatred seems to have been inferred from some of the other ethnocentric statutes. Like most people even today, Israel seems to have cared little for the well-being of its adversaries. Jesus reinterprets this law of love in a most radical manner, perhaps the most radical of all. He insists that the disciples' love must be patterned after God's love, which is given unquestioningly to the just and the unjust alike. Those who would be known as children of God must carry the family resemblance. They are expected to love as God does. If they only love those who love them but harm those who harm them, they are merely fulfilling the admonition "an eye for an eye and a tooth for a tooth."

The final exhortation succinctly sets the standard for life in the kingdom of heaven. "Be perfect as your heavenly Father is perfect!" "Perfect" *(téleios)* means complete, undivided, grown to full stature. God certainly is complete and undivided, the essence of righteousness and splendor. This is the goal toward which the disciples must strive. It is this standard that makes the interpretation of Jesus so radical.

## Themes of the Day

Jesus' instruction on the reinterpretation of the Law, begun last Sunday, continues today. Here too we realize that the new insights we gain come to us through the inspiration of the Spirit of God, who dwells within us.

### An Eye for an Eye

At times it seems we have rewritten the Golden Rule to say, do unto others before they can do unto you! In saying this we are not encouraging one another to do good but to be defensive. In fact, we may be demanding a kind of justice that is really revenge. This is not to deny the fact that some people live in circumstances that are very threatening, circumstances against which they must protect themselves. However, this particular reading of the rule tends to develop attitudes of suspicion and aggression.

While a second rule, "an eye for an eye, and a tooth for a tooth," sets limits to the reparations we can demand, Jesus radically reinterprets this law of justice. He tells us to go the extra mile, turn the other cheek, outdo ourselves in generosity, rise above the fray. He is not suggesting that we allow ourselves to be abused but that we not perpetuate the antagonism out of which mistreatment arose. He is not advocating passivity, but he is saying we should not retaliate in kind. Jesus is describing what we today would call "active non-resistance." This is the attitude taught by Gandhi and Martin Luther King, Jr. They believed in the basic goodness of all human beings, even those who wrong us. They further believed that the victim's willingness to suffer rather than retaliate would wear down the aggression of the oppressor. This is precisely what Jesus teaches. Right the wrongs by overcoming evil with good, not with revenge.

## Love Your Neighbor

We are familiar with the answer to the question: Who is my neighbor? We usually interpret it to mean those we do not particularly like, and we all know people we don't particularly like. It is important to love them, to be kind to them, to help them when they are in need. But these are not the people Jesus is talking about in today's reading. He tells us that the neighbors we are to love are those people who do not particularly like us. We are to love those who deliberately exclude us from their social circles, who talk about us behind our backs. We are to love those who make us feel we are not good enough for them, those who resent us for our accomplishments. We are to love those who exploit us or do us harm.

Once again, Jesus is not suggesting we allow ourselves to be abused, but he is saying we should not retaliate in kind. The way to turn enemies into neighbors is through kindness—go the extra mile, turn the other cheek, outdo yourself in generosity, rise above the fray. Once again we see that Jesus' interpretation of the Law is more demanding than we might have thought. However, there is ample evidence around us of the devastating effects of life lived according to the rule "an eye for an eye." We see it in our own lives and we see it on the international scene. The only way we will have peace will be through love of neighbor.

## The Work of the Spirit

One might be tempted to think this kind of love is dangerous because it counsels us to take down our defenses. It would probably be considered foolish by the standards of the world. But Jesus has overturned the standards of the world, and he claims that this kind of love is true wisdom. Paul understood this. He recognized that it is the wisdom of the world that is foolish, not this kind of love. He was convinced we can overcome our prejudices, we can get beyond our antagonisms, we can turn enemies into neighbors, because we possess the power of the Spirit of God, who dwells within us. As difficult as this kind of love might be, we can decide in its favor.

## Eighth Sunday in Ordinary Time
### Isaiah 49:14-15

Today's first reading, though it consists of two short verses, is an extraordinary exchange between the nation of Israel and God. The first verse is a lament; the second is a word of comfort. The metaphors employed are striking, perhaps even startling. Most likely, this was the effect the prophet intended by employing them.

Although Zion is the name of the mount in Jerusalem upon which the Temple was built, in poetic passages it frequently referred to the entire nation. That is the sense in which it is used here. Furthermore, as was the custom in most ancient societies, cities and nations were characterized as female. Zion identifies the God of Israel by name (YHWH) and also admits that this God is her lord, her master (*'ādôn*). She cries out that she has been forsaken (*'āzab*), forgotten (*shākah*). The first verb presumes there was some kind of relationship in the past, but despite this, Zion has been abandoned; the second verb suggests disregard on God's part. The lament is quite terse, a piercing cry from the midst of desolation. The cause of such desolation is not given; however, its grounding in reality is challenged by God's response.

Though not explicitly stated in the text, it is God who speaks. The metaphor the prophet uses to characterize the love God has for this people is extraordinary. We must remember that, like all societies of the time, ancient Israel was a patriarchal (the father was the head) society distinguished by androcentric (male centered) values. The characterization of the people as female and God as male (lord) is evidence of this. In the face of all this, the metaphor employed by the prophet is the relationship between a mother and the nursing child (*'ûl*) of her womb. Such a metaphor could have been considered presumptuous had it not been placed by the prophet into the mouth of God.

The word for tenderness or compassion (*rahămîm*) comes from the word for womb (*rehem*). The imagery is striking for two reasons. First, it exemplifies the intimacy of the bond that unites God and the People of God. Not only is the child at the mother's breast, suggesting that Zion finds its sustenance in God, but this is a child who has come forth from the mother's body, further suggesting that Zion's origin was from God. For some, the most startling feature of this metaphor is its feminine nature. The love God has for the people is characterized as the love of a woman for the child of her womb, an intimacy peculiar to a woman.

The words of God continue. It is improbable, though possible, that a woman would forget the child of her flesh. Still, God will never forget this people. Therefore, though Zion may feel abandoned and forgotten it is only a feeling; it is not a fact. God's attachment to the people will never be severed.

## Psalm 62:2-3, 6-7, 8-9

The responsorial psalm is a classic expression of trust in God. Written in third-person description, it is more a testimony to the psalmist's devotion than a prayer directed to God. In fact, in the closing verse (v. 9) the psalmist addresses the community, exhorting them to a comparable trust in God.

The first two stanzas of this response (vv. 2-3, 6-7) are almost identical. They speak of the profound calm the psalmist has found in God. There is a suggestion that God was not the first refuge the psalmist sought. However, God is the only true refuge the psalmist found. The Hebrew word that is translated "soul" *(nepesh)* really refers to the living and life-giving dimension of the entire person. In other words, it implies that there is calm in the deepest part of the psalmist's being, a trusting calm that will not be disrupted.

God is described as a rock and a stronghold, a place of salvation. The first two metaphors suggest the kind of stability and defense one finds in a military installation; the third implies rescue from danger. All these images suggest the extreme peril that faced the psalmist and the extraordinary deliverance that God provided. It appears that the psalmist was caught in the throes of some kind of threat, that the psalmist sought safety but failed to find it and eventually came to see that safety could be found only in God. The peace the psalmist now experiences is undisturbed because it is rooted in the stability that God, who is rock and stronghold, provides. The psalmist not only rests in this peace now but also trusts that it will endure (v. 6).

A very interesting chiastic structure reinforces the psalmist's sentiments of confidence (v. 8):

    (a) God      (b) my safety and glory
               (b¹) my rock, refuge    (a¹) God

The final testimony of confidence is followed by an exhortation directed toward others. To this point the psalm response has acclaimed the salvation God has granted the psalmist. This testimony is now used to encourage others to turn to God in like manner. They are told to trust in God and to pour out their hearts, to hold nothing back in their devotion to God. If God has saved the psalmist, surely God will save others as well.

## 1 Corinthians 4:1-5

In last Sunday's reading from the letter to the Corinthians Paul once again condemned the Christians for pitting person against person, group against group. He insisted that men such as himself, Apollos, and Cephas were servants of Christ and stewards of God's mysteries, not party leaders who rallied followers around them and their religious platforms. Paul continues this argument today.

The word for "servant" *(hypērétēs)* originally referred to the "under-rowers," those who worked the oars in the bowels of the ship. It eventually came to denote the secondary servants of those in official positions. Here it identifies as "servants of Christ" those who assist in the work of Christ, which is the proclamation of the gospel. The "steward" *(oikonómos)* was the one responsible for the equitable distribution of the goods of the household. Once again the designation denotes someone who works under the jurisdiction of another. In this context the ministers are "stewards of the mysteries of God." Paul has already identified the death and resurrection of Christ as the mystery of God (cf. 1 Cor 2:1-5, Fifth Sunday). On this Sunday he is probably alluding to all the blessings that flow from that primary mystery.

The remainder of the reading addresses the question of ministerial accountability and judgment. It stands to reason that anyone responsible for the goods of the household of another must be trustworthy. Paul claims that as such a steward he is indeed trustworthy. He has committed himself wholeheartedly to the proclamation of the gospel, to the distribution of the mysteries of God, and he stands by this claim regardless of what others might think. This could sound like Paul is exempting himself from judgment. This is hardly the case, for he acknowledges that he is obliged to give an account of his stewardship: he insists it is the Lord who will be his judge. Such judgment is bound to be much more demanding that mere human judgment. Human beings can be wrong, but the Lord knows the motives of the heart.

There is an eschatological dimension to the judgment of which Paul speaks. It will take place at the appointed time, the *kairós,* or decisive moment of history, when the Lord comes. This last reference is probably to the *parousía,* the coming of Christ at the end of time. This will be the time of ultimate revelation. What is now hidden will then be disclosed. Even our secret motive will be laid bare. Ministerial commitment is not an opportunity for self-aggrandizement. Rather, it requires extraordinary self-emptying.

## Matthew 6:24-34

The gospel reading for this Sunday opens with a statement about absolute loyalty. Jesus insists that one cannot serve two masters. Of all of the things that could rival our commitment to God, he singles out wealth. The Greek word used *(mamōnás)* appears in the New Testament only on the lips of Jesus (cf. Luke 16:9-13) and is always used to contrast earthy goods with heavenly realities. Jesus does not appear to be opposed to possessions in themselves but to inordinate attachment to their materialistic character. This point becomes clear in the admonition that follows.

Jesus is not naive about the human need for food and clothing and shelter and material support. Nor does he advocate passivity or laziness in the face of hard work. He is talking about setting one's priorities straight; appreciating humankind's place in the natural world; trusting in the goodness and providence of God. He uses two examples from nature to demonstrate what he means. Such an instructional technique is used by Wisdom teachers universally. They choose a particular characteristic from the broader natural world to illustrate some feature in human life. The two objects may be totally different in all other ways, but they hold this specific feature in common.

First Jesus compares the human need for food with that of the birds. They follow their nature, which does not include the kind of sowing and reaping and gathering required of humans. And in the scheme of things, God provides for them. The challenge for human beings is to trust that God will provide for them as they live according to their nature, a nature governed by laws over which they have little control. Jesus then compares the human need for clothing with the raiment of the ephemeral field flowers. They too follow their nature, which clothes them in apparel more beautiful than the royal splendor of Solomon. The challenge for human beings is the same, to trust that God will provide for them as they live according to the nature God has fashioned for them. Using the rabbinic argument "from the lesser to the greater," he then puts his disciples' faith to the test. If through their respective natures God provides for these simple creatures, how much more will God provide for you through your nature.

The point of this Wisdom teaching is confidence in God. As stated earlier, Jesus is obviously not suggesting passivity or laziness. Such attitudes are really contrary to the human drive to work for food and clothing and shelter. But human beings must trust that God will provide opportunities for them to procure what they need. The images Jesus employs suggest this teaching applies to both men and women. Sowing and reaping and harvesting are occupations normally associated with men, while spinning is generally considered a woman's work. Both women and men are prone to become anxious about having their needs met; both women and men need to be reminded they are precious in God's eyes and they, even as they toil, must learn to trust in God's providence.

## Themes of the Day

During these Sundays of Ordinary Time we have been with the disciples in the presence of Jesus, listening to his instructions about discipleship. Today we are given yet another lesson in the meaning of discipleship.

## Servants and Stewards

Disciples work under the jurisdiction and direction of the master. They are not independent agents; it is God's kingdom, and they will always be accountable to God. The metaphors used to describe the disciple might suggest the position is one of inferiority, but given the context within which they are used here, what they describe is reason to boast. The disciple is one who assists in the proclamation of the gospel. The disciple is also in charge of the distribution of the goods of God's household. These roles are both essential for the upbuilding of the reign of God. They both require individuals who are trustworthy and who are committed to the interests of the master.

What can be more noble than the upbuilding of the reign of God? What could deserve our commitment more than the proclamation of the gospel? What greater privilege could be ours than acting as agents of the blessings of God? Disciples are called to just such privileged roles. And where are these disciples to be found? They spend their lives in classrooms and in factories, in offices and in hospitals. They serve in families and in businesses, in restaurants and in shopping malls, in banks and in grocery stores. They answer telephones, they protect us from harm, they build our roads, they repair our plumbing. Disciples upbuild the reign of God in whichever form of life or occupation they have chosen.

## Do Not Worry

Although we embark on a life of service with great enthusiasm and genuine commitment, it does not take long before the enormity of the task becomes apparent, and we might begin to doubt ourselves or doubt the call itself. With such a scenario in mind Jesus exhorts us to trust in God. Since upbuilding the reign is God's plan in the first place, and since God knew our strengths and weaknesses and called us nonetheless, we should have confidence that God will see us through the task that has been given us. All is in the hands of God; for our part, we have only to trust.

Of course this sounds much easier that it really is. Our own limitations and sinfulness often get in the way of our ministry. Then there are forces in society that seem bent on undermining our every effort at discipleship. In addition to this, the people to whom we commit ourselves can be ungrateful or actually want no part at all of us or of our service. At other times the obstacles seem to come from the Church, its structures, and its personnel. In the midst of such darkness, we hear the voice of Jesus gently but firmly saying: Do not worry! Trust! God cares for the birds and the grass, surely God will care for you.

## The God We Trust

All the metaphors found in today's readings describe the trustworthiness of God. God is characterized as a rock, a stronghold, a refuge, and our salvation. Each bespeaks reliability. The responsorial psalm ends with an admonition to trust in God. The gospel reading does not have explicit metaphors for God other than Father, but God is depicted as sowing and reaping crops and spinning cloth, roles stereotypically associated with men and women respectively. In these ways God feeds and clothes the birds. We are so dear to God, surely we will be cared for at least as well as God cares for these birds.

Perhaps the image that most instills trust in us is that of the woman who nurses the child to whom she has just given birth. We are so used to masculine metaphors that many of us have come to think of God as male and are shocked when female imagery is used. But what better metaphor to speak of God's total commitment to our needs than a mother suckling the child of her womb? There is an intimacy here that can be compared with nothing else; there is a complete giving of oneself. This is the kind of bond with which we are attached to God. This bond is the basis of our trust.

## Ninth Sunday in Ordinary Time

### Deuteronomy 11:18, 26-28

In the first reading for this Sunday, Moses acts as the leader of the people. He has delivered God's word to them and has instructed them in ways of faithfully following God's will. He now directs them to commit themselves totally (heart and soul) to God. Elements in this short passage resemble a covenant renewal ceremony. First, there is a veiled reference to entering into covenant in the first place. In such a pact the parties pledge themselves to each other. Here mention is made of turning away from that commitment to follow the way of another deity (v. 28). The mention of rewards and punishments (blessings and curses) for obedience or disobedience to the Law (*miṣwâ*) is another feature of covenant making (cf. Deuteronomy 28). Each covenant enactment included witnesses who corroborated the pledging. This passage alludes to no such witnesses, but there is a visible sign, an external sign of the words of the pledge, that will mark the commitment and will be observed by all. Finally, the thrice-repeated phrase "this day" (vv. 26-28) suggests a ceremonial commitment or recommitment.

The blessings promised for fidelity to the Law generally included numerous progeny and a good name; abundant crops and a multitude of flocks; peace and security from enemies. Curses often included childlessness and premature death, family illness and diseased flocks, pestilence and drought, defeat by another nation and devastation of the land. Whenever the covenant was renewed, the people renegotiated the terms of their commitment as well as the rewards and punishments that followed in the train of their behavior. This reading hints at such a process.

Moses directs that the words he has previously delivered be somehow bound on their wrists and displayed as a pendant on their foreheads. This custom is associated with covenant making (cf. Deut 6:8). Even today specific passages from Scripture are placed in small leather cubes worn by men during morning services of days others than the sabbath and holy days. They are strapped to their left arm and to their foreheads. This both identifies them as observant members of the covenant community and reminds them of their responsibility to commit themselves mind and heart to the covenant and to live out this commitment.

## Psalm 31:2-3, 3-4, 17, 25

The theme of trust permeates this psalm response. It opens with a testimony to the psalmist's conviction that there is refuge in God. The metaphor suggests that the psalmist (identified as a male servant, v. 17) is fleeing some kind of peril and turns to God as a sanctuary in this flight. A second metaphor (rock) reinforces this image of divine protection.

The covenant relationship between God and the psalmist is apparent in several places. First, the appeal is to God's justice or righteousness *(ṣᵉdāqâ)*, a characteristic of the covenant. This appeal also suggests the innocence of the psalmist. He would hardly beg to be rescued by God's justice if he were in any way guilty. Evidence of the relationship can also be seen in the way the psalmist identifies both God and himself: I am your servant (v. 17). Finally, the psalmist appeals to God's lovingkindness *(ḥesed)*, a technical term describing covenant loyalty. It is clear this relationship is the reason for his confidence; it is why he flees to God.

The plea of the psalmist is expressed in four ways: protect me; save me from shame; rescue me; hear me. Although the opening statement about taking refuge in God is often associated with seeking asylum at the shrine or in the Temple, there are no explicit cultic references in the passage. The imagery used here suggests the focus is on the safety God will afford the psalmist and not on the specific location where this will take place. The fact that the righteousness rather than the mercy of God is called upon suggests the petitioner is an innocent sufferer.

Complete confidence in God does not prevent the psalmist from pleading with God. His first concern is being saved from shame (v. 2). The shame of which he speaks is not an inner attitude or state of mind. It refers to public disgrace. In many Eastern societies it is referred to even today as "losing face." It is the opposite of possessing honor, an attribute more important than riches. A man without honor is an outcast in society, and for many people death is preferred to such disgrace. The psalm does not clearly explain what might be the cause of the psalmist's loss of honor. In a society that believed suffering was the consequence of wickedness, it could have been almost any kind of misfortune. Honor was a fundamental value, and so to be shamed or to lose one's reputation could actually be life-threatening.

The psalmist prays that God's face might shine upon him. Since the face identifies the person and reflects the attitudes and sentiments of that person, seeing the face of God would be a kind of divine manifestation. The psalmist is probably not asking for this kind of revelation but rather for the light that comes from God's face. In other words, he is asking for God's good pleasure. His last words are an exhortation to others to trust in God as he has. To the end, his confidence will not be swallowed up by any disgrace he might have to endure.

## Romans 3:21-25, 28

The reading from the letter to the Romans introduces three of the principal theological themes treated by Paul as well as the relationship that exists between them. Contrary to what some scholars have contended, Paul does not establish an antithesis between righteousness and the Law. Instead, he maintains that one does not flow from the other; adherence to the Law does not produce righteousness. Rather, it is faith that yields righteousness.

The passage clearly states that righteousness is revealed, not gained. This is the heart of Paul's teaching. It is clear from the text that righteousness is of God, which can mean that it belongs to God or that it issues from God. Whichever the case, its origin is in God. The term itself is borrowed from the law courts and implies that one is declared righteous. But on what grounds? Paul insists it is not on the grounds of conformity to the Law through works of the Law but through faith in Jesus Christ. Continuing the law-court image, he further claims that the Law and the Prophets, a phrase that refers to the Scriptures of Israel, testify to the truth of this. In this case he does not cite specific passages, but the language suggests the theme of covenant. The Hebrew term *ṣedeq* (rightness), a characteristic of the covenant, is frequently linked with the deliverance of the people. Both deliverance and covenant were freely given by God to the Israelites. This cluster of theological themes underscores the point Paul is making, namely, that all is a gift from God.

Paul allows for no distinction. All have sinned; all fall short of the glory of God. For this reason all are in need of redemption *(apolýtrōsis)*. The word comes from the verb meaning "to pay ransom for" or "to buy back." It and the verb for "justified" are passive in meaning. Redemption and justification are received, not earned, and they are received precisely when one is a sinner. This justification is given gratuitously, freely, without cause. By its very name, grace *(cháris)* is an undeserved gift.

Paul turns again to his Jewish roots. On the top of the ark of the covenant was a plate of gold called the "mercy seat" *(kappōret* in Hebrew, *hilastērion* in Greek). On the Day of Atonement the high priest would sprinkle this mercy seat with the blood of a sacrificed bull. Paul is referring to this ritual and to the theology it signifies when he identifies Jesus as the *hilastērion.* There are two ways of understanding this ritual. It can be seen as an act of propitiation, an appeasing of the wrath of God, or as an act of expiation, the covering over of sin. There is no reason to choose one understanding over the other. What is important to remember is that in either case it is God who effects the atonement through the blood of Christ.

Paul does not actually dismiss the importance of works of the Law. He knows that obedience is very important. He himself insists on a way of living that conforms to certain Christian principles. He maintains that no way of life can earn righteousness. It is given to us by God. What is required of us is faith, a radical openness to receive what God wishes to give. This openness demands an acknowledgment of need, and it is often very difficult for human beings to admit to such fundamental insufficiency.

## Matthew 7:21-27

Jesus concludes his instructions to his disciples by insisting that their service must be grounded in solid commitment to him. The performance of extraordinary feats is not enough. There must also be conformity to the will of God as interpreted by Jesus himself. The reading for this Sunday contains a definite eschatological tone. Jesus alludes to the day of judgment, when the lawless ones will be dismissed from his presence (cf. 25:41).

Although the Septuagint, the Greek version of the First Testament, uses "Lord" *(kýrios)* as a substitute for YHWH, the personal name of God, the word is also a common title of respect. This second use is probably the way the word is meant to be understood here. Jesus' status as leader is being recognized by those who call on him. They claim to have prophesied, to have exorcized demons, and to have performed miracles all in his name. However, Jesus himself insists this is not enough. In fact, he characterizes himself as judge before whom these people stand, hoping to enter the eschatological kingdom of heaven. Rather than reward them for their accomplishments, he condemns with a rebuke frequently found in rabbinic literature: I never knew you. Depart from me!

Jesus insists that what is essential for entrance into the reign of heaven is adherence to his words, not signs of respect, forms of religiosity, or spectacular deeds. Discipleship requires a life of righteousness, not merely charismatic activities. Using a teaching technique from the Wisdom tradition to illustrate the point he wishes to make, he contrasts the way of the wise with the way of the foolish. The former built the house on the solid ground of Jesus' words. With such a firm foundation none of the vicissitudes of life were able to destroy it. On the other hand, the fool's house was constructed on sand, which provided no solid foundation at all. It was unable to withstand adversity, so it collapsed. The word that identifies the first builder as wise is *phronímo*. This refers to practical wisdom, the kind that comes from having reflected on experiences of life. It suggests that both builders should have considered the buffeting their houses would have to endure and then planned accordingly. Only one acted in this way.

The implications of Jesus' words are quite clear. He has just delivered an extended sermon interpreting the religious tradition anew and outlining the kind of behavior required of those who would follow him. In order to be his disciples one must follow Jesus' instructions carefully and faithfully. Those who do will be invited into the reign of God. Those who do not will be barred entrance. While this may sound like a hard saying, Jesus has been very clear in laying out the requirements of discipleship. Those who do not follow them do so out of choice.

## Themes of the Day

Today Jesus concludes the private schooling of his disciples. He places a choice before them, and he places it before us as well. Will we be his disciples? Will we follow him and by our lives testify to the choice we have made?

### Signs of Discipleship

Being a disciple of Jesus requires more of us than an interior response to a call from God. Discipleship is more than merely an inner commitment. For it to be authentic it must be concretized in some way. The signs of discipleship must be as obvious to others as a tattoo on the arm or a pendant worn on the forehead. As with the markings on a slave, these signs indicate to whom the disciple is committed. Somehow, the way we live out our commitment must be this obvious to others. This is a challenge to all of us. What do our life-styles say about our discipleship? Can people tell to whom we are dedicated simply by the way we live our lives?

Besides being obvious to those who see us, our discipleship must be firmly established, like a house built on rock. It may face hardships and attack, it may be besieged and buffeted, so it must be able to stand resolutely. If Jesus the Lord is the rock upon which our discipleship is built, we will be able to withstand anything life has to offer. This is not to say we will be preserved from the storm, but grounded in him, we will be secure within the storm.

## Grounded in Faith

Sometimes it is very difficult to separate discipleship from the ministerial works in which we are involved. These works are definitely important because they are the works of God. However, if our discipleship is determined by these works and not by the faith out of which the works flow, we are like people who have built our house on sand. If our discipleship is not built securely, we may not be able to endure criticism and failure; we may not be able to survive the rain and the floods and the wind and the buffeting. However, if we are grounded in faith in Jesus we will be able to understand that our hardships are our participation in the sufferings of Christ, and we will be able to call on his strength for endurance.

## The Choice Is Ours

We are called to discipleship, but the choice is ours. The people of ancient Israel were given the choice to enter into covenant or not, to accept the Law or not. The choice was theirs. Jesus held out options to his disciples. They could listen to his words and act upon them, or they could dismiss his words and go their own way. The choice was theirs. Paul told the Romans they could accept justification through faith in the blood of Jesus or they could be deceived into thinking that works of the Law could justify them. The choice was theirs.

The readings for today hold out the same options for us. Will we choose a discipleship grounded in faith in Jesus, or will we rely on our own talent and determination to accomplish our tasks? Will we build the house on rock, or on sand? The choice is ours.

# Ordinary Time (Part Two)

| | First Reading | Psalm | Second Reading | Gospel |
|---|---|---|---|---|
| **Tenth Sunday** | Hosea 6:3-6<br>I desire love, not sacrifice | Psalm 50:1, 8, 12-13, 14-15<br>I do not need your sacrifices | Romans 4:18-25<br>Righteous through faith | Matthew 9:9-13<br>Matthew, follow me |
| **Eleventh Sunday** | Exodus 19:2-6a<br>Kingdom of priests, holy nation | Psalm 100:1-3, 5<br>The sheep of God's flock | Romans 5:6-11<br>Reconciled through Christ's blood | Matthew 9:36–10:8<br>The Twelve are sent out |
| **Twelfth Sunday** | Jeremiah 20:10-13<br>Terror on every side | Psalm 69:8-10, 14, 17, 33-35<br>LORD, answer me | Romans 5:12-15<br>The gift outstrips the transgression | Matthew 10:26-33<br>God cares for you |
| **Thirteenth Sunday** | 2 Kings 4:8-11, 14-16a<br>Elisha, a man of God | Psalm 89:2-3, 16-17, 18-19<br>Sing the goodness of the LORD | Romans 6:3-4, 8-11<br>Buried with Christ in baptism | Matthew 10:37-42<br>Who receives you, receives me |
| **Fourteenth Sunday** | Zechariah 9:9-10<br>Your king comes to you humbly | Psalm 145:1-2, 8-11, 13-14<br>The LORD, gracious and merciful | Romans 8:9, 11-13<br>The Spirit of God dwells in you | Matthew 11:25-30<br>I am meek and humble of heart |

| | | | |
|---|---|---|---|
| **Fifteenth Sunday** | | | |
| Isaiah 55:10-11<br>My word will not return void | Psalm 65:10-14<br>God has watered the land | Romans 8:18-23<br>Creation awaits with eager expectation | Matthew 13:1-23<br>A sower went out to sow |
| **Sixteenth Sunday** | | | |
| Wisdom 12:13, 16-19<br>God's might is the source of justice | Psalm 86:5-6, 9-10, 15-16<br>LORD, you are good and forgiving | Romans 8:26-27<br>The Spirit intercedes with us | Matthew 13:24-43<br>Let them grow together |
| **Seventeenth Sunday** | | | |
| 1 Kings 3:5, 7-12<br>An understanding heart | Psalm 119:57, 72, 76-77, 127-128, 129-130<br>LORD, I love your law | Romans 8:28-30<br>Conformed to the image of Jesus | Matthew 13:44-52<br>Sell all for the kingdom |

# Ordinary Time (Part Two)

## Initial Reading of the Ordinary Lectionary (Part Two)

*Introduction*

The readings for this section of Ordinary Time reinforce the idea of ordinary. We are not in the midst of a specific liturgical season, nor are we anticipating one. We are in Ordinary Time. Although both epistles and gospels are continuous readings, the first readings are more an assortment of various religious themes.

*First Testament Readings*

The first readings may appear to be a collection of random passages from various books of the First Testament. There is a sampling of readings from the Pentateuch (Exodus), the historical books (1 and 2 Kings), Prophets (Hosea, Isaiah, Jeremiah, and Zechariah), and a Wisdom book (Wisdom). At times a theme seems to correspond to a similar theme in the second reading or the gospel. At other times this is not the case. What we have is an unspecified gathering together of discrete passages, each of which contributes a unique insight into our rich and broad religious tradition.

The reading from Hosea insists on the priority of love over ritual observance. Exodus describes God's invitation to Israel to establish a covenantal relationship. Jeremiah is torn between the suffering that has come upon him as a result of his being a prophet and the desperate need he has to proclaim the word that is within him. In Kings we read about a prophet who repaid a good deed with the promise of a child and a king who was abundantly rewarded by God for having asked for the wisdom needed to rule justly. Zechariah envisions a humble king who will establish peace throughout the world; Isaiah compares the power of the word of God to that of the rain, whose prerogative it is to engender fertility on the earth; Wisdom acclaims the justice of God.

Though discrete in themselves, together these readings create a kind of family scrapbook. We see the inner landscape that defines us, certain family traits we too possess, reminiscences of family gatherings, and images of friends we have met along the way. It is good to bring such a scrapbook out occasionally so we can remember who we were, who we are, and who we might yet become.

## Psalms

The psalm responses are as diverse as are the first readings. Chosen as responses to these readings, they provide us with a prayer book of great diversity. They include a covenant renewal ceremony that underscores the message of Hosea; a hymn that praises God for the invitation into covenant; a lament that could have been found on the lips of Jeremiah; a hymn that extols God's power such as was exercised through Elisha and one that praises God for the water that gives life to the land; a psalm that characterizes God as merciful and gracious; and a Wisdom hymn that corresponds to the account of Solomon's prayer. This diverse collection suggests there is no occasion when prayer is inappropriate. It also demonstrates the variety of prayers we have at our disposal.

## Epistles

The excerpts from Paul's letter to the Romans not only provide an overview of that great epistle but also create a mini-epistle in themselves. The major theme that threads itself through these readings is the indispensable role Christ plays in the justification of believers. Paul's knowledge of Scripture and skill in rabbinic methods of interpretation serve him well in this regard. He first appeals to Abraham as an example of how faith rather than obedience is the source of justification. Having established this, he explains how Jesus accomplished our justification through the shedding of his blood. Paul points to the universal significance of the sin of Adam to demonstrate the universal scope of the grace achieved by Christ.

Paul next turns his attention to the implications Christ's sacrifice has for the lives of others and the way believers can have access to this grace. Believers participate in the death and resurrection of Jesus through baptism. In it they die to their old lives of sin and rise to a new life in Christ. Paul does not limit this transformation to women and men alone. Since all creation was carried with Adam into sin and death, all creation will be carried with Christ into this new life.

Paul brings this teaching to conclusion by turning again to the workings of God, insisting it is God who accomplishes our justification. In fact, the Spirit of God works within us and prays within us. Finally, Paul argues that God has called all human beings to conform to the image of Christ.

*Gospels*

The portions of Matthew's gospel read in this segment of Ordinary Time show the care Jesus took in instructing his disciples. Although he spoke to the crowds in parables, it was to his disciples he explained these parables.

The readings begin with the account of the call of Matthew, whose name in Greek (Matthaios) itself suggests disciple *(mathētēs)*. In this liturgical reading Matthew becomes the representative of all disciples. We are told that the needs of the world prompted Jesus to send his disciples out into that world so they would continue the wondrous deeds he himself had begun. They were to proclaim the good news, cast out unclean spirits, and heal the sick. Jesus knew the dangers they would face in such ministry so he warned them, distinguishing mere physical suffering from everlasting suffering. Finally, he laid before them the nature of the self-sacrifice that would be exacted of them. Experiencing success in the ministry, they came to know the cost. At the end, Jesus exclaims, Come to me; take my yoke; learn from me. The initial invitation is extended again.

The disciples' formation continues in Jesus' parabolic instructions. With the crowds they hear the teaching of Jesus, but away from the crowds they learn its fuller meaning. The message of the parables is as much for the crowds as for them. However, it is only to them that the mysteries of the kingdom are revealed. Their eyes are opened because it will be their responsibility in the future to proclaim this same message to others. Jesus is very careful in preparing them for this task.

*Mosaic of Readings*

While there are many themes in the readings of these Sundays in Ordinary Time, two principal ones stand out: our justification in Christ and our call to discipleship. Together, they suggest we have been called in by God and then sent out by Christ. The other readings can be viewed through this twofold lens.

# Readings

## Tenth Sunday in Ordinary Time

### Hosea 6:3-6

There are two parts to the first reading for this Sunday. In the first part (v. 3) it is the people who speak; in the second (vv. 4-6) it is God. The major theme is loyalty to covenant commitment. The reading addresses both disloyalty to this commitment and restoration of the covenant bond. The very vocabulary reveals this: the passage speaks of judgment *(mishpāt);* covenant commitment or lovingkindness *(ḥesed);* sacrifice *(zebaḥ)* and holocaust *('ōlôt).*

The affliction the people suffer is probably the consequence of their disloyalty (v. 3). However, the verse indicates a change in disposition, for "to know" *(yāda')* suggests a knowledge that flows from communion. In the setting of this passage, it suggests a call to accept the LORD as covenant partner. The double verb (know; strive to know) marks the determination behind the action. The people are resolute in their intent on returning to God. They employ metaphors from nature to describe God's working in their lives. The dawn and the light of day are not only essential, but their advent is both reliable and consistent. One can be sure that the day will dawn and that it will do so each day. By using this figure of speech the people profess their faith in the constancy of God.

Comparing the coming of God with the coming of the spring rains is quite daring for a prophet who lived in the circumstances in which Hosea found himself. His major battle centered on the claims of the Canaanite people that their god Baal was the source of fertility and life. Baal was himself characterized as the storm god who controlled the rain and all the other life-giving waters that come from the heavens. Perhaps using that image was Hosea's way of deposing Baal and placing the God of Israel in this prominent position. The metaphor itself implies that God provides the refreshment needed for survival. Describing God in this way was an act of faith on the part of this people, who are now repenting of their sin.

The second part of the reading begins with words of frustration from God: What am I going to do with you? Although Hosea prophesied exclusively to the people of the northern kingdom, both that kingdom (named Ephraim after one of the sons of Joseph) and the southern kingdom (Judah) are addressed here. This was probably to ensure that the message would apply to the People of God in its entirety. God's frustration stems from the unreliability of their piety *(ḥesed)*, as fleeting as an ephemeral morning cloud or as transitory as early mist, both of which will evaporate in the heat of the sun. Because their covenant commitment was so unreliable, they were punished. A parallel construction describes their fate:

> I smote them through the prophets  
> I slew them by the words of my mouth

The word for "smote" might be better translated "hewed" *(hāsēb)*, the action of cutting down a tree or carving out a cistern. "To slay" *(hārag)* is to put to death, the ultimate curse passed on those who have violated their covenant commitment.

The words of God are harsh, but they do not end here. The final statement clarifies the people's failure and offers the possibility of hope. It suggests that the people have indeed fulfilled some of their obligations. They have offered sacrifice, but this action seems to have been purely in external conformity to ritual obligations. Covenant fidelity requires *ḥesed,* lovingkindness, commitment of heart and soul. It requires the knowledge of God that stems from personal interior commitment. This is the kind of loyalty God desires.

## Psalm 50:1, 8, 12-13, 14-15

Certain elements within this responsorial psalm suggest it is a cultic theophany, an experience of God that took place during some liturgical event. This included divine speech (v. 1), reference to sacrifice (vv. 8, 13, 14), and fulfillment of vows (v. 14). These features suggest that the cultic setting is probably a form of covenant renewal. The extraordinary character of this theophany is seen in the threefold identification of God: *ʾēl,* and *ʾĕlōhîm,* both yielding the translation "God" though only one appears in this version of the text; YHWH, the personal name of the God of Israel, translated as "LORD." A fourth title, "Most High" *(ʿelyôn),* the name associated with the god worshiped in Jerusalem before David captured the city, was eventually appropriated by the God of Israel.

The passage itself is a form of rebuke, a judgment against the people who have gathered to offer sacrifice. As an integral part of this rebuke, God calls on the earth to witness the divine judgment. The phrase "from the rising of the sun to its setting" can be understood in two ways. It can be read literally, suggesting that during the entire day the earth and all its inhabitants will witness God's judgment of the worshipers. The phrase can also be a spatial reference, a figurative way of including everything from east to west. Whichever way it is interpreted, it is meant to sketch the vast scope of the earth's witnessing.

The sacrifices themselves are rejected by God, and the motives for which they seem to have been offered are condemned. Although both the more generic term "sacrifice" *(zebaḥ)* and "holocaust" *(ʿōlâ)* are mentioned in the psalm response, the burnt offerings are a particular focus of attention. As part of this ritual the bodies of sacrificed animals were burned and in this way offered to God, as if God were hungry and in need of food. Such a conception of God corresponds to that of various other religions of the region. The gods who were worshiped in them were dependent upon their clients for nourishment. On the other hand, the God of Israel was dependent upon no one and in need of nothing. The people of Israel should have known this. Such a false notion about God would have been especially inappropriate during a covenant renewal ceremony, a ceremony that celebrated God's miraculous deliverance of the people from bondage in Egypt.

The divine pronouncement next outlines the components of true sacrifice, the kind of sacrifice pleasing to God. It consists of praise (the Hebrew has *tôrâ* [law], which in other translations is rendered "thanksgiving"). The immediate mention of fulfilling vows suggests that this practice along with offering praise are responsibilities that accompany covenant commitment. All God wants is fidelity. If those who have come to worship remain faithful to their covenant responsibilities, they will be able to call upon God and God will rescue them. The reversal of roles is striking. Rather than God being dependent upon their sacrifices, they are dependent upon God's protection. They will glorify God for having delivered them. This is the proper attitude to have when approaching God in worship.

## Romans 4:18-25

The relationship between faith and righteousness, which we read about last Sunday, is further developed in today's reading. Paul appeals to the well-known story of Abraham. That ancient Israelite tradition opens with God promising to make Abram a great nation (cf. Gen 12:2). Paul refers to two episodes in this story that provide the basis of his argument, both elaborations of God's initial promise of posterity. In one, Abram's name is changed to Abraham, which means "father of many nations" (Gen 17:5). In the other, God points to the stars in the night sky, the number of which is impossible to count. God then promises, "Thus shall your descendants be" (Gen 15:5). The promise is reassuring, but it stands in opposition to the fact that both Abraham and his wife Sarah were advanced in years and still had no child. The night scene closes with the statement that Abram (Abraham) believed God's promise and "it was reckoned to him as righteousness" (cf. Gen 15:6).

This ancient tradition lends itself perfectly to the theology Paul is developing. He sees Abraham as more than a model after whom the Christians should pattern their lives. Using typology as a method of interpretation, he proposes Abraham as a type, a symbol of something in the future. The Christians would then be the antitype, that something in the future that was foreshadowed by the type. This kind of interpretation presumes that the first reality was intended for the sake of the second. Paul actually states his adherence to such a presumption: "It was not for him alone that this was written . . . ; it was also for us" (vv. 23-24).

Although Abraham's faith is simply mentioned in the Genesis account, Paul embellishes it in his explanation. Because Abraham relied on the promises God had made, he was able to trust these promises would be fulfilled despite the apparent impossibility of the situation. The role death plays in this tradition should not be overlooked. Paul says that Abraham's body was already dead, as was Sarah's womb. At issue is whether God can bring back to life what is already dead. Thus Abraham is not only a type of faith, he is also a type of life out of death.

Paul moves immediately to the point of his instruction, which is the heart of his gospel, namely, faith in the death and resurrection of Jesus. Paul's manner of argumentation now becomes clear. Just as the justification of Abraham resided in his belief that God could bring life out of death, so the justification of the Christians resides in their belief that God has brought life out of death.

The conclusion of the reading may have originated in an early Christian confessional creed: Jesus died for our sins and was raised for our justification. Having developed his argument from typology, Paul provides an interpretation of the Abraham story that underscores the role faith plays in justification.

## Matthew 9:9-13

The account of the call of Matthew is very brief, but the implications of Jesus' selection of him are far-reaching. Matthew appears to be a customs officer, not one who collects individual taxes. Nonetheless, the populace regarded tax collectors of any kind with the same disdain. Custom posts were normally set up at borders, where taxes on goods in transit could be collected. This suggests Jesus has moved from one district to another. Tax collectors were accountable to officials of the occupying nation but were usually recruited from the native population. Therefore they were looked down upon by their overlords and despised by their own people. Their job required they submit a certain percentage of the taxes they collected. Their own livelihood was derived from whatever else they could exact from the people. Some collectors were quite demanding. For this reason they were all considered thieves. Furthermore, tax collectors used pagan money in their transactions and dealt with Gentiles. Such actions rendered them ritually unclean and ineligible for temple worship. Matthew was one such man, and Jesus chose him as a disciple.

As if this were not enough, Jesus was joined at table with other tax collectors and sinners. The Pharisees, who were known for their insistence on fidelity to the smallest detail of the Law, used the designation "sinner" for anyone who disregarded the strict observance they cherished. To associate with such people was to risk contamination. Jesus not only associated with them but he dined with them, presumably eating from the same dish, thus establishing an intimate bond with them. It is no wonder the righteous Pharisees would question his actions, thereby really questioning his religious integrity.

They pose their question to Jesus' disciples, not directly to him. They refer to Jesus as "your teacher," alluding to the close relationship between the rabbinic teacher and his disciples or students. In that tradition the conduct of one reflected on the character of the other: the disciples were judged in the same light as was Jesus. Why the Pharisees addressed the disciples is not known.

Perhaps they were trying to intimidate them, to undermine their loyalty. Perhaps it was feigned respect for the teacher. Whatever the reason, Jesus responds, since it is his integrity that has been challenged. In a society where honor and shame play such an important role, it is important that he not only defend his honor but that he enhance it by shaming his opponents. This is what he does.

Jesus acknowledges the questionable character of those with whom he is associating, but he declares he has come to help those who need help. Using the formulaic language of the rabbinic schools, he directs his detractors to go and study the Scriptures. The quote from the prophet Hosea (6:6) states that God desires the covenant disposition of lovingkindness (the Hebrew is *ḥesed*) rather than ritual conformity. In this regard, Jesus' behavior is sharply contrasted with that of the Pharisees.

The last verse can be understood on different levels. Jesus says he has come to save sinners. Because of their strict observance, the Pharisees may well have considered themselves righteous, with no need of salvation. However, the reference from Hosea would suggest that because they have no mercy they are definitely in need of salvation.

## Themes of the Day

The ruling theme for this Sunday is the call from God. We can look at it as an ongoing reality rather than a once for all event, or even a "born again" experience. This is a call to new faith and constant conversion.

### *The Continuous Call*

This second set of readings for Ordinary Times begins with a call narrative. We have already seen that the call to discipleship is extended to all the baptized. It is not a special grace given only to those who have chosen a particular style of life. The response to this call can unfold in any life, at any age, under any circumstances. It is a call to follow Jesus and to proclaim his gospel in the life situation in which we find ourselves.

Baptism may be the one defining call for the Christian, but as our lives unfold we discover that at its major junctures we are invited again and again to commit ourselves anew to the gospel and to discipleship. When we are young and filled with enthusiasm and daring, we are called to a particular life-style and to a life work; as naiveté matures to realism and we begin to question the decisions we have made, we are called to recommit ourselves with open eyes and faithful hearts; when life takes turns for which we were not prepared, we are called to set aside what we had worked for and trustingly to readjust our plans; finally, failing health and age call us to adjust our sails so we can catch the power of God. Each of these moments of grace has its own authentic call, an opportunity to follow the path to which Christ beckons us.

## A Call to Faith and Conversion

The call itself is a call to faith and conversion. It is a call to turn our lives around and to open them to God's refreshing grace. It is a call from a life of selfishness to one of generous giving to others. It is a call from unbelief to faith. At each juncture of life the call may make a distinctive demand. In the beginning we might resemble Matthew, in awe of the wonder of the experience and willing to sacrifice all to follow Christ. As we move through life we may become bogged down by its demands and its hardships. Our own observance of religious practices might lead us into false security. As with the people at the time of Hosea, the call might come to us by way of affliction. As we pass what we consider our most productive years, we may think conversion is behind us. Then, like Abraham, we are called to begin anew, believing God will indeed accomplish new things in us. In each of these cases it is not conversion that grants us faith. Rather, it is the faithful responsiveness to the call, which is expressed in conversion of life.

## Those Called

Some mistakenly believe only those are called who seem deserving of the call. Today's readings should disabuse us of this misconception. The call to discipleship is offered to sinners, to those who appear unacceptable, to tax collectors and prostitutes, to those outside the circle of respectability. Only such people realize how gracious God is in bringing them into the circle of acceptability. The call to discipleship is offered to those who are sick and impoverished. Only they realize how desperately they need God's grace. Only such people are able to acknowledge their own powerlessness. When they do accomplish great things, they know that everything was achieved by the power of God working through them.

## Eleventh Sunday in Ordinary Time
### Exodus 19:2-6a

Israel's journey through the wilderness brings the people to the foot of Mount Sinai. There they pitch their camp, while Moses ascends the mountain to receive directives from God. The theophany consists of a kind of "messenger call." God not only calls to Moses but also appoints him as messenger to the people. It is he who is to deliver God's words to the Israelites: the words Moses will eventually speak will have divine authority. The message itself is reminiscent of a covenant formula current in the ancient Near Eastern world of the time. In this formula the suzerain, or sovereign overlord, reminds the people of the wonderful deeds accomplished in the past for their benefit. The people are then required to show their fealty to this suzerain by observing the injunctions laid down for them.

The words of the LORD spoken to Moses can be understood in two ways. First, they describe events that transpired in the lives of those being addressed ("You have seen for yourselves"). Second, if this passage was ultimately part of Israel's covenant renewal ceremony as many commentators believe, it is a ritual anamnesis, a liturgical remembering that makes present for a new generation the past events being remembered. Three sets of events are mentioned: God's defeat of the Egyptians as God delivered the Israelites from Egyptian bondage; the guidance and protection ("on eagle's wings") God provided as the Israelites journeyed through the wilderness; their arrival at this mountain of divine presence, where they were invited into covenant with God. It is important to note these are all actions of God. The covenant formula would suggest that Israel did nothing to warrant these blessings.

Although God's goodness appears to be unconditional, covenant membership is not. This is not a unilateral covenant in which God makes promises and asks for nothing in return. This is both bilateral (both parties assume certain responsibilities) and conditional. "If" God's voice is heeded, and "if" the people comply with the covenant responsibilities, they will enjoy the privilege of covenant partnership. Three images are used to characterize this partnership. First, they will become a special people among all other people. The technical covenant phrase found in other passages describes this relationship well: You will be my people, and I will be your God. This moving phrase describes the unique election Israel always claimed. Second, the people are further told they will be a kingdom of priests. This means that, like priests, they will become agents through whom God's presence is made known to the whole world. Third, they will be a holy nation, holy in the cultic, not the moral, sense. They will be a people set apart from the profane, intended for God's special use.

Although the covenant carries very definite obligations, there is still a dimension of freedom. The people are invited, not forced, into the covenant. They are free to choose partnership or not. (There is an ancient rabbinic tradition that recounts how two other nations were invited to enter into covenant with God. They declined. Israel was then invited and accepted the invitation. While the tradition was intended to remind Israel of its lowly state, it also underscores the dimension of freedom.) The reading ends on a note of anticipation. Will the people accept the invitation?

## Psalm 100:1-2, 3, 5

The few verses in this responsorial psalm come from a hymn of praise that calls Israel to worship its God. There is also a universal dimension of this call: it is further addressed to all the lands. It may be that the summons goes out to all, but the God to whom the praise is directed is clearly the LORD, the God of Israel. ("LORD" is a way of circumventing the use of YHWH, the personal name of God.)

In this response the call includes three imperatives: "serve," "come before," "know." Each verb can be understood in its own distinct way, but all three can also be viewed as different ways of saying basically the same thing. "Serve" can be understood in a very general way as the function of a servant or a slave. In this sense it is quite appropriate to call people to serve God. It is also used in the context of worship, which is a particular kind of service. "Come before" implies entering the presence of God, clearly a reference to communal worship rather than individual devotion. The addressee is invited to enter the sacred precincts in order to give praise to God. Finally, "know" can mean simple recognition; however, when used of God it carries a confessional connotation. We do not so much know God as we know the works of God, works of creation or salvation, both of which elicit praise from us. A summons to know God is a call to acknowledge the wonderful works of God. Since any summons to praise is itself a call to worship, all three of these imperatives do convey the sense of worship.

The psalm uses two major characterizations of God, both of which reveal something of Israel's faith. God is described as Creator and shepherd (v. 3). The first image highlights the sovereignty of God, who as sole Creator conquered the primordial forces of chaos and continually holds these forces at bay. The second image portrays the tender, provident care of God. In the ancient world shepherds devoted all their time and energy to the care and protection of their flocks. Because of the responsibility they had for the well-being of their people, kings were often characterized as shepherds. To refer to God as shepherd is to acknowledge divine providence but also to make a political statement. God, not some human ruler, is really the one to whom allegiance is owed.

The response concludes with a description of God that consists of attributes associated with the covenant: goodness, lovingkindness, faithfulness. "Good" has a variety of meanings. It is normally used in the very general sense of pleasant, favorable, or beneficial. Its precise meaning here will depend upon the meaning of the two words with which it is associated. "Lovingkindness" (*ḥesed*) describes God's loyalty to covenant obligations. It includes dimensions of providence, mercy, and deliverance. As a divine attribute, it flows from God's fundamental goodness. The psalm declares that this lovingkindness endures forever *('ôlām)*, a word that can refer to either the remote past or the distant future, therefore, to perpetuity. "Faithfulness" *('ĕmûnâ)* refers to God's total dependability, a dependability grounded in God's nature and underscored by God's covenant commitment. It is only right that we praise a God who is characterized as Creator and shepherd and described as forever good, kind, and faithful.

## Romans 5:6-11

Paul's teaching on justification is complex and sometimes difficult to understand. However, the particular focus he takes in this passage is clear. He insists that our justification was won for us through the blood of Christ. Paul uses three verbs to explain the marvels God has worked on our behalf: "justified" *(dikaióō)*; "saved" *(sōzō)*; and "reconciled" *(katallássō)*. While in many ways these verbs are synonymous, each offers a slightly different perspective on God's action.

Paul tells the Christians in Rome they have been justified through the action of Christ; they have not justified themselves. The verb itself *(dikaióō)* is relational. It is based on the righteousness that originates in God, a righteousness that gives and sustains life, security, and well-being. Human beings can only be righteous if they are in right relationship with God and, through this relationship, share in God's righteousness. "To be saved" means to be delivered from serious peril. Paul does not use the word to speak of deliverance from the perils of life. He generally uses a different verb for that *(rhýomai)*. Here he is speaking about deliverance from the ultimate peril, the peril after life. Since God is the one who metes out the punishment due to sin, God is the only one who can save the sinner from this peril.

The word for reconcile means "to change or exchange." Paul uses it to describe the transformation that takes place in the human-divine relationship. According to Paul we have no right to this relationship with God. It has been given to us, won for us by the Lord Jesus Christ. In fact, we did not even deserve it. We were sinners, alienated from God, when Christ died for us and gained access for us to the grace that changes us, that places us in right relationship with God, that makes us righteous. Paul tries to explain the astonishing character of this gesture when he says it is hard enough to die for a good person but to die for someone who is not good is almost unthinkable. Yet that is exactly what Christ did. He died for us while we were yet sinners; he died for us before we had been justified. His dying made us righteous, saved us from ultimate peril, reconciled us with God.

Two other themes in this passage demand our attention, namely, *kairós* and justification by the blood of Christ. The first word, *kairós*, alerts us to the eschatological significance of Christ's death. The word means "decisive moment" and is used to indicate the dawning of the new age of fulfillment. Here it implies that this dawning is also the moment of our justification, our salvation, our reconciliation with God. The second, justification by the blood of Christ, recalls the Jewish sacrifice of expiation offered by the high priest. In that ritual the guilt of the one offering the sacrifice was believed to be transferred to the victim and destroyed along with the victim, whose blood was poured out on the altar. Through his own death Christ accomplished this expiation for us.

Although the passage treats the efficacious nature of the death of Christ, it ends on a hope of resurrection. Paul claims that if such wondrous things can be accomplished through Christ's death, how much more will we be blessed through his resurrected life.

## Matthew 9:36–10:8

The scene described in today's gospel reading reveals both the sentiments of Jesus and the character of the messianic ministry he shares with some of his disciples. The sight of the crowds moved Jesus profoundly. The verb *(splanchnízomai)* refers to agitation in the innermost part of the person's body, the emotions of the womb or the loins, the kind of emotion one has for someone who has come from one's own body. Jesus did not merely feel sorry for the crowds; his compassion sprang from his profound love for them. Seeing their predicament, this love cried out in compassion. They were unprotected and without guidance, like sheep without a shepherd (cf. Ezek 34:30). Their great need and the urgency of the moment prompted Jesus' words and actions.

What was the urgency of the moment? It was the urgency of harvest. In Jewish and subsequent Christian eschatological thinking, the final judgment was frequently characterized as a time of harvest. At that time all people would be gathered in, and the wicked would be separated from the righteous. Although there is no mention of judgment in the passage, reference to the harvest certainly suggests this theme. In eschatological thinking the harvest marked the close of this age. There is an underlying urgency in Jesus' words. This time is approaching, and there may not be enough laborers to ensure the harvest will be brought in. (To shift the metaphor, he would be concerned that the scattered sheep might not be gathered together.) Before Jesus appoints his disciples to address this need, he makes it clear that the harvest is God's to bring in. They will only be harvesters, and they are told to pray. This attitude will become particularly important once they begin to see the marvels they are able to perform. They must be reminded that it is the power of God working in them.

This is the only place in Matthew's gospel where the author uses the word "apostle" *(apóstolos)*. Its use here is fitting, since the account describes the apostles being sent out *(apostellō)*. They are given authority *(exousía)*, authority that not only gives them the right to perform an action but also the ability to do so. They are given the ability to cast out demons or unclean spirits and to heal diseases. The ancients believed the reason such evils were in the world in the first place was that evil itself held sway in the world. They further believed that when the reign of God was established the reign of evil would come to an end. For this reason they viewed exorcisms and healings as evidence that God's reign was indeed taking hold in the world. The commission given the apostles in this narrative is twofold. They are told first to proclaim the arrival of the reign of God (the same message proclaimed by John the Baptist [cf. Matt 3:2] and Jesus himself [cf. Matt 4:17]) and then to demonstrate the truth of their proclamation through wondrous acts.

The injunction delivered to the apostles to stay out of pagan territory and to concentrate their efforts with the lost sheep of Israel has been a point of contention for many interpreters. It sounds as if Jesus is concerned only with the Jews. (In a later passage Jesus will limit the scope of his own ministry to these same lost sheep of Israel; cf. Matt 15:24.) In this regard it is important to note the ties the author makes with the Jewish eschatological worldview. Most obvious is the selection of twelve apostles, the number of the tribes of Israel. This tie was most likely intended to imply that the apostles would fulfill the eschatological role the tribes were to accomplish. The reference to the lost sheep of Israel also focuses the concern described here. This focus was meant to suggest the fulfillment of expectations rather than the exclusion of concern. (The final commission is evidence of this. It directs the disciples to baptize *all* nations [cf. Matt 28:19].)

The final statement prohibits the apostles from peddling their power as some of the wandering teachers of the day seem to have done.


## Themes of the Day

This Sunday we are again faced with the themes of call and discipleship. Today we view call from a slightly different perspective, and we see more clearly the demands discipleship places on us.


### God's Special Possession

So often when we consider something to be special we judge it to be somehow better. When God chooses someone, it is not because that person is better but because that person can be useful in the plan of God. Israel was weak and vulnerable when God chose it to be God's special possession, so God picked Israel up and carried it away from danger. God called it into covenant, and it was its relationship with God that made it special.

So it is with us. Most of us are rather insignificant in the eyes of the broader society. And even those who are well known or in some way famous are still just simple human beings with needs and fears and dreams like the rest of us. In a very real sense we are special in the eyes of those who love us. And the first one to love us is the God who brought us into being, who sustains us in life, and who has invited us into an intimate relationship with God. God cares for us in much the same manner as a shepherd cares for the sheep. This is what makes us special. It is to this we have been called.

## Called to Be Justified

Paul picks up this theme in his development of justification. We are not justified because we in ourselves are special; we are special because when we were still sinners we were justified. Again and again we are told that all has come to us as a pure gift from God. We have earned nothing through our own merits; we deserve nothing as reward for our good works. It is God who calls; it is God who chooses; it is God who justifies. If we are to boast, we must boast in God.

## Give As We Have Been Given

Works do not gain faith. It is the other way around. It is faith that manifests itself in works. In the gospel we see that the disciples are sent out to give others the gift of faith that had been given to them. They proclaim the gospel, the good news that the time of fulfillment has come, and then they perform mighty works that demonstrate what they preach.

So it is with us. We have been called to discipleship; we have been made God's special people; to us has been entrusted the good news of salvation. We must proclaim this good news to others. We must be the healing touch of Christ in our world. We must comfort those who mourn, bring back to life those who are in despair, embrace those who have been ostracized by society, drive out anger and fear and hatred. We must heal the rifts in our families, in our communities, and in our workplaces. We have been reconciled with God so that others can be reconciled through us. The kingdom of God has been opened to us; now we must lead others into it with us.

## Twelfth Sunday in Ordinary Time
### Jeremiah 20:10-13

These few verses from the prophet Jeremiah follow the classical pattern of the lament. The reading begins with a complaint about some misfortune (v. 10), which is followed by sentiments of confidence that God will intervene and rescue the one who is suffering (vv. 11-12). This confidence leads the petitioner to praise God, who has already taken steps to remedy the situation (v. 13).

Jeremiah describes himself as the innocent victim of slander, of entrapment, and of vengeance. Even his friends, those whom he should have been able to depend upon, seem to have turned against him. He is alone, bereft of support and attacked on every side. It is important to remember that Jeremiah is in such dire straits precisely because he has announced the judgment of God on the people. The enemies who persecute Jeremiah are therefore really the enemies of God. In attacking the prophet of God, they are rejecting the God of the prophet. However, it is Jeremiah who carries the burden of the prophetic office, and so he complains to God.

Despite his distress, Jeremiah is confident. God is on his side as a mighty and awe-inspiring champion *(gibbôr)*, a warrior who will fight for his cause. This military imagery is also present in the title "LORD of hosts." This title calls to mind the cosmic war that God waged against evil, the battle in which God was victorious (cf. Ps 24:9-11). The title was also used of God during wars against other nations, when God was believed to be the commander of the army of Israel (cf. 2 Sam 5:10). In these battles too, God was triumphant. With such a God on his side, Jeremiah is confident of deliverance and protection. His trust is not misplaced. He is certain God will turn the plans of the prophet's assailants upside down. They have been watching for Jeremiah to misstep, but God will cause them to stumble; they have been hoping to prevail *(yākōl)* over the prophet, but they will not triumph *(yākōl);* they have wanted to take vengeance on God's servant, but God will take vengeance on them. Finally, they will be put to shame and confusion, a fate that in an honor-shame society is sometimes worse than death.

Some contemporary readers might be troubled by the prophet's prayer for vengeance. This must be understood within the context of the society of the prophet. It is not a prayer of bloodthirsty revenge but a plea for justice, for correcting inequity. Israel believed the justice of God was the source of authentic vengeance ("Vengeance is mine," Deut 32:35). What should be noted here is that the prophet turns to God for justice. He does not attempt to avenge the wrong himself.

The passage ends with a short hymn of praise. The prophet is confident of deliverance, confident that God has already begun the process of righting the wrong, correcting the inequity. Since the needy were no match for the wicked ones, God stepped in. This is reason for song.

### Psalm 69:8-10, 14, 17, 33-35

Elements of a psalm of lament can be detected here. There is the cry of lament itself (vv. 14, 17); the reasons for the lament (vv. 8-10); expressions of confidence that God will heed the psalmist's plea (vv. 33-34); and an expression of praise, presumably for having been heard (v. 35). Unfortunately we are not accustomed to cry out to God in lament. Perhaps some think it is unseemly to complain to God. However, a lament is a statement of profound faith. It acknowledges that God has power over the circumstances of life, and it is an expression of humble faith that God will come to the aid of those who cry out.

The cry of lament (vv. 14, 17) contains several words closely associated with the theme of covenant. The technical covenant term lovingkindness (*ḥesed*) appears in both verses. In addition we find truth (*ʾĕmet*); salvation (*yēshaʿ*, translated "constant help," v. 14); and passionate love (*raḥămîm*), love like that of a woman for the child of her womb (v. 17). By arguing in this way, the psalmist is bringing the strength and the personal dimension of the covenant to the plea for deliverance. The petitioner is not merely someone who has fallen on hard times. This is a member of the covenanted community. Surely God will turn an understanding ear to this plea.

This passage begins with a statement of the reasons for the lament. The psalmist suffers reproach and shame as well as family alienation, and all for the sake of God. Such suffering is a serious matter in a society structured on kin relationships and significantly influenced by questions of honor and shame. The zeal the psalmist experiences for the house of God could be an expression of profound personal devotion or a commitment to cleansing the Temple of all the sinful practices that have defamed it. Since personal devotion that does not infringe on the lives of others is seldom the cause of the kind of suffering the psalmist describes, the reference here is probably to some kind of temple reform. This is substantiated by the fact that the psalmist must also endure the reproaches directed toward God. The people who afflict the psalmist also disdain God.

The psalmist is somehow identified with the lowly ones or the poor, the very people who are called on to experience the goodness of God. This raises the question of what has come to be known as "God's preferential option for the poor." The biblical tradition certainly seems to suggest that God is particularly inclined to hear their cry. But why should they be so privileged? The answer is found in covenant theology. Implied in this sacred agreement are two major issues: a promise by God to care for the needy, and the responsibility of humans to care for one another. Israel believed that when someone within the covenant community was disadvantaged and not cared for by other members of the community, God would step in and redress the imbalance. The psalmist seems to be counting on a display of such divine justice.

Confidence in God's being faithful to covenant promises and hearing the plea for deliverance is evidence of the psalmist's faith. Even before there are clear signs of deliverance the psalmist praises God, thus fittingly concluding this powerful hymn of lamentation and confidence.

## Romans 5:12-15

The point of the teaching in this passage is the incomparable nature of God's salvific grace. In order to illustrate the scope and force of this grace, Paul uses a diatribe, a form of argument used by the Greek Stoics. He sets up a comparison between the universal effects of sin and death and the all-encompassing power of forgiveness and life. He does this by contrasting the actions of Adam, "the type of the one who was to come," and Christ, his unrivaled counterpart. While it may appear the contrast is between Adam and Christ, it is really between the epochs each inaugurated. Adam inaugurated the era of sin and death; Christ established the eschatological era of acquittal and life. At each stage of Paul's comparison we see the surpassing power of the salvation won by Christ.

Although the name "Adam" often refers to the individual depicted in the creation accounts, throughout this passage the corresponding Greek word for "man" is *ánthrōpos* (humankind) rather than *anēr* (singular male). His use of this collective word indicates Paul is not talking about Adam simply as the first man but as the individual who represents the entire race of women and men.

The epoch Adam inaugurated is sketched first. Paul uses both the account of the first sin (Gen 3:6) and the common experience of all people to explain the pervasive presence of sin and death in the world. Adam may have been the first to sin, but subsequently all have sinned. In one sense there is no transgression if there is no Law to transgress. However, according to Paul the power of sin and death are independent of the Law. He maintains that indeed there was sin in the world before Moses received the Law. It entered the world through Adam. The evidence of this is the universal reign of death, which, according to the Genesis narrative, follows sin. All die; therefore all must have sinned.

Paul uses an *a fortiori* argument to make his point about the excellence of Christ: if this is the way it was with sin, how much more it is with grace (v. 15). Although Paul earlier insisted that all have sinned, his primary comparison is between Adam and Christ. As death for all entered the world through the sin of one—Adam, so grace was won for all through the gift of one—Christ. However, there is a significant difference; grace is much more powerful than sin. Grace does not acquit merely the sin of Adam; it acquits all sin.

## Matthew 10:26-33

In today's gospel passage we continue our reading of the instructions Jesus delivered to his disciples. Various themes are prominent: the responsibility disciples have for proclaiming the good news; the loving care God has for human beings; the role Jesus plays in determining one's eschatological future. The underlying issue that links these themes is fear.

The passage opens with an exhortation: Fear no one! Neither those who might resist their proclamation of the gospel nor those who have the power to put them to death. What they should fear is total destruction in Gehenna and rejection by God. At the core of this instruction is an acknowledgment of the weighty responsibilities disciples bear and the cost fidelity to these responsibilities might exact. Jesus insists it is now time for the gospel to be proclaimed openly and boldly. The doors have been flung open:

> what was concealed, must be revealed;
> what was secret, must be made known;
> what was said in darkness, must be spoken in light;
> what was whispered, must be shouted.

The shift that must take place is both clear and dramatic. From the context of the passage we can conclude this shift will not only be difficult to accomplish but dangerous as well. There will be reason to fear those who reject the challenge of the gospel message. Jesus does not minimize the danger, but he does redirect the fear of the disciples. The theme of eschatology is introduced here. Jesus contrasts physical death, which only afflicts the body *(sōma)*, with ultimate death in Gehenna, which destroys body and soul *(psychē)*. Gehenna is the name given to the Valley of Hinnom, which lay just southwest of Jerusalem. It was used for burning garbage. Both the fire and the stench that rose from it led to its being characterized as hell, the fiery place of eternal punishment. Jesus tells the disciples they should not fear those who can inflict physical death on them, but they should fear the one who can cast both body and soul into the fires of Gehenna.

Jesus then says that suffering should not be seen as proof God is disinterested. Using a Jewish method of argument known as "from the light to the heavy," he offers two examples to demonstrate this point. If God cares for the insignificant sparrows, how much more is God concerned for the disciples? If God can count the number of hairs on their heads, how much more knowledgeable is God about their needs? Jesus uses these examples to encourage the disciples to trust in God despite the hardships they might have to endure. He again exhorts them not to fear, for they are valuable in the sight of God.

The eschatological theme returns in the last verse. One's attitude toward Jesus determines one's ultimate fate. Those who are willing to make a solemn declaration of faith in Jesus before others will be acknowledged by Jesus before God. Those who deny knowing or having any dealings with him will be similarly denied before God. In all of this Jesus is assuring those who suffer in his name that it is better to endure misfortune, even death, than to have to endure rejection by God in the world to come.

## Themes of the Day

As glorious and as much of an honor as discipleship may be, it can also be very difficult. The strength needed to continue on the chosen path despite its hardships can come only from God.

### The Hardships in Discipleship

We live in a world where money is usually the standard of success. It is a world of competition where there is only one winner and everyone else is a failure. It is a world that values possessions more than commitment, shrewdness more than integrity. It is a world where some races and cultures and the natural environment itself are secondary to the desires of those in power. This is a world that desperately needs to hear the call to conversion, but it is a world that is either deaf to it, or hearing it, may persecute the one who delivers the message. This is a world subject to the death that entered it through the sin of Adam.

Those who respond positively to the call of God may well have to face the hostility of this world, because their values and their commitment to righteousness threaten its moorings. They may encounter this hostility in friends and neighbors. They may even have to face it from family members. What may be particularly difficult is the feeling of having been rejected by the very ones to whom one commits oneself in service. Disciples may experience "terror on every side." This can happen in both major and minor situations. One can be maligned or one can feel marginalized. To commit oneself to the reign of God is to challenge the reign of the world, and this can make one very unpopular.

### Fear No One

In the midst of this suffering we can find strength in the promises of God, and we believe God is faithful to these promises. We have not been created and then thrown into the world to fend for ourselves. God cares for us more than for the sparrows. God knows everything there is to know about us: our fears and aversions, our thoughts and dreams. Why is it so hard for us to believe we are cared for by God? Have we not learned that God's care can be operative side-by-side with hardship? Or do we expect God will swoop into our lives and rescue us from whatever causes our pain? Why do we think God should preserve us from pain rather then strengthen us in it? Is the latter not perhaps the greater show of divine power? We have God's promise, but do we really believe God will be faithful to that promise? Or are we not satisfied with that promise and want a different one?

*The Gracious Gift of God*

Only half of this picture is bleak. The other half is radiant with hope. Paul assures us that the gracious gift God offers us is far greater than the transgressions brought on by sin. This gracious gift is Jesus Christ himself. The gift exceeds anything for which we might have hoped. He is the comfort that will carry us through our disappointments. He is the strength that will enable us to endure the misunderstanding and hardship that come with discipleship. We are called to acknowledge him before the world, and we are promised that if we do he will acknowledge us before God. There is light even in the midst of darkness. There is hope even in the midst of suffering.

## Thirteenth Sunday in Ordinary Time
### 2 Kings 4:8-11, 14-16a

At first glance the story of the Shunemite woman looks remarkably similar to one found in the Abraham cycle, namely, the promise of a son (cf. Gen 18:9-11). A closer look at the story will show that the two narratives are really quite different. In this story the principal character is a woman, not a man as in the account about Abraham. In fact, the woman's husband does not even appear on stage in this passage. It is to her the promise is made. Furthermore, it is made as a reward for her generosity to the prophet and not to further the story of the People of God. Although both births are considered extraordinary, in the case of Abraham it was Sarah who was said to be beyond childbearing years. Here it is the husband of the woman who is advanced in years. The gender reversal is striking, particularly when we remember this is a patriarchal society.

Shunem was not a major Israelite site, so the identity of the prophet was probably not well known in this area. Despite this, the woman recognized Elisha as a holy man of God. This passage does not tell us how she was able to do this, but in the end she is shown to have been correct in her judgment. She is described as a woman of influence who was able to convince the prophet to dine with her (cf. Lydia in Acts 16:15). She was also a women of means, for she and her husband were able to afford to add a room to their home and furnish it so the prophet might stay with them on a regular basis. It is this generosity that the prophet feels compelled to reward. This last detail is precisely one of the more unusual features of the account. The woman is rewarded not because of her faith in God but because of her kindness to the prophet. Furthermore, the prophet seems to act in a manner independent of divine direction. Elisha consults his servant in this matter, not God.

The promise made to the Shunemite woman is the same as the one made to Abraham: By this time next year she will have a son. There is no magic here, no divination. The only way Elisha could have made a promise that would eventually be fulfilled would have been through the power of God. Despite the fact that this man did not seem to conform to the expectations we might have of prophetic activity, he did exercise divine power. Abraham's son would be unique because he was the hope of a future nature. The son of the Shunemite carried no such national importance. He was the reward for kindness to a prophet.

## Psalm 89:2-3, 16-17, 18-19

The verses of today's responsorial psalm come from a royal psalm that praises God's faithfulness to the promises made to David (cf. 2 Sam 7:16). The shift between second- and third-person pronouns here has been the source of much confusion. Although some consider this shift as evidence of a change in direction of the address or of the one speaking, most scholars today recognize it as a simple poetic device known as *enallage,* a technique found frequently in the poetry of the ancient world.

Today's response contains certain themes that are very important in the Davidic theology. Lovingkindness *(ḥesed)* and faithfulness *(ĕmûnah)* are technical terms for covenant fidelity. It should be noted it is God's love that lasts forever and God's faithfulness that is praised through all the ages. The promises that are a part of this covenant are pure gift from God. Unlike the covenant made with the people through the mediation of Moses (cf. Exodus 19–21), an agreement that required their compliance to God's Law, this covenant imposes no added responsibilities on David or his descendants.

The psalmist wants to remind God of the pledge made to David. One of the first items mentioned is "steadfast love" (v. 3a). This is unconditional love, and God promises such love will endure forever. This love should not be confused with emotional attachment, a sentiment that can fade or even completely disappear. Instead, it is a firm and unalterable commitment. God has chosen David, and God will not renege on this choice. Joined to this constant love is "covenant faithfulness" (v. 3b), a loyalty that will stand as long as the heavens stand. The psalm describes the bond that joins God and David as one that transcends the historical. It is outside of any specific time; it extends through all the ages. It also stretches beyond the confines of earth, even into the heavens. It is as if the choice of David was determined by God at the time of creation, and it will last as long as the created world lasts.

The attention of the psalmist turns from the promises made to the king to the people themselves (vv. 16-17). A macarism is used to describe them as "blessed." The reason for this blessedness is threefold. They walk in the light of the LORD's countenance, a metaphor that means they enjoy the good favor of the LORD. They rejoice in God's name, and since one's name contains part of the very essence of the one named, this suggests they praise God for God's excellence. They exalt in God's justice, that is, they are recipients of God's righteousness. All these blessings flow from the covenantal lovingkindness *(ḥesed)* and faithfulness *(ʾĕmûnah)* mentioned earlier.

The last verses (vv. 18-19) are praise of God. Every good thing the people enjoy comes to them from God. Their strength is rooted in God, and any blessing they enjoy is theirs because God has looked favorably on them. A parallel construction closes the response on a Davidic note:

a) Lord                      b) our shield
a¹) Holy One of Israel       b¹) our king

To God, who is known as the Holy One of Israel, belongs the king, who is the protector of the people. All the blessings described in the psalm come to the people from God but through the king. He is both the mediator and the one responsible for dispensing God's goodness.

## Romans 6:3-4, 8-11

In today's reading from the letter to the Romans Paul explains how baptism has enabled the Christians to participate in the death and resurrection of Jesus. The ritual is itself the reenactment of his death and resurrection. As they were plunged into the water, they were buried with Christ in death; as they emerged from the water, they rose with him into new life. Paul's real purpose in drawing these lines of comparison between the death and resurrection of Jesus and the baptism and new life of the Christians is ethical exhortation. He seeks to encourage them to set aside their old manner of living and to take on a new life of holiness.

While the descent into baptismal waters can symbolize Christ's descent into death, there is another dimension of the water imagery that strengthens Paul's argument. According to an ancient tradition the cosmic waters were chaotic, therefore death-dealing (cf. Genesis 6–9; Job 22:11; Ps 73:13-14; Isa 27:1). To be engulfed by water was to be swallowed up into chaos and death. This symbolism lends itself to describing both the death of Christ and the baptism of the Christians. Christ was plunged into the chaos of death; the Christians are plunged into the death of chaos. By the power of God Christ rose to a new life of glory; by the power of God the Christians are raised to the glory of a new life.

Just as death had no lasting power over Christ, so sin need have no lasting power over the baptized Christians. They now have the power of the resurrected Lord to withstand the assaults of sin. However, Paul is not naive about the struggles of life. He knows they will demand the constant vigilance and self-denial of every follower of Christ. Crucifixion is a fitting image for both Christian conversion and ongoing fidelity, not only because of the role it played in Christ's death but because the torment it entails exemplifies the suffering that a change of life will exact of the Christians. However, as is evident in the case of Christ's death and resurrection, the cross is the only way to new life.

## Matthew 10:37-42

The passage from Matthew's gospel consists of an instruction on both the demands (vv. 37-39) and the rewards (vv. 40-42) of discipleship. The demands are quite radical; the rewards are remarkable.

Jesus offers three examples of the cost of discipleship. Two of them reflect the family setting; the third is taken from the context of Roman execution. In all three cases Jesus insists that if the disciples are not willing or able to measure up to the demands he makes they are not worthy to become his disciples. The first example challenges the ties of kinship that are marked by natural love or affection *(philéō)*, universally the principal bonds of relationship in society. Jesus insists these bonds must take second place to commitment to him. (A similar statement claiming teachers have claims that supersede those of parents is found in rabbinic writings [*M.Bab.Metzia* ii:11].) Such a demand not only causes suffering and a sense of loss, it could also alienate disciples from their loved ones.

Reference to carrying the cross is probably an anachronistic allusion to Jesus' own crucifixion. Although the disciples would have been very familiar with this form of Roman execution, they would hardly have grasped the import of this demand before Jesus' own death. However, the main point of the symbolism would not have been lost on them, especially because of the discussion of life and death that follows. Jesus plays with the idea of finding and losing. To "find" one's life means to live only on one's own terms and in one's own self-centered framework. This can give only temporary satisfaction; it cannot guarantee a life of ultimate fulfillment. On the other hand, a life of self-sacrifice, lived unselfishly for the sake of Christ and the gospel, will be rewarded with ultimate life.

The tenor of the instruction shifts. Jesus sketches some of the benefits disciples will enjoy, but he does so in a way that seems to be instruction for other people, those who are approached by disciples. He first shows the link between the disciples and both Jesus and the one who sent Jesus. Since Jesus was the agent of God sent into the world to accomplish God's plan, and since the disciples are agents of Jesus sent into the world to continue that mission, those who are open to the disciples are also open to Jesus and to God. It is clear the disciples are accorded a privileged position in the society, one of the rewards of faithful discipleship. This privileged position brings with it the assurance of others' hospitality, another reward of discipleship.

Jesus next speaks to those who offer hospitality, characterizing the disciple as prophet, righteous person, and "little one." Not all disciples received the special gift of prophecy. However, a prophet always delivered the word of God, and the traveling disciple ministered in the same way. Therefore, the designation was an appropriate one. Disciples were not the only ones who were righteous, but if they were faithful it was because they lived righteous lives. This designation was appropriate as well. "Little ones" probably refers to the inferior social status of the disciples. Two characterizations of them, found elsewhere, confirm this. They are referred to as servants (cf. Matt 10:24-25) and as children (cf. Matt 18:2-4), two groups of people who lack status. "Little ones" refers to the humble and unassuming way the disciples were to consider themselves.

Although hospitality was presumed in this society, Jesus promises that hospitality shown a disciple will not go unrewarded. The exact nature of this reward is not clear. Does it come from the person shown the hospitality? Is it the same kind of reward that person would receive for faithful service? Or is it a reward commensurate with the importance of that person? What is clear is that hospitality will be rewarded.

## Themes of the Day

The themes for this Sunday are similar to those of last Sunday. We are faced again with the cost of discipleship, but we are also comforted by the promise of the providence of God. The difference between the Sundays is that here we see these themes through the lens of baptism. It is not by accident these themes reoccur at this time, for our natural fear of hardship underscores our ongoing need for encouragement.

### Baptized into His Death

Who are called to be disciples, to become the new creation, to be prophets in the world? Who are called to be sent, to share the gift they have received from God? Who are the chosen ones, the special people, the kingdom of priests, the holy nation? All who have been baptized, who by the grace of God have been freed from sin.

Baptism is for us both death and life. Through it we enter into Christ's death and we die to lives of selfishness and sin. Through it we rise with Christ to a new life freed from everything that previously held us down. As glorious as this new life might be, it requires death to our old ways of living, and this is always difficult. It is not easy to put the needs of others before our own, especially when everything around us encourages us to think first of "Number One." It is not easy to refrain from acting as if we know more or better than others. It is not easy to show interest in the concerns of others, especially when we judge them to be trivial. It is not easy to forgive slights or oversights, to say nothing about deliberate assaults. These are all patterns of thinking to which we must die if we are to rise to new life, and these are very difficult deaths to undergo.

## The Cost of Discipleship

The cost of discipleship cuts right to the core of our being; it lays bare the very structures of kinship. Baptism re-creates us as children of God; through it we are given a new life and born into a new family. The bonds of discipleship are now even stronger than the bonds of blood. This means a radical divestment has occurred, a divestment which may or may not be tested but which has occurred nonetheless. Lest we think this is too much to ask, we should remember that marriage requires a similar transfer of loyalties from the family of origin to the new family being created, and because of the love they share, a couple is eager to make this transfer. Discipleship is no less demanding. In fact, it requires the primary loyalties now be directed to the Lord, and we are to live out all other loyalties in the context of that primary relationship.

Discipleship requires our very lives. As disciples we can no longer put ourselves first. We must be willing to spend ourselves and to be spent, to serve others in the day-to-day unfolding of life. As disciples we must demonstrate our commitment in whatever we do regardless of how insignificant the task may seem. We must be honest when we shop; we must be truthful in our speech; we must be considerate when we drive; we must be patient with members of our family. As disciples we must be open to the needs of all people. Wherever we are and in whatever we do we must be committed to peace in the world, to economic justice, to the integrity of creation. If disciples are not so committed who will attend to these matters? We may find such commitment very demanding, but that is part of the cost of discipleship.

## The Prophet's Reward

God promises that such wholehearted commitment will be rewarded. If we lose our lives in this way, we will really gain them. If we are unselfish in the way we share ourselves with others, we will be enriched through our generosity. If we spend ourselves and are spent in our service of others, we will be filled with blessings unimaginable. We all know people who are so committed, whose lives radiate goodness, whose hearts are open to all. This is the promise set before us. This is the reward of the prophet.

## Fourteenth Sunday in Ordinary Time

### Zechariah 9:9-10

These two verses constitute a very rich oracle of salvation, one of the many passages memorialized by Handel's oratorio *Messiah*. The prophet proclaims the words of the LORD: Rejoice greatly! Shout for joy! The words are addressed to the people of Jerusalem: "daughter Zion; daughter Jerusalem." In the ancient world walled cities were often characterized as female, encompassing the inhabitants as if in an embrace or within her womb. The designation "daughter" connotes an intimate relationship. The introductory exclamation along with the following description of the approach of the king suggest some kind of procession. If it is not itself liturgical, as some commentators believe it is, it certainly is the inspiration of a liturgical procession.

The oracle itself is an idealized picture of an Israelite king and the peaceful kingdom over which he will rule. Though this is a vision of the future, the verbs are prophetic perfect, indicating that in God's time the future is already present. This king is righteous or just *(ṣaddíq)*, and he himself is saved *(nôšā; the Hebrew has a passive form, suggesting the king is able to save others only because God has first saved him)*. He is meek *(ʾānî)* because he has little reason to be proud. If he has been victorious, it is because the victory is given him by God. He is seated on the foal of an ass, a purebred animal born of a female ass rather than a mule. While this may be a depiction of a victory march, it is devoid of military ostentation.

The three-part description of the banishment of the armaments of war is balanced by a three-part description of the future kingdom (v. 10). Most English translations follow the Greek version, which employs the third-person singular form of the verb for "cut off" or "banish," implying it is the king who is responsible for the conditions for peace. However, the Hebrew has a first-person singular form *(hīkᵉrattî)*, suggesting that the elimination of the chariot, the war horse, and the warrior's bow is truly God's doing. This latter version is preferred by most commentators because it emphasizes the mighty power of God and provides the reason for the king's humble demeanor. Mention of both Ephraim, a name for the northern kingdom of Israel, and Jerusalem, the capital of the southern kingdom of Judah, implies that war has been banished from both kingdoms.

The verb-forms change. It is the king who proclaims peace, not only to a united Israelite people but to all nations. This king will be the agent of God's blessings to all people. The description of the extent of his reign reflects the scope of the ideal realm of the messianic king (cf. Ps 72:8). The phrase "from sea to sea" indicates total range; "the River" is probably the Euphrates. The prophet had the whole world in mind.

## Psalm 145:1-2, 8-9, 10-11, 13-14

The responsorial psalm for today is both a hymn of praise of the greatness of God and a hortatory instruction. It opens with a declaration of praise, followed by the reasons for praising God. In the third and fourth sections the psalmist speaks directly to God again, praying that all of God's works will give thanks and proclaiming the LORD's universal and everlasting reign.

The passage opens with an acclamation closely associated with the revelation of God and an acknowledgment of God's name, revealed at the time of the reestablishment of the covenant (cf. Exod 34:6). In these two verses covenant language abounds. God is described as gracious *(hannûn)* and compassionate *(rahûm)* and filled with lovingkindness *(hesed)*. It should be noted that this divine goodness is not reserved for Israel alone but is extended to all God's works. These include all people and nations and also all of natural creation. The covenant has been expanded to a universal embrace.

The works of the LORD include everything God has made as well as everything God has done, everything God has fashioned as well as everything God has accomplished. There is a comprehensiveness to this call for praise (vv. 10-11). The psalmist cries out to all the wonders of the created world, whose very existence testifies to the magnificence of the Creator. More than this, the God before whom the psalmist stands in awe is also a savior who has performed marvelous deeds on behalf of the people. God has delivered them from bondage, has provided for them in their need, has established them as a people, and has promised them a secure and prosperous future. As they unfold in the sight of all, these acts of graciousness themselves celebrate the LORD.

The faithful of the LORD are those who are holy *(hāsîd)*, those who are bound to God in covenant loyalty. Whether their holiness is the result of God's faithfulness to them or their faithfulness to God is not clear. It does not seem to matter to the psalmist, who is preoccupied with the praise of God and not with extolling others. These faithful are summoned to bless the LORD, to praise or honor God in reverence and awe. God is characterized here as a monarch who rules over a kingdom. The word for glory *(kābôd)* means "heavy" or "weighty." Used here it implies that God's kingdom is substantial, distinguished because of its magnitude, comprehensive in its splendor. The character and extent of God's rule demonstrate the essence and scope of God's power.

The final section of the psalm extols God's reign and God's care for those who are burdened. The idea that gods ruled as kings was quite common in the ancient world, so to characterize the God of Israel in this way was not unusual. What are unique are the exclusive claims made about the reign of Israel's God. It is resplendent, as one would expect. But it is also universal, encompassing all, and it is eternal. In this light, the covenanted faithful ones are called not only to praise God for the wonders God has accomplished in and for them but also to announce the glory of God's rule to the entire human race, to all the children of Adam. It seems it is not enough that they enjoy the privilege of belonging to God's kingdom. Through them, God invites the entire universe to participate as well.

## Romans 8:9, 11-13

Paul contrasts two ways of living: life in the flesh and life in the spirit. Although "flesh" and "spirit" can refer to two distinct aspects of human nature, each can also connote the whole human being, but from a distinct point of view or with a distinct life-direction. When Paul refers to the flesh, he is not thinking of specific sexual behavior. He is speaking of human nature in all the limitations that sometimes incline one away from God. By "life in the spirit" he means a life attuned to God. The spirit is, in fact, that dimension of the human being that can be joined to the very Spirit of God.

Paul's denunciation of life in the flesh is unqualified. It cannot please God. Life in the spirit, on the other hand, is a form of union with God. He assures the Christians they are in the spirit if the Spirit of God dwells within them. He likens the Spirit of God to the Spirit of Christ, and he maintains it will be through the same Spirit that raised Jesus from the dead that their own resurrection is promised. Their own eschatological fulfillment is contingent on the indwelling of the Spirit.

The real point of this passage is the resurrection of those who are in union with God. Paul speaks of life and death in two ways. Reversing the metaphor slightly, he states that those who live in the Spirit have Christ living in them. This is the same Christ who, through his own death, vanquished the powers of death. Though sin can still exact physical death, it cannot quench the spirit that lives because of righteousness. It is this spirit that, through the power of the Spirit of God, will live on. Just as Christ conquered death and lives anew, so those joined to Christ will share in his victory and through the Spirit will enjoy new life.

Paul does not deny that Christians are under the same sentence of death as are all other people. However, he contends that sin and death are not the ultimate victors. The Spirit of God raised Jesus, and that same Spirit will raise all those who here and now live in the Spirit of Christ.

## Matthew 11:25-30

From the point of view of structure, the gospel reading for this Sunday can be divided into three parts: a hymn of thanksgiving for revelation (vv. 25-26); a christological statement that explains Jesus' role in this revelation (v. 27); an invitation and appeal (vv. 28-30). In the midst of this there seems to be one overriding theme, namely, wisdom. Both in structure and in content the reading shows an affinity with the book of Sirach. The reading opens with an expression of thanksgiving that echoes a prayer found in Sirach (cf. Sir 51:1), and it closes with an invitation similar to one in the same chapter of that book (cf. Sir 51:23).

Jesus addresses God as Father. Many people today are troubled by this male characterization. While we cannot deny that Jesus was a member of a patriarchal society, it is important to note the intimacy implied in the Aramaic form of the word (*'Abbā'*), the form Jesus probably used. God is further addressed as Lord of heaven and earth, a title that denotes universal sovereignty. Jesus appeals to the Wisdom tradition to explain why he is grateful to God. That tradition contrasts the wise and the foolish. This passage demonstrates how God has reversed the expectations of the world. The hidden things of God are not revealed to the worldly wise, those who are aware of their own knowledge and who are, as a result, quite self-sufficient. Instead, they are revealed to the immature (*nēpios*), those who are unself-conscious, dependent on others, and consequently receptive. It is clear that in this case God's gracious will and the designs of the world are quite different.

Jesus describes the intimate relationship he shares with God in terms that can only be considered a high christology, an emphasizing of his divine rather than his human nature. Principles that undergird the Wisdom tradition come into play again. This tradition states that wisdom, or knowledge, comes from reflection on experience. To really know something presumes some form of experiential knowledge. To know another implies intimate knowledge of that other. Jesus here claims that only God can really know him, because only God has this kind of experiential knowledge of him. Correspondingly, only he can really know God, for only he has experiential knowledge of God. If anyone else knows God, it is only because Jesus has revealed God to that person. In this sense, Jesus is the mediator of knowledge of God.

The invitation Jesus extends to the weary is reminiscent of the invitation to submit oneself to Wisdom (cf. Sir 6:24; 24:19). Such submission suggests the image of a yoke. There are various levels on which one can understand the significance of the yoke. While it certainly could be a sign of oppression and subjugation, it was also worn by free people for the purpose of distributing the weight of the burden they were carrying. Finally, the "yoke of the Law" was a common expression in rabbinic teaching (cf. *P. Aboth* 3:6; later in this gospel Jesus will allude to this characterization of the Law).

Most likely, each of these meanings somehow comes into play in Jesus' use of the image. He invites his hearers to take his yoke, to accept the responsibilities he will lay on them. Compared to the burden the Law had become, his yoke is easy. His hearers are to learn from him, the one who is meek and humble of heart, the one who, in the eyes of the world, is lowly and insignificant. This description brings us back to the reference to those to whom the hidden things of

God are revealed. If Jesus' hearers will conform themselves to this model and take on his yoke, they too will be blessed with the revelation of God.

## Themes of the Day

The readings for today engage us in a reflection on the nature of the Trinity as well as the ways we are enriched by each of the divine Persons.

### The Triune God

There is absolutely no way we can comprehend the concept of a triune God. All we have are pieces, individual glimpses into aspects of God, and we try to fit these pieces together into a coherent whole. Even though the father-son language, which is so much a part of trinitarian discourse, describes the likeness in nature and intimacy of relationship between the first two Persons, the traditional gender imagery has become a stumbling block to many people. A broadly acceptable solution to this matter is not yet on the horizon. Still, this should not prevent us from trying to understand the concepts we use to speak about God.

The first reality the gospel acknowledges is the sovereignty of God. This is followed immediately by mention of the handing over of all things to Jesus, making him a kind of vice-regent of God. Finally, Jesus and God have intimate and exclusive knowledge of each other. All this indicates they are not the same but enjoy a singular relationship and share on a level that is divine. Paul speaks of the Spirit, clearly a divine reality, but different from Jesus and the one called God. According to Paul this Spirit is the Spirit of Jesus and the Spirit of God, implying that somehow both Jesus and God claim the Spirit. It is this Spirit who raised Jesus from the dead, and it is this same Spirit who dwells in Christians. It is clear the Spirit does nothing independent of God, whose Spirit it is. What does all this tell us? All we can be sure of is that we are dealing with something totally beyond our ability to comprehend.

### The Grace of God in Our Lives

We are not completely lost in oblivion, however. The grace of this triune God touches our lives in some ways that are tangible and in other ways that demand faith. The most tangible manifestation of God is Jesus himself. We know he was a man of flesh and blood, one who walked on our earth, breathed its air, and ate its fruits. We know he touched the lives of others through his words and deeds. It is these very words and deeds that reveal something about God that we can understand. They reveal unselfish love and unfailing compassion; they reveal universal acceptance and concern for human needs; they reveal a passion for life and all things human. It was in Jesus that the divine characteristics extolled in the psalm are made manifest. He was gracious and merciful; he was slow to anger and of great kindness; he was compassionate and faithful and committed to all who are bowed down.

God has been revealed to us through Jesus. While Jesus was a tangible person, our acceptance of him as the manifestation of God requires faith, and this faith is no easier today than it was at the time of Jesus. But if we have this faith, we will believe that the Spirit of Jesus dwells in us, directing our lives after the pattern of the life of Jesus. This Spirit will free us from lives of pettiness and self-centeredness, greed and arrogance. This Spirit will enable us to open our arms to all and forgive those who have caused us pain. If we have this faith, we will be able to live fully in the Spirit.

## Learn from Me

The overriding disposition of these readings is humility. Jesus, the human manifestation of the divine, is meek and humble. This tells us something else about God. It tells us that high station does not result in pride. On the contrary, Jesus is humble; the king depicted in the reading from Zechariah is humble; the true disciple is called to be humble. A second disposition is placed before us: grateful praise. We turn again to the psalm, and we praise and bless God; we extol God's holy name. In Jesus we have known the tender touch of God, and we are grateful.

## Fifteenth Sunday in Ordinary Time
### Isaiah 55:10-11

This short reading from the prophet Isaiah is really an extended metaphor. The workings of the natural world become the vehicle for saying something about the word of God. Only by looking carefully at what is said about the world can we come to an understanding of what Isaiah is claiming about the word of God.

Isaiah has provided us with a glimpse of what ecologists today would refer to as the "integrity of creation." He limits his focus to one element of the natural world, precipitation in the forms of rain and snow, and he traces the cycle it takes. His knowledge of this cycle comes from observation of nature itself, the primary source of wisdom. The rain and the snow originate in the heavens; they water the earth, making it fertile; and then they return to the heavens, having accomplished their purpose.

This simple description lays bare several characteristics of the integrity of creation. The first is the interrelationship that exists between the various spheres. Without water the earth would not be fertile; without the fruits of the earth human beings would not have food to eat. A second characteristic, not expressed but presumed, is the consistency of the workings of the natural world. There an order persists that is reliable, an order we can trust. Finally, contrary to anthropocentric arrogance, it is clear that human beings are totally dependent on the fertility of the natural world and the laws that govern it. These three characteristics constitute the tenor of the metaphor: the features that belong to the natural world applied to the word of God.

Speaking through the prophet, God declares: So it is with my word! A cause-and-effect relationship exists between the word of God and the outcome it accomplishes; the word of God is consistent and reliable, and human beings are totally dependent on it. The effectiveness of the word of God originates in its performative nature. There is a kind of speech known as performative speech, which effects what it describes. Examples of this include the pronouncement of vows and the proclamation of a juridical sentence. When the words are spoken, the deed is done. This is the way the word of God was understood. When God said, "Let it be," it was. Here God says, "My word . . . shall do my will." The metaphor used here assures us that we can be as confident of this as we can be of the working of the natural world. Just as nature produces miracles upon which we can rely and because of which we can survive, so the word of God will effect miracles upon which we can rely and because of which we can live.

## Psalm 65:10, 11, 12-13, 14

The responsorial psalm picks up the theme of nature from the first reading for this Sunday but develops it in a different direction. Whereas the previous reading concentrated on the unfolding of the life processes within nature itself, this passage describes God as directly involved in these natural workings. This difference in perspective may spring from the difference in literary form. The prophetic reading is a discrete metaphor, applying to one subject the characteristics of another; the response is a hymn of praise, exalting God for the wonders God has accomplished in nature.

The psalm praises God for the natural wonders that make the world fertile, the source of nourishment for living things. (The fact that the imagery comes from the world of agriculture rather than from a maritime setting says something about the context of the original audience.) Behind the praise of God's control of the water may be a polemic against the fertility god Baal. The Canaanites believed this god regulated the heavenly waters that rained down upon the land, fertilizing it and making it fruitful. In the land of Palestine autumn rains soften the land, allowing it to be malleable enough for plowing and cultivation, while the spring rains nourish the plants and provide growth. The psalmist claims it is the God of Israel who exercises power and control over all of these processes.

God not only governs the heavenly waters, but God reigns over the land as well, bringing the much needed water to it and preparing it for planting. In the Canaanite mythological world a different deity held sway in this realm. However, the God of Israel has neither rival nor companion. This God prevails over every aspect of the world. Precipitation and prepared land have little value for living things if there is no growth on which they can feed. Here too God is depicted as directly involved in the processes of nature. God oversees the rich yield, the bountiful harvest. Another consequence of such abundance is extensive flocks. Animals like human beings require fertile fields off which they can live. Where there is such land, herds will flourish.

Because of its frequent mention of harvest and abundant yield, the psalm lends itself to prayer at the time of harvest festivals. At that time the fields and the valleys, now ripe with growth, join in the joyful praise of God. Although the psalm is a hymn of praise, the exaltation is also a form of thanksgiving.

## Romans 8:18-23

Paul's teaching on eschatology takes a very interesting turn: he maintains that the new life of which he speaks is not limited to the human sphere. Rather, all the created world participates in this transformation. He begins by insisting there is no comparison between the sufferings we are forced to bear now and the glory that will be ours in the eschatological age of fulfillment. The word he uses for "present time" is *kairós*, the decisive moment. The sufferings of which he speaks were referred to in Jewish eschatological thinking as the "birth pangs of the Messiah" (cf. Matt 24:8; Mark 13:8). They are the afflictions that accompany the transition from the present age to the age of fulfillment. The time of suffering is the time in between. As is the case with a woman in labor the pains may be intense, but just as hers are forgotten when the child is born (cf. John 16:21), so will the present afflictions pass.

According to Paul the entire created world is somehow swept up with humankind into this eschatological drama. It awaits the revelation that will be granted the children of God, not as spectators but as participants. Frustration or vanity *(mataiótēs)* is the inability to fulfill one's intended purpose. Creation was subjected to this kind of frustration when, in the beginning, it was cursed because of human sin (cf. Gen 3:17). Now, just as it fell under the punishment imposed on humankind, it will be transformed along with it. The only way one can understand this statement is if one posits some kind of bond between the natural world and humanity. And of course there is. Humankind is not separate from the natural world; it is a unique expression of it. Ecologists today say that human beings are the consciousness of the universe, the natural world reflecting upon itself. This modern idea corresponds with the ancient notion that creation suffers because of human sin.

Paul sees the world as suffering but fundamentally good and redeemable. He was not like the Gnostics of his day, who considered the world to be evil and something to escape. From the point of view of interrelationship one could argue that if all creation suffers the consequences of sin along with human beings, then it will also be redeemed along with them. Paul insists that creation too is enduring the birth pangs; surely it will be able to rejoice in the new life as well.

The reading ends on a note of eschatological hope. Paul assures the Christians they already possess the firstfruits of the Spirit, a pledge or deposit that guarantees there is more to come. What this is, the reading does not say. All we know is that it is a pledge that assures them they will indeed be brought into full transformation. By implication, all creation will be brought along with them.

## Matthew 13:1-23

What is identified in the text as the parable of the sower might better be understood as the parable of the soil. The role played here by the sower is unremarkable. As was the custom of the time, the sower merely walks along a path and throws the seed out as he goes. Nor is the focus in this parable on the seed, although its importance as the "word of the kingdom" cannot be denied. The parable is about the varying receptivity of the soil. The passage read this Sunday falls into three distinct sections: the parable itself (vv. 1-9); the reason for speaking in parables (vv. 10-17); the explanation of the parable (vv. 18-23). The author of the gospel uses the expression "kingdom of heaven" rather than "kingdom of God." This may reflect the Jewish practice of avoiding the use of the personal name of God.

Jesus' teaching moves out of the privacy of a house into the public arena. He is no longer speaking merely to his disciples. Crowds have gathered, and he now addresses them in parables. Parabolic teaching was a very common pedagogical technique. It was neither unique to Jesus nor to his time in history. Isaiah used it when he characterized the people of Israel as a vineyard (cf. Isa 5:1-7). As is so often the case in Wisdom thinking, nature provides examples from which to gain insights into human life. The parable itself is straightforward. Because seed was simply strewn along the way, if fell on all kinds of soil. Some lent itself to cultivation and some did not. Jesus describes this in a way that would be quite familiar to his hearers. Taken at face value, it was not a difficult story to understand. But what did it really mean?

Jesus concludes his teaching with a cryptic statement: Whoever has ears ought to hear. In a sense this statement captures the underlying meaning of the parable. Those who have ears, those who are open, ought to hear and understand. Those who have this openness will gain understanding of the parables; those who do not will experience the parables as a source of confusion or misunderstanding. In the explanation Jesus gives to his disciples he points to the enigmatic character of metaphorical language. While it can be understood on the level of its literal meaning, its real meaning is much deeper and must be discerned. Sometimes this deeper meaning is more obvious than at other times. All the parables of Jesus address some aspect of the kingdom of heaven, the mysteries of which will be concealed from those who are not open to receive them. The prophet Isaiah faced similar hardheartedness in his day (cf. Isa 6:9), and Jesus refers to this as he explains his use of parables.

Jesus calls the disciples' attention to the privilege that is theirs. They have been given the opportunity to see and hear (understand) what righteous women and men of the past longed to see and hear. He then provides an allegorical interpretation of the parable. It should be noted that in each case described the word that was sown was actually heard; to some extent it was accepted. Jesus is not referring here to outright rejection from outsiders but to the way followers receive the word of God. Sometimes the word does not take root at all; sometimes it does not take lasting root; sometimes it takes root but does not bear fruit. In other words, there are failures.

There are also successes. The word produces various percentages of yield. One can understand this from two points of view. It can be seen as disappointing that some of the seed appears to have been wasted and, even when it had taken root, there was not a better harvest. On the other hand, it can be very gratifying that the seed produces the remarkable yield it does. God's word will indeed bring forth the reign of God. When one understands the meaning of the parable, one is apt to wonder: What kind of soil am I? How receptive am I to the word of God?

## Themes of the Day

The readings for this Sunday call us to a kind of self-examination. The gospel describes various levels of receptivity. Today we are challenged to look into our own lives in order to discover how receptive we are.

### *Levels of Receptivity*

Receptivity is the willingness to allow ourselves to receive from another, to be influenced by that other, perhaps even to be transformed. Receptivity came very naturally to us when we were children. We instinctively knew we were needy. As we grew and matured we became more and more independent and self-directed and less inclined to be influenced by others. This situation is natural, but it does have its drawbacks. The more independent we are, the less likely it is we will be open to others and, consequently, less receptive to their ideas.

By definition disciples are receptive to the one they are following. Because of the independence into which so many of us have grown we can experience a major problem here. To be a disciple of Jesus requires receptivity, so it is important that we scrutinize ourselves to discover the extent to which we are open. Is our openness superficial, like the rocky ground? Is it fickle, like the thorny ground? Or are we really receptive to the word of God, like the ground that produces? And finally, are we as productive as we might be?

## The Word of God

To what should we be receptive? To the words of Scripture, the words of the liturgy, the words of the sacraments, the living tradition of the community. God's word is sown in many forms and under many guises. It is easy to receive what agrees with our own thinking, with our own point of view, with our own theological stance. What is difficult is to be open to statements or insights or practices that stretch or challenge us, that may force us to reevaluate what we hold dear. At issue is not the character of the seed but the disposition of the soil.

It makes little difference who sows the seed. God works through both the well recognized and the most unlikely of sowers. It might be a legitimate leader of the community or one of its otherwise ordinary members; it could be a child or an elder; it might even be someone from the outside, someone with whom we are not familiar, someone we don't particularly like. God moves through life indiscriminately, sowing the seed prodigally. How will we receive it?

## The World of God

The people of biblical times were aware of the revelation of God in and through the natural world. Isaiah employs this realization in his teaching about the effectiveness of the word of God. The psalmist uses the natural world to describe God's work of salvation. Paul claims that eschatological fulfillment will include all creation, not merely humankind. Unfortunately, the more sophisticated we have become, the less concern we have shown to the very matrix of life. We seem to have closed our eyes to the needs of the natural world, stopped our ears to the cries of the earth, hardened our hearts to the world of which we are merely a part. Yet the word of God will accomplish the end for which God sent it; the creation that was made subject to futility still waits with eager expectation; those who hear this word will bear fruits and yield a harvest for us all.

## Sixteenth Sunday in Ordinary Time
### Wisdom 12:13, 16-19

Although this passage from the book of Wisdom is directed to God, it is meant to be a lesson to be learned by the people of Israel. The author lists several forceful divine characteristics and then seems to temper them with traits that could be considered their opposites. In the first verse he brings divine care and condemnation together (v. 13). The principal theme of this verse is an acknowledgment of the total and exclusive providence of God. Only the God of Israel exercises care, and God exercises it over all. It is because God has neither peer not rival that God is accountable to no one for the manner of justice practiced. There is no one who can lodge a complaint of injustice against God.

God's might is the second characteristic discussed. This trait is tempered by leniency. Divine justice springs from this might, justice that requires that righteousness be rewarded and wickedness punished. It is actually because God is so powerful that God can decide to be lenient. A weaker God could not risk being lenient, reducing the burden of judgment that should rightfully be imposed. On the other hand, a strong or powerful God can be merciful without placing order in jeopardy. God manifests divine power when it is questioned. When it is not questioned, it is not manifested. The righteous ones trust in the power of God at work in the world and in them as well. However, those who are fearful are so because they do not trust in divine power. Their temerity springs from this mistrust. It is their mistrust that is rebuked by God. God judges and governs with might tempered with mercy and with power tempered with clemency.

God's manner of dealing with the people of Israel becomes a lesson to be learned by them. They are exhorted to pattern their treatment of others after God's treatment of them, to temper their own might with leniency, to regulate their own justice with kindness. God's kindness in the past gives them reason to hope for mercy in the future. However, they are expected to act in this same manner toward others.

### Psalm 86:5-6, 9-10, 15-16

Parts of an individual lament are singled out for this psalm response: a prayer to be heard by God (vv. 5-6); expressions of praise (vv. 9-10); and a plea for mercy (vv. 15-16). The structure of the first section is the same as that of the third: God is extolled in the first verse (vv. 5, 15). Presuming on the attributes expressed there, the psalmist makes a fervent plea (vv. 6, 16). Today's passage does not indicate the reasons for the psalmist's petition. Rather, it concentrates on the psalmist's perception of God.

Covenant language throughout these verses explains the reason the psalmist believes God will respond positively. God is described as abounding in lovingkindness *(ḥesed),* the kind of steadfast love associated with the covenant The psalmist calls God "good and forgiving," most likely because of the way the psalmist has experienced God in the past. If God acquitted the psalmist of previous violations of the covenant, surely God will look with pardon again. The parallel construction reinforces the entreaty:

> Harken        to my prayer
>       attend        to the sound of my pleading

The supplication gives way to a paean of praise. The excellence of the God of Israel is extolled. This God is recognized as Creator of all and for this reason receives the homage *(shāḥaḥ)* of all the nations. The psalmist also declares there is no other god, and consequently the LORD has no rivals. It is no wonder all nations praise the name of the God of Israel. It is not clear to which of God's wondrous deeds the psalmist refers. The Hebrew word used *(pālāʾ)* suggests achievements considered impossible to accomplish. The reference could be either to cosmic feats or to historical exploits. Since there is mention of God as Creator, the allusion could be to the wonders of creation, certainly reason to sing God's praise. However, the sentiments of the psalm are principally those of supplication. The psalmist is pleading for help and in this pleading makes an appeal to God's covenant commitment. This action suggests the wondrous deeds were those God performed in history on behalf of the people of Israel. There is really no need to choose one connotation in favor of the other. In fact, the psalm is richer if both cosmic and historical connotations are kept in the background of one's interpretation.

Already identified as the only God to whom all nations pay homage, God is further described with the same confessional faith as is found in the account of Moses' encounter at Sinai: compassionate *(raḥûm)* and gracious *(ḥannûn),* slow to anger and filled with lovingkindness *(ḥesed).* That earlier tradition reports that the people had sinned by worshiping the golden calf, but God willingly reestablished the covenant with them (Exod 34:6). Quoting this passage, the psalmist both acknowledges personal guilt and appeals to divine steadfastness. It is from the same Hebrew word for "turn" *(pānâ)* that "face" is derived. The psalmist is asking for the blessings that flow from facing God. Chief among them is mercy *(ḥannûn),* a covenant trait. Finally, the psalmist designates himself as a servant *(ʿebed)* of God, yet another example of covenant language.

The nations may bow down before the God of Israel, who alone is the Creator, but the psalmist pays homage because, despite his own sinfulness, he relies on the steadfastness with which the God of compassion and grace clings to the covenant.

## Romans 8:26-27

In the two verses that make up the epistle reading for today Paul provides us with a bold and moving explanation of prayer to God. In it he describes human limitation and how the Spirit comes to the assistance of human beings precisely in this limitation.

Paul first acknowledges human weakness. The reference here is not merely to physical frailty but to the totality of the human condition. Human beings are weak, limited, prone to ignorance and to making mistakes. Paul maintains that women and men do not know how to pray as they ought. This can mean either that they do not know how to engage in the practice of prayer or that they do not know for what they should pray. Still, such weakness need not prevent them from accomplishing great things. Paul refers to those weak human beings who are committed to Jesus as holy ones, saints. Such a reference itself reveals something about his understanding of holiness, specifically, that human weakness is not an obstacle to it.

The verb that tells of the Spirit's activity in the face of human need is a compound verb with the preface *syn* (with). It suggests that the Spirit does more than merely offer aid; it implies that the Spirit identifies with this weakness, takes it on, and in that capacity comes to our assistance. This is an important point to appreciate, for it means that it is the Spirit's identification with us that makes it possible for us to pray. According to Paul the Spirit acts as intermediary between God and humankind. As Spirit of God there is a divine connection; in solidarity with human weakness there is a human connection. The Spirit of God knows the will of God, and so the Spirit intercedes for us. Identified with our weakness, the Spirit is also identified with our inability to pray, groaning with sighs too deep for words.

It is God who searches hearts, and so God knows the Spirit in making intercession for Christians. This passage gives us a glimpse into Paul's thinking. Believers pray to God and seek to do God's will, but human limitation clouds their eyes and obstructs their inner eyes. The Spirit of God takes hold of them and empowers them to pray and to do God's will. However, it is really the Spirit within them that enables them to act in this way. God has a purpose, and though we do not know what that purpose is, the enabling Spirit of God moves us toward it.

## Matthew 13:24-43

The gospel reading for today once again casts Jesus in the role of Wisdom teacher, using metaphorical techniques to makes his points (cf. Matt 13:1-3, Fifteenth Sunday). Jesus employs three parables to illustrate aspects of the growth of the reign of God, or kingdom of heaven: the field sown with weeds; the mustard seed; the yeast in the dough. As was the case in the gospel reading for last Sunday, so the passage for today falls into three distinct sections: the parables themselves (vv. 24-33); the reason for speaking in parables (vv. 34-35); an explanation of the first and longest parable (vv. 36-43).

The first parable describes circumstances known to all farmers. Good seed is sown, but weeds grow up along with the crops. The parable highlights two important points. The first point underscores the disappointment such circumstances create. Despite all the dedicated work that goes into the establishment of the kingdom of God, there will not be a perfect yield. At issue here is not the size of the yield but its quality. It will include both the good and the bad. The second point is eschatological. The time of growth is the period of this life, and the harvest represents the end of this age. In the parable the servants are dismayed by the character of the mixed growth, and they offer to purge the field of the weeds. It is the owner who demonstrates patience and wisdom. He tells them this is not the time for such a radical response, and purging should be delayed. They are told to let everything grow. The time of harvest will come, and that will be the time for separation.

The second and third parables both address the unimpressive beginnings of the kingdom of heaven, its gradual and imperceptible growth, and the extraordinary yield it will ultimately produce. Although universalism is not the primary point of the parable of the mustard seed, the phrase "birds of the sky" has traditionally been understood as a reference to the Gentiles who will find a home in the kingdom. It should be noted that Jesus chooses one parable that describes a man working to establish the kingdom (v. 24) and another in which a woman plays the principal role in its establishment (v. 33). The details of the respective parables may mirror stereotypical gender roles of the time, but each depicts God working through the agency of the individual. The gender balance is significant.

Although it possesses a prophetic tone, the biblical citation that is used as an explanation for Jesus' teaching in parables is really taken from Ps 78:2. The point being made is twofold. First, the teaching of Jesus fulfills the promises found in the teaching of Israel's prophets. Second, this particular passage suggests the disclosure of meaning rather than its concealment. Furthermore, what are disclosed are those mysteries that were hidden from the beginning of time. The eschatological thinking of the day included belief that at the beginning of time the ultimate purpose of creation was written on a scroll, which was then sealed. At the end of time this seal would be broken and the secrets revealed. Jesus is here declaring that he is indeed inaugurating this end-time.

The parables Jesus taught to the crowds in public were explained to his disciples in private. His allegorical interpretation is straightforward, and its eschatological significance is clear. The reward for righteousness and the punishment for sin is striking. In agricultural practice of that day weeds were bundled up and burned for fuel. The fate of the righteous is reminiscent of a passage found in the book of Daniel (12:3). In that reference the wise are promised a prize that is apocalyptic in nature. When the kingdom of God comes in its ultimate fulfillment, their radiance will be like that of the cosmic bodies. This teaching ends with a solemn admonishment: Whoever has ears ought to hear and understand this.

## Themes of the Day

The messages found in the readings for today do not easily hold together. We hear about the role played in our lives by the Spirit of God; the composition of the kingdom of God; and the ultimate graciousness of divine judgement.

### The Spirit

We have been considering discipleship and the receptivity required if we are to produce fruits of righteousness in our lives. We might think it is not fair that some people are open to the seed and some are not. We might even think it is not their fault. If we think this, we would be wrong. The Spirit of God dwells in all of the disciples, not merely a few of them, so those who fail to be receptive have failed to open themselves to the Spirit. The Spirit helps us in our weakness, in our inability to pray, and in our difficulty in understanding the parables of Jesus. The first disciples had Jesus to explain the parables to them; we have the Spirit to enlighten us. It is the Spirit who helps us to interpret the teachings of Jesus and to be receptive to the challenges that they pose.

### Let Them Grow Together

One particular teaching of Jesus that is often a stumbling block for good and decent people is the presence of sinners in the kingdom of God. They may not say it bluntly, but in their hearts they believe there is no room for murderers, sexual offenders, public officials who have violated the people's trust, religious leaders who have committed some shameful sin. They seem to believe the kingdom of God is only for the righteous or those whose sins are minor. They operate with some kind of gauge that measures acceptability by the degree of innocence. In a sense we can't blame them. We are all a bit afraid to live close to those we consider sinners. We might fear they will take advantage of us in some way. We certainly don't want them to be an evil influence in our lives, particularly not in the lives of our children. There is probably a bit of this kind of resistance in all of us.

The parable we hear today shows that God has a different point of view. God knows that if sinners are expelled now some of those who are basically good will be cast out with them. There will be a time for separation and judgment, but the time is not now. This means the righteous will have to live with the sinner and, even more challengingly, show them the same kind of concern they show others. The presence of sinners does not necessarily erode the quality of the kingdom. Instead, it provides disciples an opportunity to rise to the occasion of generosity and forgiveness.

## Divine Judgment

There are two images of judgment in the readings. The one in the gospel is terrifying and decisive. The wicked are bound together into bundles and readied for burning. We must remember that this is a parable. In this story, weeds will always be weeds, so there is no chance of change. The image found in the first reading is quite different. There the justice of God is said to be lenient, clement, and kind. The power of God is demonstrated not in retribution but in mercy. God is said to be "merciful and gracious, slow to anger and abounding in kindness and fidelity," and repentance is a very real possibility. This is the image that gives us hope.

## Seventeenth Sunday in Ordinary Time
### 1 Kings 3:5, 7-12

The "wisdom of Solomon" is a phrase that is well known even by those unfamiliar with most of the biblical tradition. The passage read today is an account explaining the origin of that wisdom. It reports an exchange between God and the king. The encounter took place in a dream, an avenue believed to be a vehicle of divine revelation. It is God who initiates the exchange, inviting Solomon to request whatever he desires. No reason is given for God's generosity. That in itself is a point to remember. God gives because God is generous.

In response, Solomon describes both himself and the people he rules. He begins by humbling himself before God, identifying himself as God's servant, admitting that he is king because of the favor of God. This favor came about through God's double initiative. First, it came to pass because God promised Solomon's father, David, that a son of his would rule the people of Israel (cf. 2 Sam 7:12). Second, Solomon himself states that of all the sons that David fathered, God chose him as successor. The king humbles himself further by declaring that he is an insignificant youth with no experience. This is probably less a reference to his age than to his inexperience in the role of leadership. This self-description sets the stage for the favor Solomon will ask of God.

Solomon next describes the people he will rule. Their most important feature is their election by God. Solomon realizes the seriousness of his situation. He has been selected to rule over God's chosen people. His allusion to the size of the population may be exaggerated, but it does reflect the success David achieved in annexing neighboring lands and peoples. Such rule is no mean task, and the king seems well aware of his responsibilities.

In the face of this Solomon asks for an "understanding heart." The heart was considered the seat of thought and understanding. The Hebrew modifying word is *shōmē'a*, which can be translated "listening" or "obedient." The king is asking for understanding that is docile, that is open to the direction of another, presumably God. He asks for this kind of understanding so he can judge the people appropriately and decide what is good for them. His request shows that his concern is with God's people and not merely with his own well-being.

It is no wonder God is pleased with Solomon. There is an interesting shift in perspective at work here. Solomon asks for wisdom, but this in itself was a shrewd request. In Wisdom thinking of the day, wise choices were thought to warrant prosperity and peace. This is precisely what happens here. Solomon makes a wise choice and receives the blessings that flow from it. His request is granted; he is given a wise *(ḥākām)* and understanding *(nābôn)* heart.

The last verse of the passage reinforces the tradition of Solomon's wisdom. It claims that no one before him nor anyone after him could compare with him. It must be remembered, however, that the wisdom of which this passage speaks is not experiential wisdom, the kind that stems from reflection on experience. This wisdom is really a gift from God. Just as God chose Solomon to be king, so God equipped him to rule wisely.

## Psalm 119:57, 72, 76-77, 127-128, 129-130

This is a psalm that glorifies the Law of the LORD. Almost every verse contains the word "law" or a synonym for it. It would be incorrect to say this betrays a legalistic mentality. Rather, it demonstrates the reverence in which the Law was held. The word "law" *(tôrâ)* means "instruction." It refers to the directives given to the people to enable them to live life appropriately. The creative genius of the psalmist is seen in the innovative ways in which the Law is extolled, each verse expressing a slightly different idea.

The distribution of land was an important concept in Israelite thinking. This can be seen in the earliest accounts of the allotment of tracts of land to the various tribes (cf. Joshua 13–21). Land gave people not only a sense of security and belonging, it also gave them their identity as a people. In poetic expressions of the Bible, God rather than land is said to be the cherished portion of the people (cf. Pss 16:5; 73:26). The Hebrew of verse 57 can be read in this way. Following the lead of these other psalms, some translate this verse as: My portion is the LORD, I will keep your words. The lectionary reading has: My portion, Lord, is to keep your words. Both versions are faithful translations of the Hebrew; however, the version used here is more in line with the locus of this particular psalm. It makes obedience to the Law the reason for the people's security and sense of belonging, and it gives them their identity. This notion is reinforced by the accompanying verse (72), which extolls the Law's value.

We miss the true meaning of the Law if we do not situate it squarely within the theology of covenant. Doing this, we can then appreciate the goodness of God, who has not only invited us into covenant but has also shown us how we can faithfully live out this covenant commitment. As we have seen again and again, both lovingkindness (*ḥesed*) and compassion (*raḥămîm*) are intimately associated with covenant (vv. 76-77).

The last two stanzas of this responsorial psalm return to the theme of the value the psalmist accords the Law. It is more precious than fine gold, because it secures for us much more than mere worldly possessions. It provides us with reliable direction on the way to live, thus ensuring us a right relationship with God and the blessings that flow from it. The Law is the treasure of all people, wise and simple alike. All are invited to follow it and to attain the favors it promises. All are enlightened by the wonders it contains. It is clear from this psalm response that the Law is anything but a burden. Rather, it is a trusted guide from God, a treasure beyond compare.

## Romans 8:28-30

Two significant themes are found in today's reading from the letter to the Romans: all things working for good and the nature of divine predetermination. Although these themes may be familiar to most, they are complex and often misunderstood.

The first theme, that all things work for good, should not be misunderstood as meaning "everything will work out in the end." This latter sentiment suggests that the misfortune that befalls every life and the suffering each of us must endure will ultimately be corrected by God. Far from saying this, the expression suggests a profound trust in God, who can bring good even when adverse circumstances are not altered. Those who love God believe God loves them and desires what is in their best interest. Though they may not know what this might imply, they believe God does, and they trust God will draw good out of misfortune.

The second theme is also widely known and perhaps even more misunderstood. Using but a few words Paul lays out the entire plan or purpose of God from the pretemporal age to the period of glorification: God foreknew, predetermined, called, justified, and glorified. Although the verbs are in the past tense, the actual unfolding of this divine purpose is believed to be an ongoing reality. A careful examination of each of these verbs will throw light on the essence of this divine purpose. To have foreknowledge is to know what will occur long before it comes to pass. Even before the beginning of time God knew the plan that would bring all things to their final conclusion. However, it was not enough to know this purpose. God also has the power to bring it about. This effective power is what predetermination means.

The theme of divine call is common in the Scriptures. The pressing question here is twofold: Who is called? And, to what are they called? Paul is very clear about the answer to the second question. They are called to conformity to the image of God's Son. The entire Christian tradition provides the answer to the first question: All are called. It is precisely at this step in the divine plan or purpose that most misunderstanding occurs. Who is called, and to what are they called? Nowhere does Paul suggest that some are predestined to salvation and others to perdition. Rather, he argues that all are called to conform their lives to the image of Christ, who is the firstborn Son of God. (In classical theology human freedom is always viewed as compromised by this predetermination. Paul does not seem worried about this.) If believers conform themselves to the image of their elder brother, they will themselves become children of God. It is this conformity that will result in their being justified, and their justification will be the source of their glorification.

## Matthew 13:44-52

Using parables, Jesus continues to teach his disciples about the kingdom of God. The reading for this Sunday contains three of these parables. The first two (the treasure in the field and the pearl) point to the inestimable value of the kingdom. The third (the net) treats the diverse composition of its membership. The reading closes with a short dialogue between Jesus and his disciples.

The parables of the treasure in the field and the pearl of great price are similar. Both suggest the kingdom of God is present though unperceived. Only the very shrewd discover it. When they do discover it, they sacrifice everything to possess it. As is the case with all metaphorical language, the focus of a parable is limited. The point of the comparison in the first parable is the value of the treasure itself, not the possibility that the purchase of the field might have been a fraudulent transaction. Those who first heard that parable would have rejoiced with the man who found the treasure. The one who found the pearl was probably a professional trader of pearls rather than merely a retailer. His eye would recognize the value another might overlook. He too would be applauded by Jesus' original audience.

The parable of the net is quite different. It resembles the parable of the wheat and the weeds (cf. Matt 13:40b-42; Sixteenth Sunday). The dragnet described here probably had floats on its top edge and weights on the bottom. After it was cast out it would be drawn in by ropes, with the fish caught in the net. This kind of indiscriminate fishing required sorting once the fish had been hauled to shore, but no sooner. Those who heard this parable would have been familiar with the scene it describes. The eschatological character of the parable is seen in the mention of the end *(syntéleia)* of the age and the role of the angels at the time of final judgment, when the good will be separated from the evil.

While the exchange between Jesus and his disciples addresses the parables that precede it, it can also be considered the conclusion of Jesus' entire parabolic instruction (cf. Fifteenth and Sixteenth Sundays). Jesus asks if the disciples understand what he has been teaching them. Their response is affirmative. This could be true either because the parables just proclaimed are easy to understand or, as in the case of the other Sundays, because Jesus explains their meanings. The scribes of whom Jesus speaks probably did more than copy the scrolls. They were the interpreters of the Law. Jesus considers his disciples interpreters of the Law, instructed (made disciples, *mathēteúō*) in the kingdom. Just as a householder brings out treasures old and new, so they are able to understand that Jesus' teaching is grounded in the original tradition yet is radically different.

## Themes of the Day

Two themes seem to weave through the readings for this Sunday: treasure and delight. The treasure is the extraordinary gift that comes from God; the delight is the joy we experience when we realize the treasure is ours. A third theme, found in the first reading, picks up a theme we have considered several times during this period of Ordinary Time, namely, service of others.

### The Treasure

The treasure is the kingdom of heaven, the reign of God. It is the realization of knowing that we belong to God, that we are cherished and cared for, that we have been called to commit ourselves to the noblest values of the human heart. It is the prize that gives meaning to the present, and its fullest delight draws us into the future. It feeds our hungers; it satisfies our thirsts; it piques our curiosity. The kingdom of heaven excites us as a child is excited at Christmas or a bride on the morning of her wedding. It has the calming touch of a nursing mother, the warmth of a lover's embrace, the approving smile of a good friend. The reign of God is the fulfillment of our deepest desires and our fondest hopes. Nothing in the world can compare with it, and that is why we are willing to sacrifice everything to attain it.

The treasure we find is really a gift that is given. We need not work to attain the kingdom, nor can we earn it in any way. It is given to us by God; all we have to do is accept it. There is something about the kingdom that resembles God's offer in today's first reading. Appearing to Solomon, God invites him to ask for whatever he would like. This demonstrates the generosity of God. In a sense the kingdom of God is ours for the asking. Unfortunately we do not always recognize its value, and we do not ask for it.

## *The Gift Received Is a Gift Given*

The gospel concentrates on the treasured character of the kingdom. The first reading adds another dimension to our consideration. Having been given the opportunity to choose any blessing he might desire, Solomon chose to be of service to others. In this he is a model for disciples to follow. We have discovered the treasure in the field; we have found the pearl of great price; we have been blessed with the kingdom of God. What we have been given, we must now give to others. We can be assured that it will be with us as it was with Solomon. In giving we will lose nothing. In fact, we gain an abundance of blessings. All things work for good, and God is glorified in all. Such is the character of the kingdom of God.

# Ordinary Time (Part Three)

| | | | |
|---|---|---|---|
| **Eighteenth Sunday**<br><br>Isaiah 55:1-3<br>Come to the water | Psalm 145:8-9, 15-16, 17-18<br>You satisfy every desire | Romans 8:35, 37-39<br>What can separate us<br>from the love of Christ | Matthew 14:13-21<br>They ate and were satisfied |
| **Nineteenth Sunday**<br><br>1 Kings 19:19a, 11-13a<br>God was in the whispering sound | Psalm 85:9, 10, 11-12, 13-14<br>The LORD proclaims peace | Romans 9:1-5<br>Cut off for the sake of my people | Matthew 14:22-33<br>Let me come to you on the water |
| **Twentieth Sunday**<br><br>Isaiah 56:1, 6-7<br>I will bring all to my<br>holy mountain | Psalm 67:2-3, 5, 6, 8<br>Let all nations praise you | Romans 11:13-15, 29-32<br>God's gifts are irrevocable | Matthew 15:21-28<br>Woman, great is your faith |
| **Twenty-First Sunday**<br><br>Isaiah 22:19-23<br>The key of the house of David | Psalm 138:1-2, 2-3, 6, 8<br>Your kindness endures forever | Romans 11:33-36<br>Inscrutable are God's judgments | Matthew 16:13-20<br>You will bind and loose |
| **Twenty-Second Sunday**<br><br>Jeremiah 20:7-9<br>Like fire burning in my heart | Psalm 63:2, 3-4, 5-6, 8-9<br>My soul is thirsting for you | Romans 12:1-2<br>Your bodies are a living sacrifice | Matthew 16:21-27<br>Take up your cross |

| | | |
|---|---|---|
| **Twenty-Third Sunday**<br><br>Ezekiel 33:7-9<br>A watchman for the<br>house of Israel | Psalm 95:1-2, 6-7, 8-9<br>Harden not your hearts | Romans 13:8-10<br>Love fulfills the Law | Matthew 18:15-20<br>Be reconciled with others |
| **Twenty-Fourth Sunday**<br><br>Sirach 27:30–28:7<br>Forgive your neighbor | Psalm 103:1-2, 3-4, 9-10, 11-12<br>The LORD is kind and merciful | Romans 14:7-9<br>We are the Lord's | Matthew 18:21-35<br>Forgive seventy-seven times |

# Ordinary Time (Part Three)

## Initial Reading of the Ordinary Lectionary (Part Three)

*Introduction*

During this period of Ordinary Time the lectionary readings seem particularly focused on issues and concerns of ordinary life. While there is continuity in the readings from the letter to the Romans and in the gospel, the first readings appear to have been chosen in random fashion. But this is the way life is. Ordinary Time is for the ordinary life of ordinary people. The lessons to be learned are lessons about everyday discipleship and the kind of community this discipleship creates.

*First Testament Readings*

The first readings for this section of Ordinary Time provide us with a kind of collage, an artistic creation composed of diverse snippets from various sectors. Three themes contribute color and texture: God's self-revelation, the service of God, and the forgiveness of others.

On the Eighteenth and Nineteenth Sundays of the year we stand in awe of divine gentleness. We are invited to approach God even though empty-handed, not with resources with which to buy what we need. The invitation is tender: Come! Come to the water! Come to me! We may look for God in the majestic events of the world, but God is finally revealed in a gentle whisper. These readings tell us God may be awesome, but God is not awful.

On the Twentieth through the Twenty-Third Sundays we are given glimpses into some of the ways God is served. All these readings come from prophetic books, thus suggesting an eschatological dimension to our activities as servants. In other words, these roles might find fulfillment in the future. We are told that the service of God is not the privilege of some elite group. All people, even those we might consider foreigners, are called to the mountain of God, there to participate in the worship of God. We also discover that privileged positions of service can be lost if we do not faithfully fulfill the responsibilities that accompany these positions. The office of prophet makes special demands on the one who holds it. Even when these burdens are more than the individual can carry, this person still experiences a burning need to proclaim the word of God. Finally, we see that one is not a prophet for oneself. Regardless of the difficulty of the task, the word of God must be spoken. If it is not, the misfortune of those who never heard the word intended for them will be on the conscience of the one who refused to proclaim it.

This collection of readings closes with an exhortation to forgive those who have offended us just as God has forgiven us.

## Psalms

All of the psalm responses acclaim some characteristic of God that benefits human beings. This can be compassion, kindness and truth, justice, strength, the blessings of a banquet, salvation, or forgiveness. There is praise and gratitude for God's providence and generosity. There is confidence God will continue to shower blessings on those who cry out for them. As with so much of the theology contained in the Bible, so also in the psalms: God's past blessings become the ground for trusting God will bestow blessings in the future. In the face of all of this goodness on the part of God, the psalmist calls believers to live lives that reflect that goodness.

## Epistles

The continuous reading from the letter to the Romans develops three major themes. The first is found in the first reading of this collection. It underscores the enduring bond that exists between Christ and those who follow him in faith. Nothing can sever this bond—nothing in this world and nothing in the next. This should be reassuring for those who are suffering or who are in doubt.

The next three readings address the question of the destiny of the people of Israel who have not accepted Christ as their Messiah. Paul's devotion to them is obvious. However, this devotion does not merely spring from common ethnic origin. It is grounded in the fidelity of God, who makes promises and does not renege on them. It was to the Jewish people that God gave such wondrous blessings; it was from the Jewish people that Christ entered into human history; it was because of the Jewish people that the gospel was preached to the Gentiles. Who can imagine what blessings the rest of the world will experience when the Jewish people finally accept Christ?

The last three readings contain some of Paul's teaching regarding the manner of life required of Christians. They must reject the standards of the world and conform themselves to the standards of the gospel, the entire ethical program of which can be summarized in the admonition to love. Finally, the collection of readings ends where it began, with a statement about the intimate relationship that exists between Christ and those who have chosen to be his disciples.

## Gospels

Three of these gospel narratives report demonstrations of Jesus' miraculous power, while the other four depict him instructing his inner circle of disciples. In the case of the miracles he responds to human need. He never performs miracles merely to put on a show of power. Instead, he acts in response to human need. He feeds the multitude because they need food; he draws Peter to safety because he is sinking; he heals the sick Canaanite child because her mother pleads for her recovery. Jesus touches the lives of others because they are in need, and this need fills him with compassion.

In the rest of the gospel readings Jesus continues his instruction of his disciples. His schooling of them is beginning to show its fruits, but only beginning. Acting as spokesperson of the group, Peter acknowledges that Jesus is indeed the Messiah for whom they have been waiting. Immediately upon this testimony of faith Jesus announces that Peter will be the foundation rock of the believing community Jesus will establish. Whether this privilege emboldened Peter or his devotion to Jesus was quickened at the thought of Jesus' suffering, Peter's misunderstanding of the character of the Messiah reveals that he and the other disciples still have much to learn.

In the final Sunday of this cluster of Sundays we hear again from Peter. He appears to be willing to go far beyond the forgiving spirit required of him by the religious culture of his day. However, Jesus declares that even this is not enough. The standard by which we must judge ourselves is the limitless compassion of God.

## Mosaic of Readings

The readings for this time of year move easily from one area of life to another. These readings do not contain trivial themes. On the contrary, they address many of the realities of everyday life, realities frequently overlooked because of their ordinariness. "Ordinary" does not mean banal. It is the warp and woof of life; it is the normal place we encounter God. Even if we take a vacation from the responsibilities we carry throughout the year, we are reminded by several of the readings that there is no vacation from our responsibilities of Christian living.

# Readings

## *Eighteenth Sunday in Ordinary Time*

### Isaiah 55:1-3

This powerful prophetic oracle contains some of the most moving sentiments placed in the mouth of God. God is cast in the role of a street vendor who offers food and drink at no cost, both to those who are able to pay (v. 2) and to those who are not (v. 1). All are invited to come to the LORD to be refreshed and nourished. The invitation is similar to that of Woman Wisdom, who calls those in the streets to enter her house and partake of the banquet of her table (cf. Prov 9:5-6). The generosity of God is seen in the offer of water, grain, wine, and milk. While water is essential regardless of the climate or topography of the land, it is particularly important in the climate of Mediterranean Palestine. Grain, wine, and milk are staples of the Near Eastern diet and imply here abundant harvests and healthy flocks. These necessities are offered by God free of charge. What God has to offer is satisfying and will be long lasting compared to all else for which people seem to spend their money.

The prophet's reference here is probably to something more than ordinary food and drink, since those called are also told to listen *(shāmaʿ)*. This is the same verb that introduces Israel's important prayer: Hear, O Israel! It suggests not only hearing but also heeding the words that are heard. The oracle is implying that the word of God is itself a source of nourishment and rejuvenation. It is comparable to the richest part of the meal. It is, in fact, the source of life itself.

The real object of the invitation is God's announcement of the reestablishment of a covenant bond (v. 3). This harkens back to the royal covenant, the one God made with David and his house (cf. 2 Sam 7:12-16). That was a unilateral covenant, a free gift from God with no requirements placed on the human partner. However, that covenantal privilege did not exempt the kings from observance of the Law, which was associated with the Mosaic covenant. At the time of the establishment of that covenant God had said that those kings who were not faithful to the Law would be punished but would not lose the kingdom as Saul before them had done. This oracle suggests the covenant had been violated, and now God was eager to restore the severed bond.

### Psalm 145:8-9, 15-16, 17-18

The responsorial psalm for today is a hymn of praise of the greatness of God. In the first section the psalmist speaks about God, extolling divine mercy and compassion. In the second section the psalmist speaks directly to God, inviting all God's works to give thanks and proclaiming the LORD's universal providence. In the third section the psalmist prays that all God's works will give thanks and proclaim the LORD's universal and everlasting reign.

The passage opens with an acclamation closely associated with the revelation of God and the acknowledgment of God's name, revealed at the time of the reestablishment of the covenant (cf. Exod 34:6). In these two verses covenant language abounds. God is described as gracious *(hannûn)* and compassionate *(rahûm)* and filled with lovingkindness *(hesed)*. It should be noted that this divine goodness is not reserved for Israel alone but is extended to all God's works. This includes all people and nations, but also all of natural creation. The covenant has been expanded to a universal embrace.

Next is celebrated divine providence, one of the most prominent of God's characteristics (vv. 15-16). Everything that has been created relies on this providence. A vivid image is used to depict both the dependence of all living creatures and the generosity of God. All of life stands needy and trusting before God, in whose hands is found the sustenance upon which life depends, and God is openhanded in satisfying this need. The image bespeaks the confidence creation has in God and the tender concern God has toward creation.

Finally, the basis of God's loving attention is proclaimed (vv. 17-18). God's covenant commitment is revealed as justice *(ṣedeq)* and lovingkindness *(hesed)*. These constitute the source of God's provident care and the firm foundation upon which the faithful ones can trust. A third covenant characteristic is truth *(ʾĕmet)*. Here it refers to the firmness or constancy with which the faithful rely on God. They can rely on God because God has entered into a solemn agreement with them, has made serious promises to them, and can be depended upon to be faithful. In order to experience the benefits of this covenant one needs only to call upon God, who is always there to hear.

## Romans 8:35, 37-39

The question Paul poses is a rhetorical question; it is clear he believes there is nothing that can separate believers from the love of Christ. But why would he pose the question in the first place? He is probably not merely encouraging them, countering the idea that they will turn away from Christ to avoid any suffering that might flow from their commitment. Instead, he is challenging the long-standing theory of retribution, which held that good would be rewarded and evil punished. This point of view argues that a person's misfortune is the consequence of some misdeed. Paul turns this understanding upside down by insisting the opposite is true, namely, that the righteous, precisely because they are righteous, enter into the sufferings of Christ. In other words, misfortune does not separate them from Christ; it unites them with him.

Several of the hardships Paul lists have been associated with the tribulations ascribed to the end-time. They are not ordinary hardships but the kind that arise because of one's commitment to Christ. Affliction *(thlípsis)* is the kind of ordeal associated with the transition into the final age; distress *(stenochōría)* refers to a kind of confining oppression; persecution *(diōgmós)* suggests religious persecution; famine and nakedness are consequences of disastrous social disruption, thought to accompany the end-time; peril is a very general term but is used infrequently by Paul; in this context the sword probably refers to execution rather than war.

If these hardships are indeed references to the final tribulation, the pangs that precede the birth of the final age, then they surely do not separate believers from, but rather unite them with, the love of Christ. These misfortunes are not indications believers have been overcome but rather signs they are overcoming the forces of this age. They are empowered by the God who loves them. Victory is accomplished not because believers have clung to Christ but because Christ has clung to them. The military imagery is striking. It suggests that believers are waging war, which, if the reference is to the final struggle, is an apt image.

Paul draws up yet another list of realities that have no power to separate believers from the love of God. They include both physical dangers and superhuman powers. He begins by juxtaposing life and death. This includes all of human existence in this world. Neither the sufferings of this life nor death itself has power over this bond of love. Angels, principalities, and powers are names of supernatural beings. Angels were regarded as intermediaries between heaven and earth; principalities were heavenly rulers; powers were heavenly beings known for their might. None of these supernatural beings can threaten the bond of love. Neither the evils of the past nor those that might exert power in the future have any control. Height and depth were astrological terms denoting a star's closest and farthest point from its zenith. Their mention implies there is nothing in the broader cosmos that can interfere with the bond of love. The concluding statement encompasses all creation. Nothing can separate us from the love of God in Christ Jesus our Lord.

It is important to note several points. First, what predominates is God's love for us. Second, it comes to us through Jesus. Third, this Jesus is the Christ, which means the "anointed one." Finally, Christ Jesus is the Lord to whom we give our allegiance.

## Matthew 14:13-21

The gospel reading opens with mention of how the death of John the Baptist prompted Jesus to seek a place where he might be by himself. Some have suggested Jesus was attempting to escape the fate that had befallen John. However, the text gives no reason for Jesus' action. If he was trying to hide from danger, the miracle of multiplication certainly did thrust him into public attention. The deserted place *(erēmos)* was not an arid desert, for it had grass upon which the crowd was directed to recline. It probably did hold great symbolic meaning, for it would have reminded the people of the formative period of their past in the desert where God had entered into covenant with them. A return to the desert was often a time of recommitment. Furthermore, this place was close enough to populated areas that the disciples could suggest that food and lodging might be procured.

Jesus' departure did not deter the crowds, who seemed to know where he was going and who arrived there before he did. Seeing them, Jesus was moved with pity *(splanchnízomai),* a word meaning "profound inner emotion," which is used only by or about Jesus and which has messianic significance (cf. Matt 9:36; 15:32; 20:34). Jesus responded so intensely because he was moved by the plight of the people. He cured their sick, but he obviously had something else in mind as well.

Bread and fish was the basic diet of poor Galileans. However, five loaves and two fish would hardly have constituted a meal for Jesus and his disciples, much less for the crowd said to have gathered on this occasion. Yet that was the fare the disciples were told to distribute. The crowd was told to recline, the customary position taken at a banquet. Although only the men seem to have been counted, the author admits the presence of women and children. Jesus' actions over the food are brief but significant. He took it, he blessed it, he broke it, and he gave it as food. The eucharistic overtones are obvious (cf. Matt 26:26-27). The prayer said over the food was probably more a thanksgiving to God than a blessing of the food itself. If it was the typical Jewish blessing of the time, it might have resembled the following: "Blessed are you, O LORD our God, Ruler of the universe, who brings forth bread from the earth" *(Ber* 6:1).

It is difficult to know whether the historical Jesus actually spoke these words and if so, whether it was done with a proleptic eye to his Last Supper, which was itself a foreshadowing of the final messianic banquet. However, we can be certain the gospel writer wanted these connections to be made. In fact, the episode recalls other feeding traditions that must have been called to the writer's mind on this occasion. The most obvious is the miraculous feeding in the wilderness with manna (cf. Exod 16:15; it appears the Jews believed manna would return with the coming of the Messiah [2 Bar 29:8; cf. Rev 2:17]). There is also a story in the Elisha cycle in which the prophet feeds a smaller crowd with loaves of bread, some of which were also left over (cf. 2 Kgs 4:42-44).

A sometimes overlooked detail in this feeding account might allude to the final messianic banquet for which the Jews waited with great anticipation. According to a tradition in Jewish apocalyptic lore, the primordial beasts of chaos, having been decisively conquered, will be served at the eschatological banquet. (Such a final elimination of enemies is quite common in mythological literature.) These beasts were the sea monsters Behemoth (cf. Job 40:15) and Leviathan (cf. Job 41:1; Ps 104:26). Is it merely coincidence that this gospel narrative with its eschatological nuance adds fish to the menu? The miracle in the wilderness described in today's gospel seems to have gathered together traditions of the past as well as expectations of the future, all of which point to the ultimate eschatological banquet.

The role played by the apostles cannot be overlooked. They were the ones through whom the crowds experienced the munificence of Jesus. They distributed the food and, most likely, collected what was left over into twelve baskets. The author of the gospel shows by this that Jesus provides for his people through the agency of the Church.

Over the years there have been attempts to explain what really happened in this event. Was food really multiplied? Or did people bring out their own provisions and share them with others? Any attempt to explain away the miracle completely misses the point of the narrative. Its many-leveled meaning rests on the miraculous abundance God provides through Jesus.

## Themes of the Day

### The One Who Nourishes

Jesus is the one who nourishes us, who provides us with the sustenance we need. Bread and fish may have been the diet of peasant fisherfolk of first-century Israel, but they represent all the ways that we, the needy people of the contemporary world, are sustained by him. In a world fraught with meaninglessness he offers purpose; to a world stumbling in darkness and confusion he provides direction. He satisfies the hungry heart; he enlivens the drooping spirit. Those who follow Jesus will never be left to languish in the desert.

When we follow Jesus wholeheartedly, we are surprised at the ways in which we are sustained. While there may be times we feel that a banquet of rich food has been set before us, we are usually nourished with simple food, the ordinary fare of daily life. A student of years gone by thanks us for our commitment and our kindness. Our words turn the fear in the eyes of a patient to relief. We are warmly welcomed into a gathering of friends. We are touched by the sentiments of a season: the warmth and glow of Christmas; the joy and hope of Easter. Jesus nourishes us with the simple things of life.

### Bread That Satisfies

If we but open our eyes we will be amazed at the bountifulness of the nourishment provided for us. We will discover that there is more than we will ever need; that God is magnanimous, even prodigal in giving; that God's generosity exceeds all our expectations and also our understanding. So often the hunger we experience is really dissatisfaction. Because we want richer fare, we overlook the simple yet substantial bread within our reach.

A second characteristic of this bread should not be overlooked. It comes to us in a community of disciples. We are nourished by God through the ministry of one another. Again, this happens through very simple actions: distributing bread and gathering up the fragments; visiting the sick and consoling the grieving; caring for a child and giving aid to an elder; bagging groceries and directing a choir. If we but open our eyes we will be astounded at how ordinary actions can satisfy our hunger and the hunger of others.

### Without Cost

Perhaps what astounds us most about the goodness of God is that it is given freely, without paying and without cost. There was no thought of requiring payment from the multitude on the mountain. Isaiah insists that God simply invites: All you who are thirsty come . . . come, receive grain and eat! Of course, we have to acknowledge that we are needy. We have to reach out our hands to receive. But when we do, we are sustained, and we discover that a bond is established that endures. Jesus had compassion on the multitude. This compassion was not a fleeting emotion; it is an enduring attitude. He is always concerned about our welfare and our needs. This will never change. We will never be sent away to find nourishment for ourselves. Nothing can separate us from the love of Christ.

## Nineteenth Sunday in Ordinary Time
### 1 Kings 19:9a, 11-13a

The description of the prophet Elijah's experience of God draws on several earlier Israelite traditions. The first is the location of its occurrence. It happens on Horeb, the mountain of God. Because of their majestic appearances mountains were considered sacred places by many ancient peoples. Their peaks were the closest points to the heavens, and for this reason the highest mountain was believed to be the dwelling place of the deity and the logical place for offering sacrifice. In the literature of ancient Israel there are various versions of the story of God entering into covenant with the people on a mountain. In one tradition Sinai is the name given to the mountain on which this occurred (cf. Exod 19:1-6); a second tradition identifies the mountain as Horeb (cf. Deut 4:10-15a). The story of Elijah's experience belongs to this second tradition.

Both traditions describe the theophany, or revelation of God, as having been accompanied by spectacular meteorological phenomena. There is piercing thunder and brilliant lightning; the mountain is engulfed by a thick cloud and it shakes violently; God descends upon the mountain in a blaze of fire (cf. Ps 29:3-9). Such an impressive display of nature was not unique to Israel's worldview. The Canaanites believed their own weather god Baal was manifested in precisely the same way. In fact, they believed that Baal was the god of the storm. Perhaps the Israelite storytellers related the event of the establishment of the covenant in this way in order to show that it was their God and not the god of the Canaanites who was announced with such fanfare and who governed the powers of nature.

In today's reading we see that Elijah has retreated into a cave, but God calls him from this place of shelter and darkness to stand "before the LORD," out in the open. Unlike Moses, who actually asked for a glimpse of God (cf. Exod 33:18), Elijah received the revelation at God's initiative. Elijah witnessed the wind, the earthquake, and the fire associated with a theophany, but he did not experience God within these natural marvels. It was only when he heard a tiny whispering voice *(qôl)* that he was gripped with the realization that God was present. In response he covered his face in an act of reverence and stood at the entrance of the cave. This was not an experience of oral revelation; no divine words were delivered. The voice itself was the experience. When Moses had asked to see the glory of God, he was told that he would not be able to look upon God's face. He would only be granted a glimpse of the back of this glory after it had passed by. Here Elijah was also granted limited revelation—a wordless voice.

Most commentators maintain that this revelation points out that usually the small and insignificant events of life are the stage upon which the revelation of God is enacted. It is so easy to be awed by the spectacular and overlook the ordinary. Yet most lives are made up of the ordinary, and it is there the "tiny whispering voice" of God will be heard, if we are attuned to it.

### Psalm 85:9, 10, 11-12, 13-14

The verses of this passage presume a community waiting for God's word, a prophetic oracle that will announce peace (v. 9). Presumably the people are in distress or they would not be hoping for a word of peace. There is no direct appeal to God here. These verses depict the people awaiting a reply to a plea they must have made elsewhere. Their confidence that God will respond rests in the conviction that they are God's own people; they are faithful people; they trust in God. There is great expectancy here. The people have done what they can to get God's attention. The next move is God's.

These people are not in total despair. They do believe in salvation, and they maintain that the salvation for which they wait is near to them. At least, it is near to those who are loyal (v. 10). The salvation described here is associated with prosperity, suggesting the people's distress has something to do with economic misfortune. The hoped-for prosperity will be bounteous, filling the whole land. It seems these people have suffered a serious setback, one they cannot remedy by themselves. In faith they had already turned to their God for help. After having made their petition, they wait confidently for God's response.

Lovingkindness, truth, justice, and peace (v. 11) are characteristics of the covenantal relationship described here. The people are living agents of this relationship. Lovingkindness is covenant loyalty; truth is covenant faithfulness; justice is the covenantal righteousness that comes from God; peace is the wholeness or harmony that results from the covenantal relationship. It is not clear whether it is God who possesses these virtues or whether it is the people. In either case they are salvific powers, and their union is a sign of the time of fulfillment. When they meet and embrace, salvation is complete. In order further to characterize the scope of this saving event, the psalmist singles out one partner of each of the two pairs, thus creating another figurative description. Truth springs up from the earth, and justice comes down from heaven. All creation, from earth to sky, shares in the benefits of the salvation by God.

In the final verses the psalmist returns to the theme of prosperity (vv. 13-14), confident that God will reestablish the wealth of the people and that the land once barren and forsaken will yield an abundant harvest. Although the image is of an actual harvest of the fruits of the earth, the reference can stand for any situation that brings forth life and prosperity.

Finally, justice and good fortune join the LORD in triumphal procession, with justice in the lead and good fortune bringing up the rear. The procession is really a theophany, a glorious manifestation of the LORD. The four covenantal virtues are the telltale marks of this manifestation. They are present only because God is there revealing them, making them real in the lives of the people. This revelation of God is in fact the salvation for which the people long, for which they wait in confidence.

## Romans 9:1-5

The seriousness of the message Paul declares in the reading for today is evident in his threefold proclamation: I speak the truth; I do not lie; the Spirit testifies to the witness of my conscience. The issue of which he speaks is his ardent attachment to his Jewish compatriots, his kindred according to the flesh. Although Paul turned from proclaiming the gospel to the Jewish people and devoted himself to the conversion of the Gentiles, he never ceased loving the people from whom he came. It is this very love that causes him such anguish, because his own people have not accepted Jesus as the Messiah that God first promised and then sent them.

The depth of Paul's distress can be seen in the radical solution he proposes. He is willing to be considered cursed *(anáthema)* and cut off from Christ for their sake. We read just last week that Paul believed nothing could separate us from the love of God in Christ Jesus. Therefore, while Paul's sentiment here is certainly genuine, the intensity of this sentiment prompts him to propose something that should not be taken literally. Paul was not the first leader to be willing to forfeit his future with God for the sake of the people he loves. Moses had made the same suggestion after his people had sinned by worshiping the golden calf. Fearing that their future as God's people was in jeopardy, Moses had offered himself as a kind of vicarious sacrifice (cf. Exod 32:32). It is in this light that Paul's proposition should be understood.

After declaring his own attachment to the Jewish people, Paul proceeds to list seven prerogatives they enjoy as the chosen people of God. First he calls them Israelites, not Jews. "Israelite" is the name that identifies them as descendants of Jacob/Israel, the covenanted people of God. Although nowhere else are they referred to as adopted children of God, they do enjoy the designation "firstborn" (cf. Exod 4:22). The "glory" of God refers to the extraordinary way God's holiness was manifested to the Israelite people. It appeared in the cloud that led them through the wilderness (cf. Exod 16:19), and it settled in the Temple (cf. 1 Kgs 8:11). This glory indicated that God was present with the people in a very special way. It was with the Israelites that God entered into covenant, first through Abraham (cf. Gen 15:18; 17:2), then through Moses (cf. Exod 19:5), and then through the house of David (cf. Ps 89:3-4). To them was entrusted the sacred Law (cf. Exod 20:2-17; Deut 5:6-21) and the precepts of divine worship (cf. Leviticus 17–26). The promises were made through their ancestors (cf. Gen 12:2-3).

The greatest boast of this people is that the Christ, the anointed one of God, was to come from their line. This boast is directly linked to Paul's' anguish of heart, for the people do not realize Christ's true identity. But Paul does. He acknowledges Christ's sovereignty over all. The last phrase of the text is obscure. It can be an acclamation of God, who is blessed forever, or its juxtaposition with a description of Christ would suggest Paul is actually calling Christ "God." If the first interpretation is the correct one, the Greek construction is quite awkward. The second version fits both the Greek construction and the sense of Paul's argument. In other words, from the Jewish people came Christ, who is sovereign over all and who is God, blessed forever.

## Matthew 14:22-33

The gospel reading for this Sunday consists of four related episodes: Jesus sends his disciples across the water while he goes up the mountain to pray (vv. 22-24); Jesus walks on the water (vv. 25-27); Peter attempts to walk on the water (vv. 29-31); the disciples in the boat declare the identity of Jesus (vv. 32-33).

The first episode sets the circumstances for the rest of the reading. This episode follows the report of the feeding of the five thousand (cf. Matt 14:13-21, Eighteenth Sunday). Jesus sends the disciples on ahead, he dismisses the crowd, and he goes up a mountain to be by himself and to pray. Scene one closes.

In the meantime, the disciples are struggling in the boat. Lake Gennesaret, also known as the Sea of Galilee, is well known even today for the sudden and violent storms that arise on it. The disciples' boat was already well into the sea, far from shore. To add to their distress the light was not in their favor. Since according to the Roman military the night was divided into four watches of three hours each, this episode occurred during the fourth watch, sometime between 3 A.M. and 6 A.M. In the pre-dawn dimness the disciples saw Jesus walking toward them on the water. They knew that what they saw was a physical impossibility, and so they mistook him for a ghost *(phantasm),* and they cried out in fear. Jesus' response was the typical response to fear in the face of an experience of the divine: Do not be afraid! To this he adds the theophanic exclamation: It is I; I am *(egō eimi)!*

In the ancient Near East not only was water cherished because of its importance for sustaining life, but it was also feared because of the devastation wrought by the overflow of unruly lakes and rivers. For this reason it became an apt symbol for chaos. Several creation myths recount how a valiant warrior-god battled the forces of cosmic chaos and emerged victorious. Although chaos was never quite destroyed, it was held in check by this mighty god. To portray Jesus walking on the chaotic water as a stouthearted conqueror was to cast him in the guise of this creator-god, who alone governed the waters.

Not quite sure about what he sees, Peter exclaims: "If it is you, command me to come." Peter accepts Jesus' invitation to come, and he begins to walk on the water. His faith upholds him. However, his faith is not strong enough to overcome his fear of the chaotic waters, and so he sinks. Peter is a model of both faith and lack of faith. He believed that he would be able to walk on the water, and he did; he doubted that he would be able to withstand the chaos, and he did not. Ultimately, it was faith that won out, for Peter cried out to Jesus, knowing that Jesus had the power to save him, and he did.

All the theophanic elements of the story come together at its end. Jesus walks over chaotic water in the manner of a conqueror. He responds with a standard expression to the kind of fear brought on by an experience of the divine. He saves Peter from the unruly waters. Although the text does not say Jesus calmed the wind, it does subside when he gets into the boat. Finally, those in the boat pay him homage, identifying him as the Son of God. The entire event is a manifestation of the extraordinary power that resides in Jesus.

### Themes of the Day

Today we continue the christological reflections begun last Sunday. Once again we are awed by the mysterious power of Jesus and, as was the case last Sunday, we are invited to participate somehow in that power.

### The Whispering Sound

The first theme repeats the major theme of last Sunday. Although divine power is manifested in dramatic ways, it is also present in the unassuming. Traces of God can be seen in the delicacy of a violet, in a cool summer breeze, in the blush of innocence, in the fiery eyes of justice. Every one of us lives in the midst of God, breathes the breath of God's life, and is constantly touched by the exquisite artistry of God's creativity. Life itself is a mountain experience of God.

### Subdue Chaos

As wonderful as life is, it can also be frightening. There may well be order in the natural processes of creation, but many times human beings are unaware of that order or, for any number of reasons, do not live in harmony with it. What results can only be described as chaos. In addition to this, misunderstanding and rancor, jealousy and vindictiveness, greed and hunger for power, are but a few of the causes of social discord. Finally, our personal lives themselves can come unraveled, and we can feel that we are genuinely "at sea." Every human being is tossed about by the exigencies of life.

It is at times like these that we need faith in Jesus. Even though we do not recognize him, he is there in the midst of our chaos. Having the power of God, he is the definitive champion of all chaos, and so he is able to allay our fears and calm the sea. In so many ways he has already shown us the love he has for us, so why do we doubt? Why do we hesitate? Perhaps it is because we are so used to depending upon ourselves. In this regard, the gospel underscores a very important point. It is not enough to acknowledge Jesus or even to step into danger for his sake. We are able to do this only if we have faith in the power that comes from him. If we rely solely on our own devices, we are liable to sink even deeper into chaos.

### Concern for Others

Since the general context of the readings for Ordinary Time is the character and responsibilities of discipleship, it is appropriate to use this context to show the relationship between the disciple's experience of God and the implications of this experience for discipleship itself. This can be stated in a phrase that has been used frequently in the reflections for Ordinary Time: What has been given must now be shared. We find this sharing exemplified in the reading from Paul, who was willing to offer himself in exchange for God's graciousness toward Paul's own people.

A true experience of God, whether it be in the ordinariness of life or in one of life's tribulations, is both transformative and effusive. It affects us in a way similar to the way we are affected when we hear about the birth of a child or the end of a war. This is news that cannot be contained; it must be proclaimed. This last theme reminds us that disciples must be ready to do what they can in order for the good news of God's revelation to be made known to others.


## Twentieth Sunday in Ordinary Time

### Isaiah 56:1, 6-7

There are two major themes that determine the contours of this passage. The first is the inclusive nature of the believing community; the second is the reciprocal character of the relationship between God and those who belong to this community.

The reading opens with a double imperative: Observe justice *(mishpāt)*; Do righteousness *(ṣᵉdāqâ)*! This word-pair enunciates Israel's primary ethical obligation, which is social responsibility. This imperative is followed by a form of divine promise, which is also twofold: Salvation *(yᵉshûᶜâ)* is to come; Righteousness *(ṣᵉdāqâ)* is to be revealed. A covenant relationship is presumed here, as the language indicates. Justice and righteousness are associated with law. Righteousness, which describes the quality of a relationship, is really a divine characteristic. It is only appropriated by human beings when they are in right relationship with God—clearly a covenant attribute. The promise of salvation suggests the people are in some kind of desperate straits, and God, the people's covenant partner, promises to intervene.

The message of the first verse pertains to members of the covenant community. The message of the verses that follow pertains to those who are presently outside this community but who have shown their desire to become part of it. They have joined themselves to the Lord, probably by becoming proselytes; they minister *(shārat)* to God, most likely by participating in certain forms of worship; they love the Lord's name, an expression implying allegiance to God; they have become servants or devotees of the Lord. These four forms of attentive behavior demonstrate their commitment to the God of Israel. In addition, they have committed themselves to Sabbath observance and fidelity to the covenant and its responsibilities. These people may be foreigners, but both internally and externally they are one with the community of believers.

In response to their fidelity, God invites them into the liturgical life of the community. They are encouraged to proceed to God's holy mountain, the site considered the dwelling place of God on earth. The word "holy" (*qādôsh*) calls to mind all the prescriptions that determine what is worthy of being dedicated to God and what is not. Foreigners, who at another time would have been prevented from approaching the holy place, will be brought to it. The shrine or temple is considered a house of prayer, and these worthy foreigners will be allowed to rejoice here as members of the praying community. Finally, their sacrifices and burnt offerings will find the same favor with God as do those of the bloodline of Israel. Their participation in the life of prayer and sacrifice is the crowning act of their acceptance.

The final phrase is worthy of note, because with only a few words God dismantles the entire concept of ritual holiness as exclusively Israel's prerogative. Now the temple is designated as a house of prayer for all people, not a national shrine reserved for the elect. Now God is accessible to all, not merely to those of the bloodline of Israel. Salvation and righteousness embrace all.

## Psalm 67:2-3, 5, 6, 8

The verb-forms in this psalm make it difficult to be categorized. Some commentators believe the verbs are in past tense, and they classify the psalm as a prayer of thanksgiving for blessings already received. Others consider them a form of wish or bidding prayer, a moderate request for blessings not yet enjoyed. However the verbs are read, it is safe to consider the psalm as a prayer of blessing.

The psalm begins with a slight adaptation of the first words of the blessing used by Aaron and the priests, who were descended from him (v. 2; cf. Num 6:24-26). This use of the Aaronic blessing in a congregational prayer suggests the favors once promised to that particular priestly family are now sought for the entire people. The metaphor of God's shining face refers to the favorable disposition a smiling countenance reflects. The psalmist asks that God look favorably upon the people, that God be benevolent toward them.

God's goodness toward this people will redound to God's reputation among other nations. They will see the people's good fortune and will interpret it as the fruit of God's saving power on their behalf and God's continued rule over them. Those other nations will conclude that only a mighty and magnanimous God would be able to secure such good fortune. Here prosperity is not used as leverage against others. Quite the contrary, it benefits even those who may not be enjoying it. It does this because it is perceived as coming from God and not merely as the product of human exploits or ingenuity.

The psalm moves from an acknowledgment of divine rule over one people (v. 3) to an announcement of universal divine governance (v. 5). All nations will not only rejoice over God's goodness, they will also be guided by that same God and ultimately will praise that God (vv. 6, 8). In other words, the good fortune of one nation is testimony to the salvific activity of God. This in turn becomes the occasion of salvation for all the earth. One nation is the source of blessing for all. This is the fulfillment of a promise made to Abraham (cf. Gen 12:2-3).

The psalm ends with a prayer for continued universal blessing. The past tense of the verb in this verse has led some commentators to conclude that the blessings referred to earlier were also bestowed and enjoyed in the past. They maintain that the plea here is that God continue to bless the people so all nations will continue to revere God. Whether past or future, the psalmist believes all good fortune comes from God. Others see this and praise God, and in this way God is made known to all the earth.

## Romans 11:13-15, 29-32

Speaking directly to the Gentile converts in the Roman community, Paul continues his discussion of the privileged position occupied by the Jewish community in the plan of God. Paul is proud to be known as the "apostle to the Gentiles." However, lest those in his audience erroneously think their acceptance of Christ has made them superior to the Jews who have not been converted, Paul continues to argue in favor of Israelite privilege. Without in any way diminishing the salvific import of the conversion of the Gentiles, Paul maintains that it also serves a secondary purpose. Namely, the Jewish people will envy the way the Gentiles have been caught up in the embrace of God, and they themselves will turn to the gospel. The reversal of fortunes is clear. It was because of the rejection of the gospel by the people of Israel that Paul turned to the Gentile mission; now it is because of the acceptance of the Gentile world that the Jews will be converted.

The significance of the Jewish community is underscored by Paul's next comment. Although the formula is not explicitly stated, Paul uses an *a fortiori* argument. (If this is how it is in this situation, how much more so will it be in that one?) If the Jews' rejection of the gospel has brought reconciliation with God to the rest of the world, how much more will their acceptance of the gospel effect? Paul answers this final question: Their acceptance will bring about life from death. Although there is some dispute about the meaning of this phrase, most commentators believe the reference is to the final consummation, the final judgment and resurrection at the end of time. If this is true, then Paul is claiming that once again the future of the human race lies with the fate of Israel. The present age will end only when this people has accepted

Jesus as its Messiah. Such a claim may be bold and exaggerated, but it certainly shows Paul's continued commitment to the well-being of the people to whom he belongs according to the flesh.

Paul both reiterates the irrevocability of the privileges God bestowed upon the people of Israel (cf. Rom 9:1-5, Nineteenth Sunday ) and elaborates on the reversal of fortunes described above. They were the ones called to be God's special people, and it was to them God granted extraordinary gifts. The Gentiles have no reason to feel superior, for they had begun as disobedient sinners, and they have been granted divine mercy only because of the disobedience of the Jews. Now it is the Jews who are disobedient, and, Paul argues, if God has shown mercy to those who originally had worshiped other gods, surely God will show mercy to the nation that was called to be God's own people. No one is in a position to boast; both Jew and Gentile have sinned. Both are shown mercy not because they have earned it but because God is gracious.

## Matthew 15:21-28

The story of the Canaanite woman addresses several important and interrelated issues. They include the question of crossing territorial and cultural boundaries and that of women and men in public social exchange. To these cultural questions should be added two theological matters: the Christian mission to the Gentiles and the issue of faith. In addition to its rich thematic complexion, the narrative raises important questions. Why does Jesus enter pagan territory in the first place? Why does he initially withhold his healing power?

It should be noted that it is Jesus who crosses over into Gentile territory. He is the one who initially disregards boundaries. We are not told why. The region of Tyre and Sidon was between thirty and fifty miles northwest of the Lake of Gennesaret. It was considered pagan territory, and there was no reason for Jews to venture into it. According to the thinking of the time, important boundaries were anything but arbitrary. They were set by God, and they determined the rightness or wrongness of reality. Israel's land was considered holy because it belonged to God; it was properly apportioned to various tribes to care for in God's stead. To cross into pagan territory was to leave God's own holy land.

The woman is called a Canaanite, a designation not generally used at this time in history. It calls to mind the people who occupied the land before the Israelites took control of it. Throughout the entire history of ancient Israel the Canaanites were one of the primary enemies of the Israelites. Not only did this woman's residence in pagan territory make her unclean, but she was a member of one of the nations ancient Israel had hated the most. Finally, she was an unattended women. This in itself constituted her as a threat to Jesus' respectability.

Jesus disregarded territorial boundaries, and now the woman disregards appropriate social decorum; she speaks to a strange man. However, her reason for doing so is given. Like any mother would, she pleads for the healing of her daughter. With his own words Jesus indicates that gender is not the issue here, rather, ethnic purity is. His ministry is not to the Gentiles, whom the Jews of the day derisively referred to as "dogs." It is to the lost sheep of the house of Israel.

The woman is not deterred by what appears to be Jesus' chauvinism, for the well-being of her daughter is at stake. She is not defensive either; she accepts the secondary role that Jews accorded Gentiles, and she turns to her own advantage the words intended to belittle her. After all, Jesus had come into her territory; she had not pursued him. Once he was there, she felt she had a right to elicit from him the same wondrous power she must have heard he freely bestowed elsewhere.

The woman has shown remarkable faith. She recognizes Jesus' power to heal. More than this, she calls him "Son of David," a title with messianic overtones. After he first seems to ignore her and then to insult her she pays him homage, bows down before him. Moved by her faith, Jesus yields to her wishes and heals her daughter. Jesus probably came into the territory with no thought of healing the sick, but the scope of his ministry was expanded through the insistence of a woman whose love for others could not be thwarted by apparent disdain. This forced Jesus to move beyond the limited confines of his own cultural experience.

## Themes of the Day

The overarching theme derived from today's readings is the question of insider-outsider. We see here that the divisions and barriers that emerge out of human experience have been shattered by the graciousness of God.

### *A Human Reality*

In order to define itself, every religious, social, or political group must delineate clearly what it is and what it is not. Those who wish to be members of these groups must conform themselves to these cultural definitions, which determine who is in the group and who is not. Having such definitions is not inappropriate. In fact, it is necessary. However, when these definitions determine not only membership within a particular group but acceptability generally, they begin to function in ways that are biased and discriminatory and harmful to all involved.

We do not usually consider the limitations of culture when we think of the incarnation. We find it difficult to entertain the possibility that Jesus was ever in any way biased. This is unfortunate, because this tends to make Jesus less than human, and it minimizes the extraordinariness of those of his actions that break through the limitations of his culture. Jesus entered deeply into human reality, becoming a man of his own limited time and culture. At the same time, he was open enough to break out of the limitation of his cultural identity. In today's gospel this was accomplished through the agency of one whose gender, culture, and religious commitment made her unsuitable according to the standards of Jesus' culture. This should teach us not to marginalize people because of our cultural biases, for we may thereby be forfeiting an offer of God's grace.

## Prophetic Fulfillment

Jesus' openness to "the other" finds a precedent in the prophetic tradition. Isaiah spoke of a time when outsiders would join insiders in worshiping God, thus dissolving the categories of insider and outsider. He was, of course, referring to the age of eschatological fulfillment. This age dawned with the coming of Jesus. He himself moved out of the constraints of his own cultural worldview, and he directs us to do the same.

The issue here is not merely universalism. Rather, it is unity in the diversity of that universalism. In the kingdom of God one group does not force another to conform to authentic yet humanly determined standards. Instead, people are accepted along with their own cultural profiles. The readings for today show us the outdatedness of exclusionary distinctions. Unfortunately, they are still operating in our communities today. People are either excluded because of gender, culture, or religious perspective, or included only because they are able and willing to conform to discriminatory standards. We still have much to learn in this area.

## God's Universal Embrace

Even Jesus was rejected because he did not conform to the image of Messiah prevalent in his day. One might think such rejection would result in rejection of those perpetrators by God. However, such was not the case. God's embrace enclosed even those who rejected Jesus, and God's plan of salvation unfolded in a new way. An invitation to enter the kingdom was issued to the Gentiles, those who had been considered outsiders. If outsiders are now insiders, what has happened to the former insiders? Paul insists they are still insiders. God has not simply shifted the identifying boundaries; God has dissolved them. In the interim between the dawning of the eschatological age and the end of time, the invitation to be included remains open to all.

## Twenty-First Sunday in Ordinary Time
### Isaiah 22:19-23

The role of leadership among the People of God is a most important position. In ancient Israel those in office had religious as well as political responsibilities. Today's first reading narrates the transfer of such authority from one man to another. Shebna is identified here as master of the palace, probably a kind of majordomo. Elsewhere he is said to be a scribe, perhaps secretary of state, and Eliakim is master of the palace (cf. Isa 36:3, 22; 2 Kgs 18:18, 37). This latter passage enables us to conclude that the men probably had exchanged places. However, the exchange appears to have been done forcibly; therefore, honor and shame are involved. Since as master of the palace Shebna had charge of all the goods of the royal household, it is safe to presume some form of mismanagement or even deceit had taken place, and so he was deposed.

The phrase "on that day," usually pointing to the eschatological time in the future, here refers to a moment in the immediate future. However, the flavor of eschatological fulfillment remains: the phrase still suggests a new period of time. Furthermore, since the royal house of David is involved, there are also messianic connotations. Finally, Eliakim is the son of Hilkiah, the high priest who had found the copy of the book of the Law, which prompted Josiah's reform of the nation (cf. 2 Kgs 22:8). The presumption is that the son possesses the same integrity as does the father.

The description of the transfer itself resembles a ritual of investiture. The robe and sash are probably official garb that mark the office. The act of clothing Eliakim in this ceremonial attire symbolizes his being clothed with the authority of his new position. The extent of his authority is remarkable. It goes beyond management of the household. Three metaphors characterize it: father of the people, key to the house, and tent peg. With the father metaphor he is given jurisdiction over all the people of the southern kingdom. The key to the household is a symbol of full authority; not only does this person control the goods of the household, he also decides who comes in and who goes out. Just as a tent peg holds the structure in place, so the one in this position guarantees the stability of the household. Finally, the prestige of this position will bring honor to the house of his father, meaning his entire family.

Even if this passage does not reflect an actual historical occasion, an interpretation held by many commentators, the picture it sketches is significant. The oracle itself promises a person who will provide the order and stability the kingdom of Judah must have needed. If he was not himself a messianic figure, he was needed to ensure that the kingdom that would produce such a figure would survive.

### Psalm 138:1-2, 2-3, 6, 8

The responsorial psalm for this Sunday follows the general structure of the individual prayer of thanksgiving. Addressed directly to God, it begins with sentiments of thanksgiving, followed by a statement of the reason for being thankful (vv. 1, 3). It ends with a declaration of confidence in God's enduring faithfulness.

Evidently the psalmist had previously been in dire straits, had called upon the LORD for help, had been heard, and had been inwardly strengthened. This is the reason for the prayer of gratitude. The temple setting suggests the psalmist has come there to worship and publicly to witness to the goodness of God. The presence of the angels (*'ĕlōhîm*) suggests the court of heaven. In ancient Canaanite myths this court was made up of minor deities who stood in reverence around the throne of the principal god. As it developed its monotheistic understanding of God, Israel merely demoted these deities to angels, supernatural beings that were still under the dominion of the God of Israel. Thus the sovereignty of this God was enhanced by the homage they gave. Since the Temple was thought to be the earthly representation of the heavenly divine dwelling, it was not unusual for Israel to believe these beings were somehow in the same kind of attendance in the Temple on earth. Therefore, standing in the Temple in the presence of God, the psalmist would also be in the presence of the attending angels. The reason for the psalmist's gratitude is God's faithfulness to covenant commitment. This is clear from the presence of the technical covenant language, lovingkindness (*ḥesed*) and truth (*'ĕmet*). The promise referred to could be a pledge God made specifically to the psalmist or it could be a reference to the general promise of protection and beneficence associated with the covenant God made with the nation as a whole. In either case God has been faithful, and the psalmist publicly witnesses to this faithfulness with gratitude.

The psalmist acknowledges that the LORD is exalted, lifted high in glory, yet attentive to those who are humble or of mean estate. We have already seen that God's goodness springs from covenant commitment. The psalmist concludes the prayer of thanksgiving on a note of confidence that this commitment will endure forever. God is not only faithful to past promises but will be faithful into the endless future.

### Romans 11:33-36

Paul breaks out into rapturous praise. It is interesting to note that, in a manner uncharacteristic of Paul, there is no trace of christology in this prayer. He seems to be speaking directly out of Jewish thought:

> O Lord, my Lord, who can understand your judgment? Or who can explore the depth of your way? Or who can discern the majesty of your path? Or who can

> discern your incomprehensible counsel? Or who of those who are born has ever discovered the beginning and the end of your wisdom? *2 Apoc. Bar.* 14:8-9

Paul should not be regarded here as returning to his former understanding of faith. On the contrary, as we saw in the reading for last Sunday (cf. Rom 11:13-15, 29-32) Paul is talking about the mysterious ways of God in the plan of salvation, and therefore it is fitting that he direct his praise to God. After all, it is God who saves. God does it through Jesus Christ, but salvation is divine activity. It is appropriate to praise God for this graciousness.

As we saw last Sunday, it is through the rejection of one people that salvation is open to others. Paul argues further that it will be through the very salvation of these others that the first people will be brought to the gospel. This seems to be the way God works. God's ways do not follow the path of human logic. It is this divine judgment that is inscrutable; it is this way of saving that is unfathomable.

The sapiential tradition of Israel teaches that wisdom comes from reflection on the experience of life. However, it also teaches that the fundamental questions of life, questions of origin and meaning and destiny, cannot be adequately answered by experience alone. The tradition then turns to the Creator, who fashioned reality as it is, in whose mind reside the meaning and purpose of all creation. This is the divine wisdom of which Paul speaks. Even though human beings cannot grasp God's plan, it has meaning and purpose, and God's plan for all creation will unfold in God's way. The mysterious ways of salvation have brought Paul to praise the incomprehensible wisdom that determined them.

Paul's praise of God concludes with a finely honed doxology. It extols God the Creator, who is the source of all that is; it acclaims God the sustainer, through whom all creation continues to be; it celebrates God the goal, for whom all things were made and to whom all things proceed. It is to this sovereign God that all glory belongs. Paul is certainly grounded in a very Jewish understanding of God. What is unique, however, is the way he has interpreted this theology. It is here that Christ holds a constitutive place.

## Matthew 16:13-20

This reading consists of two distinct yet related themes. The first is christological (vv. 13-16); the second is ecclesiological (vv. 17-20). Only after Simon Peter proclaimed Jesus to be the Christ, the anointed one of God, does Jesus announce that his own church will be founded on Peter.

Jesus asks the disciples what people are saying about him: Who do they think he is? He applies to himself the messianic apocalyptic title "Son of Man." The question is not self-serving. Jesus seeks to discover how his words and actions are being understood by the people, and he is preparing the disciples for their own assessment of him. The answers given to his questions are telling. Some believe he is John the Baptist; others that he is Elijah; still others that he is one of the other prophets. All these religious figures have already died. The people seem to believe that Jesus is a prophetic figure who has come back from the dead.

It is not clear why Jesus should be associated with John the Baptist, since in both their life-styles and their central messages they were so different. The connection may have been made simply because the memory of this exceptional man was fresh in the minds of the people. Many had set their hopes on John, and with his death they transferred them to Jesus. Elijah had been the mysterious prophet whose return would herald the advent of the reign of God. Since Jesus had launched his ministry with the announcement that the long-awaited reign was now at hand, it is understandable that people would link him with Elijah. In some way, all the prophets had looked forward to the coming of this reign, so the people's general reference was not inappropriate. Simon Peter speaks in the name of the others when he proclaims that Jesus is the Christ, the Messiah, the anointed one of God. To this he adds the divine title "Son of the living God."

Using a macarism (Blessed are you), Jesus opens his discussion of the role Peter will play in the assembly of believers. Jesus insists that the only reason Peter could make such a testimony of faith was that Jesus' identity had been revealed to him by God. With a play on Greek words, the author has Jesus declare that Peter (*Petros*) is the rock (*petra*) upon which Jesus will establish his church. Although the image of a rock suggests stability and endurance, we should not presume these characteristics are natural to Peter. "Church" (*ekklēsía*) is probably a reference to the assembly of people, not the building within which they gather.

Jesus promises that the forces of the netherworld will not be able to encircle this church. It is clear this promise is not based on any strength of Peter's. It is solely a gift from Jesus. For his part, Peter will exercise the power of the keys. As we saw in the reading from the prophet Isaiah, controlling the keys is a sign of authority. However, here the symbol of keys refers to a different kind of authority, one that is more judicial or disciplinary than managerial. Peter is given the authority to enforce laws and to exempt from their obligation. This does not suggest that Peter legislates. Rather, he interprets the Law, determining when it should be binding and when not. In a sense, Peter is cast in the role of chief rabbi.

The answers to Jesus' query at the opening of this reading reveals that there were many different messianic expectations current at the time. This fact is probably behind Jesus' charge not to reveal his identity as the Christ, the Messiah. We will see next Sunday that not even the disciples understood the meaning of Messiah.

## Themes of the Day

The readings highlight yet another christological theme. As was the case with other Sundays in this section of Ordinary Time, our understanding of Christ carries implications for an understanding of discipleship.

### Who Do You Say I Am?

Our christological reflections reach a climax in the question posed to the disciples: Who do you say I am? In this liturgical context, the same question is posed to us. Who is this one who multiplies loaves of bread, who walks on turbulent waters, who breaks the boundaries that separate insider from outsider? It is none other than the Messiah. When Peter testified to Jesus' identity, it was a relevant religious and political statement, for messianic expectation was a burning question at that time. But what does it mean for the average Christian today? Many believers consider messianic expectation a theological theme that belongs to the past. They feel that it is difficult to get excited about the coming of someone we believe has already come and gone.

If Jesus were to pose this question today, how would we answer? And what would be the implications of our answer? You are the Messiah, the one who will establish justice on the earth, and I offer my services to you in this venture. You are the Messiah, the one who will ensure that the vulnerable of society will not be exploited, and I will stand in their defense. You are the Messiah, the one who will usher in the kingdom of peace, and I commit myself to the practice of peace. You are the Messiah, the one who will refashion us into a holy nation, and I open myself to this transformation.

### The Character of the Disciple

On the Nineteenth Sunday we saw Peter step out of the boat and attempt to walk on the tempestuous waters toward Jesus. It did not take long before we became aware of the inadequacy of his faith. This Sunday Peter testifies to the identity of Jesus. It is natural to wonder whether the faith he proclaims has deepened or if this is just another demonstration of bravado. Like Peter, we too may have good intentions, but when they are put to the test we realize that was all they were—good intentions. Still, we should not be discouraged by our weaknesses, for just as Peter's failure did not deter God from entrusting him with power and authority, so ours need not be obstacles to God's grace in our lives. We watch God entrust the Church to individuals who are weak and undependable, and we realize that judgments are inscrutable and God's ways unsearchable.

The first reading assures us that God chooses Peter, and others like him, not simply because there is no one else to whom responsibility can be given. On the contrary, God works through those who are weak so there will be no question about the source of any success they may experience. This penchant on God's part also prevents us from using our own weakness as an excuse for not committing ourselves to the service of God and others. We are asked to open ourselves to God regardless of our limitations and weaknesses. The rest is in God's hands.

## Twenty-Second Sunday in Ordinary Time
### Jeremiah 20:7-9

These words of complaint consist of some of the most pathos-filled sentiments of the prophet Jeremiah. Directed to God, they begin with a searing accusation. The verb *(pātâ)* can mean both "duped" and "enticed." The first meaning suggests God misled the prophet when he was called to deliver the word of the LORD. Jeremiah did allow himself to be misled, but this only happened because he was inexperienced and naive. God had promised to be with him, and Jeremiah took this promise seriously (cf. Jer 1:5-8). The verb also carries the meaning of seduction, of being overpowered. While there is no sense here of sexual exploitation, the text does state that Jeremiah struggled to withstand God's power but was unsuccessful. His may not have been a physical struggle, but there certainly was coercion.

Jeremiah is caught between fidelity to his vocation as a prophet of God and his own natural inclinations. He did not seek this calling. In fact, he resisted it from the start. He has been called to deliver a message of violence and destruction to the people of whom he is a member. It is his nation that will be racked with violence and will face destruction. Jeremiah recoils from this responsibility. As if delivering such a message was not enough, he must also face the ridicule of his compatriots. Relying on the promises God had made to the house of David, that it would endure even if it had to be chastised (cf. 2 Sam 7:14-16), they view Jeremiah's oracle of doom with disdain, and they consider the prophet himself a laughingstock. Jeremiah is forced to bear a threefold burden. He must deliver a message of doom to his own people; he is mocked by those to whom he has been sent; he receives no comfort from God.

The last words of Jeremiah's complaint are the most poignant (v. 9). He can no longer endure the burden, so he decides never again to speak in God's name. As if it has happened in the past, Jeremiah knows what to expect when he makes this decision. Like a roaring fire, the words seem to burn within him. He cannot restrain their fury. He must speak. It is as if the prophet is helpless before the word of God. He can neither determine the message he is to proclaim nor decide whether or not it will be proclaimed. He is simply the messenger. All he can do is complain. He complains because of the mockery of the others, and he gets no support from God; he complains because he cannot contend with God, and he gets no comfort here; he complains because the words themselves are aflame within him, and there is no relief in sight. Jeremiah is indeed a man of sorrows.

## Psalm 63:2, 3-4, 5-6, 8-9

Three religious sentiments are present in this psalm of confidence. It begins with expressions of longing, followed by a short hymn of praise, and it concludes with words of confidence. Flesh *(bāśār)* and soul *(nepesh)* are two dimensions of a human being that constitute the totality of that person (cf. Gen 2:2). The metaphor used to portray the intensity of the psalmist's longing is arid land. This metaphor not only makes the longing concrete, it also suggests that the need for an experience of God is as natural and basic to a human being as water is basic and essential for life itself. Without such an experience the person is devoid of the source of life, just as parched land is devoid of the source of its life.

Several elements of this passage suggest its setting is cultic or somehow liturgical. Most obvious is mention of the sanctuary. Added to this is a description of the psalmist praying with uplifted hands, a traditional stance of prayer. The prayer itself (calling upon God's name) could be offered anywhere, at anytime, so it is not explicitly liturgical. However, given the other cultic features, it certainly can be understood in this way. The verb for "seek" (v. 2) might be better translated "seek early," suggesting early morning prayer after keeping a night vigil. Finally, the psalmist actually does pray for some kind of theophany, a physical manifestation of God (v. 3) that would take the form of divine power *('ōz)* and glory *(kābôd)*.

The psalmist contrasts the arid life without God with the sumptuous life with God. The satisfaction that comes with the experience of God is compared to marrow of bone and fatness of flesh, parts of an animal that are not only tasty but also contain life-giving properties. While in reality such a rich banquet satisfies physical need, it is to be understood here figuratively as characterizing the satisfaction the soul experiences. Regardless of the importance of life and the joys one might receive when that life is lived in union with God, the psalmist insists the authentic covenant bond of lovingkindness *(ḥesed)* is more precious than life itself. The psalmist's trust in being heard by God is rooted in this covenantal bond.

The passage ends with several images that characterize the psalmist's trust in God. First, God is proclaimed as the psalmist's help *('ēzer)*. This is not a hope for the future but rather a present experience. Next the text depicts the psalmist under God's protective wings, a reference to the eagle that spreads its wings over its young. Finally, the psalmist clings to God and is upheld by God's right hand, a stereotype that signifies God's power. The psalmist has turned to God for life and security, and God has responded with the requested protection.

## Romans 12:1-2

Usually when Paul issues an ethical injunction, he grounds it with an appeal to his apostolic authority. That is not the case in the reading for this Sunday. Nor is the injunction based on moral principle. Instead, Paul appeals to the mercies of God as the basis of his admonition. And what does he ask of the Christians of Rome? Making a veiled reference to the sacrificial system of ancient Israel, Paul exhorts them to offer themselves as a living sacrifice.

The Greek uses the word for body *(sōma)*, which refers not only to the person but to that individual's corporeality or concrete relationship with the world. It is because we have bodies that we are able to experience this world. Yet it is precisely this experience that Paul is exhorting the Christians to offer up as a living sacrifice—a disciplined life, not a sacrificial death. Such an offering will be holy (set apart) and pleasing to God because it is a total gift of oneself. Although Paul is not requiring a holocaust of the physical *sōma,* he is asking for an offering no less demanding, no less total. Rather than a bloody sacrifice, this offering will be a rational or spiritual *(logikós)* service *(latreía).* The very language used points to the cultic character of what Paul is describing. This suggests the worship he is recommending is as efficacious as were the sacrifices that ancient Israel offered to God.

Most likely, the strongest exhortation in the passage is the one that is framed negatively: Do not conform to this age. Through faith in Jesus Christ, the Roman Christians have entered into the eschatological age of fulfillment. They have been saved through the blood of Christ, and filled with the Spirit of God, they are being transformed into Christ. They have put aside the standards of this world in order to take on the standards of Christ and of the reign of God. Here we see the transformation and renewal of which Paul speaks. He would have the Christians bring their transformed and renewed minds into conformity with the will of God. The closing words return us to the language of the cult. This offering of oneself will be good and pleasing to God and perfect.

## Matthew 16:21-27

Two distinct yet related episodes make up today's gospel reading. Jesus predicts his own suffering, death, and resurrection, and then he discusses the need for the disciples to follow him by bearing their own suffering. Both episodes are dependent upon Jesus' teaching about his impending suffering.

He underscores its necessity *(deí)* and that it must take place in Jerusalem, the center of Jewish religious and political life.

Mention of the elders, chief priests, and scribes is significant. These were three groups that made up the Sanhedrin, the highest court of the Jewish nation, which, with permission from Rome, was allowed to exercise religious authority. We must be careful in our interpretation of this passage. Too often the opposition of these people to Jesus has led Christians to hold an attitude of anti-Judaism. Instead, we should recognize here the gospel writer's way of showing that Jesus was rejected for religious as well as political reasons. The unrest he caused may well have been a political threat to Rome, but the bold claims he made greatly troubled the religious leaders.

Much to the chagrin of Peter, Jesus states he will be rejected, will suffer and die, but will rise again. This perception of the Messiah does not appear to conform to the expectations of the people, at least not to Peter's. Jesus' insistence on this understanding could jeopardize his acceptance by the people. Peter's rebuke exemplifies this. The Greek text has "God be gracious to you" (God spare you this fate). From a human point of view it is natural for Peter to be concerned about the fate of his master. According to Jesus, that is precisely Peter's problem; he is speaking from a human point of view and not from the perspective of God. Using very strong language, Jesus points this out to him. He addresses Peter as Satan, the one who acts as an obstacle *(skándalon)* to the unfolding of God's will. Peter may have recognized Jesus as the Messiah (cf. Matt 16:13-20, Twenty-First Sunday), but he had not yet learned how Jesus was going to fulfill this role.

Turning to the other disciples, Jesus provides them with yet another lesson about discipleship. Those who follow him must, like him, deny themselves of self-interest and self-fulfillment. Those who take up the cross must do so realizing their fate is sealed, since one never puts the cross down again. There is a play on the words "save" and "lose." Those who selfishly save themselves from the sufferings of the cross really lose in the arena of eschatological judgment, while those who unselfishly offer themselves are saved from this judgment. This is what following Jesus means. The seriousness of this choice is seen in the fact that it will determine one's final judgment. In referring to himself as Son of Man, Jesus recalls the apocalyptic image of this mysterious figure coming on the clouds at the end of time (cf. Dan 7:13-14). The disciples may not fully understand what Jesus has just told them, but both his and their destinies have been laid out before them.

## Themes of the Day

Reflection on christological themes continues. Last week's profession of faith in Jesus as the Messiah is followed immediately by the announcement of his impending death.

## A Suffering Messiah

The one who fed the multitude, who calmed the waters, who broke down social barriers by healing the daughter of a Canaanite woman is also the one who will suffer greatly and be put to death. Throughout his encounters with the leaders of the people Jesus always prevailed. As he enhanced his honor, he put them to shame. It is understandable that their wrath against him would have been inflamed. Still, all of his wondrous deeds demonstrated the extraordinary power that was at his disposal. Why would he not use it in his own defense? Perhaps that it is key. The power was meant for the upbuilding of the reign of God, not for his own self-aggrandizement. As difficult as this may be for us to fathom, Jesus is going to be killed.

The gospel does not say Jesus will gallantly step forward and take suffering upon himself. This would be a demonstration of his power. Instead, his fate will be a demonstration of his vulnerability. He will be taken forcibly and will suffer at the hands of others. He will do this willingly, but not as a volunteer. Jesus will be a victim. The manner and extent of his torment will be decided by someone else.

## Follow Me

As we saw in previous Sundays, our christological understanding carries implications for discipleship. Today Jesus is very explicit about this. Whoever follows him must follow him to the cross. If we participate in his success we must also share in his shame. Disciples have a choice to follow or not to follow, but if they choose in his favor they must be ready for suffering and humiliation.

Paul exhorts us to reject the standards of the world. This is a very difficult path to follow, especially when it seems that those who do conform to this age prosper much more than we do. Furthermore, following Christ can place barriers between ourselves and others. If we no longer share their values and their interests we may feel alienated. Suffering is bound to invade our ministerial lives as well. We must remember that Jesus' message antagonized many people in his day. Those who proclaim the same message in their own contexts must be prepared for a similar reaction.

## Have We Been Duped?

After witnessing all the marvelous feats Jesus accomplished, we discover he is going to suffer and be put to death. How can this be? With Peter we protest. With Jeremiah we wonder: Have we been duped? Perhaps the "high christology" is meant to enable us to commit ourselves to him in his suffering. The realization that we too will have to suffer becomes a crucial test of our faith. As we reflect more deeply on this mystery we may discover it is not God who has duped us. Rather, the power Jesus demonstrated so captured our imagination that we have duped ourselves. We may have expected the same manifestation of power, the same miraculous interventions in our lives without realizing that his power may take a different form with us. Rather than transform the circumstances that cause us distress, it transforms us by enlightening our minds and strengthening our hearts.

## Twenty-Third Sunday in Ordinary Time
### Ezekiel 33:7-9

Most prophetic pronouncements are either oracles of salvation or oracles of judgment and doom. The oracle that constitutes today's reading is an oracle of appointment. It was not given to the people through the prophet. Rather, it was a very personal message to the prophet himself. The phrase "son of man" does not mean the same here as it does in the well-known passage from the book of Daniel (cf. Dan 7:13-14). In that passage the word for "man" is ʾĕnôsh, which has the connotation of weakness or vulnerability. It is a word that underscores the divide between the human and the divine. The one who comes on the clouds is said to be like the offspring of human weakness or vulnerability. However, in the present passage, the word for man is ʾādām, the generic term that is translated "humankind." Thus, when God calls Ezekiel "son of ʾādām," he is simply identifying him as a member of the human race, not as an apocalyptic or eschatological figure.

The role to which the prophet has been called is that of watchman. Sentinels of various kinds stood watch to protect homes or cities from the attack of enemies. This role becomes a metaphor for the responsibilities assigned by God to the prophet. In place of watching over a city or an individual dwelling, Ezekiel is entrusted with keeping watch over the entire house of Israel. The enemy that might undermine the security of that house is the wickedness that threatens to undermine the nation. Ezekiel fulfills this function when as a prophet he proclaims God's words of warning. Such a proclamation is the defense he uses to protect the people. He is told that God will hold him responsible if he does not protect the people by means of his proclamation. If he is faithful to his charge but the people refuse to heed his message, he can rest assured that he has fulfilled his responsibility. They will be punished, but he will not be.

The wording of the oracle implies there is still time for the people. The sinner can still be called back from sin. However, in a very real sense this all depends upon the fidelity of the prophet to his call to be watchman.

### Psalm 95:1-2, 6-7, 8-9

The responsorial psalm combines an invitation to praise, a plea for openness, and a word from God. The invitation is given three times: Come, let us sing joyfully (v. 1); Let us come into his presence (v. 2); Come, let us bow down (v. 6). Together they seem to be a reenactment of a liturgical movement. There is the initial summons to praise, followed by an invitation to enter the presence of God (presumably the Temple), there to bow before God in worship. God then addresses the reverent community.

The relationship that exists between God and the people is characterized by means of several metaphors. God is the rock of their salvation (v. 1). A rock is solid and secure. It affords grounding for whatever relies on it. Natural formations of rock also provide refuge and shelter from inclement weather and various dangers. It is an apt image to refer to God as the protector of the people. God is also clearly identified as Creator (v. 6). This can be a reference to God as the Creator of the universe and everything within it, or it can be a more personal reference to the fashioning of a disparate group of individuals into a coherent community. The image that follows suggests the latter interpretation.

The psalmist identifies the community as the flock and God as the shepherd (v. 6). In a pastoral community such a relationship was quite intimate. Shepherds took total responsibility for their sheep, caring for them and protecting them even at the risk of their own lives. For reasons such as this, "shepherd" became a fitting metaphor to describe the monarch, who was expected to act in this same way on behalf of the people of the realm. In this psalm the images of rock and shepherd illustrate the people's perception of God as protector.

Having depicted God as a caring and devoted protector, the psalmist turns again to the people and issues a serious plea that they be open to the voice of God. This plea suggests that "today" the people who have been gathered together will hear God's voice. Since this gathering is clearly liturgical in character (v. 6), it is safe to conclude that the word from God will be a part of the actual liturgical celebration. The people have come to worship God and to receive some word from God that will comfort them or set a direction for their lives.

The word that follows is an appeal by God to respond positively to God, not in the spirit of rebellion that governed their ancestors while they were in the wilderness (cf. Exod 17:1-7; Deut 6:16). During that earlier time, the people had demanded signs that would prove the presence and power of God acting on their behalf, despite the fact that they had witnessed God's gracious deliverance of them from Egyptian bondage. God desires hearts that are open, not hearts that have been hardened by selfishness or lack of faith. "Today" the descendants of those rebellious wanderers are called upon to respond with open faith and willing obedience.

### Romans 13:8-10

Most people consider that John the Evangelist is the Christian writer who emphasizes love as the centerpiece of his teaching. They would seldom associate Paul with this message. However, the epistle reading for this Sunday shows that Paul teaches the very same message of love. Again and again we have seen that Paul never really repudiates the Law. Rather, he argues that keeping the Law is not a requisite for faith but that faith is a requisite for keeping the Law. In this reading he takes a slightly different tack. The reading begins and ends with the same bold statement: Love fulfills the Law.

The passage opens with a double negative *(mēdeni mēdén)*. This construction provides emphasis to Paul's injunction. Paradoxically he tells the Christians of Rome that on the one hand they should owe nothing, while on the other hand they should owe everything, for love requires total self-giving. The debt of love is not an obligation that can be paid once for all. It is more like interest for which we are always liable. Paul cites several commandments taken from the Decalogue. The order of these commandments follows the Septuagint version of Deut 5:17-21. As with his argument about the superiority of faith over obedience, so also here Paul does not dismiss the importance of fidelity to these commandments. Rather, he maintains that they are fulfilled in the act of loving.

Love will take different forms, depending upon the circumstances. Love is faithful to its commitments, and it respects the commitments of others, so adultery or any other form of sexual infidelity will be out of the question. Love holds life in high regard; it overcomes anger and revenge, and so it cannot entertain any thought of killing. Love respects the property of others and so it will not condone stealing or dishonesty or any kind. Love honors the rights of other people, and so it does not entertain thoughts of covetousness. Paul singles out only four commandments, but he insists that love covers all other commandments as well. When one truly loves another, one desires only what is good for that loved one. This is precisely what Paul is saying here. Love is the fulfillment of the Law.

There is no explicit biblical injunction to love oneself, since few people need to be taught how to pursue their own good. The promotion of healthy self-love is a contemporary concern. However, there is a rabbinic tradition that resembles Paul's injunction to love others as we love ourselves. The great Rabbi Hillel (ca. 70 B.C.E.–10 C.E.) advises: What you would not want done to you, do not do to someone else. The positive expression of this has come to be known as the Golden Rule. Paul insists this consideration should be the standard that determines the way we treat each other.

Finally, Paul most likely understands "neighbor" as Jesus interpreted the word. It is not limited merely to kinfolk, or ethnic compatriots, or companions in the faith. As Jesus explained to the lawyer who asked who his neighbor might be, the neighbor is also one with whom we have very little in common, perhaps even a former enemy (cf. Luke 10:29-37). Following the teaching of Jesus, the love Paul exhorts is to be extended to all people without exception. It is no wonder he can say that love is the fulfillment of the Law.

## Matthew 18:15-20

The issue addressed in this gospel reading is the procedure to be followed when dealing with an erring member of the community. Reconciliation within the community is such a pressing concern that its maintenance becomes a matter of church discipline. It is important to note this is a procedure entered into by the entire community, not just the leaders.

The process, which consists of three steps, has roots within the Jewish tradition. First, the one who is erred against goes privately to the erring one in an attempt to resolve the situation. The same strategy is stated in the passage in Leviticus that enjoins love of neighbor (cf. Lev 19:17). What is suggested in both passages is that such correction is a form of love. If this approach is not successful, the injured one, in the company of one or two community members, should return to the erring one. The situation has now moved from an exchange between two people to one that is somewhat formal and juridical (cf. Deut 19:15). If the situation is still not resolved, it is to be brought before the entire church assembly. If the erring one remains recalcitrant, a severe punishment is exacted. The community is directed to treat this person like an outsider, like a heathen or a tax collector. Heathens and tax collectors are not singled out because of any particular bias. On the contrary, they are merely symbolic of those people who have been disdainful toward the message of the gospel. Any community member who remains adamant throughout this process of reconciliation demonstrates the same kind of disdain and should thus be treated with the same kind of separation.

The importance of the community in this process of reconciliation is apparent in two important ways. First, it is the entire band of disciples, not merely its leader, that exercises disciplinary power within the community. They are the ones who do the binding and loosing (cf. Matt 16:13-20, Twenty-First Sunday). Second, Jesus declares that any agreement arrived at by two members of this band will be heard. He is not talking about prayer in general but prayer for guidance in coming to a decision that will affect community well-being. A similar idea is found in early Jewish writings: "If two sit together and the words of the Law [are] between them, the divine Presence (the *Shekinah*) rests between them" (*Mishnah Aboth*, 3:2). By means of this statement Jesus promises to be present in his Church if the members turn to him for guidance.

### Themes of the Day

The call to take up one's cross, which we considered last Sunday, can carry a variety of meanings. This Sunday we examine some practical ways in which disciples are required to do this.

### Accountability

One of the crosses disciples will have to bear is the exercise of accountability. It is not always easy to call people to an accounting of their performance. It is hard enough for parents and teachers to do this, but it is especially difficult when those over whom we exercise this responsibility are otherwise our peers. Yet sometimes this is what disciples are required to do. This can be particularly difficult for those who are in positions of leadership. It is an unenviable responsibility of pastors in the parish, coordinators of religious education, members of the parish council, principals in the school, and directors of liturgical ministry, to name but a few. Not everyone will take direction kindly, and they may be subject to resentment and even opposition. This is a heavy but necessary cross to bear.

### Reconciliation

Disciples must also engage in the very difficult process of effecting reconciliation. Differences of opinion, misunderstandings, and actual offenses tend to alienate people. If this bad feeling is allowed to continue bitterness may set in and actual division result. We see this happen in families, in neighborhoods, in parish communities, in workplaces. It is not enough to say we must try to forgive from our hearts. The process of reconciliation requires significant movement toward the admission of guilt as well. Both the one offended and the offender must be willing to be transformed. As disciples, we must not only be agents of the reconciliation of others but especially must do our part in repairing the rifts in our own lives. This can be a very difficult task to accomplish.

### Prayerful Collaboration

Gathering two or three together in prayerful collaboration is not as easy as it sounds. It has been said that the ministerial cross of the present day is committees. This is the case not just because they take up our time but because they require so much more of us. If collaboration is to be effective we have to be open and honest about our own opinions and our biases and also respectful of the opinions and even the biases of others. We must work for the common good and not merely for what we personally think is best. We must be willing to accept and implement decisions with which we may not totally agree, and we must live with them gracefully. Working collaboratively can be a real burden.

### Genuine Love

We normally acclaim love as the highest form of human expression, and it is. However, as glorious and satisfying as love may be, it is more demanding than anything else in life. Taking the passage from Romans as guide for our comments, we must admit that love fulfills the entire Law only when we honor our personal commitments and the personal commitments of others regardless of the contrary passionate attractions we may experience; when we value the life, dignity, and reputation of others even when we are on the brink of hatred and vindictiveness; when we respect the possessions of others despite the fact that we desperately desire them for ourselves. It is only because love is so demanding that it covers all our responsibilities. However, when we truly love we are willing to carry the crosses that discipleship requires.

## Twenty-Fourth Sunday in Ordinary Time
### Sirach 27:30–28:7

The Golden Rule, "Do unto others as you would have them do unto you," covers not only external actions but interior dispositions as well. This passage from Sirach reflects the sentiments of that rule as well as some that are found in the Lord's Prayer, specifically, "forgive us as we forgive others." Finally, divine retribution is the basis of Sirach's teaching here.

The book of Sirach belongs to the Wisdom literature of ancient Israel. Most of its teaching consists of insights gained from reflection on the experience of life. The tone of this passage is set in the first verse. Wrath and anger may be instinctive responses to situations in life, but they are abhorrent if they are permanent dispositions of mind and heart. Sirach does not say that we may not experience these sentiments but that we should not cling to them. He identifies those who do so as sinners. The gist of his teaching is the need to forgive others. The basis of his exhortation is not social order, although it will not be able to survive if we harbor attitudes of revenge. Nor is it generosity of soul, which frequently expands to overlook the offensives of others. Rather, it is our own need to be forgiven. We are all sinners; we have all offended others. Therefore we are all in need of forgiveness. If we are not willing to forgive those who have offended us, how can we hope to be forgiven our own offenses?

In this reading the basis of forgiveness is not mutual compassion or mercy. The point is not forgiveness by others but forgiveness by God. If we are vengeful, we will suffer God's vengeance. If we nurture anger, we cannot expect to enjoy God's healing. If we are not merciful, mercy will not be extended to us. But if we do forgive, our own prayers for forgiveness will be heard. In various ways Sirach insists it is our own need for forgiveness from God that should prompt us to grant that same forgiveness to others and not whether those others have earned our forgiveness.

Sirach appeals to human frailty and mortality. The certainty of death should prompt us to set aside any anger or wrath we might experience. Life is too short to bear attitudes that can undermine our spirits. More importantly, we have all been brought into the embrace of God's covenant. As partners with one another in that covenant, we must be willing to extend to others the same gracious compassion God has extended to us.

## Psalm 103:1-2, 3-4, 9-10, 11-12

The responsorial psalm begins with a summons to bless the Lord. Although the word "bless" is often used as a benediction, a prayer for God's presence, or a grace for the future, in this case it is a call to praise or thank God for blessings already received. The call to "bless the Lord" is normally addressed to someone other than the psalmist. Here it is a self-address (vv. 1-2). The Hebrew word translated "soul" *(nepesh)* comes from the word for breath. It yields over twenty meanings, chief among which are life-breath (or soul), life, living person. The reference here is probably to that center within the person from which all one's life forces flow. This is not merely a spiritual or immaterial reality; it encompasses every aspect of the person. This understanding is corroborated by the phrase "all my being."

In the biblical world a person's name was an expression of that person's unique identity. In many ways names held more significance for people then than they do today. One could exercise power over another simply by somehow controlling the name of that person. There were times during Israel's history when, in their attempt to show great reverence for God, the people paid homage to God's name rather than directly to God (cf. Deut 12:11, 21; 14:23f.; 16:2, 6, 11). Even when they did this they were careful to avoid using the divine name itself. Today we show the same respect when we merely use the consonants YHWH or substitute Lord (small upper-case letters) rather than the divine name itself.

The reason for praising or thanking God, the benefits to which the psalmist refers, is God's willingness to pardon, to heal, and to redeem or save. These are all acts that flow from God's lovingkindness *(ḥesed)* and compassion *(raḥămîm,* vv. 3-4). It is out of this mercy God acts, not requiring the harsh punishment the sins of the people would warrant.

Two images that denote immeasurable distance are used to describe the breadth of God's devotion. These are the expanse between the heavens and the earth, and the area between east and west. The heavens could refer either to the sky, the height of which is incalculable, or the dwelling place of God, which is in an entirely different realm than the home of human beings. The extent of God's covenant commitment is further sketched in the figure of speech "east to west," which denotes immeasurable distance. Human eyes can only envision a fraction of the stretch that lies between the horizons. What is perceived is only infinitesimal; the reality is beyond comprehension. Using these images, the psalmist is claiming the same limitlessness for God's lovingkindness. Out of covenant love, God puts our transgression so far from us that the distance cannot even be imagined. This is ample reason to praise and bless the LORD.

## Romans 14:7-9

In some of the earliest biblical traditions we see that while the ancient Israelites believed God exercised absolute rule over all that was living, they did not have a clear idea of God's sovereignty in the land of the dead (cf. Pss 6:5; 115:17). Only gradually did they come to realize that both life and death were in the hands of their God. This meant that death could not sever the covenant bond that united them to their God. This ancient Israelite idea is the basis of Paul's statements in today's short reading. Paul maintains that Christ, in virtue of his death and resurrection, exercises the same power over life and death. In like manner, those who are joined to Christ are joined permanently. Nothing, neither life not death, can separate them from the love of Christ (cf. Rom 8:38).

The specific aspect of this tenet of faith Paul is arguing here is the total lordship of the risen Christ. He insists that in every aspect of life and even in death Christians are under the lordship of Christ. Whether they live or die they belong to Christ and are accountable to Christ. Their lives and deaths must demonstrate this. In a very real sense, this understanding is the bedrock of Christian ethics. Christians do not live for themselves. For them there is no radical individualism or self-fulfillment independent of Christ. Having conquered death by means of his resurrection, Christ has gained lordship over all.

## Matthew 18:21-35

The issue treated in today's gospel reading is forgiveness. However, both Peter's question and the setting of the parable Jesus recounts indicate that the context of this forgiveness is the community. Peter asks about a brother (*adelphós*), a member of the believing community; the debtors in the parable seem to belong to the same household. These details indicate forgiveness within the community is the specific focus here.

The rabbis taught that the duty to forgive had been fulfilled if one forgave an offender three times. Peter must have thought he was being extraordinarily generous if he forgave seven times, a number that carried overtones of completeness. However, Jesus indicates that not even this was enough for members of his community. With a veiled reference to the excessive primitive vengeance of Lamech (cf. Gen 4:24), Jesus insists that an offending member of the community was to be forgiven seventy-seven times. Although the Greek is also translated "seventy times seven," the point being made is the same. There is no limit to the number of times we must be willing to forgive those who have offended us.

Jesus employs a parable to illustrate the extent to which his followers must be willing to forgive and the consequences that will befall them if they are not. The parable describes the manner in which forgiveness operates within the kingdom. Details of the story reflect ancient Near Eastern customs. Oriental kings frequently exercised power over life and death, as is suggested here. The Greek text tells us that the first debtor owed ten thousand talents, while the second debtor owed a hundred denarii. Since one talent was equivalent to six thousand denarii, the second man's debt was only one-six-hundred-thousandth of the first man's debt. The ludicrous contrast demonstrates the difference between the mercy of the king and the hardheartedness of the first debtor.

Punishment for not paying debts was meted out in proportion to the debt owed. Since the first man owed an outrageous amount his punishment was quite severe. He was threatened with being sold along with his wife, his children, and all his property. In other words, he would lose his membership in the household and his status of freedom in the kingdom. Since the second man only owed about three months' wages there was a possibility of his debt being paid, if not by him, then by his family. Both men fell at the feet of the one to whom they owed the money, and with exactly the same words. They begged for patience. Neither asked that the debt be forgiven. They both promised to pay it back, although neither seems to have had the means to do so. The stage has been set for the message Jesus wishes to teach. The story will answer Peter's question: How often must I forgive?

With one simple statement Jesus draws a connection between the generosity of the king and that of God. The debts owed to them can never be repaid. Moved with compassion (*splanchnízomai*) they forgive the entire amount. We who correspond to the debtors have this compassion as an example after which we should pattern our relationships with one another. If God is willing to forgive the exorbitant debt we owe God, surely we can forgive the paltry debts owed us. Jesus' final statement is sobering; if we are unwilling to show mercy, the mercy already shown us will be taken back, and a severe retribution will be exacted.

## Themes of the Day

It has been said that one of the most distinctive features of Jesus' teachings is the exhortation to forgive those who have offended us. Jesus was very explicit about this, and he left us his own example by forgiving his executioners while he hung dying on the cross.

### Forgiving

Quite a bit is being written today on the question of reconciliation. Until recently we have thought the process begins with the offender repenting of the offense and then asking for forgiveness. Those who have done serious research in the area disagree. They believe that the process must begin with the one offended offering forgiveness and that this willingness to forgive transforms one from being a victim to being a survivor. Furthermore, such magnanimity is what may touch the heart of the offender, who may thus be transformed from being an offender even to becoming a friend.

It is very difficult to forgive someone who has offended us, because it may be that our honor is at stake or that our very person has been threatened. Very deep feelings are involved. When we have been hurt, we want to inflict pain in return; we want to even the score. Most people would not blame us for feeling like this. In fact, they would even encourage us in our retaliation. However, retaliation is the way of the world and not the way of the Lord. Once again the disciples of Jesus follow a less-traveled road.

### Being Forgiven

Today we have yet another example of how disciples must give what they have been given. The gospel suggests that nothing another owes us can compare with what we owe God. If God has been so generous in forgiving us, surely we can be generous in forgiving others. How many times must we be willing to forgive? As many times as God is willing to forgive us. If we cannot forgive others, perhaps we have not been transformed by God's forgiveness of us. It may be we have not yet been transformed enough. The process of becoming a forgiving person takes time. For some it may take a lifetime. Only little by little are our pettiness and indignation reduced and our desire to strike back diminished. Perhaps we need to be forgiven seventy-seven times before we can forgive once, but as disciples we are expected to give the forgiveness we have been given.

### Pay What You Owe

Lest we think forgiveness provides an easy way out for offenders, we are reminded that ultimately justice will prevail. If we remain untransformed by

God's forgiveness of us, as demonstrated by our unwillingness to forgive others, then we are liable to judgment. And this judgment often springs from within us. Our unwillingness to forgive can eat away at us, and we can carry hurts from childhood far into adult years. A slight from a co-worker can bore itself so deeply into our consciousness that we become obsessed by it. Forgiving others, as difficult as that may be, is in the long run much easier than bearing the weight of resentfulness, vindictiveness, and unresolved frustration. When we forgive we truly begin to be healed.

# Ordinary Time (Part Four)

| | | | |
|---|---|---|---|
| **Twenty-Fifth Sunday**<br><br>Isaiah 55:6-9<br>My thoughts are not your thoughts | Psalm 145:2-3, 8-9, 17-18<br>The LORD is gracious and merciful | Philippians 1:20c-24, 27a<br>Life is Christ; death is gain | Matthew 20:1-16a<br>Laborers in the vineyard |
| **Twenty-Sixth Sunday**<br><br>Ezekiel 18:25-28<br>The virtuous who sin will die | Psalm 25:4-5, 6-7, 8-9<br>Your ways make known to me | Philippians 2:1-11<br>Christ humbled himself | Matthew 21:28-32<br>A man had two sons |
| **Twenty-Seventh Sunday**<br><br>Isaiah 5:1-7<br>My friend had a vineyard | Psalm 80:9, 12, 13-14, 15-16, 19-20<br>The vineyard of the LORD | Philippians 4:6-9<br>Have no anxiety | Matthew 21:33-43<br>Kill the son and acquire the vineyard |
| **Twenty-Eighth Sunday**<br><br>Isaiah 25:6-10a<br>The Lord provides for all the people | Psalm 23:1-3a, 3b-4, 5, 6<br>The LORD is my shepherd | Philippians 4:12-14, 19-20<br>I can do all things in him who strengthens me | Matthew 22:1-14<br>Come to the wedding feast |
| **Twenty-Ninth Sunday**<br><br>Isaiah 45:1, 4-6<br>I am the Lord; there is no other | Psalm 96:1, 3, 4-5, 7-8, 9-10<br>Sing to the LORD a new song | 1 Thessalonians 1:1-5b<br>Our gospel came to you in power and the Holy Spirit | Matthew 22:15-21<br>Give to Caesar what is Caesar's, to God what is God's |

| | | | |
|---|---|---|---|
| **Thirtieth Sunday**<br>Exodus 22:20-26<br>Care for the widow, the orphan, and the alien | Psalm 18:2-3, 3-4, 47, 51<br>I love you, LORD, my strength | 1 Thessalonians 1:5c-10<br>You turned from idols to serve the living God | Matthew 22:34-40<br>What commandment is the greatest? |
| **Thirty-First Sunday**<br>Malachi 1:14b–2:2b, 8-10<br>A curse upon the priests | Psalm 131:1, 2, 3<br>LORD, my heart is not proud | 1 Thessalonians 2:7b-9, 13<br>Gentle as a nursing mother | Matthew 23:1-12<br>Do what they say, not what they do |
| **Thirty-Second Sunday**<br>Wisdom 6:12-16<br>Wisdom is found by those who seek her | Psalm 63:2, 3-4, 5-6, 7-8<br>My soul is thirsting for you | 1 Thessalonians 4:13-18<br>The dead in Christ will rise | Matthew 25:1-13<br>The kingdom is like ten virgins |
| **Thirty-Third Sunday**<br>Proverbs 31:10-13, 19-20, 30-31<br>The valiant woman | Psalm 128:1-2, 3, 4-5<br>Blessed are those who fear the LORD | 1 Thessalonians 5:1-6<br>Like a thief in the night | Matthew 25:14-30<br>He entrusted talents to his servants |
| **Thirty-Fourth Sunday**<br>Ezekiel 34:11-12, 15-17<br>I will look after my flock | Psalm 23:1-2, 2-3, 5-6<br>The LORD is my shepherd | 1 Corinthians 15:20-26, 28<br>Christ, the firstfruits of the dead | Matthew 25:31-46<br>I was thirsty, you gave me food |

# Ordinary Time (Part Four)

## Initial Reading of the Ordinary Lectionary (Part Four)

### Introduction

Ordinary Time is a time for us to listen to the teachings of Jesus and to look into our own lives to see what kind of disciples we have become. It is not a period of high liturgical drama but one of the day-to-day struggle to be faithful. As we move toward the end of the Liturgical Year our reflections become more serious. The exhortations seem to have greater urgency. The gospel stories show Jesus in more conflict. Even the prayers in the psalms are solemn. Before we can think of a new beginning, we must consider the end.

### First Testament Readings

The majority of these readings are hortatory in nature. If we set aside the reading for the last Sunday, we see that the others are bracketed by Wisdom teaching. The opening Isaian passage reminds us of the inscrutability of the ways of God and counsels us to seek God's ways rather than those of the scoundrel. The readings for the Thirty-Second and Thirty-Third Sundays praise Wisdom herself and the valiant woman who is the exemplar of wisdom. Within this *inclusio* we find prophetic instruction.

Ezekiel insists that God is not unjust in punishing the fallen righteous person or in blessing the repentant sinner. In the Isaian poem of the vineyard we see how devastating God's punishment can be. However, this picture of God's wrath is tempered the next two weeks with glimpses of God's attentiveness. As God has cared for us, we are told, in the passage from Exodus, to care for the most vulnerable in society. The reading from Malachi brings us back to the theme of retribution. The priests, the spiritual leaders of the community, are condemned for their failure to live up to their noble calling. This shows us that the call to live lives of righteousness cannot be taken lightly.

351

On the last Sunday of the Liturgical Year we are left with a portrait of God the Good Shepherd. Since the major focus of this Sunday is the end-time and the judgment it brings, such a picture is comforting.

## Psalms

An interesting fact emerges as we look at the forms of the psalms employed as responses at this time. We find an acclamation of God as ruler of the universe, and two psalms are linked with the monarchy, but there are no hymns of praise. Instead, there are two laments, four hymns of trust, and a Wisdom psalm. The tenor of these responses is quite serious, an appropriate note on which to end the Liturgical Year.

## Epistles

Taken as a group, the epistle readings begin and end with statements about the efficacy of the resurrection of Christ. If we read them in successive order we can detect a definite theological movement. The first epistle opens with a moving statement about Paul's desire to be even more intimately united with Christ. However, for the sake of the ministry he chooses to continue his earthly mission regardless of the difficulties involved. It is this ministry and the fruits of Paul's labors that are discussed on the Twenty-Eighth through the Thirty-First Sundays. Finally, the readings for the last three Sundays contain powerful eschatological themes, as befits the last Sundays of the Liturgical Year.

## Gospels

There is a definite pattern in the gospel readings of this last section of Ordinary Time. The gospels from the Twenty-Fifth through the Thirtieth Sundays all contain parables of the kingdom of God. Furthermore, these parables are eschatological in character. Though the stories read on the first four Sundays differ greatly, their underlying themes are similar. They all depict situations in which those who appear to be in privileged positions are passed over in favor of people who appear to be undeserving.

Jesus' conflicts with the leaders of the people are featured on the Twenty-Ninth through the Thirty-First Sundays. On the first two Sundays we see them trying to trip him up by some misinterpretation of the Law. If he had failed the tests they set, he would have lost honor in the sight of the people, and he would no longer have been considered a legitimate teacher from God. Not only did Jesus pass their texts, but he snared them in the very traps they had set for him. Although he criticized these leaders, he still respected the authenticity of the roles that they held, and he taught his followers to do the same.

On the last three Sundays Jesus teaches his disciples how they are to live their lives as they await the dawning of the eschatological age. This message challenges us as well. Since we do not know exactly when the Lord will return we must be vigilant; we must be prepared; and we must be industrious.

## Mosaic of Readings

The readings that carry us to the end of the Liturgical Year are both comforting and challenging, particularly in the way God is characterized and the focus the teachings of Jesus take. While there is frequently mention of the judgment that will take place at the end-time, God is depicted as provident and caring. Again and again the parables of Jesus warn us against being smug in our righteousness. It is God who justifies, and God seems to be partial to those who humbly acknowledge that they are the beneficiaries of the mercy of God.

# Readings

## Twenty-Fifth Sunday in Ordinary Time

### Isaiah 55:6-9

The oracle of salvation read today includes a call to worship and a call to conversion. The call to worship is seen in the prophet's exhortation of his hearers to seek and to call upon the LORD, in other words, to approach God. However, the primary focus here is on the call to conversion. This second call is a summons to forsake wicked ways and evil thoughts and to (re)turn to the Lord. The word "[re]turn" *(shûb),* with all its forms, is the twelfth most frequently used verb in the First Testament. It means "to turn from evil and to turn toward the good." The verb implies that those who have sinned were once in relationship with God but have turned away. The exhortation is to turn back. These are not suggestions. The verb-forms indicate they are imperatives. The people are summoned to worship and repentance.

The prophet describes the sinfulness of the people. He perceives a pattern of sin, not merely isolated offenses. They have embarked on a way *(derek)* of life that has taken them away from the God with whom they have entered into covenant. This is nothing short of total betrayal. The word employed here for sinfulness usually refers to external behavior. Here it is coupled with the word for "thoughts" or "plans" *(maḥăshābâ)*. The sinners have not only chosen a course of action opposed to the Laws of God, but they have devised plans contrary to God's plans. In the face of this, the prophet assures them God will still be compassionate *(rāḥam)* toward them. He can promise this because he firmly believes that God does not merely forgive once. Rather, God is gracious in forgiving, pardoning sinners again and again.

The difference between the thoughts and plans of God and those of the wicked are next compared with the vast expanse between the heavens and the earth. The comparison is ludicrous, for there is no comparison. These few verses do not explicitly explain what these thoughts and plans might be. However, they can be surmised. We find depicted, on the one hand, wicked thoughts and the way of the scoundrel, on the other hand, compassion and forgiveness. This oracle both exhorts sinners to turn away from their evil lives and assures them that having turned away they will enjoy the salvation of God. Certainly the difference between these two dispositions is incalculable, like the distance between heaven and earth.

## Psalm 145:2-3, 8-9, 17-18

The responsorial psalm for today is a hymn of praise of God's greatness. In the first section the psalmist speaks directly to God, celebrating this greatness. The second and third sections are addressed to unknown hearers. In the second section, the covenant characteristics of divine mercy and compassion are extolled. In the third section, the psalmist describes God's universal and everlasting reign.

The passage opens with verbs that describe the devotion of the psalmist (vv. 2-3). "Bless" *(bārak)* implies bending one's knee in submission or reverence; "praise" *(hālal),* though it is sometimes used to refer to human beings, is most frequently used as a call to praise God. The psalmist exclaims that he will offer blessings and praise all his days. As is seen so often in hymns of praise, it is the name of God that is lauded, the name somewhat removed from God yet an expression of the very essence of God. To extol God's name was a way of showing both reverence and praise. The reason for this praise is the greatness of God. It is unfathomable, beyond human understanding. All one can do is stand in awe of God and give praise.

The second stanza (vv. 8-9) is an acclamation closely associated with the revelation of God and the acknowledgment of God's name revealed at the time of the reestablishment of the covenant (cf. Exod 34:6). In these two verses covenant language abounds. God is described as gracious *(ḥannûn)* and compassionate *(raḥûm)* and filled with lovingkindness *(ḥesed).* It should be noted that this divine goodness is not reserved for Israel alone but is extended to all

God's works. This includes all people and nations, also all of natural creation. Here the covenant has been expanded to a universal embrace.

Finally, the basis of God's loving attention is proclaimed (vv. 17-18). God's covenant commitment is revealed as justice *(ṣedeq)* and lovingkindness *(ḥesed,* translated "holy"). These characteristics constitute the source of God's provident care and the firm foundation upon which the faithful ones can trust. A third covenant characteristic is truth *(ʾĕmet).* Here it refers to the firmness or constancy of God, on whom the faithful can rely. They can do this because God has entered into a solemn agreement with them, has made serious promises to them, and can be depended upon to be faithful. In order to experience the benefits of this covenant, one needs only to call upon God, who is always there to hear.

## Philippians 1:20c-24, 27a

Paul shares with the Christians of Philippi his own inner struggle regarding life and death. The phrase "in my body" *(sōma)* (v. 20c) indicates he is talking about physical life and death and not speaking metaphorically. This is no idle intellectual exercise on his part. Paul would not be grappling with this issue if imminent death were not a real possibility for him. Nor would he ever take steps to hasten his end. Therefore we can conclude that when writing this Paul's life was somehow in jeopardy. Although the decision of living or dying was probably not in his hands, it is his attitude toward these options that is of importance. Having said this, we should note that Paul does not consider death a way of escaping the misfortune he may be suffering. His own physical safety or comfort plays no part in his considerations. Rather, he weighs the religious and ministerial advantages of both living and dying. At issue is the extent to which Christ will be glorified, either through Paul's continued life or through his death.

For Paul, union with Christ is what gives primary meaning to life. This is what he means when he says that for him "life is Christ." Living in Christ and with Christ and for Christ is uppermost in his mind. Paul believes that neither life nor death can separate him from Christ (cf. Rom 8:39). Continued life will give him opportunities for strengthening this union, and death will allow him to become fully united with Christ. This latter situation is the gain of which he speaks. Although Paul prefers dying and being with Christ, he can see advantages for himself either way.

Paul next considers his ministry. Death might offer him the kind of union with Christ that he really desires, but it will probably not be as advantageous for others. If he continues "in the flesh *(sárx)*" he will be able to further the preaching of the gospel, and his ministry will continue to enrich those to whom he has already preached, to say nothing of future fields of mission. Paul's unselfish commitment to the welfare of his converts is clear. He seems willing to postpone the joyful union with Christ for which he yearns and of which he is certain in order to spend and be spent for the benefit of those who would hear the gospel from him.

The part of Paul's speech that is read today merely draws the lines of his dilemma. It does not indicate if or how it was resolved. However, the final verse provides us with a hint of his final inclination. In it, Paul exhorts the Philippians to live lives that conform to the gospel message he has preached. It lays bare his overriding concern for their spiritual well-being. Even when he is facing the possibility of his own death, when he is looking forward to ultimate union with Christ, Paul puts aside any thought of personal gain in favor of commitment to the service of others.

## Matthew 20:1-16a

Many of the parables Jesus taught are somewhat shocking, but the one selected for today's gospel reading is particularly startling. As strange as it may seem, this parable clearly shows how the graciousness of God can be easily mistaken for injustice. On the one hand, it does not seem fair to pay all of the laborers the same wage regardless of the amount of time they put into the work. On the other hand, all of the laborers received exactly the amount for which they had contracted when they were first hired, and so from this point of view there was no injustice.

The details of the story are clearly narrated. The hiring practice described is quite common in many areas of the world, even today. In order to procure the best workers, hiring crews go early to the site where potential workers gather. If the workday described here was divided into twelve hours from 6 A.M. to 6 P.M., then hiring occurred at 9 A.M., noon, 3 P.M., and 5 P.M. as well. One wonders why some had not been hired by 3 P.M., even more so, by 5 P.M. It could not have been because their labor was not needed, for the master of the household *(oikdespótēs)* kept going out throughout the day to enlist more laborers. Perhaps they were known to be incompetent or lazy. Whatever the case, they were unwanted. This is a very important point in the story.

The reckoning at the end of the workday calls to mind the judgment that will come at the end of time. It is in this part of the story we find the shift in perspective we have come to expect in the parables of Jesus. There are actually two such shifts. When he pays the laborers a denarius each, the owner of the vineyard demonstrates the eschatological reversal: the last shall be first. There is nothing wrong with this practice. In fact, it is necessary for the drama of the story. It enables us to see that the laborers who were chosen first, who bore the heat of the day and the brunt of the work, embraced the principles of retributive justice: payment according to work done. However, they expected more because they gave more.

The real paradox of the narrative is seen in the payment policy of the owner of the vineyard. The justice with which he pays the laborers is superseded by his generosity. What is almost scandalous is that he is most generous toward the workers who were unwanted by others. Those who were hired first did what they had agreed to do, and they were recompensed as they had been promised, but they were dissatisfied with the method of payment. It is clear that they did not grumble when they saw how the others were being paid. They were only unhappy with their own wages. Most likely they would have been satisfied if the generosity of the owner had been meted out in proportion to the work done. However, justice and grace do not always fit well together. The parable shows that the reign of God is based on the latter, not the former.

The reply of the owner of the vineyard to the grumbling of these laborers is much stronger in the original Greek than in most translations: Is your eye evil because I am good? In many societies the "evil eye" is a superstitious power attributed to certain people, giving them the ability to inflict bad luck on others. The reference suggests a connection between the evil eye and envy, jealousy, or lack of generosity. The owner's final words were dismissive: Take what is yours and go.

## Themes of the Day

Our attention shifts slightly in these last Sundays of Ordinary Time. We turn from concentration on the character and responsibilities of discipleship to reflecting on the import of the end of time. As we move toward the close of the Liturgical Year, we are invited to consider the final coming of Christ and the Last Judgment. When themes of christology and discipleship appear, they do so within the context of the eschatological age of fulfillment.

### Final Justice

The idea of the end of time brings thoughts of judgment. Actually, our eschatological tradition says there will be two judgments, a personal judgment immediately after our death when we are confronted with the specifics of our individual lives and the final judgment at the end of time when all things will be laid bare. The thought of one judgment is enough to strike fear in the hearts of many, to say nothing about having to face two judgments. We sometimes waver between the idea of divine justice, which requires that good be adequately rewarded and evil be appropriately punished, and the idea of the mercy of God, which we hope will be generously extended to us. As we begin today to consider the end of time, we are invited to look closely at the character of God's judgment.

At the outset we must remember that we have no firsthand way of knowing anything about either the individual or the final judgment. We may have some insights into the experience of dying but nothing about what happens after death. However, our religious tradition is quite consistent in its teaching on this matter. As evidenced in the readings for this Sunday, both testaments insist that the justice of God does not conform to the standards of human justice. This does not imply it is capricious. Rather, it is incomprehensible, and it is so because its foundation is mercy. This suggests that God takes into consideration the circumstances and the weakness of human beings and does not demand strict and exact retribution. However, something is required. The first reading exhorts sinners to repent and amend their ways; in the second those invited into the kingdom are expected to act appropriately within that kingdom.

## Lives of Generosity

We all find consolation in this view of divine judgment because we all want to be recipients of divine mercy. However, our hearts are not always generous enough to rejoice in the mercy extended to others. It is almost as if we feel we have been cheated in some way, as if God is required to apportion mercy according to merit and we are the ones who determine standards for this apportionment. Those of us who persist in our demands for such strict retribution face not only frustration with God but bitterness of heart toward those we think have received more than they deserve.

As disciples of the kingdom of God we are called to announce the good news of the gospel. It seems inconsistent of us to proclaim the mercy of God and then be filled with resentment whenever others experience it. That same divine mercy can work in us to abolish our pettiness and indignation and replace it with generosity of heart. Furthermore, it can transform us so completely that we too can extend mercy toward others rather than exact retribution from them. Judgment belongs to God, and God exercises it mercifully. We are called to conduct ourselves with the same kind of generosity, the same kind of love, the same kind of mercy. Paul is an example of this kind of generous giving.

## Twenty-Sixth Sunday in Ordinary Time
### Ezekiel 18:25-28

The first reading for this Sunday paints a very interesting scenario. The people of Israel seem to have challenged the justice of God. The issue is the question of retribution, the manner in which God rewards righteous living and punishes wicked behavior. This passage does not include the specifics of Israel's accusation, but it does sketch clearly God's response to it. This response opens with a counter accusation: It is not God's ways that are unfair but the ways of the house of Israel.

Two situations are described. Both of them portray a change in behavior. In the first situation a righteous person sins; in the second a sinner repents. (The Hebrew suggests these are two separate individuals.) God metes out punishment in the first situation and grants a reward in the second. Is this injustice on God's part? Is God expected to forgo deserved punishment in the first case because of the good deeds performed earlier by the one who is now a sinner? Is God only to remember the past sinfulness of the person in the second case and not reward a significant change in that person's life-style? These two situations show us that the justice of God is not dispensed according to the merits that have accumulated throughout one's past history. Rather, it corresponds to the character of one's present manner of behavior, to the kind of person one has become. When it comes to retribution, only the present seems to count. Is this injustice on God's part? Exactly how did the house of Israel want God to act?

What is described here is not the unlikely case of a person who has lived righteously throughout all of life but dies immediately after having committed one isolated serious sin and now suffers the consequences of that one violation. The text says this person actually turns away from virtue. Having chosen another path, this person now suffers the consequences of that choice. Dying is probably not a reference to physical death but a symbol of separation from God, who is the source of life. In like manner the sinner, who turns away from wickedness and chooses the path of righteousness and justice, will live united with God, the source of life. Is this injustice on God's part?

## Psalm 25:4-5, 6-7, 8-9

The psalm response opens with a prayer for divine guidance. The word "way" has very close association with the Wisdom tradition and refers to a manner of living, specifically the way of righteousness or the way of evil. The term often designates movement or direction on a road rather than the road itself. Here it could refer to a style of life. "Path" appears in parallel construction with "way" and also refers to a style of life. When this expression is used in reference to God, it can mean either God's own ways of acting or the ways God teaches humankind to follow. This psalm seems to allow for both meanings.

Understanding the words from the perspective of God's way of acting makes us attentive to the salvation accomplished by God (v. 5), to God's covenantal commitment (v. 6), to God's own uprightness (v. 8). Regarding the first theme, the psalm gives no indication as to the character of the salvation wrought by God. Was the psalmist in physical danger? Was the deliverance from personal misfortune? Coupled with the reading from Genesis, the threat could have been cosmic annihilation. Whatever the case, the psalmist asks for insight into God's saving ways, presumably in order to sing God's praises and to offer thanks for God's goodness.

Covenant language is very strong in the second stanza (vv. 6-7). "Compassion" comes from the word *rāḥam* (womb) and might be translated "womb-love." It refers to a deep and loving attachment, usually between two people who share some kind of natural bond. "Lovingkindness" *(ḥesed)* denotes loyalty to covenant obligations. Following the Hebrew, some translations contrast God's calling to mind the covenant commitment with the psalmist's former sins. The plea that God remember may be the psalmist's way of asking God's forgiveness.

The final stanza comments on the righteousness of God (vv. 8-9), which is attentive to both the sinners and the *anawim* (humble). Both groups are taught the way of the LORD, the way God acts toward people's infidelity and loyalty. Presumably the first group will be taught that wickedness will be punished, while the second will be assured their righteousness has not gone unnoticed.

The phrase "way of the LORD" can also refer to the manner of living God expects of humankind. Here it is probably a reference to the Law, for it is there the will of God is to be found. The psalmist would then be asking for guidance to discern God's will in order to live in accord with it. This interpretation does not negate the preceding explanation; it simply gives it a slightly different perspective. God's saving action calls for a response. Having been saved, what responsibilities do we now have? How should we live so as not to fall back into the situation from which we were saved? If God has established a covenant with us, what are our covenant obligations? What have we taken upon ourselves on entering into this relationship? Finally, if God is just, what kind of lives should we be living? The psalmist prays: Teach me your ways. Show me how you have acted; show me how I should behave.

## Philippians 2:1-11

Today's reading contains one of Christianity's most exalted hymns of praise of Christ. Most people recognize the christological importance of this hymn. However, we may fail ro remember that Paul offered this magnificent vision of Christ's self-emptying not simply as a profound statement of faith but, more immediately, as a stirring incentive for the Philippians' own attitudes of mind and heart. The message Paul is preaching here is unity within the Church.

There is a fourfold basis for Paul's appeal for unity. The first and fundamental reason for unity is the Christians' common experience of Christ. Regardless of their differences, they should find comfort in the love Christ has shown them.

The third reason is their communion *(koinōnia)* in the Spirit. Finally, there is the compassion *(splánchnon)* and mercy *(oiktirmós)* of Christ. After listing the communal bonds that flow from their union with Christ, Paul appeals to their debt to him. He sought to form a community that would be like-minded, sharing the same values. Seeing such commonality in them would give him great joy. Unity in this church would be manifested in their common outlook, in their lack of selfish ambition, in the consideration they show to one another. Having exhorted the Philippians to live in such unity, Paul offers Christ as their model.

This christological reflection on the nature and mission of Jesus can be divided into two parts. In the first (vv. 6-8) Jesus is the subject of the action; in the second (vv. 9-11) God is. The first part describes Jesus' humiliation; the second recounts his exaltation by God. Christ Jesus, who was in the form of God and equal to God, did not cling to the dignity that was rightfully his. He did not use his exalted status for his own ends. He freely gave up the right to homage that was his.

The verb used here is significant. Not only did Christ relinquish his Godlike state, he emptied himself of it. Though in the form of God, he chose the form of a servant or slave. Without losing his Godlike being he took on the likeness of human beings. He did not merely resemble a human being; he became one. "Likeness" points to the fact that he was human like no one else was human.

Christ humbled himself and became obedient. Having taken on the form of a slave, he made himself vulnerable to all the circumstances of that station in life. Obedience is the determining factor for a slave. The extent of Christ's obedience is striking. Compliance with God's will in a world alienated from God puts one's life in jeopardy. In a sense, Christ's death was inevitable. Crucifixion was common punishment for slaves, the nadir of human abasement. Such ignominy was a likely consequence of emptying himself and taking on human form.

The exaltation of Christ is as glorious as his humiliation was debasing. While Christ was the subject of his self-emptying, his super-exaltation is attributed directly to God. In exalting Jesus, God accords his human name a dignity that raises it above every other name. It now elicits the same reverence the title "Lord" *(kýrios)* does. Every knee shall do him homage and every tongue shall proclaim his sovereignty. The entire created universe is brought under his lordship. This includes the spiritual beings in heaven, all living beings on earth, and even the dead under the earth. All will praise Christ, whose exaltation gives glory to God.

## Matthew 21:28-32

Once again we see Jesus with the leaders of the Jewish people in a struggle over reputation. This is a significant kind of encounter in a society governed by principles of honor and shame. Each of the competitors must retain status within the community in order to win the loyalty of that community. Although the word "parable" is not used in the text, Jesus recounts a parabolic story and then turns its interpretation against his opponents.

Stories of two siblings are common in folklore. They usually represent two ways of life or two ethnic groups. Examples include Cain and Abel (cf. Gen 4:1-16), Jacob and Esau (cf. Gen 25:23-28). Although the folktales generally feature male characters, sometimes the siblings are sisters (cf. Ezek 23:1-49). The sons in this story represent two ways of responding to a father's command. The first son outrightly refuses to obey. This is a serious breach of protocol in a patriarchal kinship structure. It could also be dangerous, for the head of such a household frequently held the power of life and death in his hands. These details were well know by those in Jesus' audience, and they contributed to the portrayal intended by Jesus. However, the headstrong son repents *(metamélomai)* and eventually does as his father charged him to do. The second son does not disrespect his father by refusing to go as he was directed, but neither does he obey him.

Jesus turns to his adversaries and asks them for an interpretation of the Law: Which one did the father's will? Without knowing it, they condemned themselves with their own answer. They were the ones who prided themselves of their righteousness and piety. They even looked down upon those whose situations in life frequently prevented them from adhering strictly to various prescriptions of the Law. In his response Jesus tells them that tax collectors and prostitutes, known sinners, will enter the kingdom of God before these, who appear to be righteous, will. Jesus does not suggest that they will be refused entrance, simply that the others will be preferred. In a paradoxical fashion Jesus shifts the focus of the story from the question of obedience to one of acceptability. He asked: Who was obedient? He illustrates: Who is acceptable?

The people's openness to the message of John the Baptist becomes the litmus test of their openness to the message of the kingdom. As precursor of the promised one, John had admonished his hearers to choose the way of righteousness. Those who were considered public sinners made that choice; those who considered themselves righteous did not. The ones who knew they were needy were open to God's grace; the ones who considered themselves observant and pious did not see their need of repentance. The story demonstrates how fidelity to God's will is more than a question of words; it is a matter of deeds. Jesus has tricked his opponents into condemning themselves. In shaming them he himself has gained honor in the eyes of the people.

## Themes of the Day

*Choose*

Throughout our considerations of the character and responsibilities of discipleship, the words "must," "should," and "require" have appeared again and again. Such language could make us think that following Jesus only makes demands on us. Without in any way minimizing the fact that there are indeed responsibilities that come with discipleship, it is important to remember that this does not deny us our freedom. We are called to discipleship, and there may well be an urgency in this call, but it is an invitation that is to be accepted only freely. Nor is the decision to be a disciple a once-for-all choice. As is the case with life itself, options are placed before us all the way along the road. We are invited to choose in favor of the reign of God, or we are free to ignore the invitation. Furthermore, the invitation always remains open to us. Because we decline it on one occasion does mean it will never be offered again. God's desire for our acceptance is persistent and enduring.

## Obedience and Disobedience

In every life there is a struggle between obedience and disobedience, and this struggle takes various twists and turns. At times we are willing to conform to regulations set from the outside; at times we are not. Even in this we are not consistent. Those who are fundamentally righteous have sometimes fallen from grace, and people considered evil to the core have been known to reform their lives. Taking another perspective, we see that in some situations we promise to be submissive but then do not carry through with our promise. In other situations we refuse to comply, but later we change our minds and do what we have been asked to do. What ultimately count are not the promises one makes but the actions one takes. In every life there is a struggle between obedience and disobedience.

## Commitment in Community

Ultimately the choice set before us is the imitation of Christ. The specific characteristic of Christ offered for our consideration today is his humility. Paul is concerned about the character or disposition of the community. He warns against the members' inclination to demand their rights, to expect that others show them the deference they believe they deserve. Such attitudes can undermine the loving quality of the community, so he offers them the example of Jesus for their imitation.

It is clear that whichever aspect of discipleship we examine, some aspect of community is present. To be a disciple of Jesus is to follow him as a member of a believing community.

## Twenty-Seventh Sunday in Ordinary Time
### Isaiah 5:1-7

The piece of poetry that constitutes the first reading for this Sunday is a parable of great artistry. On the most obvious level it employs the metaphor of a vineyard representing the house of Israel. On the level of literary form it moves quite easily from a poem of love (vv. 1-2) to an indictment of sin (vv. 3-4) to a proclamation of judgment (vv. 5-6), thus reviewing the entire sweep of the major portion of Israel's history from its election to the time of the prophet Isaiah. The last verse explains the meaning of the parable.

The love song tells the story of the prophet's friend. The word for "friend" *(yādad),* which is also translated "beloved," is generally used to describe individuals who are greatly loved by God. The second word translated here as "friend" or "beloved" is *dôd,* the word with which the woman in the Song of Songs refers to the man she loves. In that collection of love songs the vineyard is one of the places where the lovers met (cf. Cant 7:12). The similarities between this poem and the Song of Songs would certainly not be lost on Isaiah's hearers.

The attentiveness of the vineyard owner is clearly sketched. Each step of the viticultural process is carefully accomplished. Anyone familiar with planting and caring for vines can attest to the backbreaking nature of such a venture. The psalmist's friend was certainly devoted to his vineyard. Everything was done to guarantee a bountiful harvest but to no avail. The love song ends on a discordant note. Not only was there no abundant harvest, but what came forth were wild grapes. This unnatural yield was not the result of poor cultivation on the part of the grower. On the contrary, the vineyard itself had failed.

The speaker now changes. No longer is the prophet describing his friend; it is the owner of the vineyard who turns to the inhabitants of Jerusalem and Judah for some form of judgment. This owner declares that all the steps necessary to ensure a bountiful yield were taken. One might be able to offer some reason for a paltry harvest, but how does one explain a crop of wild grapes? The only answer is deliberate treachery or rejection of all of the careful attention provided. The indictment of sin has been issued.

Judgment is now passed on the unnatural vineyard. Some of the steps taken to ensure its productivity will be undone. The protection that would have fended off the assaults of predatory animals and the theft of the crops is removed, and the vineyard is now vulnerable to any form of defilement and devastation. Natural enemies will overrun the carefully cultivated land and plants, and all will fall into ruin. The real identity of the owner is disclosed in the final verse of the condemnation. The clouds will be commanded to withhold necessary life-giving rain. Since only God has such power over nature, the prophet is obviously telling a parable about God and a vineyard God loved dearly. This becomes clear in the explanation of the parable.

As is so often the case with parabolic teaching, the meaning of this parable turns a situation in life upside down. Here, the owner of the vineyard has just turned to the people of Jerusalem and Judah for a judgment about the case placed before him. They did not know the judgment they would pass would be directed back upon them. God, through the prophet, decodes the meaning of the parable: the owner of the vineyard is God; the vineyard, the cherished plant, is the house of Israel. With a double play on words, the prophet describes the heinousness of the people's offense. God looked for judgment *(mishpāt)*, but found bloodshed *(mispāḥ)*; for justice *(ṣedeq)*, but found an outcry *(ṣᵉᶜāqâ)*. God had invested so much in the future of this people, and they scorned the attention of the beloved vineyard owner. What began as a love song ends as a message of doom.

## Psalm 80:9, 12, 13-14, 15-16, 19-20

This responsorial psalm is a communal lament. Using the metaphor of vineyard, the psalmist sketches the history of Israel's origin, its growth, and its collapse. In this state of ruin the psalmist cries out to God for restoration and promises fidelity in the future.

It is clear that this vineyard is the nation of Israel. It was rescued by God from oppression in Egypt and brought into the land of Canaan after the original inhabitants had been driven out. Under the reign of David, Israel expanded its influence from the Mediterranean Sea to the great River, the Euphrates. The psalmist reminds God of the special care shown this people in the past in the hopes God will look kindly on them in the difficult straits in which they find themselves. Hope for future salvation is often based on the fact of past blessings.

The misfortune the people are suffering may have been at the hands of other nations, but it only came to pass because of God's will. In fact, it was God who actively broke down the nation's defenses so it became vulnerable to outside forces of destruction. Boars and beasts of the field were wild animals and consequently considered unclean. Therefore the nation has not only been assaulted, it has also been desecrated. In agony the psalmist cries out: Why have you done this?

This communal lament contains striking images of God: cultivator of vines and military leader. Though deeply dissimilar, these images are brought together here. Cultivating a vineyard is demanding and tedious work, and it takes a long time to bring a vine to maturity. Vinedressers must be dedicated, patient people. They deal with living things that follow their own laws of growth, which the ones tending cannot control. Vinedressers must be willing to forgo their own comfort in the face of long hours and inclement weather. This image represents the tender solicitude with which God cared for the people in the past.

"LORD of Hosts" is a military title. Hosts refer to divisions of the army, so the hosts of God would be the heavenly defenders who fight cosmic battles and who claim God as their military leader. Israel believed God would marshal these forces of heaven and would fight for Israel (cf Isa 40:26). Here the psalmist maintains that this divine fighter who rules from the heaven is the same God who cultivated Israel as a choice vine. Convinced of this, the psalmist cries out: "Look down from heaven; take care of this vine!" The psalmist prays for the nation (the vine) as well as for the king (son of your right hand). This reference signifies the place of honor the king enjoys. "Son of man" is a reminder that despite this royal privilege the king is a child of Adam just like everyone else.

It is not until the final promise that we are given the reason for the nation's misfortune. It was not simply caused by the wrath of God. Rather, the people had turned away from God. Now, through the agency of the psalmist, they promise not to do this again. They ask for a second chance so they can recommit themselves to the LORD of Hosts. Their prayer is twofold: Give us new life! Restore us! They are confident that if God looks kindly on them again they will be saved.

## Philippians 4:6-9

The tenderness with which Paul regards the Christians of Philippi is evident in this reading. Something is causing them to be anxious, and Paul offers them encouragement and direction. The passage itself can be divided into two parts: encouragement in the face of anxiety (vv. 6-7) and an exhortation to ethical living after Paul's own example (vv. 8-9).

Anxiety suggests a lack of confidence in one's ability in a certain situation. It is a common experience of all people. From a religious point of view, it can also imply a lack of confidence in God's concern and protection. It is the latter attitude that Paul addresses here. Rather than be anxious about something, the Christians are admonished to turn to God in prayer. Paul's counsel does not suggest that the circumstances that caused the anxiety will be corrected but that the anxiety will be relieved. Paul does not lead his hearers to believe prayer is some kind of magical exercise that will right every wrong. It is, rather, an openness to God, which itself can help people bear trying circumstances. Paul counsels prayer in general and petition in particular. We should take note that he tells them to offer this prayer with thanksgiving. Such gratefulness will be evidence of their confidence that God will hear their prayer.

Paul next assures the Philippians that if they surrender their anxiety in favor of this thankfulness, they will know the peace only God can give, the peace that surpasses all understanding. Using a military term, he promises that this peace will stand guard *(phrourá)* over their minds and hearts in Christ Jesus. This latter phrase, a favorite of Paul's, identifies the context within which Christian life unfolds. It suggests that Christians live principally in relation to Christ and through Christ.

The moral instruction has two distinct parts. The first consists of three pairs of ethical qualities followed by two comprehensive attributes. They provide Christians with directions for judging the worthiness of things. In other words, they tell them how to think. Although these qualities resemble the moral philosophy of the day, Paul interprets them from within his own Christian worldview. This is followed by an admonition to righteous living. This second message tells them what to do. Authentic Christian living stems from the union of these two imperatives.

The source of the first list may have been Greek moral thinking, but the source of the second exhortation is Paul himself. It was from him the Philippians learned the message of the gospel; it was from him they received the tradition that was handed down. His own life is the example placed before them as a model for theirs. Paul's attitude appears to be the complete opposite of that of the Philippians. They lacked self-confidence and trust in God; Paul is confident in his own Christian authenticity because it is grounded "in Christ."

Just as the first section that addressed the issue of anxiety ended with a promise of the peace of God, so does this ethical exhortation conclude. Both Christian thinking and Christian behavior will open the believer to the kind of peace only God can give.

## Matthew 21:33-43

In this Sunday's gospel reading we find Jesus once again sparring with the leaders of the nation. He challenges them with another parable about a vineyard. In this one the master of the house himself planted the vineyard, built the protection around it, and constructed the winepress to be used at the time of vintage. After the hard work was finished he leased to tenants who had only to care for the vines until the grapes were ready for the press. He left the country and acted as an absentee landlord. The scene is set for the drama to unfold.

Many commentators believe Jesus intended an allegorical interpretation of this parable, one that would be understood clearly by his audience. This is certainly a credible way of interpreting it. First, there was a long-standing tradition in Israel in which the People of God were characterized as a vineyard (cf. Isa 5:1-7). In such a context God would be understood as the owner of the vineyard, and the leaders of the people would be the tenant vinedressers to whom the vineyard was leased. To these leaders God periodically sent prophets to announce God's designs. Israel's history records how both the leaders and the people refused to listen to the prophets and even put some of them to death (cf. Isa 52:13–53:12).

Failing all else, the son of the owner is sent with the full authority of his father. The reasoning of the tenants may seem puzzling. Why would they think killing the son would make them eligible for inheriting the vineyard? There may have been a provision stating that in the absence of an owner property could be claimed by those who were able to secure immediate possession. With the son dead, the tenants might be able to lay claim on the vineyard if they could ensure the absence of the owner. Continuing the allegorical interpretation, the parable suggests that God sent Jesus with full divine authority, and the leaders of the people put him to death outside the city. Whether Jesus actually predicted his own death or whether this prediction reflects the parable's later reshaping by a Christian community, the detail is an important feature of the story as it has come down to us.

When Jesus finished recounting the parable, he turned to the leaders and asked them to provide a legal ruling on the situation. They must have known the parable was highlighting their own resistance to God's directives, and further they would have known that whatever judgment they might suggest would fall on their heads as well. The sentence they passed was quite harsh, but it was no harsher than the conduct of the wretched tenants.

The final verses contain a series of loosely connected themes. The rejection of the son calls to mind the passage from Scripture about the rejected stone that becomes the cornerstone (cf. Ps 118:22-23). Just as the vineyard is taken from the wicked tenants and given to others, so the kingdom of God will be taken from the leaders and given to people who will produce fruits. We must be careful not to interpret this passage in an anti-Judaic fashion. It was the leaders who were condemned by Jesus, not the entire people.

The effect this parable produced resembles the effect produced by the parable read in last Sunday's gospel. The leaders condemn themselves with their own words. They are thereby shamed in the sight of the people, while Jesus' honor is enhanced.

## Themes of the Day

### Vineyard

Vines are sturdy plants. While they are usually found in mild to warm climates, they can also thrive is less clement regions. They can grow wild and yield grapes of the same nature, or they can be cultivated and thereby produce fruit that is more abundant and sweeter to the tongue. The fruit of the cultivated vine both nourishes and delights. From it we get grapes that can be eaten, dried as raisins, or crushed into wine. It is no wonder both ancient Israel and the early Christians employed the metaphor when speaking of the reign of God.

Today the metaphor describes a cultivated vineyard that must be tended and protected. In order that its life force be put to the best possible advantage, it needs to be watered and pruned and protected from whatever might hamper its growth. What is also necessary is protection from predators and from those who might rob the owner of its produce. The metaphor suggests that while the vines themselves might be hardy, they are also vulnerable. So is the reign of God. It must be tended and protected from what might endanger it so that it can produce abundant and delectable fruit.

## Treachery

We do not slip out of the reign of God by accident. We deliberately step out of it. Just as we freely choose it; so we freely reject it. The first reading and the gospel describe two attempts at thwarting God's plans for the kingdom. In both instances there is deliberate treachery. The first reading describes the tender and solicitous care God has taken on behalf of the vineyard/kingdom. God worked tirelessly to ensure that it would thrive and be a source of enjoyment and prosperity. Despite all God's plans and effort it produced an unacceptable crop. There was no mistake here. God was in no way remiss in planting or tending. The vineyard was rebellious.

The metaphor functions differently in the gospel account. Here the fault is not with the vineyard. It produces an abundant crop. In fact, it is the very productivity of the vineyard that sets the stage for the treachery described. In this case, those who were trusted stewards turn out to be traitorous usurpers. They want the vineyard for themselves, and they are willing to use any means to acquire it.

Without interpreting either of these metaphors allegorically, we can see ourselves in each instance. There are times when, regardless of what God seems to be doing for us, we simply rebel against God's plans. We stand in defiance and cry out: I will not serve; I will do what I want. There are other times when we who are disciples of Jesus act as if the kingdom is ours, to direct or to manage it as we see fit. We might even marginalize or force out others with whom we do not agree, so that we have sole control. Unfortunately, we may not be above such treachery.

## Recompense

When we consider the justice of God, it is important we place it within the right context, lest we create a picture of God that is false and misleading. It is because of God's tender love for the vineyard that treachery cannot be tolerated. If we have produced unacceptable fruits, it is for our own good that God steps in and dismantles the structures that enabled us to produce as we did. If we attempt to usurp the kingdom in order to exercise our own control over it, it is appropriate that God snatch it from our grasp and entrust it to one who will faithfully carry out God's plans.

Along with themes such as these, today we are provided with an exhortation to righteousness and a psalm that speaks of repentance. Paul's words, though challenging, are nonetheless consoling. He promises that if we live lives of integrity the God of peace will dwell with us. The psalm describes a new situation after a time of infidelity. Once again God will care for the vine, and it will rejoice in its new life. As terrifying as God's judgment may appear to be, there is always the hope of another chance.

## Twenty-Eighth Sunday in Ordinary Time

### Isaiah 25:6-10a

The scene depicted in this passage from the prophet Isaiah is one of permanent victory, abundant feasting, and life without end. The setting is a high mountain, presumably the mountain of the LORD, for this is where both the power and the munificence of God are made manifest. It is on this mountain that a sumptuous feast is prepared, most likely the eschatological banquet. The rich foods mentioned are symbols of the fullness of life. It is also on this mountain that God destroys death, along with the pall and shroud that are symbols of death.

There are other features that support the claim that the vision depicted here is eschatological in nature. The first is the universal character of the vision. All peoples, not only the tribes of Israel, will feast on the mountain, and the pall of death that covers all people will be removed from them. It seems that the whole earth is burdened with the reproach of God's special people, for that reproach will be lifted from all the earth. The diminished distinction between peoples and earth should not be overlooked. Eschatological fulfillment embraces not only the entire human race but the natural world as well. The second eschatological feature is the use of the phrase "on that day." It usually refers to the time when all promises are kept, the time of ultimate fulfillment. Here, "that day" is the day of salvation. Finally, there is the promise that death itself will be destroyed, something that will only happen at the end of time as we know it. This last feature recalls the Canaanite myth that tells the story of the primal cosmic battle, wherein the young warrior god is victorious over Môt, the god of death. A lavish banquet followed this cosmic victory. The title

LORD of hosts *(s<sup>e</sup>bā<sup>ʾ</sup>ôt)*, which identifies God as the commander of a large company of warriors, conforms to this mythological tradition. The ancient myth was symbolically renewed as part of the yearly celebration of nature's victory of new life at springtime over the seasonal death of winter. The dying and rising was an annual event. Here death itself is destroyed, never again to hold sway. What was an important myth of cyclic celebration for the Canaanites is a rich metaphor for eschatological finality in this Isaian oracle.

Once death is destroyed there will be no cause for tears. Instead, there will be rejoicing. We have seen that the pall and shroud of death that covered all peoples will also be destroyed. Here death does not refer merely to the final demise but includes anything that diminishes life. The reproach of God's people certainly diminishes their full life. Lifting that reproach is another cause for rejoicing.

Finally, on that day of eschatological fulfillment the people will acclaim the God to whom they looked for salvation. Although salvation is mentioned only at the end of this passage, the entire vision is one of salvation. The hand of God, the symbol of God's power, will rest on this holy mountain, bringing to fulfillment all of God's promises and blessings.

## Psalm 23:1-3a, 3b-4, 5-6

The responsorial psalm is one of the most familiar and best loved psalms of the entire Psalter. It paints vivid pictures of a carefree existence, peaceful rest, and abundant fruitfulness. Although "shepherd" suggests a flock rather than merely one sheep, here the focus is on the individual. In addition to this image God is characterized as a host, one who supervises a banquet and within whose house the psalmist ultimately dwells.

The psalm opens with a metaphor that sets the tone for the entire song. It is the responsibility of the shepherd to find pastures that will provide enough grazing and abundant water for the entire flock, to lead them there without allowing any of the sheep to stray and be lost, to guard them from predators or dangers of any kind, and to attend to their every need. To characterize the LORD as a shepherd is to trust that God will discharge all of these responsibilities. The personal dimension of the psalm shifts the care given to the entire flock to concern for one individual, making God's care a very intimate matter. Not only are the physical needs of the psalmist satisfied, but the soul, the very life force *(nepesh)* of the person is renewed.

The guidance of the shepherd is more than provident, it is moral as well. The psalmist is led in the paths of righteousness (v. 3), and this is done for the sake of the LORD's name. Since one's name is a part of the very essence of the person, this indicates that the way of the LORD is the way of righteousness. Following this, we can say that the magnanimous care shown by the shepherd flows from enduring righteousness rather than from some passing sentiment of heart. This is confirmed by the reference to the covenant kindness *(ḥesed)* that surrounds the psalmist (v. 6). In other words, the divine shepherd's tender commitment to the flock, and to each individual within it, is as lasting as God's covenant commitment.

The psalmist is confident of the LORD's protection, as demonstrated in his mention of the shepherd's rod and staff, which were used to ward off wild animals as well as poachers. The valley of "deep darkness," can be a reference to the darkest part of the terrain or to the gloom that can overwhelm an individual. However, it also has a mythological connotation and is frequently interpreted as death. Whichever meaning is intended, the psalmist claims to be unafraid, for the presence of the LORD is reassuring.

The image of the shepherd securing nourishment for the flock suggests another metaphor, that of the host who prepares a lavish banquet for guests. Many societies have a very strict code of hospitality. They are obliged to provide the very best provisions they have, even for their enemies. The LORD spreads out such a banquet here, which not only affords nourishment but also is a public witness to God's high regard for the psalmist, who will continue to enjoy God's favor in God's house. Whether this indicates the Temple or is merely a reference to the place where God dwells, the fundamental meaning is clear. The psalmist has been under the loving guidance of the LORD and will remain there forever.

## Philippians 4:12-14, 19-20

The word that identifies the situation of which Paul speaks in this reading is "distress" *(thlípsis)*. Paul is not here speaking of the ordinary trials and sufferings that invade every life. Nor is he merely thanking the Philippians for meeting some of his physical needs. Rather, he is talking about the tribulations that will engulf all people at the onslaught of the end-time, the apocalyptic suffering known as the "birth pangs of the Messiah." This is the distress the Christians share *(synkoinōnéō)* with him. There may well be physical misfortune thrust upon believers, but the misfortune of which Paul speaks stems from the apocalyptic conclusion of this age. And what is the avenue through which Paul enters into this time of tribulation? It is the burdens of the ministry.

Paul insists that the demands of the ministry have taught him to be adaptable in every circumstance. He has experienced the humiliation that often comes to the ministers of the gospel as well as the adulation it frequently generates. He can live with and minister in the midst of either one of these situations. There have been times when he has had enough to eat, either as a result of his own ingenuity or because of the generosity of others. There have been other times when he has known hunger. Sometimes his physical needs have been satisfied, and other times they have gone unmet. However, these have all been external matters, matters that hold very little importance for Paul. He is convinced that his commitment to ministry was inspired and directed by God, so he is confident God will provide whatever he needs to fulfill his responsibilities in this matter. He is sure that his own human limitations in ministry will be supplemented by the grace and power of God.

Paul does not make light of the help the Philippians must have offered him. They probably did meet some of his physical needs. However, this should not be seen as merely philanthropic assistance. In acting in this way, they actually participated in his ministerial endeavors, and he is grateful for this.

Acknowledgment of the Philippians' assistance when he was in need leads Paul to comment on their own needs. God met Paul's needs, and because of their participation with Paul, God will meet their needs as well. As with Paul, this good fortune must be understood within a theological and not merely a humanitarian context. The glorious riches in Christ Jesus, from which they will be supplied, are much more than food and drink and shelter. This may be a reference to the glory that will be revealed to all at the end of this age. In a very real sense, by participating with Paul in his own distress the Philippians themselves are entering into the tribulations of the end-time. Therefore, they are promised a share in the glory of the new age as well.

Paul concludes his teaching with a doxology. The glory of which he speaks is the glory that belongs to God. It has been God's from the beginning and will continue to be God's from age to age. It is out of the graciousness of God that human beings are invited to participate in it.

## Matthew 22:1-14

This is the third Sunday in succession that the gospel presents Jesus in confrontation with the leaders of the people. Again Jesus uses parables that describe the unfaithfulness of those who have a special relationship with God. Each Sunday's reading had a particular focus. On the Twenty-Sixth Sunday we saw that repentant sinners will enter the kingdom before the supposedly righteous ones. In last Sunday's gospel those responsible for the supervision of the vineyard plotted to appropriate it for themselves. Today we are shown the severe consequences of refusing the invitation to a royal wedding banquet.

This parable lends itself to an allegorical interpretation that highlights various theological aspects. The king is certainly God, who has planned the eschatological celebration; the king's son is Jesus. The servants are the prophets and other religious leaders who serve God by calling others to union with God. This mission cost some of them their lives. The first set of guests, those who were originally invited, appear to have been respectable people who, when the final call came, were preoccupied with their own affairs. Their culpable negligence or indifference was no insignificant matter. To refuse the invitation of the king was tantamount to political insubordination. The people who finally filled the wedding banquet hall were picked up at random. They were street people, both good and bad. They may not have enjoyed the social status of the first group of invitees, but they at least accepted the invitation. Commentators disagree about the meaning of the wedding garment. It probably represented some aspect of righteousness. It shows that even though the invitation is given freely, there are still standards for its enjoyment.

The eschatological character of this parable is unmistakable. The practice of employing the banquet as a metaphor for the delights of the age of fulfillment can be traced as far back as the ancient prophetic tradition (cf. Isa 25:6). There appears to be an interim between the initial invitation to the wedding banquet and the announcement that the banquet is ready. This interim resembles the period of time between the invitation to participate in the age of fulfillment and one's entrance into that age. Finally, the punishment meted out by the king calls to mind the final judgment and the distress that will accompany it.

The final saying (v. 14) captures the essence of the entire parable. The invitation to the wedding banquet was an offer to all. However, a much smaller number of people actually enjoyed participating in the celebration. Although in this episode Jesus does not engage the leaders of the people, it is clear he tells the parable for their benefit. The point Jesus makes is that enjoyment of the eschatological time of fulfillment is open to all but guaranteed to none.

## Themes of the Day

The end-time is depicted as a banquet, a time of great happiness. It will be like a feast of the richest food and most satisfying drink. Every morsel will be relished and every sip savored. There will be rejoicing, as at the time of a wedding when all enmity is put aside and love is the order of the day. We will not have to work for this banquet; it will have been planned for us. God will set the table, and God will invite us to the feast. It is up to us to respond.

### I Cannot Come

As incredible as it may seem, some people turn down the invitation. They either ignore it completely or become so involved in their own concerns they have no time for it. Other people actually attack those who have been sent to deliver the invitation. This is the case not only in the parable but also in our world today. An invitation to the eschatological banquet does not seem to be as interesting as a sports event, the latest movie, or some social affair. So much of our time and energy is spent either climbing the economic ladder or just trying to keep our heads above water. It is not that the concerns of our lives are ignoble; they are not. But even if we are interested in the banquet, we do not seem able to afford the time and energy it might require. And so we send our regrets: I cannot come.

What a shame! We seem to have forgotten that everything is tending toward the end; life itself is moving toward the time of the banquet. All of our plans, all of our interests, all of our distractions will cease. Only the banquet will remain, and we will have turned down our invitation.

### The Guests Who Came

It is the street people who fill the banquet hall. The feast will be enjoyed by the ones who lack respectability, the ones who do not conceal their hunger. True, they may have had nowhere else to go, but they could have chosen to stay on the streets. Instead, they came and probably came gladly. They would certainly have enjoyed the feast, thus greatly pleasing the one who provided the food and drink and even the appropriate wedding attire. The people who finally came are not necessarily better than those who turned down the invitation. However, they are the ones who recognized the value of the invitation, and they were also well aware of their own need. It seems that all God asks of us is that we receive the blessings that have been prepared for us. We need not work for them. In fact, we cannot work for them on our own. All we can do is enjoy them.

### Dependent on God

One theme seems to connect all the readings for this Sunday. That theme is our total dependence on God. We have already seen it is God who spreads the table and invites the guests. It is also God who will punish those who are indifferent to or antagonistic toward the eschatological banquet. Paul testifies that it is God who supplies whatever we need in whatever circumstances. We do not have to bargain with God or make reservations. All we have to do is accept what God has to offer.

## Twenty-Ninth Sunday in Ordinary Time
### Isaiah 45:1, 4-6

The first reading for this Sunday resembles a royal decree, a formal statement wherein God addresses a king in order to authorize him for some task, empower him to function in the capacity of that task, give legitimation to decisions he may make or to a plan of action on which he might embark, or instruct him in the art of ruling. This particular royal decree is made extraordinary by the fact that in it the God of Israel addresses a Persian king. The contents of this decree reveal the instrumentality of a non-Israelite in the salvation of the people of Israel. Cyrus was the Persian ruler who permitted the Israelites to return from captivity in Babylon to their homeland and there to rebuild their Temple (cf. Ezra 1:1-8). In this passage he is called "God's anointed," a title ascribed to kings, but to Israelite kings and particularly Davidic kings. Thus a Persian inherits the role and function of the descendants of King David.

Several artifacts from the ancient world depict a ceremony wherein a god reaches out to one who would be king. The act of grasping his hand was seen as conferral of royal authority. This human king would then rule in the place of the god. Here that same action probably represents the conferral of power and authority on Cyrus. It gives divine legitimation to the role Cyrus will play in the history of Israel. It is not by accident that Cyrus plays this role. He has been especially chosen by God, called by name as was Israel (cf. Isa 43:1). This call occurred even though Cyrus did not know the God of Israel. Here we see that God works through people without their even knowing that it is really God who is directing the events of history.

Cyrus subdues nations, releases captive kings so they might serve him unfettered, throws open locked doors and barred gates in a spirit of freedom. All this is done for the sake of the Israelites (Jacob-Israel). The unfolding of this process is interesting. Cyrus the foreigner is the agent of the release of the Israelites, but their release is for the sake of the enlightenment of the foreign nations. It is one thing for God to work through the Israelites. But if the God of one people is seen to work marvels through the instrumentality of another people, it is easy to conclude there is but one God who works through all. This is precisely what is stated in this reading. There is no other God but the God of Israel. It should be noted that it was Israel's need for salvation, not any of its many successes or triumphs, that brought the people to the profound theological insight of monotheism.

"The rising and the setting of the sun" mark the boundaries of the day. Used here the phrase implies that throughout the entire day God will be revered as the only God. The self-declaration, "I am the Lord, there is no other," seems to be a standardized expression (Cf. Deut 4:35, 39; I Kgs 8:60), particularly in the writings of Isaiah (cf. Isa 45:5, 6, 14, 18, 21, 22; 46:9). This expression could well be God's primary self-identification.

### Psalm 96:1, 3, 4-5, 7-8, 9-10

This psalm calls for praise of God for the wonderful deeds God has performed (vv. 1, 3). Twice the psalmist calls for this praise, each time highlighting a different aspect of the song. First, the song is to be a new one. This suggests the old ways have passed away. Some kind of transformation has taken place. Second, it is to be directed to all the earth or all the lands (ʿeres, vv. 1, 9). While the primary meaning of the word designates the earth in a cosmological sense, a second and equally significant sense denotes a particular territory. One can conclude that in this psalm both the natural world and the human society within it are called to praise God. The glory *(kābôd)* of God refers to the visible manifestation of God's splendor. While it is usually revealed in the Temple (v. 8), here it is also associated with the wondrous deeds God has accomplished.

Once the nations have seen the wonders God has performed on behalf of Israel, they too are summoned to praise the LORD. In fact, all the earth *(ʿeres)* is actually called to worship the LORD, who has been revealed in such a wondrous manner. The essence of their homage is the cultic cry: The LORD is king! This cry was frequently used during celebrations of the kingship of God. These either followed military victory or took place at the new year, when God's primordial triumph over the forces of chaos was reenacted. It was believed that after the primordial victory both heaven and earth would acclaim God's dominion; during a cultic celebration the people at worship would proclaim the cry with joy.

The primary focus of the psalm is the superiority of the God of Israel, who reigns as king over all the world. All the gods of the other nations are worthless idols *(ʾĕlîl)*. Worship of them is futile. On the other hand, the God of Israel is great. The God of Israel is the one who made the heavens that stretch over the entire earth, demonstrating the scope of God's reign. This is the God who should be feared. The summons to worship this great God is clear: Bring gifts or tribute to the Temple. It is not clear whether it is the LORD who is in holy attire (divine glory, v. 3) or those who are officiating at the temple worship. In either case, the scene described is magnificent, befitting so great a God.

God's reign is acclaimed in three ways. First, the exercise of divine kingship is ascribed to the LORD. Second, the created world and all the societies within it are summoned to worship this God. Third, as king the LORD will govern or judge *(dîn)* the people in the manner they deserve. Thus sovereign, universal, and equitable rule are attributed to the God of Israel.

### 1 Thessalonians 1:1-5b

At the time of Paul formal letters followed a definite format. It is clear from his writing that Paul was familiar with this pattern, though he adjusted it slightly for his own use. Today's epistle reading is the introduction to Paul's first letter to the Thessalonians. In it Paul's adherence to a model can be clearly seen. First the senders are named; then those to whom the letter is sent are identified. This is followed by a greeting. Where the Hellenistic letter included a wish for good fortune, Paul has a statement of thanksgiving. The message itself then unfolds in the body of the letter.

Paul writes in his own name and in the names of two missionary companions, Silvanus and Timothy. Apparently these three men were the ones who founded the church in Thessalonica, and now they are writing back to their own converts. Silvanus is the Latin form of Silas, the name of Paul's constant companion during his second missionary journey (cf. Acts 15:40–18:5). Timothy, his junior colleague, also traveled with him. In his address to the Christians, Paul reminds them that through their baptism they are now living in God and in Christ Jesus. His greeting to them is a combination of the customary Greek wish "grace" *(cháris)* and "peace" *(eirēnē)*, the Greek equivalent for the Hebrew *shālôm.*

Paul speaks for all three men when he tells the Thessalonians how grateful the missionaries are for their fidelity to the gospel that was preached to them. In fact, the Thessalonians are always in their prayers. The converts are remarkable for their show of faith, love, and hope. Theirs is an active faith, one that produces fruits. Probably the most significant expression of their faith is the love they show others. Finally, fidelity to the gospel frequently brings on the wrath of the unrighteous. Most likely the Thessalonians would not be spared this suffering. The faith in which they were grounded has also found expression in trust. For all of this the Thessalonians are praised.

Paul's praise can function in various ways. First, it is simply praise of the Thessalonians for their faithfulness to the gospel. High praise is also an incentive to continue on the way of righteousness and, if possible, to excel on that way. Finally, their commitment is evidence of the success of Paul's own ministry. If there is anyone who knows the extent to which the Thessalonians have been transformed through the gospel and have been faithful to its message, it is Paul. He knew how they had been chosen, and he was witness to the effects of the love of God in their lives. Paul had much for which to praise his converts.

Having praised them, Paul reminds the Thessalonians of the circumstances of their conversion. They accepted the gospel primarily though Paul's preaching but also through the power of the Holy Spirit. They had the example of the missionaries to strengthen them, but it was divine power that grounded them. Though spiritual children of Paul and his companions, the Thessalonians really belong to God.

### Matthew 22:15-21

Once again Jesus is in a battle of wits with the religious leaders of the people. This time they are the ones who initiate it. While the purpose of the encounter is the entrapment of Jesus, the underlying issue is the possibility of being faithful both to God and to a secular state. The Pharisees did not seem to approve of the Gentile rule over the Jewish people. The Herodians, on the other hand, were Roman loyalists. Within the ranks of the people, the Zealots vehemently opposed the occupation, while many others had made their peace with it and sometimes even benefited from it. Roman taxation was an issue that could easily cause people to take sides. It was with this very issue that the Pharisees hoped to ensnare Jesus.

They begin with words of flattery, which are intended to set the trap. If Jesus is as forthright in his speech and as free of human respect as they describe him, he will certainly speak his mind clearly and ensnare himself. Regardless of how he answers, he is bound to alienate some of his hearers and to be shamed in the sight of all. The ploy is certainly a clever one. Having set the trap, they offer him the bait. They ask him for an interpretation on a point of Roman law: Is it lawful for a Jew to pay taxes to Rome? The tax in question is probably the poll tax paid directly to Rome, evidence of political subjugation. If Jesus answers no, he can be accused of political insubordination of the type that might incite others to respond in kind. If he says yes, he will appear to have relinquished Israel's boast of being a people bound only to God.

Jesus is not taken in by their flattery. He knows what they are trying to do, and he knows what is at stake. They not only want to shame him in the eyes of the people, they are placing him in political jeopardy as well. In response to them he first shames them by calling them hypocrites, and then he unmasks their ploy. He asks for a coin that can be used to pay the poll tax. The coin itself was abhorrent to the Jewish people, for it contained the image of Caesar along with titles that accorded him both political honor and divine status. Both of these features violated Jewish Law. In deference to Jewish sensitivities, imageless copper coins were used in ordinary commercial exchange. Jesus does not seem to have one of the questionable coins, but without hesitation his antagonists are able to produce one. Just by having one in their possession they have been caught in their own trap.

Jesus responds to their initial inquiry with a question of his own, thus putting them on the defensive. They have produced the coin, and now they acknowledge that it contains the image of Caesar. Jesus directs them to "give back" or "repay" *(apodídōmi)* what is owed to both Caesar and God. Besides exonerating him from possible political or religious reproach, Jesus' response suggests that one can indeed be loyal both to a religious tradition and to a secular power. It may be very difficult at times, especially when their claims seem to conflict, but it is possible. Once again Jesus gains honor in the sight of the people, while his antagonists are disgraced.

## Themes of the Day

### All Peoples

The frequency with which we consider the question of insider-outsider is an indication of how important universalism and the breaking down of boundaries is within our religious tradition. All peoples, all lands, are called on to praise God. And all of the major religions of the world do just that. Human beings have always realized that, in comparison with the grandeur and expansiveness of the universe within which they live, they are weak and vulnerable creatures. This has led them to believe in and offer homage to a divine being, or beings. Praise of God has always been an expression of awe and gratitude as well as humility.

Our religious tradition further tells us that just as all reality originated from the mystery we call God and is held in existence by this same God, so all reality will ultimately be brought together again in the embrace of God. From various points of view this embrace has been called salvation or enlightenment or fulfillment. However it is characterized, there is something within the human heart that draws us to God and to this definitive realization. In this there are no outsiders, all are insiders.

### Insider-Outsider

It is human beings who categorize people as insiders or outsiders. They are the ones who define and then draw boundaries based on gender, race, age, class, culture, talent . . . the list could go on and on. God does not abide by such lists. God cares about and cares for all people (cf. Isa 19:25), and God works through all people to accomplish good in the world. Even ancient Israel, as ethnocentric as it was, acknowledged this. Its return from Babylonian exile, an event that was characterized as a second exodus and that marked the rebirth of the nation, is credited to Cyrus, a Persian ruler.

In our day we have witnessed the non-violent overthrow of a mighty nation through the agency of Gandhi, a diminutive Hindu of Indian origin, and the extraordinary peaceful resistance to racial discrimination led by Martin Luther King, Jr., a Baptist minister. Susan B. Anthony struggled to ensure that women in the United States were enfranchised, and Nelson Mandela did the same for black Africans in South Africa. Each one of these individuals was an outsider in her or his society, yet God worked through them to break down these barriers of separation. The outsiders have become insiders and have brought others inside with them.

## Criteria for Deciding

If neither gender, nor race, nor age, nor class, nor culture qualifies one for being an insider, what does? Today's readings suggest it is service of others. Whether Cyrus was aware of the implications of his foreign policy or not, he issued a decree allowing captive peoples to return to their homelands. Paul and Silvanus and Timothy gained entry into various communities of the ancient world as they preached the good news of the gospel to those people of cultures not their own. In breaking down the walls of prejudice, the social activists of our own age liberated not only the oppressed groups to which they belonged but also those who had oppressed them. The lives of these dynamic people show us that service of others draws them into our circles and encircles us in theirs.

There is an underside to this issue. There are those who by their conduct make themselves outsiders to the group. They refuse to help, or, even worse, they seek the undoing of others. Those who tried to trip Jesus are an example of this. By birth they belonged to the People of God, but their actions belied the covenant relationship of which they boasted.

With open arms God invites all into an embrace of love. As we have been embraced by God, so we are called to embrace all others.

## Thirtieth Sunday in Ordinary Time

### Exodus 22:20-26

The passage that is read today comes from the law codes of ancient Israel. It reveals the humane nature of that law. It exhorts the Israelites to be especially attentive to those within their community who are the most vulnerable, defenseless, and disadvantaged. It singles out the alien, the widow, and the orphan.

Ancient Israel was a patriarchal society based on the rights of free adult men. Women were under the jurisdiction of and benefited from the rights that belonged to their fathers, their brothers when their fathers died, their husbands when they married, and their sons when their husbands died. The term "widow" was generally used only of childless women whose husbands had died and who could not return to the jurisdiction of their families of origin. These woman were frequently reduced to begging, a life that was always dangerous but particularly so for woman. Orphans were those children who had no legal male guardians. They too were utterly vulnerable and relegated to lives of begging. The aliens *(gēr)* referred to here are not merely those who are passing through the land but those who live among people who are not their relatives. Because they do not belong to these people, they do not enjoy the privileges that flow from kinship.

The laws of Israel forbad taking advantage of those who were already un-protected by social structures. A special reason is given for consideration of the alien. The Israelites themselves had been resident aliens in Egypt. They knew the hardships this life entailed. It was precisely those hardships that led to the revelation of their God as the God of the dispossessed. They came to know God in this way, first from their own experience and now through this divine decree. God is particularly attentive to the needy. This special care is also extended to widows and orphans. If these vulnerable are further op-pressed and they cry out to God, God will hear their cry just as God heard the cry of the Israelites when they were in bondage in Egypt (cf. Exod 3:7). The punishment for afflicting them is severe. The guilty ones will be killed, their wives and children will be forced to endure the plight of the widowed and the orphaned. The latter part of this sentence reveals the society's patriarchal bias. Despite the offensiveness of this threat, it is clear that the God of Israel is the God of the oppressed.

The Law is also concerned with those within the community who are bur-dened with financial hardship. This burden must not be exacerbated. Interest-free loans should be made so that the needy can get out from under their burden. Every attempt must be made to ensure they undergo no added humili-ation or distress and no unreasonable dependency on another. Since one's outer garment was also used as a blanket against the evening chill, to demand that cloak as a pledge was to deprive the person of protection. Once again God promises to hear the cries of the dispossessed and vulnerable. The reason God gives for this kind of concern is: I am gracious *(ḥannûn)!* I am compassionate! I am concerned about those who are vulnerable! God is the God of the oppressed.

## Psalm 18:2-3, 3-4, 47, 51

This psalm of praise for deliverance is a composite of direct address to God and description about God addressed to someone else. Perhaps the most note-worthy aspect of the psalm is the array of metaphors employed to characterize God. They include: rock, fortress, deliverer, shield, horn of salvation, strong-hold. Although each has its respective meaning, they all embody some aspect of deliverance.

Rock, fortress, and stronghold depict God as an impregnable bulwark against which no enemy can triumph. Shield and horn of salvation are mili-tary accouterments that protect the soldier from harm. A deliverer *(miplāt)* is one who rescues someone from a calamity such as war. All of these characteri-zations imply that the psalmist is protected by God from grave danger of every kind. In a world where people feel they are always at risk and where violence is the common response to threat, the idea that a powerful God will step in and act as defender is very consoling.

The word that is translated "love" *(rāḥam)* is very unusual. It comes from the word for "womb," and it denotes the kind of intimate love a mother has for the child she is carrying or has already borne. It conveys the sense of elemental connection, a connection with something that has come forth from one's very being. This word is usually employed to characterize the extraordinary, even incomprehensible, love that God has for human beings. The claim to love God with this kind of devotion is a bold claim indeed.

The victory cry "The LORD lives!" is a cultic formula that extols God's dynamic activity. Because the psalm speaks of the psalmist's need for defense and deliverance, the reference is certainly to God's saving activity in history. What began as a hymn of thanksgiving has now become a doxology, a prayer in praise of God's mighty accomplishments.

The last verse of this response introduces a royal theme. The God who has been the defense of the psalmist has also secured victory for the king. It may be the king is another one of the people saved by the LORD, or perhaps the king and the psalmist are one and the same. Since the point of the psalm is the secure defense offered by God, either interpretation would be acceptable.

## 1 Thessalonians 1:5c-10

As Paul speaks to the Christians of Thessalonica he sketches the route taken by the gospel message as it passes from one people to another, one group to another, one generation to another. As important as the transmission of teaching may be, the gospel is really handed down by the example of life-style. Today's reading from Paul develops this theme. The process begins with Paul and his missionary companions. Their manner of living among the Thessalonians converted the latter to the life-style of the former. This conversion made such an extraordinary effect on their lives that they in turn made a comparable impact on the lives of others. The gospel message takes shape in the lives of believers and elicits a positive response from those with whom they have contact. Francis of Assisi taught this message when he exhorted his followers: Preach the gospel at all times; if necessary, use words.

Paul challenges the Christians to follow his example and that of Jesus. At first glance this might seem to be an arrogant directive. However, a closer look at the text shows that he has a particular circumstance in mind when he says this. The converts received the word of the gospel in the midst of affliction *(thlípsis)*, the tribulations associated with the end-time. It was within such circumstances the missionaries proclaimed the word; it was within such circumstances the Thessalonians accepted it; and it is within such circumstances they give witness to others. The reputation of the Thessalonians has spread throughout Macedonia and Achaia, Roman provinces in the eastern part of Greece. There is no need for Paul to boast about them to others.

It seems that even the details of the conversion of the Thessalonians are well known. Paul uses what may have been a creedal formula to describe how they turned from idols to the worship of the living and true God. Jesus is depicted as the one who was raised from the dead by God, the one who will come from heaven to save them: Christ has died; Christ is risen; Christ will come again. The promise of Christ's future coming brings us back to the theme of the distress at the end of time. Paul believes that those who are faithful amidst the tribulations of this life will be spared the final wrath of God. He is not painting a picture of doom. Rather, he is giving meaning to the hardships the Christians are presently enduring, and in so doing he is assuring them of a hopeful future.

## Matthew 22:34-40

The credibility of Jesus is again under attack. He has just succeeded in silencing the Sadducees, the priestly and aristocratic group that was in sympathy with Roman occupation. Now the Pharisees, a lay group that exerted significant influence among the people because of their knowledge and piety, set out to trick Jesus. One of them, a lawyer, or expert in the Law, asks Jesus to identify the most important commandment. This question was an issue of considerable interest to rabbis at the time, about which there seems to have been little agreement. While the discussion in rabbinic circles was probably carried on for the sake of clarification, in the present hostile context the question is posed in order to put Jesus to the test *(peiráō)*.

By this point in history the Law included 613 commandments, 365 prohibitions (one for each day of the year), and 268 prescriptions (one for each bone in the body). Although all laws were considered binding because they had been delivered by God to Moses, some were regarded as "heavy," or very important, and others were looked upon as "less weighty." Presumably the lawyer, whose very profession consisted of the interpretation of the Law, would have understood this better than Jesus, who was not a scribe. Despite the fact that this was a disputed question, whatever priority Jesus would proclaim would most likely be challenged by some. If it appeared he was annulling a part of the Law, he could lose his status in the community as a teacher.

Jesus' answer is faithful to his own Jewish faith. He does not single out any particular statute but rather endorses the summons that constitutes the *Shemʿ*, the most significant prayer of the Israelite religion (cf. Deut 6:5). To the injunction to love God with all one's heart and soul, Jesus adds "with all your mind," probably for the purpose of emphasizing the total engagement of the person. This is his way of saying the love of God must occupy one's entire being and not be simply a superficial allegiance.

Jesus was asked to identify one commandment, and he offers two. The second, which is said to be like the first rather than second in importance, is a citation from the book of Leviticus (19:18). Twice Jesus has reached into the biblical Law in order to answer the question posed to him. By bringing these admonitions together as he does, he shows that, though not identical, they are interrelated. Placing his answer within the context of the *Shema'*, he makes the proclamation that there is no other God but this God the controlling theme in his response. From this proclamation flows the responsibility to love God with one's entire being and to love one's neighbor as oneself.

With his final statement Jesus demonstrates that singling out a dual commandment in no way abrogates the other commandments. He is not judging between the "heavy" and the "less weighty" requirements. Instead, he is asserting that the entire religious tradition, identified as the Law and the Prophets, is dependent upon this commandment of love. In other words, there is no genuine fulfillment of the Law that does not flow from love of God and love of others.

## Themes of the Day

### Created in Love

Our religious tradition is founded on love. Actually, life itself is grounded in love, a love that is open and generous. We may not always feel this love, but if we are honest and we allow ourselves to reflect on life, we will realize this truth. We have been called into being and we are sustained in existence for no other reason than loving generosity. We are the recipients of unbounded generosity; for some reason we are loved. It was out of love that we came from nothing or, as modern cosmology insists, that we came from reordered chaos. We certainly did nothing to deserve this love. All we can conclude is that we are loved because the source from which we came is loving. This is precisely what the Bible tells us again and again (cf. Jer 31:3; Matt 10:31; 1 John 4:8).

The universe springs from this love; we have been called by this love; and we will only be happy if we live in this love. Therefore, when we are directed to love God and love one another, we are not being asked to do something contrary to our nature. Rather, we are being told to live in accord with the nature out of which we have been fashioned. We come from God who is love, so it is in our very nature to love and to be loved.

### Love of God and Neighbor

We may sometimes think it is easier to love God than to love others. It may actually be just the opposite. Other people are tangible. We can see and hear them, interact with them. Their influence in our lives can permeate our consciousness. That is not the way it is with God. Like Moses on the mountain, we can only see the traces of divinity as God passes by (cf. Exod 33:23). However, we show we love God by loving what God loves; we show we love God in the way we love our neighbor. Our religious tradition goes so far as to say we really do not love God if we do not love others (cf. 1 John 4:20).

It is true that we love God when we love those who are such an intimate part of our lives, but love like God's love must be more expansive that this. If our love is open and generous like God's love, we will care for the widows and the orphans and the aliens; we will feed the hungry and visit the sick; we will alleviate the misery of those suffering with AIDS or mental illness; we will include those who have been forced to the margins of society. If our love is open and generous like God's love, we will do what we can to provide decent living conditions for people trapped in the prison of poverty; we will work to ensure clean water and air and a healthy world for those who will come after us. If our love is open and generous like God's love, we will treasure God's world and God's people within it.

### The Witness of Love

Love, which is the foundation of the reign of God, is contagious. When we love others, the reign of God spreads throughout the world. It was the goodness of their lives that made the Thessalonians renowned in the neighboring territories. The compassion that we show toward others is a form of evangelization. It proclaims much louder than any words could ever do that the reign of God has been established. When we love like this, we truly love with the openness and generosity of God.

## Thirty-First Sunday in Ordinary Time
### Malachi 1:14b–2:2b, 8-10

The words of the LORD as spoken through the prophet Malachi are condemnatory and searing. They are a denunciation of the priests of Israel who not only have defiled the office of priesthood but also have led the people astray with their faulty teaching. Their infidelity is particularly heinous because of the privileged position they had enjoyed in the community. With the exception of the Davidic kings, no other group within the nation of Israel could claim a special covenant relationship with God (cf. Num 10:13). Furthermore, their lives were circumscribed by matters of holiness (cf. Lev 21:6), and they were the ones who interpreted the Law for the people (cf. Deut 17:8-11).

The judgment speech opens with a divine self-identification. The LORD of hosts (*sᵉbā'ôt*) claims to be a great king whose name is feared by all nations.

God's name would only be feared if God's power had somehow been manifested. This power could well have established God as a mighty king. The military term "host," when used in the title for God, usually refers to a vast company of celestial warriors. This title identified God both as the one who conquered the primordial forces of chaos and as the champion of the armies of Israel. Feats accomplished by such fearsome forces would certainly fill the hearts of the nations with reverential fear.

The honor granted the name of God by the nations is in sharp contrast with the dishonor accorded it by the priests of Israel. The list of their many and grievous sins begins with mention of personal transgressions, moves to offenses against others, and concludes with reference to the infidelity directed toward God. The "way" from which they had turned is probably a reference to the moral and religious life-style expected of all of the People of God, not to the behavior required of the priests. They had also violated the trust of the people who came to them for a word of direction *(tôra)* but were led astray instead. Besides misdirecting the people, the priests also had attempted to curry the favor of some by making decisions based on partiality. Finally, they had abrogated the covenant made by God with them.

The commandment *(miṣwâ)* given the priests is expressed as a threat, with mention of the punishment exacted if it is not followed. If they do not reform their lives and thereby give glory to God's name, they will suffer the curse of God. The blessings referred to could be the riches they had been able to accrue during the time they served as priests, the benedictions they had pronounced when officiating in the priestly role, or their original commission to priesthood. If the latter, it would seem that what was initially a privilege has, because of their sinfulness, become a curse. Besides experiencing this curse, the priests will also be shamed before the people, a fate considered by some to be worse than death itself.

There is a change of speaker in the last verse. Perhaps it is the prophet who appeals to community solidarity by reminding the priests that all come from the same Creator and all the people of the covenant claim the same ancestors. This is reason enough to keep faith with one another.

The reading for today does not tell us whether or not the priests took this condemnation to heart and reformed their lives. For us it serves as a reminder that privileged positions within the community bring with them serious responsibilities. Failure to fulfill these responsibilities will meet with profound consequences.

### Psalm 131:1, 2, 3

These three verses constitute the entire psalm. It is difficult to classify it because it is primarily descriptive rather than exclamatory. What is described are the sentiments of someone who is devoted to the LORD. Each verse of the psalm has its own character. The first verse is a self-description of humility; in the second verse the psalmist is characterized as a child at peace in its mother's presence; the third verse is a call to Israel to trust in the LORD.

The psalmist describes his humble bearing in various ways. His heart, which is really his mind, or the seat of his understanding, is not pompous; he does not think vainglorious thoughts. Such thoughts would lead to egotistical behavior, and this has not been his practice. The psalmist's eyes are not lofty; he does not look disdainfully on others. Finally, he does not engage himself in matters beyond his comprehension or ability. All of this indicates that he has neither an inflated concept of himself nor a desire to impress others with a false idea of his importance. In other words, when the psalmist lists what he is not, he is also describing indirectly what he is. He is a man with an honest and straightforward heart, a man who can look someone in the eye without minimizing the other, a man who has a realistic view of who he is and what he can do. This is an example of genuine humility.

The image sketched in the second stanza is one of tenderness and complete security. While it may not be correct to claim that God is characterized as a woman whose weaned child sits tranquilly beside her, it is certainly true that the confidence God inspires is compared with that of the woman. There is no relationship that can be compared with that of a mother and her suckling child. The child not only takes shape from her substance but continues to depend upon her milk for years after birth (the normal period in Israel was three years). It is no wonder the child experiences absolute calm in her presence. This is the kind of trust and serenity the psalmist experiences in the presence of God.

The psalmist turns to the people of Israel and entreats them to place their trust in this same God. One might conclude that as God has encircled the psalmist with tenderness and concern, so God will embrace the entire people. The situation with the mother and child illustrates that a relationship formed in such loving circumstances will not only endure throughout life, it will deepen and grow stronger. Israel is called to this kind of confidence.

## 1 Thessalonians 2:7b-9, 13

This short reading provides us with a glimpse into the deep affection with which the missionaries hold their converts. Paul uses the metaphor of a nursing mother to represent these sentiments. He speaks first of gentleness. This calls to mind the tenderness with which the mother holds the suckling child to her breast, a gesture both calming and reassuring. With a comparable love, the missionaries had embraced the Thessalonians, holding them tenderly and protectively. Born anew in Christ, the converts were indeed infants in the faith, in need of care and tender sheltering. The metaphor suggests that the missionaries' love preceded the Thessalonians' acceptance of the faith; it was not a reward for it.

The image of a nursing mother also effectively characterizes the apostolic self-giving of which Paul speaks. The woman's love for her child prompts her to give to that child both what she has and literally what she is. The child was first fashioned of her very substance and is now nourished from her body. Analogously, the missionaries have wholeheartedly shared the gospel with the Christians and have magnanimously given of their very selves. If this metaphor is carried further, we might say it refers to a unilateral relationship, it does not include the notion of reciprocal giving. Both the mother and the missionary spend themselves with no thought of receiving anything in return other than the satisfaction of having given themselves out of love.

The appropriateness of this last point is confirmed by Paul's next comment. Caring for the physical needs of traveling preachers seems to have been the custom of the day (cf. Luke 10:7). Thus Paul and his companions would have been within their rights to expect such hospitality from their converts. However, they chose to forgo this prerogative. They worked at their respective trades (cf. Acts 18:3) earning their own keep, being a financial burden to no one. They proclaimed the gospel as they saw fit asking for nothing in return.

The passage ends on a note of gratitude. The recompense the missionaries receive for their ministry is the religious maturity of their converts, and for this they are grateful to God. Though new to the faith, the Thessalonians accepted the gospel for what it was, the word of God, not the words of the men who delivered it. In other places Paul may have had to argue that his preaching was not a fabrication of his own making (cf. Gal 1:11-12), but not here. The gospel has taken root in the minds and hearts of these converts, and it is already producing fruit.

## Matthew 23:1-12

Addressing the crowds and his disciples, Jesus issues a scathing denunciation of the scribes and Pharisees. His mention of the chair of Moses could be a reference to the honorary chair set up in the synagogue in which sat the chief interpreter of the Law, or it could simply refer to the position they held as the legitimate successors of Moses. While Jesus recognizes the authenticity of their office, he criticizes them for the disparity that exists between what they teach and how they live. This disparity is evidence of the duplicity of their lives. He counsels his hearers: Listen to them, but don't follow their example.

Jesus' criticism focuses on two Pharisaic practices. The first is their casuistic method of interpreting the Law. It was their devotion to the Law that prompted the Pharisees to develop the vast array of detailed minor rules, referred to as the "hedge around the Law," meant to ensure obedience to the commandments. This collection, the number of which eventually reached 613, came to be a heavy burden for the people to carry, and the scribes and Pharisees did nothing to alleviate this onus.

The second feature for which they are criticized is their love of praise. Devout men scrupulously adhered to the admonition to bind the Scriptures on their hands and foreheads (cf. Deut 6:8). This led to the practice of placing scriptural passages in small leather boxes called "phylacteries" and binding them on their foreheads and upper left arms. In a second practice, tassels with blue cord were attached to the four corners of the outer garment (cf. Deut 22:12). The scribes and Pharisees widened the former and lengthen the latter, thereby suggesting that they were more devout than most.

In addition to this outward display, they sought other ways to be treated with deference and to enjoy privilege. At banquets they coveted the places of the honored guests who flanked the host, the most honored sitting at the right, the second most honored at the left. In the synagogue the congregation sat on benches facing the chest that contained the sacred scrolls. The Pharisees sat in the front benches, which were the most important seats. In public settings it was customary for those of inferior station to salute the more important members of society—the more important the person the more elaborate the salutation. The scribes and Pharisees loved ostentatious greetings.

Jesus declared that such pomposity should have no place among his followers. His is to be a community of equals, and so his followers must shun titles that implied status. They are not to be called "Rabbi," which means "my great one," because there is only one great rabbi and they are equal disciples of that teacher. The title "father" suggests a patriarchal structure with one autocratic head. This is not the kind of community Jesus desires. They have a Father in heaven; on earth they are all sisters and brothers. Finally, they are to consider no one their master *(kathēgētēs)*, the great guiding mind of the community; they have one master, and it is Christ.

The passage concludes with a reversal of fortunes, the kind of shocking statement so characteristic of the teaching of Jesus. The great ones in the community should be the servants of all. Those who exalt themselves now will experience eschatological humiliation; those who humble themselves now will enjoy eschatological exaltation.

## Themes of the Day

The quality of a community and the depth of its love are often determined by the character of its leadership. As we approach the end of the Liturgical Year the readings invite us to examine the character of leadership in the community of believers.

## Leadership Roles

Since Vatican II the responsibilities of leadership have been spread throughout the community in various ways. This has not happened simply because there are fewer and fewer priests and religious to do the work, although the shortage is keenly felt. Rather, it has occurred primarily because the council itself insisted that by virtue of their baptism all Christians are called to discipleship, and this includes active participation in the mission of the Church. While those who are ordained continue in specialized forms of leadership, other people have stepped forward to assume their newly recognized responsibilities. And sometimes these people have more influence in the Church than do the ordained. Leadership is no longer the exclusive domain of priests and bishops.

Post-Vatican parishes are more often than not administered by a parish staff consisting of the pastor, pastoral associates, principals of schools, liturgical leaders, directors of religious education, ministers of the sick, and youth ministers, to name but a few. Important decisions can no longer be made without the involvement of the parish council. All of these people set the tone of the parish. In a very real sense, they are leaders. What kind of leaders are they? Are we?

## Hypocritical Leaders

It is from Jesus' description of the Pharisees in today's reading that we derive the connection between pharisaical and hypocritical. His condemnation of them, along with the condemnation of the priests in the first reading, should be a warning to all of us who in any way exercise leadership. We must always be on guard lest we become ensnared by the trappings of leadership and fail in our covenantal responsibilities toward God and the community we serve. We can become satisfied with externals, with buildings completed, lessons taught, or liturgics performed; we can aspire to places of honor and invitations to events where we can associate with important people; we can look for recognition and praise. Even worse that these signs of vanity, we can use our positions of trust to exploit others, whether their resources, their emotions, or their physical persons. Unfortunately all this can be done under the guise of "what is best for the community."

## Authors of Life

There is another mode of leadership, one that is faithful to the very meaning of authority. It is a way of leadership that authors life. Paul's striking image of a nursing mother who both gives and sustains life characterizes such leadership.

It flows from the love we must have for one another. It does not impose heavy burdens on others. This kind of leadership is both strong and gentle: it is strong in its commitment to the gospel, and it is gentle in its consideration of others. Those who exercise leadership in this way will fashion a community where life is fostered, not stifled; where talents serve all the members; where the talents of all the members are invited to serve. Such a community will not only nurture its members, it will itself be the author of life in the world.

## Thirty-Second Sunday in Ordinary Time
### Wisdom 6:12-16

All societies have some type of Wisdom tradition. Israel was no exception. Most of the tradition is composed of the insight gleaned from the reflection on life experience. Human beings who search for meaning and understanding realize, however, that human wisdom cannot plumb the depths of reality. The deepest questions of life do not seem to be satisfied with answers derived from experience. Still, the order discerned in life suggests there is meaning or purpose behind or within everything. This meaning or purpose is considered a form of divine wisdom. In the tradition of Israel this wisdom is personified as a woman. Wisdom in this feminine personification is not exactly a divine characteristic, but she is very close to it (cf. Wis 7:25-26). It is this Wisdom that the author of the book of Wisdom, known as Pseudo-Solomon, applauds in the reading this Sunday.

A bold claim is made here, namely, that Wisdom is perceived by those who love her, found by those who search for her. Actually, the love of Wisdom (*philo-sophía*) and the search for Wisdom are evidence that one is already wise. The search at dawn shows that the desire for Wisdom is uppermost in the minds of the wise. It should be noted that while people search for Wisdom, Wisdom is also in search of them, moving through the highways and byways of life. She looks for devotees at the gate of a city because the city is the center of commerce and communication. It is there decisions are made; it is there people are met. Wisdom is at the heart of human activity because that is where life is lived.

There seems to be a paradox here. Human beings are always in search of Wisdom because she is just out of their reach. And yet Wisdom is always available to them, waiting for them, calling to them. Although she permeates all of reality she resides at its deepest level, so only those who venture into the deepest realms of experience will find her. However, those who find Wisdom find peace and security, meaning and fulfillment. And once she has been found, one will be able to see her everywhere.

### Psalm 63:2, 3-4, 5-6, 7-8

Three religious sentiments are present in this psalm of confidence. It begins with expressions of longing, followed by a short hymn of praise, concluding with words of confidence. Flesh *(bāśār)* and soul *(nepesh)* are the two dimensions of a human being, which constitute the totality of that person (cf. Gen 2:2). The metaphor used to portray the intensity of the psalmist's longing is arid land. This metaphor not only makes the longing concrete, it also suggests that the need for an experience of God is as essential for a human being as water is essential for natural life itself. Without such an experience the person is devoid of the source of life, just as parched land is devoid of the source of its life.

Several elements of this passage suggest its setting is cultic or somehow liturgical. Most obvious is mention of the sanctuary. Added to this is a description of the psalmist praying with uplifted hands, a traditional stance of prayer. The prayer itself (calling upon God's name) could be offered anywhere, at anytime, so it is not explicitly liturgical. However, given the other cultic features it certainly can be understood this way. The verb for "seek" (v. 2) might be better translated "seek early," suggesting early morning prayer after keeping a night vigil. Finally, the psalmist actually does pray for some kind of theophany, a physical manifestation of God (v. 3) that would take the form of divine power *('ōz)* and glory *(kābôd)*.

The psalmist contrasts the arid life without God with the sumptuous life with God. The satisfaction that comes with the experience of God is compared to marrow of bone and fatness of flesh, parts of an animal that are not only tasty but that also contain life-giving properties. While in reality such a rich banquet satisfies the physical need, here it is to be understood figuratively as characterizing the satisfaction the soul experiences. Regardless of the importance of life and the joys one might receive when that life is lived in union with God, the psalmist insists that the technical covenant bond of lovingkindness *(hesed)* is more precious than life itself. Actually, the psalmist's trust in being heard by God is rooted in this covenantal bond.

The passage ends with several images that characterize the psalmist's trust in God. First, God is proclaimed the psalmist's help *('ēzer)*. This is not a hope for the future; rather it is a present experience. Next the text depicts the psalmist under God's protective wings, a reference to the eagle that spreads its wings over its young. Finally, the psalmist clings to God and is upheld by God's right hand, a stereotype that signifies God's power. The psalmist has turned to God for life and security, and God has responded with the requested protection.

### 1 Thessalonians 4:13-18

Paul begins this passage in a way he frequently introduces new material (cf. 1 Cor 10:1; 12:1; 2 Cor 1:8). The subject of his instruction is the final coming (*parousía*) of the Lord. It seems the Christians are troubled by the death of some of their members. The expression "fallen asleep" was a euphemism for death that was common in antiquity, just as the expression "passed away" is common today. The issue does not appear to be the sadness they experience because of their loss. Paul wants to prevent their suffering the kind of grief that proceeds from hopelessness. What might cause them to be hopeless? Perhaps they share a belief current at the time that death is indeed the end of all life. This point of view would not prevent them from also believing that as Christians they had died with Christ and risen with Christ to a new life. Their concern over the death of other Christians suggests that they believed living this new life in Christ would exempt them from physical death. When this did not happen, they must have questioned either the authenticity of the faith of the deceased or the trustworthiness of this new life.

Before Paul offers a description of the events that constitute the final coming of the Lord, he explains the nature of the union that exists between the risen Lord and those who are joined to him in faith. His argument is based on faith in the resurrection of Jesus. First, Jesus died and rose from the dead, thus conquering the control death had initially exercised over him. Next, through the victory of Jesus those joined to him are also delivered from the power of death, for neither life nor death can separate them from the love of Christ (cf. Rom 8:38-39). Finally, at the end of time all believers will be decisively joined with the Lord. Paul testifies to the truth of this on the strength of the word of the Lord.

Paul draws on elements from the apocalyptic tradition of Israel to describe the events that will take place. Clouds, angels, and trumpet blasts frequently accompany a theophany, or manifestation of God. Their appearance at the time of the *parousía* indicates that this final coming is precisely such a theophanic event. Everything will begin with a mighty word of command, with the voice of an archangel (a rather highly ranked angel in Hellenistic Judaism's classification of celestial beings), with the thundering blast of a trumpet. Then Christ will descend from heaven, where he is enthroned in glory with God. The Thessalonians will be comforted to know that the Christians who have already died will be first in the procession to rise and meet the Lord. Paul seems to say that those who are still alive at this time will be taken up as they are. We must remember that Paul's real concern is the interpretation of an apocalyptic tradition in such a way as to comfort his audience, not a precise prediction of the future. His immediate concern is to encourage those who are not only struggling with the death of a loved one but with questions of faith.

### Matthew 25:1-13

The parable of the ten virgins is told against the background of Palestinian wedding customs. In that culture a marriage unfolded in various stages. It began with the betrothal (cf. Matt 1:18). At that point the couple were technically married, but they still lived apart. After all the financial matters between the two families were settled, the bridegroom went in procession to be joined with his bride. Only then did the feasting begin. Most likely the virgins in the parable were part of the bridal procession, waiting for the arrival of the bridegroom. There is no mention of the bride, not because the woman lacked importance but because the point of the parable is the virgins' degree of preparedness in anticipation of the arrival of the bridegroom. It should be noted that it is the role played by women in the wedding procession that lends itself to a comparison here.

Several features of the parable mark its eschatological character. The most obvious is the banquet itself. In the tradition of ancient Israel it served as a symbol of eschatological fulfillment (cf. Isa 25:6), and Jesus himself used the metaphor of a wedding banquet to teach lessons about the end-time (cf. Matt 22:1-12, Twenty-Eighth Sunday). A second eschatological feature is the idea of waiting in darkness for an event to occur without knowing exactly when it will come to pass. Finally, there is an ultimate separation that cannot be altered. Jesus may be recounting a parable that describes circumstances surrounding a wedding, but he is teaching a lesson about the end-time.

There is no difference in the status of the virgins. They all came with torches, and they all fell asleep as the night drew on. The difference is in their preparedness. Half of them had made provision for the possible delay of the bridegroom, the other half had not. It was their responsibility to be ready at any moment. Their vigilance was determined by their preparedness, not by their ability to stay awake. They all fell asleep, and no one was reprimanded for having done so. This is not a parable about generosity, so the virgins who are considered wise should not be censured for refusing to share their oil with those who did not have foresight. This particular aspect suggests that what is required for entrance into the banquet cannot be loaned or given by another. It must be procured by oneself.

The fate of the virgins who came after the door was locked is quite harsh. However, we must remember that as a story about eschatological reality, this parable recounts the passage from the present age to the age of fulfillment. One is either able to cross that threshold, or one is not. The crossing is decisive. The virgins were left behind not by accident but through their own negligence.

At the end of the passage Jesus concludes the parable and turns to his audience. His exhortation is simple but strong: Be alert (*grēgoréō*)! You do not know when the end will come!

### Themes of the Day

A significant shift in our reflection on the reign of God takes place today. For the past Sundays we have considered the nature of the kingdom, characterizing it as a banquet, a vineyard, and a community committed to justice. Today we fasten our gaze on the end of time, and we consider the goal of the kingdom.

## The End

At what age do we genuinely realize we will some day die? Children may be struck with the realization of death when a grandparent dies. But then, grandparents are old people who have lived their lives, are worn out, and don't seem to be enjoying life anyway—so children might think. We have to entertain some feeling toward people to miss them when they die. And then frequently what we are feeling is our own loss, not theirs. Do the dead experience the loss of life? Is life really lost? Or is death a transition from life to another form of existence? Do we have to die before we are able to realize what death really is?

The early Christians thought these questions had been answered with the resurrection of Jesus. Having entered into his death and resurrection through baptism, they believed they would now share in his victory over death. When loyal Christians began to die, not only did the old questions come back, but the community was plagued with new and difficult ones. Was it possible that those loyal Christians had not been loyal after all? Or worse, were the promises made by Jesus empty promises? Had his death been as final as have been all other deaths, and was the report of his resurrection an illusion?

No, Paul assures us. It is all true. Christ has died; Christ is risen; Christ will come again, and all the faithful will be joined with him. *How* it will happen, we do not know. *When* it will happen, we do not know. *That* it will happen, we are sure.

## Court Wisdom and Be Vigilant

We cannot live as if the end is already upon us; yet we must live as if the end is imminent. How are we to do this? The readings for today give us insight into this paradox. The only way to live life fully is to live it in the present. What we have from the past is the wisdom we have gleaned from it. We cannot be sure about the future because so many circumstances can overturn the plans we have set. All we have is the present. However, we cannot live myopically in the present. We must bring the wisdom of the past to bear on the present, where we live with an eye to the future.

The wisdom we have culled from life becomes the treasury from which we can bring out the prudence and insight needed to negotiate life's paradoxes. It throws light on our strengths and our weaknesses; it enables us to discern what is important and what is not; it directs us to bring extra oil for lamps. Life and the wisdom we have acquired through it have taught us that we can indeed trust the promises of God. They have been fulfilled in the past, and wisdom assures us they will be fulfilled in the future.

It is wisdom that cautions us to be vigilant, to be ready to adjust our plans. It is wisdom that prepares us for the night watches of life. It is wisdom that assures us that while we may not know the exact time of the coming of the Lord, he will indeed come into every life, perhaps at the time we least expect. It is wisdom that instructs us to be ready, even while we sleep.

## Thirty-Third Sunday in Ordinary Time
### Proverbs 31:10-13, 19-20, 30-31

The poem praises a woman who traditionally has been described as virtuous or worthy. The Hebrew adjective *ḥayil* has a much stronger sense. It denotes might or strength, the kind of valor found in armies. It is in this sense that the woman is worthy. The poem opens with a rhetorical question that suggests such a woman is extraordinary, not in the sense that valiant women cannot be found but in the sense that among all valiant women this one is remarkable. It has been said that the description of this woman is from a male point of view, highlighting the characteristics men would find pleasing. It is better to say that, as with all of Scripture, it betrays a particular cultural point of view that might be considered inadequate according to the standards of today.

The woman exemplifies the virtues needed in a self-sufficient household, particularly industry, versatility, trustworthiness, constancy, and general goodness. In patriarchal societies a man is judged primarily on his ability to manage his own household. This poem describes the woman as in charge of the household, not in the subservient way a housewife has stereotypically been understood by some but in the self-sufficient manner of the one in charge. This characteristic is linked with the reference to the man's heart. Although it includes the idea of emotion, in Hebrew the word for "heart" *(lēb)* refers primarily to the mind or will. It is the richest biblical term for indicating the totality of a person's inner or immaterial nature. To say the woman's husband has entrusted his heart to her is to say she is privy to his inner reflections and is thus competent, even without his guidance, to assume a responsibility that is really his. This is an unusual situation in a patriarchal society.

The woman's industry has made the household prosperous. There are resources that can be shared with people who are less fortunate. Here too the woman is in charge. She herself is described as reaching out in order to give. Poor and needy people usually gather in places where many people pass by so they might receive help from those who cross their paths. If this is where the woman distributes her alms and offers her care, she has a role in public life as well as in the privacy of the household.

It is in the last verse of the poem that we discover the basis of this woman's virtue and the real reason for the praise accorded her. She is one who fears the LORD. In the Wisdom tradition it is not worldly competence or beauty or charm that is the mark of the wise person. As cherished as these characteristics may be, they are vain and empty (*hebel,* cf. Eccl 1:2). Rather, it is fear of the LORD that is the basis of wisdom (cf. Prov 1:7). It is correct to say that this woman is the model not primarily of the good wife but of the wise person generally. She is virtuous and successful because she possesses the wisdom that flows from fear of the LORD. Her husband has entrusted his heart to her for the same reason. This is why she should be praised at the gates of the city, the place where the business of the community was transacted. Among all women, the one who fears the LORD is truly valiant.

## Psalm 128:1-2, 3, 4-5

This psalm is classified as a Wisdom psalm. It is clearly descriptive instruction that teaches rather than an address directed to God in praise or thanksgiving. The psalm contains some of the themes and vocabulary associated with the Wisdom tradition. Examples include reward and punishment; happy, or blessed; ways, or path. It begins with a macarism (v. 1), which is a formal statement that designates a person or group as blessed (or happy). This statement includes mention of the characteristic that is the basis of the happiness and then describes the blessings that flow from that characteristic. In this psalm those called blessed are the ones who fear the LORD, who walk in God's ways (vv. 1, 4), and the blessing that flows from this attitude of mind and heart is a life of prosperity (vv. 2-3).

In the Wisdom tradition, fear of the LORD is the distinguishing characteristic of the righteous person. It denotes profound awe and amazement before the tremendous marvels of God. While this may include some degree of terror, it is the kind of fear that accompanies wonder at something amazing rather than dread in the face of mistreatment. The one who fears the LORD is one who acknowledges God's sovereignty and power and who lives in accord with the order established by God. If anyone is to be happy and enjoy the blessings of life, it is the one who fears the LORD.

The blessings promised here are both material good fortune and a large and extended family. Large families, like vast fields, were signs of fertility and prosperity. They not only provided companionship through life and partnership in labor, they were also assurances of protection in a hostile world. The promise of future generations (v. 6) guaranteed perpetuity for the family; its bloodline and its name would survive death and would endure into the next generation. Although the androcentric bias in the psalm is seen in its reference to the fruitful wife and numerous children (the Hebrew reads "sons"), the concern is really with the family as a cohesive and abiding unit.

The last verses of the psalm (vv. 12-14) redirect the focus from the good fortune of the individual to the blessing enjoyed by the nation. Mention of Zion, Jerusalem, and Israel are indications of this (vv. 12-14). The reference to children's children holds both familial and civic importance. It bespeaks long life and the continuation of the family, but it also implies that the nation is prospering and that it will endure. The blessings come from God, but God resides at the heart of the nation in Jerusalem, the city of Zion (v. 5). The good fortune of the individual is really a share in the good fortune of the nation.

The final statement (v. 6b) is less a prayer than an exclamation: "Peace upon Israel!" Peace, *shalom*, is fullness of life. This includes personal contentment, harmony with others and the rest of creation, adequate material resources. And all of this is the result of right relationship with God. The psalm begins and ends on the same note: "Happy are those who fear the LORD" and "Peace."

## 1 Thessalonians 5:1-6

As we approach the end of the Liturgical Year we continue reading Paul's discussion of the final coming of the Lord. In the passage for today he links the two Greek words for time, "times" and "seasons" *(chrónos* and *kairós)*. The first word denotes successive, measured time; the second refers to a decisive moment in time. While some commentators consider this expression simply a pleonasm with no special significance, others maintain Paul is telling the Thessalonians there is nothing about either kind of time that requires explanation to them. The first kind needs no explanation; the second kind has no explanation. This statement is followed by Paul's discussion of some of the characteristics of the "Day of the LORD."

Several of ancient Israel's prophets spoke about this mysterious day (cf. Amos 5:18-20; Isa 2:12; Ezek 7:10). It was considered the day of fulfillment. It represented the time when the justice of God would be revealed on the earth, so it was thought to be a day of rejoicing and vindication for the righteous but of reproof and lamentation for the wicked. It gradually came to be considered the period of time between this age and the coming age of fulfillment. As the in-between time, it was a period both of anticipation and of anxiety. As the liminal passage from one age to the next, it was a time of dispossession and suffering.

Paul employs two powerful metaphors to describe this day of the Lord: a thief in the night and the birth pangs of the Messiah. Two features of the first metaphor are particularly fitting. The first is the sudden and unexpected nature of the approach of this day. It does not belong to chronological time, so it cannot be scheduled. It comes upon us when we least expect it. The day of the Lord is a kairotic moment, a decisive moment totally out of our control. It may be that events in time are leading up to this moment, but because of its kairotic nature we may not be able to recognize this. It is as if we are walking in darkness. Like a thief in the night, it comes upon us unexpected and unrecognized. For our part, we are called to vigilance.

Appealing once again to the Israelite prophetic tradition, Paul warns that like false prophets of old, some people will interpret the signs of the times incorrectly and will announce their erroneous predictions to the people. They will proclaim "peace" when disaster is on the horizon (cf. Jer 6:14; Ezek 13:10). The second metaphor (birth pangs of the Messiah) was frequently used to refer to this disaster. The metaphor characterizes the suddenness of the suffering that will come, and it also calls our attention to the fruit of that suffering. As agonizing as birth pangs may be, they give way to new life. So too will the birth pangs of the messianic age.

Finally, Paul uses the light-darkness, day-night dichotomies to describe both the situation within which the Thessalonians find themselves and the vigilance this situation demands of them. Unlike the thief in the night, they are children of light and of the day. (The categories of children of light and children of darkness are also found in the literature of the Qumran community.) As such the Thessalonians must not be found sleeping. Instead they must be alert, always on the watch, so that when the day of the Lord comes, they are not found unprepared.

## Matthew 25:14-30

The gospel reading for today continues the theme of preparedness begun in last Sunday's gospel. Though the details of the parables differ considerably, their general outline is the same: the curtain rises on people waiting for the arrival of one who will bring all things to a conclusion; this arrival is delayed and the exact time is unknown; some of those who are waiting make provisions for the arrival, others do not; the anticipated one arrives unexpectedly; there is a final accounting. This basic structure clearly marks the parable as a lesson in eschatology. What makes this Sunday's gospel different is its focus on the manner in which one is expected to use the time before the long-awaited one returns. An allegorical interpretation of the parable is not considered beneficial here. In a certain sense, the parable speaks for itself.

The initial behavior of the man who goes on a journey indicates he has great confidence in all three of his servants, for he gives each one a significant amount of money. Since a talent amounted to about six thousand denarii, and since one denarius was equivalent to a day's wage, even the servant who received only one talent was entrusted with a sizable sum of money. The one referred to as "Master" was not showing favoritism in entrusting the servants with unequal amounts of money. On the contrary, he was sensitive to their varying abilities, and he distributed the financial responsibility accordingly. The stage is now set, and he departs on his journey.

When the man finally returns from his journey, he settles accounts with his servants. The first two show that during his absence they have been very industrious, doubling the amount entrusted to them. It is the behavior of the third servant that throws light on the meaning of preparedness. He excuses himself by stating that he was intimidated by the demanding character of the master. In response to this attempt at self-justification, the master turns the excuse against the unproductive servant himself. He tells him that the realization of the character of the master should have spurred him on to do something with the money. The servant is called wicked or worthless *(ponérós)*, lazy *(oknērós)*, and useless *(áchreîon)*, and he is forced to forfeit the talent originally entrusted to him. Now he has nothing. As if this were not enough, the useless servant is cast out of the household. The master's judgment is swift and unrelenting.

This parable throws light on the meaning of preparedness. It is not a disposition of passive waiting or non-engagement because of the fear of possible failure. Rather, the preparedness rewarded here stems from the realization that one is a steward of the goods of another, and knowing the disposition of that other, one seeks to maximize the potential of those goods. The time of waiting is a period of opportunity, of active engagement, of creative growth. One's eschatological future does not rest on the extent or quality of one's talent but on how one utilizes that talent as one waits for the master to return.

### Themes of the Day

Last Sunday we saw that the delay of the coming of the Lord requires that we be vigilant. This Sunday we are encouraged to live industriously.

### *Good and Faithful Servant*

It is not enough that we wait patiently. The reign of God that we anticipate expects that we be industrious as we wait. We have all been entrusted with talents, talents that really belong to God. As we live in the interim between the Lord's departure and his final return, we are required to use these talents to the best of our ability. We are required to invest ourselves in the here and now. It makes no difference what our talents may be or how many talents we may have. They have been intrusted to us as the possessions of the master are entrusted to a servant.

The ideal Wisdom figure in the first reading is an example of industriousness. She has a broad scope of interests and responsibilities, and she faithfully pursues each one of them. Her worth is not principally in her productivity but in the fact that fear of the LORD governs her life. This fear is not servile; it enriches her, unlike the fear that seemed to immobilize the third servant in the gospel story. It is her commitment to God that results in her resourcefulness. Even the psalm praises the one who fears the LORD.

## Willingness to Risk

Fidelity to the reign of God requires that we be willing to take risks. The time of the coming of the Lord is not known to us, so there will have to be a kind of tentativeness to all our plans. We will never be certain that they will be brought to fruition. We must spend and be spent without the assurance that we will be able to reap the rewards of our investment. Yet we must make plans and set out to accomplish them; we must invest our time, our talents, our very selves in this life that is both tentative and contingent.

To refuse to risk oneself is to refuse to trust. It is to require absolute certitude and knowledge of the future, or at least a certain control over the circumstances of life. To refuse to risk is to require the assurance that we will never fail. We cannot hope to stand before the Lord on the last day and claim that we have done nothing because we were afraid we might not succeed. We will never know how successful we might be if we refuse to risk.

## The Judgment

The judgment of the household is swift and exacting. If we have been wise and have industriously employed the Lord's talents that were entrusted to us, we will be richly rewarded. However, if we have not realized the potential that is possessed by our talents, and if we have not employed them in the way they were intended to be employed, we will be punished. If the latter is the situation, if we have not faithfully engaged the talents, we will not be able to blame the Lord for the suffering we will have to endure. We will have brought the misfortune on ourselves. The foolish man in the gospel knew the householder was exacting. He had some idea of what to expect. He made his choice, and he had to accept the consequences of that choice.

## Thirty-Fourth Sunday in Ordinary Time (Christ the King)
### Ezekiel 34:11-12, 15-17

On this last Sunday of the Liturgical Year we are given for our meditation the image of God as the Good Shepherd. This metaphor aptly characterizes both God's concern and God's personal intervention in the shepherding of the flock. The reading describes how God fulfills the role of shepherd primarily in two ways: by caring for the sheep and by separating the good from the bad. "Shepherd" is a male metaphor, because in patriarchal societies such as ancient Israel women were seldom placed in charge of the flock. The public and unprotected nature of the occupation placed them in jeopardy. They could too easily be kidnapped, and the reproductive potential of the family would be depleted. The passage itself opens with the prophetic message formula: Thus says the LORD! The content of the first part of the reading (vv. 11-12, 15-16) leads to its classification as an oracle of salvation, while the last verse contains a note of judgment and possible doom.

God's first words are self-proclamation: I will tend my sheep. There is no intermediary here; God is immediately involved. Since the flock is described as scattered, one can presume those who were formerly responsible for the sheep failed to carry out their responsibilities. They were not attentive to their charges, so the owner of the flock now steps in to shepherd the flock personally. The rest of the oracle of salvation confirms this. The good shepherd first states that he will "carefully look for" *(dārash)* and seek *(bāqar)* the sheep, implying that they must first be found before they can be cared for. Although all translations do not include it, the word "day" *(yôm)* appears twice in the verse that speaks of gloom and darkness (v. 12). The simple reference "the day," along with the further characterization of that day as one of gloom and darkness, and the final depiction of separation, suggest the eschatological Day of the LORD, the day of final judgment.

Once the scattered sheep have been rescued and brought together, the attentive shepherd feeds the flock and provides them with the security and rest they need (v. 15). He appears to be particularly interested in the most vulnerable sheep of the flock, those that were lost or have strayed away, those that are injured or sick. One gets the sense that these sheep are not responsible for their predicaments; the former shepherds are. These negligent shepherds should have been attentive to the sheep; they should have protected them from harm and cared for them when they were sick. The reasons for their delinquency are not given. All we know is that they were derelict in their duty, and the sheep suffered the consequences. Now, however, the sheep are under the supervision of the owner, who is a good shepherd.

The last two verses of the reading probably pertain more to the interpretation intended by the prophet than to a dimension of the referent of the metaphor itself. The curious statement about destroying the sleek and the strong members of the flock is the first case in point. Since God is the shepherd and the weak flock is the People of God, those within the flock who are strong are probably those within the community who take advantage of their strength at the expense of others. They will be treated very harshly. The Hebrew says that God will "feed them with judgment" *(mishpāt)*. The final scene is also one of judgment *(mishpāt)*. Even those who have been under the care of the shepherd will face an accounting on that day of gloom and darkness. This last theme brings us back to where we began, that is, the last Sunday of the Liturgical Year.

## Psalm 23:1-2, 2-3, 5-6

This responsorial psalm is one of the most familiar and best loved psalms of the entire Psalter. It paints vivid pictures of a carefree existence, peaceful rest, and abundant fruitfulness. Although "shepherd" suggests a flock rather than merely one sheep, here the focus is on the individual. In addition to this image God is characterized as a host, one who supervises a banquet and within whose house the psalmist ultimately dwells.

The psalm opens with a metaphor that sets the tone of the entire song. It is the responsibility of the shepherd to find pastures that will provide enough grazing and abundant water for the entire flock, to lead them there without allowing any of the sheep to stray and be lost, to guard them from predators and dangers of any kind, and to attend to their every need. To characterize the LORD as a shepherd is to trust that God will discharge all these responsibilities faithfully. The personal dimension of the psalm shifts the care given to the entire flock to concern for one individual, making God's care a very intimate matter. Not only are the physical needs of the psalmist satisfied, but the soul, the very life force *(nepesh)* of the person, is renewed.

The guidance of the shepherd is more than provident, it is moral as well. The psalmist is led in the paths of righteousness (v. 3), and this is done for the sake of the LORD's name. Since one's name is a part of the very essence of the person, this indicates that the way of the LORD is the way of righteousness. Following this we can say that the magnanimous care shown by the shepherd flows from enduring righteousness rather than from some passing sentiment of the heart. This is confirmed by the reference to the covenant kindness *(ḥesed)* that surrounds the psalmist (v. 6). In other words, the divine shepherd's tender commitment to the flock and to each individual within it is as lasting as is God's covenant commitment.

The image of the shepherd securing nourishment for the flock suggests another metaphor, that of the host who prepares a lavish banquet for guests. Many societies have a strict code of hospitality. The people are obliged to provide the very best provisions they have, even for their enemies. The LORD spreads out such a banquet here, which not only affords nourishment but also is a public witness to God's high regard for the psalmist, who will continue to enjoy God's favor in God's house. Whether this indicates the Temple or is merely a reference to the place where God dwells, the fundamental meaning is clear. The psalmist has been under the loving guidance of the LORD and will remain there forever.

## 1 Corinthians 15:20-26, 28

This reading from Paul's Corinthian correspondence brings together several of his most treasured theological themes: the efficacy of Christ's resurrection; human solidarity in Adam and in Christ; the sequence of eschatological events; the victory of Christ; and the ultimate reign of God. At the end of the Liturgical Year the reading carries us back through time to the primordial period of beginnings and then forward to the end of time and the eschatological age of fulfillment.

Christ is identified as the firstfruits of those who have fallen asleep. In double fashion the expression speaks of the end-time. "Fallen asleep" is a euphemism for death, and firstfruits refers to harvest. It was believed the first-fruits of a crop functioned in two ways: they contained the most forceful expression of the life of the plant, and they stood as a promise of more yield to come. As the firstfruits of the dead, the risen Christ is the most forceful expression of life after death, and his resurrection contains the promise of resurrection for all who are joined to him.

It is fair to say that, like all others, Paul considered Adam the first human being. However, Adam also stands for the entire race. The Hebrew word itself (*'ādām*) yields both a singular and a collective meaning. Here Paul is referring to human solidarity in Adam when he declares that one man sinned and brought death into the world, and that one man stands for all of humankind. In an analogous fashion, Christ is the person Jesus, and joined in faith all believers participate in the resurrected life of Christ. This is clearly meant by the phrase: Death came through a human being *(ánthrōpos);* resurrection from death came through a human being *(ánthrōpos).* In both instances it is through one who stands for all.

The eschatological events Paul is describing will transcend time. Every aspect of these events is grounded in the resurrection of Christ. First he is raised; then at his final coming *(parousía)* those who are joined to Christ are raised. Only when this has taken place will the end *(télos)* come. This end is the fulfillment, the goal, toward which all reality tends. Paul seems to be suggesting there is an interval between the *parousía* and the final end, when Christ will hand over everything to God. During this time all of Christ's enemies will be vanquished. This eschatological perspective corresponds to the Jewish apocalyptic worldview of his day. Paul does not indicate how long this interval will last. We can only presume it will last as long as it takes to achieve a decisive victory. When this happens, Christ will bring the fruits of his victory to God. At the final consummation, God will be all in all. All came from God; all returns to God. From the beginning God was the purpose and end of all things. At the end, all purposes will be realized. All reality will have come home.

## Matthew 25:31-46

The scene of the Last Judgment as it unfolds before us today is both sobering and surprising. It is a scene of apocalyptic splendor and majesty, a scene of separation of the righteous from the unrighteous, a scene of reward and punishment. The gospel account brings together a context that is clearly apocalyptic and events that are commonplace.

A vision of the eschatological future is sketched here. The coming of the Son of Man, the angels, the universalism, and the glorious throne from which the Son of Man will make decisions are all reminiscent of the apocalyptic scene of the coming of one like a Son of Man (cf. Dan 7:14). All people are brought before him for judgment and sentencing. The image of the shepherd separating the sheep from the goats would have been quite familiar to Jesus' original audience. The sheep are preferred because they are more valuable, and so they are placed at the Son of Man's right hand, the place of privilege. This scene is sobering because one gets the sense that there is no way of escaping it.

What is surprising is the reason given for the judgment. It is not the accomplishment of some phenomenal feat. Rather, people are judged on whether or not they meet the very basic human needs of others. Frequently this criterion has been misunderstood to mean the basic human needs of anyone, but that is not what the text says. The gospel is not talking here about humanitarian service, regardless of how unselfish it might be. Jesus reserved the term "brethren" for his disciples. Furthermore, he referred to them as "little ones" (cf. Matt 10:42), those who are insignificant in the eyes of the world. Finally, he promised a reward to anyone who gave a cup of water in the name of a disciple (cf. Matt 10:42). All of this suggests that the throng of people gathered at this eschatological event will be judged according to the way they treated the disciples of Jesus.

The identification of Jesus with the disciples is based on the very concept of apostle. (Although Matthew employs this word only once [cf. Matt 12:2], he uses "disciple" in the same sense.) An apostle is one who is sent with the authority of the sender: "Whoever receives you, receives me" (cf. Matt 10:40, Thirteenth Sunday). To reject the apostle is to reject the one who sent the apostle. The guilt of the people being judged in this passage is not found in the wrong they have done but in their failure to accept those who were bringing the kingdom of God to them. To reject them is to reject the kingdom. The sentences passed hinge on their openness to this kingdom. The righteous are invited into the kingdom, where they will enjoy eternal life; the wicked are cast into the punishment of eternal fire. The choice they made was decisive; the sentences passed are binding.

## Themes of the Day

### Judgment

We have now come to the end of the Liturgical Year. This is the point that marks the transition from one period to another. Throughout our consideration of the responsibilities of discipleship we have seen how important love of neighbor is, particularly the neighbor who is in need. Today we see that this responsibility is brought to completion. It is precisely the attention we give to those who are less fortunate than we are that becomes the determination of our future.

The kingdom of God is an inclusive kingdom. Its embrace is as comprehensive as is the embrace of God. Criteria for membership are not based on obedience to the commandments or on conformity to ritual obligation, but on the covenantal bonds that unite us to one another. These are bonds of love and concern, bonds that reach deep into the human heart. The gospel story lays bare the genuineness of such concern. Assistance is given whenever and wherever there is need. It is given in ordinary acts: in giving food and drink, shelter and clothing; in spending time with someone who might be lonely or afraid; in patiently waiting for an elderly person; in thanking people for their service. The kingdom of God is established, brick by brick, through these simple acts of kindness. If this is the kingdom we establish during our lifetime, this will be the kingdom into which we will be welcomed at its end.

### You Did It for Me

What we do for others we do for Christ because Christ is identified with those in need. We seldom see the face of the glorified Christ in the faces of the needy; it is more often the face of the disfigured Christ that is turned to us. We see his fear and his shame, his brokenness and sense of loss. It is very difficult to look into such eyes, and unfortunately we frequently turn away from them. What is even worse, we sometimes help only those we consider to be the "worthy poor," those who fit the standards we have set. The rest we consider the "refuse of the earth," the unavoidable flotsam of life's misfortune. These are precisely the ones with whom Christ is identified. He looks out to us through their eyes. It is his hand that reaches out for assistance. He is the one who tests our patience and generosity. It is through them that we enter the kingdom of God.

### The End

In the end, Christ will have conquered all. Having entered into the frailty of human nature, having identified himself with the needy of the world, having handed himself over to death, Christ will have conquered all. It is a curious kingdom he has won. It is not a kingdom of the strong but of the weak. Hence he has turned the standards of the world upside down. He has shown that it does not take strength to ignore or to exploit the needy, but it does take strength to overcome our own selfishness in order to serve them. The kingdom Christ hands over to God is a kingdom of love and care.

The one in whose hands the kingdom resides, the one who will act as judge, is characterized as a shepherd. These readings, which contain hard themes such as Christ's death and punishment in eternal fires, depict God as a tender and loving shepherd. This shepherd does not punish those who are lost but instead seeks them and lovingly carries them to safety. Jesus, who is our king and our judge, is this shepherd who has given himself for his sheep. The Liturgical Year ends on a note of tender solicitude.

# Solemnities and Feasts

The commentary for the solemnities and feasts is different from the rest of this book in several ways. Each feast has its own identity, which usually determines the selection of the readings. Therefore there is no continuous reading of an epistle or gospel. In fact, many of the feasts fall into other units such as Ordinary Time part 3 or part 4. They interrupt the sequence of readings to provide special considerations for the meaning of the various feasts. Consequently, neither a chart nor a section describing the feast as a unit is included here.

## The Solemnity of the Most Holy Trinity
### Exodus 34:4b-6, 8-9

The report of Moses' encounter with God is rich with covenantal language and meaning. It should be noted that it is God who initiates the encounter and it is God who reveals the divine name and its meaning. Moses is told to go up onto Mount Sinai, and then God descends upon the mountain in a cloud. This cloud both reveals and conceals the presence of God. Throughout the people's journey in the wilderness the presence of God was signified by the pillar of cloud, which they followed (cf. Exod 13:21). In this sense the cloud was revelatory. However, it was merely a symbol of the presence of God, it did not really reveal God or the essence of God. In this sense it concealed the divine.

Unlike the account recorded in an earlier passage (cf. Exod 3:13-15), Moses does not ask for God's personal name. Nonetheless, God reveals it: YHWH (the LORD)! Since names were believed to contain within them part of the very essence of the person named, what follows is considered by most commentators to be an explanation of what God's personal name means. The explanatory phrase, which eventually became a creedal recital (cf. Pss 86:15; 103:8; 145:8; Num 14:18; Joel 2:13; Nah 1:3; Neh 9:17; Jonah 4:2), is not really an interpretation of the name itself but a description of the divine essence. God is merciful, gracious, slow to anger, rich in lovingkindness and truth (v. 6).

All of these adjectives are relational and somehow associated with the covenant. This means that they identify the dispositions of God toward covenant partners.

Merciful *(raḥûm)* is womb love, the kind of attachment one has for the child of one's own body or for those who issued from the same womb from which one was born. This is the kind of love God has for covenant partners. Though it does not carry the same familial connotation, "gracious" *(ḥannûn)* is frequently used as a synonym for "compassionate" or "merciful." God is also said to be slow to anger, reluctant to rain divine wrath on those who have violated the covenant relationship. Lovingkindness *(ḥesed)* and fidelity or faithfulness *(ʾĕmet)* characterize the steadfastness with which God clings to the covenant partners.

Moses' response to this spectacular revelation is worship. He prostrates himself on the ground in profound adoration. Appealing to the favor *(ḥēn)* he trusts is his in God's eyes, he pleads for the people. Moses admits they are a difficult people, stiff-necked or stubborn. They do not easily follow directives. They are the kind of people who will test those extraordinary dispositions that characterize God. Though Moses has found favor with God, he nonetheless identifies with this sinful people ("our company," "our wickedness," "receive us"). He begs for pardon. The covenant already established Israel as God's special people. Here Moses pleads that they be God's own inheritance *(naḥālâ)*. This appeal suggests the covenant relationship has been severed or is in jeopardy.

In this theophanic exchange God has revealed some characteristics of divine love, and Moses immediately speaks to them.

## Daniel 3:52, 53, 54, 55

The liturgical character of this doxology is evidenced by the refrain repeated after every phrase: Praiseworthy and glorious above all forever! This refrain is a call for praise and at the same time an expression of praise. It bespeaks the superiority of God (above all) as well as the eternity of God (forever). As it is arranged, one person in the congregation would proclaim one of the divine attributes, and the congregation would respond with the refrain. Although each phrase focuses on a specific divine characteristic, it is really God who is praised.

God is first praised for having been the God of the ancestors. The reference here is probably to the promises God made to Abraham and to his family (cf. Gen 12:1-3; 17:5-8). All the rights and privileges the people of Israel have claimed for themselves spring from this initial promise. It certainly deserves the praise of the people. This is followed immediately by the mention of God's holy and glorious name. Since the name somehow contains within itself part of the very essence of the one named, to praise God's name is to praise God. The name of God is mighty and awesome, certainly worthy of the praise of the people.

Next God is praised in the Temple, the focal point of the religious life of the nation. The Temple itself was considered the *axis mundi,* or center of the universe. It was there that the glory of the LORD resided on earth. It was to the Temple that the people traveled to celebrate the important feasts of their religion. It was there that they offered their sacrifices. The Temple of Israel was known for its impressive structure and splendorous decoration. Everything about it heralded the power and majesty of God.

Although God was believed to be present in the Temple, God was really enthroned above the heavens. In ancient Near Eastern mythology, after the primordial cosmic battles had been won and the universe ordered (in many myths creation was an ordering of cosmic chaos), a palace was built for the victorious conqueror and a throne surrounded by a heavenly court was set up. Enthroned on high, this creator god ruled over all creation. While Israel did not celebrate such cosmic events in its religious rituals, it did retain many of the mythological expressions in its poetry. Traces of this characterization are found in the prayer for today.

In addition to sovereignty over the earth and the heavens, God holds sway over the depths. In ancient Israelite literature this is a reference to chaotic waters, the very waters that constituted the initial cosmic upheaval. This primordial enemy was conquered but never completely abolished. It was restrained by the triumphant God who ruled from heaven, but it would always be a threat to the ordered universe. For this reason the God who ruled from heaven would have to keep close watch on the depths lest they overflow and swallow up all of life.

## 2 Corinthians 13:11-13

This short passage contains various characteristics of the form Paul used in concluding his letters. It begins with the typical Pauline exhortation. This is followed by greetings to the members of the community from other Christians. Paul closes his correspondence with some form of benediction. His epistolary conclusions are also characterized in another very interesting way. In them Paul frequently incorporates elements that reflect the principal message of the letter itself. This is certainly the case here.

Paul's exhortation is fivefold. He begins with a summons to rejoice. The joy he advocates is not simply the human sentiment of delight. Rather, he would have the Corinthians rejoice in the Lord, find their delight in Christ Jesus. The joy he champions stems from commitment to the Lord Jesus Christ. Paul next admonishes them to mend their ways. Behind this admonition is the implication that they have been living in a way that is at variance with their commitment. This gives us a clue to the character of his Corinthian correspondence. He then tells his converts to encourage one another, to be a comfort rather than a concern.

It is perhaps the next admonition that throws the clearest light on the situation in the Corinthian community to which Paul addresses so much of his letter. He exhorts them to be of one mind. This is not an idle counsel. While it is quite common to find a variety of opinions and interests in every community, rancorous disagreement can cause serious divisions. If this turns into factionalism, it can cause the entire fabric of community to unravel. Most likely the oneness of mind of which Paul speaks is agreement in matters of faith and community order, not in matters of mere personal preference. The exhortation concludes with a summons to live in peace, a peace that can embrace difference on one level because there is common faith on another, deeper level.

Paul promises that if the Corinthians follow his admonitions and live in the way he counsels here, they will experience the presence of the God of love and peace. Lest we think he is suggesting God's presence is their reward for fidelity, we must remember that he always insists it is precisely the grace of God that enables Christians to be faithful in the first place. Therefore, if they live lives of love and peace, it will be because the God of love and peace is in their midst. Finally, Paul urges the Corinthians to greet one another with an expression of this love.

Paul reinforces his exhortation to community unity by reminding the Corinthians of the much broader community of believers with whom they are united. The designation "holy ones" or "saints" *(hágioi)* is a common reference to members of the Christian community, those who have been joined to Jesus through faith and baptism. Paul says that the Christians who are with him in the place from which he is writing join him in greeting the Christians in Corinth.

The blessing with which Paul ends is trinitarian in character. It notes the gift of grace, which is received through Jesus Christ; the love God has for all of creation, which is the source of all good things; and the community of the Holy Spirit, within which believers are rooted. There is no more meaningful benediction with which Paul might end his letter.

## John 3:16-18

The extent of God's love is drawn in bold lines in two different but very significant ways. The first is the scope of divine love; the second is the price God is willing to pay because of that love. Ancient Israel continually marveled at the love God had for this chosen people. While this love can be seen throughout the religious tradition, it is particularly evident in the writings of the prophets. Christian writers also spoke of God's love, but their main interest was with those who had committed themselves in faith to Jesus Christ. This passage is remarkable in its explicit declaration of God's love for the entire world.

The author maintains that God's love for the world is so deep and so magnanimous that, for the world to be saved, nothing is spared, not even God's only Son. God gave/sent this Son, first in the incarnation and again in his saving death. This plan of salvation, tragically and inevitably, became judgment for some. While the word for judgment really means "to make a judicial decision," it is generally used to indicate a negative ruling. Such momentous decisions are made on the basis of certain criteria. In this passage faith in the Son of God is the pivotal criterion. Those who believe are saved; those who do not believe call down judgment upon themselves.

The world *(kósmos)* can be understood in three ways. It can refer to the totality of natural creation, the inhabited world generally, or the inhabited world in its sinfulness. Although the passage speaks of salvation, it is set in contrast with judgment and perishing. This indicates that here the world is understood in the third way, as subject to and guilty of sin. The world was created as good, but it often stands in opposition to God and consequently is in need of being saved. Such is the situation presumed here, since otherwise there would be no need for salvation. It is this sinful world that God loved (v. 16); it is into this sinful world that God's only Son was sent (v. 17).

The passage says that God both gave *(dídōmi)* and sent *(apostéllō)* God's only Son. The first verb indicates that this Son was truly a gift from God. It underscores God's immense and unparalleled generosity to the world. The second verb indicates that the Son had a sacred, all-encompassing mission to perform. It highlights the serious responsibility on the part of the Son. In both cases it is the world, in desperate need of deliverance and salvation, that benefits from God's actions.

## Themes of the Day

On this feast of the Trinity, we praise our God who is present with us on earth, who rules over all from the heavens, and in whose hands is control over chaos. The readings for this feast do not directly explain the doctrine of the Trinity as we have come to know it. We will have an opportunity to proclaim that faith when we recite the Nicene Creed later in the liturgical celebration. Rather, they offer us glimpses into the nature of our triune God.

### Praise

The psalm response suggests that our primary response to God should be one of praise. God is full of blessing and has bestowed this blessing upon us for no other reason than that God loves us. The psalm is an example of total doxology, total praise of God's praiseworthiness. There has never been a time when this was not true, from the time of our ancestors to our own day. There is no place over which God does not gloriously rule: in the heights, over the depths, in the Temple on earth, from the throne of heaven. Words cannot explain God's wonder; all they can do is repeat our praise. Our inability to express adequately this exaltation is itself praise of God. It is an acknowledgment of God's surpassing glory.

### Gracious and Merciful

The God who is beyond our comprehension is also the God who has reached down into the chaos of our world in order to save us. We see this in both the first reading and the gospel. The covenant language in the reading from Exodus underscores God's unfathomable goodness. God's graciousness and mercy are not rewards for our fidelity. They are instead extended to us in our sinfulness. It is God's saving grace that transforms us, not any merit on our part. In the gospel we are assured that Jesus was sent into the world to save it, not to condemn it. Such openness and love is so unlike human sentiments. It is no wonder that all we can do is stand in awe before a love that will not be dismissed.

### A Trinity of Unity

The trinitarian phrase found in the letter to the Corinthians is so expressive of the love God has for us that it has been incorporated regularly into the liturgy. It declares that through his death and resurrection Jesus has opened for us the treasury of divine grace. It also proclaims that the love of God has forged the bonds of community that unite us. Created in the image and after the likeness of this God, we are called to unity among ourselves. As incomprehensible as it may seem, it is primarily through the unity we share that we will manifest the unity that exists in God.

## The Solemnity of the Most Holy Body and Blood of Christ (Corpus Christi)

### Deuteronomy 8:2-3, 14b-16a

A careful reading of the Scriptures will uncover a method of theological argumentation that is both interesting and effective. This method is a form of retrieval. The audience is told to remember the past in order to act in a certain way in the present. This technique is usually employed to call to mind either the blessings God bestowed upon the ancestors or the punishment God imposed because of the sinfulness of those same ancestors. The purpose of such recalling is, in the first case, to encourage the people to trust that God will be no less generous in blessing them, and in the second case, to warn them that punishment will follow their sinfulness as well. There is some ambiguity in the way the time line has been drawn here. While it appears that Moses is directing the people to remember events as if they had taken place in their own past, he is probably talking to the subsequent generation of Israelites (forty years symbolized a generation or a lifetime). Traditional people frequently believe that through the agency of their ancestors they too experienced events of the past. Reference in the last verse to these ancestors shows this is the perspective here.

The reading for today concentrates on the blessing of God. However, it also shows that with this blessing comes responsibility. While God is gracious, this graciousness is not to be squandered. Moses directs the people to remember events of their past. Though the time of their sojourn in the wilderness is over, there are still lessons they must learn from it. The principal lesson to be learned now is the same as it was in the past, namely, total confidence in God. Mention of the commandments indicates that the people had entered into a covenantal relationship with God. God is the one who initiated the covenant; God is the one who promised to care for the people. For their part, they are expected to live in a way that shows they are committed to God. The trials in the wilderness do not so much test their obedience to the commandments as their total dependence on God.

The details of the story of the manna (cf. Exod 16:1-30) are intended to illustrate its extraordinary character. It was probably the hardened excretion of certain insects which feed on the sap of the tamarisk tree. However, the Israelites were astounded by it and cried out: What is it *(mān hû')?* The substance gets its name from their question. Their hunger had brought them to a realization of their own meager resources, and they were thrown on the providence of God. This was the lesson they had to keep learning. This experience was meant to teach them another lesson, namely, that the source of their life is not merely the bread, but the promise of God.

A recital of various examples of the providence of God completes this reading. The people were delivered from bondage, guided through the wilderness, protected from its hazards (cf. Num 21:6), miraculously given water (cf. Num 20:8), and provided mysterious food. Once again Moses exhorts them to remember these things. Originally the lesson to be learned was total dependence on God, whether God appeared to be working through natural processes or had suspended the laws of nature to perform some miraculous feat. Surely the purpose of this recital is the same. God has promised to care for us; can we live on the strength of that word?

### Psalm 147:12-13, 14-15, 19-20

The passage is from the final stanza of a hymn of praise of God. It highlights God's protection of and solicitude toward the people of Israel. Both Jerusalem, the capital of the nation, and Zion, the mount upon which the city was built, came to represent the people. They are called upon directly to praise God (v. 12). This summons is followed by a listing of some of the many wonderful works of God that elicit such praise. All of them point to the uniqueness of the bond that holds God and this people together.

God protects the people by fortifying the city. The ancient practice of building walls around cities provided them with a defense against attack and gave them a vantage point from which to observe the activity outside the walls (v. 13a). As strong as these walls might have been, the gates of the city put it in jeopardy. These gates, necessary to provide the normal traffic into and out of the city, for travelers and traders, and for those who farmed outside the walls rendered the city vulnerable. The psalmist calls the people to praise God, who has strengthened them precisely at this their most vulnerable spot (v. 13).

Walls also act as borders. They define the limits of personal property and they determine the sweep of the city. Protected as they are, the people of Jerusalem/Zion are truly blessed. They can go about their daily lives with a sense of security, for the fortification provided by God has assured them of peace (v. 14). Furthermore, this peace has enabled them to prosper, since they do not have to invest time or resources into defense measures.

Prosperity is symbolized by the wheat, which is abundant and of the finest quality. Both characteristics represent the blessing bestowed by God. The abundance suggests either expansive fields that were never ravaged by wild animals or invading enemies, or an extraordinary yield from a smaller plot of land. In either case the people would consider themselves singularly blessed by God. The exceptional quality of the wheat demonstrates the fertility of the land. Again, this is land that has been spared the despoiling that usually accompanies war. This is a land that has known peace.

The psalmist paints a dynamic picture of the powerful word of God. It is like an emissary who runs swiftly throughout the earth, both proclaiming and bringing about what has been proclaimed. God speaks, and God's word is accomplished. God promises to protect and to provide for the people, and the promise is realized.

This same powerful word is spoken to Israel but with a different emphasis and with different consequences (vv. 19-20). It is God's special word, God's law, the law of life, that will ensure God's continued protection and care. Just as Jerusalem/ Zion (the people) is singled out for special consideration, here Jacob/Israel (the nation) is chosen for a unique relationship. No other nation has been so blessed. No other nation has been given God's law of life. This is the People of God. This privilege is the reason to praise God. The psalm ends as it began: "Praise the LORD!"

## 1 Corinthians 10:16-17

Paul's discourse on the Eucharist not only identifies the symbolic potential of the substances of bread and wine but also describes actions that are rich in symbolism. It is not clear why he treats the cup before the bread, since bread and wine are equally important.

"Cup of blessing" was a common Jewish expression for the cup of wine taken at the end of the meal. The blessing referred to was probably some form of the following: "Blessed are you, Lord God, King of the universe, who created the fruit of the vine." At the Passover meal, the third of the four cups that were taken is called "the cup of blessing," because when it is poured, a blessing is said over the meal. In a very real sense, it is the act of blessing that is important, not the wine that is being blessed. Paul adds dimension to this explanation of the effectiveness of the act of blessing: It is by sharing the cup that is blessed that one participates in the blood of Christ. The significance of the cup of wine is not in its material substance but in its incorporation *(koinōnia)* of the partakers in the blood of Christ. Blood often symbolized life itself (cf. Gen 9:4). However, the reference here is probably to Christ's blood as it was poured out in death. Thus, it is through his blood (death) that we participate in his blood (life).

Throughout the Middle East eating food with another establishes a bond of companionship, a bond that includes mutual obligations. Regardless of any elaborate formalities that are enacted, the meal only begins when the host breaks bread and shares it with those seated around the table. Here again we see the importance of the symbolic action. Furthermore, community is established with the breaking of the bread, not with the subsequent eating of it. Paul further develops this aspect of *koinōnia* in what follows. When we eat, we incorporate our food into ourselves. The opposite is true with regard to the Eucharist. When we partake of that bread we are transformed into it. Breaking bread together may form us into a community, but sharing eucharistic bread forms us into the body of Christ. In both statements the word for "body" is *sōma,* suggesting that in neither case is Paul speaking merely about physical substance. In the first instance he has Christ's total being in mind; in the second he is referring to the ecclesial (mystical) body of Christ.

Whenever the actions of blessing a cup of wine and breaking a loaf of bread are performed in a community that boasts Jewish roots, those present will certainly understand the ritual significance of these actions. Paul has here provided profound and heretofore unimaginable soteriological and ecclesiological dimensions to them.

## John 6:51-58

In today's reading Jesus identifies his flesh as the bread of heaven, and he alludes to his death given for the life of the world. The thought of feeding on the flesh of another was repulsive to some of his hearers, as it most likely is to many people today. Such a bold assertion demands some kind of explanation, and Jesus offers it.

In unmistakable language Jesus declares that his flesh is food and his blood is drink. Lest this claim go unnoticed, he states it four times (vv. 53-56). The phrase "flesh and blood" is rich in meaning. On a literal level, it is a common way of characterizing a human being. When applied to Jesus, it is a proclamation of faith in the incarnation. He was indeed "flesh and blood." On another level, it calls to mind the victim of sacrifice that is first slaughtered (flesh and blood) and then shared at a cultic meal (food and drink). Jesus is "flesh and blood" in this way as well, first as the sacrificial victim on the cross and then as food and drink.

The christological interpretation of the manna has taken on new meaning here. The flesh and blood of Jesus have become the source of life for those who partake of it. In other words, eternal life comes from feeding on Jesus, not simply from believing in him. Jesus goes one step further in his teaching on eternal life. He implies that it is not something believers merely hope to enjoy in the future. Rather, those who share in this meal already possess eternal life. What the future holds for them is the fullness of life that will be enjoyed after the general resurrection on the last day. The course through which eternal life passes from God to us is simply sketched. The living God, whom Jesus calls Father, is the source of this life; Jesus already enjoys it because of his intimate union with God; believers already enjoy it because they feed on Jesus, who is the bread of life.

Jesus develops the eating metaphor still further. He maintains that just as we and the substance we eat and drink become one, so Jesus and those who feed on him form an intimate union. In a mutually intimate way, they abide in him and he abides in them. The Greek word used here *(ménō)* means "to stay in a place," "to abide forever." This implies that Jesus not merely visits those who feed on him, but he really stays with them; he dwells there permanently. Union with Jesus is as intimate as the act of eating, and the mutual indwelling that results from it is just as personal.

There should now be no question in the minds of his hearers. Jesus, not manna, is the bread that came, not from the sky but from the very being of God. Those who ate manna died; those who feed on Jesus will live forever.


## Themes of the Day

This feast harkens back to the celebration of Holy Thursday. Its readings do not offer an explanation of the doctrine of transubstantiation. Rather, by way of the metaphors of food and drink, they provide us with a look at the mystery of divine presence.

## God Who Feeds

Our God is a God who feeds. In the past God set a table in freedom and then provided food that enabled our ancestors to survive. They may not have been deserving of God's care, but they were hungry and were threatened with extinction, and God came to their aid. God feeds those who are needy, not those who claim to be worthy. Jesus offered sustenance to the crowds that gathered around him. It was not manna from heaven he offered but his own flesh and blood as food and drink. As with the Israelites in the wilderness, there was scepticism. However, the Israelites eventually recognized God's goodness in the bread from heaven, while many in the crowds that came to Jesus were scandalized by his offer.

Today we are offered the real bread from heaven, Jesus' flesh and blood as food and drink, the real presence of Jesus in the Eucharist. This food and drink not only sustain life, they are the pledge of eternal life. As in the wilderness and at the time of Jesus, faith is required to realize this is indeed food sent from God as a guarantee of life.

## One Bread, One Body

Those who eat this bread and drink this cup are caught up in a profound unity with God, a unity not envisioned in the wilderness experience. There is a new overlay of significance. Jesus' claim to give his flesh and blood was a bold one, Paul's seems even bolder. He states that partaking of the bread and the cup not only joins us with Christ, but actually makes us participants in the body and blood of Christ. Humanity and divinity are joined as one. The Eucharist is a sign of unity in another way. Joined to the body and blood of Christ, we are joined to one another. We are one body, and that body is Christ. The Eucharist is truly a celebration of thanksgiving, thanksgiving for our transformation and thanksgiving for our unity.

# The Presentation of the Lord (Feast)
# February 2

## Malachi 3:1-4

This passage describes a messenger of God. The very name Malachi (*mal'ākî*) means "my messenger." It is the LORD of hosts who speaks here. Commentators are not in agreement as to the actual identity of the messenger. What seems to be of more significance to the author is the role this messenger will play. Several themes mark the passage's strong eschatological character: the future coming of the LORD, the present day of the LORD, and the idea of judgment.

Although the passage states that the LORD of hosts is coming, it really focuses on the messenger who will precede God. The first thing he will do will be to prepare the way that God will use to approach the people. It is a very common custom to prepare for the coming of a dignitary. Even today we clean and repair the streets and neighborhoods through which such prominent people will pass. Everything must be in proper order as befits the station of the visitor. Isaiah vividly described such comprehensive improvements (cf. Isa 40:3-4; 57:14). Also part of the preparation for such an event is the announcement of the actual approach of the dignitary. Isaiah depicts this aspect as well (cf. Isa 52:7).

It is very common in the Bible for the coming of God to be in some way delayed. Those who anticipate this momentous event are told to be vigilant and to wait patiently. Such is not the case here, Instead, God declares this messenger will come suddenly. There is something ominous in this statement. It is almost as if the messenger will come before the people have a chance to complete the necessary repairs. Furthermore, the messenger is coming to the Temple. His destination is a clear indication of the particular focus of the eschatological events that will unfold.

Translations may not always indicate that the word for "Lord" (whom you seek) is *ʾādôn,* a common word that can refer to anyone whose status demands our respect. It is not the personal name of God, which is frequently rendered as "LORD." This is important to know because it is used to refer to the messenger described in this passage. Parallel construction illustrates this:

|  |  |
|---|---|
| the Lord | whom you seek |
| the messenger of the covenant | whom you desire |

It is this messenger, not God, who comes to the Temple. Since fidelity to the covenant is the standard by which the people are judged, it will be the character of their fidelity that determines whether they will be rewarded or punished. In the Isaian passages mentioned above, the LORD will come with salvation and blessing. Here the messenger of the covenant will come with judgment and affliction.

Judgment is passed on the priests, the sons of Levi. The punishment is among the harshest described in the Bible. Their purification will be searing. Two striking metaphors are used to describe the agents of this purging: the inferno that refines ores, and the lye used by fullers to whiten cloth (cf. Zech 13:9). The messenger will supervise the purification that will serve to transform these priests, making them worthy to offer sacrifice once more. There is no thought of their total destruction, only of their purification. There is a note of hope at the end of this passage. The sacrifice of the people, offered at the hands of the priests, will once again be pleasing to God.

## Psalm 24:7, 8, 9, 10

There are few themes more central to the faith of ancient Israel than that of the kingship of God. While "king" is the prominent title accorded God in the responsorial psalm for this feast, other titles throw light on the nature of God's kingship. The idea of king is itself a metaphor that comes from a world where royalty held sway. It represents power and majesty, authority and dominion. When applied to a deity it could refer to the rule exercised over people or the sovereignty wielded over other gods. In monotheistic Israel, God's kingship functioned in both ways.

Besides being referred to as king, the LORD is also described in military terms. Since hosts *(ṣᵉbāʾôt)* are army divisions, the title "LORD of hosts" would suggest that God is the commander of military forces. Such a characterization recalls the ancient Near Eastern myth of creation. In it a young and vibrant warrior god first defeats the cosmic powers of chaos and then reorders the universe. A shout of victory rings out over all creation: Such-and-such is king! As is fitting for such a demonstration of power, a palace for this victorious god is constructed in the heavens. From there the mighty warrior rules as sovereign over all. In this psalm, the God of Israel is praised as LORD of hosts and king of glory, who is strong and mighty in battle.

There is a liturgical dimension to this response. Since the psalm clearly depicts God as king, and since kings seldom travel without some kind of entourage, it is safe to conclude that the approach of the king as described in this psalm is a form of a procession. What appears to be a question-answer dialogue can be explain by a custom practiced in walled cities. Individuals were able to enter these cities through a small door in the much larger gate. This door was usually narrow enough to allow passage in and out of the city to be monitored by guards. However, military or celebrative processions had to go through the gate. Before entrance, a sentinel would require some form of identification. The sentinel on the city wall would shout out the questions; and the people on the ground would shout back the answers. The exchange in the psalm reflects this practice. The titles used here suggest that God has been victorious, and so as the people shout out their answer to the sentinel's question, they are also proclaiming God's glory.

## Hebrews 2:14-18

When we think of Jesus as a high priest, we generally think of him as majestic and accomplishing our salvation with the power of God. The author of the letter to the Hebrews invites us to fasten our gaze on Jesus' humanity. He argues that Jesus is one with all women and men, because he fully entered into the human existence of flesh *(sárx)* and blood *(haíma)*. He did not merely appear to be human, as some down through the centuries have erroneously claimed. He was genuinely human. It was necessary that it be so, for if he was to conquer death, he would first have to be subject to it. Only under such circumstances would his victory have any power in the lives of others. One would expect God to be triumphant over death, but one would never expect someone subject to mortality to have such power.

The author draws lines of conflict between Jesus, who has the power of life, and the devil, who holds the power of death. In vanquishing death, Jesus has neutralized the power of the devil. According to this author, it is the devil who tempts human beings to sin, and it is their sin that leads to their death. Through his death Jesus has conquered this process of perdition. What is astounding is that he accomplished this not for himself but for us. He became human so that through the death of his human body he might deliver all human beings from the ravages of human death. It is natural to fear death, but it is also natural to die. Understanding human weakness because it is his weakness as well, Jesus' death put an end to the fear of death. No longer need human beings think of death as the enemy that lurks in the darkness. It can now be seen as the necessary passageway that leads into a new life.

The death of Jesus did nothing to benefit the angels, not because they did not need his help but because he was not one of them. He did not share physical solidarity with them as he did with human beings. The author of the letter refers to the human race as descendants of Abraham, a common boast made by the Israelite people. Perhaps the author did not trace their common ancestry back to Adam because the traditions about Adam are associated with myth, while descent from Abraham might be traced through lines of kinship.

After having examined what it means to be human, the author turns to Jesus' role as a high priest. Jesus knows all about human weakness, for he was tested like everyone else. This prompts him to be merciful. His own integrity prompts him to be faithful. As victim on the cross, he has offered himself for the salvation of all. As high priest he offers a sacrifice of expiation for the sins of all. He is truly a merciful and faithful high priest.

## Luke 2:22-40

This account of the presentation of Jesus in the Temple is a celebration of piety—the piety of Mary and Joseph, of Simeon, and of Anna. It is clear that Jesus was raised in an observant family. Five times the author declares that the parents of Jesus conformed to the ritual prescriptions of the Law (vv. 22, 23, 24, 27, 39). Just as they had complied with the imperial decree to be enrolled in the census (2:1-5), so now they observe the religious requirements of purification (cf. Lev 12:1-8) and redemption of the firstborn (cf. Exod 13:2, 12).

The first ritual requirement sprang from the belief that the life-power within blood was sacred and belonged to God. Because of the mysterious nature of its power, it was to be kept separate from the secular activities of life. When separation was not possible, the people and the objects that came into contact with the blood had to be purified. It is obvious why birth and death were surrounded with many purification regulations. The second ritual requirement was a way of reclaiming the firstborn male child who, they believed, really belonged to God. Buying back the child was a way of acknowledging God's initial claim.

Simeon, like the prophets of ancient Israel, had been seized by the Spirit of God (cf. Isa 61:1). Three times the author states that it was the Holy Spirit that directed him (vv. 25, 26, 27). The consolation of Israel for which he waited probably referred to the time of messianic fulfillment. Seeing the child, he recognized him as the object of his longing, the one who was both the glory of Israel and the light for the rest of the world. He also predicted the opposition that Jesus would inspire. Some would accept him and others would not.

This latter scene must have taken place in an outer court of the Temple, where women were allowed, for Simeon explicitly addressed Mary. This was very unusual behavior, for typically men did not speak to women with whom they were unfamiliar, especially in public. His words are somewhat enigmatic. It is clear why the rejection of her son would be like a sword in Mary's heart, but what this might have to do with the thoughts of others is not as obvious.

Another woman joins the group, Anna the prophetess. She is old and a widow, constantly in the Temple praying and fasting. As with Simeon, her entire life was an advent, awaiting the fulfillment of messianic promises. She probably witnessed the meeting with Simeon and heard what he said, for she is convinced of the identity of the child, and she proclaims this to all those who cherished messianic hopes.

Though neither Simeon nor Anna belonged to the ranks of formal temple personnel, they were the ones who recognized the divine child, while the others did not. This should not be seen as an anti-Judaic bias. It points to the fact that religious insight comes from fidelity and genuine devotion rather than official status or privileged role. God and the ways of God are revealed to those who have open minds and open hearts. The piety of this man (v. 25) and this woman (v. 37) disposed them to the unexpected revelation of God.

The family returns to Nazareth to resume its unpretentious life, but it is not the same. Even though the child grows up like other children, he is merely waiting for his time to come.

## Themes of the Day

Traditionally this is the fortieth day of Christmas. Even though the Christmas season closed with the feast of the Epiphany, this feast brings us back to some of the Christmas themes. However, the feast is also on the edge. This makes it a kind of hinge between the seasons of Christmas and Lent.

### *The Temple*

The Temple is not merely a building where believers gather to worship God. It is sacred because it is the dwelling place of God on earth. It symbolizes God's presence among us. The advent of God to the Temple was always a time of great anticipation and excitement. It promised blessing and rejoicing.

Today's readings hold a Christmas and a Lenten theme in balance. In the gospel the child Jesus is brought to the Temple to fulfill the requirements of redemption. By right he belongs to God, since he opened his mother's womb. Here for the price of two turtledoves he will be redeemed and returned to his parents. His willingness to submit to the religious traditions of his people adds a dimension of legitimation to these traditions that they had not previously enjoyed. The child enters the Temple quietly, not with the fanfare proclaimed in the responsorial psalm. However, the sentiments found in the psalm are still appropriate. This child is indeed the king of glory, the strong and mighty one. Simeon recognizes this, as does the prophetess Anna. Do we recognize the Lord of the Temple in the unassuming? The poor? The vulnerable?

The scene depicted in the first reading is startling in its contrast. It announces that God will indeed come to the Temple in might and power. However, this advent will be terrifying. God will come not be to purified but to purify with fire and lye. The Temple has been violated; the sacred precincts have been desecrated. Devotion to the Temple requires that it be cleansed and reconsecrated. Only then will it be a suitable place for God to take up residence again. This picture of purification is modified by the reading from the letter to the Hebrews. There we see that the purging and refinement are accomplished in the self-sacrifice of Christ. He has expiated sin through the shedding of his blood (clearly a Lenten theme). His death was the ultimate act of purification.

### *A Light to the Nations*

It took the eyes of an old man and the faith of an old woman to recognize that the Lord had indeed come into the Temple. These two had been waiting for his coming, as the world had waited for thousands of years (the Church marks this waiting during the season of Advent). Ritually, it was the child who was redeemed. In fact, it is the world that will be redeemed. This child will be the light that shines in the darkness of the world (clearly a Christmas theme). He will enlighten all people, Jew and Gentile alike. This feast shares the theme of universality so prominent on the feast of the Epiphany. Having come to a backwater nation, the king of glory opens the portals for the entire universe to enter.

## The Nativity of St. John the Baptist (Solemnity)
## June 24

### Isaiah 49:1-6

The first reading for this feast is a "prophetic speech" (The LORD said to me). In it God refers to the speaker as "my servant." Hence the designation "Servant Song." The actual identity of this servant is quite mysterious. At first reading it sounds like the prophet is the servant (The LORD said to *me:* You are my servant.). But then the servant is identified as Israel. Even this causes confusion, because the servant is called to accomplish the return of Jacob, the gathering back together of Israel (vv. 1, 5). Because the speaker is said to have been formed as a servant from the womb, reminiscent of the call of the prophet Jeremiah (cf. Jer 1:5), some think the servant is Isaiah himself. Commentators are hard pressed to discover the precise identity of this mysterious individual. Most of them direct the reader to lay aside the search for the exact identity of the servant and instead to concentrate on his mission.

The passage opens with a summons to the many peoples of a vast expanse of land. This could be an instance of universalism. However, the servant's task of gathering Israelites suggests they have been scattered as a result of the deportation and exile. This summons is followed by a self-description of the servant. Beyond being called from birth, he was named while yet unborn. It is as if he had been formed in the womb precisely for this mission. His prophetic message is identified as sharp, cutting. However, he is hidden by God until the appropriate time arrives. This prophetic vocation is not a chance occurrence. God planned it and nurtured it.

The text states that Israel is the servant, and it is through this people that God will be glorified *(pā'ar)*. Since the verb suggests a kind of boasting, we can say that God boasts through Israel. But why? "Jacob" and "Israel" are two terms that refer to the entire nation. The poem states that Jacob will be brought back and Israel will be gathered together. The prediction presumes that at this time the people are at some distance from their home; they are scattered. This is probably a reference to the Exile. It will be the mission of the servant, whoever that is, to bring them back to the LORD. The accomplishment of this mission will make the servant glorious in the sight of God. This is the cause for the boasting mentioned earlier. The spectacular return of the scattered exiles and their reestablishment as a people will be seen as the work of God. The glory will shine forth not from their own accomplishments but from what God has accomplished in them through the agency of the servant.

The commission of the servant shifts dramatically (v. 6). Once again it is the LORD who speaks, so the words are authoritative. Gathering the dispersed people of Israel, as important as it may be, is a matter with too narrow a scope. Therefore, the mission of the servant will be expanded to include all the nations, that is, to the ends of the earth. A mission that originally focused on the rebirth of one nation has been broken open to include the salvation of all. It is noteworthy that a people struggling with its own survival after its defeat at the hands of a more powerful nation should envision its God as concerned with the salvation of all, presumably even the nation at whose hands it suffered. Yet this is precisely what "light to the nations" suggests.

## Psalm 139:1-3, 13-14, 14-15

Regardless of the level of sophistication in a society, it frequently has a rather uncomplicated understanding of justice. It maintains that reality unfolds according to a certain pattern, and for the good of society every member of the group must conform to that basic pattern. When there is unexplained misfortune, it is necessary to discover the guilty person or persons so that a remedy can be applied. One technique of discovery is trial by ordeal. The suspected person is submitted to a test, usually one with great physical danger. The outcome of the ordeal is seen to be the judgment determining that person's innocence or guilt. This seems to be the situation that generated the sentiments of the psalmist.

The words themselves reveal confidence, first in the psalmist's own innocence and then in God's omniscience. It is God who is doing the probing, and God has intimate knowledge of the inner dispositions of the psalmist. The scope of God's investigation is described in several ways. "Sitting down and rising up" and "journeys and rest" are expressions each of which includes every aspect of waking life. They are similar to the pairs "night and day," "up and down," "north and south," all of which denote totality. In other words, there is nothing about the psalmist's life that is beyond the ken of God.

The second and third stanzas of the response explain why God possesses complete comprehension of every aspect of the psalmist's life. It is because God is the one who created the psalmist in the first place. The psalmist's attention now moves from God's comprehensive knowledge to divine ingenuity in creating. The imagery used to describe the act of creation suggests both tenderness and artistry. The "inmost being" of which the psalmist speaks is really the kidneys (*kilyâ*), the seat of profound emotions. The psalmist's physical being was carefully knit together in the womb or belly *(beten)* of his mother. Since creation is a personal activity and takes place in secret, the knowledge God has of human beings is privileged knowledge. Only God knows how the psalmist was formed; consequently, God would know whether or not the psalmist is innocent.

To the image of being formed in the womb, the psalmist adds the idea of being formed in the lowest part of the earth. Some commentators see here an allusion to chthonic (under the earth) mythology. While Israel did not teach that human creation took place with the earth, it certainly insists that it took place from the earth (cf. Gen 2:7).

## Acts 13:22-26

Paul provides a brief summary of some of the stages in the unfolding of God's plan of salvation. He does this by highlighting the importance of two biblical figures, David and John the Baptist. David was a virtual unknown, the youngest of seven sons. Even in his own family he held an unimportant role. When the prophet Samuel came to his father looking for a possible king, Jesse never considered David as a candidate (cf. 1 Sam 16:1-13). Here is another example of how God seems to prefer the insignificant things of the world to confound the prominent. Despite this, it was David who consolidated the tribes into the monarchy; it was David who expanded the territory that comprised the kingdom. Most important to the author of the Acts of the Apostles, it was David who established the royal dynasty from which came the Messiah.

As the appointed time approached God continued to ready the world for the advent of this Messiah. This was accomplished through the preaching of John the Baptist. His message was one of repentance, a sign the people had strayed from their appointed course. But then, the fact that a Messiah had been promised was a sure indication that the human situation was not as it should be. Although both John and Jesus called for repentance (cf. Mark 1:4, 15), their fundamental message was quite different. John declared that "one is coming"; Jesus announced that "the time is fulfilled" (cf. Mark 1:15). Though John attracted followers from far and near, he knew that he was only the precursor; he was not the long-awaited one. The measure of John's greatness can be seen in his willingness to draw people to himself only to step aside and point them to another. It was with prophetic insight and profound humility that John would declare that the one for whom he was preparing the way was far greater than he himself was.

Paul's purpose in reminding his hearers of the roles played by these two men was to place his own preaching squarely within this tradition. Just as God had chosen David as an instrument in the development of the messianic tradition, and just as God had called John to lead the people to Jesus, who was the fulfillment of the promises made to David, so now Paul has been appointed by God to proclaim this message of salvation. Although Paul's ministry was primarily to the Gentiles, here he is speaking to people who are either themselves Jewish or who are Godfearers, a name given to those who were sympathetic to the teachings of the Israelite religion. It was clear from the beginning that the audience was made up of Jewish people and potential converts, for only they would have appreciated his references to David, and, most likely, only they would have had some acquaintance with John the Baptist.

## Luke 1:57-66, 80

In many cultures the act of naming a child is viewed as giving that child its identity. Some societies even believed an unnamed child was not fully human. In Israelite society circumcision was the boy's initiation into the community of the People of God (cf. Gen 17:9-14). The gender bias of this ritual is obvious, since it presumes that the female participates in the community only indirectly, through her father, brother, husband, or son. In this narrative the two initiatory ceremonies have been combined. There does not seem to be any general rule determining who names the child. Sometimes it is the father (cf. Gen 21:3), at other times it is the neighboring women (cf. Ruth 4:17). In this episode it is the neighbors and relatives. The communal character of this society is evident. It is clear the parents are not the only ones who have a stake in a new child.

Since the name given is somehow linked with the person's identity, the name put forward reveals what the namer expects of the child. The neighbors and relatives presume the boy will be called Zechariah after his father. They see his identity and destiny linked with his family, his kin group. The boy's parents both insist he will be called John, a name that means "God is gracious." The name could refer to God's goodness in granting this child to a couple who were advanced in years (cf. Luke 1:7), or it could be a promise of future blessings. The name was given by the angel. Since it came from heaven, it is correct to say this child's destiny would be a heavenly destiny.

There is evidence in the reading that this was truly a chosen child. At his birth the neighbors and relatives rejoiced that God had shown great mercy (*éleos*), not simply kindness (*chrēstótēs*), toward his mother Elizabeth. This suggests she was in great need and God took pity on her, making the child particularly cherished. Furthermore, his father Zechariah was given back his speech when he confirmed that the child was to be named John. He is but eight days old and already he has been a source of blessing for both his parents. While Zechariah blessed God for the marvels that had been performed, the neighbors were frightened by them. They did not know what to make of these events, but they were convinced God had great designs for this child.

The last verse of the reading shows their impressions were correct. John had indeed been set apart by God for a mission to the people of Israel. In preparation for this, he spent his days in the wilderness, the place traditionally considered a testing ground. It was there that he was strengthened in spirit for the task before him.

## Themes of the Day

### A Cosmic Hinge

Like the feast of the nativity of Jesus, this feast falls on one of the solstices, a hinge point in the cosmos. Some of patristic writings tell us that the birth of Jesus was placed in the calendar when, in the Northern Hemisphere, the days begin to lengthen. So this day was chosen to celebrate the birth of John precisely because the days were getting shorter. This calendric decision exemplified John's declaration: He must increase while I must decrease (John 3:30). This is the time of seasonal change, of cosmic reversal. The entire universe has been alerted. Something new is about to happen.

A nativity is always a dramatic entry into history, whether this be the birth of a child of note or of a simple laborer. Each new birth is a new beginning for the entire human race. Parents either hope the child will enjoy a life that will be richer than their own, or they believe the child will effect a change in the lives of others. Hopes are always high at new births. Some births are believed to change even the movements of the heavens. Many people believe we are influenced by the astral arrangements under which we are born. Others are convinced that the stars themselves proclaim the significance of the new birth.

The meaning of John's birth may well hinge on the meaning of the birth of Jesus, but it is significant enough to make us step out of liturgical Ordinary Time for a moment and reflect again on the entrance of God into ordinary human time. John's birth shares in the meaning of the incarnation.

### An Eschatological Hinge

John the Baptist is the hinge between the old age and the new eschatological age of fulfillment. John himself was never a disciple of Jesus; he did not enter the age that he heralded (cf. Matt 11:11; Luke 7:28). He was the trumpet that sounded the coming of the king; he was the rooster that announced the dawning of the new day. He brought the people to the threshold of the new age, but he himself never stepped over into it. The idiosyncratic character of his life caught the attention of the crowds, but he did not keep this attention on himself. Instead, he used it to point to Jesus, who appears to have been so commonplace that he might have been overlooked had not John cried out. It was John's prophetic destiny to be the sharp-edged sword, the polished arrow. He was the voice that cried in the wilderness: Hear me! Listen! Behold, he is coming!

### The Hand of the Lord

From the beginning the hand of the Lord was on John. His conception had been extraordinary (cf. Luke 1:7); his name had been announced by the angel (cf. Luke 1:13); like many prophetic figures, he had been chosen from his mother's womb; his father had been struck speechless and remained so until his name was proclaimed to others (cf. Luke 1:22, 64). Everything about this child pointed to a divinely determined destiny. His almost appears to be a thankless role, but it was not. His was the last prophetic voice that challenged the people to prepare; he was privileged to see the one that others did not see. John opened the door to the future and then stepped back so that the voice from the future might call us forth.

## SS. Peter and Paul, Apostles (Solemnity)
## June 29

### Acts 12:1-11

The execution of James and the imprisonment of Peter demonstrate again how the reign of God is embroiled in the political circumstances of the day. The Herod of this episode is Herod Agrippa I, the grandson of the hated Herod the Great. He was a child when his father was executed, so his mother sent him to Rome, both for the sake of safety and to procure a Roman education. There he grew up with various members of the imperial family. This explains both the privilege he enjoyed with his Roman overlords and the disfavor in which he was held by the Jewish people. It was because of the former that he was able to expand the scope of the territory over which he ruled; it was because of the latter that he seemed always eager to curry the favor of the leaders of the Jewish people.

Belonging to an occupied people, the Jewish leaders had only as much power and authority as was granted them by their occupiers. However, since Herod Agrippa was always trying to please them, they exercised a considerable amount of influence. Both James, who appears to have been the leader of the Christian community in Jerusalem, and Peter, the recognized leader of the apostles, become victims of the antagonism of the Jewish leaders and the pusillanimity of the king. James is put to death, and Peter faces the same fate. He is still alive only because it is the feast of Unleavened Bread and executions are unlawful during festivals. Unleavened Bread began on the fourteenth of Nisan, the evening of Passover, and it lasted a week. The similarity between Peter's imprisonment and impending execution and the circumstances surrounding the death of Jesus is striking.

The restraints Peter was forced to endure suggest that this similarity was not lost on Herod. He was probably afraid the supporters of Peter might try to release him. Most likely Peter was kept in the Tower of Antonia, the headquarters of the Roman garrison in Jerusalem, which was northwest of the temple area. Roman night guard was divided into four three-hour watches with a squadron of four soldiers assigned to each watch. Peter was chained on each side to a soldier, while the other two kept watch outside the cell. Although the Christians prayed for his release, there was little chance this would occur.

The author provides all these details so the miraculous character of Peter's release will stand out boldly. Peter himself is completely passive throughout the incident. On the eve before he is to be put to death, he is awakened from sleep, told to dress and to follow the one who is freeing him. Even as the events unfold, Peter is not fully conscious of what is transpiring. His deliverance is all God's doing, enacted by an angel of the Lord. It is clear that the future of the Church is being directed by the hand of God and not by the political maneuverings of human potentates.

## Psalm 34:2-3, 4-5, 6-7, 8-9

The psalm response is part of an acrostic, a poem whose structure follows the order of the alphabet. Although the content of this type of psalm may vary, the form (the entire alphabet) always signifies the same thing, completeness. This psalm is less a prayer than an instruction. Its teaching is the conventional understanding of retribution: the righteous will be blessed and the wicked will be punished. In this first part of the poem the psalmist thanks God for having been delivered from distress, and he invites others to join in praising God. The attitude of the psalmist gives witness to others and develops into a pedagogical technique, teaching others to act in the same way.

The psalm begins with an expression of praise of God and an acknowledgment of the appropriateness of blessing God. This praise probably takes place in some kind of liturgical setting, for it is heard by the lowly *('ănāwîm)*, those who live in trust and dependence on the LORD. They are here invited to join with the psalmist in rejoicing and in praising God's name.

Normally in psalms of thanksgiving the reasons for gratitude are recited. Without going into detail, the psalmist confesses having been in distress, having turned to the LORD, and having been rescued. This is the reason for gratitude. This is why the psalmist glorifies God and bids others to do the same.

The congregation is now given explicit directions. They are encouraged to look to the LORD so they too may rejoice in gratitude, their faces radiant and not filled with shame. One's face, we should remember, is the expression of one's dignity, of one's status in the community, and to lose face is to lose honor or to be shamed. The companions of the psalmist are encouraged to attach themselves to God and thereby to enjoy the blessings this ensures. The fate of the psalmist is placed before them as an example to follow.

An image that might be unfamiliar to us is used to demonstrate this. An angel or messenger from God pitches a protective camp around those who fear the LORD, who stand in awe and reverence of God's majesty and power. Thus they are guarded by the power of God against anything that might endanger them.

The passage ends with an admonition. The congregation is encouraged to taste God's goodness, to partake of it a little, to sample it a bit. The psalmist is saying that if only they put God's goodness to the test they will see for themselves how delectable it is, how satisfying it can be. They have the psalmist's witness. It is now time for them to experience God's goodness for themselves.

## 2 Timothy 4:6-8, 17-18

Paul is aware that his days are numbered, that his death is imminent. He does not resent it, but neither does he run toward it eagerly. He faces it with the calm resignation that springs from deep faith. He uses moving imagery to characterize his death. The first metaphor is taken from the context of the cult. There we find the rite of pouring out wine as a kind of drink offering (cf. Num 15:5, 7, 10). This practice may have been introduced into the ritual as a substitute for blood libation. Paul states that he is being poured out like this sacrificial blood. Not only is every ounce of life being exacted of him, but his offering of it is viewed as a sacrificial act.

A second metaphor is no less poignant. Paul views his death as a departure, a kind of leave-taking (*análȳo*, a compound derived from *lȳō*, meaning "to loose") associated with sailors who weigh anchor or soldiers who break camp. Like them, Paul has completed a demanding tour of service and is now preparing to return home. The references suggest eager anticipation. In none of these metaphors is Paul in control. The cultic image suggests he is poured out by another. Although the sailor and the soldier perform important roles in their leave-taking, they certainly did not make the decision to leave on their own. They were merely carrying out the decisions made by another.

Finally, Paul uses imagery derived from athletic competition to evaluate the course of his ministerial commitment. He has competed well; he has finished the race. To this he adds that he has kept the faith, an idiomatic expression that means remaining loyal to one's oath. He has done what he could.

Now he has only to wait for the conferral upon him of the crown promised by God. The reference is to Christ's eschatological manifestation. For a moment Paul moves away from focusing solely on his fate in order to anticipate joining with all the others who will be awarded the victorious crown. He claims no special privilege. This man, who is facing death at the hands of others, is looking forward to a time of communal fulfillment.

Paul compares the trustworthiness of God with the unreliability of human companions. It seems everyone had deserted him during one of his trials, perhaps because they would have been putting themselves in jeopardy had they stood with him. Whatever the case, Paul is not resentful, for God was there to strengthen him when all others fled. Throughout this discourse, he extols the marvelous deeds God has done on his behalf. He even maintains that the gospel benefits from his adversity. His imprisonment and trial have provided an opportunity for him to proclaim the good news to the people involved. Because of it he is able to spread the word even more broadly, despite the difficult circumstances in which he finds himself.

Paul is confident that just as God had previously rescued him from peril, so God would rescue him again. He is not speaking of being freed from prison but of being preserved from anything that might threaten his spiritual well-being and prevent him from being led safely into the kingdom of heaven.

## Matthew 16:13-19

This reading consists of two distinct yet related themes. The first is christological (vv. 13-16); the second is ecclesiological (vv. 17-19). Only after Simon Peter has proclaimed Jesus to be the Christ, the anointed one of God, does Jesus announce that his own Church will be founded on Peter.

Jesus asks the disciples what people are saying about him; Who do they think he is? He applies to himself the messianic apocalyptic title "Son of Man." The question is not self-serving. Jesus seeks to discover how his words and actions are being understood by the people, and he is preparing the disciples for their own assessment of him. The answers given to his questions are telling. Some believe that he is John the Baptist; others that he is Elijah; still others that he is one of the other prophets. These religious figures have already died; the people seem to believe Jesus is a prophetic figure who has come back from the dead.

It is not clear why Jesus should be associated with John the Baptist, since in both their life-styles and their central messages they were so different. The connection may have been made simply because the memory of this exceptional man was still fresh in the minds of the people. Many had set their hopes on John, and with his death they transferred them to Jesus. Elijah had been the mysterious prophet whose return would herald the advent of the reign of God. Since Jesus launched his ministry with the announcement that the long-awaited reign was now at hand, it is understandable that people would link him with Elijah. In some way, all the prophets had looked forward to the coming of this reign, so the people's general reference was not inappropriate. Simon Peter speaks in the name of the others when he proclaims that Jesus is the Christ, the Messiah, the anointed one of God. To this he adds the divine title "Son of the living God."

Using a macarism (Blessed are you), Jesus opens his discussion of the role Peter will play in the assembly of believers. Jesus insists that the only reason Peter could make such a testimony of faith was that Jesus' identity had been revealed to him by God. With a play on Greek words, the author has Jesus declare that Peter *(Petros)* is the rock *(petra)* upon which Jesus will establish his church. Although the image of a rock suggests stability and endurance, we should not presume that these characteristics are natural to Peter. Also, "church" *(ekklēsía)* is certainly a reference to the assembly of people, not the building within which they gather.

Jesus promises that the forces of the netherworld will not be able to encircle this church. It is clear this promise is not based on any strength of Peter's. It is solely a gift from Jesus. For his part, Peter will exercise the power of the keys. Controlling the keys is a sign of authority. However, here the symbol of keys refers to a special kind of authority, one that is more judicial or disciplinary than managerial. Peter is given the authority to enforce laws and to exempt from their obligation. This does not suggest that Peter legislates. Rather he interprets the Law, determining when it should be binding and when not. In a sense, Peter is cast in the role of the chief rabbi.

## Themes of the Day

This feast celebrates the two pillars on which Christianity was built. Peter is associated with the community in Jerusalem and Paul with the Gentile converts. Together they represent the universality of the Church. The red vestments worn on this day remind us of the price that the commitment of these men exacted of them. The focus here is not on the offices either of them might have held within the community but on the character of their witness of faith.

### Who Do You Say I Am?

The church is rooted in the identity of Christ. His followers have come from every race and culture, every generation and social class. It is not a common culture that has drawn them together but a common faith. They do not consider Jesus the reincarnation of some great personage of the past. Rather, they profess him to be the Christ, the Son of the Living God. Today the successors of these two great apostles sometimes struggle with the appropriate response to the proclamation of the gospel. This may be due in part to the fact that there are so many cultural ways of expressing one's Christian faith. However, there is no question about the identity of Jesus. He is the same yesterday, today, and forever.

### I Have Kept the Faith

Today we remember that throughout the ages the Church has been strengthened by the blood of the martyrs. This was the case in its earliest years, and it is the case even today. Both Peter and Paul are examples of how God can take those who are weak in faith and transform them into champions for the cause of the gospel. Once transformed, each of them threw himself wholeheartedly into the mission that was his. Their fate should not surprise us, for they were disciples of one who gave his last breath for the life of the world.

In so many places in the world today modern martyrs are called upon to pay the ultimate price for their faith. We see this in Latin America, in many African countries, in the Middle East, and in Asia, to name but a few areas. Although the word "martyr" usually refers to one who dies for the faith, the Greek word *(mártys)* really means witness, one who gives testimony. Like Peter and Paul, the martyr is one whose life gives witness to the faith. However, when this witness becomes too much of a challenge to the world, the witness's life is placed in jeopardy. Peter and Paul call us all to this kind of testimony to faith.

### The Transfiguration of the Lord (Feast)
### August 6

#### Daniel 7:9-10, 13-14

An apocalyptic vision unfolds before the seer. Visions and dreams were traditionally thought to be avenues of divine revelation. The seer is usually on earth, while the vision itself takes place in heaven. Everything about this vision bespeaks revelation, yet it is symbolic, with all of the ambiguous traits of symbol. It reveals only the symbol. The seer must be able to interpret it. The reading for today comprises two scenes, both of which take place in the throne room. The two major figures are the Ancient One and the one like a Son of Man.

The description of the Ancient One is not only brilliant in itself, but its contrast with the flames of fire only exaggerates the brilliance. The name given this heavenly being is telling. "Ancient One" implies both eternity and great wisdom. Therefore it demands reverence, respect, and obedience. Enthroned in the heavens presumes that the Ancient One rules wisely over all that is. White clothing implies purity and luminosity. Since often exquisite white linen was worn by kings, here it might also be an indication of royal raiment. White hair is a symbol of the age and wisdom of this ruler. It reinforces the notion of eternity.

Only the Ancient One was seated, an honor reserved for rulers. Presumably the throngs that attend him are standing around the throne, as is the practice with all royalty. The throne itself is reminiscent of the fiery chariot in Ezekiel's apocalyptic vision (cf. Ezek1:15-21). Flames of fire suggest a divine theophany (cf. Exod 19:18). The scene depicts the courts of heaven at the end of the ages, as is clear from the mention of the books that are now opened. At creation, according to ancient Near Eastern mythology, the destinies of the nations were written in books, which were then sealed and kept secret. Only at the end of time would these seals be broken and the fates of all revealed (cf. Revelation 5–9).

The one who comes on the clouds is described as one like the Son of man (in Aramaic *bar enash*). Its literal translation is "son of weak man." Of itself it denotes a limited human being. However, this figure is not really a human being; he only resembles a Son of man. The picture painted here is colored with both mythic and royal tones. The figure comes with the clouds, which are the most frequent accompaniment of a theophany, or revelation of God. He comes riding them as one would ride a chariot (cf. Ps 18:10). He is presented before God in the manner of courtly decorum, where one would not simply approach the ruler but would be presented by an attendant. This is no ordinary man.

The mysterious figure is installed by God as ruler over the entire universe. The authority and dominion that belong to other nations is handed over to him. Unlike other kingdoms that rise and eventually fall, his will be an everlasting kingdom, granted by God, not attained by means of conquest or political alliance. Finally, his dominion will be exercised on earth. The one like a Son of man may have been in heaven when he received his commission, he may even rule from some exalted place in the heavens, but his kingdom belongs to the earth.

## Psalm 97:1-2, 5-6, 9

The psalm opens with the traditional enthronement declaration, "The LORD is king!" Behind this exclamation is the theme of divine kingship. The ancients believed the gods were always vying with each other for power and status. The god that could be victorious over this chaotic situation, if only for a time, was enthroned as king over all. There are echoes of this mythology in the responsorial psalm. The god who rules is the LORD, the God of Israel.

The exclamation is appropriately followed by an exhortation: "Let the earth rejoice!" God's victory and rule call for celebration, one that extends beyond the confines of Israel to many islands, an image denoting the furthest parts of the world. God's throne is established on a firm foundation. Unlike other regimes built on brute force or military victory, both of which might fail and result in dethronement, God's rule is constructed in the permanence of justice *(ṣedeq)* and judgment *(mishpāṭ)*. It is not only impregnable, it is immutable. It stands secure, enabling God to govern undisturbed by any threat and assuring reliable protection to all those under God's jurisdiction.

With three phrases the psalmist declares the sovereignty of the LORD. First, the reference to the heavens includes all the celestial beings once thought to be gods themselves, now merely luminaries or winds or forms of rain. No longer is there any vying among them. Instead, they are all intent on praising God's justice; the order that was set after the primordial battle had been won. Second, not only Israel but all people see God's glory *(kābôd)*, the splendor that shines from God's holiness and that is usually a characteristic of divine theophany or manifestation. Third, all other gods are prostrate before the LORD in an attitude of utter subservience. Actually, the verb *(bôsh)* means to put to shame or to lose face before the other. In a society where honor and shame play such important roles, this is a significant point. The universal kingship of the LORD is beyond question.

The passage from the psalm ends with a proclamation of praise addressed directly to the LORD. It captures the essence of the preceding verses. God is exalted above both heaven and earth. There is no threat of future upheaval or rebellion. God has no rivals. The divine king has been enthroned, and the rule of this God will last forever.

## 2 Peter 1:16-19

A defensive tone seems to surface in this reading. The authenticity of the gospel message preached by the author appears to have come under attack, and he counters with two arguments. The first one is based on personal experience, and the second one, on the revelatory nature of the Scriptures.

A myth is a creative literary form that expresses some of the mysteries of life and of the broader universe. Its very creativity enables people to enter into the depths of the mysteries it describes. Because it is an imaginative rather than a scientific or historical way of conceiving reality, the richness of a myth will be diminished if it is forced into one of these other categories. A myth must be understood on its own creative terms. Those who would understand it in a literal fashion, which is really to misunderstand it, might be tempted to say it is not true because the universe does not work in the way the myth describes it. In a similar manner, reality itself can be misunderstood. It does not fit into a neat pattern. Those who try to force it to do so might be tempted to dismiss as impossible or untrue whatever does not fit the patterns of their understanding.

This seems to be the issue with which the author is struggling. The extraordinary, even incomprehensible, character of the final coming *(parousía)* of the Lord Jesus Christ has led some to denounce it as myth. One can almost hear them exclaim: That could never happen! The author counters the denunciation: Oh yes it did, and I was an eyewitness to it. The event of which they speak is the transfiguration of Jesus. His full and solemn title is used in this report of his wondrous manifestation *(megaleiótōs)* of divine glory. This glory is probably a reference to the cloud from which the voice was heard. Those who were with him on the mountain were witness both to his glory and to God's affirmation of him. If Jesus could have been so transformed during his lifetime, surely this same Lord can return in the same glory.

The second witness to which the author appeals is the Scriptures, the prophetic message that foretold the coming of the Messiah. The Christians inherited these Scriptures from the Jewish community, and they held them in the same esteem as the inspired word of God. The prophetic words acted as beacons in the darkness, guiding the people through trial and doubt. If the detractors will not believe the testimony of the eyewitnesses, they should at least accept the reliability of these sacred words.

Two very powerful metaphors are used to describe the *parousía* of the Lord, both of which characterize it as the coming of light out of darkness. They are the dawning of the day, the eschatological day of fulfillment, and the rising of the morning star. The latter image recalls the messianic prophecy spoken by the Moabite prophet Balaam: "A star shall come out of Jacob" (cf. Num 24:17). The Christian community placed the fulfillment of this prophecy on the lips of Jesus: "I am the root and the descendant of David, the bright morning star" (cf. Rev 22:16). The Scriptures themselves bear witness to the veracity of the gospel message.

## Matthew 17:1-9

The gospel narrative recounts a theophany, a self-revelation of God. There are really two dimensions of this event: the experience of Jesus himself and the experience of the apostles who accompanied him up the mountain. Several elements in the account place the event squarely within the company of other significant theophanies. The first characteristic is its location. It takes place on a mountain whose significance is less in its name than in its height. High mountains were thought to be places where the gods dwelt. Hence people often traveled to such spots in order to have some experience of the god who resided there. It was on a mountain that Jesus was transfigured. There a bright cloud engulfed the apostles, and a voice from the cloud addressed them.

Jesus is transformed before Peter, James, and John, the apparent inner circle of the apostles. The Greek verb *metamporphóō* can refer to a change that is merely external or to one that is actually a change of state or being. The once popular interpretation of this account as a post-resurrection story read back into the time of the public ministry of Jesus has been challenged by most commentators today. In its place is the opinion that the account is not a vision of the future glorification of Jesus but an insight into the identity that was his during his public life. From this point of view the transformation would be a change that took place when Jesus' inner reality shone forth and transfigured his outer appearance. Like Moses before him (cf. Exod 34:35), Jesus' face shines brightly. In this instance, his attire is also brilliant. Jesus is seen to be conversing with Moses and Elijah, the representatives of the Law and the Prophets, respectively. These are the men who stood for the entire religious tradition of ancient Israel. The topic of their conversation is not given. However, their presence confirms the authority of Jesus and the legitimacy of his teaching.

The importance of this teaching is evident in the words that were spoken from the cloud: Listen to him! As with other incidences in the biblical tradition, the cloud symbolizes the presence of God (cf. Exod 40:35). The description of the cloud is curious. One would expect a brilliant cloud to illuminate everything upon which its rays fell. Instead, it is said to have cast a shadow. Furthermore, it is not clear over whom this shadow is cast. Presumably, it is the apostles. Whatever the case may be, from this cloud God both identifies Jesus as Son and gives authority to his teaching. While Moses and Elijah converse with Jesus, the voice from the cloud speaks to the apostles. They are the ones who seem to need the identification of Jesus and the directive from God.

The apostles' response to this two-dimensional experience is also twofold. They would like to prolong Jesus' transfiguration and conversation with the ancient heroes, and they seem eager to participate in such a venture. At least Peter, who acts as spokesperson, is of this mind. However, the voice from heaven strikes fear in their hearts, and they fall prostrate. They may have witnessed Jesus' initial transformation, but they seem not to have seen his return to normal appearance. Using words that frequently accompany an awe-inspiring experience of God, the Jesus they have always known reassures them: Do not be afraid. Identifying himself as the mysterious Son of Man, he directs them to remain silent about this experience until after his resurrection. It should be noted that the transfigured Jesus was identified as Son of God, while it is as Son of Man that he will be raised from the dead. Though very different, both titles boast an aspect of divinity.

## Themes of the Day

In the midst of Ordinary Time we are invited to join Peter, James, and John as they behold the transfiguration of Christ. By some horrible coincidence we recall Christ's brilliance on the day the world marks another cosmic event, the anniversary of its birth into the atomic age at Hiroshima. The paradox of these events should not be lost on us. The white light that shone from Christ was a mere suggestion of the divine splendor that is beyond human comprehension; the flashing light from the atomic explosion was an omen of the destructive force that is within human grasp. It is imperative that the horror of the latter be brought under the control of the glory of the former.

## Transfiguration

The transfiguration of Christ was not a simple metamorphosis. Christ was not changed from a terrestrial human being to a celestial divine one. Rather, his transfiguration was a moment in time when the divine glory he had always possessed broke through his humanity and shone with a brilliance that was blinding. Nothing could prepare the apostles for this experience, and there was no way to describe it except with cosmic imagery. The brightest light flashed forth from his countenance, like the birth of a new star. His hair, his garments, everything about him shone like the sun. Moses and Elijah stood as witnesses to his glory, and the voice of God confirmed his divinity. It is no wonder the apostles fell prostrate.

## Eyewitnesses

Who would believe such an explosion of power and might would have taken place? We sing of this glory time and again in the psalms. We proclaim that nothing can stand before the splendor of the LORD; even mountains melt like wax. Yet when it really appears we can hardly believe it ourselves. The readings outline three moments when this glory was revealed. The first was reported by the visionary in the book of Daniel. He was granted a glimpse of the throne room in heaven. In that scene it is the Ancient One who shines forth with indescribable radiance. The second moment was the scene of the transfiguration. The third is hidden in the testimony of the author of the letter of Peter. The pseudonymous author of the letter was probably a second-generation Christian who may or may not have shared in the actual vision of the transfigured Lord but who was a witness to faith in his divine glory. The splendor of God is manifested in each generation of believers.

## We Possess the Prophetic Message

We are the ones who today possess the prophetic message; we are the present-day eyewitnesses of Christ's majesty. We too have moments when we might behold his glory and hear the voice proclaiming his identity, but we need eyes of faith and ears that are open. We really never know when God will choose to reveal a glimpse of divine glory. The disciples probably thought Jesus was merely taking them up a mountain to pray, as he had done on other occasions. Like them, all we can do is follow Jesus and open ourselves to whatever God has in store for us.

## The Assumption of the Blessed Virgin Mary (Solemnity)
### Revelation 11:19a; 12:1-6a, 10ab

Several mythological themes lie behind the apocalyptic vision that unfolds before us. The basic one is the primordial cosmic battle. The principal opponents in that battle are a sea monster or dragon and a young warrior god. Although the dragon is fearsomely powerful, victory goes to the warrior. A second very common tale found in the folk literature of many cultures is the story of someone who seeks to usurp the position of an unborn prince. His plan to kill the prince at his birth is thwarted by attendants who snatch the child from him and carry the baby to safety. These two myths have been superimposed in this vision. The complex interweaving of detail from both myths along with the fact that this is an apocalyptic vision should caution us not to force an allegorical interpretation on it.

The vision is not only apocalyptic, it is also eschatological. After it had been installed in the Temple, the earthly ark of the covenant was approached only by the high priest and only on the Day of Atonement. In this vision, the heavenly ark is revealed to all. The Israelites believed this revelation would take place only at the time of eschatological fulfillment. Two signs appear in the heavens: a pregnant woman and the cosmic dragon. She is no ordinary woman. Rather, she is depicted as an astral deity, superior even to the moon. The twelve stars symbolize the signs of the zodiac. The seven-headed dragon is a composite of the cosmic monster (cf. Pss 74:13-14; 89:9-10; Isa 27:1) and the evil empire drawn from the vision of Daniel (cf. Dan 7:7). The diadems on its head represent its blasphemous claims to sovereignty. While it waits for the birth of the child, the dragon engages in cosmic battle and is relatively successful. However, complete victory is not yet in sight. It fact, ultimate victory is denied.

· The child is described in royal terms. He is destined to shepherd (*poimaínō*) all of the nations. Because of the responsibility they had for their subjects, kings were often thought of as shepherds. This newly born king will rule with a rod of iron, which is an image of harsh punishment. Finally, he will exercise this authority universally, over all the nations. Upon his birth he is rescued from the threat of the dragon and caught up to the throne of God. His mother is also protected by God, but she flees into the wilderness.

The passage ends with a great exclamation of praise. The accomplishments of God's anointed one are described in four phrases. He has brought salvation; he has manifested his power; he has established the kingdom of God; and his own authority has been revealed. It is not clear whether this acclamation is referring to the ultimate fulfillment in the future or to the fulfillment this anointed one has inaugurated, which is unfolding in the present.

## Psalm 45:10, 11, 12, 16

The verses of this response have been taken from a royal psalm, specifically a royal wedding psalm. All attention is given to the queen. Each verse of the response treats a different aspect of her person. The change in pronouns suggests the psalmist is talking first to the king (v. 10) and then to the queen herself (vv. 11-12, 16).

We are directed first to three characteristics of her royal dignity. She is identified as a queen, an indication that she and the king are already married. She stands at the king's right hand. Although she is standing, the proper sign of respect when in the presence of the king, she holds the place of honor at his right hand. Finally, she is arrayed in gold. We may also note that although Ophir's reputation as a source of gold is referred to several times in the Bible, its exact location is not known.

The psalmist next turns directly to the woman, and gives her advice or direction as a Wisdom teacher might: Hear and see! Listen to my words and realize their value! The title "daughter" fits well with the theme of kinship. The patriarchal custom of the woman leaving the household of her father to become part of the household of her husband is clearly reflected. The psalmist encourages the woman to conform to this practice.

The king is characterized as the lord (*ʾādôn*) of the woman. This probably refers to his royal role and not to his role as husband. Were the latter situation the case the word used for "lord" would probably be *baʾal,* which is also translated "husband." There is surely a sexual connotation in the reference to his desire for her beauty. Since it is the king who desires her and not merely her husband, one could conclude that he wishes to incorporate her into his harem. This idea may be repugnant to contemporary sensibilities, but in the ancient Near Eastern world it would have been considered the highest honor to which a woman might aspire.

The final verse alludes to the wedding procession that was part of most marriages. Usually the bride and her attendants walked in procession to the home of the groom. The high station of this wedding couple is seen in the fact that the wedding entourage is carried into the palace, probably on exquisitely decorated litters. Once the bride arrived, the feasting would commence. From this point on the bride would reside in the home of her husband.

### 1 Corinthians 15:20-27

This reading from Paul's Corinthian correspondence brings together several of his most treasured theological themes: the efficacy of Christ's resurrection; human solidarity in Adam and in Christ; the sequence of eschatological events; and the victory of Christ. The reading carries us first back through time to the primordial period of beginnings, and then forward to the end of time and the eschatological age of fulfillment. Christ is identified as the first-fruits of those who have fallen asleep. In double fashion the expression speaks of the end-time. "Fallen asleep" is a euphemism for death, and firstfruits refers to harvest. It was believed the firstfruits of a crop functioned in two ways. They contained the most forceful expression of the life of the plant, and they stood as a promise of more yield to come. As the firstfruits of the dead, the risen Christ is the most forceful expression of life after death, and his resurrection contains the promise of resurrection for all who are joined to him.

It is fair to say that, as did his contemporaries, Paul considered Adam the first human being. However, Adam also stands for the entire race. The Hebrew word itself *(ʾādām)* yields both a singular and a collective meaning. Here Paul is referring to human solidarity in Adam when he declares that one man sinned and brought death into the world, and in that one man is all of humankind. In an analogous fashion, Christ is the person Jesus, and joined in faith, all believers participate in the resurrected life of Christ. This is clearly meant by the phrase: Death came through humankind *(ánthrōpos);* resurrection from the death came through humankind *(ánthrōpos).* In both instances the deed is accomplished by one *ánthrōpos* who stands for all.

Paul sketches a picture of the risen Christ with his foot on the neck of death, his vanquished enemy. This picture of victory was common in the ancient Near Eastern world. The enemy could be either dead or merely quelled. Whichever the case, the enemy was conquered.

The eschatological events Paul is describing will transcend time. Every aspect of these events is grounded in the resurrection of Christ. First he is raised; then at his final coming *(parousía)* those who are joined to Christ are raised. Only when this has taken place will the end *(télos)* come. This end is the fulfillment, the goal toward which all reality tends. Paul seems to be suggesting there is an interval between the *parousía* and the final end, when Christ will hand over everything to God. During this time all of Christ's enemies will be vanquished. This eschatological perspective corresponds to the Jewish apocalyptic worldview of his day. Paul does not indicate how long this interval will last. We can only presume it will last as long as it takes for Christ to accomplish the decisive victory. When this happens, Christ will bring the fruits of his victory to God.

### Luke 1:39-56

The gospel reading falls naturally into two parts: the account of Mary's visit to Elizabeth (vv. 39-45); and Mary's prayer of praise (vv. 46-56). Mary's greeting to Elizabeth is a customary salutation *(aspázomai),* but its effect is profound. It causes the child in Elizabeth's womb to leap with joy *(skirtáō).* This is reminiscent of the joy that filled David as he leapt before the ark of the covenant, the symbol of God in the midst of the people (cf. 2 Sam 6:14-15). Elizabeth is filled with the Holy Spirit and proclaims her faith in the child Mary is carrying. In the cases of both David and Elizabeth's unborn child, it is their realization of being in the presence of God that cause them to rejoice. It is as if Mary is the ark and the child within her is the glory of God.

In response to this wondrous experience, Elizabeth exalts first Mary and then her child (v. 42). She recognizes the blessedness they possess and she praises it. This blessedness is derived from the dignity of the child, a dignity Elizabeth acknowledges by referring to him as her Lord *(kýrios).* As David had wondered how the ark of God could come to him (cf. 2 Sam 6:9), so Elizabeth wonders how the mother of her Lord should come to her. Mary is here called "blessed" *(makários)* for having believed what had been spoken to her by the Lord, a reference to the annunciation (cf. Luke 1:26-38). In this case it is faith, not some work of righteousness, that is extolled. She believed she would conceive and bear a son, and it has come to pass. It is this son she carries in her womb that precipitated the events recorded in this passage. The way the good fortune will be manifested in Mary's life is not stated; she is merely called blessed.

Mary's hymn of praise has strong parallels in the victory hymns of Miriam (Exod 15:1-18), Hannah (1 Sam 2:1-10), and Judith (Jdt 16:1-17). She does not deny the greatness of the things that will be accomplished through her. On the contrary, the more magnificent the things accomplished, the clearer will God's power and might be seen, for only God could bring about such wonders. She praises God for having singled out the lowly and for having reversed their fortunes. This is the way God has acted from age to age, offering mercy to those who are open to it, to those who stand in awe of God's greatness.

While the first section of the prayer describes the great things God did to Mary, the last verses list some of the past blessings enjoyed by Israel. First is the reversal of fortune that had happened so often in the past: the hungry are filled, while the rich are sent away empty (v. 53). The choice of Mary is another example of God's preference for those who do not enjoy abundant prosperity. The reference to the promise made to Abraham places all God's blessings within the context of the covenant associated with this prominent ancestor (Gen 15:1-21; 17:1-14). These promises included a pledge that they would be a great nation; that they would be given a land of their own; and that they would live prosperous and peaceful lives, secure from outside threats. The history of Israel is an account of the people's infidelity to their responsibilities and God's mercy in the face of their failures. Mary's hymn of praise suggests that the marvels accomplished in her are a final example of God's mercy. The salvation of the people has finally come.

## Themes of the Day

In the Western Church this feast celebrates the assumption of Mary into heaven; in the East it commemorates her dormition, or falling asleep. However, the readings invite us to reflect on the role she plays in the mystery of our redemption. Whatever we honor in Mary in some way points to her Son.

### The Celestial Woman

Over the centuries devotion to Mary has been expressed in forms taken from the culture out of which it developed. Sometimes she is pictured as a humble peasant girl. At other times she is depicted as a queen, robed in gold of Ophir, who rules from heaven. Probably the most familiar pose is that of a mother with her child. Just as Christian theologians have reached into various religious traditions to explain some dimension of christology, so have they appropriated various images in their development of Mariology. Perhaps the most dramatic of these themes is that of the celestial woman from the vision found in the book of Revelation. It is because of the cosmic significance of Jesus that this tradition has been applied to Mary.

Reading this passage on a Marian feast suggests a Marian interpretation. The woman, now interpreted as Mary, brings forth her child, who is destined to rule all the nations. Mythological themes from other traditions take on new meaning here. For example, the mythic enmity between the dragon and the child recalls a similar enmity between the serpent in the garden of Eden and the offspring of the primordial woman. This cosmic vision places Mary in the heavens at the outset of God's plan of redemption. This feast declares that upon the completion of her role in this plan, Mary returns to heaven triumphant.

### A Prophetic Voice

The gospel reading for this feast characterizes Mary in a very different way. Here she is a simple peasant woman intent on offering service to another. However, the words placed in her mouth belie this unassuming picture. They are words of prophetic challenge. She announces the great reversals of God's good news. The structures of privilege and discrimination will be overturned. The dispossessed and the needy will experience the goodness of God. Mary did not presume that she would accomplish such great feats. Rather, they would be accomplished by the child she was carrying. Once again we see that the greatness of Mary is a reflection of the greatness of the Son of God, whom she bore. He was the firstfruits of salvation. He was the victor who won the kingdom. Her part in this victory was to bring him to birth and into maturity.

## The Exaltation of the Holy Cross (Feast)
### Numbers 21:4b-9

The setting of this episode is the wilderness. In the tradition of Israel the wilderness can be understood in two ways, which are diametrically opposed to each other. On the one hand, it is considered a place of love and intimacy, the site where God and the people first entered into a covenant relationship (cf. Hos 2:14). On the other hand, it is a place of testing, and for Israel, a place of failure. It is the second understanding that is operative in this passage.

There is something astonishing about the murmuring of the people. They acknowledge that God had brought them out of Egypt. They admit that they do have food (probably the manna). Still they complain. Their experience of deliverance from bondage should have grounded them in trust in God, but it did not. Besides this, they have been miraculously supplied with sustenance, and they complain about the quality of the food. It is no wonder they are punished. The text says the people grew impatient, when the only attitude appropriate for them would have been gratitude. Given all that God had done for them, it was God who should have been impatient with them.

The account of the bronze serpent brings together various themes that originally may have had little if anything to do with one another. First, there may have been actual snakes in the wilderness whose bite caused a terrible burning sensation. If this was the case, the people would certainly have looked for some kind of remedy. Second, there is evidence that either this bronze serpent or a replica of it called "Nehushtan" was set up in the Temple, and the people made offerings to it (cf. 2 Kgs 18:4). The similarity in sound between copper (*nᵉḥōšet*) and serpent (*nāḥāš*) cannot be denied, adding a level of credibility to the connection. The bronze serpent did not prevent the people in the wilderness from being bitten. Rather, it healed them from the deadly effects of the snakebite, and it only healed those who looked toward the bronze serpent in faith and repentance

This narrative brings the desert serpents together with the Nehushtan in a cause and effect relationship. Most likely the relationship really worked in the direction opposite the one described in the narrative. In other words, the wilderness tradition developed in order to explain why a monotheistic people would have installed a talisman in their Temple. If they could persuade people that the construction of this image had been directed by Moses as a means of curing people of the venom of the serpents, then perhaps its presence in the Temple might stand not as a blasphemous fetish but as a reminder, both of the punishment that they would have to face if they sinned and of the mercy of God that was always at hand if they repented.

## Psalm 78:1-2, 34-35, 36-37, 38

Each phrase of the introductory verses of this psalm response contains language that clearly identifies the didactic character of the psalm. The parallel construction only serves to underscore this:

| | |
|---|---|
| a) harken | b) my teaching (*tôrâ*) |
| a¹) incline your ears | b¹) saying of my mouth |
| | |
| a) I will open my mouth | b) parable (*mashāl*) |
| b) I will utter | b¹) riddles (*hîdâ*) |

*Tôrâ*, which is usually translated "law," is more instruction than legislation; *mashāl* is the generic word for "wisdom saying," but it also refers to the particular form of proverb; *hîdâ*, or mysterious saying, is one that draws one into an intellectual adventure. In such a context it is clear to see that the sayings are to be understood as specifically Wisdom sayings.

Again, it is the vocabulary that sets the context for understanding what follows. Three words in particular should be noted: steadfast or faithful (*'ēmūn*); covenant (*berit*); and compassionate (*raḥûm*). The psalm shows that God upheld the integrity of this intimate bond even when the people did not. Without naming specific incidents, the psalm sketches a bit of the history of the people. They turned to God only after they had been severely punished. Several times God allowed enemy forces to overtake the Israelites, but only one time does the text say that it was God who slew the people. That occurred when many people died from the bites of the fiery serpents God had sent, the incident referred to in the first reading. It seems the people only clung to God when their very survival was at stake. Their commitment was not sincere; their promises of fidelity were empty. Yet, despite the untrustworthiness of the people God's commitment was unfailing. Even as the text proclaims God's compassion, it recounts their guilt. They sinned, but God forgave them. God held in check the anger and wrath that were justifiably provoked by the people's disloyalty.

This is a Wisdom psalm; a very clear lesson is to be learned here. The past is offered as an example of what can happen in the present and the future. And what is that? Both judgment and salvation. Take heed! Harken! When our ancestors sinned, they were punished; when they repented, even if it was half-hearted repentance, God was merciful.

## Philippians 2:6-11

This christological reflection on the nature and mission of Jesus can be divided into two parts. In the first (vv. 6-8), Jesus is the subject of the action; in the second (vv. 9-11), God is. The first part describes Jesus' humiliation, the second recounts his exaltation by God.

The first verse sets the tone for the actions of Christ Jesus. He did not cling to the dignity that was rightfully his. Two phrases identify this dignity: he is in the form of God; he is equal to God. The form of something is its basic appearance, and from this its essential character can be known. Hence, since Christ is in the form of God, he enjoys a Godlike manner of being. The parallel phrase restates this in a slightly different way: he is equal to God. The verb reports that Christ did not cling to this prerogative; he did not use his exalted status for his own ends. Christ freely gave up the right to homage that was his due.

Once again the verb plays an important role in this recital. Not only did Christ relinquish his Godlike state, he emptied himself of it. The contrasts drawn here are noteworthy. Though in the form of God, he chose the form of a servant or slave. Without losing his Godlike being, he took on the likeness of human beings. This does not mean he only resembled a human being but really was not one. Christ did take on human form, but the qualification suggested by "likeness" points to the fact that he was human like no one else was human. Although the word "Lord" (*kýrios,* a word that is also applied to God) is not found in these early verses, the contrast between "Lord" and "servant" stands conspicuously behind them.

Christ emptied himself and took on the human condition. The final verb states he then humbled himself and became obedient. Having taken on the form of a slave, he made himself vulnerable to all the particulars of that station in life. For a slave, obedience is the determining factor. The extent of his obedience is striking. Compliance with God's will in a world that is alienated from God requires that one be open to the possibility of death. In a sense, Christ's crucifixion was inevitable. It was a common punishment for slaves, the nadir of human abasement. Such ignominy was a likely consequence of emptying himself and taking on human form.

The exaltation of Christ is as glorious as his humiliation was debasing. It is important to note that while Christ was the subject of his self-emptying, his super-exaltation is attributed directly to God. Once again there is a play on words and ideas. Just as form and appearance denote being, so name contains part of the essence of the individual. In exalting Jesus, God accords his human name a dignity that raises it above every other name. It now elicits the same reverence the title "Lord" *(kýrios)* does. Every knee shall do him homage and every tongue shall proclaim his sovereignty.

The extent to which Christ is to be revered is total. The entire created universe is brought under his lordship. This includes the spiritual beings in heaven, all living beings on earth, and even the dead under the earth. Distinctions such as spiritual or physical, living or dead, are meaningless here. All will praise Christ, whose exaltation gives glory to God.

### John 3:13-17

Nicodemus was the leader of the Jewish people who was interested in the teaching of Jesus but who came to him at night, presumably out of fear of being detected. The lesson Jesus provides for him was well worth his effort.

Just as healing came to those in the wilderness who looked upon the bronze serpent Moses raised up before them (cf. Num 21:8-9), so life eternal comes to those who believe in the "Son of Humanity" (the Greek has *ánthrōpos*, which means "humankind"), who is raised up in both ignominy and exaltation. The image of something raised up suggests Jesus was tied to a pole, as was the effigy of the serpent. However, the verb used means "to be raised in exaltation." Choosing this verb with its various meanings, the evangelist is saying it was precisely in his humiliation that Jesus was glorified. This thought calls to mind the Suffering Servant in Isaiah, who also suffered for others and who, in his affliction, was "raised high and greatly exalted" (cf. Isa 52:13).

"Son of Humanity" is a Semitic idiom that refers to a symbolic figure who will inaugurate the last days (cf. Dan 7:13-14). Given the way the thought is developed here, one is led to conclude that this Son of Humanity is also the only begotten Son of God (vv. 14-16). The juxtaposition of these two titles brings together the diverse and rich theologies each represents. As different as these representations may be, there is one characteristic they hold in common: both the Son of Humanity and the Son of God are agents of eternal life for all.

The extent of God's love is drawn in bold lines in two different but very significant ways. The first is the scope of divine love; the second is the price God is willing to pay because of that love. Ancient Israel continually marveled at the love God had for this chosen people. While this love can be seen throughout the religious tradition, it is particularly evident in the writings of the prophets. Christian writers also spoke of God's love, but their main interest was with those who had committed themselves in faith to Jesus Christ. This passage is remarkable in its explicit declaration of God's love for the entire world.

The author maintains that God's love for the world is so deep and so magnanimous that for the world to be saved nothing is spared, not even God's only

Son. God gave/sent this Son first in the incarnation and again in his saving death. This plan of salvation tragically and inevitably became judgment for some.

The world *(kósmos)* can be understood in three ways. It can refer to the totality of natural creation, the inhabited world generally, or the inhabited world in its sinfulness. Although the passage speaks of salvation, it is set in contrast with judgment and perishing. This indicates that here the world is understood in the third way, as subject to and guilty of sin. The world was created as good, but it often stands in opposition to God and, consequently, is in need of being saved. Such is the situation presumed here, since otherwise there would be no need for salvation. It is this sinful world that God loved (v. 16); it is into this sinful world that God's only Son was sent (v. 17).

The passage says that God both gave *(dídōmi)* and sent *(apostéllō)* God's only Son. The first verb implies that this Son was a gift from God. It underscores God's generosity to the world. The second verb indicates that the Son had a mission to perform. It includes the notion of serious responsibility on the part of the Son. In both cases, it is the world that benefits from God's actions.

## Themes of the Day

This feast recalls the exaltation of the cross, which we celebrated on Good Friday. It is through feasts such as this that the major themes of our faith are woven in and out throughout the Liturgical Year. The feast itself marks the finding of relics of the true cross by the mother of the emperor Constantine. Today we concentrate on the power of the cross in our lives.

### He Emptied Himself

The cross is the ultimate demonstration of the nature of God. The reading from Paul's letter to the Philippians describes the kenosis, the emptying of Christ. He gave of himself even to death on the cross. This is characteristic not only of the man Jesus but of the Godhead. Creation is the first example of divine emptying; redemption is the ultimate example. Unlike Good Friday when we stand before the stark cross and mourn the death of our innocent Messiah, today we stand before the glorious cross and praise God for God's incomprehensible goodness toward us. God's graciousness is poured out indiscriminately, prodigally, as only profound love can be given. Such is the nature of our God, and the cross is the symbol of this nature.

### The Sign of Healing

The readings play with the symbolism of the pole on which the bronze serpent hung. In the wilderness it was merely a pole. Jesus compares it to the cross that becomes the source of our healing. As painful as life's crosses may be, they serve to transform us. They strip away what is superficial and they give us insight into the true meaning of life. They are the testing ground of virtue, the fire within which we are refined. The cross may at times be bitter medicine, but it can combat the human weakness that eats away our goodness. It can be our hope in the midst of pain and suffering and brokenness, because it promises to carry us into new life.

## Our Access to God

It was through the cross that Jesus conquered sin and death and won for us access to God. It is through the cross that we die to sin and rise to new life in Christ. Through the goodness of God, which has been poured out for us, we have been granted eternal life. It is incomprehensible to think that death is the way to life, but that is the message of this feast. The cross, which is a sign of shame and misery, is now a symbol of glory and exaltation.

## All Saints (Solemnity)
### Revelation 7:2-4, 9-14

John the seer relates two extraordinary apocalyptic visions that were granted to him. Although they differ, placed together as they are here the second adds a dimension to the first. The events of the first vision seem to unfold on earth; those of the second take place in heaven. Both visions depict vast assemblies of the righteous.

The signing angel comes from the east. Because of all the symbolism associated with the rising of the sun, this is the direction from which salvation was expected. The seal was probably a kind of signet ring used to mark official documents or personal possessions. It belongs to God, signifying that those sealed are God's possession. Finally, God is the living God, not the God of the dead. Obviously the author felt it was important to state that death does not play a significant role in the drama unfolding here. In fact, this angel commands those destroying angels to desist so that the vast assembly can be sealed with the seal of God and, presumably, preserved from the suffering these angels bring to the earth. The singing is reminiscent of a similar mandate reported in the writings of the prophet Ezekiel. That narrative recounts how, at the outset of the destruction of Jerusalem, a sign was placed on the foreheads of some of the inhabitants, protecting them from the disastrous fate of the city (cf. Ezek 9:4-6). Here the sign has the identical function.

The number 144,000 is clearly symbolic. It is the number twelve squared and then multiplied by a thousand. Twelve stands for the number of the original tribes of Israel. Since the Christian community appropriated to itself the identity of the People of God, the reference here is probably to them. Both the squaring of twelve and the multiplication by a thousand are ways of indicating completeness. These also suggest that the number is impossible to count.

The second scene is the divine throne room in heaven (the throne represents the divine presence). The multitude gathered there came from every nation, every race, every people, and every tongue. The universality is complete. They are described in terms that denote victory: white robes and palms. Their exclamation acknowledges that they did not win this victory through their own merits. Rather, they are recipients of blessings received from God through the agency of the Lamb. Next the angels, the four elders (cf. Rev 4:4), and the four living creatures (cf. Rev 4:6) pay their homage to God and to the Lamb. Their exclamation of praise begins and ends with the acclamation "Amen"—So be it! It is true! The divine attributes they praise are proclaimed in traditional songs of praise (cf. Rev 5:12).

When John the seer is asked about the identity of those who constitute the multitude, he employs in his reply two themes from ancient Israel's tradition. The first is the eschatological concept of the great tribulation *(thlípsis)* that will precede the dawning of the age of fulfillment. The second is a reference to the atoning efficacy of the blood of the sacrificial lamb. There is no suggestion in the text that these people are martyrs. Rather, they are those who have survived eschatological distress because they were purified through the blood of the sacrificial Lamb. This distinction certainly entitles them to participate in the eschatological celebrations.

## Psalm 24:1-2, 3-4, 5-6

The psalm response consists of a hymn of praise of God the Creator (vv. 1-2) and a section suggesting the question-response ritual associated with a liturgical pilgrimage (vv. 3-6). An interesting feature of this response is the variety of images of God that it contains: Creator, savior, patron deity.

Behind the imagery of the opening verses is ancient Near Eastern cosmology. In various myths from that tradition we find a primeval struggle between gods of chaos and deities who would establish order. Chief among the former were Yam (the Hebrew word for "sea") and Nahar (Hebrew for "river"). In the myths a vibrant, young warrior-god conquers the chaotic waters, establishes dominion over the universe, and assigns the celestial bodies their places in the heavens. The similarities, both linguistic and in content, between such a myth and the picture painted in the psalm response are obvious. However, in this psalm response the focus is the earth, which the ancients believed floated like a saucer on the cosmic waters. This earth and all those who live on it belong to or are under the protection of the LORD. Such a claim would not be made if there were any doubt about the LORD's sovereignty. This is the deity who exercises dominion, and this would only be the case if the LORD were the victorious warrior who conquered the chaotic cosmic force.

The liturgical portion of the response opens with an exchange of question and answer. In the mythological tradition the high god dwelt on the highest mountain. In Israel's liturgical tradition Jerusalem with its Temple was identified with this high mountain. Therefore, as the pilgrims approached the walls of the city, certain persons (probably priests) inquired about the suitability of those who would enter the sacred precincts. According to the strict regulations in Israel's cultic tradition, only those who conformed to the prescriptions of holiness, or cultic purity, were allowed to enter. These prescriptions generally governed external regulations. Hands that had not touched forbidden objects were considered "sinless." However, here external conformity is not enough. An appropriate inner disposition is required as well. The polarities of chaos-order have been transformed into those of unclean-clean and then unworthy-worthy.

The male bias in Israel's liturgical participation is seen in the reference to those who receive blessing. This notwithstanding, God is identified as the God of Jacob and savior of the chosen people, clear allusions to both the ancestral and exodus traditions of Israel. These epithets are not only divine titles, they are also reminders of God's special election and care of this people. Fidelity to the prescriptions of the religious tradition was the primary way of living out faithfully one's role as covenant partner of God—the covenant associated either with the ancestors (cf. Gen 17:2) or with the exodus tradition (cf. Exod 19:5). The blessing and reward flowed from such fidelity, from the people's desire to seek the face of God, to be united to God through commitment and devotion.

One very important final point must be made. The two sections of this psalm response may at first glance appear to be quite separate. However, joined together as they are, they interpret each other. In other words, the God who first called and then saved Israel is none other than the Creator who vanquished the cosmic powers of chaos; the God who exercises dominion over all creation is the one who established an intimate covenant with this people.

## 1 John 3:1-3

These few short verses are brimming with theological meaning. The first and more important point is the love God has for believers. A second theme is eschatological fulfillment. Although the latter is dependent upon the former, it is also a direct result of it.

The love *(agápē)* of which the author speaks is generative; it is transforming; it makes believers children of God. Everything that happens in the lives of believers is a consequence of their having been re-created as God's children. A related theme is introduced. As children of God they are a new reality, and thus they are not accepted by the world, the old reality. Certain similarities between Jesus and the believers are drawn. The world, the entire inhabited world that is subject to sin, recognizes only its own. It did not recognize the only begotten Son of God, and it does not recognize these new children of God. The implications of this are clear. Believers should not be surprised if they encounter the same kind of rejection, even persecution and death, that befell Jesus.

The reading does not identify what it is about Jesus and the believers that is so difficult for the world to comprehend. However, it is probably the manner of living that flows from their relationship with God, a manner of behavior that contradicts the life-style promoted by the sinful world and that results in the world's rejection of what it cannot claim.

The "now but not yet" of Christian eschatology is clearly stated. As a consequence of God's love believers have already been reborn as children of God. However, transformation has not yet been completed, nor has it been fully made known to them. All of this is dependent upon a future manifestation. It is not clear from the text whether this will be a manifestation of Christ or of God. Although the Greek construction is ambiguous, the theological intent is not. Actually, any manifestation of the risen Christ is a manifestation of God, and in like manner, the ultimate manifestation of God is found in the risen Christ.

Having been made children of God, the community of believers is promised an even fuller identification with God. They will see God as God is, for they will be like God. The Hellenist influence here is obvious. Widespread in the ancient world was the notion that a reality can be understood only by another reality similar to it. For their part, believers must do what they can to pattern their lives after the purity of God. The basis of their hope is the ultimate vision of God, a vision denied believers "now" but promised for "later."

## Matthew 5:1-12a

The preaching and miracles of Jesus attracted crowds of people, making it necessary for him to take his disciples up a mountain. There he taught them. The instruction known as the Sermon on the Mount was directed to his close followers, not to the broader crowds. The first part of that sermon, the Beatitudes, constitutes the gospel reading for today. By form and content the Beatitudes are wisdom teaching, not Christian law, as is sometimes claimed. Most if not all the sentiments expressed are found somewhere in ancient Jewish teaching.

The beatitude, or macarism, is a literary form belonging to the Wisdom tradition. It takes its name from the Greek word *makários* (happy or blessed). It is a descriptive statement intended for purposes of teaching. Like most Wisdom literary forms, it describes a life situation that draws a connection between a particular manner of behavior and the consequences that flow from such behavior. Though it is a simple description, it is meant to encourage the behavior if the consequences are satisfying and to discourage it if they are not. The Beatitudes follow this pattern exactly: a group of people who act in a particular way are said to be happy; the blessings they will enjoy are stated.

It is important to remember that while the teachings of Jesus are all in some way directed toward the establishment of the reign of God, the type of behavior or of values he advocates is frequently the opposite of that espoused by society at large. This fact offers us a way to understand the challenges set before us in the Beatitudes. Perhaps the way to interpret them is to look first at the blessings promised. We may see that the behavior that Jesus is advocating is at odds with what society would say will guarantee the blessing we seek.

The first and third beatitudes are very similar. They treat the notion of power, which is often determined by the extent of one's material possessions. Societies are usually ruled by those with power and means. The reign of God, however, will be in the hands of the powerless (the meek) and those who have no means with which to exert power (the poor). The second and fourth beatitudes promise the alleviation of some form of inner turmoil. A strict reading of the theory of retribution insists that suffering is usually the consequence of sin or some kind of inappropriate behavior. According to that theory, those who grieve do so because of something they have brought on themselves, and those who hunger for justice need only live justly to enjoy it. On the contrary, the Beatitudes suggest that those suffering are innocent of anything that would result in their misfortune, but the situations in which they find themselves will be remedied for them.

The fifth, sixth, and seventh beatitudes treat aspects of religious piety. Mercy is the disposition God has for sinners (cf. Exod 34:6). Those who seek this attitude from God are exhorted to extend it to others. Already in Israel's religious tradition we read that it is not ritual conformity but a simple yet open heart that gives one entrance to the presence of God (cf. Ps 24:4). Finally, peace and tranquil order have been God's desire for us from the beginning. It is sin that disrupted this order and destroyed the peace. Those who overcome evil with good in order to reestablish peace are doing God's work and will be known as God's children.

The last beatitude very clearly underscores the reversal referred to above. Commitment to Jesus and to his cause are bound to bring insult and persecution. When this happens, the disciples should rejoice, knowing that the world is persecuting them because they belong to a kingdom that is not of this world, a kingdom with values that are the reverse of those espoused by this world. It is clear that each beatitude invites us to turn the standards of our world and our way of life upside down and inside out.

### Themes of the Day

Today we celebrate the memory of all the baptized who have gone before us and whose lives were virtuous. It is the memory of all these people that we keep, not merely of those who have been made models of virtue through the process of canonization. Though we do remember those officially considered saints by the Church, we celebrate the lives of all those who have been marked with the sign of faith, those we have known personally, those whose names we do not know.

## *The Saints of God*

The saints of God are all those who have been baptized into Christ, who have washed their robes in the blood of the Lamb. Sanctity is not an accumulation of merit. It is a gift that comes with baptism to be nurtured throughout life. We are made saints when in baptism we are made children of God. We all know people whose lives were steeped in genuine holiness. We remember the unselfish love of our parents, the heroism of members of the armed forces, the piety of our colleagues, the patience of those who suffered intensely. The life of every one of us has been blessed by the holiness of others. This is a day for us to remember and to celebrate their holiness.

## *Children of God*

As earthy and human as our saints may have been, there was a genuine mystical sense to their sanctity. They are children of God, sharing the very life of God. They were so during their lives, and they continue to be so even after death. What this means is beyond our comprehension, but Paul insists that it is truly the case. This identity carries with it a challenge for us to live life in terms of our identity as children of God. The saints who have gone before us met this challenge. Their lives revealed the family features. They lived their lives in terms of who they were as children of God.

## *Blessed Are You*

In the Beatitudes, listed in today's gospel, we are given examples of what it means to live lives of holiness. Those who live such lives are said to be truly blessed. It is important to remember that this gospel really does not present a blueprint for holiness. Rather, it offers a series of snapshots that demonstrate the holiness that is ours by virtue of our baptism. Those who have gone before us lived such lives. Today as we remember them, we hold up their lives as examples of holiness and models for our imitation. The sentiments expressed and the commitment illustrated in the Beatitudes clearly stand in opposition to the standards of the world. Their radicality may be more than some can understand, but theirs are traits that are recognizable by those who belong to the family of God, for theirs are genuine Godly traits.

## *The Commemoration of the Faithful Departed (All Souls)*
### Daniel 12:1-3

The apocalyptic scene described in this reading is part of the revelation granted to the prophet Daniel. It depicts the final struggle of human beings at the end of time and their subsequent resurrection to a life of glorification or one of horror. The prophetic phrase "at that time" appears three times in the very first verse and marks the future-oriented character of the event described. It seems that in the ancient Near Eastern world each nation had an advocate in the heavenly court who came to its defense, whether in battle or in a court of law. Michael, whose name means "who is like God," is the patronal guardian of Israel (cf. 10:23).

The reading says that Michael rises up but does not explain why he does so. It may be as protector of Israel while the nation faces the distress of the end of time. Since the judgments meted out to the righteous and to the wicked are described later in the reading, one might conclude that Michael stands prepared to present those under his charge (Israel) to the judgment seat of God or to participate in some way in the judgement itself.

The distress that is to come is unparalleled. It is probably the final tribulation that will come to pass before the appearance of the eschatological reign of God. This suffering was considered by some to be the "birth pangs of the Messiah," the agony that must be endured if the reign of God is to be born. Daniel is told that those whose names appear in the book (presumably the Book of the Righteous) will be spared. They will have to endure the agony of the end-time, but they will escape ultimate destruction.

The allusion to some kind of resurrection from the dead followed by reward and punishment is clear. Since the idea of the end-time sets the context for this passage, the resurrection referred to here is the general resurrection believed to be coming at the end of time. Death is described as sleeping in the dust of the earth, and resurrection is an awakening. After they have been raised the dead must give an account of the record of their deeds. This is the basis upon which the separation takes place: some are rewarded with everlasting life, others are punished with horror and disgrace.

Within the circle of those granted everlasting life, some are singled out for further distinction (v. 3). The verse is structured after the pattern of poetic parallelism, suggesting the reference is to one group and not two. Elements from astral religion are employed to characterize the reward of the wise. Previously they had been a source of illumination in the lives of others. In the new age they will continue to shine, but then their brilliance will be seen by all. They will be like the stars in the heavens.

This vision is a message of hope and challenge for those who are undergoing great distress. The righteous are encouraged to remain steadfast in their commitment. They are promised a spectacular reward if they do. The reading also warns the reprobates of the fate that awaits them. The choice is theirs.

## Psalm 23:1-3a, 3b-4, 5, 6

This responsorial psalm is one of the most familiar and best loved psalms of the entire Psalter. It paints vivid pictures of a carefree existence, peaceful rest, and abundant fruitfulness. Although "shepherd" suggests a flock rather than merely one sheep, here the focus is on the individual. In addition to this image God is characterized as a host, one who supervises a banquet and within whose house the psalmist ultimately dwells.

The psalm opens with a metaphor that sets the tone of the entire song. It is the responsibility of the shepherd to find pastures that will provide enough grazing and abundant water for the entire flock, to lead them there without allowing any of the sheep to stray and be lost, to guard them from predators or dangers of any kind, and to attend to their every need. To characterize the LORD as a shepherd is to trust that God will discharge all of these responsibilities. The personal dimension of the psalm shifts from the care given the entire flock to concern for one individual, making God's care a very intimate matter. Not only are the physical needs of the psalmist satisfied, but the soul, the very life force *(nepesh)* of the person, is renewed.

The guidance of the shepherd is more than provident, it is moral as well. The psalmist is led in the paths of righteousness (v. 3), and this is done for the sake of the LORD's name. Since one's name is a part of the very essence of the person, this indicates that the way of the LORD is the way of righteousness. Following this, we can say that the magnanimous care shown by the shepherd flows from enduring righteousness rather than some passing sentiment of the heart. This is confirmed by the reference to the covenant kindness *(ḥesed)* that surrounds the psalmist (v. 6). In other words, the divine shepherd's tender commitment to the flock, and to each individual within it, is as lasting as is God's covenant commitment.

The psalmist is confident of the LORD's protection, as demonstrated in his mention of the shepherd's rod and staff, which were used to ward off wild animals as well as poachers. The valley of "deep darkness," can be a reference to the darkest part of the terrain or to the gloom that can overwhelm an individual.

However, it also has a mythological connotation and is frequently interpreted as death. Whichever meaning is intended here, the psalmist claims to be unafraid, for the presence of the LORD is reassuring.

The image of the shepherd securing nourishment for the flock suggests another metaphor, that of the host who prepares a lavish banquet for guests. Many societies have a very strict code of hospitality. The people are obliged to provide the best provisions they have, even for their enemies. The LORD spreads out such a banquet here, which not only affords nourishment but also is a public witness to God's high regard for the psalmist, who will continue to enjoy God's favor in God's house. Whether this means the Temple or is merely a reference to the place where God dwells, the fundamental meaning is clear. The psalmist has been under the loving guidance of the LORD and will remain there forever.

### Romans 6:3-9

Paul explains how baptism has enabled the Christians to participate in the death and resurrection of Jesus. The ritual is itself the reenactment of this death and resurrection. As the Christians were engulfed in the water, they were buried with Christ in death; as they emerged from the water, they rose with him into new life. In drawing these lines of comparison between the death and resurrection of Jesus and the baptism and new life of the Christians, Paul's real intent is ethical exhortation. He seeks to encourage them to set aside their old manner of living and take on the new life of holiness.

While the descent into baptismal waters can symbolize Christ's descent into death, there is another dimension of the water imagery that strengthens Paul's argument. According to a long tradition cosmic waters were chaotic, therefore, death-dealing (cf. Genesis 6–9; Job 22:11; Ps 73:13-14; Isa 27:1). To be engulfed by water is to be swallowed up by chaos and death. This symbolism lends itself to describing both the death of Christ and the baptism of Christians. Christ was plunged into the chaos of death; the Christians are plunged into the death of chaos. By the power of God, Christ conquered death and rose to a new life of glory; by the power of God, the Christians participate in Christ's victory and are raised to the glory of a new life.

Paul characterizes their former lives as slavery to sin. Through baptism this old enslaved self has been crucified. Just as death had no power over the resurrected Christ, so sin now has no power over the baptized Christians. They now have the power of the resurrected Lord to withstand the assaults of sin. However, Paul is not naive about the struggles of life. He knows that these call for constant vigilance and self-denial. Crucifixion is a fitting image for both Christian conversion and ongoing fidelity, not only because of the role it played in Christ's death but because the torment it entails exemplifies the suffering that a change of life will exact on the Christians. However, as is evident in the case of Christ's death and resurrection, the cross is the only way to new life. So it is also for the Christians who are united with Christ.

## John 6:37-40

In this discourse, Jesus assures his audience that those who are joined to him will never be separated from him. This assurance is grounded in the mission God gave to Jesus and the faithfulness with which Jesus intends to carry out his responsibilities. The fulfillment of this divinely appointed mission was the reason Jesus came down from heaven and assumed human flesh in the first place. If any of these disciples were lost, it would be seen as failure on Jesus' part. This was unthinkable, because the incarnation occurred so God's plan of salvation would be realized. Jesus repeats this teaching in various ways throughout this short reading.

God's plan of salvation has two related purposes. The first is that those to whom Jesus was sent might believe in him. The second is that their faith might grow deeper and deeper until the last day, when they will be blessed by him with the gift of eternal life. This twofold purpose reflects the Christian paradoxical teaching on eschatology. The age of fulfillment has dawned already in faith, but it has not yet unfolded completely. However, the first depends upon the second: eternal life comes with faith already dynamic during this life, not merely at the end-time. Since faith is the passage from condemnation to acceptance, we can see how it is also a passage from the death of sin to the new life that will not end. It is because of their faith that believers in Jesus will not be driven away. It is because of their faith that they will be raised up with Jesus on the last day.

## Themes of the Day

This particular feast has no specific readings assigned to it. Pastoral judgment allows us to choose any readings for the Masses for the Dead. The readings that appear here are those that have been recommended for use in the United States. The following themes come from the readings analyzed. The readings themselves do not speak of the doctrine of purgatory. However, they invite us to think of all those who, through the mercy of God, continue the journey of purification en route to the face of God.

### *Remnants of Sin*

By virtue of our baptism we are given a rich inheritance. We have died with Christ to sin and we have risen with him to new life. However, if we are honest we will have to admit we do not always live out of that gift. Though baptized into Christ's death, we do not fully die to sin. In fact, there are many times in our lives when we live in sin, when we actually cling to sin. We do not follow the example of the saints, which we celebrated yesterday. Instead we capitulate; we give in to our baser nature; we live lives of selfishness and greed, hatred and immorality. We lose the battle against the forces of evil in the world and we settle for the easier road.

What happens to those who die in that state? They may not have turned completely away from the goodness of God, but they have not been faithful either. The remnants of sin cling to them, making them somewhat unfit to stand before the face of God. Are they lost? Or are they saved?

### Divine Mercy

Even though we may not always live in the strength of our baptism, there is still a burning desire on the part of God to save us. In God there is mercy in abundance. It seems that Jesus is not willing to lose anyone. Therefore, the power of Jesus and the strength of his promises give us hope that even after death there is the possibility of purification and pardon. We have no idea of when this might happen or how it will happen. All we know is that the lovingkindness of God far surpasses any infidelity of which we might be guilty. We do not deserve this mercy, but then we have never deserved God's mercy. It is a gift freely given. Even to the end we believe God will not abandon us to ourselves.

### The Good Shepherd

The image of Jesus the Good Shepherd is a very comforting image. It assures us that he not only feeds us and gives us drink, but he also protects us as we travel through the dark valley into the fullness of life. He is there at our side as we continue the journey of purification to the face of God. Though we are weak and vulnerable, we can rely on his rod and his staff.

The feast of All Souls is not a feast of sadness but one of great hope and confidence. It invites us to entrust our dead to God, because we know they are really God's dead. We know that if we have loved them, God has loved them more. They are in God's care, and God will lead them to peace.

## The Dedication of the Lateran Basilica (Feast)
### Ezekiel 47:1-2, 8-9, 12

Ezekiel recounts a vision of the temple that was granted to him. He is brought to the door of the temple, and from there he is able to observe a stream of water flowing from the threshold of the temple and growing in force until it is a mighty river. Temples were constructed in such a way as to face the east, the direction from which, according to ancient tradition, salvation comes because it is the horizon above which the new dawn of promise rises. The course the water takes is quite complicated. More important for this reading are the meaning of its source and the effects it is able to achieve.

The waters flow from the east to the Arabah *('ărābâ),* a desert plain that stretches south into the Rift Valley, where it becomes the southern depression of the Dead Sea. It is into this sea that the waters flow. The Dead Sea, the lowest point on the surface of the earth, is thirteen hundred feet below sea level. Seven million tons of water flow into it daily. Because it has no outlet, the constant evaporation of water results in a high concentration of salt, chlorides, and bromides. In this vision, the waters that flow from the temple miraculously purify these stagnant waters, allowing living creatures to live within them and to thrive. Plants too are able to grow on the banks of the sea and to produce fruits. What was once a place of death is now a place of burgeoning life and productivity. This picture recalls the primordial river that flowed out of Eden. It too divided into four branches, and it watered all the surrounding land, making it fertile (cf. Gen 2:10-14).

The last verse of the reading makes an ever greater claim. Not only is the water that flows from the temple itself transformative, but the fruits it produces share in its transformative power. The fruits themselves serve as food; the leaves of the trees that produced the fruit possess curative powers. The saving power of God goes out from the temple in a series of concentric circles: first the water from the sanctuary itself; then whatever the water touches; and finally the fruits produced by that which the water touched. The power of the presence of God radiates throughout creation.

## Psalm 46:2, 3, 5-6, 8, 9

This psalmist employs various metaphors to encourage the people to trust in God. The metaphors can all be understood on both an experiential level and a mythological level. The psalmist appears to be describing a natural disaster (vv. 1-3) and extolling the glories of the city of Jerusalem (vv. 5-6, 8-9). However, mythological themes lie beneath these metaphors. It should be noted that each stanza of this response contains a distinct title for God, each one suggesting a distinct characterization.

Mountains are symbols of strength and stability. However, if they are subject to an earthquake, they can break into pieces and tumble into the sea. God is a different kind of refuge and strength, one that will never fail, one that is not subject to stronger forces. Behind this metaphor is the mythological story of primordial creation. There we see that the victorious God has conquered the sea (v. 3) and firmly established the mountains (cf. Ps 65:6-7). With God as our help in distress, we have nothing to fear.

We discover many documents of ancient mythology stating that the gods live on the mountain tops. This stands to reason, for such places would be the closest spots to the heavens. The theme of mountain calls to mind Zion, the mountain upon which the city of Jerusalem was built and within which the Temple was erected (vv. 5-6). We know this is Zion because the title for God is Most High *('elyôn)*, the name of the god who was worshiped in the Jebusite city Jerusalem (cf. Gen 14:18-19). After David captured that city the Israelites appropriated much of the religious culture of the city and incorporated it into their own tradition. They insisted that their God was the Most High. They also believed this mountain was not only sacred but also secure, because God dwelt on it in a very special way. Dawn, the time when darkness was finally conquered, would reveal that it was this God who had been their protector.

"LORD of Hosts" is a military title. It is found in the accounts of Israel's military conflicts (cf. 1 Sam 1:3; 15:2; Ps 24:10). It is also a reference to the primordial conflict between the mighty warrior God and the evil waters of chaos. Whether we see the title as referring to ancient Israel's military encounters with its enemies or to the cosmic battle between the forces of good and the forces of evil, it is still the God of Israel/Jacob who is victorious. The astonishing feats this God has accomplished can be either the victories that God has won or the works of creation that God has wrought.

The psalmist calls all those who can hear to behold the marvels of God. Their magnificence should instill both gratitude and confidence in the hearts of all.

## 1 Corinthians 3:9c-11, 16-17

Paul characterizes the community at Corinth as the temple of God. He first describes the preliminary steps that are taken in constructing the building, and he then extolls the excellence of this temple, which is the community of believers. Speaking without pride but from the humble acknowledgment of God's goodness, Paul declares that by the grace of God he was chosen to be the wise architect *(sophós architéktōn)* responsible for the temple. It cannot be denied that every step in the building process is important. None is more pivotal that the laying of the foundation. The entire structure is dependent on it. Paul boldly claims this is precisely what he did through his preaching of the gospel. He laid the foundation, and the foundation is Christ. Every other minister builds on Paul's initial work.

Paul next extols the excellence of this building. In doing so he uses a method of argumentation that resembles the Greek rhetorical style of diatribe. He addresses his audience, referring to assumptions they share but do not seem to be living out. These assumptions have to do with the holiness of the temple of God. It is clear that Paul is not thinking of a material building. He is, rather, referring to the collection of people who gather in God's name. Paul declares that the Corinthians are this temple. This notion was not original with Paul, for it is found in the literature of the Qumran community as well. There we find the members referred to as a "holy house" (*bêt qôdeš*, cf. 1 QS 5:5; 8:4). However, at Qumran the general community was only the "holy house," while the priestly members were considered the "holy of holies," the inner sanctum where the presence of God resides. The word Paul uses for "temple" *(naós)* refers to the sanctuary rather than to the broader temple precincts. Thus, in his thinking the entire assembly is the "holy of holies" of this temple. Just as the presence of God made the Temple in Jerusalem holy, so it is the presence of the Spirit of God that makes this new temple holy, and the Spirit dwells in all of the members.

Those who defiled the Temple in Jerusalem were liable to death. Outside the inner court of the Temple a sign was posted that excluded Gentiles from entering and warned of severe consequences for violation of this prohibition. Why such a harsh penalty? Because the Temple of God is holy, and only those people and things that have been set aside as holy can enter it. With this regulation in mind Paul plays with the meaning of the Greek word *phtheírō*, which can be translated both "to corrupt" and "to destroy." Those who corrupt or defile God's temple will be destroyed. It is up to the Corinthians to determine whether the temple of God, which they are, will continue to be holy or whether it might be defiled.

## John 2:13-22

The reading revolves around the theme of temple. Jesus' actions there are acted-out prophecy, and his play on words constitutes prophetic forthtelling. The episode takes place at the time of the observance of the Jewish feast of Passover in the city of Jerusalem. Themes from each of these important details are woven together and used by Jesus.

At first glance it seems that Jesus' intensity was aroused by the erosion of temple decorum and the diminishment of religious fervor this represented. Roman coins, the currency of the day, were stamped with the head of Caesar, who was considered a deity, and sometimes with the images of other pagan gods. This made them unfit for temple use, and so money-changing became indispensable. The Jews, who came from around the world for major feasts, probably did not bring along animals for sacrifice. Thus, the sellers provided a second necessary service. All of this took place in the temple precincts, a vast area that included the outer court and the Court of the Gentiles, but not the sanctuary or Temple proper. Why was Jesus so irate? He accused the merchants of making the Temple a marketplace. But a part of it really was a marketplace. The transactions were legitimate; they were conducted in the appropriate temple area; and they were essential supports of the temple service. The explanation of his behavior is found both in an allusion to a passage from the prophet Zechariah (14:21), who said that at the end-time there would be no need for merchants in the house of the LORD, and in a psalm text remembered by the disciples. This latter passage states that zeal for the house of God makes the psalmist vulnerable to the scorn and abuse of others (cf. Ps 69:9).

Jesus makes a double claim. First, by driving the merchants out of the temple precincts, he announces that the time of fulfillment has come. Second, identifying God as his Father affirms his right to make such a claim and to act in accord with it. The Jews, most likely the temple authorities, demand that Jesus justify his actions. His words here, translated into Greek, convey this by means of a clever use of language. Two words for temple are used in this passage. Only *hierón* appears when the entire temple area is intended (vv. 14, 15), and Jesus uses *naós* when he is referring to his body (vv. 19, 21). The Jewish authorities mistakenly use *naós* in a general sense, though in Jesus' words, it is used here very specifically.

Since Jesus is portrayed as using *naós,* the word for temple proper or sanctuary, in referring to his body, he is actually predicting his death and resurrection. This corresponds to the earlier allusion to Zechariah and the replacement of the temple sacrifice by his own suffering. His challengers take his words literally and believe he is speaking about the Temple within which they stand and which is still under construction. This encounter ends with a second statement about the disciples remembering. It would require their experience of the risen Lord for them to be able to gain insight into this last saying.

### Themes of the Day

The basilica of St. John erected on the Lateran Hill is the cathedral of Rome, the mother church of all Roman Catholic churches. When we celebrate the dedication of this church, we celebrate all other churches as well.

### The Temple

The Temple was important because it was believed to be the place on earth where God dwelt in the midst of the people. It was God's presence, not the worship performed by human beings, that made this a sacred site. There is something incarnational about the presence of God. It is not merely an abstract reality. It allows itself to be manifested in the concrete, in something that has shape and character. This presence reveals itself in the various cultural forms of the people, and the people respond to God's presence in their own cultural ways.

## We Are the Temple of God

As important as the temple building may be, it is only a building. Paul insists that we are the temple of God; we are the manifestation of God in the world today. The Spirit of God dwells in us, making the believing community the living temple of God. This is an indescribable privilege as well as an exacting challenge. If we do not obscure this reality, the glory of God will shine out from us. The community, not the building, will be the place where prayer and sacrifice are offered to God. It will be within the community that others will experience God's saving presence. They will come to the community to be sanctified, to be made holy.

## A Den of Thieves or Life-Giving Water?

Today's readings provide us with two pictures of the temple of God, two characterizations of the community of believers. The picture in the gospel is a sobering one. The Temple has become a marketplace; the community has become so preoccupied with the business of the world that it has forgotten its identity. In a fury, Jesus upsets the worldly order that had been established and drives it out of the house of God. The vision from Ezekiel offers a very different picture. There we see water from the temple transforming everything in its path. As water flowed from the temple in Ezekiel's vision, so grace flows from the temple that is the People of God.

Which image more closely characterizes the community of which we are a part? Are we able to refresh what was once brackish? Can we transform the wilderness into a place teeming with life? Can we make all things productive and fruitful? Can we heal what has been threatened with death? Is the community truly the presence of God in the world today? Or is it a simply a site where ritual is performed but the concerns of God take second place to the affairs of the world? Will the zeal of Jesus be unleashed on us? Do we need to be overturned in order to be reformed? As we celebrate the dedication of this sacred place, we are reminded that we are the temple of God, that we have been dedicated, that the Spirit of God has made us a living temple.

# Index of Scripture Readings